THE UNITED STATES, GREAT BRITAIN, AND BRITISH NORTH AMERICA
FROM THE REVOLUTION TO THE ESTABLISHMENT OF PEACE AFTER THE WAR OF 1812

THE RELATIONS OF
CANADA AND THE UNITED STATES

═══

A SERIES OF STUDIES
PREPARED UNDER THE DIRECTION OF THE
CARNEGIE ENDOWMENT FOR INTERNATIONAL PEACE
DIVISION OF ECONOMICS AND HISTORY

JAMES T. SHOTWELL, *Director*

THE UNITED STATES
GREAT BRITAIN
AND
BRITISH NORTH AMERICA

FROM THE REVOLUTION TO
THE ESTABLISHMENT OF PEACE
AFTER THE WAR OF 1812

BY

A. L. BURT

PROFESSOR OF HISTORY, UNIVERSITY OF MINNESOTA

NEW YORK: RUSSELL & RUSSELL

1961

EDITOR'S INTRODUCTION

THE recent march of events has given a peculiar importance to this volume in the Canadian American Series. Never was the old Greek saying that history is philosophy teaching by experience more applicable to any section of the annals of the New World than to the story which is unfolded in these pages. The theme is that of the continuing relation with Great Britain and its colonies of the newly established United States of America, which had formerly been the most important part of the overseas empire. The recognition of American sovereignty by the British government upon which the American commissioners concentrated their diplomatic effort in the peace negotiations left many questions unsettled. There was above all the delimitation of the frontiers running through untracked wildernesses where the forgotten men of the negotiations, the American Indians, bitterly fought back against the advancing settlement. There was the commercial conflict of the mercantile system in which England had so large an initial advantage, and there was the continued use of the old military system with its mercenary soldiers and impressed seamen. More difficult still were the problems of the North Atlantic fisheries, which had plagued the relations of half a dozen European and North American communities since the end of the fifteenth century, and some of which have not yet been satisfactorily settled. The full story of the international economy thus involved has been set forth in another volume of this series, *The Cod Fisheries*, by Professor H. A. Innis. Finally, there were habits of mind shaped on the one hand by imperial and commercial needs and on the other hand by the challenge of the greatest opportunity that had ever opened before any people in history. Under these circumstances it was perhaps inevitable that the pathway should be marked by many blunders and that the misunderstandings thus created should last on in the traditional history of both the United States and the British Commonwealth of Nations. The application of the scientific method to the historical research of these issues, which were so hotly in debate and ultimately provoked another war, is in itself a contribution to statecraft, because with impartial mind it explores the causes of events in the terms in which they were presented to the actors themselves. Its judgments are not misplaced wishful thinking in the light of the world today but the full statement of how things happened in their own time, when men had other interests to keep in mind than those which seem so important to us now.

War always leaves a heritage of misunderstanding; the period which Professor Burt covers in this volume comprises two wars and deals with the immediate liquidation of both. In the first of them we see the weakness of a United States to carry on foreign relations until a stronger union was set up by the adoption of the Constitution, and even then that "more perfect Union" functioned most effectively in foreign affairs when the executive risked taking a strong initiative. As for the British North American colonies, the day was still far off when a united Dominion was to develop into a free nation of the British Commonwealth. Instead of from the comparatively single direction possible today, policy emerged from an intricate interplay of British Cabinet, Colonial Office, and colonial governors; now one and now another provided the dominant influence. The commonly accepted idea that the United Empire Loyalists worked hand in glove with the governors to maintain a reactionary regime is now seen to be not half the truth, for this first mass migration of Americans took with them a point of view conservative, it is true, but by no means lacking in insistence upon the heritage of freedom which had been their birthright as Britons. This interplay in the social as well as the political structure of Canada and the United States is a theme of inexhaustible interest.

The canvas on which Professor Burt paints the opening drama of the two English-speaking North American nations is enriched with the constant reminder of these springs of action, but the drama itself is that of political decisions of lasting importance in shaping the destiny of the North American continent. The history of this process brings to light the fact that arbitration of the issues inherent in the rise of the new sovereignty on the North American continent here for the first time in the history of international relations became a recognized and practised substitute for war. The outstanding symbol of this process was that agreement which paved the way for an unarmed frontier across the continent, the provision for disarmament on the Great Lakes which had been the scene of more than one battle in the War of 1812. It is a conclusion for which the reader is hardly prepared because on this critical issue the diplomatic jockeying for position which filled so much of the story of negotiations made way for what even the statesmen of the day recognized to be pure common sense. In the century which followed the technique of the old diplomacy continued to play its full part and the provisions for peace between the two countries remained undeveloped or at least informal, a fact which ultimately became of little importance because peace could be taken for granted. The record presented here shows how much this first great step in the actual history of disarmament owes to the Secretary of State who guided the foreign affairs of the United States through the troubled period of the war and one of whose first acts as President was to propose the ratification of the settlement with Britain, James Monroe. It would surely seem appropriate that in the present effort to give greater political reality to the principles underlying the Monroe Doctrine his services in linking the United States with the country to the north under conditions that helped to ensure permanent peace should not be forgotten. But without the generous realism of Castlereagh no such agreement could have been reached. Moreover, as has been shown in other volumes in this series, disarmament only becomes a symbol of real peace in proportion as the pacific settlement of international disputes is adequately provided for and consistently followed. It is to be hoped that this lesson of history will be more definitely applied in the great test which is today being made of the institutions of liberty.

This book, however, was planned and largely written before the present crisis began the momentous test of the fiber of the British Commonwealth on the one hand and the statesmanship of the United States on the other. In it Professor Burt continues the history which he opened up in his other comprehensive volume which dealt with the old Province of Quebec. Here there is the same sure touch of original investigation, and new and authoritative conclusions on the basis of the research.

                                                    J. T. S.

AUTHOR'S PREFACE

I HAVE attempted to reconstruct the story of the relations between the United States and its British neighbors, since combined in the Dominion of Canada, from the time they parted political company until they settled down to live in peace together. Because these neighbors were British, I could not explain the story fully without expanding it to be almost a history of Anglo-American relations during the period under review. Some readers may think that it embraces too much, and others too little; but the nicely calculated less or more will always haunt the diplomatic historian as well as other writers. If critics assail me for the long lumbering title, I would of course ask them how I could help it. I might also suggest that they think of the rose. They may find a further parallel in thorns scattered through the leaves.

This study owes its existence to Professor James T. Shotwell, Director of the Division of Economics and History of the Carnegie Endowment for International Peace. He asked me to undertake it for publication in the series on the Relations of Canada and the United States; and he has greatly enhanced the value of what I have done by securing for it a generous equipment of maps. My first thanks therefore go to him and, for its support, to the Endowment. I am also much indebted to the Graduate School of the University of Minnesota for grants in aid of research which have enabled me to gather original material built into this work; and, in building it, to my colleagues in the History Department of this university for their stimulating intercourse. Another institution to which I am particularly beholden is the Public Archives of Canada. In previous prefaces I have acknowledged my appreciation of the unfailing courtesies which the members of its staff have extended to me through many summers spent in their midst, and now I do it again. Here, too, I must express my gratitude to Professors Allan Nevins and J. Bartlet Brebner of Columbia University, Lester Burrell Shippee and George M. Stephenson of the University of Minnesota, and Gerald S. Graham of Queen's University for critically reading all or part of my manuscript; and to Mr. Arthur E. McFarlane, editorial reader for the Carnegie Endowment, for correcting many a flaw in the text. These gentlemen, needless to say, are entirely innocent of any of the sins of omission or commission which mar the following pages; and so also is another person to whom I must refer, a person who pushes, or is pushed, into many a preface—the author's wife. This one, the best critic I have ever known, has delayed the completion of this volume by making me improve at least one passage in almost every paragraph.

A. L. BURT

Minneapolis,
  June, 1940.

CONTENTS

MAPS

ABBREVIATIONS

A.C.: *Annals of Congress* (Washington, 1854, volumes cited).

Adams: *History of the United States*, Henry Adams (New York, 1889–1891).

A.S.P.F.R.: *American State Papers, Foreign Relations* (Washington, 1833–1834, volumes cited).

A.S.P.I.A.: *American State Papers, Indian Affairs* (Washington, 1832).

A.S.P.M.A.: *American State Papers, Military Affairs* (Washington, 1832).

C: Public Archives of Canada, C Series (Military Papers, originals).

Castlereagh: *Correspondence, Despatches, and other Papers of Viscount Castlereagh*, ed. the third Marquess of Londonderry (London, 1848–1853).

C.O. 42: Colonial Office Papers, Series 42 (transcripts in Public Archives of Canada).

D.C.U.S.: *Diplomatic Correspondence of the United States, 1783-1789* (Washington, 1833).

F.O. 5: Foreign Office Papers, Series 5 (photostat copies in the Library of Congress and the Public Archives of Canada).

G: Public Archives of Canada, G Series (despatches from the Colonial Office to the governments of Upper and Lower Canada, originals).

J.C.C.: *Journals of the Continental Congress* (Washington, 1904–1937).

King: *The Life and Correspondence of Rufus King* ed. C. R. King (New York, 1894–1900).

Madison: *The Writings of James Madison* ed. G. Hunt (New York, 1900–1910).

New Brunswick A: Public Archives of Canada, Series New Brunswick A (correspondence between the government of New Brunswick and the Colonial Office, transcripts from the Public Record Office).

Nova Scotia A: Public Archives of Canada, Series Nova Scotia A (correspondence between the government of Nova Scotia and the Colonial Office, transcripts from the Public Record Office).

P.A.C.R.: *Public Archives of Canada Report* (Ottawa, annually).

Q: Public Archives of Canada, Q Series (the correspondence of the Colonial Office with the government of the old Province of Quebec and the governments of Upper and Lower Canada, transcripts from the Public Record Office).

Q, . . . in M.P.H.C.: Extract from Q in *Michigan Pioneer and Historical Collections*.

R.D.C.U.S.: *The Revolutionary Diplomatic Correspondence of the United States*, ed. Francis Wharton (Washington, 1889).

S.P.: *The Simcoe Papers*, ed. E. A. Cruikshank (Toronto, 1923–1926).

THE UNITED STATES, GREAT BRITAIN, AND BRITISH NORTH AMERICA

CHAPTER I

THE PARTING OF THE WAYS

THE American Revolution created the problem of Canadian-American relations by tearing the thirteen colonies away from the British Empire and leaving two contiguous colonies behind: the old Nova Scotia, out of which New Brunswick was presently carved, and the old Canada, which was then officially known as the Province of Quebec and should not be confused with the modern province of that name. From 1713 the peninsula of Nova Scotia had been united under the same sovereignty with the English colonies on the Atlantic seaboard. For fifty years of this period they had been separated by French territory on the mainland, but in 1763, when France ceded the rest of Acadia, Nova Scotia was enlarged to make its boundary march with that of New England. At the same time France transferred her title to Canada, whose political association with the English colonies to the south was thus of much shorter duration. Why did these neighbors part company? A complete answer to this question would of course include a full statement of all the causes of the Revolution, which are so well known that there is no need to repeat them here, even in summary. Nor is it necessary to give a detailed account of the war as it affected Canada and Nova Scotia. For the purpose of this study, a sufficient answer may be found in an examination of the action and reaction between these two surviving colonies and the revolutionary movement.

The British conquest of Canada precipitated the American Revolution, which in turn threatened to engulf the colony on the St. Lawrence. Because Canada commanded the back doors of the thirteen colonies, it had long inspired fear in American hearts, and it continued to do so. Though the conquest killed one fear, it gave birth to another. In place of the old one which had kept them loyal to the mother country, arose a new one which made them fight her in Canada, where Britain seemed to have stepped into the shoes of France. The new danger assumed more menacing proportions than the old one, for France had been able to strike them only in the rear whereas Britain, with her sea power, could also smite them in front.

Though the passage of the Quebec Act[1] has often been cited as a cause

1. For a fuller discussion of the Quebec Act and its relation to the Revolution, see A. L. Burt, *The Old Province of Quebec* (Minneapolis and Toronto, 1933).

of the American Revolution, and the coming of the Revolution as the explanation of the Quebec Act, there is good reason for rejecting both interpretations of these events. The American upheaval would in all probability have come independently of the act, and the main features of the act were determined by Canadian conditions long before the incidents which provoked the famous penal legislation with which it has been confused. The complicated reason for the extension of Canada to include all the territory north of the Ohio will be explained in the next chapter, where it is necessary for an understanding of the settlement of the international boundary in the treaty of 1783. Here, however, we should note a passage which Americans, even to this day, have often overlooked when reading the act. It stipulated "that nothing herein contained, relative to the Boundary of the Province of Quebec, shall in anywise affect the Boundaries of any other Colony." By this saving clause, the old colonies' claims to the interior were preserved *in toto*.

The other sections of the act were designed to solve the peculiar problem of government in Canada. In 1763, partly out of ignorance and partly out of false expectations,[2] the authorities in London had assumed that the newly acquired country would fit into the traditional pattern of a British colony with the laws of England and an elected assembly. Orders were accordingly issued, and the result was disastrous. The French Canadians, who were solidly Roman Catholic, had a treaty guarantee of their religion, but the laws of Great Britain excluded them utterly from any share in the government. This was an impossible situation because they numbered more than sixty thousand at the time of the conquest and they were increasing rapidly, whereas the newly arrived English-speaking population, totaling scarcely two thousand and confined to the towns of Quebec and Montreal, was relatively stationary. As only the latter could sit in an assembly, the governor refused to call one; and thereby he deprived the colony not only of a legislature but also of a revenue. English criminal law was administered without difficulty, but the Canadian people could not be made to regulate their private affairs in accordance with the strange civil law. The failure jeopardized their individual property rights. There were also disquieting doubts about the material foundation of their church. Could it hold property, and could it collect tithes under British rule? In 1766, the British government began to turn away from the futile and dangerous policy that had been adopted for Canada in 1763.

The Quebec Act was the product of years of investigation, and was an honest effort to provide this foreign colony with a constitution adapted to

2. That a considerable English-speaking population, from a surplus of the old colonies, would pour into Canada; and that the Canadians would easily be persuaded to become Protestant.

its nature, for only thus could it be incorporated into the Empire. Given a government that was Canadian in character, a government that would leave no grievance to rankle in Canadian breasts, the new subjects would be weaned from their old allegiance and, though they might never become English, they would become truly British. This was the purpose of the act. It embodied a new sovereign principle of the British Empire: the liberty of non-English people to be themselves. Here is the reason why Canada got Catholic emancipation more than half a century before the mother country. Here is the reason for the recognition of the old civil laws, which protected the property of the church as well as that of the people and also preserved the tithe.

This legal restoration, however, was to be qualified out of consideration for the English-speaking newcomers. It was explicitly enacted that the Roman Catholic clergy could not collect tithes from Protestants, and the governor was instructed to have the legislative council modify the civil law so that the British minority would lose as little as possible—to preserve for them the right of habeas corpus and the laws of England governing torts and "personal actions grounded upon debts, promises, contracts, and agreements, whether of a mercantile or other nature." This included jury trials for civil suits. The act did not abolish trial by jury for criminal cases.

An assembly was out of the question. It was an English institution which the French Canadians neither understood nor desired. Nor were they to be trusted with one, for they were newly conquered subjects of doubtful loyalty. The small racial minority had clamored for an assembly, but they did not want it unless they were allowed to control it—an intolerable condition. Yet the country could not do without a legislature and a revenue. Was there any better way out of the impasse than that which the British government found: a nominated council, intended to comprise the leading members of both races, which was endowed with only a limited legislative authority because it was not elected; and the employment of Parliament's taxing power to raise a revenue in the colony?

Because British officials had to wrestle for years with the novel and complex problem in Canada before they worked out this solution, it is not surprising that the whole business was entirely beyond the comprehension of people in the old colonies. Under any circumstances they would have misinterpreted the reversal of British policy on the St. Lawrence, and at that time their imagination was already so disordered by their own resistance to imperial measures and by the home government's retaliation that they were sure to see wild visions in anything that Britain did short of yielding to their every demand. They naturally leaped to the conclusion that the Quebec Act was a dastardly blow aimed through Canada at them. By extending the Canadian boundary down the Ohio, did it not threaten to coop them up on the narrow Atlantic seaboard? Did it not reëstablish Roman Catholicism, the religion of tyranny? Did it not deny popular government, the very article of their political faith? What was the meaning of all this unless Britain was beginning to forge in Canada a weapon with which she would strike them in the back? Thus the Quebec Act innocently revived the terror of bygone days, and thereby caused the American Revolution at the very outset to thrust a fiery arm up into Canada.

The invasion of Canada might never have occurred and the Revolution might have been nipped in the bud if the British government had been intent on using Canada against the old colonies. As early as February, 1767, Guy Carleton had urged from Quebec the erection of a great stronghold there, another in New York, and the secure linking of these two *points d'appui* by the restoration of the crumbling walls of Crown Point, Ticonderoga, and Fort George. He had a penetrating eye for strategy, and he would have given British military power a stranglehold on America. But this masterly advice fell on deaf ears. Shortly afterwards he began to plead with the home government to raise one or two French-Canadian regiments for the regular army, and he repeated this prayer for years. His avowed motive was not anti-American but pro-Canadian. He would purchase the support of those whom France had employed and Britain was neglecting. In September, 1774, after an absence of four years in England, he returned to Quebec with his prayer unanswered. But he was not greatly concerned over what was withheld because he saw a good substitute in the Quebec Act, which evoked a chorus of praise from noblesse and clergy. Indeed he now felt so little need for soldiers in his province that he promptly sent off two of his four regiments to Boston. This was in response to a letter he received the day after his arrival. It was from Gage, whose attempt to apply the recent penal legislation had roused popular defiance which he was too weak to crush. The commander-in-chief also inquired if the governor could raise a body of Canadians and Indians for service against the old colonies if necessary, and the latter replied that the Canadians would be delighted to form a regiment were they allowed to do so and that the appearance of a Canadian unit would encourage the Indians. "But," he added by way of caution, "you know what sort of people they are." When copies of this correspondence reached London, the permanent undersecretary reported to his chief: "I thought this idea of General Gage's so expressive of his own timidity and weakness as well as so likely to excite popular resentment here, should it get abroad, that I have taken care to keep the letters secret in the office." [3] Meanwhile Carleton was left with less than eight hundred effectives in detachments which were scattered all the way from Quebec to Michilimackinac. He had virtually denuded the colony of troops.

There were other reasons why the door of Canada was wide open for the Revolution to enter. The English-speaking population were largely an offshoot from that of the old colonies; their traditions and connections drew them to sympathize with the American cause. They were undoubtedly thinking of poor Boston in the fall of 1774 when they sent a thousand bushels of wheat from Quebec and a big bill of exchange from Montreal to help feed the poor of Boston. The punitive measures of the British government had quickened their American patriotism, and something else was pushing them toward rebellion. They found themselves in an alarming predicament which gave them more justification for denouncing Britain's tyranny than had any people in the old colonies outside the capital of Massachusetts. In 1763 the King had promised them an assembly, but Parliament had canceled the royal word. This was a hard blow, but they might have borne it philosophically if it had not been followed by another which convinced them that the British government was purposely robbing them of their British birthright. For some reason which is not yet fully clear, Carleton did not let them have even a hint of the instructions mentioned above, and thereby he drove them to the natural but false conclusion that the home government intended to make a clean sweep of English civil law with its habeas corpus and jury trials.

The mass of the French Canadians did not share the enthusiasm of the clergy and the noblesse for the Quebec Act. Carleton had persuaded London that these two classes, if won, would pull the people after them. Here he made a curious blunder. Though he repeatedly pointed out that the broad conditions of life in America made for democracy, he had failed to observe how these very conditions had produced in New France a society fundamentally different from that of old France. He fondly imagined that the habitants had been hewers of wood and drawers of water for the priests and the seigniors, and he sought to restore what had never existed on the shores of the St. Lawrence—a well-ordered society controlled through these leaders. The clergy, who were in closer contact with the masses and were not to receive any new power, were more discreet than the noblesse. But the jubilation of the latter, whom he would place in the saddle where they had never sat, stirred uneasy feelings among the people.

Before Americans appealed to arms, they tried the effect of words to

3. Knox to Dartmouth, Nov. 15, 1774, Patshull MSS., unpaged, in P.A.C.

neutralize the dreaded Canadians.[4] In October, 1774, the Continental Congress addressed a long letter to them. It proclaimed their rights as British subjects to government by their own elected representatives, to trial by jury, to habeas corpus, to free tenures, and to liberty of the press; it pointed out how Parliament had violated these fundamental liberties by imposing a government composed of tools of the governor who, in turn, was the tool of the British government; it informed them that they were even in danger of having the inquisition thrust upon them; it invited them to join in an eternal brotherhood of liberty and to begin by forming a provincial congress which would send delegates to the next Continental Congress in the following May; and it warned them that if they would not be friends they would be treated as foes. It mattered little that the only point which the unlettered habitant could grasp was the last one. The Revolutionary gospel carried up from the south found in the English-speaking minority eager missionaries who knew how to shape it for French-Canadian consumption, for they were familiar with the country. Then Jean Baptiste was reminded that he had taken an oath not to bear arms against the English, which of course included their American brethren; he discovered that the *Bastonnais* were "as numerous as the stars" and would blast his country if he opposed them; and he learned to his horror that wicked Britain was going to drag him off to fight her battles under distant skies. These and other wild rumors flew through the valleys of the Richelieu and the St. Lawrence during the winter and spring, rousing untold hopes and fears.

Within a month of the outbreak of hostilities in the spring of 1775, the only obstacles to a military advance on Canada were swept away by insurgents who surprised Ticonderoga and Crown Point and seized control of Lake Champlain by capturing the one armed vessel upon it. Colonel Guy Johnson, the nephew and successor of Sir William, offered to retaliate by loosing his savage hordes upon the revolting colonies, but Carleton, to his lasting honor, flatly refused. He would remain on the defensive. Attention was then focused upon St. Johns on the Richelieu, the back door of the colony. The governor bent all his energies to bar it while American forces gathered to batter it down. To hold the fort, he put almost all his soldiers in it, and he lost them when it fell early in November.

The invaders, who numbered several thousand, were then free to overrun the country, but that was not their purpose. They wanted to go home. Having signed up for only a few months, their term of service was

4. Gustave Lanctot (ed.), *Le Canada-Français et ses voisins du sud* (Montréal, 1940) contains, *inter alia*, interesting materials concerning French-Canadian responses to the American Revolution.

expiring and they had to get back to attend to their own affairs. Moreover they had accomplished the object of their campaign. With the Declaration of Independence and official war against Britain still in the future, the appeal to arms was as yet designed only to repel the immediate danger and, if possible, to teach wisdom to a stupid government in

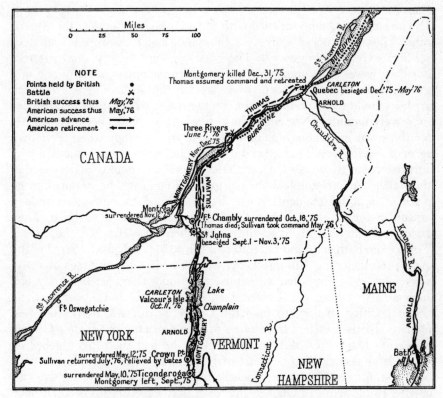

The American Invasion of Canada, 1775–1776

London. Canada was no longer a sword of Damocles. The victorious army dissolved. Some eight hundred, however, reënlisted until the spring. They did it at the behest of Richard Montgomery, their able general, whose plans were suddenly changed on the day he entered Montreal, where he had expected to spend the winter unless he went home too.

What changed Montgomery's mind was the news that Benedict Arnold had appeared before Quebec. This adventurer, having conceived the idea of surprising Quebec while all the British troops were imprisoned in St. Johns, had led an expedition up the Kennebec and down the Chaudière, losing half his men and all his baggage on the terrible journey. He arrived with no guns, little ammunition, and less than seven hundred ragged recruits. Montgomery felt committed to join him and take command; but, being obliged to leave garrisons behind, could bring down only half as many men as Arnold had before the citadel of Canada.

The siege of Quebec opened with the odds heavily against the Americans. These numbered scarcely a thousand, and they were all amateur soldiers except their general. The garrison were mostly amateurs too, but they were more numerous and their commander was only one of a group of professional officers who directed the defense. The American artillery could make no impression on the walls, where more and heavier guns were mounted. Nor could the besiegers reduce Quebec by blockade, for the town had enough supplies to last until spring, when their own term of service would expire and British relief was sure to come. Only by surprise could they take Quebec. They hoped for some treachery within the walls, but Carleton had already guarded against that by purging the place of doubtful elements. One chance seemed to remain—a sudden assault under cover of darkness and, if possible, of a snowstorm. They tried it on the last night of the year, when they attacked the Lower Town from both ends and ran into two traps. More than a hundred of the assailants, including Montgomery, were killed and four times as many were captured. They had attempted the impossible. Even if they had succeeded in taking the Lower Town they would have been in little better position, if any, to take the Upper Town, which was the real fortress. British writers have often praised Carleton for saving Canada by saving Quebec on this occasion, but if he had then lost Quebec he would have deserved to be court-martialed and Canada would not have been lost, for the armament which Britain sent out in the spring was calculated to blow out of Quebec any force that the Americans could have placed in it.

The one astonishing thing about the siege is that it was not broken by this terrible repulse. Reduced by more than half and smitten by smallpox, the investing force clung to their hopeless task partly out of bravado and partly out of fear of what might happen to them if they retreated, for the country people were now much less friendly. A vigorous sortie might have ruined the pitiful fragment of an army that lay outside the walls, but Carleton remained steadily upon the defensive, and after a few weeks the besiegers began to receive recruits. The Continental Congress was determined to retrieve the disaster and to complete the conquest. But this too was impossible.

Though fresh American troops were rushed north as fast as they could be collected, they were fatally short of supplies and lacking in discipline. Smallpox swept through their ranks as they inoculated themselves to escape duty or to gain immunity. The colonial army in Canada became a churning mass of confusion; and congressional commissioners, led by Benjamin Franklin, who went up to Montreal to regulate the occupation threw up their hands and headed for home.

The population was also turning against the invaders. In the beginning, the Canadians had been most hospitable, and several hundred of them—more than rallied to Carleton's call—turned out as companions-in-arms to fight for American liberty, whatever they may have thought it meant. The fortuitous friendship, based on no mutual understanding, melted away under several influences. The obvious incapacity of the Americans ruined the habitants' hopes that their new-found friends might win salvation for them. The exhaustion of American money and supplies let the weight of the invasion fall more and more heavily upon the Canadians. For their goods and services, worthless paper was thrust upon them who, of all people, were the least willing to take it because the dying French regime had recently plundered them with it. Religious antipathy was another powerful dissolvent. Being Protestants in a Roman Catholic land, the invaders could not conceal their bigotry; and the clergy of Canada, being convinced that their church would be much safer under British rule, threw all their weight against the Americans.

Much more decisive was what Carleton and the home government had done. When the Americans first swarmed round St. Johns, he had written to London again pressing his plan of cutting the old colonies in two, observing that there was no better base of operations than the St. Lawrence and a completely equipped army of ten or twelve thousand men sent out in the spring "might greatly change the face of things on this continent." This appeal, followed in a few weeks by news that St. Johns had surrendered and Quebec was being invested, stirred the ministry to do exactly as the governor advised. The army was dispatched early in 1776, Britain's main military effort for that year in America.

Had this great blow been directed at the seat of the war instead of being thus diverted to the periphery, the Revolution might have been crushed. Therefore it may appear that the invasion of Canada, though a tactical failure, was a great strategic success which made possible the achievement of American independence. This is the way events worked out, but the diversion was not the effective cause of this strategic victory. A closer examination of what followed the sending of this large force to the St. Lawrence shows that the crucial turning point came afterwards.

Carleton held the fate of the Empire in his hands in the early summer of 1776. The Americans scuttled away from Quebec when they saw two sails approaching on May 6, though they had no idea that a mighty armament from Britain was coming. They thought they were fleeing from a much smaller reinforcement sent from Halifax. Recovering from their panic and strengthened by the arrival of more troops from the south, they halted their retreat at Sorel and advanced on Three Rivers, only to fall into a snare which caught some and from which none could have escaped had not Carleton strangely opened the way for them by recalling a contingent that hemmed them in on the southwest. Even then he had all the Americans in the country at his mercy; for, still ignorant of his overwhelming strength, they were loath to abandon Sorel. He ordered Burgoyne to follow but not to press them up the Richelieu while he himself conducted the main body up the St. Lawrence to Longueuil and thence marched across to St. Johns to catch them in the rear. He was at Varennes, just below Montreal, on the afternoon of Saturday, June 15, and he could have reached his objective on Sunday while the retreating Americans were still many miles below. But he sat still and they scrambled on. Late Monday evening they tumbled into St. Johns. On Tuesday, their boats having just come up from the south, they departed. Burgoyne arrived as the last of them drew out of range. Carleton and his army did not appear until next morning, Wednesday!

Had Carleton sprung his trap according to plan, he could have done much more than capture the whole body of the invaders. He could have seized their boats, which would have immediately given him what cost him the rest of the campaigning season to procure by building—the command of Lake Champlain and the means of moving his army up it. Then he could have struck straight down the Hudson to New York, according to his original idea and the home government's intention, for the conditions which were to entangle Burgoyne when he attempted it in the following year had not yet developed. The cut right down the middle of the old colonies, coming on top of the complete loss of their northern army, might easily have destroyed the Revolution before it had gathered headway. Carleton's amazing delay in reaching St. Johns led to Saratoga; this precipitated France into the war; and French sea power tipped the scales against Britain. Carleton presented the Americans with their strategic victory. There should be a public monument to him in Washington.

Why did this British general refrain from applying his own commanding strategy when, at his own request, he was fully equipped to carry it out? Apparently the statesman in him had suddenly risen to overrule the soldier. This explanation is suggested by his generous treatment of the prisoners he had taken, and by various passages in his letters of that time. In common with many other prominent Britons, he pitied the "rebels" and regarded them as "deluded subjects" led astray by designing congressional leaders. He wanted to prove, as he said, that "the way of mercy is not yet shut," and to give "such testimonies . . . of the humanity and forbearance with which His Majesty's just resentment towards his revolted subjects is tempered as may serve effectually to counteract the dangerous designs of those desperate people whose fatal ascendency over them has already conducted them to the brink of ruin." As the Declaration of Independence was still in the future, he may well have imagined that in letting them all go he was holding his hand from pushing them over the brink. He may also have thought that the blow which he ought to have struck could be delivered with telling effect at a later date should his humanitarian calculations prove vain. Neither he nor anyone else could foresee that the military opportunity which he was throwing away was being forever lost.

The entry of France into the war revived the project of conquering Canada. What the Americans had not been able to do by themselves, they might accomplish with the aid of their ally. This ally had more soldiers than Britain, a fleet that qualified her command of the sea, and the ability to exert a tremendous pull upon the Canadian people, who were bound to her by ties of race and religion. In the autumn of 1778, the Continental Congress adopted an elaborate plan, which originated with Lafayette, for conquering Canada in the spring of 1779. American armies were to advance upon Detroit, Niagara, Oswego, and Montreal, while a French expedition was to sail up the St. Lawrence to capture Quebec. Already the foundations of British rule in the north were shaken by the news that France had declared war on Britain. Borne on the wings of the wind, the tidings flew from village to village, awakening old memories and new hopes in Canadian hearts. They leaped at the call of the blood. Now the French admiral in American waters spoke directly to them. A few days after the above congressional decision, he published an appeal in which he said, "Vous êtes nés François, vous n'avez pu cesser de l'être"; and mysterious hands soon posted this proclamation at the church doors throughout Canada. The two classes upon whom Carleton had relied to confirm the masses in their new allegiance were themselves being drawn back to their old allegiance. Sedition was seething on the shores of the St. Lawrence and the days of Canada as a British colony seemed to be numbered.

Washington intervened, condemning the scheme before the French government could pass judgment upon it. In a letter to the Continental Congress, he raised all manner of practical objections which he summed up by saying that the plan was "not only too expensive and beyond our abilities, but too complex." The real reason for his opposition, he explained privately to the president of the congress. Would French troops surrender the key of Canada if they got it? France reëstablished on the St. Lawrence and Spain, her ally, controlling the mouth of the Mississippi would be in a position to throttle the United States. The ambitious but dangerous plan was shelved in January, 1779. Later, however, Washington changed his mind about the designs of France and came to think that such a plan might add Canada to the United States. In the spring of 1780, and again in 1781, after the surrender of Cornwallis at Yorktown, he proposed it. Then the French vetoed it, the first time on the ground that the proper American objective was the British headquarters in New York, and the second time with the excuse that Louis XVI had joined the Americans in arms to help them win independence, not conquests. The underlying but unavowed reason for the French refusal was the calculation that Canada in the hands of Britain would keep the Americans dependent upon France, just as it had kept them dependent on Britain until she conquered it. Neither of the allies wished the other to get this colony. Each preferred Britain to keep it. Thus it happened that the alliance which made Canada almost fatally vulnerable was politically, though not physically, incapable of striking the combined blow which might have wrested it from the Empire.

Turning to the problem of Nova Scotia during the Revolution,[5] we find a very different set of circumstances. Despite the fact that the imperial association of this province with the "old thirteen" had been much longer than that of Canada, Nova Scotia had little in common with them until about the time that Canada fell, when a complete change in the nature of its population occurred and, as a consequence, an assembly was established in Halifax. The expulsion of all but a fragment of the Acadians in 1755 obliterated the French character of the colony and cleared the ground for British settlers. At once New Englanders began to move in. Twenty years later, they constituted three-quarters of the population, and their political sympathies were naturally with the land of their birth. Only a fraction of the other quarter, the English and the Scots, could be expected to evince an active loyalty to Britain during the war, for the remainder were Acadians, Germans, and Irish. There was such an official distrust of the popular temper that the assembly which had been elected in 1770 was not dissolved until 1785—a colonial Long Parliament. Why, then, was Nova Scotia not drawn into the Revolution?

It has been suggested that the interest of the province, and particularly

5. For the most recent treatment of this subject, see J. B. Brebner, *The Neutral Yankees of Nova Scotia* (New York, 1937).

that of its capital, operated to preserve this portion of the Empire. The material profits of the imperial connection greatly outweighed the cost, and the war magnified the favorable balance. Over against the prospect of moderate taxation by Parliament stood the annual parliamentary grant, upon which the government of the province depended for revenue; the local expenditure of British money on naval and military establishments, which might now be multiplied; and, according to some, the possibility of supplanting New England in the valuable West Indian trade as well as in the fisheries, from both of which the rebellious colonies were excluded by parliamentary enactment. But other colonies had likewise been receiving extensive financial aid from the mother country, and yet they revolted. They also experienced the conflict between commercial motives and the revolutionary urge, but they succumbed to the latter. As for the West Indian trade and the fisheries, Nova Scotia had been relatively uninterested in the former and could not begin to supply its demand for grain and flour; and the fisheries now attracted so many men from Massachusetts to establish legal residence in Nova Scotia as to rouse official British fears of political contamination.

In Halifax, it is true, the mercantile community was so identified with the official class that together they formed a solid body which dominated the town and commonly controlled the assembly, where they were over-represented and attendance was difficult for the country members. But the capital, the only real town, was a small place of only eighteen hundred inhabitants, and this diminutive oligarchy had little influence over the rest of the province. "The hand of Halifax was never very heavy beyond the Bedford basin during the Revolution." [6] This was inevitable because the population of the province lived in more or less isolated communities scattered around the long indented coast with scarcely any land communication between them.

Here we touch upon the real explanation of the problem. The very factor which inhibited Halifax from holding these dispersed settlements within the British fold also inhibited them from leaving it. In Nova Scotia, as in the colony on the St. Lawrence, geography and the national character of the people determined the history of the province during the imperial crisis. A glance at the only overt attempt to draw Nova Scotia into the Revolution brings out the point clearly.

The story of this attempt begins in Machias, a fishing and lumbering settlement founded in 1763 by a handful of New Englanders who seven years later secured a grant of the township from Massachusetts after vainly applying to Nova Scotia. The latter, it should perhaps be observed, was then commonly regarded as a colony of the former and was

6. *Ibid.*, p. 344.

separated from it by a boundary of uncertain location. To Machias in 1771 came the Reverend James Lyon of the College of New Jersey, and he became the revolutionary as well as the religious leader of the flock. He had spent several years as a parson in Nova Scotia, and now he preached its conquest for the Revolution. In August, 1775, a Machias proposal to dispatch an expedition of a thousand men who would rouse the revolutionaries and subdue the Tories in Nova Scotia was submitted to General Washington, who commended the spirit of the promoters but politely condemned their scheme as impracticable because any force that invaded that province could be cut off by sea. Neither he, nor the Continental Congress, nor the legislature of Massachusetts, would send such a force though the appeal was renewed and reinforced by a growing cry for deliverance which came from Americans in Nova Scotia. But Jonathan Eddy, one of the New Englanders who had settled in Cumberland County, was not to be denied.

In the autumn of 1776, Eddy set out from Machias to take Fort Cumberland on the isthmus. Though he started with only twenty recruits, he was confident of gathering many more on his way and of rallying most of the population on his arrival. As he proceeded, his following grew to seventy-two; and after they disembarked from their small boats and canoes at the head of the Bay of Fundy they were joined by about a hundred New Englanders and Acadians, but not all of these local insurgents ever appeared in arms at the same time. The population was little encouraged by the slim prospect of capturing the fort held by two hundred regulars. The filibuster wrote back to Boston, begging for guns and men; but the only reinforcement that came was for the garrison—two companies of marines accompanied by a man-of-war. A night attack destroyed the camp of the besiegers and blew them away in the greatest disorder. Some three score inhabitants, too compromised to remain, followed Eddy on his flight back to Machias. The cry for deliverance continued, but there was no further answer save words.

Divide et impera. The dispersion of the Nova Scotian population in small settlements isolated from one another rendered them powerless in the days which tried their souls. But even if they had been living in close mutual contact, still they would have been powerless. The New Englanders of Nova Scotia, though the bulk of the population, were too few to try conclusions with the British garrison, which could be augmented when and as necessary; and they were too inaccessible from the old colonies for any revolutionary army to rescue them. Like their Acadian predecessors in this land, they were unwilling prisoners of British power and they likewise pleaded for permission to remain neutral. When the militia was called out for the defense of the province, which was infested

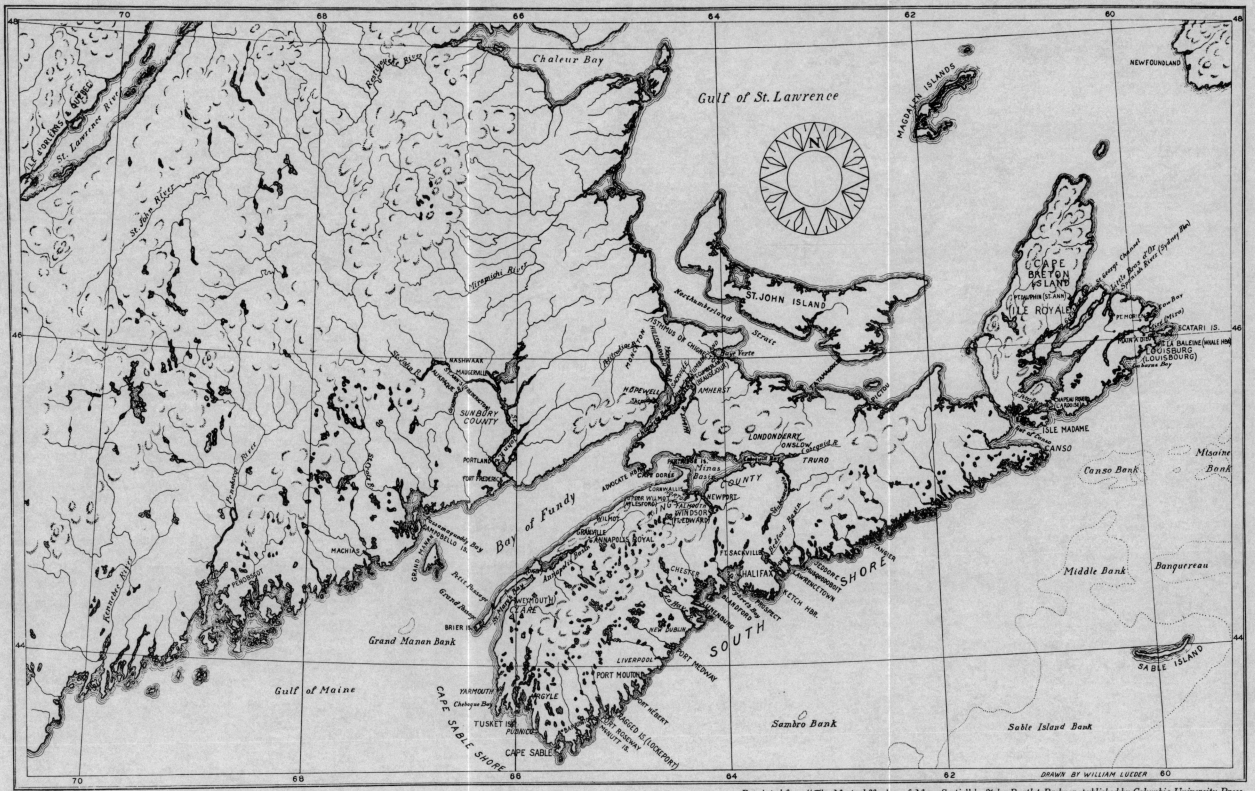

Nova Scotia at the Time of the American Revolution

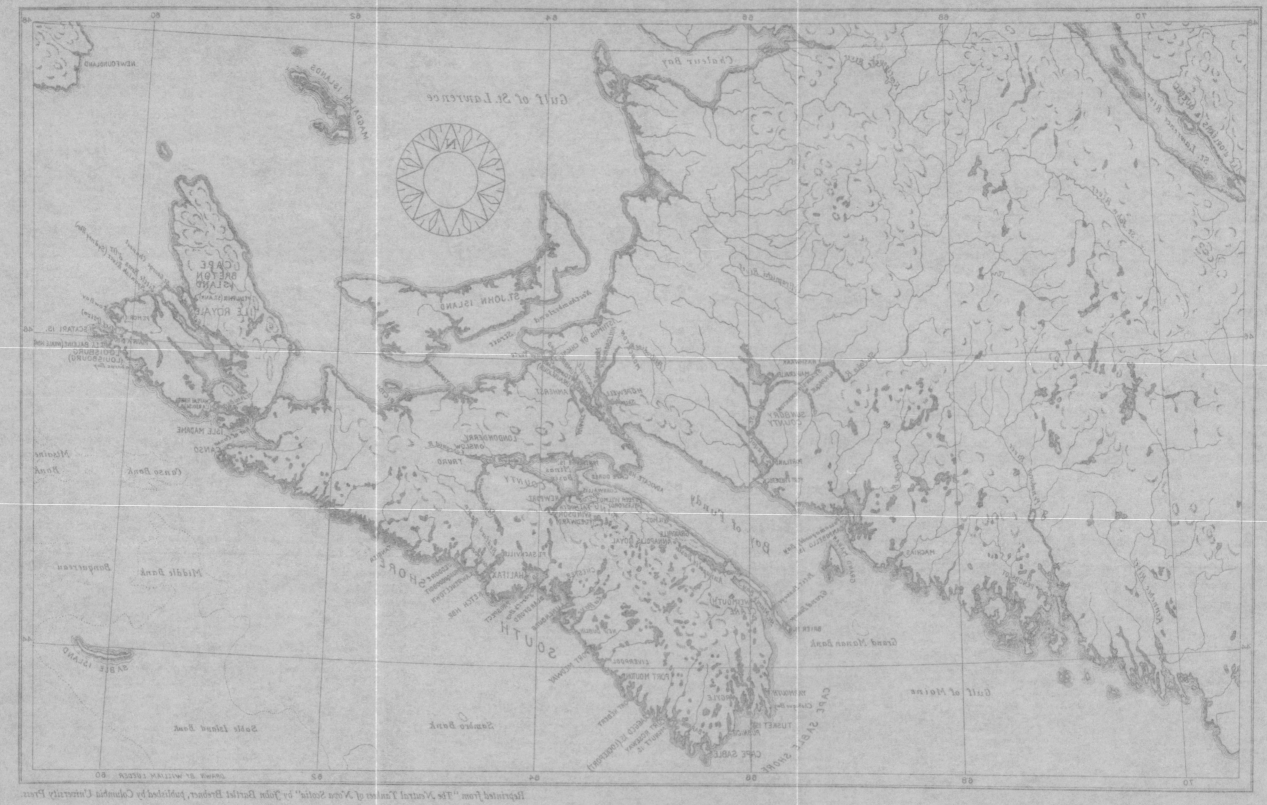

by privateers, most of the people were recalcitrant and their suppressed feelings were voiced by the inhabitants of Yarmouth who submitted a memorial to the governor saying, "We were almost all of us born in New England, we have Fathers, Brothers & Sisters in that country, divided betwixt natural affection to our nearest relations, and good Faith and Friendship to our King and Country, we want to know, if we may be permitted at this time to live in a peaceable State, as we look on that to be the only situation in which we with our Wives and Children, can be in any tolerable degree safe."[7]

Before the close of the war which severed the provinces of Quebec and Nova Scotia from their American neighbors, the Continental Congress prepared a constitution which provided for the inclusion of the former but not of the latter in the new independent union. The distinction may seem curious in light of the fact that the rejected colony had a New England population whereas the other was completely foreign in character. But again geography supplies the explanation. No protecting arm of the sea separated the United States from Canada, and for almost another generation Americans continued to live in fear of a British attack from that quarter. Nova Scotia, on the other hand, had never appeared as a menace to them, and it was clearly beyond their reach.

In concluding our examination of the reactions between the Revolution and these two surviving colonies, we should not fail to observe that the former left upon the latter an indelible British stamp which thenceforth colored the relations between the United States and British North America. In 1783, the old Nova Scotia experienced a change of character as great as that of 1755, and it came just as swiftly. The "neutral Yankees of Nova Scotia" were swamped by a flood of Loyalists, thirty thousand of them, who had been stripped of their worldly possessions, driven from their homes, and expelled from the land of their birth. They had as little love for the United States as Americans had for Britain. They founded New Brunswick, which was carved out of Nova Scotia in 1784, and they dominated the society in the rest of the old province. The Revolution was also responsible for extending settlement and altering the composition of the population of the old Province of Quebec, which was therefore split into Upper and Lower Canada in 1791. A thousand Loyalists were absorbed in the lower province, and more than five times as many laid the foundations of Upper Canada in 1784.

7. *Ibid.*, p. 310.

CHAPTER II

THE DIVIDING LINE

To understand the definition of the international boundary in the peace treaty of 1783, we have to begin with a document published twenty years earlier: the royal proclamation of October 7, 1763. Only two of the things it did are pertinent here: it defined the geographical limits of the old Province of Quebec, which was then created, and it announced the establishment of a huge Indian reserve in the heart of the continent.

Hitherto Canada had possessed no fixed boundaries, for Britain and France could never agree upon a dividing line between their empires in America;[1] but as soon as they were united, by conquest and cession, definition became possible. Thus it fell to the British Crown to draw the first boundary around old Canada. Two stretches of this boundary were to acquire an unforeseen and lasting international importance. That which ran along the forty-fifth parallel of latitude from the St. Lawrence eastward, and then followed the highlands separating the waters flowing into the Atlantic from those flowing into the St. Lawrence, was copied with slight variation by the Quebec Act of 1774, and was recopied by the Treaty of Paris in 1783. This portion of the present international border, then, comes straight from the definition in 1763, and therefore it is interesting to recall the original purpose of this particular line. It sprang from the solid French character of the newly conquered colony. The authorities in London were consciously cutting off unoccupied territory to the south in order to preserve it for English-speaking settlement.[2]

Less permanent but much more important was another section of the boundary described in the proclamation of 1763. From the point where the forty-fifth parallel intersects the St. Lawrence, it pursued a direct course to the southern end of Lake Nipissing. Of what is now Ontario, only a narrow ribbon of land lying along the Ottawa remained to Canada. Much more than the whole of modern Ontario was severed, for the hinterland of Canada under French rule stretched out to the Mississippi and down the Ohio to join Louisiana. Though the English colonies had certain paper claims to parts of this enormous territory, these were no better than the corresponding French claim, and the French claim was

1. Max Savelle, *The Diplomatic History of the Canadian Boundary*, 1749–1763 (New Haven, 1940).
2. Adam Shortt and A. G. Doughty (eds.), *Documents Relating to the Constitutional History of Canada*, 1759–1791, pp. 140–142.

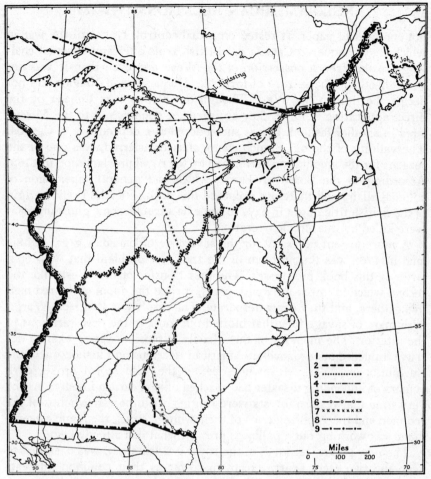

The Evolution of the Boundary in the Negotiations for Peace, 1782

1. The southern boundary of the old Province of Quebec as defined by the Proclamation of October 7, 1763.

2. The "Proclamation Line" limiting white settlement, October 7, 1763.

3. The "Fort Stanwix Line" defined by the Treaty of Fort Stanwix, November 5, 1768.

4. The southern and western boundary of the old Province of Quebec as defined by the Quebec Act, 1774.

5. Line prescribed by the Continental Congress in the Instructions of August 14, 1779. (From Lake Nipissing it was to run straight to the source of the Mississippi, then unknown but supposed to lie much farther north than it is.)

6. Possible boundary according to Gouverneur Morris, 1781(?).

7. Western line proposed by Aranda, August 3, 1782.

8. Western line proposed by Rayneval, September 6, 1782.

9. The northern boundary of the United States, with alternatives between the St. Lawrence and the Mississippi, as defined in the preliminaries of November 5, 1782. (With the elimination of the alternative along the forty-fifth parallel, it became the line of the preliminaries of November 30, 1782, and of the definitive peace treaty, September 3, 1783.)

not confined to paper. It rested on actual control. Not until the war in which they conquered Canada did British arms offer any effectual challenge to the French possession of the West, and even then it was not very effectual. The seizure of forts like Duquesne and Niagara did not decide the title to the West. Though the British took Canada by the direct application of force, they acquired the country out to the Mississippi in another fashion. It was surrendered as a dependency of Canada. The validity of the old French claim, thus transferred, was one of the reasons for the amputation performed by the royal proclamation in 1763. According to the Board of Trade, which had general supervision of colonial affairs and therefore prepared this document, the French origin of the British title might in days to come be a troublesome ghost unless it were killed by this simple operation.

A more urgent necessity for the severance of Canada's great hinterland in 1763 was the problem of the Indian, a problem that will loom large as this book progresses. The first transfer of the West, like the second which followed in twenty years, spelled the doom of the red men living there, and they grew desperate. The result was Pontiac's War, a nightmare of savage fury that blotted out most of the new garrisons in the interior. The memory of this ghastly explosion was to exert a decisive influence upon Canadian-American relations on the morrow of the Revolutionary War. Meanwhile, before the wild storm broke, dark rumors of impending disaster had reached official ears in London. At the very time the western forests were ringing with the war whoops of the red men and the agonized cries of their white victims, the home government was working out a policy to prevent what had already begun.

The new policy, set forth in the royal proclamation, was designed to keep the two races apart, except in so far as their common interests would bring them together. The heart of the continent was to be a great Indian reserve. Settlers were not to encroach upon it, but traders might enter freely to provide red society with the goods it needed and white society with the furs it wanted. Britain's colonies were to be confined to the eastern margin of America. Though some men in England urged such a restriction for imperial reasons, and others in America have suspected such a motive, it is very doubtful if the proclamation was intended to cramp the colonies. The proclamation itself provided for the day when they might need some of the land thus set aside. Such territory as the Indians would then be willing to abandon was to be purchased from them in formal council by a representative of the Crown. What Britain was really trying to do was to protect her own children by protecting her dusky wards in their ancestral hunting grounds.

To implement this noble policy, a line of demarcation was necessary.

Hence the Canadian boundary from the St. Lawrence to Lake Nipissing. At the same time the royal proclamation gave a definite boundary to the newly acquired Florida, divided into two colonies; and it adopted the watershed between the Mississippi and the Atlantic as the limit between the new reserve and the old colonies. This general definition, of course, was subject to revision by negotiation; and five years later, Sir William Johnson concluded an agreement which shifted the line. By this famous Treaty of Fort Stanwix in 1768, the Indians renounced all claim to territory southeast of a wavering line drawn up the Ohio and Allegheny rivers and across country to the upper Mohawk, and the King of Great Britain guaranteed to the red men secure possession of the lands on the other side of this new frontier. The most significant thing about this agreement was the change, not in the geographical position, but in the character of this portion of the Indian border. It was reinforced by a treaty. Britain thereby assumed an obligation which would continue legally to bind her until she secured a release by the formal consent of the other party, the natives.

Returning to a consideration of the Indian policy of 1763, we should observe another essential. Some effective provision was necessary for the maintenance of justice and order in this immense reserve, where white traders would be forever coming and going. In 1764, the Board of Trade produced a fine plan for the administration of the interior, and a tentative effort was made to apply it after Pontiac's revolt was crushed. But further investigation raised the prospective cost until, under the circumstances of the day, it became prohibitive. Unwilling to thrust the burden upon British taxpayers and unable to impose it upon American taxpayers, the home government threw up its hands in 1768 and called upon the colonies to regulate their own trade with the West. If each went its own way, disaster lay ahead, and they knew it. Therefore the New York assembly proposed a joint conference of delegates from the colonies most vitally concerned, the provinces of Quebec, New York, and Pennsylvania, to prepare a program of concurrent legislation. The Quebec council accepted the invitation to send representatives to meet with the others in New York at the close of 1771, but they never went. London interposed a veto for obvious reasons. This action need cause no regret for the loss of the project. The conference could have accomplished nothing, because it would have encountered an insuperable obstacle. A coöperative American administration needed money, which New York proposed each colony should raise by levying taxes on dry goods and rum sold in the interior; but Quebec, unlike New York and Pennsylvania, had no assembly and therefore no taxing power.[3] The impossi-

3. A. L. Burt, *The Old Province of Quebec*, p. 179.

bility of launching this American plan, coming after the foundering of the British plan, left the West without a government. This condition could not be allowed to continue. Here was a huge heaven for outlaws at the back door of the colonies. Nor was this the only menace. French traders working up the Mississippi were penetrating the region of the Upper Lakes, threatening to steal the trade if not the country itself; and the competition between British traders, unrestrained by civilized authority, was driving them toward their own destruction and, perhaps, to lighting a wilder native conflagration than had yet been seen.

The problem was most pressing in the country north of the Ohio, for the chief seat of the fur trade was around the Great Lakes; and, by elimination, only one practicable solution remained. That was to extend an existing government over the derelict land by annexing it to some colony, and there was only one choice. There could be no question of thus enlarging any of the old colonies. At first glance, it may appear that their growing quarrel with the mother country eliminated them from consideration; but closer examination reveals a more fundamental reason for what was done. The British government still adhered to the Indian policy of 1763 as essential; and this was incompatible with annexation to an old colony, which would have placed the red men at the mercy of white settlers. Reunion with Canada, on the other hand, would provide an administration for the reserve without destroying its character. No assembly would impede the hands of the Quebec governor in dealing with the Indians; the Canadians, small in number and living far away, would never press upon their hunting grounds; and the new polity de-signed to meet Canadian needs and wishes would serve as a sufficient deterrent to English intrusion, for pioneers in the old colonies would be repelled by the prospect of living under the Quebec Act, which denied representative government and recognized the privileged position of Roman Catholicism. Therefore the Quebec Act of 1774, in addition to giving Canada a new constitution, restored the hinterland that had been cut off by the proclamation in 1763.

The new Canadian boundary as defined by Parliament in this act did not coincide with the frontier already laid down for the Indians. The former ran up the St. Lawrence, over Lake Ontario and the Niagara to Lake Erie, along the western side of Pennsylvania to the Ohio, down it to the Mississippi, and thence northward to the domain of the Hudson's Bay Company; the latter wandered in wide curves overland from the Ohio to the upper Mohawk, where it stopped. The divergence deserves more attention than it has received, and this for two reasons. It left a sort of no man's land, a fragment of the derelict reserve. This was not entirely neglected, for it was the home of the Six Nations, over whom Sir William Johnson exercised a paternal sway. Nevertheless the partial neglect of 1774 foreshadows the more fatal neglect of 1783, to be discussed later. The other reason for drawing attention to the divergence lies in the motive behind it. If the new boundary of Canada had been carried along the Fort Stanwix line, New York and Pennsylvania might have risen in arms immediately. This isolated patch of Indian territory is patent evidence of the fact that the British government had no intention of robbing the old colonies of their landed inheritance. Indeed, as was observed in the previous chapter, the act was very explicit on this point, stating "that nothing herein contained, relative to the Boundary of the Province of Quebec, shall in anywise affect the Boundaries of any other Colony."

Fortunately for the United States and unfortunately for Canada, as later events proved, the Quebec Act appeared in vicious company. It was rushed through Parliament along with the famous penal legislation which was intended to cow the colonies into submission but only drove them headlong into revolution. Heated American imaginations at once saw a wicked design peering out of almost every clause of the innocent act. The whole Quebec Act was anathema to them. The hysteria which it aroused cannot be dismissed as simply the natural product of those hectic times. It was to leave its mark for all time, when the war was over.

This mark is the present international boundary from the northwest corner of the Lake of the Woods down to the point where the forty-fifth parallel cuts the St. Lawrence. To most people today, this line seems as fixed in nature as the watercourse it follows; but it was not so in 1783, when Britain and the United States adopted it in the Treaty of Paris. In accepting this line, Britain did two surprising things. One concerned the red men immediately. She completely ignored them, and, as a consequence, she found herself tied up in conflicting obligations. The guarantee she had given the Indians in the treaty of 1768 clashed with the agreement she made with the United States in 1783. She made no effort to secure release from the first bond before signing the second, nor did she try to word the latter so as to transfer the responsibility she had assumed in the former. Her neglect cost many lives and endangered many more. It nearly involved Canada in a war between Britain and the United States.

The other surprising thing concerned Canada and the United States in the more distant future, and how surprising it is becomes apparent only when we go back in mind to the time of the Treaty of Paris. Britain seems to have lightly abandoned an immense territory which she had a strong right to keep. The country north of the Ohio was not part of the inheritance of the United States. It was a dowry promised, though not paid, in 1783. Historically it belonged to Canada, from which it had not been severed until the close of the French regime, and then only for eleven years before being reunited. Geographically it was tied to Canada by the great system of natural highways that converged upon the St. Lawrence, and for many years to come it remained much less accessible from the Atlantic seaboard of the United States. Economically it was almost wholly dependent upon Canada, for its only value then was in the fur trade it supported, and this was focused in Montreal. A whole genera-

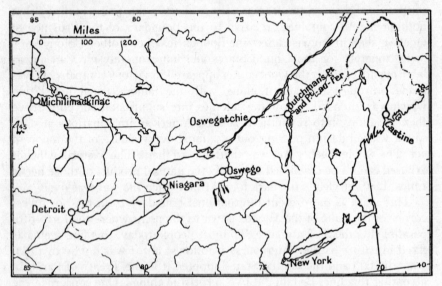

Places Held by British Forces in Northern United States
at the Close of the Revolutionary War

tion was to pass before this commercial link was broken. Of course these claims could have counted for nothing if Britain had lost the country during the war; but she had not. Only in the southwest corner had Americans, led by George Rogers Clark, gained a foothold, and that only temporarily. Contrary to the assertions of his later admirers, he added not one inch to the geographical stature of the United States. The Revolutionary War closed with Britain still in actual or virtual military possession of the "Old Northwest." Moreover, as will presently appear in a discussion of the peace negotiations, Britain was subject to secret temptations to take a firm stand on these open grounds. This might have greatly enlarged the scope of Canada's development and restricted that of the United States.

Of the two factors which actually governed the settlement—the

American demand and the British yielding to it—the former is easier to explain, though it is by no means simple. It passed through several phases which suggest startlingly different possibilities. The United States nearly got much more than it received and might have accepted much less.[4]

The roots of the American demand strike back to the royal proclamation of 1763. Had not this instrument cut off the natural hinterland of Canada, she might have secured more of it twenty years later. The restoration of 1774 was too recent and too intimately associated with the explosion of the Revolution to stand unchallenged. Though we can now see that the thirteen colonies would have revolted when they did without any Quebec Act, this piece of legislation stirred such a furor that it was popularly regarded as a major cause of the war and therefore a major obstacle to its termination. In March, 1778, Benjamin Franklin apparently suggested the repeal of the act as an essential condition for peace. A few weeks later, Sir George Saville urged his fellow members in the House of Commons to repeal the act "upon the ground of its being odious and inimical to the Americans, and consequently an obstacle to our attempts to make an accommodation with them"; and fifty-four voted for the motion, which was defeated by a majority of forty-two. In the summer of 1779, the Continental Congress, being more practical, seized upon the point made by these two representative men. Then appeared the instructions under which John Adams was later commissioned to negotiate peace, and these instructions naturally contained a definition of the boundaries of the United States. In making the definition, Congress adopted the line prescribed by the royal proclamation and extended it from Lake Nipissing straight to the source of the Mississippi. In other words, Congress cited the British government against itself.

Benjamin Franklin advanced with a bolder note in the spring of 1782. Under a new commission and new instructions, both dated June 15, 1781, he was opening informal negotiations in Paris with Richard Oswald, Lord Shelburne's agent. The wily Philadelphian then demanded the surrender of all Canada as a solid pledge of peace. From the days of his futile sojourn in Montreal, he seems to have cherished the idea of adding Canada to the United States. In July, 1782, when he knew that London had refused to listen, he pitched his tune in a softer key, suggesting cession as a counsel of perfection; and at the same time he retired to the position laid down by Congress in 1779, for the new instructions referred to the old instructions as setting forth "the desires and expectations of

4. The best account of the peace negotiations is S. F. Bemis, *Diplomacy of the American Revolution* (New York, 1935), an admirable piece of work.

Congress." The Nipissing line as a boundary was thus one of the conditions for peace which he then proposed. Though John Adams and Henry Laurens, his colleagues who had not yet joined him, were also indulging in sweet summer dreams of winning at the conference table what their countrymen had failed to win by arms, and though Oswald was bewitched by Franklin into advising the cession of Canada, there is no evidence that the British government ever considered such a surrender. For a while, however, it was willing to give away more than it did in the end.

When Franklin announced his terms in July, 1782, he was standing alone. Only one of the other American peace commissioners, John Jay, had yet reached Paris, and he was laid low by an attack of influenza. On his recovery, London learned that he was more openly hostile to Britain than his colleague had been, and thus the American position seemed to stiffen. The upshot was an important decision of the cabinet, delayed until August 29 by the difficulty of collecting its scattered members. The decision was to conclude peace on the above terms, of which the 1763 proclamation line was one. The future of what is now the thickly populated portion of Ontario seems to have been trembling in the balance, without Franklin's or Jay's realizing that perhaps a little pull would bring it down on their side.

At the same time the British government was prepared to concede another American demand which, though it is not at first obvious, had an important influence in determining the boundary. It was the formal recognition of American Independence before the actual negotiation of the peace terms. Franklin understood that Britain was ready to grant it when he handed his conditions to Oswald in July. Then a change of administration in London disturbed his belief. The new government desired to postpone recognition to make it the first article of the treaty. At once the legal mind of Jay caused both colleagues to boggle. The recognition of independence was, according to their instructions, the first and only absolute essential. It might escape them if deferred to a treaty. This might hedge it with conditions. Moreover, this was to be only one of a series of interlocking treaties, for the American war had developed into an international struggle, and contingent negotiations might cover a British withdrawal of recognition confined to a draft of the projected treaty. They suspected some British trick. They sniffed it in the preparation of Oswald's commission to treat with them. A draft of this document, submitted for their consideration early in August, spoke of "colonies," instead of "the United States," and a peace or truce with all or any of them. The perplexed commissioners consulted Vergennes, the French minister. He told them that, if independence were an article of the treaty, the form of Oswald's commission would be immaterial.

They could commit Britain by the mere exchange of powers, Oswald accepting theirs as plenipotentiaries of the United States. It would have been well for their country if they had accepted this advice. But Jay suspected a French trick to make American independence wait upon French and Spanish interests, and neither he nor his colleague felt free to waive the requirement of a preliminary recognition of independence. That was then impossible to get. Parliament, in the recent act authorizing negotiations, had not empowered the government to give it, and Parliament was no longer in session, having been prorogued on July 11 to September 3. However, the cabinet also agreed on August 29 that the King should ask Parliament "to acknowledge the Independence of the thirteen Colonys absolutely and irrevocably" if Oswald reported the Americans unwilling to treat without such action.[5]

Franklin and Jay thus appear to have been in a position to get all they had demanded, but they were not. The time at their disposal was too short. England was then gravely worried over the fate of Gibraltar, where a little garrison was holding out against a huge land and naval armament of France and Spain. The dispatch of a relieving fleet under Lord Howe encountered all manner of exasperating difficulties, and rumors flew back that the place had fallen. On September 13, before Howe's arrival, the allies put forth their supreme effort. They were confident of victory, but they suffered disastrous defeat. In the early afternoon of September 30, London learned that Gibraltar was safe. This joyful news raised the British price for a settlement above the level of August 29.

Within this interval, the Americans had no chance of securing a binding agreement on the terms which they had demanded and Britain was willing to concede. The explicit preliminary recognition was absolutely impossible because the date for the meeting of Parliament arrived some days before Oswald could report from Paris and, there being no other necessity for commencing the session so early, a further prorogation on September 3 put off the opening to October 11. The Nipissing line was also out of the question, though not so completely. This becomes apparent if we make a simple examination of the time-table, remembering, of course, how slowly things moved in those days. Oswald's new instructions, based on the cabinet meeting of August 29, reached him on September 4. His immediate task was to discover if the Americans still insisted on an explicit preliminary recognition, which would prevent him from doing business with them. To proceed, they would also have to accept his commission to which, in draft form, they had objected. By the tenth, they informed Oswald that they would be satisfied if he got a new

5. Sir John W. Fortescue (ed.), *The Correspondence of King George the Third*, VI, 118.

commission empowering him to treat with the commissioners of the thirteen United States. They were substituting an implicit for an explicit
preliminary recognition, though Congress had once defeated a motion to
permit such a change.[6] Though Oswald immediately sent off an urgent
demand for the new commission, over a week elapsed before the cabinet
in London decided to order it, and still another eight days before he had
it in Paris on September 27. As if to preserve the rhythm, the negotiators then rushed their work, and after yet another eight days Jay produced a draft of the preliminary articles. These, including independence
and the proclamation line, were to come into force upon the signature of
the preliminaries between Britain and France, a condition arising from
the Franco-American alliance of 1778. On October 7, Oswald forwarded
a copy to London, where it arrived on the eleventh. It has been suggested
that the American hesitation during the five or six days following the
receipt of Oswald's new instructions was crucial.[7] But the mere elimination of these days in the middle of the time-table would not have sufficed
to clip off more than double that number at the end. The real "slip between the cup and the lip" was the time spent over Oswald's new commission, seventeen days. This delay was caused by the firm belief of
Franklin and Jay that they had to secure a preliminary recognition in
some form from Britain. Their insistence on "the point of independence," together with the resistance of the little garrison in Gibraltar, deprived the United States of the Nipissing line as a boundary.

With confidence based on the solid rock, the British cabinet decided
on October 17 that Oswald should demand "the Back Country" unless
"the United States shall make a just provision for the Refugees" or unless some equivalent for the Loyalists could be extracted in the negotiations with France and Spain.[8] In reality, the American commissioners had
no alternative. They had to abate their boundary demand, and they were
both able and willing to do it. They were able because they were not tied
to any particular boundary. Even the stiffer instructions of 1779, since
superseded, had not made the Nipissing line an ultimatum. If that could
not be obtained without continuing the war, they had provided for an
agreement upon some other line, the only limit being that it should nowhere lie south of the forty-fifth parallel. The new instructions of 1781,
as stated above, prescribed only one *sine qua non*—the recognition of independence. Everything else the commissioners were to arrange as best
they could with the coöperation of France. This sweeping delegation of
power was an astonishing act. "Never in history has one people voted to

6. *R.D.C.U.S.*, III, 270.
7. Bemis, *op. cit.*, pp. 213–214.
8. Fortescue, *op. cit.*, VI, 144.

put its entire destiny more absolutely, more trustfully, under the control of a foreign government."[9] Some patriotic Americans hoped that the victory of Yorktown, a few months later, would inspire the members of Congress to withdraw or modify their declaration of dependence; but they were not to be moved. Too many of them were still under the spell of the French ambassador, La Luzerne. Vergennes had sent him across the Atlantic to tie the United States to the apron strings of France, and he had done it deftly.[10] Yet the knot which Americans refused to undo at home, other Americans cut in Europe. These were the peace commissioners, who scented an international plot to rob their country of all its hinterland. This is why they were willing to abandon their insistence upon an irrevocable preliminary recognition and also to abate their boundary demand.

How this Franco-Spanish "plot" threatened to establish a much more southerly Canadian-American boundary than what we have today is the only part of this far-reaching intrigue that calls for explanation here. To begin with, we should observe the existence of clear indications that Congress would have accepted much less territory than the treaty finally gave. These indications commenced in June, 1781, when Congress threw overboard the 1779 decision to prescribe definite geographical limits for the new country, and they continued with the persistent rejection of every motion that aimed at the adoption of a boundary ultimatum. In addition to these formal votes, there are the expressions of some influential individuals. On January 7, 1782, three months after Cornwallis surrendered at Yorktown, the Secretary for Foreign Affairs, Robert R. Livingston, wrote Franklin a letter in which he contemplated the possible failure of the United States to get the interior. He suggested, as a last resort, that the territory might be erected into a buffer native state which "should enjoy its independence under the guarantee of France, Spain, Great Britain, and America, and be open to the trade of those whose lands border upon" it.[11] Also about this time Gouverneur Morris, having departed from Congress where he had presided over the committee that proposed the Nipissing line, drafted suggestions of much more modest boundaries. One of these undated papers is particularly interesting. Internal evidence suggests that the new committee consulted the chairman of the old one and this was his sketch of what might be submitted to Congress for its adoption as an instruction to the peace commissioners in Europe. In this, he proposed that they might accept, if

9. Bemis, *op. cit.*, p. 190.
10. Adams was convinced that France had caused the cancellation of his commission of 1779. *R.D.C.U.S.*, VI, 58.
11. *Ibid.*, V, 90.

"expressly required by our good ally the King of France," a line leaving Lake Ontario at

the mouth of Oswego or Onandaga River—thence up the same river southwardly to the latitude of forty-three degrees North—thence in that latitude along the northern Boundary of Pensilvania to the western Boundary thereof—thence along the same to the southern boundary thereof, and along that boundary Easterly to the Western boundary of Maryland—thence to Lord Fairfax's Line —thence southwardly along that line to the high grounds which divide the waters falling into the Atlantic from those which fall into the Mississippi— thence along those grounds to the southern boundary of Georgia as settled by the proclamation of 1763—and thence along that boundary to the Atlantic."[12]

As already intimated, the hidden hand of France had a share in prompting the above votes of Congress. The same influence was behind the election of Livingston as Secretary for Foreign Affairs and may very well have given occasional guidance to his official pen. Too much credit, however, must not be given to La Luzerne. Gouverneur Morris' later well-known hostility to westward expansion is enough to suggest that other forces were already at work. There was thus an inherent American weakness on the question of boundaries, and France was ready to manipulate it for her own and her Spanish ally's advantage.

In the late summer and early autumn of 1782, the "plot" came to a head in Europe; and Jay, who then bore the chief burden of representing the United States because Franklin fell ill,[13] was the first to smell it. In the beginning of August, he approached Aranda, the Spanish ambassador, to whom he had been referred on leaving Madrid, in the hope of settling the Spanish-American boundary. Aranda spread out Mitchell's large map of North America and asked Jay what he proposed. He demanded the Mississippi down to the thirty-first degree of latitude, where the American claim was stopped by the recent Spanish seizure of West Florida. Discussions with the government in Madrid had led him to believe that Spain admitted the American right to the Mississippi boundary,[14] and therefore he was taken aback by what followed. Aranda at once launched into a long argument against any such extension of the United States. As he did not commit himself to any particular line, Jay requested him "to mark on the map the line he proposed, and to place it as far to the west as his instructions would possibly admit." In a few days the American received the map with the proposed Spanish limits marked

12. Quoted by Bemis at the end of his excellent article on "Canada and the Peace Settlement of 1783" in *Canadian Historical Review*, XIV, 265–284.
13. *R.D.C.U.S.*, V, 875.
14. *Ibid.*, VI, 46.

in red ink. The line ran round the south shores of the Upper Lakes from the western tip of Superior to the western end of Erie and thence almost straight south to Florida. On August 10, in company with Franklin, Jay carried the map to Vergennes, who had hitherto supported the American claim to the Mississippi as a boundary. Now the French minister "was very cautious and reserved" and his principal secretary, Rayneval, who was present, said that the Americans were claiming more than they had a right to.[15]

During the next few weeks these two Frenchmen, hand in glove with Aranda, apparently tried to play the role of "honest" broker between Spain and the United States. On August 26, Aranda insinuated the idea of a buffer state when, to quote Jay's account of his interview with the Spaniard, he "asked what right we had to territories which manifestly belong to free and independent nations of Indians." Some days later Rayneval posed the same question and cited the royal proclamation of October 7, 1763, to disprove the American claim. Yet he suggested a compromise line to divide the disputed territory between Spain and the United States, with a provision that trade should remain free to both parties. Here the significant thing to note about this line is that the Frenchman refused to extend it north of the Ohio, giving as his reason the British title to everything north of that river.[16] Jay's natural alarm at this startling injection of Britain into the discussion was almost immediately increased by his discovery that Rayneval, under pretense of retiring to the country, had secretly slipped over to England. The conclusion seemed obvious—that France was ready to betray her American ally to her Spanish ally and their common foe. Though the western boundary was not a chief object of this secret visit, Vergennes' secretary took advantage of his opportunity to intimate to Shelburne that Britain had a better right than the United States to the country north of the Ohio. Neither then, when Gibraltar was in peril, nor later, when that fortress was secure, did the British seize the bait.

Jay, however, was fearful lest the government in London yield to this temptation, and therefore he sought to counteract it immediately by offering another. To prevent the mediation of France from bringing Britain and Spain together to share at American expense, he would induce Britain to share with the United States, to the exclusion of Spain and behind the back of France. He entered upon the scheme without presenting it to his colleague, who, he thought, still reposed too much trust in French integrity, though Franklin was probably the cannier of the two. Be this as it may, Jay hurried a confidential agent off to London on

15. *Ibid.*, p. 23.
16. *Ibid.*, pp. 25–27.

September 11, with a nice argument for Shelburne's ear. It was "the obvious interest of Britain immediately to cut the cords which tied" the United States to France by a prompt recognition of American independence and acceptance of peace terms. Britain might share with the United States in a more profitable way than by drawing a boundary through the interior. The United States, in return for securing the ownership of the whole West out to the Mississippi, would allow the growing trade of this territory to be a British monopoly "by consenting to the mutual free navigation" of American lakes and rivers, including the Mississippi. These facilities, together with the possession of Canada, would open to Britain "an inland navigation from the Gulf of Mexico by means of which the inhabitants west and north of the mountains might with more ease be supplied with foreign commodities than from ports on the Atlantic." In "this immense and growing trade," Britain might build up a commercial empire to replace the territorial empire she had lost.[17] Incidentally, the United States would enlist the aid of Britain in breaking Spain's strangle hold on the Mississippi.

Jay's plot, if such it can be called, was largely a work of supererogation. The British cabinet was still anticipating peace with the Nipissing line for a boundary, and the younger American was repeating a secret move already made by the elder. Franklin had not told him what he had done in July. He had then suggested to Oswald, who reported to Shelburne, that the treaty should provide for complete reciprocity between Britain and the United States in trade and navigation, that the resumption of such a beneficial intercourse might finally lead to a federal union between them, and that meanwhile Britain "ought to take care not to force" the United States "into the hands of other people." Jay, however, strengthened this earlier suggestion by repetition, and he probably contributed something new.

The idea of British-American reciprocity, propounded by Franklin, was not the property of any man. The natural product of the times, it was in the air on both sides of the Atlantic. All the Englishmen and all the Americans who were involved in the peace negotiations believed in it. What Jay did was to stretch the idea, to give it a continental as well as a maritime application. Accordingly the fourth article in the October preliminaries[18] provided for the free navigation of the Mississippi from its source to its mouth, mutual free navigation of other British and American waters, and free trade between the United States and the British Empire.[19]

17. *Ibid.*, pp. 30–32.
18. See *supra*, p. 26.
19. "For very obvious reasons," as Jay said, the articles "were not communicated to the Count de Vergennes." *R.D.C.U.S.*, VI, 47.

The discovery of the danger in the West explains why the American commissioners were willing to abate their boundary demand when their agreement with Oswald foundered on the Rock of Gibraltar. The question was then how much they would have to yield in order to secure the rest. Oswald was instructed to urge the boundary laid down in the Quebec Act, and he told Jay that Henry Strachey, sent by Shelburne to strengthen his hand, talked of a longitudinal line east of the Mississippi. But the American plenipotentiaries, reinforced by the arrival of Adams from the Hague on October 26, were not to be intimidated by what appeared to be a British echo of a Franco-Spanish conspiracy. Fish, debts, and Loyalists stirred more interest than the boundary during the week of feverish negotiations that covered Strachey's stay in Paris, for neither Oswald nor his backer pushed very hard to advance the British line. They simply accepted what the Americans offered. According to the new draft of the preliminary articles with which Strachey departed for London on November 5, the boundary was to continue straight west along the forty-fifth parallel from the St. Lawrence to the Mississippi. This would have given southern Ontario to the United States and corresponding portions of Michigan and Wisconsin to Canada. That much was obvious at the time, but more was at stake than anyone could have then foreseen. Canada would not have been denied the access to the waters of the Mississippi intended in the treaty, and when the time came to carry the boundary beyond, this might have continued along the same parallel instead of the forty-ninth, giving to Canada a huge belt of territory that now belongs to the United States. But the forty-fifth parallel was not to be projected westward from the St. Lawrence, for the American commissioners were not wedded to this straight line.

As an alternative the Americans offered the crooked line which, being substituted in London, became the present boundary up the St. Lawrence, through the Great Lakes, and on to the northwest corner of the Lake of the Woods. It was to have been carried thence straight west to the Mississippi, the source of which was then supposed to lie still farther north. Exactly why the British government chose the alternative is not clear. The best explanation that has yet been given was made by Jay in a memorandum to Grenville when they were negotiating the treaty of 1794. If the American had been far wrong the Englishman might have corrected him. It was as follows: "As the waters would form a line which could never be mistaken, and afforded great conveniences to both parties, the line of the waters was preferred by both."[20]

Associated with the boundary was another feature of the final treaty which appeared when this draft was being prepared. It was the almost

20. *A.S.P.F.R.*, I, 491.

entire omission of the interesting fourth article of the October preliminaries. All that remained was the stipulation that the navigation of
the Mississippi from its source to the ocean was to be forever free and
open. Britain had no objection to this, and there was a good American
reason for keeping it. But the rest of the article, designed to establish
complete reciprocity, after being accepted by Oswald in Paris, had struck
a big snag in London. Under examination there, the American offer
looked very like a Greek gift. This article would make Britain give much
more than she could ever get, for it would turn the navigation laws inside
out, to the utter ruin of British trade and shipping. Britain would still
bear the whole burden of her restrictive commercial system, and the
United States would reap all the benefits. Naturally the government
eliminated the sweeping provisions for reciprocity, and shelved the subject for treatment in a supplementary commercial treaty, which, Oswald
was to tell the Americans, the King desired to conclude.[21] An Englishman endowed with half Jay's suspicions might have concluded that the
American had attempted to play a diabolically clever trick, but he had
harbored no such intention. As intimated above, he was thinking of much
more than relations along the new boundary. Like many other Americans of that day, he was gravely concerned for the whole trade and shipping of his country, and he sincerely believed that the greatest possible
reciprocity between Britain and the United States would be as advantageous to the former as it seemed necessary for the latter. Many Englishmen also believed it.[22]

No further change in the boundary was made or even attempted; and,
throughout the later stages of the peace negotiations, the Mississippi
stipulation was preserved as the only vestige of the concomitant article
on trade and navigation. This second draft of preliminaries was for other
reasons rejected in London, necessitating a third set. In this final draft,
the boundary option preferred by Britain and the provision for the freedom of the Mississippi raised no question. Since this document, unlike its
two predecessors, was of British authorship, it did not have to be referred back to England for acceptance after being signed in Oswald's
Paris lodgings on November 30, 1782. It came into force with the completion of the Anglo-French preliminaries on January 20, 1783.

During the subsequent negotiation of the definitive treaty, signed in
Paris on September 3, both sides vainly sought to supplement the above

21. Fortescue, *op. cit.*, VI, 144.

22. In 1779 Congress commissioned and instructed Adams to negotiate not only a treaty of
peace but also a treaty of commerce. This, however, was not to give Britain anything not already granted to France. Its main object was to preserve American rights to share in the
British North American fisheries. Thus the idea of a separate commercial treaty was not new,
though the great expansion of its purpose was.

conditions. Adams, with prophetic foresight, was prepared with an article to prohibit fortifications on the northern boundary of the United States and armed vessels on the Great Lakes, though he does not appear to have fought for its inclusion.[23] But at the last moment he and his colleagues did make a formal demand for something else of great importance in the years to come. It was the opening of the whole St. Lawrence to free navigation by Americans, by the enlargement of the article on the Mississippi to make it apply equally to both rivers.[24] Apparently the American commissioners did not press very hard for this amendment, which would have given only a superficial symmetry to the article as it stood. The United States might be enabled to break through the Spanish barrier by interesting Britain in the Mississippi, but Britain had no corresponding reason for admitting Americans to the St. Lawrence. Moreover, this privilege then meant relatively little to the United States, and its insertion would have been out of place in the peace treaty. Whether Britain should share the St. Lawrence was really part of the larger question of reciprocity, which, revived in long and futile discussions to be noticed presently, was again shelved on the understanding that it would be settled in a supplementary commercial treaty.

To complete the explanation of the establishment of the great central portion of the boundary which, after the lapse of a generation, governed the location of the long border farther west, it is necessary to examine the other factor controlling the issue—the astounding complaisance of Britain toward the American demand for territory. She had an excellent title to the country north of the Ohio, she was still in possession of it, and she was tempted by France and Spain to keep it. Why did she give it up so easily? And why did she betray the Indians, her allies and wards, to whom she had pledged her word, by undertaking unconditionally to deliver their hunting grounds to the Americans, their foes? The answer to the second question is terribly simple. No evidence has yet appeared to suggest that the British government had the least idea of doing anything that concerned the red men. Amidst the distractions of a falling empire, it forgot them completely, until it was too late. In the parliamentary debate on the preliminary articles in February, 1783, the opposition exposed the criminal negligence of the government; but the signature of the French preliminaries had already committed Britain to the terms of the American preliminaries. Here is one of the most striking blunders in the whole history of British imperial policy.

The fundamental reason for the British weakness on the boundary question was the British revulsion from the war. The people were thor-

23. Bemis, *Diplomacy*, p. 251.
24. *R.D.C.U.S.*, VI, 603.

oughly sick of it. The House of Commons, reflecting public opinion, tied the hands of the government by adopting without a division the resolution moved by General Conway on March 4, 1782. It branded as enemies of their country all who should advise or attempt the further prosecution of the war in America. When one belligerent publicly announces that it will fight no longer, the other can get almost any terms it desires. This, however, is not the whole explanation of Britain's attitude. It also rested upon some shrewd calculations.

Though Franklin and Jay were primarily concerned with advancing the interests of their own country when they argued in favor of Britain's granting generous terms to her old colonies, they were putting their fingers on an obvious British interest. Shelburne could not help seeing the possible advantage of thus weaning the United States from France, Britain's chronic foe, and of laying the foundations of a lasting peace with the new republic. Had he seized the Franco-Spanish bait and driven a hard bargain for territory in the West, he might have got much more for British North America, but at what a price to Britain and her remaining colonies!

Still another reason for the absence of any haggling over the boundary was that it seemed of little consequence to the government in London. Of course the Montreal merchants were in a panic. They monopolized the fur trade, which gave to the wilderness north of the Ohio the only value it then possessed, and any international line drawn through it was to them a catastrophe. They and their influential creditors in England brought all the pressure they could to bear upon the government to push the boundary south. They might as well have addressed their prayers to the moon. According to later gossip, Oswald broke down and wept when some merchants demonstrated to him that he had signed away the chief trading posts and the country from which they drew their peltries, but the story is apocryphal. He and his superior knew what they were doing. They were by no means neglectful of the fur trade, but they could not view it with the narrow eyes of Montreal.

The annual profits of the fur trade were as dust in the balance when weighed against the annual cost of the military posts and garrisons maintained in the interior during the late war to protect that trade. The vouchers to prove it Shelburne had in his pocket when he defended the treaty in Parliament. But even if the private gain had greatly outweighed the public expense, there were other considerations to be taken into account. However much the peace might break Montreal's monopoly by opening other routes into the interior, the furs would still find their way to London, the world's market; and England, in the absence of competing American industries, would still supply the natives with manufactured goods. What line on a map could make any difference to the Indians? Through their native forests they would pass and repass at will, taking their peltries to the traders who attracted them most. Shelburne and his agent were disciples of Adam Smith and believers in the doctrine of free trade. They had no use for monopolies and artificial trade restrictions, and the American commissioners agreed that there should be no barriers to the movement of men and goods across the dividing line. Hence the official British indifference in the days when the boundary was defined by the preliminary articles.

Though Shelburne fell from power in February, 1783, and therefore played no part in the negotiations leading to the definitive treaty, the change of ministry brought no change in the official British indifference. Fox, who became responsible for negotiations, and Hartley, whom he substituted for Oswald, were if anything more eager for the establishment of the freest intercourse between the British Empire and the United States. Of their sweeping ideas for a new commercial union to succeed the Old Colonial System, nothing need here be said; but we may observe some of the suggestions which were advanced during the final discussions in Paris for implementing the reciprocity proposal in the interior. Among the additional articles proposed by Hartley was one for the common use of all carrying places and navigable waters along the boundary, and another to forbid the imposition of any tax on articles of commerce passing through the country. The American commissioners agreed that all waters divided by the boundary should be equally navigable by British and Americans, but said that the regulation of all communications by land or water wholly within the jurisdiction of Britain or the United States, and also the question of freedom from any tax or impost, should be left for a commercial treaty. Some weeks later they submitted a draft of a treaty which, in addition to the article placing the St. Lawrence on a parity with the Mississippi, contained another providing for the freedom not only of the boundary waters but also of the adjacent carrying places, where there was to be no tax or restraint of any kind unless imposed equally upon British and Americans.

No such provisions were written into the treaty because Fox cut the discussions short, thrusting forward the provisional treaty slightly reworded to make it definitive. He may have been influenced by the fact that his coalition with North was none too firm, but he was able to give a sound reason for his precipitate action. He said that the arrangements for a closer understanding between Britain and the United States should not, like the negotiations for peace, be concluded under the eye of France. A commercial treaty should follow the peace treaty. Fox's move was facilitated by the ratification of the preliminaries by Congress on April 15.

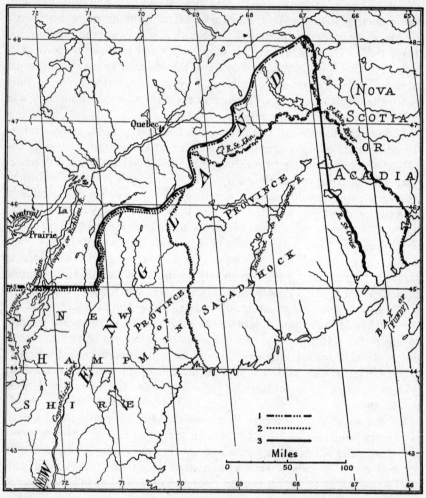

The Northeastern Boundary in the Negotiations for Peace, 1782

Redrawn with permission of the American Geographical Society from Charles
O. Paullin and John K. Wright, *Atlas of the Historical Geography of the United
States.*

1. *Line prescribed by the Continental Congress in the Instructions of August 14, 1779.*
2. *Possible boundary according to Gouverneur Morris, 1781 (?).*
3. *Boundary described in the definitive treaty, September 3, 1783.*

The Americans in Paris were loath to sign, for their signatures would terminate their commission, leaving much of their business unfinished. But they were already reconciled to the prospect of a supplementary commercial agreement, and they had information that the administration in London was tottering. Further delay might be disastrous, and therefore they decided to get what they could when they could. By signing the treaty on September 3, 1783, in Hartley's lodgings, they got more than was intended. The boundary from the Lake of the Woods to the point where the forty-fifth parallel of latitude cuts the St. Lawrence was lightly accepted by Britain because, according to mutual understanding, it was to be lightly drawn. Though traced on the map, it was not to cut into the continent. It was to be no dividing line, no real boundary at all. But, contrary to expectation, this is precisely what it became because the modifying supplement was not added. The responsibility for this momentous failure lay not in the United States but in England. There, as will be explained later,[25] a strong tide of opinion, already rising, soon swept away the mutual understanding on which this boundary was based.

It will have been observed that the above discussion has dealt with only two of the three portions of the present Canadian-American boundary which have their origin in the Treaty of Paris of 1783; namely, those which separated the United States from the old Province of Quebec. The third part divided the United States from the old Province of Nova Scotia, which then included the present Province of New Brunswick. If the boundary of Nova Scotia had been as definitely settled as that of Quebec in 1763, it would probably have given rise to no more difficulty in 1782 than did that section of the line which ran along the forty-fifth parallel and the highlands.

The history of the Nova Scotia boundary, though more ancient, is less certain. It begins with the early Stuart grant to Sir William Alexander, which extended to the St. Croix River and an imaginary straight line drawn northward from its source, but this definition had little meaning. Not until the Treaty of Utrecht in 1713 did Nova Scotia finally pass to Britain, and for another half century the French effectively confined it to the peninsula. The British claim that it stretched over the mainland to the north could not be made good until France was defeated in the Seven Years' War and obliged to surrender New France by the Treaty of Paris in 1763. Then, on November 21, 1763, an undoubted authority spoke. On that day appeared a royal commission appointing a new governor for Nova Scotia and defining his jurisdiction. It reads in part as follows: "Although our said Province has anciently extended and does of

25. *Infra*, pp. 56–59.

right extend as far as the River Pentagoet or Penobscot, it shall be bounded by a line drawn from Cape Sable across the entrance of the Bay of Fundy to the mouth of the River St. Croix,[26] by the said River to its source, and by a line drawn due north from thence to the southern boundary of our Colony of Quebec." Subsequent commissions did not repeat the unnecessary reference to the Penobscot. It was a gratuitous offense to Massachusetts, whose ancient claim to the country as far as the St. John River was nullified by the formal promulgation of the St. Croix line.

It is not surprising, therefore, that the instructions adopted by Congress in 1779 prescribed the St. John without any mention of the St. Croix, but contemplated the possibility of failure to secure this extension for the Bay State. In that event, Congress authorized its minister plenipotentiary to agree to a later adjustment of the eastern boundary by special commissioners. Though not legally bound by these instructions, Franklin and his colleagues had to regard them as representing the wishes of their country. They demanded the St. John along with the Nipissing line, and at first they were successful. The draft sent off by Oswald on October 7, 1782, named the St. John River; but immediately afterwards, on that or the very next day, he persuaded Franklin and Jay to leave the boundary in this quarter for settlement "by Commissioners as soon as conveniently may be after the war."[27] Thus the St. John River was only momentarily and tentatively accepted by Oswald. The British government did not reject it, because it did not have to consider it. The amendment followed hot on the heels of the original, and several days passed after their arrival in London before the cabinet met for any decision. The important minute of October 17, which inferentially denied the Nipissing line by ordering a demand for "the Back Country," called for directions to Oswald "to insist upon as large an extension as can be obtained to the South West of Nova Scotia." "Rather than agree to a bad boundary," he was to have the question referred to commissioners as already stipulated.[28] Even with the assurance that Gibraltar was safe, the government in London was prepared to close with this American proposal. Why, then, was it not written into the treaty?

Perhaps the best answer that can be given to this question is an intimation of what might have happened. Had commissioners been appointed after the peace, they would have faced the problem of deciding between conflicting claims. We have seen the extent of the American

26. This definition followed the line laid down in the grant to Sir William Alexander in 1621.

27. R.D.C.U.S., V, 808.

28. Fortescue, op. cit., VI, 144.

claim, the St. John, but not the potential British claim. There is reason to believe that it might have been more ambitious than what the royal words of 1763 suggest. The commission to the governor of Nova Scotia then stated that the province "has anciently extended and does of right extend" as far as the Penobscot, but it did not say that Nova Scotia had never rightfully extended farther. Apparently Shelburne contemplated stretching the British claim beyond: for his instructions to Strachey, whom he sent to strengthen Oswald, refer to the inclusion of the old Province of Maine in the Province of Nova Scotia.

Strange as this claim may seem today, it was then in accord with fact, for the British, by holding the mouth of the Penobscot, were in virtual control of most of Maine. Though American commissioners might have stood out resolutely against surrendering the whole, it is quite possible that they might have been driven to yield a great part of it. A suggestive passage, referring to a line forty miles and more to the west of the Penobscot, occurs in one of the undated papers which Gouverneur Morris drafted, apparently as a sketch of instructions for the negotiation of peace. It reads as follows: "With respect however to the Eastern boundary of the Province of Maine, as that has never yet been ascertained, we conceive it to be open to negotiation; but not so as to be carried westward farther than the river of Kennebeck."[29] Though Franklin and Jay had already made a concession in abandoning their insistence upon the St. John, it is highly doubtful if they or Adams, who had just joined them, thought they were making a second concession at the close of October or beginning of November when they proposed a definition of the St. Croix as the limit of the United States[30] instead of leaving the question for later settlement. The American trio probably saw that post-treaty commissioners could hardly get more for their country and might easily get less. At least the New Englander harbored an apprehension that the British government would reject the St. Croix proposal and, encouraged by French suggestion and precedents, insist upon Nova Scotia's reaching as far as the Penobscot and possibly to the Kennebeck.[31]

Adams' fears were unfounded. London was satisfied with the adoption of the St. Croix boundary in the preliminaries of November 5, and, like the western river and lake line, it was repeated without question in the final preliminaries of November 30, and in the definitive treaty of September 3, 1783. The agreement upon this part of the dividing line,

29. Bemis, *art. cit.*, *Canadian Historical Review*, XIV, 283.

30. It was Adams, apparently, who made the substitution. He reported to Livingston that he had "arrived in a lucky moment for the boundary of Massachusetts, because I brought with me all the essential documents." *R.D.C.U.S.*, V, 839. See also *ibid.*, pp. 873–876.

31. *Ibid.*, pp. 856–857, 866.

copied from the royal commission of 1763, seems so natural that we may surmise it would have been made in the beginning if the 1779 instructions had not tied the hands of the American commissioners by implying its exclusion.

The only flaw in the agreement was hidden from all the negotiators. They used Mitchell's map, the best of the day, on which the St. Croix River, known from Champlain's day, was clearly but wrongly marked. They had no inkling of that tragic cartographical inaccuracy which was soon to cause international disputes over a definition designed to prevent all disputes.

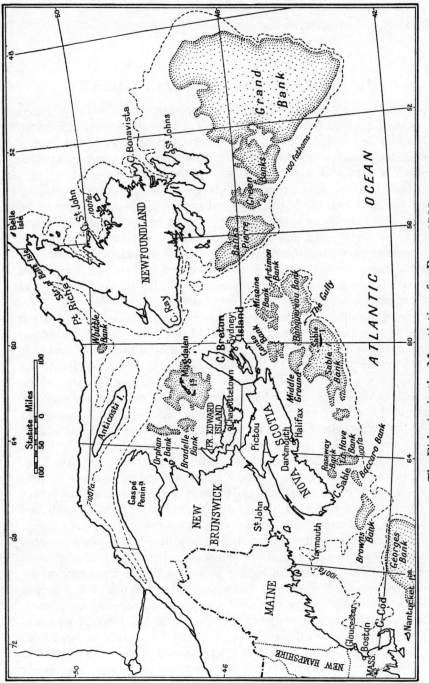

The Fisheries in the Negotiations for Peace, 1782

Adapted from H. A. Innis, *The Cod Fisheries.*

CHAPTER III

THE FISHERIES IN THE PEACE TREATY

UNTIL the present century, disputes over fisheries troubled the relations between Canada and the United States. The difficulty emerged from the American Revolution, though its roots go back another century and a half to the founding of New England. The seventeenth century saw the growth of a race of hardy fishermen, the mainstay of New England's economic life. For generations they played a leading part in developing the fisheries in that ideal region for cod created by the foundering of the northeastern corner of this continent. The American Revolution thrust forward a fundamental and complicated problem for these men to face. On withdrawing from the Empire, they would automatically lose their right as British subjects to share in the British fisheries. The prospective loss was bound to be great, perhaps disastrous; but its exact extent was hard to calculate, for these rights had never been clearly defined.

The best guide to the uncertain maze lies in the treaties of 1713 and 1763, by which the subjects of Britain and France shared the fisheries and the subjects of Spain were entirely excluded. By the Treaty of Utrecht in 1713, France recognized British sovereignty over Newfoundland, but her people continued to enjoy, for fishing and drying, the use of the shores of that island north of Cape Bonavista on the east and north of Point Riche on the west. Was this a residual right or a fresh concession? Was the use of this "French Shore," as it came to be called, intended to be exclusive, or was it to be shared with British fishermen? The treaty gave no answer. By that same instrument, for the benefit of New England, Britain forced France to cede Nova Scotia and to renounce all fishing rights within thirty leagues of its shores. Fifty years later the Treaty of Paris, which transferred New France to the British Empire, continued the 1713 provision for fishing and drying on the French Shore as a *liberty*. By accepting this word, whether she intended it or not, France accepted the British answer to the above questions. This treaty also allowed French subjects the *liberty* of fishing in the Gulf of St. Lawrence on the condition that they would not fish within three leagues of any British coast, excepting of course the Newfoundland shore already mentioned. The prohibition to fish within thirty leagues of Nova Scotia was continued by reference to the earlier treaty; and the waters within fifteen leagues of Cape Breton, then ceded, were closed to the French. Neither the Grand Bank of Newfoundland nor any other banks were specifically mentioned, but those within thirty leagues of Nova Scotia or fifteen of

Cape Breton were reserved for exclusive British use by the above restrictions.

Though the world then recognized the principle of territorial jurisdiction extending beyond the actual shore, there was no international consensus of opinion on where the line of demarcation should be drawn between territorial waters and the high seas and, in the absence of such a general rule, states were left to make claims and agreements as best they could. By the above treaties, France had recognized an exclusive British dominion over specific territorial waters varying in width from three to thirty leagues, and the whole Gulf of St. Lawrence might be regarded as a "closed sea" because the word "liberty" had been used, and because this liberty had been made conditional. There was also the possibility that France and Britain might combine, for such was their interest, to include in the same category the banks where they shared the fishery to the exclusion of Spain.

Though France had leagued herself with the United States, one of the reasons for her entry into the war was to better her position in the fishery,[1] and she caught the Americans napping. The treaty of 1778, far from guaranteeing them any right in the fisheries, actually implied a curtailment of their old rights. One article looked forward to the French acquisition of territory, fishing off which was to be reserved for the French exclusively, American poachers being liable to the confiscation of their vessels. By another article, the United States recognized the French claim to the exclusive right to the French Shore.

When Congress turned its attention to the conditions on which the war should be ended, the New Englanders pressed for definite terms to protect their fishery interest. After some heated discussions it was decided in 1779 to leave the fisheries question out of the peace negotiations, and to have it settled in a subsequent commercial treaty. The settlement was to stipulate that Britain would not "molest or disturb the inhabitants of the United States of America in taking fish on the banks of Newfoundland and other fisheries in the American seas anywhere excepting within the distance of three leagues of the shores of the territories remaining to Great Britain at the close of the war if a nearer distance can not be obtained by negotiation." This "nearer distance" was to be sought in the Gulf of St. Lawrence "and particularly along the shores of Nova Scotia." A further provision to be desired was "that even the shores [of Nova Scotia] may be occasionally used for the purpose of

1. For this subject, see D. Irvine Dallas, "The Newfoundland Fishery; A French Objective in the War of American Independence," *Canadian Historical Review*, XIII, 268–284. For a good study of the fishing industry, see H. A. Innis, *The Cod Fisheries* (New Haven and Toronto, 1940).

carrying on the fisheries by the inhabitants of these States."[2] We can at once dismiss the first and more general point about the Banks of Newfoundland, because it had no bearing on Canadian-American relations. Our concern is with the other two points, the admission to British territorial waters and the use of British shores. Far from claiming either of these things as a right, the words of Congress rested on the assumption that Britain was entitled to withhold them.

It is also interesting to speculate on what would have been the relations between the United States and British North America if the decision to relegate fisheries to a subsequent treaty had been adhered to. The new republic would have commenced its existence without any British guarantee regarding fisheries, and then would it not have been difficult or even impossible to extract such a guarantee? Would not Britain have had the whip hand? Could she not have excluded the New Englanders from their profitable haunts in British territorial waters and on British shores? The apparent weakness of this initial American position cannot be explained away by appealing to any hope of including Nova Scotia in the United States, for at this very time Congress explicitly stated that its desire for peace precluded a demand for such an acquisition.

For two years the question lay dormant. The commission and the instructions of 1781 were silent upon it. Congress did not tie together what it had separated in 1779. The new instructions simply referred the peace commissioners to the old instructions for guidance on "disputed boundaries and other particulars."

Then a strident voice arose in New England. It was that of Samuel Adams. He "could not have used a fitter engine than the fisheries for stirring up the passions of the eastern people," reported Barbé-Marbois, the secretary of the French legation in Philadelphia. This shrewd observer of the seasoned politician went on to say, "He has raised the expectations of the people of Massachusetts to an extraordinary pitch; the public prints hold forth the importance of the fisheries; the reigning toast in the east is, May the United States ever maintain their right to the fisheries. It has often been repeated in the deliberations of the general court, No peace without the fisheries."[3] Another Philadelphian echo of this storm in the northeast may be found in Livingston's long letter of January 7, 1782, giving directions to Franklin on the conduct of negotiations. The Secretary for Foreign Affairs developed a strong general argument in favor of American fishing rights, and he reinforced it by pointing out how largely the people of Massachusetts and New Hampshire were dependent upon what they brought home from the sea. But

2. *R.D.C.U.S.*, III, 303.
3. *Ibid.*, V, 239. Bemis, *Diplomacy*, p. 220n.

his whole argument was confined to operations on the Newfoundland banks. He made not the slightest reference to using British shores or territorial waters. As will presently appear, the American right to these two things, which caused so much trouble in the nineteenth century, was injected into the negotiations rather furtively.

It was Franklin who introduced into the peace negotiations the principle that the fisheries were a *sine qua non*, thereby improving upon his instructions. He did it in conversation with Oswald in the early summer of 1782, and he did it in words that were purposely rather vague. All he demanded was freedom of fishing on the Newfoundland Banks "and elsewhere." The Englishman was innocently vague in his notions of what was involved. He wondered why the American "should have thought it necessary to ask for this privilege," yet he observed that drying on Newfoundland had not been mentioned.[4] Having been thus introduced, the fisheries question retired into the background until thrust forward by a startling American discovery. It was another French trick. True to her own interest, France had no intention of allowing her American alliance to be used for prying open the British fisheries for the benefit of New England. She shared part of the fisheries with Britain, and she relished the prospect of excluding the Americans, now that they had ceased to be British. She might then be able to get more for herself. In August, the French government intimated to the British government that American fishing rights other than on the high seas were, and ought to be, limited to American territorial waters. Thus France tempted Britain to cling to her rights in the fisheries as well as in the interior of the continent. This bait was also offered in vain.

Jay scented the danger in the east almost as soon as he smelled it in the west. On September 10, the day after he learned of Rayneval's secret departure for London, he received from British hands a translation of an intercepted French dispatch from America. It was Barbé-Marbois' report to Vergennes, which has been quoted above for its description of the vigorous agitation stirred up by Samuel Adams. Here the significant thing to note is that the young Frenchman, after describing this agitation, proposed means for stifling it. Jay at once conjectured that one of Rayneval's objects in going to London was to sound Shelburne on the fisheries, and that is exactly what Rayneval did. He repeated the suggestion that Britain should share them with France to the exclusion of all others.[5] Meanwhile, as mentioned in the discussion of the western boundary,[6] the suspicious American sent his own confidential agent to

4. *Ibid.*, p. 207.
5. *R.D.C.U.S.*, V, 822.
6. *Supra*, pp. 29–30.

counteract the machinations of the Frenchman. There was no possibility of combating this French temptation by holding out an American one. Only a threat would serve the purpose, and Jay was ready with it. The Americans could not make peace if their countrymen were to be shut out of the fisheries while Frenchmen were admitted to them. An attempt to force such a settlement upon the United States would only lead to more irritation and every possible measure of retaliation.

When Oswald received his new commission on September 27, and the plenipotentiaries at last plunged into the business of preparing the preliminary articles, they seem to have had little difficulty in handling the fisheries problem. Oswald allowed Jay to wrap it up in his all-embracing reciprocity blanket. According to the third article of the draft completed early in October, both Britons and Americans were to "continue to enjoy unmolested the right to take fish of every kind on the banks of Newfoundland and other places where the inhabitants of both countries used formerly . . . to fish and also to dry and cure the same at the accustomed places," whether they now belonged to Britain or to the United States, and each government would "extend equal privileges and hospitality" to the fishermen of the other. Here it is worth observing that the habits of the fish were such that the projected partnership would be almost wholly one-sided, the Americans contributing practically nothing of value and the British everything.

The French still hoped to defeat the American desire to share in the fisheries. On October 24, the day after news reached Paris that London had refused to accept the first preliminaries, Jay and Rayneval dined with Franklin at Passy, and the conversation turned to diplomacy. The Frenchman asked, among other things, what the Americans demanded concerning fisheries, and they told him. He tried to discourage them, and made insinuations against the New England agitations. They replied that the right to share with Britain was essential to peace, and Franklin enlarged upon the importance of fish to his countrymen. Rayneval then softened his manner and deftly sought to reverse their argument. After observing that France naturally wished to favor the United States more than did their common foe, he pointed out that Britain would of course be disinclined to share her "great nursery of seamen" and he wished as few obstacles to peace as possible.[7]

The arrival of Strachey and Adams two days later brought relief and encouragement to Franklin and Jay. The fresh instructions from England, carried by Strachey, were not those of a government determined to shut out American fishermen from all their former haunts; and Adams was a stanch New Englander who believed that the French had secured

7. *R.D.C.U.S.*, VI, 47–48.

the cancellation of his 1779 commission "as an attack on the fishery."[8] His influence was soon felt by Strachey. It is also probable that the recent conversation at Passy had a valuable effect upon the Americans, for in the new negotiations they tempered their boldness with caution. One thing was now clear to them. They could not recover the right to land and dry on the shores of Newfoundland. There had been such trouble between French and English fishermen there that the government in London decided to keep them apart, though it would not formally recognize the exclusive claim to the French Shore.[9] This decision was soon reflected in the peace treaty with France, whereby the French renounced their right to use the eastern shore from Cape Bonavista to Cape St. John in return for an extension on the western shore to Cape Ray. Having had this experience with the French, Britain had no desire to repeat it with the Americans. After a great deal of conversation, to quote Strachey's report, Franklin "agreed it might be proper not to have a mixture of their people with ours for drying on Newfoundland."[10]

A price was paid for this American acquiescence. It was the right to land and dry elsewhere. With the Bostonian at his elbow, Franklin pleaded the plight of American fishermen "when they happened to be so far from home as that their fish might run some risk of being spoilt before they reached their own shores." He professed the belief that "only on such occasions" would they exercise the privilege, and "even then . . . only for a partial drying and salting, so as to prevent the fish spoiling before they went home and delivered them to their wives and children to complete and finish the drying." He "supposed there would be no inconveniency in throwing on shore their fish for a few days, on an unsettled beach, bay, or harbor on the coast of Nova Scotia." This remarkable man who could combine the innocence of a dove with the cunning of a serpent also said, "I observe as to *catching fish* you mention only the banks of Newfoundland; why not all other places, and amongst others the Gulf of St. Lawrence? Are you afraid there is not fish enough, or that we should catch too many; at the same time that you know that we shall bring the greatest part of the money we get for that fish to Great Britain to pay for your manufactures?"[11]

It is not surprising that the preliminaries of November 5 repeated the third article of the October preliminaries with slight revision. In place of the general provision for drying and curing, which had covered Newfoundland, it stipulated the right to use "the shores of the Isle of Sables,

8. *Ibid.*, V, 58.
9. Dallas, *art. cit.*
10. *R.D.C.U.S.*, V, 868.
11. *Ibid.*

Cape Sables, and the shores of any of the unsettled bays, harbors, or creeks of Nova Scotia, and of the Magdalen Islands": and the phrase, "also the Gulf of St. Lawrence," was inserted after "the banks of Newfoundland" as a place where fishing was free. No change was made in the way the article was expressed. It was still ostensibly a reciprocal agreement,[12] though its real purpose was one-sided.

When setting out for London with this draft of preliminaries, Strachey carried with him the impression that the American insistence on the fisheries concession was not too strong to be conquered by resistance in London. Yet he who had been sent to stiffen the pliant Oswald on boundaries, Loyalists, and debts was himself returning with two arguments for yielding on the fisheries. The American people would not like a refusal, and it would be difficult to restrain them.[13]

On November 11, 1782, the British cabinet considered the fisheries question along with the other details of the preliminaries. At this meeting it was decided what the United States might get. Instead of acting upon Strachey's intimation that the Americans would perhaps yield before a firm refusal, by insisting on the exclusive British right to the inshore fisheries, the government merely recommended "that Mr. Strachey should object to any Privileges being granted to the Americans of drying Fish on the Shores of Nova Scotia," though at the same time he was directed "to insist" on personal security for all Loyalists. The cabinet minute registered no protest against the concession to fish anywhere or to dry on other shores.[14] Apparently the government in London was prepared to concede what the Americans in Paris were demanding. But there was to be no weak surrender. Strachey was sent back to France, after a personal interview with every member of the cabinet, to put up a last desperate struggle. Meanwhile Adams had been pressing inquiries in all possible quarters to collect from American merchants and sea captains in Europe exact and detailed information about the fisheries,[15] and he was well armed for the battle about to open.

Strachey fired the first shot in Oswald's lodgings on November 25, when he and his host faced the Americans with a revised set of articles fresh from London. That on the fisheries was surprisingly bold. It avoided all use of the word "right," employing "liberty" instead, and it granted almost nothing that Britain had to give. In addition to the liberty to fish on the Newfoundland Banks and in the Gulf of St. Lawrence, which could hardly be denied to Americans, it permitted them to

12. *Ibid.*, p. 852.
13. *Ibid.*, p. 869.
14. Sir John W. Fortescue, *Correspondence of King George the Third*, VI, 155.
15. *R.D.C.U.S.*, VI, 91–92.

dry and cure on the shores of Sable Island and of "the unsettled bays, harbors, and creeks of the Magdalen Islands, in the Gulf of St. Lawrence, so long as such bays, harbors, and creeks shall continue and remain unsettled." Here was the only real concession offered, and it was less than the crumbs dropped from the rich man's table. The privilege to dry on Sable Island and the Magdalen Islands was to be enjoyed only on the severe condition that citizens of the United States did not fish within three leagues of the coasts of British North America, whether within the gulf or outside, nor within fifteen leagues of Cape Breton.[16]

Adams at once let loose a veritable bombardment. "I could not help observing," he recorded in his journal for that day, "that the ideas respecting the fishery appeared to me to come piping hot from Versailles." He continued:

I related the manner in which the cod and haddock came into the rivers, harbors, creeks, and up to the very wharves, on all the northern coasts of America, in the spring, in the month of April, so that you have nothing to do but step into a boat and bring in a parcel of fish in a few hours. But that in May they began to withdraw. We have a saying in Boston, that "when the blossoms fall, the haddock begin to crawl," i.e., to move into deep water; so that in summer you must go out some distance to fish; at Newfoundland it was the same. The fish in March and April were in shore, in all the creeks, bays, and harbors, i.e., within three leagues of the coasts or shores of Newfoundland and Nova Scotia; that neither French nor English could go from Europe and arrive early enough for the first fare; that our vessels could, being so much nearer—an advantage which God and nature had put into our hands; but this advantage of ours had been an advantage to England; because our fish had been sold in Spain and Portugal for gold and silver, and that gold and silver sent to London for manufactures; that this would be the course again; that France foresaw it, and wishes to deprive England of it, by persuading her to deprive us of it.

There were three lights, he said, in which the fisheries might be viewed.

1st. As a nursery for seamen. 2d. As a source of profit. 3d. As a source of contention. As a nursery of seamen, did England consider us as worse enemies than France? Had she rather France should have the seamen than America? The French marine was nearer and more menacing than ours. As a source of profit, had England rather France should supply the markets of Lisbon and Cadiz with fish, and take the gold and silver, than we? France would never spend any of that money in London. We should spend it all, very nearly. As a source of contention, how could we restrain our fishermen (the boldest men alive) from fishing in prohibited places? How could our men see the French admitted to

16. *Ibid.*, pp. 76–77.

fish, and themselves excluded by the English? It would then be a cause of disputes, and such seeds France might wish to sow.[17]

Adams displayed a letter from one of his correspondents, a certain Captain Coffin, who wrote from personal experience. According to this seafaring man, New England fishermen frequently fished around the Strait of Belle Isle and cured on the adjacent shores of Newfoundland and Labrador, delivering their catch to vessels which arrived in the fall, bound for Spain and Portugal. The letter also described the three regular fares.

From Cape Sables to the Isle of Sables, and so on to the banks of Newfoundland, are a chain of banks extending all along the coast, and almost adjoining each other, and are those banks where our fishermen go for the first fare, in the early part of the season. Their second fare is on the banks of Newfoundland, where they continue to fish till prevented by the tempestuous and boisterous winds which prevail in the fall of the year on that coast. Their third and last fare is generally made near the coast of Cape Sables, or banks adjoining thereto, where they are not only relieved from those boisterous gales, but have an asylum to fly to in case of emergency, as that coast is lined from the head of Cape Sables to Halifax with most excellent harbors.

Still another branch of the industry mentioned by Coffin was the sea-cow fishery which

was before the present war, carried on to great advantage, particularly from Nantucket and Cape Cod, in and about the river St. Lawrence, at the Island St. Johns[18] and Anticosti, Bay of Chaleurs, and the Magdalen Islands, which were the most noted of all for that fishery. This oil has the preference to all others, except spermaceti.[19]

During the next four days there were hot arguments over fish. The climax came on the twenty-ninth in Jay's rooms, where the American commissioners fought with Oswald, Strachey, and Fitzherbert, who was in charge of the Franco-British negotiations. Adams then presented a new article which he had drafted on the previous day. In substance it was almost the same as that in the preliminaries of November 5. It recognized the mutual *right* of British subjects and American citizens to fish in all the accustomed places, and it allowed Americans to dry and cure "on the shores of Cape Sables, and of any of the unsettled bays, harbors, or creeks of Nova Scotia, or any of the shores of the Magdalen Islands, and of the Labrador coast." They were also to be permitted in time of peace

17. *Ibid.*, pp. 72–73.
18. Prince Edward Island.
19. *R.D.C.U.S.*, VI, 85.

to lease land from the legal proprietors for the erection of necessary stages and buildings.[20]

It will be observed that, when defining the shores where Americans could dry and cure, Adams dropped Sable Island, added Labrador, and lifted the restriction to unsettled bays on the Magdalen Islands. Much more important than these changes was the substitution of a new word to cover American drying and curing on British shores. No longer did it appear as a *right*, which the British would never admit. With good sense, the New Englander substituted *liberty*. He lost nothing by this implied admission, though it seems to have inspired Strachey with the hope of winning a further concession. He proposed to leave out the word "right" entirely and to make fishing a "liberty" too, and Fitzherbert backed him by adding that the former was an obnoxious expression.

This was more than Adams could bear, and he exploded.

When God Almighty made the Banks of Newfoundland at three hundred leagues distance from the people of America, and at six hundred leagues distance from those of France and England, did He not give as good a right to the former as to the latter? If Heaven, in the creation, gave a right, it is ours at least as much as yours. If occupation, use, and possession give a right, we have it as clearly as you. If war and blood and treasure give a right, ours is as good as yours. We have been constantly fighting in Canada, Cape Breton, and Nova Scotia, for the defence of this fishery, and have expended beyond all proportion more than you; if then the right cannot be denied, why should it not be acknowledged, and put out of dispute?[21]

The Englishmen played for time, suggesting that all the other articles be settled, leaving that of the fisheries to be adjusted in the definitive treaty. Adams parried by offering to wait until a courier could bring a definite statement from London, and Fitzherbert countered by saying that a reference to England would lay everything "loose before Parliament" and be like "going to sea again." Franklin then made a feint by pulling from his pocket a paper presenting claims for goods carried off by British armies from Boston, Philadelphia, and the plantation states. Any messenger to London would have to transmit this additional claim. The American commissioners also threatened hostile legislation unless the fisheries were opened. The United States would pass an act of navigation prohibiting the export of American produce in British bottoms.[22]

Most effective, perhaps, in beating down the British resistance were the heavy blows struck by the sturdy Bostonian. He insisted that he

20. *Ibid.*, pp. 85–86.
21. *Ibid.*, p. 86.
22. *Ibid.*, pp. 86–88, 94.

would never put his hand to any articles that did not give satisfaction on the fisheries. That was the price of peace. He also asserted, to quote from his journal again,

that if we were forced off, at three leagues distance, we should smuggle eternally, that their men-of-war might have the glory of sinking now and then a fishing schooner, but this would not prevent a repetition of the crime, it would only inflame, and irritate, and enkindle a new war, that in seven years we should break through all restraints and conquer from them the Island of Newfoundland itself, and Nova Scotia too.[23]

Fitzherbert, who "always smiled," might turn away the New Englander's wrath; but neither he nor his two colleagues could any longer stand out against the great strength of the American argument, and therefore they quickly reached an agreement.

This agreement was not a mere acceptance of the draft by Adams. He had made a mistake in claiming the fisheries generally as a *right*. His opponents very properly insisted on distinguishing between the fisheries within territorial waters and those outside. They were willing to concede a right to share the latter but only a liberty to share the former, and he was obliged to yield. In yet another way he had overshot the mark. He had even sought to use Britain as a cat's-paw on the French Shore, by insinuating to Fitzherbert that Britain should insist on her right to its concurrent use. The Englishman replied that he hoped to avoid the direct issue with France, and he pertinently suggested that if he could gain the point for his own country it would profit the United States nothing, because the Americans had already officially recognized the "exclusive" right of the French to fish there. Adams had therefore to abandon the American claim to share that section of the inshore fisheries. Two other readjustments which he was persuaded to accept concerned the liberty to dry. It was everywhere, not just in Nova Scotia, to be limited to unsettled parts of the shore. Of course this did not apply to Newfoundland where, as already understood, there was to be no American drying at all. Adams also abandoned his proposal for leasing land for erecting stages and buildings on British shores. With these exceptions, he won everything he had demanded.

According to the third article of the preliminaries signed on November 30, 1782, which became the definitive treaty in the following year, Americans were to continue to enjoy unmolested the right of fishing on the banks of Newfoundland, in the Gulf of St. Lawrence, and at all other places *in the sea* where they were wont to fish; they were to have the liberty to take fish "on such part of the coast of Newfoundland as British

23. *Ibid.*, p. 93.

fishermen shall use (but not to dry or cure the same on that island) and also on the coasts, bays, and creeks of all other of his Britannic Majesty's dominions in America," and to "dry and cure fish in any of the unsettled bays, harbors, and creeks of Nova Scotia, Magdalen Islands, and Labrador, so long as the same shall remain unsettled." A final clause, however, provided for a continuance of this liberty to dry after settlement if the fishermen secured "a previous agreement for that purpose with the inhabitants, proprietors, or possessors of the ground." [24]

The pretense of reciprocity was dropped in the wording of this final agreement. Previous drafts had referred to mutual British and American fishery rights, but this said exactly what was meant. Adams had himself observed that the only time the fish abounded in the territorial waters of the United States was early in the spring before English fishermen could arrive, and even then the Americans preferred British waters. But it would be a mistake to assume that the idea of reciprocity, having served its purpose of advancing American interests, had vanished. It simply did not apply in this particular, where the United States had much to get and nothing to give. The concept was much broader, and it still presided over the whole negotiation of peace. As mentioned in the last chapter, both sides still looked forward to a generous reciprocal arrangement which would, as far as possible, reunite the economic tissues that war had torn apart. To achieve this splendid purpose, it was necessary for Britain to cultivate American good feeling. The bonds between the United States and France must be severed. Thus there was much in common between Britain's yielding on the fisheries and her yielding on the interior boundary. There was also a difference. Strange as it may seem, the government in London apparently felt that British rights in North America were more secure far from the sea than along its shores. No evidence has yet suggested that fear of invasion played any part in persuading Britain to accept less than she might have secured in the middle of the continent, but there is little doubt that a realization of the practical impossibility of keeping Americans out of the inshore British fisheries contributed to this British surrender. [25]

Samuel and John Adams served their country well; and perhaps they

24. *Ibid.*, p. 92.
25. Professor G. S. Graham of Queen's University has drawn my attention to an item in the Chatham Papers. It is an unsigned memorandum which points out that, as Europeans could not get out in time to take advantage of the early spring fishery, from February to April, Great Britain "could not prevent the Americans pursuing this branch without sending out Men of War in winter on purpose to prevent their coming nearer than the proposed distance of three leagues. The American government altho' they had agreed to this restriction would not have been able to keep their people precisely to their distance; so that it would have been in vain to have insisted on this restraint."

did Britain a good turn too, though not intentionally. Had they not forced her to pay their price in 1783, she might have had to pay more in the end. Swarming New England fishermen might have wrecked the peace long before 1812. Then Britain would have been caught in the midst of the great European struggle, instead of at the end of it; and the United States would not have been divided in an attack on a helpless British North America.

CHAPTER IV
COMMERCIAL DIVORCE

"Our respective territories are in vicinity, and, therefore, we must be inseparable. Great Britain, with the British power in America, is the only nation with whom, by absolute necessity, you must have the most intimate concerns, either of friendship or hostility. All other nations are three thousand miles distant from you. You *may* have political connexions with any of these distant nations, but with regard to Great Britain it *must* be so. Political intercourse and interests will obtrude themselves between our two countries, because they are the two great powers dividing the continent of North America."[1]

Thus spoke David Hartley to the American peace commissioners in the summer of 1783. His prophetic words expressed what he rightly called "an awful and important truth," and they did not deny it. They heartily agreed with him and with every other Briton who had a share in framing the treaty that whatever seeds of discord might lie in it should be smothered by a most generous application of reciprocity. But the commercial agreement which they envisaged as the vitalizing supplement of the peace treaty was never reached. Already a storm was gathering in England to blow it away.

On January 27, 1783, the government laid the preliminaries of November 30 before Parliament. Great uneasiness at once arose because, though the preamble talked of establishing reciprocity, the rest of the document contained no provision for reopening trade with the lost colonies. Prohibitory legislation, passed on the outbreak of the war, was still in the statute book. Would not other countries, led by France, seize the opportunity to capture the American trade? Even if it were repealed, the navigation laws would raise a formidable barrier. Mercantile voices, particularly in London and Glasgow, cried out for action, and members of Parliament expressed their impatience. To allay the widespread fears, Shelburne's Secretary of State for Home Affairs, Thomas Townshend, moved on February 21 for leave to introduce a bill to make provisional regulations for the resumption of the trade so that it would not have to wait upon the preparation of a permanent system. He excused himself from entering into details lest they stir discussion which might interfere with the important business of the day, and the motion was straightway carried. Then followed the memorable debate upon the preliminaries which lasted until after three o'clock on the following morning, when the

1. *R.D.C.U.S.*, VI, 483–484.

House adopted by a narrow margin a vote of censure upon the government for the peace it had concluded. The purpose of the vote was to upset Shelburne but not the treaty. Two days later he resigned, and for over five weeks the country had no administration. Meanwhile the posthumous child of the late ministry was born. On March 3, the bill announced by Townshend was ushered in by William Pitt, who temporarily continued to serve as Chancellor of the Exchequer.

The bill was one of the boldest ever submitted to Parliament. In addition to opening British ports to Americans in the same manner as to other foreigners, it granted citizens of the United States enormous privileges withheld from all others. Beginning with a sweeping repeal of all legislation affecting American commerce, and a statement that intercourse between Britain and the United States "should be established on the most enlarged principles of reciprocal benefit to both countries," it admitted to the ports of Great Britain and of her possessions in the New World American goods in American bottoms on the same terms as British goods in British bottoms; it continued "the same drawbacks, exemptions, and bounties" on exports from Britain to the United States as had been given in colonial days; and it placed American vessels on the same footing as British ships in exporting any merchandise from British American ports to the United States.[2] For all practical purposes, the United States was to recover the advantages and yet be free of the disadvantages of being included within the charmed circle of the British commercial system. Though Americans, as foreigners, were not to share British privileges in Britain's other foreign trade nor in the internal trade of the sadly shrunken Empire, these were channels which few Americans had ever sought before the Revolution; and the foreign trade they had once pursued in a clandestine manner could now be openly developed.

Weeks of heated debate followed the introduction of this bill. The commercial and the West Indian interests were strong for it, and the shipping interests were stoutly hostile. The clash of these opposing groups was reflected in the House of Commons, but there the issue was raised to a higher level. The attack upon the measure was led by William Eden, later Lord Auckland, who admitted that the measure was framed "on a principle which had, in some degree, been encouraged by the whole house" and that he had himself been forward in seeking a renewal of commercial intercourse "on very liberal terms."[3] As the days passed, the orphaned proposal was overwhelmed by powerful arguments.

2. Lord Sheffield printed a copy in an appendix to his *Observations on the Commerce of the United States* (London, 1783).

3. *Parliamentary History*, Vol. XXIII, col. 603.

It would ruin Ireland's newly developed provision trade with the West Indies by giving free admission to American produce. By overriding the navigation laws in Britain, it would undermine them in Ireland, and there the action would be irrevocable. The recent Irish act adopting them stipulated that they would cease to bind Ireland when they ceased to bind Great Britain, and now that Ireland enjoyed legislative independence there would be no chance of reënactment. It would disrupt Britain's foreign trading relations with other countries, by cutting across existing commercial treaties containing most-favored-nation clauses. "Was Parliament prepared to consent to the admission of all the world as British subjects?" asked Eden.[4] Another criticism leveled at the bill was that its provisions were one-sided. Britain would be giving everything and the United States nothing. There should be a *quid pro quo*, and it was considered doubtful if the new republic could give anything in return. The Franco-American alliance[5] and the sovereignty of the component states tied the hands of Congress. The greatest evil to be apprehended from the proposed measure was the effect upon Britain's security. It would ruin her carrying trade, the "great nursery for seamen" which supplied the lifeblood of the Royal Navy. The country might for a while grow richer, but the new prosperity would be most unhealthy because bought at a fatal price. Yet most of the members seem to have been agreed that something special should be done to keep the loss of the colonies from entailing the loss of their trade. The dependence of British West Indian planters upon American supplies also pointed to the necessity for some special arrangement. Therefore the bill, though mutilated, was not killed. It was only laid aside in the hope that a better solution was at hand.[6]

After the formation of the Fox-North coalition ministry on April 2, Fox turned his attention to Paris. He believed it possible to negotiate a far-reaching reciprocity agreement for insertion in the peace treaty, and for that purpose he dispatched David Hartley who, in the preceding debates, had urged the freedom of trade with the United States. Meanwhile, to meet the apparent emergency, Fox secured the repeal of the prohibitory legislation and persuaded Parliament to empower the King in Council for the next six months to make such temporary regulations as might seem necessary. Under this authority the government issued an order-in-council on July 2, reopening direct trade between the United

4. *Ibid.*, col. 606.

5. V. G. Setser, *The Commercial Reciprocity Policy of the United States,* 1774–1829 (Philadelphia and London, 1937), p. 19.

6. The *Parliamentary Register* gives a fuller report of the debates than does the *Parliamentary History.* Occasional details given in neither may be found in the reports of parliamentary proceedings in *The Gentleman's Magazine.*

States and the British West Indies. This measure checked the new operation of the old restrictive laws which would have severely pinched the island planters. Though advertised as an indulgence to the people at both ends of the trade, what was conceded to the Americans was clearly incidental to what had to be granted to the West Indians. The renewed intercourse was not to be as free as that of prewar days. It was limited to a number of specified articles which did not include the important items of American fish and meat, it was confined to British subjects, and it was restricted to British vessels. The last of these three conditions dwarfed the other two. The exclusion of American shipping was a body blow to American hopes of reciprocity, then being fed by Hartley. To him, the news from London seems to have come like a stab in the back. Obviously the British government was bending before the storm which had been blowing up ever since the introduction of the bill by Pitt in the beginning of March. The break came when Fox precipitately abandoned his effort to write reciprocity into the peace treaty and put off the question of commerce for a supplementary agreement.[7]

John Baker Holroyd, Lord Sheffield, was riding the storm, and he was riding it hard. This patriotic soldier, accomplished scholar, wealthy landowner, and member of Parliament for Coventry had at first followed Eden in the attack upon Pitt's bill, but he soon forged to the front of the fray and stood out as the doughty champion of the navigation laws. Not content with speeches in Parliament, he addressed the public in a fuller and more telling manner. His *Observations on the Commerce of the United States* struck a new note that inspired many a disheartened Briton of that day. There was no need, he said, to go courting the Americans to win back their trade. Britain could make them eat out of her hand. All she had to do was to cling to her commercial system. The Americans had practically no industries, and Britain had the best in the world. She could sell elsewhere, but they would have to come to her for most of the manufactured goods they needed. They had to buy on credit, her merchants could and did give it, but those of European countries could not. She offered the best market for their produce, yet was not dependent upon them because she had other sources of supply. By clinging to her navigation laws, under which she had grown great, Britain could make the Americans pay her for their own political independence. What they lost in the West Indian trade, the most valuable part of their commerce, would be gained by Canada, Nova Scotia, Newfoundland, and Ireland; and British shipping would increase at American expense. His arguments could not be dismissed as vain boasting. He was bursting with facts and figures gathered by painstaking researches which made him an

7. *Supra*, p. 35.

outstanding authority on matters of trade. He strengthened his appeal by the scrupulous care with which he pointed out how, in this or that particular, European rivals could attract American commerce and hold it.

Sheffield's influence[8] in rallying the country round the navigation laws is not to be wholly explained by the logic of his appeal, as outlined above. An important psychological factor has already been suggested. He revived his fellow countrymen's self-confidence, so rudely shaken by the loss of the best part of the Empire. His influence was all the greater, also, because of the peculiar political conditions of the time. For a whole year from the time this storm began to blow, the ship of state was floundering. At first, for almost a month, there was no government at all. The Fox-North ministry, which was then organized, was little better than no government. It was based on an immoral political combination, and it was distrusted by the public almost as much as it was detested by the King. When, in December, he dismissed this coalition and appointed Pitt to form a new administration, the drifting continued. This young captain had to fight for his life against a hostile crew in the House of Commons. Not until after the general election which followed the dissolution at the end of March, 1784, was he able to seize the helm with a firm hand. Even then he was not always capable of steering a steady course, for he ran into cross currents and contrary winds.

What happened in England at the end of the Revolutionary War may, in a way, be compared to what happened in the United States at the end of the World War of 1914. Once peace was signed in 1783, all the talk about reciprocity and a commercial treaty came to nothing, because British politicians were as little anxious to face the issue as, in a later day, were American politicians to consider membership in the League of Nations. The storm had been too violent.

8. Sheffield's book was a great success. It ran through two editions in 1783 and reached a sixth in 1784. A few years afterwards, as literary executor of his intimate friend Edward Gibbon, Sheffield may have found some added satisfaction in discovering the following reference to himself in the historian's autobiography: "The sale of his *Observations on the American States* [*sic*]was diffusive, their effect beneficial; the Navigation Act, the palladium of Britain, was defended, and perhaps saved, by his pen; and he proves, by the weight of fact and argument, that the mother-country may survive and flourish after the loss of America." A better witness, possibly, is David Macpherson, whose four huge volumes of *Annals of Commerce* appeared in 1805. He also mentions another author who quickly followed Sheffield into print, preaching the same vigorous gospel in a work entitled *Opinions on Interesting Subjects of Public Law and Commercial Policy Arising from American Independence.* This was George Chalmers, a Scottish lawyer who had been driven home from Baltimore by the Revolution and became a well-known antiquarian and political writer. According to Macpherson, "the press teemed with pamphlets written in support of these new maxims of commercial policy" for treating Americans as if they were still British subjects, and "the government was like to be carried away with the stream" until Sheffield spoke out, followed by Chalmers. Macpherson, *op. cit.*, IV, 18–19.

Thus it came to pass that the separation of the United States from the adjoining British North American colonies was much more complete than had been contemplated. It was actually more complete than the severance of the revolted colonies from the West Indies and the mother country, though they were much more remote. The temporary act empowering the Crown to regulate British-American commercial relations was straightway used to permit a considerable liberty of American trade with Britain as well as with her West Indian possessions, and this liberty was continued by an annual renewal of the act. But the Old Colonial System was allowed automatically to close in on the remnant of the Empire lying closest to the United States. Neglect does not explain the difference. According to the best opinion that officials in London could gather, a great future was in store for British North America. These colonies, whose population was so largely increased by the influx of the Loyalists, would soon be able to replace the United States as a source of supplies for the West Indies. Hence the temporary character of the indulgence to American trade with the plantation islands. When the substitute was ready, Britain had merely to withdraw her hand. The old law would then rush in to block the hole she had made in the wall around her colonies. But the hole was never stopped, for British North America did not live up to these British expectations. Indeed other breaches, albeit smaller ones, were made in the wall which divided the United States from the Maritime Provinces and Canada.

Their governors were impelled to take the law into their own hands to open a traffic with the neighboring Republic; and the home government had to intervene in order to limit and regularize this intercourse. The problem was more pressing in the Maritime Provinces than in Canada because the latter received a much smaller number of Loyalist refugees and it already had a much larger population. Geography also made communication with the United States easier for the Maritime Provinces.

During the first winter of the peace, Governor John Parr of Nova Scotia admitted supplies from Boston in small American craft. He did it with the advice of his council, and he justified his action by saying that it averted a serious shortage of provisions. By March, 1784, he thought his province could dispense with the services of American shipping, for he then wrote, "We are now our own carryers."[9] He was too sanguine. Presented with petitions for a continuance of this liberty, as well as with some against it, he and his council decided that they should not put an end to the irregular traffic with New England. In September, he reported this decision to the Secretary of State in London, observing that it gave

9. *P.A.C.R.*, 1921, Appendix E, pp. 4–5.

satisfaction to everyone except some Halifax merchants who were holding flour at £3 10s. a hundredweight and some farmers who were demanding high prices for their cattle. On January 2, 1785, he wrote home
that the people would have starved without this relief.[10] Governor
Thomas Carleton of New Brunswick, which was carved out of Nova
Scotia in 1784, also yielded to popular pressure early in March, 1785,
when he issued a proclamation allowing Loyalists to import their effects
in other than British bottoms.[11] In both provinces, the license thus
granted seems to have been stretched to cover more than a few commercial sins.

Meanwhile the home government was awakening to the necessity for
intervention. On April 8, 1785, an imperial order-in-council, issued
under the temporary act mentioned above, decreed that only livestock,
grain, and lumber could be imported into the Maritime Provinces, and
then only in British ships and on a governor's proclamation that their admission was necessary for the inhabitants. With one slight change in
1793, this was long to remain. It rested on an annual order-in-council,
following the periodic renewal of the parent act, until 1788 when the act
was made permanent.[12]

It is well-nigh impossible to give an exact description of the traffic
between the Maritime Provinces and the United States during this
period. It was both a little less and much more than the law allowed.
Carleton thought his people could dispense with American lumber, and
therefore did not admit it until 1791, when he found they were getting it
not only for their own use but also for shipment to the West Indies.[13] In

10. Nova Scotia A, CVII, 4.
11. New Brunswick A, I, 160–162. Thomas Carleton's proclamation was designed to encourage the further immigration from the United States of people who were anxious to live
under British rule.
12. 28 George III, c. 66.
13. "The lumber which has been sent to the West Indies Islands in vessels belonging to
this Province has been mostly taken from the American States, but no part of that lumber could
be legally imported for the supply of the Inhabitants, and hence the price here became an inducement to hazard an illicit importation, which, in our situation, is next to impossible to prevent. The temptation was in this case, the stronger on account of the heavy port charges which
are imposed by the States on all British Vessels, and which enhance the expense of collecting
cargoes of lumber in their ports by vessels of sufficient size for the West India navigation; but
these exorbitant charges may, it seems, be avoided, by employing a sort of small craft in
bringing the Lumber into one of our nearest Ports, and there putting it on board of either British Ships or provincial Vessels for the West India Market.

"Under all these circumstances, we found it necessary to follow the example of Nova
Scotia in permitting the importation of this among the Articles allowed for the supply of the
Inhabitants; and it appeared otherwise expedient, as the only means of preventing an illicit
traffic, in which the Americans would undoubtedly, in some measure, share the profit of carry-
ing their Lumber, which it is of so much importance for us to prevent." Carleton to Sydney,
July 15, 1791, New Brunswick A, V, 30–31.

December, 1785, the two houses of the Nova Scotia legislature adopted a joint address for the limitation of American imports to flour, wheat, rice, corn, and rye meal; and in July, 1786, the assembly urged the governor to curtail the trade with the United States, asserting that it injured the province which already produced a sufficient surplus of lumber, potatoes, peas, beans, etc. for export.[14] A good comment on these legislative resolutions is to be found in the imports of 1790, when Nova Scotia received from the United States 80,000 bushels of grain, 40,000 barrels of bread and meal, 54,000 staves and headings, 16,000 hoops, 285,000 shingles, and nearly 1,000,000 feet of boards. "This importation," said Macpherson, "affords a clear proof, after a trial of seven years, that Nova Scotia is very far indeed from being able to supply the West-Indies with provisions; and, what is more surprising in an uncultivated country covered with trees, that it even stands in need of lumber for building houses, and making casks for the fish, which are likely to continue the principal article of its trade."[15] In 1787, Parr was reprimanded for licensing the introduction of three hundred barrels of American pitch and tar.[16] But he was vindicated after his death, for the needs of the shipbuilders were not to be denied. The circuitous importation of pitch, tar, and turpentine, as required by law, would have caused prohibitive prices had it not been for the illicit trade which Carleton observed in New Brunswick and drew to the attention of the authorities at home. He wished to prevent it, but the only way that he could see was to make it licit, for the trade would go on. After some hesitation, the home government passed an act of Parliament adding these articles to the list of livestock, provisions, and lumber.[17] This was the slight amendment of 1793. The addition of molasses and tobacco was also sought, but in vain.[18] American rum poured into Nova Scotia and New Brunswick during these years. It was cheaper than the domestic manufacture, which in turn was cheaper than the British West Indian product laid down in Halifax; and there was no keeping it out when fishermen of the United States were allowed by treaty to hover around these British shores and even to land and dry with the permission of the inhabitants. The conditions suggest a heaven for smugglers. Such was the intimacy between the Maritime Provinces and New England that Parr's successor asked permission to provide himself with an armed ves-

14. See Beamish Murdoch, *History of Nova Scotia* (Halifax, 1867), III, 45, 49.
15. Macpherson, *op. cit.*, IV, 212.
16. Parr to Sydney, July 4, 1787, Nova Scotia A, CIX, 89–90. Sydney to Parr, Sept. 20, 1787, *ibid.*, pp. 136–137.
17. 23 George III, c. 50.
18. Nova Scotia A, CIX, 4–11; CXVII, 295–301; CXVIII, 77.

sel to keep this intimacy within legal bounds. He got the permission from England, and the vessel from the United States.[19]

No such trade, legitimate or illegitimate,[20] linked Canada with the United States in the early years of their peaceful separation. Not until 1787 was there any commercial intercourse between them. Then only a little chink was made in the wall, and the pressure which effected it came from the American side of the line. The people of Vermont were cooped up in the interior and threatened with economic suffocation, for the treaty of 1783 severed them from the British Empire and the hostility of New York excluded them from the United States until 1791. During the war, from which they soon withdrew because they saw the awkwardness of their position, they had flirted with Britain, discussing the possibility of a political reunion with the Empire. Both parties naturally dropped this discussion when peace came, but Vermont could not end the flirtation. She had to find a way of escape. Therefore she knocked at the door of Quebec and held out temptations of commercial reunion. The suggestion was not so strange as it may seem to some people today, for the outlet which Nature provided for the dwellers by Lake Champlain was along the course of its waters down to the sea.

From Quebec, the discussion was referred to London, where it was enlarged into an examination of the possible economic relations between the colony and the neighboring Republic. The investigation was the work of the privy council committee which had taken over the duties of the defunct Board of Trade. Their lordships called in Sir Guy Carleton and Governor Haldimand.[21] Sir Guy could not see Canada needing lumber or provisions from across the line. Tobacco of an inferior quality was produced by the habitants, but it suited their taste. Rice could not be grown in the St. Lawrence Valley and therefore might be imported from the south, but its admission would discourage Canadian agriculture by encouraging the use of a substitute for Canadian grain. Haldimand advanced similar views, and, as these were the two men in all England who were most familiar with the colony, the committee's report followed

19. See Murdoch, *op. cit.*, III, 122.

20. Some furs were smuggled out of Canada up the Richelieu, and not inconsiderable quantities of lumber came down that river from Lake Champlain. P.A.C. Legislative Council Minutes, Vol. E, p. 235. The price of rum in the colony was just too low to encourage illicit import. A. L. Burt, *The Old Province of Quebec*, p. 457.

21. Then in England on leave; he never returned to Quebec.

For a good article on the relations between Vermont and Canada down to the War of 1812, see W. A. Mackintosh, "Canada and Vermont: A Study in Historical Geography," *Canadian Historical Review*, VIII, 9–30 (March, 1927); and for a scholarly and delightfully written study of the whole subject of the St. Lawrence serving as the main channel for the trade of the continental region drained by it, see D. G. Creighton, *The Commercial Empire of the St. Lawrence* (Toronto and New Haven, 1937).

their advice.[22] The upshot was an order-in-council of April 8, 1785, forbidding the importation of any American produce into the province by sea, and an additional instruction of May 26 to the governor in Quebec. The instruction, after calling attention to the order-in-council, stated that it was necessary to regulate the foreign intercourse of Canada by land and inland navigation, and to this end directed the governor to propose to the legislative council the passage of an ordinance prohibiting the export of peltry and the import of foreign rum or spirits, and, unless coming from Britain, of foreign European or Asiatic manufactures.[23]

This instruction deserves close scrutiny, for it contained rather startling implications arising from the peculiar position of the old Province of Quebec. This peculiarity was new, being a by-product of the American Revolution; it was unprecedented in the history of the Empire; and it was unexpected, for it had been masked by the confident talk about reciprocity. Cut off from the sea for five months out of every twelve, the old Province of Quebec was really an inland colony. Only through a foreign country, the United States, could it have communication with the outside world during the whole year. Here was a condition not contemplated by the navigation laws. Having been framed with only maritime colonies in view, they were silent on land communication and inland navigation. Hence the striking contrast between the order-in-council, which confirmed the old prohibition in its new application to intercourse with the United States by sea, and the instruction, which implied that the ban did not legally apply along this novel land frontier of the colonial Empire. If it had applied, there would have been no sense in asking the colonial legislature to do what Parliament had already done. The instruction also implies doubts about the wisdom of extending the Old Colonial System to make it operate under these new conditions. Otherwise, why did the home government seek a local ordinance instead of issuing an order-in-council, the direct and certain method of accomplishing what was desired? The legislative council could not act immediately and might not act at all. Moreover, why was the ordinance to be so limited in scope? Was there to be freedom for the passage of goods which were not thus barred? Or was such traffic to be regulated, and, if so, by what authority? The instruction suggests that London was groping in the dark along an unfamiliar way and might follow where Quebec would lead.

The possibility of a breakdown of the Old Colonial System in the interior of America, and the need of guidance from Canada, were more distinctly recognized by the British government in the following year. Sir

22. G. S. Graham, *British Policy and Canada*, 1774–1792 (London, 1930), pp. 120–121.
23. A. Shortt and A. G. Doughty, Eds., *Documents Relating to the Constitutional History of Canada*, p. 733.

Guy Carleton, elevated to the peerage as Lord Dorchester, was sent back to Quebec as governor in 1786, with instructions to report on certain broad questions of policy. One of these arose from the contemplated division of the old Province of Quebec into two distinct colonies, Lower and Upper Canada. The somewhat peculiar colonial situation of the Province of Quebec would then be made complete in Upper Canada, which would have no access to the sea whatever except through Lower Canada or the United States—like Vermont.

Though Upper Canada was connected with Lower Canada, geographically by the St. Lawrence and politically by common allegiance to the British Crown, there were reasons for thinking that its natural economic affiliation might be with the United States. Thence had come its people; they were still coming; and they would continue to come. Here we note a striking contrast. The home government smiled on post-Loyalist immigration in Canada[24] though frowning upon it in the Maritime Provinces, and there was much more to attract smiles than to draw frowns. Unlike the refugees down by the sea, whom few old associates wished to join, the settlers in the West were followed by large numbers. These "late loyalists," as they were called, were relatives and friends whose professions of allegiance to the Crown were attested by their predecessors, believed in Quebec, and accepted in London. A new English-speaking Canada was thus arising beyond the old French Canada, from which it wished to cut loose in order to have a government suited to its own distinct character. Finally, as the years passed, this new colony would come to be half surrounded by American settlements; and the boundary, being a line drawn along a natural highway, might tend to unite rather than divide the people on either side.

It is not very surprising, therefore, that Dorchester was asked to give his opinion on whether "the inhabitants of the province so to be erected may not be supplied with European and other produce and manufactures with greater facility and upon easier terms by the subjects and through the territories of the United States of America than by our subjects and through our province of Quebec, and thereby a connection and intercourse between the subjects of the two countries be unavoidably promoted and encouraged."[25] Here one may detect lingering hopes of reciprocity along the inland border. But the vision of 1786 was different from that of 1782. British trade was to follow another course to another end. Instead of curving round to the American interior via the St. Lawrence, it would cut through the United States from the Atlantic seaboard to the British interior. Yet the old idea of attaching part of the

24. *Ibid.*, p. 829.
25. *Ibid.*, p. 815.

United States to Britain by commercial ties was still apparent, and it probably overshadowed the new idea of Upper Canada's economic dependence upon the United States as a channel of supply. What was thus desirable may also have appeared inevitable. Geography might emancipate Upper Canada if Britain would not allow it to remain outside the Old Colonial System.

The instruction containing this highly interesting suggestion apparently drew no direct reply from Dorchester, possibly because he saw that American settlement was still too remote from the western Loyalist communities to make the question a practical issue, and because he could not reconcile himself to the prospect of his province's being cut in two. But there may have been another reason; for he likewise paid no attention to the additional instruction of May 26, 1785, though its consideration had been deferred by the council in Quebec until his arrival.[26] As an administrator of government, he was careless of details and given to procrastination. This is also why, apparently, he sailed from England without having secured from the home government any understanding of what he might do about opening the border to trade, or how he should do it. As a result, he experienced some embarrassment.

The Vermont proposal might be bogged in England but not in Canada. In the fall of 1786, only a month after he landed in Quebec, the governor received a memorial from Levi Allen, asking permission to bring in free of duty any produce of Vermont for sale in the province or for export in British bottoms to Great Britain or the British West Indies and to bring back British goods in exchange.[27] Nor was Allen the only interested party in the colony. Ever since the peace, the merchants of Quebec and Montreal had been tantalized by the offer of this trade which was held just out of their reach. One can imagine how eagerly they responded to an invitation to assist a committee of the council in the winter of 1786–87 to prepare a report on the commerce of the country. As the Vermont proposal was specifically referred to the committee, the merchants were like children who can stretch their arms far enough to touch but not to pluck a luscious fruit. The fever of their eagerness infected the committee.

The council committee's report urged the wisdom of opening the province to trade with Vermont "upon the most liberal and friendly foundation." How this was to be done, the members did not say. They evidently hoped that an appeal to London would not be necessary, even

26. P.A.C. Legislative Council Minutes, Vol. D, p. 308.
27. Q, XXVIII, 7. Jay, who was then Secretary for Foreign Affairs, got wind of this Vermont negotiation and suspected that it had a political character. He wrote to John Adams, then minister in London, to investigate the rumor. The information gathered by Adams was in accord with the nature of the negotiation as explained above. D.C.U.S., III, 134; V, 142, 235.

though they shared an opinion then current in the province that all inter-course with the United States was outlawed by the order-in-council. They should have known better, because three of the four who signed the report had been present at the council meeting of a year before when the instruction of May 26, 1785, was examined and shelved. To avoid the obstacle of their own imagining, they pointed out that the order-in-council did not apply to traffic with Vermont for the simple reason that Vermont was not part of the United States. Their cleverness was wasted on the governor, who saw the limitation of the order-in-council. He favored opening the door, and he too wished to avoid the long delay of a reference to London; but he was uncertain how to proceed.

After some hesitation, Dorchester opened commercial intercourse with the "neighboring states" by way of Lake Champlain on April 18, 1787. He did it by a written order to the collector of customs, who re-sided in Quebec, to permit the free import of lumber, naval stores, hemp, flax, grain, provisions, and livestock, the produce of those states, and the free export of any product, save furs, of Canada or of any other dominion of Great Britain. Five days later, he asked the council to pass an ordi-nance allowing the free import of leaf tobacco and of pot and pearl ashes from the same source for reëxport to Britain, and the council complied with alacrity. In exchange for the above articles, Vermont of course took British manufactures.[28]

Dorchester's falling back upon an ordinance to enlarge his order im-plies a suspicion about the regularity of the order, and his dispatch home reporting what he had done suggests an uneasiness about the whole business. He there defended his admission of American produce into the province by the specious argument that British shipping could not be forbidden to carry from the St. Lawrence what American vessels were allowed to bring into Britain direct from the United States. The privy council committee, to whom his action was referred, inferentially con-demned the method, though not the object, of the order, and also the neglect of the instruction of May 26, 1785. Their lordships' report clearly stated what had been left unsaid two years before, that the regu-lation of intercourse by land or inland navigation between the Province of Quebec and the adjoining states should be entrusted to the governor and council. The report also repeated the injunction of 1785 against the export of peltries or the import of foreign spirits or foreign European manufactures, and it enjoined a general conformity to the laws of the mother country. On receiving a copy of this document, Dorchester cor-rected himself by having the council transform his order into an ordi-

28. Burt, *op. cit.*, pp. 448–453.

nance in 1788 which prohibited the import of all goods not specifically admitted.[29]

In 1789, a serious food shortage in Canada moved the governor to take the law into his own hands. In January, he ordered the naval officer at St. Johns on the Richelieu, the port of entry for the trade opened in 1787, to admit bread, biscuit, and flour of any grain; and early in April, for the relief of the Loyalist settlements, he proclaimed the free import of foodstuffs by any inland waterway west of St. Johns, provided they were brought in British craft. Both the order and the proclamation were to be effective only until August, but in July a further proclamation extended the time to the end of the year. Bolder still was a step he took in June, when, on the advice of the council, he authorized importation of American foodstuffs by sea until the close of navigation. He did it knowing that he was violating an imperial statute as well as an imperial order-in-council; but he felt that it was necessary and he trusted the home government to provide the requisite legal cloak, which it did.[30] By the end of the year, the emergency had passed and these temporary measures expired.

The trade over Lake Champlain, established in 1787, was disappointing. The great quantities of timber that were expected to come floating down the Richelieu did not arrive. The cost of marketing the products of Vermont's forests proved too heavy. Being thus unable to sell very much, the people of Vermont could not afford to buy anything like the amount of goods they might otherwise have taken from the merchants of Quebec and Montreal. This economic obstacle in the way of a profitable exchange was apparent by the summer of 1789, when Vermont enterprise proposed an ingenious method of surmounting the difficulty. It was presented in a memorial to Dorchester by Stephen Keyes and Jabez Gale Fitch for themselves and other traders over Lake Champlain. They would reduce the financial burden upon timber by imposing a physical burden upon it. They would use the rafts to bring down iron from "the crags of Vermont," if iron were added to the list of articles admitted to the province. A committee of the council, to whom the governor referred the petition, welcomed the idea and drafted a bill to permit the free im-

29. Here there is a little mystery which might be solved if we had detailed records of imports at St. Johns in 1788 and succeeding years. Was the ordinance of 1787 repealed by that of 1788? By construction it was, for the few articles added by the former, ashes and leaf tobacco, do not appear in the list of the latter, whose general prohibition excluded everything not in this list. Yet the former was not formally repealed by the latter, which did not even mention it. The western Loyalists had petitioned against the free import of ashes from Vermont, but they also petitioned against lumber from the same source, and lumber was still admitted. It is possible that the introduction of tobacco from Vermont met opposition from the Canadian habitant, but this is unlikely because he would not touch it and, with the aid of his family, he consumed what he produced.

30. 30 George III, c. 1.

port of Vermont pig iron. Then opposition appeared at the council board, chiefly on the ground that the colony's only manufactory, the forges of St. Maurice, should not be injured for the benefit of two unknown foreigners. The attack was so strenuous that the sponsors of the bill succeeded in passing it in April, 1790, only by adding a suspending clause postponing the operation of the ordinance until it received the royal approval. This does not seem to have been granted, which appears rather strange in the light of the mother country's willingness to remove another obstacle that stood in the way of this trade over Lake Champlain.

As Dorchester's council committee observed in their report early in 1790, the free admission into the colony of bar and pig iron, pot and pearl ashes, and lumber could not relieve these articles of the heavy foreign duty imposed on their import into Britain. Only what was certified to be the produce of British colonies could enter the mother country free of duty in British ships. The report suggested to the governor that he appeal to the home government to have Parliament abolish this discrimination. This he did on July 21, and in no perfunctory manner. If, he wrote to the Secretary of State, Britain admitted on the same terms as colonial goods "all the produce of America . . . which shall come into the ports of Quebec and Montreal by land or inland navigation" under the regulations of the provincial legislature, "three considerable advantages" would surely follow: "Canada must gain by the passage of all commodities through the country, Great Britain by an increase of her carrying trade, and both by interesting our neighbors to preserve in the hands of Great Britain this outlet to the sea and to the most profitable markets for all their produce." Quebec rather than London should control the extension of the indulgence. It should be gradual, he thought, so "that our settlers on the north side of the lakes may acquire strength and get the start of those on the opposite shore." But he looked forward to the time when there would be no restriction whatever on the importation of American produce across the border. His reference to the lakes shows that he was thinking of much more than Vermont, and his concluding words recall the query of the neglected instruction. "It appears to me highly proper to form alliances with our neighbours, as soon as all things are well matured. . . . Their own interest alone can render them zealously attached to us, and give duration to any of their engagements."[31] Dorchester's appeal was superfluous. Three weeks before he wrote this dispatch, the discrimination was ended. Levi Allen had been busy over in England, and he found an unexpected ally in Spain. The Nootka Sound affair, by stirring British fears of latent American hos-

31. *Q*, XLV, 532–534.

tility, made the government in London most sensitive to the value of Vermont's friendship. Thereupon the Secretary of State wrote the governor urging him to cultivate the good will of Vermont; and Parliament passed an act, which came into force on July 1, 1790, giving American produce legally imported into the province the same favorable treatment as British colonial produce on entering Great Britain.[32]

32. 30 George III, c. 29. For a further discussion of the effect of the Nootka Sound affair upon Anglo-American relations, see *infra* pp. 106–115.

CHAPTER V

THE DISPUTED ST. CROIX

THE international dispute over what was the St. Croix River, defined by the peace treaty as the eastern boundary of the United States, began on this side of the Atlantic before the treaty was signed on the other. It was precipitated by one who knew the country as few knew it and who had a unique interest in it. He was John Allan, a Scot who had grown up in Nova Scotia to be such a good New Englander that he early ran off to join the Revolution and then bent all his energies to stirring up the red men, New England, and the Continental Congress against the British in his old province. Getting little response beyond words of encouragement, a colonel's commission, and a congressional appointment as superintendent of Indians, he undertook almost singlehanded to use the red men to tear away from Nova Scotia the St. John Valley and the north shore of the Bay of Fundy. Having failed to win this larger territory during the war, he was eager to gain as much of it as the peace terms seemed to allow, and his quick eye soon caught an opportunity.

On August 11, 1783, Allan wrote his first epistle to the people of St. Andrews warning them that they were settling on the American side of the new international border. His challenge rested on the Massachusetts belief that the St. Croix was the river then, and still, known as the Magaguadavic, which falls into Passamaquoddy Bay on the east side; whereas the town of St. Andrews was being founded on the assumption that the St. Croix was the stream then commonly called the Schoodic, emptying into Passamaquoddy Bay on its upper west side, if indeed it was not the Cobscook, which flows into the bay of the same name far down the western side of Passamaquoddy Bay.

Behind the international dispute which thus began lay a dormant intercolonial dispute of pre-Revolutionary days. It arose at the end of the Seven Years' War, when the St. Croix was first named as the boundary of Nova Scotia in a royal commission to a governor of that province. In 1764 Governor Bernard of Massachusetts, the adjoining colony, sent a surveyor named John Mitchel[1] to survey Passamaquoddy Bay and to determine the position of the dividing river. He reported that the Indians identified the Magaguadavic as the St. Croix, but he also observed that

1. This was the way he spelled his name. Because it was commonly printed "Mitchell," a confusion arose in the nineteenth century, when the surveyor was erroneously identified as John Mitchell, the cartographer who prepared the map of 1755 for the British Board of Trade.

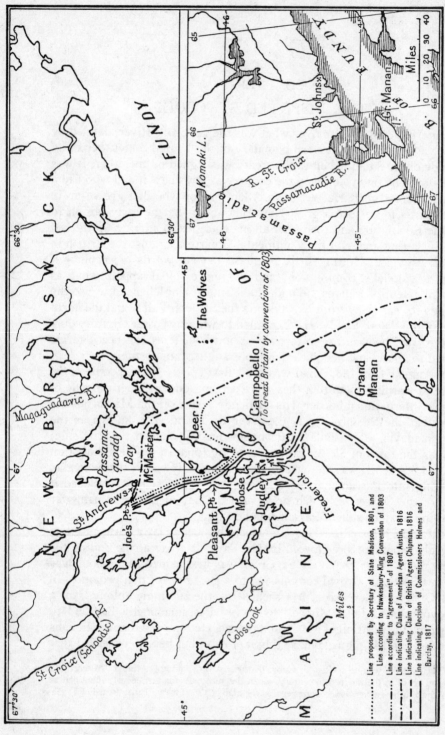

Islands in the Bay of Fundy with Inset from Mitchell's Map Showing his St. Croix and "Passamacadie" Rivers
Redrawn with permission of the American Geographical Society from Charles O. Paullin and John K. Wright,
Atlas of the Historical Geography of the United States.

this was not the river so designated by Champlain a century and a half before. That, according to Mitchel, was the little Digdeguash, which runs into the top of Passamaquoddy Bay. In the following year Governor Wilmot of Nova Scotia likewise tried to discover the limit of his authority over against Massachusetts. His surveyor-general, Charles Morris, found equally obliging Indians, who told him that the St. Croix was the Cobscook. Morris adopted their view, though he had earlier favored the Schoodic, and apparently he convinced Wilmot that Nova Scotia extended as far as the Cobscook.

The conflict between the claims of the two colonies was at once confused by a land deal which was being arranged between the two governors and was the immediate cause of their geographical curiosity. Bernard wanted to get a big block of land for himself and a few friends. He hesitated to make the grants himself in Massachusetts lest the breath of scandal blast the titles. Therefore he sought the nearest possible substitute just across the border in Nova Scotia, and he applied to his willing neighbor in Halifax. "It is for this reason," he confessed to Wilmot, "that I have been desirous of knowing the true River St. Croix: *on the East Side of which, whichever it is, I would have my friends* placed."[2] Bernard's position was somewhat embarrassing. As governor of Massachusetts he would push the St. Croix eastward; as a prospective proprietor of land in Nova Scotia he would pull it westward. Of course he realized that he might lose all if he pulled too hard, and he drew Wilmot's attention to this consideration.[3] Nevertheless in October, 1765, a grant was passed under the seal of Nova Scotia giving Bernard and his associates one hundred thousand acres between the Schoodic and the Cobscook "called the river St. Croix."

One may suspect the governor in Halifax of playing a trick upon his neighbor in Boston by enlisting his interest to support the Nova Scotian claim, but there are good reasons for rejecting this interpretation of the transaction. In this very month Wilmot passed more than a dozen equally large grants in order to gratify influential individuals who had no thought of living on their broad estates in Nova Scotia.[4] Wilmot was not a man of sharp practices, and even if he had been he would scarcely have tried them on Bernard and his friends, whom he was obviously seeking to please. Bernard was a much more powerful person than Wilmot, and

2. W. F. Ganong, "Boundaries of New Brunswick," *Royal Society of Canada Transactions,* Second Series, VIII (1901), 235. The italics are in the original.

3. "If therefore my friends should take grants on the West side of St. Croix, they might be hereafter impeached for being under the Seal of Nova Scotia & out of its boundary." *Ibid.*

4. Because these and other undeveloped grants blocked settlement, they were later escheated. For a list of escheats, see that supplied by Margaret Ells in *The Canadian Historical Association Report,* 1933, pp. 56–58.

so also were two of his associates. They were Thomas Pownall, the former governor of Massachusetts who had returned to England for further government favors, and Richard Jackson, the omniscient counsel of the Board of Trade and Plantations in London.[5] If the governor of Nova Scotia had displeased them, they might have wrecked his career.

After 1765, there was no official display of interest in determining the location of the St. Croix until 1770, when the Massachusetts claim for the Magaguadavic was restated by a commission appointed by Thomas Hutchinson, then acting governor in Boston. Two years later, by direction of the Board of Trade, an accurate survey was made of this part of the coast. The plan of the survey showed the Schoodic as the Great St. Croix and the Magaguadavic as the Little St. Croix. After another three years came the next official action. A parliamentary act passed in 1775 to punish the rebellious colonies by restraining their trade declared that "for all the purposes of this act" the boundary between Massachusetts and Nova Scotia was the river emptying into the western side of Passamaquoddy Bay commonly known as the St. Croix River.[6] This was obviously the Schoodic. It will be observed, however, that the proviso, "for all the purposes of this act," reserved the definitive question, and in any event this piece of legislation could never win American acceptance as in any way binding. With the exception of the few fitful proddings just mentioned, the intercolonial dispute was allowed to sleep until it was awakened as an international issue in 1783; and then, as we shall see, it tended to sink back into slumber.

When Allan found that his warning of August 11 went unheeded, he repeated it in further letters, which had no more effect. He also appealed to the Commonwealth of Massachusetts and the Continental Congress, with results that were slower than his burning soul could have desired. Nothing much happened for about a year. On October 3, 1783, the General Court of the Bay State asked the governor to procure an authenticated statement of facts about the settlement at St. Andrews. He seems to have done little until he received a congressional resolution of January 29, 1784, turning over the problem to him;[7] and even then he was not very expeditious. Congress recommended that he investigate the alleged British encroachment and, if he found it had occurred, request the governor of Nova Scotia to withdraw the trespassers. This reference to Boston produced a resolution of the General Court on July 7, 1784, delegating the task to three agents.[8] Generals Benjamin Lincoln

5. John Pownall, the secretary, was a brother of Thomas.
6. 15 George III, c. 10, sec. 12.
7. *J.C.C.*, XXVI, 52.
8. *A.S.P.F.R.*, I, 90.

and Henry Knox were two who were selected. They acted without the third, who was incapacitated by ill-health.

Lincoln and Knox reported on October 19, 1784, that the new British settlement of St. Andrews was actually within the limits of Massachusetts because they were satisfied that the Magaguadavic was the true St. Croix. They had it from the Indians there, whom they had visited; they had it from the aging John Mitchel, who submitted an affidavit of his findings twenty years before;[9] and they had it from the map which, they learned from Jay,[10] was the only one used by the authors of the treaty in drawing the boundary. This map, prepared by Dr. John Mitchell for the Board of Trade and published in 1755, was admittedly inaccurate, and yet it was so drawn as to indicate clearly that the Magaguadavic was the river which the framers of the treaty took to be the boundary. There Passamaquoddy, spelled Passamacadie, appears as a large square bay with a river flowing into each interior corner. These rivers undoubtedly correspond to the Schoodic and the Magaguadavic; the former, like the bay, is labeled Passamacadie, and the latter is named St. Croix. The report drew attention to the fact that the territory at stake was much wider than the distance between the mouths of the two rivers, that being scarcely more than three leagues whereas the sources were a hundred miles apart.

Though the two generals were convinced that the establishment of St. Andrews was an encroachment, they had not performed the second part of their task. They admitted that they had not communicated with the governor of Nova Scotia, and they excused themselves on two grounds. One was that they had not been in a position to do so until they had finished their inquiry, which was just completed. The other was a political consideration. Having noticed the rapid improvements made by British subjects on the banks of the Schoodic, they foresaw embarrassment in an effort to effect a wholesale removal. Therefore they suggested to the General Court the propriety of quieting in their possessions those who were "desirous of becoming inhabitants of the United States."[11]

Governor Hancock then moved without having secured any such precautionary measure. On November 12, 1784, he wrote to Governor Parr in Halifax, enclosing the congressional resolution, informing him that "a respectable committee" of Massachusetts after "a most careful examination of the evidence" had found the Magaguadavic to be the St. Croix,

9. *Ibid.*, pp. 90–91.

10. Of the three American peace commissioners who negotiated the treaty in Paris, he was the only one who had yet returned home from France. In reply to a similar inquiry, Adams later confirmed Jay's statement and added, "The river St. Croix, which we fixed on, was upon that map the nearest river to St. Johns." *Ibid.*, p. 91.

11. *Ibid.*

and requesting him to "be pleased to recall" the British subjects who had left Nova Scotia and planted themselves on lands west of that river. Meanwhile Nova Scotia had ceased to be the counterclaimant when New Brunswick was erected into a separate government. Therefore Parr simply acknowledged the communication,[12] forwarded it to the governor of the new northern province, and sent a copy home. When Governor Thomas Carleton of New Brunswick received the papers, he was less polite. For six months, he maintained an absolute silence toward Boston.[13]

There the problem was already beginning to wear a more complicated aspect as the result of a discriminating and finely tempered letter of December 27, 1784, by General Rufus Putnam, the future "father of Ohio," who had been surveying the eastern extremity of Massachusetts for the state government. He knew the country well and he had consulted at length, apparently in a most frank and friendly fashion, with the chief British surveyor in that quarter. Putnam found that whether the Schoodic or the Magaguadavic were the right boundary there would still be serious difficulty arising from the wording of the treaty. That instrument gave the United States all the islands within twenty leagues of the shores of the Republic between a line drawn due *east* from the mouth of the St. Croix and another drawn likewise from the mouth of the St. Mary's River on the border of East Florida, except such islands as were within the limits of the Province of Nova Scotia. What puzzled Putnam was the due *east* line from the mouth of the St. Croix. He agreed with the British surveyor that the mouth of the Schoodic was at Devil's Head, where the river turns southward and widens out; but he observed that a line drawn from this point would cut across the mainland and would include in the United States every island not only in Passamaquoddy Bay but also along the coast to the eastward for several leagues. This result, he added, "I can by no means suppose to be intended." For the very same reason, he argued, the line could not be drawn from the mouth of the Magaguadavic. Therefore he concluded that, whichever had been intended as the boundary river, the mouth of the St. Croix would have to be found somewhere else. "The most probable opinion" which he could form was that the peace commissioners had considered the whole of Passamaquoddy Bay as the mouth of the St. Croix. Apparently the British surveyor and his superiors had seen the difficulty involved in taking Devil's Head as marking the mouth of the St. Croix, and had sought protection in a twisted interpretation of the treaty. They, said Putnam, would run a straight line from Devil's Head down to the mouth of the St. Mary's, and would insist that the United States had no claim to

12. *Ibid.*, p. 92.
13. *Ibid.*, p. 95.

the mainland or islands east of this line, thereby cutting off the American mainland as far west as Machias. To the westward of this line, they would allow no islands to be American unless they were within twenty leagues of the coast and had not been granted by the government of Nova Scotia. "Where the gentlemen of Nova Scotia have got the idea" baffled Putnam, but he found it firmly established in St. Andrews and judged that it also ruled in Halifax. Otherwise the American could not understand on what principle the governor of Nova Scotia had recently granted Grand Manan Island, which lay south of a line drawn eastward from any mouth of the St. Croix. The British "idea" may here be dismissed, for it was too palpably absurd to appear as a factor in the boundary dispute between the British and the American governments. But the problem uncovered by Putnam—the national ownership of the islands lying south of an east line—was a real one, and no solution was found until after the War of 1812. As for the immediate dispute over the two rivers, Putnam openly admitted that both were called the St. Croix and only the peace commissioners themselves could determine which they intended to be the boundary.[14]

In the spring of 1785, the voice of sweet reasonableness spoke to the Continental Congress. It was the voice of John Jay, who was now Secretary for Foreign Affairs. On April 21, he reported in favor of immediate steps to settle all disputes with Britain over the eastern boundary of the United States. The method he proposed is worthy of note. In the instructions of 1779, Congress, under his presidency, had authorized its use for determining this very boundary if Britain would not agree to the St. John River as the dividing line, and in 1794 Jay was himself to secure its adoption. It was the international commission method. He would have Congress instruct the American minister in London, John Adams, to propose that commissioners be appointed to hear the conflicting claims and to give a final decision. Each party would name half the commissioners, and they were to be all foreigners or half were to be American citizens and half British subjects. If Britain preferred the second alternative, she was not to choose an inhabitant of the territory west and south of the Gulf of St. Lawrence nor was the American government to select anyone from Massachusetts.[15]

Six months elapsed before Congress was goaded into action on the matter. During the interval a reply at last came from the governor of New Brunswick, inspired by word from London. In striking contrast to the attitude of the American Secretary for Foreign Affairs, the British Secretary of State was intransigent. On receiving the forwarded chal-

14. *Ibid.*, pp. 92–93.
15. *J.C.C.*, XXVIII, 287–290. *A.S.P.F.R.*, I, 94.

lenge of Massachusetts, he wrote at length to Parr to prove that there could be no argument against the Schoodic as the St. Croix.[16] This conclusion, without the supporting argument, was relayed to Boston by Carleton in a letter of June 21, 1785, which was at once transmitted to Congress[17] without producing any visible result.

It was not possible, however, to ignore a disturbing letter from Passamaquoddy written on August 23 by James Avery, a Massachusetts collector of excise. He reported that New Brunswick was asserting claims to Moose, Dudley, and Frederick islands, which had been surveyed for Massachusetts by Putnam and now contained a number of worthy American settlers. Only a few days before, he said, the sheriff of Charlotte County, New Brunswick, had posted notices on Moose Island, which lies across the entrance to Cobscook Bay, requiring the inhabitants to repair to St. Andrews for jury service, much to their alarm because they were threatened with the loss of their lands if they disobeyed. The redoubtable Allan and several other individuals appealed to the American excise collector to checkmate the British sheriff, lest an acknowledgment of British authority prejudice the American title. Thereupon Avery went to the island and, as a justice of the peace, warned the people against obeying a foreign power. He later went to St. Andrews, where he saw the sheriff and other principal inhabitants. They asserted that all the islands in Passamaquoddy Bay belonged to New Brunswick and promised punishment for all who ignored the summons. They also showed him a long letter from the British Secretary of State. It was a copy either of that mentioned above or of a parallel one to Carleton, stating that the Schoodic was the boundary and that British subjects settled between that and the Magaguadavic might fully rely on the protection of their home government.[18] Avery's letter was addressed to Governor Bowdoin, who passed it on to Congress, at the same time sending Carleton a fitting protest from Massachusetts.[19]

Congress referred the incident to Jay, and three days later, on September 22, 1785, he reported. On the principle that "one unopposed encroachment always paves the way for another," he would have Massachusetts, "without *noise* or *delay*,"[20] garrison the most exposed places in the actual possession of that state. The garrisons "should not be so large as to give alarm," they should be under "select and discreet officers," and should be replaced by continental troops as soon as possible. He also

16. *P.A.C.R.*, 1894, p. 431.
17. *A.S.P.F.R.*, I, 95.
18. *Ibid.*
19. *Ibid.*, p. 96.
20. Italics in original.

pointed out the danger of mutual acts of violence on the border. Because they might produce war, he urged the necessity of an early settlement of the disputes, and to this end he drew the attention of Congress to his April report. Three weeks passed before Congress moved, and then, ignoring the suggestion of armed defense against any busy British official, it merely referred the question to Adams in London. If he could not negotiate an adjustment "consistent with the true meaning" of the peace treaty, he was to propose the appointment of commissioners empowered to reach a final decision.[21]

Only two distant echoes came back from the British capital. On July 15, 1786, Adams tucked into the end of a short letter to Jay his only report on the question of the eastern boundary. It was to the effect that Lord Carmarthen, with whom he was dealing, said he would speak to Lord Sydney, who had charge of the colonies, in order that Sir Guy Carleton, then being sent back to Quebec, "might have some instruction concerning it before he went out." [22] The other echo was from the secretary of legation in London. In a letter of September 4, he repeated a current rumor that the instruction had been given.[23] The rumor was never confirmed.

For several years afterward the dispute was almost forgotten. One lone Bostonian, a certain John Boyd, raised a cry of distress. He was the former owner of extensive lands on the east bank of the Schoodic. At the end of the war, like other proprietors of huge Nova Scotian grants, he had seen his estates escheated to make room for the Loyalists. Unlike the others, who were British and therefore could not deny the power of the Nova Scotian government to take away what it had given, he hoped to get a Massachusetts confirmation of his canceled Nova Scotian title. To this end, in the fall of 1786, he appealed to the General Court of Massachusetts against the British encroachment beyond the St. Croix, meaning the Magaguadavic. All the General Court did was to instruct the state's delegates "to recommend him to the attention and favor of Congress, and to move that honorable body to afford him such relief as they may think proper." That body did nothing. After three years of vain waiting, he directed a similar petition to the President, Senate, and House of Representatives of the United States.[24]

In February, 1790, the eastern boundary problem was temporarily revived, apparently as a result of this man's repeated efforts to repair his private fortune. Early in the month, President Washington submitted to

21. *J.C.C.*, XXIX, 753–754.
22. *D.C.U.S.*, V, 136.
23. *Ibid.*, p. 431.
24. *A.S.P.F.R.*, I, 97.

the Senate a budget of accumulated documents bearing on the Massachusetts claim; and a week later he supplemented it with a new resolution just received from that state, asserting that British subjects had been and were still guilty of encroachment upon its border.[25] The upshot was a report of a Senate committee on March 9, recommending "that effectual measures should be taken, as soon as conveniently may be," to settle with Britain all disputes about that line, and reviving Jay's suggestion of April, 1785—representations to the British government and, if they failed to secure an adjustment, the proposal of an international commission.[26] This report was fruitless. Nothing was done until Jay went to London in 1794.

This story of neglect is not surprising. Two men were chiefly responsible for raising the issue and for reviving it when it languished. One was a notorious fanatic and born troublemaker. The other conformed to the traditional type of petitioner of those days who supported his weak prayer by references to his patriotism, his large family, and his distressed circumstances. The modern reader gets the impression of an American suspicion, arising early in the dispute, that the British were perhaps right in their contention for the Schoodic. Putnam certainly suggested it in 1784; and Adams, in spite of an early letter to the contrary,[27] seems to have betrayed it. As a good Massachusetts man and one of the peace commissioners, he would surely have done more than he did in London if he had been convinced that the Magaguadavic had been intended as the boundary. At that very time, on the complaint of his state and of the Continental Congress, he made quite a fuss over the truculent behavior of a British naval officer in Boston. There might have been more American interest in the dispute if there had been more provocation from New Brunswick; but the British surveyor whom Putnam met did not follow up his wild notion of an imaginary line, and the zealous British sheriff, who played into Allan's hands, soon ceased from troubling. Governor Hancock's letter of February, 1790, to President Washington, covering the legislature's resolution, mentioned the likelihood of "a disagreeable contention" between the two people on the frontier, but the resolution said nothing about it and the governor's fears were not fulfilled. Here it should also be observed that, when the Senate committee suggested a new approach to the British government, the weary Adams had long since shaken the dust of England from off his feet and no successor had been appointed because Britain had not deigned to send a minister to the United States. There was then no official contact between the two gov-

25. *Ibid.*, pp. 90-99.
26. *Ibid.*, p. 100.
27. *Supra*, n. 10.

ernments. Diplomatic representatives were at last exchanged in 1791 and 1792, but still there was no American move to settle the question until Jay, in 1794, arranged for its solution.

Perhaps the main reason for the neglect lies in the apparent unimportance of the dispute during the decade following the war. Both sides refrained from making extravagant claims, so that the stake seemed small. When viewed relatively, the question shrinks to nothing because it was completely overshadowed by other issues.

CHAPTER VI

THE RETENTION OF THE WESTERN POSTS

BOTH Britain and the United States violated the Treaty of Paris from the very beginning. Each side entered upon this unhappy course quite independently, and then tried to cast the blame on the other. The result was a bitter controversy which might easily have involved British North America in a war with the United States. Fortunately, after several years, the quarrel disappeared from official view without recourse to arms, the causes being partly settled by a new treaty, partly removed by unilateral action, and partly abandoned. Unfortunately, even to the present day, many historians have not been as wise as their governments. Both British and American writers, with a national bias unbecoming to those who profess objectivity, have too often repeated the old recriminations, thereby renewing ill feeling that should have died long ago.

The violation of most immediate concern to Canada was Britain's refusal to surrender territory she had signed away in the treaty. Article VII stipulated that "His Britannic Majesty shall with all convenient speed . . . withdraw all his armies, garrisons, and fleets from the said United States, and from every port, place, and harbour within the same." The British commander-in-chief in America punctiliously evacuated New York before the ratifications of the treaty had been exchanged, but the advent of peace brought no order for the withdrawal of the British garrisons in the interior, which were now on the American side of the line. The chief of these posts thus held were Oswegatchie (Ogdensburg, N.Y.), Oswego, Niagara, Presque Isle (Erie, Pa.), Sandusky, Detroit, and Michilimackinac. They were only a few isolated forts on the edge of the United States and their total area was a negligible number of acres, yet they enabled Britain to retain effective control over many thousand square miles of American territory. For eleven years, Britain refused to fix any date when she would deliver these keys of the West. Until the negotiation of Jay's Treaty in 1794, which provided for their surrender in 1796, it looked as if Britain was determined to keep them indefinitely, in defiance of her pledged word.

Americans, then and since, leaped to the conclusion that this violation of the treaty sprang from a British desire to preserve the valuable fur trade that depended on these posts. The belief was natural. English and Canadian merchants interested in the trade had done their utmost to procure a more southerly boundary for this very purpose; and though this effort of big business to affect high politics failed, the merchants were assured that they would not suffer. There was to be such freedom of movement across the border that the trade would continue to flow unimpeded along its old course, and in any event the British garrisons would remain in the posts on American territory long enough to cover the withdrawal of traders who wished to liquidate their operations there. When the hope of reciprocity was sacrificed on the altar of the navigation laws, the retention of the posts appeared to be the only means by which Britain could retain the fur trade focused in Montreal.

There was no secret about the intention to delay the recall of the troops for the sake of the fur trade, reciprocity or no reciprocity. Early in June, 1783, David Hartley proposed to the American peace commissioners that the treaty allow these garrisons to remain for three years to secure the British lives and property that were at the mercy of the red men; and the Americans countered by proposing a continuance of the occupation only until Congress ordered evacuation and American garrisons arrived to take over from the British. Here the matter rested until August, when Hartley presented the draft of the definitive treaty which he was to sign forthwith if the Americans accepted it. This contained no special provision for the surrender of the western posts, though both sides had anticipated such an arrangement. Fox's precipitancy in thrusting forward the preliminary articles as the final treaty was responsible for this elimination. The posts thus came under the general clause, quoted above, providing for the removal of British forces from the United States "with all convenient speed." The American commissioners were apprehensive, for they had received official warning of how the British government might interpret this vague phrase. Nevertheless they accepted it for the sake of grasping the peace within their reach. They must therefore share the blame for the peace's turning rotten in their hands. This consideration, which has often been overlooked, makes the British violation less flagrant in its initial stages.

The oft-repeated statement that Britain continued to hold the posts for the sake of preserving her monopoly of the fur trade is a good illustration of the operation of national suspicion and prejudice. It has long been accepted in the United States as an established fact though it has never been proven. True, the original delay of orders for the withdrawal of the garrisons was frankly based on consideration for the fur trade. But this original delay was to be only temporary, three years at most if we may judge from Hartley's proposal; and the purpose was to cover the withdrawal of British trading commitments on the American side of the line rather than the continuance of the British monopoly there. It is also true that the British fur-trading interests did their utmost to effect, and greatly profited by, the further delay which put off indefinitely the surrender of the posts; but to say that this proves the old charge is to reason backward. The common American belief that Britain was actuated by an economic motive is turned inside out when pushed to its conclusion. It ignores an important calculation that was made in London during the peace negotiations and could hardly have been ignored in the years that followed. It is a balancing of the cost of keeping the posts over against the loss of the fur trade that might follow their abandonment.

The interested merchants never asserted that anything more would be lost than the trade on the American side of the line and the capital already entrusted there. According to their own estimates, London imported annually from Canada furs worth about two hundred thousand pounds, of which nearly two-thirds came from the American side of the line, and the commercial debt of the whole interior was three hundred thousand pounds.[1] We may therefore conclude that two-thirds of this amount, or two hundred thousand pounds, was owing from American territory. This was the capital in jeopardy. It was by no means certain that it would wholly disappear, but even if it did the loss would be equivalent to only twelve thousand pounds a year, 6 per cent being then good interest. Turning to the trade to form some idea of the possible annual loss, we must remember that what was at stake was not the selling price of the furs but only a small fraction of it—the profit on handling two-thirds of two hundred thousand pounds' worth of furs. Nor would all this be sacrificed. Some of the trade might have disappeared, but mercantile circles commonly assumed that the surrender of the posts would simply transfer the trade to Americans. Even if that were true, it would make little difference to Britain. Though gathered by American traders, the furs would still find their way to the world market in London, and British manufactures would still be used to pay for them because the United States had no substitutes. In short, the profit taken in Britain would be little affected. The only British sufferers would be the merchants and traders of Canada who would no longer collect their share of the profit on the trade that would cease to pass through Montreal, and, as Shelburne and others had already seen, the great natural advantages of that Canadian city would probably continue to draw a large portion of the furs gathered on the American side of the line. Of the annual profit, therefore, only a small portion would be lost. At most, it would be no more than a very few thousand pounds. Perhaps twenty thousand pounds would cover both items, the annual interest on the capital lost in the interior and the annual profit sacrificed. The total cost of keeping the posts has not yet been ascertained, but some idea of how enormous it was may be deduced from the fact that the bills presented for merchandise, provi-

1. Q, XLIX, 289.

sions, and rum purchased at Detroit during the ten months following November, 1779, amounted to nearly a hundred thousand pounds. This sum represents only supplementary costs at one post.[2] To conclude, the private gain was as dust in the balance compared with the public loss. From a purely business standpoint it was Britain's interest to deliver the posts to the Americans as soon as possible, if only the fur trade were taken into account. Therefore we must seek other reasons for Britain's violation of the treaty.

The indefinite retention of the posts was due primarily to a British blunder and secondarily to an American weakness. The blunder was the utter neglect of the Indians in the negotiation of peace with the United States. The promise Britain made to the latter clashed with the guarantee she had given to the former. The painful dilemma of having to break her word with either white or red Americans was thus of her own making, and only they could release her by reaching some mutually satisfactory agreement between themselves. It was therefore the combined interest of all three parties that such an agreement be made, but for a number of years the new Republic proved incapable of reaching this agreement. No blame attaches to the United States for not assuming the obligation which the British Crown had undertaken toward the Indians on American soil, for even if there had been no Revolution the treaty of 1768 was out of date, such had been and still continued to be the pressure of pioneers. One may say, however, that the United States brought on the ensuing trouble through the failure to work out and adopt immediately a sensible Indian policy or to create a government which could do so. It was this failure which forced the British to stay as a consequence of their earlier blunder. Then things were turned topsy-turvy by the American cry, echoed down through the years, that the British stay caused the American failure.

The war in the interior was only suspended by the advent of peace between Britain and the United States, for the red men were not bound by the Treaty of Paris. They were neither consulted about it nor mentioned in it. A supplementary peace was therefore necessary to liquidate the war in the West. For a while there were separate negotiations between individual states and neighboring tribes. Then Congress undertook a general settlement on the basis of a report by a committee to which the whole problem had been referred.

A cursory examination of this report, which was submitted on October 15, 1783, is sufficient to reveal the folly of the newly projected policy. The committee betrayed no sense of responsibility toward the Indians. The red men had levied barbarous war on the United States, and now

2. See A. L. Burt, *The Old Province of Quebec,* p. 304.

that the treaty had delivered them into the hands of the United States the red men had no rights whatsoever. The report admitted, however, that it would be extremely difficult if not impossible to clear all American soil of the Indians, and that it would be impolitic to attempt it because it would drive them and their fur trade into the arms of the British. The savages were therefore to be left on land not needed by the United States, which needed a lot. "The United States stands pledged to grant portions of the uncultivated lands as a bounty to their army and in reward of their courage and fidelity." In addition to this first bonus, new land was required to accommodate the expanding population, and for pressing financial reasons. "The public creditors have been led to believe and have a right to expect that those territories will be speedily improved into a fund towards the security and payment of the national debt." As the Indians had really forfeited their lands by their actions during the war, and therefore had no claims to be extinguished by purchase, they could have no "reasonable objections" to the American government's appropriating these lands without payment. Some compensation might be offered if necessary to avoid the risk of renewing the war "which will be much more expensive," but the committee trusted that the Indians would make no "extravagant demands" when they were informed how great were the damages they had inflicted and the expenses they had imposed upon the United States during the war. "As we are disposed to be kind to them, to supply their wants and to partake of their trade, we . . . draw a veil over what is passed and will establish a boundary between them and us." The boundary then prescribed followed the Miami River from its mouth, where the border between the present states of Ohio and Indiana reaches the Ohio River, to about Springfield, Ohio, thence about due north to the Maumee, and down that stream to Toledo on Lake Erie. This dictated settlement was to be written into one peace treaty with all the western tribes.[3]

Elias Boudinot, the able president of Congress and acting Secretary for Foreign Affairs, raised his voice in protest, but he might as well have been crying in the wilderness. He later looked back and said: "As to originating the Indian war, so far from being originated by Great Britain, I know that it originated in the false policy of Congress in 1783; I foretold it then with all of its consequences."[4] This policy was amended for the worse in March, 1784, when Congress shifted the line farther to the west and directed the peace commissioners, whom it had just elected, to pursue separate negotiations with the scattered tribes on the principle

3. J.C.C., XXV, 681–686.
4. Quoted in Justin Winsor, *The Westward Movement* (Boston, 1897), p. 237.

of *divide et impera*.[5] A combination of the tribes in the interior was already feared.

Only the possession of overwhelming force could have enabled Congress to impose such a settlement upon the Indians, and Congress had neither men nor money at its disposal. The utter impotence of the confederacy would have ruined even the best policy, for it gave free rein to the sturdy race of frontiersmen then invading the territory of the Indians. These pioneers laughed at the orders of Congress against private purchase or occupation of lands beyond the jurisdiction of any particular state. The few officers who tried to enforce the orders made no impression upon these men who pushed on, armed against all opposition, white and red.

At Fort Stanwix in 1784, at Fort McIntosh in 1785, at the mouth of the Miami in 1786, and at Fort Harmar in 1789, the agents of Congress negotiated piecemeal treaties which, added together, were to have given an approximation to a general settlement of the northern interior. But the Indians refused to be bound in this fashion. They declared the treaties worthless, and thereby made them so. Peace became more impossible as the trickle of blood along the frontier grew into an angry stream.

Turning back to the correspondence of Governor Frederick Haldimand in Quebec, we can there see clearly the painful dilemma which Britain had to face as a consequence of her own blunder, and how the pressure of this dilemma forced the emergence of the decision to retain the posts indefinitely. These dispatches therefore deserve careful scrutiny.

Toward the end of April, 1783, Haldimand received a printed copy of the peace preliminaries. This was his first intimation of what the new boundary was to be, and it came as a great shock. The startling news soon flew about, for he communicated it to the Montreal merchants that they might guide their affairs accordingly. On May 7 he reported that the people were "much alarmed at the idea of abandoning the posts in the upper country, which are no less necessary to their security than to their commerce." Then, by way of contrast, he plunged into a statement of what concerned him most:

My own anxiety at present arises from an apprehension of the effects which the preliminaries will have upon the minds of our Indian allies, who will consider themselves abandoned to the resentment of an ungenerous and implacable enemy . . . who, in the exultation of their present success, are at no pains to conceal their designs against them.[6]

5. *J.C.C.*, XXVI, 152–154.
6. *Q*, XXI, 220.

On June 2, the governor reported a visit from Joseph Brant and another Mohawk chief named John, who had been deputed by the Six Nations to learn the truth about the preliminary articles. They had heard evil rumors that disturbed them. Haldimand was also disturbed. He wrote:

I own that I was much embarrassed and wished to have had it in my power to talk to them with more certainty than I could of the measures which the government intended to take for their security and welfare. These Indians have great merit and sufferings to plead in the cause of Great Britain. It will be a difficult task, after what has happened, to convince them of our good faith; they seem peculiarly hurt that no mention is made of them in the treaty. . . . Nothing shall be neglected on my part which can contribute to give them satisfaction, or to reconcile them with the subjects of the United States of North America, tho' I must acknowledge that I foresee great difficulties. Actions not words can make impression upon them. I have therefore dispatched Major Holland, the surveyor general of the province, to Lake Ontario to examine into the state of the old French post at Cataraqui,[7] and to survey the north side of the lake, as I will endeavour to prevail upon the Mohawks to settle there, provided the country contiguous to it should be found propitious. Joseph Brant and John the Mohawk are returned with him.[8]

Three months before the treaty was signed, Haldimand thus set forth the two main objects of British policy in the interior of America. One was to persuade the red men that their real interest lay in coming to terms with the victors in the late war. A careful examination of the official correspondence that passed between Quebec and London affords convincing proof that there was a fairly consistent British effort, throughout the troubled years that followed, to effect this reconciliation. Britain was not sacrificing interest for honor. Both considerations dictated the end in view. The tragedy was that Americans, by their dealings with the Indians, defeated the British purpose which should have been their own too.

The second object proposed in Quebec and accepted in London was to restore the shattered confidence of the Indians in the British. Haldimand admitted that it would be far from easy, but he determined to do everything possible to prove to Britain's red allies that she had not forsaken them. From now on through several years, tortuous arguments and honeyed phrases were used in many councils with suspicious savages to persuade them that black was white, that Britain had not really done what they thought she had done. But these efforts probably had no more influence than the wind. Over the untutored minds of the natives, words

7. Kingston, Ont.
8. *Ibid.*, pp. 229–231.

had little power compared with deeds. The governor knew it well, and he acted accordingly. He saw to it that the customary presents were distributed liberally, and, as intimated above, he undertook immediately to provide lands under the British flag for all Indians who were expelled from their old homes in the new United States. It should not escape attention that, in preparing for this transplantation, he was contemplating the present surrender of the keys of the West, the interior posts on American soil.

The following quotations from the proceedings of Sir John Johnson's conference with the Six Nations at Niagara in the latter part of July, 1783,[9] transmitted to London by Haldimand three weeks later, give an early and good illustration of this policy in operation. Assisted by several army officers, the son and successor of the great Sir William addressed the assembled tribes on the "peace which seems to give you great uneasiness on account of the boundary line." He continued:

You are not to believe or even think that by the line which has been described it was meant to deprive you of an extent of country of which the right of soil belongs to and is in yourselves as sole proprietaries as far as the boundary line agreed upon and established in the most solemn and public manner (in the presence and with the consent of the governors and commissioners deputed by the different colonies for that purpose) by your late worthy brother and friend Sir William Johnson in the year 1768 at Fort Stanwix. Neither can I harbour an idea that the United States will act so unjustly or unpolitically as to endeavour to deprive you of any part of your country under the pretence of having conquered it. The King still considers you his faithful allies, as his children, and will continue to promote your happiness by his protection and encouragement of your usual intercourse with traders with all other benefits in his power to afford you. I therefore in the most earnest manner recommend to you for your own advantage to bear your losses with manly fortitude, forgiving and forgetting what is past, looking forward in full hopes and expectation that, on the return of the blessings of peace and [on] cool and just reflection, all animosity and enmity will cease, conciliation succeed and friendships be renewed; and as a proof of your inclination to promote that desireable end, let me once more recommend to you to collect and give up without exception all prisoners that may be yet among you, and as an inducement to comply with what I recommend, and as a proof of His Majesty's bounty, and attention to you, I have brought up a large assortment of every thing necessary to supply your wants, and I have further the satisfaction to acquaint you that so far from being neglected or cast off when your services can be no longer wanted, as has been very unjustly imagined and reported, the King has ordered out a large cargo of goods to supply your further wants as well as to afford relief to all such among you who

9. *Ibid.*, pp. 433–455.

by the fortune of war, the loss of friends, old age, or infirmities are rendered unable to support themselves.

I must recommend to you to be unanimous among yourselves and not to separate or scatter about the country and thereby weaken yourselves and lessen your consequence, and to advise your young men to desist from all acts of hostility. Otherwise they may draw on themselves the resentment of the people on the frontiers, which was very near being the case some time in May, in consequence of the Shawanese and Delawares on the waters of the Miamis having taken a number of women and children, as has been represented by their commissioner who lately left this place for Albany.

The chiefs replied:

You also have induced us to believe that by that line it was not intended to deprive us of our country of which the right of soil was in ourselves agreeable to the treaty in 1768 at Fort Stanwix. . . . We are exceedingly happy to hear your opinion on that subject. It's true we have been very uneasy, and with much reason, our fear relative to our country having given us great concern; but should the Americans molest, or claim any part of our country, we shall then ask assistance of the King our father who still considers us his faithful allies and children for we have assisted him in his battles and have done whatever was required during the war, notwithstanding the war was entirely his own and we had nothing to do with it farther than assisting him as old allies. At the commencement of the war we were told both by the commanding officer at this post and by Col. Butler that all the rebel prisoners we should take should be our own, notwithstanding which at your request we are determined to collect them all and give them to you without exception. We will moreover send messages to our younger brethren the western nations strongly recommending them to follow our example.

In concluding the conference, Johnson said:

The opinion I gave you relative to the boundary line agreed upon, I conceive to be just; and as we are yet uninformed of what secret treaties may have taken place or indeed that even the definitive treaty is as yet signed, I am in hopes that matters may turn out more favorable than we at present apprehend them to be.

Sir John was feeding his hearers with false hopes, for he was in a desperate position. He knew that Britain had betrayed the Indians, and they knew it; yet he had to persuade them to the contrary. One thing alone would have reassured them, and that was the promise of military support to maintain the integrity of the Fort Stanwix line. But that was something which neither he nor any other British official in America could give. It would commit Britain to a resumption of the war from which she had just escaped. On the other hand, it was impossible for him to say that the chiefs' request for aid would encounter refusal, for such a warning would have been conclusive proof to the red men that their

white father had deserted them. Therefore in his final oration the superintendent of Indian affairs did not even touch the explosive idea propounded by his guests.

Early in August, 1783, Major General Baron von Steuben, sent by
General Washington in accordance with congressional directions, arrived in Canada. His mission was not to demand the surrender of the
western posts. That would have been premature until after the ratification of the treaty, which was not yet even signed. Von Steuben was to
arrange with Haldimand how the posts should be delivered when the
time came, and he was also to visit them to form an opinion on how they
should be garrisoned and supported after the transfer. Seldom has a man
enjoyed a more delightful failure. In a few days Haldimand bowed Von
Steuben out of the province, and he did it so graciously that the disappointed emissary wrote back a letter of thanks in the warmest terms.
Lack of instructions from England, which the governor regretted exceedingly because he would dearly like to oblige both General Washington
and his agent, was the excuse for sending the latter back empty-handed
and for refusing to let him visit the posts. Haldimand's real motives are
to be found in his report to Lord North, dated August 20.[10] He was
afraid, not of what Von Steuben might do, but of what might be done to
him, and he was playing for time.

Tho I have been successful, by the unwearied efforts of the officer under my
command, in preventing the Indians from going to war, and am not without
hopes of being able to keep them quiet, provided the Americans are not aggres-
sors, yet I had well grounded apprehensions that the resentment and . . .
revenge . . . so predominant amongst the Indians might, at this critical moment, have been productive of great mischief either to Major Genl. de Steuben,
his suite, or to the escort which I should necessarily have given him. The risk of
such an event would at least have been great, and the good which could result
from the premature visit of the baron did not appear to me sufficient to compensate for that risk, especially as the misfortune, however unjustly, would
certainly be imputed to us. . . . Many bad, and no good consequences might have
arisen from such premature discussion [of how the posts should be surrendered].
The longer the evacuation is delayed, the more time is given to our traders to
remove their merchandise, or to convert it into furs, and the greater opportunity
is given to the officers under my command to reconcile the Indians to a measure
for which they entertain the greatest abhorrence.

Haldimand still contemplated making delivery of the posts, and he
gave his advice on how it should be done. After explaining that Congress
had proposed through Von Steuben to purchase the military stores and
provisions in the various forts, he wrote:

10. *Ibid.*, pp. 388–394.

My answer was that I had no such power or authority, and that the measure was fraught with danger. I hope no such idea is entertained in England, for such a measure would be considered by the Indians as selling them to their enemies and will, in all probability, be the signal for an attack against our garrisons and people. I wish that the orders in consequence of the definitive treaty may be to withdraw the stores and troops from the forts, leaving it to the Indians to make their own conditions with the Americans. This appears to me the measure the best calculated for the safety of His Majesty's troops and subjects who are too much dispersed to be able to resist an attack from the Indians, who are forming a general confederacy for their own security and which may be directed equally against us as the Americans.

The governor was vainly hoping that dispatches from England would bring some information, he knew not what, with which he could prove to the Indians that they had not been forgotten and thereby "render the most essential services to the United States of America by preventing the horrors and dangers of an Indian war." His uneasiness grew as the weeks passed and London remained silent while ominous news came out of the West. In the middle of October, he reported that the native tribes had "completed the general confederation from one extremity of North America to the other." [11] On November 17, just as navigation on the St. Lawrence was about to close, he at last received a dispatch from Lord North dealing with the affairs of the interior.[12] If ever he felt chagrin, he must have felt it then. Though full of praise for all he had done, the letter was empty of guidance, and it contained a passage confessing what he and his agents had been denying—the guilt of the British government. Lord North welcomed the suggestion of settling the Mohawks on the north side of Lake Ontario because "it would be far from either generous or just in us, *after our cession of their territories and hunting grounds,*[13] to forsake them." The governor was to make similar offers to any other friendly native tribes anxious to withdraw from the United States. It was to be hoped, continued the fatuous lord, that such Indians would be able to continue hunting on their old grounds and would return with their peltries to trade them in security on British soil. The Secretary of State, incapable of holding the reins, was throwing them across the horse's neck.

Within ten days Haldimand made up his mind on the proper course to follow, and he explained it in a dispatch of November 27 to Lord North.[14] This he sent by messenger down to Halifax because the last transport of

11. *Ibid.*, XXII, 5.
12. *Ibid.*, XXI, 279–287.
13. Italics inserted.
14. *Ibid.*, XXIII, 46–51.

the season had already sailed from Quebec and the contents of the letter were too important to admit of unnecessary delay. The pertinent part, which begins with some plain speaking, is as follows:

They [the Indians] entertain no idea (though the Americans have not been wanting to insinuate it) that the King either has ceded or had a right to cede their territories or hunting grounds to the United States of North America. These people, my Lord, have as enlightened ideas of the nature and obligations of treaties as the most civilized nations have, and know that no infringement of the treaty in 1768 which fixed the limits between their country and that of the different provinces in North America can be binding upon them without their express concurrence and consent. Your Lordship will observe that the object of their general confederacy is to defend their country against all invaders. In case things should proceed to extremities, the event no doubt will be the destruction of the Indians, but during the contest not only the Americans but perhaps many of His Majesty's subjects will be exposed to great distresses. To prevent such a disastrous event as an Indian war is a consideration worthy the attention of both nations, and cannot be prevented so effectually as by allowing the posts in the upper country to remain as they are for some time. . . . It would certainly be better for both nations and the most likely means to prevent jealousies and quarrels that the intermediate country between the limits assigned to Canada by the provisional treaty and those established as formerly mentioned by that in the year 1768 should be considered entirely as belonging to the Indians, and that the subjects neither of Great Britain nor of the American States should be allowed to settle within them, but that the subjects of each should have liberty to trade where they please.

This was the crucial proposal to retain the posts indefinitely, and it was made without even a reference to the fur trade as a supporting argument. Indeed Haldimand was so far from seeking to exclude Americans that he proposed to admit them to share on equal terms what was then the bulk of the trade. His motive for wishing to keep the posts indefinitely was perfectly simple. It was to prevent the awful explosion, another and perhaps worse Pontiac's Revolt, which seemed about to burst. This was likewise his single purpose in reviving the neutral-barrier project which had troubled the peace negotiations over in Europe.

London adopted the proposal from Quebec. Lord North had nothing to do with it. He had fallen with Fox long before Haldimand's letter reached the Secretary of State's office on March 7, 1784. A month later, the general election having intervened, Lord Sydney, replying to the governor's dispatches of the preceding summer and autumn, said:

The 7th Article stipulates that they shall be evacuated with all convenient speed, but no certain time is fixed, and as America has not on her part complied with even one article of the treaty, I think we may reconcile it in the present instance to delay the evacuation of those posts, at least until we are enabled to secure the traders in the interior country and withdraw their property. The management of the Indians requires great attention and address at this critical juncture, and I am persuaded that our retaining possession of those posts will not even be detrimental to America and may be the means of preventing mischiefs which are likely to happen should the posts be delivered up whilst the resentment of the Indians continues at so high a pitch.[15]

Here the fur trade creeps in again, but the reference to it should not be misinterpreted. It was merely incidental. The Secretary of State was looking forward to the present termination rather than the indefinite continuance of the British traffic south of the boundary, and he went straight on to echo Haldimand's argument that it was to the interest of the United States as well as of Britain for the latter to keep the posts while the natives were in such a dangerous mood.

Several weeks before this letter reached him, Haldimand had again to face the embarrassing question of evacuation without having received any advice from London; and then he added to the discussion a new feature which has stuck even to the present day. Early in May, 1784, a certain Lieutenant Colonel Fish, who had come and gone with Von Steuben,[16] returned to Canada in the service of Governor Clinton of New York to arrange for the transfer of the posts in that state. It was a polite request based on the ratification of the definitive treaty, and it was politely parried. Haldimand was full of regrets that he had received no orders, and of course he would obey them scrupulously when they arrived. It was in the midst of this not unpleasant visit of Fish in Quebec that the treatment of the Loyalists was first linked with the retention of the posts. Haldimand did it cautiously. In conversation only and as his mere personal opinion, he told Fish that evacuation should be delayed until the United States had executed the treaty articles in favor of the Loyalists. When reporting the whole incident to the Secretary of State, the governor suggested that this, his private idea, might be adopted as a public policy:

It appears to me that the evacuation of the posts might be delayed as the means of obliging the Congress to prolong the term of one year granted by the treaty for the Loyalists to solicit the recovery of their estates, for from the want of government and good order in the different states it has not hitherto been safe for the Loyalists to go amongst them for that purpose.[17]

Two months later Haldimand drove the suggestion home by reporting

15. *Ibid.*, pp. 60–61.
16. *Ibid.*, p. 125.
17. *Ibid.*, pp. 164–165.

a repetition of the incident. This time his guest was Lieutenant Colonel William Hull, who represented Major General Knox, the republican Secretary of War. Though Sydney's letter had arrived during the interval, it offered the governor no help beyond the information that the posts were to be held. He was itching to write the Loyalist argument into his formal reply, but he refrained from committing his government in this way without authority. He seized the opportunity, however, to talk to Hull about the Loyalists much as he had spoken to Fish about them.[18] Again London caught up the suggestion from Quebec.

Thus the British violation of the treaty quickly passed through several stages. Originally the retention of the posts was intended to be very temporary and to cover the liquidation of British fur-trading interests south of the line. Before the ratification of the treaty, until which time Britain was under no obligation to withdraw the garrisons, Governor Haldimand introduced a new and noneconomic motive which lengthened indefinitely the period of continued occupation. It was to prevent another Pontiac's Revolt which might have swallowed up the lives of many Britons, more Americans, and still more Indians. Then, having persuaded the home government to postpone evacuation indefinitely, he pointed out how this decision could be not only excused but also turned to further profit. The sufferings of the Loyalists might be used as a public justification for refusing to yield the posts, and the retention of the posts might be used to relieve the sufferings of the Loyalists. The other well-known British excuse was already being supplied by clamorous English merchants who, in their efforts to collect American debts, encountered obstacles though Article IV of the treaty promised that there should be none. Here too the retention of the posts found a use as well as an excuse. Britain held a stick with which she might coerce her debtors in America.

The American violation of the treaty in the matter of debts was so patent that only those who were particularly interested in doing so could deny it, but in the treatment meted out to Loyalists it was not so clear except to the actual sufferers and their friends. Naturally the British government laid much greater stress on debts as an excuse for holding the posts. Here, however, we should pay more attention to the lesser infraction. Canadian-American relations were affected only indirectly and temporarily by the debts question but intimately and permanently by the Loyalists. The great majority of the English-speaking population of British North America on the morrow of the Revolution was composed of these exiles from the United States. It is not surprising therefore that the revolutionary tradition in the United States has a close counterpart in the Loyalist tradition in Canada. What the one has done to American

18. *Ibid.*, p. 329.

feeling toward Britain, the other has done to Canadian feeling toward the United States.[19] This, however, was due to something more than a supposed violation of the treaty. The bitter feelings which entered into the Canadian body came straight out of the war, which was really a civil war. As the defeated faction, the Tories or Loyalists found in the terms which ended the struggle little provision for justice and less for mercy.

In Article V of the treaty, Congress promised that it would "earnestly recommend" to the legislatures of the various states that they restore the confiscated property and rights of "real British subjects" and of those people who were within the British lines in America but had never borne arms against the United States. Others—that is, Americans who had fought to preserve the British connection—were to be free to return and to remain for twelve months unmolested while they endeavored to recover their confiscated property. To assist this class of people, Congress promised to send the state legislatures two further "earnest recommendations." One was to reconsider and to revise their punitive legislation born of the war to make it "perfectly consistent, not only with justice and equity, but with that spirit of conciliation, which, on the return of the blessings of peace, should universally prevail." The second was to restore rights and properties to the Loyalists. They, however, were to repurchase at the price paid whatever had fallen into other private hands. Article VI of the treaty stipulated that there were to be no further prosecutions or confiscations arising out of anyone's participation in the war.

The fifth article was a farce, and the sixth a nullity. Congress fulfilled its duty by sending the "earnest recommendations," but for all their effect they might as well have been sent by George III. Except in South Carolina, where considerable justice was done, the "traitors" still suffered. Repeated confiscation rather than repentant restoration was the rule, and Loyalists who returned to get their property only too often got something very different. A few were killed; more were tarred and feathered; and many were again glad to escape with their lives. It is not surprising that Haldimand seized the apparent opportunity to rescue the perishing by tying them to the posts. His action was more gallant than honest, for the evil upon which he put his finger was not, strictly speaking, a violation of the treaty. The only promise in Article V, to which he referred, was that certain recommendations should be sent to the various states, and this promise was performed. Article VI, however, was violated by confiscatory state legislation after the peace, but Haldimand said

19. Americans have been much less conscious of the latter feeling than have Englishmen of the former, not because one people is naturally more sensitive than the other, but because the United States and Great Britain have been more nearly equal in strength than have British North America and the United States.

nothing about it, probably because he knew nothing about it at the time.

Most of the sufferings of the Loyalists had nothing to do with any violation of the treaty. The treaty simply did not protect them. For this defect, the opposition blamed the government when the latter submitted the preliminaries to Parliament. But the government had done its best to make protection of the Loyalists a corner stone of the treaty. It is doubtful if the effort could have succeeded without Britain's threatening to resume the war, and the government could not risk committing the country by such a move. Though Parliament rejected Shelburne, it accepted his peace in spite of this defect. Britain would compensate her own suffering children. This British acceptance of the treaty without the desired provision for the Loyalists thus offers a certain parallel with the acceptance by the American commissioners knowing that the treaty as worded would probably be interpreted to delay the surrender of the posts. Each side preferred a defective peace to the danger of renewing the war.

More fundamental was another reason which explains the American violation of the treaty as well as its defect from a British standpoint. Here debts and Loyalists can be lumped together. This treaty was peculiar in that only one of its two signatories possessed the attributes of sovereignty. America could bind Britain, but Britain could not bind America. The American party to the treaty was Congress, and Congress had only a limited power delegated by the thirteen sovereign states. It had no authority to bind them, and not one of them incurred a single legal obligation under the Treaty of Paris. The American peace commissioners did not try to conceal this fact. They rather emphasized it, because it was a shield against British demands. Yet some Canadians who should know better still blame the sad fate of the Loyalists upon the bad faith of the United States.

By the end of 1784, it was evident that the United States could not secure the western posts by applying for them in Quebec. Attention was therefore turned to London, and the first article of the instructions to the first American minister to Britain directed him to press for the surrender of these American keys to the American West.[20] On assuming his new duties in the late spring of 1785, John Adams at once found that American obstacles to the recovery of British debts had raised a British obstacle to the transfer of the posts. Thereupon he reversed the British argument by saying that the retention of the posts withheld from the United States a trade "which would have gone a great way" to assist the payment of debts.[21] He also suggested that the continuance of the British in the centers of Indian influence was leading to an Indian war which "might

20. *D.C.U.S.* IV, 158.
21. *Ibid.*, p. 206.

spread wider and last longer than any man could foresee." [22] After various informal conversations which ran round in such circles and never got anywhere, the American minister submitted, on December 8, a formal memorial demanding the evacuation of the frontier posts.[23]

When the American minister thus grew bolder, his government turned timid. In October the Secretary for Foreign Affairs, John Jay, had been a little impatient with Adams for his silence about the surrender of the posts,[24] but now he wanted to hold him back. At the end of March, 1786, he reported to Congress the danger into which their representative in London was running. A categorical refusal to yield the posts "would involve the United States either in War or in Disgrace." The country was not prepared for the former and "should if possible avoid the latter." It would also be unwise to press the question as long as the intentions of France concerning it were uncertain. Therefore Jay urged immediate instructions to Adams to spin out the negotiation and avoid demanding a categorical answer until he received further orders from Congress.[25] The Secretary for Foreign Affairs secured the directions he desired, though not immediately. His letter to the minister, based on his report to Congress, was dated May 1, 1786.[26]

The reference to France in the communication to Congress needs elucidation, for it is important. Jay had the inspiration of drafting the aid of that country by appealing to the mutual guarantee in the eleventh article of the treaty of alliance with France. On January 19, 1786, he wrote Jefferson, newly appointed minister to the court of Versailles, inquiring if France felt bound by her guarantee to insist on the surrender of the posts, and if she would second American remonstrances to Britain on that head.[27] Two months later Jay recommended to Congress the issue of definite instructions to the minister in France to approach the French government on the question.[28] Jay's move to draw France into this Anglo-American quarrel seems not to have proceeded beyond this point. Jefferson was probably responsible for stopping it. On March 12, 1786, he replied from London. He shied at the question he was asked to put, because it would awaken another which ought to be allowed to sleep. How far did the United States feel bound, by the other half of the mutual guarantee, to defend the American possessions of France? Nevertheless he would endeavor, on returning to Paris, to sound the foreign

22. *Ibid.*, p. 368.
23. *Ibid.*, pp. 453–456. This memorial is dated November 30, 1785.
24. *Ibid.*, p. 275.
25. *J.C.C.*, XXX, 147–148.
26. *D.C.U.S.*, IV, 431.
27. *Ibid.*, II, 386.
28. *J.C.C.*, XXX, 127–128.

minister without raising this ghost. He suggested that if "any thing forcible" were meditated it would be prudent beforehand to ask the good offices of France to obtain the posts, but France would probably counter by saying that the United States must first execute the treaty, which condition, added Jefferson, ought to suffice to obtain delivery of the posts without the mediation of any third party.[29] In May, Jefferson saw Vergennes and discussed posts and debts with him, but the conversation profited nothing because of the American's fear of stirring the reciprocal question.[30]

What, then, could the United States do—without French aid, without money in the treasury, without an army, and really without a government? Adams quickly noted the revolution in the British attitude toward his country since 1783.[31] Though pressing for the posts and feeling out for a commercial treaty, he despaired of accomplishing anything against the British calculation that the United States were not really united and therefore could do nothing. Turning his pressure backward, he prayed for an American navigation law.[32] But it was impossible to make the British skip by cracking a whip that could not be produced. The impotence of the Continental Congress to pass such a law was one of the reasons for the adoption of the Constitution.

The utter helplessness of the United States dominated the situation from the signature of peace until after 1789. Indeed there was a rough nemesis in the way the inability of Congress to bind the individual states, having operated to American advantage in the negotiation of a one-sided treaty, then turned into a serious American disadvantage in the execution of the treaty. In the fourth and sixth articles, Congress made promises which it could not perform, that there should be no impediments to the recovery of British debts and no postwar confiscations or other proceedings against Loyalists; and the American violation of the treaty in these particulars by certain states played into the British hands.

On February 28, 1786, in reply to Adams' demand for the posts, Lord Carmarthen, the Secretary of State, frankly admitted the British obligation to withdraw from American soil. He made no attempt to explain why the garrisons had remained, for he did not need to do it. He simply drew attention to the American failure to observe the treaty, and assured Adams "that whenever America shall manifest a real determination to fulfil her part of the treaty, Great Britain will not hesitate to prove her sincerity to co-operate in whatever points depend upon her for carrying

29. *D.C.U.S.*, III, 6.
30. *Ibid.*, pp. 50–51.
31. *Ibid.*, IV, 277.
32. *Ibid.*, p. 213.

every article of it into real and complete effect."[33] With this reply went a mass of papers to support the British charge of nonperformance by the United States.[34] Adams was convinced that it was vain to expect the posts or anything else as long as the offending laws were unrepealed. "It will appear to all the world with an ill grace, if we complain of breaches of the treaty, when the British court have it in their power to prove upon us breaches of the same treaty, of greater importance."[35]

Jay was likewise convinced, and he tried to convince Congress by his long and detailed report of October 13 on the British reply. He could be perfectly candid because he was not writing for publication.[36] The report was hidden in the *Secret Journals of Congress*.[37] Though he riddled some of the arguments and statements in the papers submitted by Carmarthen, he observed the omission of further evidence that might have been produced against the United States. But its presentation would have been superfluous, he commented, so manifest were the American violations of the treaty, particularly in the matter of debts. His cutting analysis left the United States without a leg to stand on.

In whatever light, therefore, deviations from the treaty prior to its final conclusion and ratification may be viewed, it is certain that deviations on our part preceded any on the part of Britain; and therefore instead of being justified *by*[38] them, afforded excuse *to*[38] them.

As to the detention of our posts, your secretary thinks that Britain was not bound to surrender them until we had ratified the treaty. Congress ratified it 14th January, 1784, and Britain on the 9th April following. From that time to this, the fourth and sixth[39] articles of the treaty have been constantly violated on our part by legislative acts then and still existing and operating.

Under such circumstances, it is not a matter of surprise to your secretary that the posts are detained; nor in his opinion would Britain be to blame in continuing to hold them until America shall cease to impede her enjoying every essential right secured to her, and her people and adherents, by the treaty.

Jay went even further in his correspondence with Adams and Jefferson, pointing out the American responsibility for the trouble with the Indians. On November 1, 1786, he wrote to the New Englander, "Our people have committed several unprovoked acts of violence against them."[40] In a

33. *Ibid.*, V, 7–9.
34. *Ibid.*, pp. 9–23.
35. *Ibid.*, p. 121.
36. He may have been inspired by political reasons to make the strongest possible case against his own country. He might thereby hasten the establishment of a real government.
37. *Secret Journals of Congress, Foreign Affairs*, IV, 185–287.
38. Italics in original.
39. So corrected in the 1934 edition. The 1821 edition had "fifth."
40. *D.C.U.S.*, V, 140.

letter to the Southerner, written six weeks later, he apprehended an Indian war and suspected that Britain was instigating it. At the same time, he was certain that American actions were working to produce the same result. He said:

Our Indian affairs have been ill managed. . . . Indians have been murdered by our people in cold blood, and no satisfaction given; nor are they pleased with the avidity with which we seek to acquire their lands. Would it not be wiser, gradually to extend our settlements, as want of room should make it necessary, than to pitch our tents through the wilderness? . . . Shall we not fill the wilderness with white savages, and will they not become more formidable to us, than the tawny ones who now inhabit it?[41]

The only way to get the posts was to execute the treaty faithfully, and the only way to do this was not only to bridle the state governments and legislatures but also to establish a real central government. Such was the substance of the conclusions drawn by Jay at the end of his remarkable report, and this reasoning, being absolutely sound, appealed to other political Americans of the day. Thus British pressure in the interior, as on the seaboard, contributed to the consolidation of the new Republic; and the British retention of the posts finally operated to remove its own American cause.

British policy may have simmered down to using the posts to settle debts, but this simple and secondary purpose should not be allowed to obscure the fundamental and complex problem of the interior—that of Indian relations. The two objects of the British were to recover the confidence of the natives and to reconcile them with the Americans. Both seemed necessary, and yet the relation between them made their attainment a task so delicate that it was almost impossible. Too great an effort to bring about a reconciliation with the Americans would defeat itself by destroying what little confidence the red men still had in the British; and too great an effort to recover the lost confidence would encourage the tribes to fight rather than to make peace. The first result would drive Britain from the interior of the continent; the second might drag her into war with the United States; and either would drench the whole of the West with blood. The two British objects were poised in unstable balance. Irresponsible Americans disturbed it, and responsible Britons tried to restore it by retaining the posts. When the rising tide of war in the West threatened further disturbance, the government in London contemplated something more than mere continued occupation but apparently could reach no definite decision.

Joseph Brant spent the winter of 1785–86 in England seeking com-

41. *Ibid.*, III, 138.

pensation for his losses and a promise of military aid for his people should the worst come to the worst. He achieved his first purpose but not his second, for it was obvious that the promise would make the worst come to the worst. The Secretary of State merely assured him that the King would never forget his Indian allies and would always be anxious to further their interests and happiness.

Equally vague were the instructions issued to Lieutenant Governor Hope, administrator of the Province of Quebec in Haldimand's absence. The government, said Lord Sydney in a dispatch of April 6, 1786, knew that a meeting between Indian deputies and congressional delegates would be held about the time of Brant's return, and realized that much would depend on that meeting. Official opinion in London inclined to the belief that a temporary accommodation would be reached. If this proved correct, Sydney added, "no difficulties will immediately occur." The word "immediately" is worth stressing as a reminder of the temporary nature of British policy in the interior. How Britain could finally extricate herself from the nasty tangle of her own making was an insoluble problem in London. More pressing and almost as difficult was how to avoid the evil consequences that might rise up at any time. Should the impending conference break up in discord, the Secretary of State continued, "our situation will in some degree become embarrassing"—as if it were not embarrassing already. Perhaps the nakedness of the British position on American soil was considered decently clothed by the recent communication on debts. Be that as it may, what was Hope to do if hostilities commenced? He must "at all events in the present state of this country" avoid "open and avowed assistance." But the natives were not to be abandoned to the mercy of the Americans. That would not be "consistent with justice or good policy." Out of resentment the Indians might attack the province. The conclusion of this wobbly argument was characteristic: "It is utterly impracticable for His Majesty's ministers to prescribe any direct line for your conduct should matters be driven to the extremity, and much will depend upon your judgment and discretion in the management of a business so delicate and interesting." [42] The implication was clear: if the Indians were hard pressed, Quebec was to send secret aid which London might repudiate.

The British government was still groping in the dark when Guy Carleton, as Lord Dorchester, sailed for Canada at the end of August, 1786. Apparently he was expected, though not actually instructed, to feel the way. Shortly after his arrival the new governor told Sir John Johnson that the red men should realize that he had no power to commence a war "which might involve half the globe with all the seas in

42. A. Shortt and A. G. Doughty, eds., *Documents Relating to the Constitutional History of Canada*, p. 807.

blood and destruction," and that every effort should be put forth to persuade them to make peace with the Americans.[43] A fortnight later, in a letter marked "secret," he asked the Indian superintendent to have one of his officers sound out the Six Nations on the future of the upper posts, particularly Oswego and Niagara. Did these tribes wish Britain to hold them, or were they indifferent? What would they do if they saw them delivered up, or evacuated? How would they act if the United States tried to seize them? The last question prompted Dorchester to add the following remark: "An attempt to wrest them from us, I should consider as the beginning of hostilities, and however indifferent we may be about them [the posts] yet war must be repelled by war."[44] In January, 1787, he threw up his hands and flung back the responsibility to where it belonged. Writing to the Secretary of State, he roundly condemned the government's policy of "no resolution," and he urged some definite decision. Were the posts to be retained? If so, their garrisons would have to be increased and much money would have to be spent in putting them in a proper state of defense. Or were they to be surrendered? This would help the Americans to conquer the Indians. Or were the forts to be abandoned and destroyed? This would be much better. He ended with a prayer for advice on what he should do if the Americans attacked and captured the posts.[45]

The governor and the home government were like Dr. Johnson and the lady who persisted in being "wiggle waggle" in spite of his efforts to make her categorical. Dorchester waited almost a whole year for a reply to his appeal. Then he was informed that he might spend money to put the forts in a "temporary" state of defense, the extent of the works to depend on his judgment, and if the places were seized and he thought himself strong enough to recover them he should do his best. He was reminded that, before his departure from England, he had been told that the retention of the posts was perfectly justifiable. Nothing the Americans had done since, added Sydney, had changed the government's opinion.[46] Its policy, however, had been readjusted in one particular, because the unstable balance mentioned above was threatened by the nearer approach of the American-Indian war. On April 5, 1787, weeks before the arrival of Dorchester's desperate cry, the Secretary of State wrote the governor on the more critical state of Indian affairs. His warning that "active assistance would at the present moment be extremely imprudent" echoed his words of a year before when he wrote to Hope. But now he slipped farther down the dangerous incline of encouraging

43. *Q*, XXVII, 82.
44. *Ibid.*, pp. 86–87.
45. *Ibid.*, pp. 34–36.
46. *Ibid.*, XXVIII, 28–30.

the Indians. He declared that it would not be proper to refuse the natives "such supplies of ammunition as might enable them to defend themselves." He had information that they were short of ammunition, and he directed the governor to supply them "in a way the least likely to alarm the Americans" or to incite the natives "to any hostile proceedings."[47] He did not venture to suggest what this way was, nor how the ammunition, once in the hands of the red men, was to be reserved for purely defensive purposes. Thus did he at last give substance to the American charge that the British were instigating native hostilities against the United States. If he did not see what he was doing, he was blinded by his Tory and national prejudices.

Another development of British policy which seems to have begun about this time was aimed at the permanent crippling of the United States, for hostility slides insensibly into greater hostility. The vision of a commercial empire over the heart of the continent, first conjured up during the peace negotiations to tempt Britain into an accommodating attitude on the boundary, was revived, transformed, and magnified, until at last it inspired the British government to seek a new boundary settlement that would have confined the Republic within much narrower limits. Meanwhile the new motive gave a new value to the western posts and made Britain more reluctant to surrender them.

The weakness of the United States was primarily responsible for this development. These years were the "critical period" of the young Republic, when its whole future was darkly clouded. Peace tended to dissolve the loose union born of war. The country had only the shadow of a government, and that faded away in the autumn of 1788, when the Continental Congress expired of inanition. For nearly six months there was not even a shadow of a government; and when the Constitution, ratified by only nine of the thirteen states, gave birth to the Government of the United States in 1789, there were grave doubts about the life of the new infant.

While the political unity of the Republic was thus dissolving, the population of the country was spreading over the Alleghenies, threatening something more serious than an Indian war. The older communities faced the Atlantic and the newer ones, of which Kentucky was the chief, looked toward the Mississippi as their highroad to the rest of the world. They were back to back, and pulling apart. It looked as if the country might split along the mountains. Political geography worked with physical geography toward this result. Spain sat astride the mouths of the Mississippi, the only route by which Americans west of the Alleghenies could export their rapidly increasing surplus produce. Spain could smother them by closing this door, and they had no wish to live by

47. *Ibid.*, XXVII, 44–47.

the grace of the Spanish government or the corruption of Spanish officials. Moreover Spain's possession of all the continent west of the Mississippi was attracting covetous eyes to look westward across the river.
Spain was thus the enemy of western Americans, and their feelings were
made almost explosive by not ungrounded fears that their brethren to the
east were about to betray them by some deal with Spain. Unable to
recover by reciprocity the commercial advantages they had enjoyed
while still in the British Empire, Americans on the Atlantic felt in such
desperate need of substitutes that they were inclined to purchase admission to the ports of the Spanish Empire by surrendering the American
claim to the free navigation of the Mississippi. It is small wonder that
leading Americans on "the western waters" contemplated secession
from the Atlantic states, and looked for some outside power to rescue
them by pulling Spain out of New Orleans.

The invitation, first extended to France, was repeated to Britain, and
those who made it intimated that whoever performed this service would
be richly rewarded by securing a monopoly of the commerce of the whole
Mississippi Valley. Another temptation was offered by one who had
commanded a regiment in the Revolutionary army. Having become
anxious to plant a colony by the Missouri, he suggested that Britain,
from her base on the Great Lakes, should seize the territory west of the
Mississippi, thus helping herself as well as him. These were only two of
many communications touching the state of opinion in the United States
and the uncertain future of the country which the governor received in
Quebec and forwarded to London. With the encouragement of his
superiors, he was gathering all the information he could through various
channels. The best known was a veritable conduit. He was the future
Lieutenant General Sir George Beckwith, who sojourned from time to
time in the Republic as a confidential agent and unofficial representative
of Britain. It was to him that the Missouri scheme was unfolded by its
author, apparently a Connecticut Yankee.[48] Interesting as are many of
the details of Dorchester's American correspondence,[49] there would be
little point in recounting them here, for the chief significance of the
correspondence lies not in its details but in its general effect. This seems
to have been little in the United States or Canada, but it may have been
considerable in Britain. It must have raised the potential value of the
western posts and strengthened the British determination to play a waiting game. A premature surrender of Britain's strategic position on the
Great Lakes might throw away the opportunity of winning an enormous
prize.

48. Isaac Sherman, possibly a relation of Roger Sherman.
49. *P.A.C.R.*, 1890, Note E.

CHAPTER VII
THE GROWING CRISIS IN THE INTERIOR

THE year 1789 saw two events which combined to liquidate this western business by persuading Britain to withdraw. They were the adoption of the Constitution of the United States and the outbreak of the French Revolution. The former, through its creation of a real central government for the country, undermined both the excuse and the reason for British garrisons' remaining on American soil; the latter, through the war it let loose in Europe, forced Britain to make her peace with the United States. The result was Jay's Treaty of 1794. This was five years afterwards and it came rather suddenly, for the operations producing it were slow in getting under way. Indeed they were so slow that the international situation in the interior of America grew worse instead of better, and reached a dangerous crisis on the very eve of Jay's Treaty.

In the beginning of this five-year period, however, an incident on the Pacific Ocean started a train of events that brought Britain for a short while in 1790 to the verge of abandoning the western posts, thereby giving a foretaste of what the French Revolutionary War might do when it engulfed Britain. This was the famous Nootka Sound affair, already mentioned in connection with the Vermont negotiations. The Spanish seizure of a few English merchant vessels on the west coast of Vancouver Island in the summer of 1789 was not an occasion for war, but the subsequent correspondence provided sufficient cause. Spain justified the affront by asserting her exclusive right to the Pacific coast of America, and she did more. She called upon Britain to restrain her subjects by punishing such as would encroach upon this Spanish preserve. In her own eyes and in those of the world at the time, Spain was numbered among the mighty and Britain among the fallen. Britain had just lost her Empire; Spain's seemed as great as ever. Spain secretly began to prepare for war, and so did Britain; for the issue appeared to be worthy of such a test. It was whether Britain or Spain would cease to be a great power. One of them had to step down. This threat of war in the Old World shook the balance of power in the New. The weakness of the United States had played into Britain's hands, and now the embarrassment of Britain might give an advantage to the United States.

By mere coincidence, the American government again asked for the posts at the very time the Nootka Sound affair began to worry the British government. Diplomatic relations had been severed in 1788, when Adams withdrew from London on the failure of Britain to send a minister to the United States; and as soon as Washington became President he faced the task of healing the breach with London. Without waiting until he had a Secretary of State, who should have done it, he himself wrote on October 13, 1789, to Gouverneur Morris, then in Paris on private affairs, asking him to approach the British government informally to seek an understanding on the differences between the two countries. As the President later explained to Congress, he preferred this unofficial method because, if Britain remained obdurate, the rebuff to the United States would not strike home as it would have done had Morris been invested with a public character.[1]

Of the various points which this private agent was to raise, Washington placed the posts first. Morris was instructed to begin by observing that "as the present constitution of government, and the courts established in pursuance of it, remove the objections heretofore made to putting the United States in possession of their frontier posts, it is natural to expect," from British assurances of good faith, that there would be no unnecessary delay in fulfilling this part of the treaty. In more explicit language, the new Constitution had made the treaty a supreme law which would override the resistance of individual states to its complete application, particularly in the matter of debts. The second point, which need not concern us here because it did not touch Canadian-American relations, was the American complaint that slaves belonging to the citizens of the Republic had been carried off during the evacuation of the British army though the treaty stipulated that such blacks were not to be taken away. The third point was the elusive commercial treaty so much desired by the United States, especially for the West Indian trade it would open. The freer intercourse it would bring with British North America was of very minor importance to the United States, however much it might mean to these closer neighbors. Morris was to convey the warning information that in the late session of Congress a very respectable number of both houses were inclined to impose discriminating duties against Britain and such a measure would have passed "but for conciliatory considerations, and the probability that the late change in our government and circumstances would lead to more satisfactory arrangements." In other words, British doors must open or American doors would shut. Finally, the President suggested to his agent that he might draw attention to the bad impression created by the British refusal to send a minister to the United States.[2]

On March 28, 1790, Morris reached London and called on the Duke of Leeds, formerly Lord Carmarthen. Not finding him at home, he wrote

1. *A.S.P.F.R.*, I, 121.
2. *Ibid.*, p. 122.

him a note to which he received a reply that evening arranging a meeting for the morrow. Before he saw the Englishman, the American committed a grave indiscretion. He saw the French ambassador, La Luzerne, and to him he imparted the nature of his instructions. The Frenchman straightway abused the confidence, and the American mission was prejudiced at the outset by receiving this French taint, which, however, does not seem to have affected the outcome. The interview in Whitehall on the twentyninth passed off pleasantly for Morris. Perhaps he would have been less surprised if he had been able to peep at the Spanish skeleton in the British closet. "With much warmth and gladness in his appearance," according to Morris, the Duke assured him that it was his own and the whole government's wish "to cultivate a friendly and commercial intercourse between the two countries." Morris replied, "I am happy, my lord, to find that such sentiments prevail: for we are too near neighbors not to be either good friends or dangerous enemies." He explained how the newly adopted Constitution would remove all obstacles to the recovery of British debts. Leeds professed happiness at the news and repeated what he had written to Adams, that the articles of the treaty should be performed in the order in which they stood in that document. Morris objected that neither side should wait upon the other to fulfill its obligations; and he observed that the southern states, so much blamed for obstructing the collection of British debts, did not deserve all the censure heaped upon them. They had been crippled by the removal of their Negroes in contravention of the treaty. They could not pay unless they were themselves paid. According to the American's report, the Englishman appeared embarrassed by the presentation of the claim for the delivery of the western posts and the payment for slaves carried off, and also was somewhat apologetic for not having been able to find a suitable man willing to be minister to the United States. The embarrassment of Leeds fitted in with the positive statement Morris had just received from La Luzerne, that Britain would not give up the posts.[3]

Though the duke promised a "speedy answer," he let a month pass before he wrote to Morris. He then offered several excuses for his tardiness, but the real reason was probably his own uncertainty. His government was obviously loath to part with the posts and to join in a commercial treaty. The excuse for keeping the former still held, for Washington and Morris were really anticipating the future, but there was now a prospect that the excuse would no longer hold. Therefore another was found, and Leeds advanced it in a tentative way in his note of April 28. He threw out a vague phrase about the possibility of the American delay's having made completion of the treaty impracticable, by which he meant

3. *Ibid.*, pp. 122–123.

that a strict compliance with the letter of the treaty might fail to do justice to British subjects who had suffered damage through the delay; and he declared that his government would have no scruple in further postponing British performance until redress was granted or compensation secured. To the suggestion of a commercial treaty, he replied with a governmental "sincere wish" to cultivate "a real and bona fide system of friendly intercourse." [4] Morris took the last remark as a polite dismissal and accordingly, in a note of two days later, he expressed to Leeds the hope that he was mistaken. At the same time he requested an explanation of the allusion to the lapse of time's impairing the purpose of the treaty. He said it was a new idea to him.[5] Apparently he did not know that Jay had raised it at the end of his important secret report, admitting its validity but advising that it be allowed to sleep in silence because the United States had neither the means nor the power to satisfy the requirements of "strict justice" on this score. Now that the British had found it, the idea was less likely to sleep, particularly since the United States, by the adoption of the Constitution, had thrown away the defensive plea of impotence. Morris might have felt more comfortable had he known that, on the very day he inscribed this note, the British cabinet decided to bring the hidden international crisis to a head by demanding immediate satisfaction from Spain and by rushing naval preparations to back the ultimatum.[6]

The British decision to face war with Spain had surprisingly little immediate effect upon British policy in the interior of North America. Had the United States been strong and inclined to side with Madrid, the British government might have been willing at once to buy off the American government by yielding the posts and even by granting some commercial concessions. But the Republic was still weak and the Morris mission betrayed a leaning toward London. The ministers of George III therefore determined to make the most of both conditions in pushing the old policy. Their confidence is reflected in three secret dispatches of Grenville to Dorchester dated May 6,[7] the very day the Spanish skeleton burst from its closet. The first dispatch stated that there was no apprehension of a Spanish attack on British North American possessions but there was a possibility that the United States might take advantage of an Anglo-Spanish war, and even enter it, to reach out after the posts. Therefore the governor was to remain on guard instead of coming home

4. *Ibid.*, p. 123.

5. Omitted from *ibid.*, but printed in *P.A.C.R.*, 1890, Note E, pp. 130–131.

6. For the best account of this affair see W. R. Manning, "The Nootka Sound Controversy," *Annual Report of the American Historical Association*, 1904, pp. 279–333.

7. *P.A.C.R.*, 1890, Note E, pp. 131–133.

on the leave he had requested. The second dispatch, as observed in a previous chapter,[8] urged him to cultivate the friendship of the people of Vermont. The third directed his attention to opinion in the United States, suggesting that it might be turned in favor of Britain against Spain by utilizing the American desire to see Spain pulled from the mouth of the Mississippi. The central idea of these three dispatches was the preservation of the posts.

The hot press of seamen, which began on the night of May 4, 1790, and gave the public their first intimation of trouble brewing, opened an unexpected door for Morris. Some American sailors were gathered up. This was the second incident of the kind which later caused so much bitterness. The first had occurred in 1785, when Adams procured the release of his unfortunate countrymen.[9] Morris had little difficulty in repeating the service, and in doing so he had an opportunity to advance his mission. His complaints about captive Americans brought another interview with Leeds on May 20. This was continued on the morning of the twenty-first, when Pitt was also present and the discussion broadened. The only account we have of what went on at this meeting comes from the pen of Morris, and therefore is not exactly impartial; but it is probably substantially true as far as it goes, and it is important because it is the report submitted to the President and by him to Congress. It would therefore have real significance even if it were false.

The Englishmen tried to disarm the American, who felt his position improved by the crisis, by assuring him that he had misinterpreted the passage about a commercial treaty. Morris countered by observing that the mistake was easily corrected "but it appeared idle to form a new treaty" until both parties were satisfied with the one they had. Then the issue was joined. Pitt proposed a discussion of better relations as a whole, to see "if, on general ground, some compensation could not be made mutually." At once Morris shot out, "You wish to make a new treaty instead of complying with the old one," and Pitt admitted that this was "*in some sort*[10] his idea." Coming to the point he feared, the American hinted that Britain wanted to keep the posts, and the prime minister confessed, "Why, perhaps we may." Morris argued their uselessness to Britain and their importance to the United States. "We do not think it worth while to go to war with you for these posts," he admitted, but he added a warning that his country would get them when time and circumstance permitted. When asked if he had power to treat, he coupled his negative with a remark that the United States would not

8. *Supra*, p. 70.
9. *D.C.U.S.*, IV, 461.
10. Italics in original.

appoint a minister after their late experience. Catching the obvious hint, Pitt inquired if the Republic would exchange ministers with Britain; and Morris, expressing his confidence that the United States would reciprocate, suggested the appointment of a British minister who could be detained until the appointment of his American counterpart. Resuming discussion of a commercial treaty, Morris referred to the restraint of the House of Representatives in not imposing heavy restrictions on British vessels. Pitt retorted that instead of restrictions the United States should consider privileges—in return for those accorded Americans by Britain. Morris struck back by saying that he knew of none except being pressed like British subjects, and when brought to book he replied that any favors shown were granted to serve British and not American interests. The interview closed with a British statement that the ministry would consider the question and Leeds would reply to Morris' letter of April 30.[11]

The British determination to hold the posts, still evident on May 21, showed signs of crumbling in the next few days. On the twenty-ninth Morris wrote: "I learn that Mr. Grenville has this day consulted some persons skilled in the fur trade, and that, from his conversation, it seemed probable that they would give up the posts. *My information is good.*" [12] Two days later, Haldimand was closeted with Grenville, who sought his advice on this very point; and then his old secretary, Major Mathews, was called in for the same purpose.[13] There are also records of others' being consulted, and we have a list of questions concerning the surrender of the posts which Grenville put to Captain Schank of the navy, who had commanded on the Lakes, and to a London merchant, named Inglis, whose firm was heavily interested in the fur trade.[14] Grenville was canvassing informed opinion on what would be lost by yielding the posts and how much of this loss could be prevented by establishing the garrisons in new forts on the Canadian side of the line.

Four considerations stand out in Grenville's queries. One was an inland communication with the Mississippi to implement the treaty's promise of free navigation. This, he thought, might be procured in exchange for the posts. We do not know what information he collected under this head; but it is interesting to observe that Grenville's inquiry seems to be the first official recognition of the defect of the treaty in running the boundary line from the Lake of the Woods westward to the Mississippi, and of the necessity for a new boundary definition in this

11. *A.S.P.F.R.*, I, 123–125.
12. *Ibid.*, p. 125. Italics in original.
13. *P.A.C.R.*, 1889, Haldimand's Private Diary, p. 287.
14. *Q*, XLIX, 297, in *M.P.H.C.*, XXIV, 90–91.

quarter. The second consideration was the defense of the province. This he was told would be little affected by the shifting of the troops to places on the British side of the border. The third was the control of the Lakes, on which the British had a few small merchant vessels, more and bigger naval ones, and the Americans none of any kind. The contemplated withdrawal of the garrisons meant the abandonment of naval bases, but substitutes could be found, Schank reported.[15] The remaining consideration, the fourth in number though not necessarily the fourth in importance, was the fur trade. The firm of Phyn, Ellice, and Inglis estimated that the loss would be 50 per cent and might be 75.[16] Other advice was less pessimistic. Haldimand thought that the loss would perhaps be covered by a gain in the sale of British goods to Americans. He also told Grenville that if the Americans insisted on having the posts, Britain should yield them, making a merit out of necessity. The Americans could seize them whenever they wished and Britain would not undertake a war to defend them. Such was Haldimand's belief. Mathews agreed that the posts were indefensible against the Americans, but he raised an objection to their voluntary surrender. He was still gripped by the fear of the effect upon the Indians.[17] Grenville, however, was of the opinion that the establishment of new posts on the Canadian side would be just as effective in holding the confidence of the natives as would the maintenance of the old posts on the American side.

This sudden disposition to yield the posts is a little mysterious. There was no change in the general international situation to produce it. True, a letter was received on May 25 from Beckwith in the United States telling of American armaments in the interior, to be mentioned presently; but the letter concluded with the assurance that they were not anti-British in design.[18] Possibly there were fears that they might become so, if they were not already, when the United States awoke to the opportunity presented by the Spanish crisis, for Beckwith had written on April 7, four weeks before even Londoners learned of it. Such fears would be a natural development of the apprehension of an American attack expressed in the first of Grenville's dispatches to Dorchester on May 6. That the sudden change was only an illusion, created by a division in the cabinet between Grenville on the one hand and Leeds and Pitt on the other, is theoretically possible but historically improbable. The fact seems as clear as the reason for it is obscure, that, at the close of May, 1790, the Nootka Sound affair made the British government seriously

15. *Ibid.*
16. Statement on the Western Posts, May 31, 1790, *Q*, XLIX, 289–290.
17. Mathews to Nepean, July 9, 1790, *ibid.*, pp. 315–316.
18. *Ibid.*, pp. 283–286.

consider turning the western posts over to the United States. Morris was wrong in believing that war between Britain and Spain was inevitable, but he was apparently right in reporting to Washington that Britain would be willing to pay a good price for American neutrality.[19]

The American counterpart of the British suspicion of an impending attack upon the posts was the suspicion that Britain contemplated a further violation of the territory of the United States by a military advance from the western posts upon Spanish America. Both were unfounded and yet very disturbing. When Grenville's dispatches of May 6 reached Quebec, whither Beckwith had returned, Dorchester rushed him back to the United States to sound opinion and if possible to bend it in favor of his country.[20] On arriving in New York early in July, this confidential agent at once approached Hamilton, with whom he had established close relations on previous visits, assuring him that the Canadian governor was restraining the western tribes, and arguing that the true interest of the United States was to join Britain in a war against Spain. His conversation, immediately relayed to President Washington, confirmed the impression already received from Morris that war was imminent, and brought the administration to consider what American policy ought to be on the outbreak of hostilities, particularly what answer should be returned to Dorchester if he requested permission to move British troops across American soil to attack Spanish Louisiana, and what should be done if he tried to move them without permission. Some members of the administration may have been at least dimly aware of western American encouragement of such a British venture, for this was the time the Missouri scheme mentioned in the last chapter[21] was forwarded to London.

The opinions which the President gathered from his chief advisers reflect the first troubling of the American mind by the pursuit of an elusive neutrality. Jefferson, the Secretary of State, would ignore the demand or else grant it to both parties. He would protest an unauthorized march, and would postpone entry into the war as long as possible. Vice-President Adams would refuse the demand and protest a march lest acquiescence be misconstrued. Chief Justice Jay would be more tolerant because the posts from which the attack would be made and the territory over which it would move were British in practice though American in theory. Henry Knox, the Secretary of War, did not give the direct answer of a soldier. He said there would be no war unless France supported Spain, and then France would try to involve her American ally.

19. *A.S.P.F.R.*, I, 125.
20. *Q*, XLV, 518, 521. The governor's instructions to Beckwith are dated June 27.
21. *Supra*, p. 105.

He was for neutrality but saw the possibility of the United States' being drawn in by inducements offered by either side or by a realization that war was the lesser evil. Hamilton would grant the request as the easiest way out of a difficult situation, and would then explain to Spain. He was rather careless of the effect upon that country because he preferred the friendship of Britain. She could give much more benefit and also greater injury to the United States. She was fighting the cause of all trading nations, which included the American people, in standing firmly against Spain and her ideas of monopoly. Added together, these different opinions favored an irresolute and even a yielding attitude toward a bold Britain.

Each side was thus willing to give way before pressure from the other. Here was a condition the very opposite of that which produces war. Unfortunately the condition for an amicable settlement was not also present. Such a settlement might have been precipitated if the atmosphere had been made more tense by the Spanish menace, but this instead of growing blacker began to fade away. On August 5, London learned that Spain promised restitution of the seized vessels and compensation for losses incurred by their detention. This was a hopeful sign to Britain, but it was by no means the end of the crisis. It did not touch the fundamental issue, which was the British challenge to the Spanish claim of monopoly over the northwest coast. To preserve that, Spain would not shrink from war unless it was apparent that she was rushing to her own downfall. The collapse of the Spanish Empire began in Paris with the outbreak of the French Revolution. It paralyzed France, nullifying the Family Compact by which she was bound to support Spain. Without the protection of the French navy, Spain was virtually naked in 1790, because there was no comparison between her naval power and that of Britain; but it was not until October that officials in Madrid saw how their country was deserted and undone. Then the proud Spanish King bowed his head, and on November 4 Britain knew that the crisis had passed—the crisis which might have cost her the occupancy of the western posts.

The international situation in the interior of America thus took a bad turn and the weakness of the United States made things worse, for the Republic had not yet gathered the strength that could come only with years. The newly established government of President Washington tried to cut the Gordian knot of the West and succeeded in cutting itself. Before the name of Nootka Sound came to be known, American forces were gathering in the interior, as reported by Beckwith in his letter of April 7; but not until the autumn of 1790, when the Anglo-Spanish crisis was passing away, did the composite army of militia and regulars under General Josiah Harmar set out to invade the heart of the Indian territory and to build a fort on the Maumee River at the principal town of the Miami tribe. The plan was strategic; for the Maumee was the center of the native confederacy now dominated by Joseph Brant, and the Miamis, who had signed no treaty, were about the most hostile of all the western Indians. Moreover the advance of the Americans would be almost straight toward Detroit. Harmar was to impress the might of the Republic upon the minds of the savages, and to give the British a warning hint to end their trespass. He did the opposite. Unable to control his own men, much less the natives, he was surprised near the source of the Maumee and his force was driven back in disorder.

These open hostilities, which transformed a retail into a wholesale slaughter, aggravated Anglo-American feeling over the posts. In the summer of 1790, Washington and his cabinet foresaw dangerous complications with Britain arising out of their plans to subdue the Indians. Anxious to avoid this evil, the administration thought of informing Dorchester of the American preparations and assuring him that they were directed solely against the red men. Jefferson demurred, for he saw a dilemma. If the notification were early enough, the Canadian governor would withdraw the natives, thereby defeating the purpose of the expedition; if he had insufficient time to do this, he would likewise be unable to withdraw the secret aid he had given the Indians, and the notification would only encourage him to push his supposed scheme for a march across American territory against the Spaniards. Such was Jefferson's argument. It may have prevented a formal communication to Quebec, but it did not prevent an informal message to Detroit, where the senior officer of the western garrisons was in command. From General St. Clair, who had charge of all the American forces on the frontier, he received the President's assurance that the impending blow was aimed only at the red men and he was also informed of the President's confidence that the British would lend them no assistance or encouragement.[22] This friendly gesture probably acted as a restraint upon the growing tension, but it could not alter the fundamental situation. British eyes closely watched American campaigning against the Indians lest at any time it disclose a covert attack upon the posts, whose potential value increased as the menace of a Spanish war declined and vanished.

Much more serious was the reaction in the United States, where few could see their country's share in the responsibility for this ghastly warfare beyond the pale of civilization. Britain was naturally blamed for Harmar's exasperating failure, and was commonly accused of playing a dastardly game. It was difficult to doubt the guilt of Britain when so many American lives were being blotted out by savages with British

22. *Q*, I, 235, in *M.P.H.C.*, XXIV, 99–100.

arms and ammunition supplied through British-held forts on American soil. The bitterness thus engendered in the United States was poisoning the American attitude and working for a renewal of the war against Britain.

This American reaction was intensified in 1791, when General St. Clair himself attempted to wipe out the disgrace of 1790, and only piled it higher. From his base at Fort Washington, by the present city of Cincinnati, he commenced a carefully planned invasion of the wilderness. He penetrated some ninety miles northward before the red fury overwhelmed him on November 4. Nine hundred of his men were slain. The survivors, abandoning their camp and their artillery, fled in such panic that they threw away their arms as they ran. They ran for nearly thirty miles, though pursued for only four. It was a terrifying defeat. There had been nothing like it for over a generation, not since Braddock and his men were mowed down.[23]

The British attitude was also affected by the campaign of 1791. The preparations for this American effort to subdue the natives stimulated British apprehensions of a surprise attack upon the posts. Dorchester then felt the limitation of the principle he had laid down, that force must be repelled by force; and he anticipated action on the well-established rule that offense is the best defense. On April 14, he warned the officer commanding the upper posts that, in addition to seeing that they were "in a thorough state of defence," he "must be prepared to march forward should the turn of affairs render this absolutely necessary." To this end, part of the garrisons of Detroit and Niagara "with a considerable draft from the militia and some field pieces should be in readiness to move upon a short notice." [24] On May 9 the governor asked the superintendent of Indian affairs what and how advanced stations should be occupied if the safety of the posts required a forward movement.[25] Johnson appealed to his deputy, Alexander McKee, who replied on June 20. He condemned the abandonment of two posts planted on the Maumee to protect Detroit during the late war, one at the town of the Miamis and the other at the foot of the rapids; and he urged the restoration of the latter with a garrison of one hundred and fifty men.[26] Dorchester thought "this idea judicious" and on August 1 he called for a report on these two posts: what was their strength, when were they erected, by whose orders were they abandoned, and when?[27] Almost immediately he departed on leave, and his project slumbered until after his return more than two years later.

23. St. Clair's own account is in *A.S.P.I.A.*, I, 137–138.
24. *S.P.*, I, 22–23.
25. *Ibid.*, p. 25.
26. *Q*, LII, 236, in *M.P.H.C.*, XXIV, 263.
27. *Q*, LII, 256, in *M.P.H.C.*, XXIV, 301.

The catastrophic climax of the campaign of 1791 was both reassuring and disturbing to the British. The destruction of St. Clair's army rendered the British tenure of the posts so secure that no aggressive step, such as Dorchester had contemplated, seemed necessary at the time. But the capture of St. Clair's papers, which the victorious Indians turned over to those who could understand them, confirmed British fears that an attack was coming, though not immediately, and that preventive measures would be necessary. Knox's instructions to St. Clair, thus disclosed, directed the building of an American post at the town of the Miamis and admitted that it might stir British jealousy, which the general should remove by reassuring words. Obviously a clash on the Maumee was likely to come sooner or later. The Secretary of War also said that "the delicate state of affairs" might "render it improper at present to make any naval arrangements on Lake Erie." [28] Innocent as this may appear to American eyes, it struck British eyes as the notice of a vital challenge to be delivered in the future. Though Knox was honestly anxious to avoid war with Britain and he cautioned St. Clair accordingly, he added a qualification which to British readers indicated that the caution was to be only temporary. It was to hold until events of sufficient importance impressed the people of the United States and the world with "the rank injustice and unfairness" of the British. [29]

The British fears were of little consequence when compared with a British hope inspired by the American defeat. It was the hope of a new boundary treaty which would repair the blunder of 1783. The modest beginnings of this hope may be traced back to a confidential discussion between Hamilton and Beckwith in January, 1791. The former then intimated that Dorchester might persuade the Indians to accept an American settlement that would secure them their lands. It would be a friendly act toward the United States, and it would please the British traders of Detroit who complained that the war was ruining them. On receiving this suggestion, the governor instructed the superintendent of the Indian Department to discover what peace terms would be acceptable to the red confederacy, and on the same day he had his secretary write Beckwith that he, Dorchester, could take no steps to effect a general accommodation without authorization "by one or other of the contending parties." Beckwith at once delivered the hint, and Hamilton was taken aback to find his words twisted into an invitation to mediate. He had conveyed various British suggestions from Beckwith to the President, but now he replied that he could not present this proposal. Mediation, he said, might be desirable in a war with "a great or respectable nation," and then it

28. From the instructions of March 21, 1791, *ibid.*, pp. 189–191.
29. Instructions of July 14, 1791, not printed in *ibid.* but to be found in *Q*, LVIII, 123.

would be sought officially by application to some foreign government and not to any officer of that government resident abroad. It was inadmissible in this struggle with "vagrant Indian tribes" who could not be considered on the same footing as a civilized power. Hamilton softened this double rebuff by adding a double confession. He admitted that hostilities might have been "excited by our frontier people from interested motives, as an Indian war leads to the spending money in their country as well as to the gratification of their individual resentments," and that "fomenting such a war would never be any object for such a government as yours." Returning to his original purpose, he again intimated that Dorchester might bring the Indians nearer to peace if he would only let them know that it would please his government. Peace, he reiterated, was not just an American interest; it was vital to British trade in the interior.[30]

Hamilton could not kill the idea of mediation. Dorchester had planted it in the West and also in London. In the West, his orders to Johnson were carried out by the efficient McKee. It cost him much time and labor to gather and to hold together a sufficient number of chiefs to form a representative council. Not until the beginning of July did he succeed. The meeting place was near the rapids of the Maumee, not far from his own establishment. There he announced the governor's desire to mediate, and he secured a statement of the terms on which they would make peace. They demanded a boundary running up the Ohio to the Muskingum, up that river to the portage across to the Cuyahoga, on to Venango, and thence north to Lake Erie along the line dividing the Six Nations from the western tribes. This transaction, and its solemn confirmation in Quebec a few weeks later by a deputation of chiefs who insisted on going down to appeal to the governor, implied a certain moral obligation on the part of the British to press for a peace which would guarantee this line.[31]

On hearing what Dorchester had started, London had no wish to stop it. Pitt's government had at last decided to appoint a minister to the United States and had selected George Hammond. His instructions, dated September 1 and therefore before the arrival of reports of the conference on the Maumee, anticipated an opportunity for British interposition to terminate the Indian war. He was then to exert himself to that end, "taking care to adopt no measures respecting it except in concert with" the governor in Quebec. A fortnight later, on September 16, the account of the conference having arrived in England, a dispatch was

30. *P.A.C.R.*, 1890, Note E, pp. 168–171.
31. McKee to Johnson, July 5, 1791, *Q*, LII, 239. Dorchester to Grenville, No. 102, Aug. 17, 1791, and enclosures, *ibid.*, p. 259.

written to Dorchester reflecting greater eagerness. Peace was the concern of Britain as well as of the United States and the Indians. "It is but too evident that unless some means are taken to put an end to the further progress of the war, this country must sooner or later be placed in a very unpleasant and embarrassing situation." If Hammond managed to attract overtures for mediation by the governor, the latter was to open the ears of the Indians "to any reasonable propositions" that would secure them the possession of their lands in peace and quiet. If his mediation succeeded in effecting a settlement, it would "be extremely expedient" for him to participate in its execution.[32] It is fairly obvious that London liked the idea but was handling it cautiously.

The British hope of a new boundary settlement, which thus fluttered through 1791, suddenly soared when the news of St. Clair's disaster reached England early in 1792; and as it soared it took on a new and larger shape. In the middle of March the cabinet adopted an ambitious plan as the goal of British policy. There was to be a neutral barrier of exclusively Indian territory between the Republic and the neighboring British colonies. It was not to be confined to the western territory in dispute but was to extend eastward to separate completely the British and the American frontiers. The inviolability of this native reserve was to rest on the joint guarantee of Britain and the United States. Of course it was understood that the buffer territory would lie wholly on the American side of the line drawn in 1783. Here was the American contribution. The price Britain would have to pay was the surrender of the posts; and the government deliberately decided to offer it, calculating that the objection to surrender was "much lessened" by the substitution of the red men for the United States as prospective possessors.[33]

Lord Dorchester, then home on leave, was apparently the father of this scheme. In outlining it to the government, he omitted one important particular. That was where the new boundary should run when it struck east from the line demanded by the western tribes. Therefore when the government adopted the plan and began to act upon it, he was called upon to supply what was missing.[34] He then confessed that the project was not practicable along the eastern stretch of the frontier from Lake Champlain to the St. Croix, because there were "no Indians in these districts who have claims of much importance, or indeed are capable of occupying any space . . . to answer the purpose of a barrier." All he could propose for this quarter was a slight boundary rectification. Nor could he suggest any line through the ancient lands of the Six Nations,

32. *S.P.*, I, 59. Dundas to Dorchester, No. 1, Sept. 16, 1791, *Q*, LII, 206.
33. *Q*, LVIII, 59–62.
34. *Ibid.*

because that territory was not then in dispute. However, he thought it might become "the source of future hostilities between the States and the Indians," necessitating the drawing of a permanent boundary. To find what this should be, he recommended a consultation of the natives concerned. He admitted that the neutralization of the territory demanded by the western Indians was all that was necessary to extricate Britain from her present difficulties in the interior.[35]

Meanwhile the British government was going ahead with the scheme, determined to lose no time; for one country's extremity was the other's opportunity. A special messenger was already sailing to New York, where he was to give the British consul dispatches for Hammond in Philadelphia. He was then to make haste to Quebec, there to deliver dispatches for Major General Alured Clarke and Colonel John Graves Simcoe. In the absence of Dorchester, Clarke was commander-in-chief in British North America and, as lieutenant governor, was administrator of Lower Canada. Simcoe was lieutenant governor of Upper Canada, the other new province created by the division of the old Province of Quebec at the close of 1791. Hammond was to propose the plan to the American government, and the two Canadian officials were to coöperate by supplying him with information and by sending him an expert official of the Indian Department to advise on all doubtful points.[36]

Hammond did not obey these instructions. His head was older than his years, which numbered less than thirty. He realized that the American despair was not great enough to support the British hope. Already he had privately approached Hamilton, suggesting mediation, and had discovered that the government of the United States would never consider it so long as Britain held the posts, but might, if she surrendered them, accord special privileges to British fur traders on American soil.[37] Here was the first inkling of the solution to be embodied in Jay's Treaty. He also encountered an American determination to fight the Indians to a finish if that was necessary for a satisfactory peace—an anticipation of the Battle of Fallen Timbers which, joined with Jay's Treaty, terminated this ugly business in the interior.

Hammond may have drawn some comfort in his disobedience from the knowledge that his report on the American attitude would have reached London about the time his new instructions had been sent, for it arrived on the very day; but he found little comfort in the orders which followed. A dispatch of April 25 told him to press the barrier project against the "apparent disinclination" of the United States, and that the late Indian

35. *Ibid.*, pp. 86–91.
36. *S.P.*, I, 125.
37. S. F. Bemis, *Jay's Treaty* (New York, 1923), p. 119.

triumph would probably soon force American acceptance. He was also directed to urge the rectification of the boundary across Lake Champlain as proposed by Dorchester in order to give Grande Isle and Isle La Motte to Canada. These, said the dispatch, had little value to the United States except as a cheap means of buying off the British claim for heavy damages incurred by the American infraction of the treaty.[38] Again the British minister disappointed his government but served his country by using his discretion.

The British plan was never presented to the American government. If it had been, it might have let loose such a storm as would have blown Hammond home forthwith. He contented himself with putting forth more feelers. He informally outlined the proposal to Hamilton, and he engaged Jefferson and Knox in conversation on its principle. These gentlemen made it abundantly clear that the United States government would never tolerate foreign intervention in its internal affairs nor any suggestion of ceding American territory. Hammond reported accordingly, and won the approval of his government. A dispatch of August 4, 1792, shelved the impossible project.[39]

While the British minister was thus holding back out of regard for the sensibilities of the United States, he was engaged in strenuous controversy with the American Secretary of State, who tried to get the posts by demanding that Britain execute the treaty. Hammond thereupon drew up a brief against the United States for violating it; and this, Jefferson proceeded to demolish in a longer brief. The two men then had an interview which did not bring them together. Both were wrong, and they ought to have known it. Each was trying to excuse his own country by accusing the other, though there was no causal relationship between the faults on each side. This unpleasant game of recrimination, cut short by Hammond's reference to his government for instructions on how to answer Jefferson,[40] is not quite so futile to follow as it was to play, because the records contain some interesting material.

Hammond's brief, a letter of March 5 to Jefferson, reveals a shift of British emphasis from debts to Loyalists. As the former grievance was being removed, the latter was being thrust forward to screen the British violation. At the end of their interview, on June 3, Jefferson parted from Hammond with the firm conviction that Britain had no intention of yielding the posts, and also with the uncomfortable suspicion that she had still further designs on American territory.

This suspicion sprang from their discussion of the error of the treaty

38. Dorchester to Dundas, March 23, 1792, *Q*, LVIII, 86. Bemis, *op. cit.*, p. 120.
39. *Ibid.*, pp. 121–123.
40. *A.S.P.F.R.*, I, 193–198, 201–216, 237.

in running the boundary west from the Lake of the Woods to the Mississippi, an error already perceived by Grenville and now dawning upon the interested public.[41] Some revision was necessary, and the British minister proposed a cession of American territory to bring the boundary down to the Mississippi where it was navigable—to the falls of St. Anthony (Minneapolis), where it would have come had Britain accepted the projection of the forty-fifth parallel as the dividing line. Britain had no mind to play the role of the daughter who might swim but not go near water. Article VIII of the treaty guaranteed her the right to navigate the Mississippi throughout its length, and the United States must keep faith by granting her access to the river's navigable waters. The erroneous boundary was drawn on the understanding that it would do this very thing, and the understanding must be preserved. Thus argued Hammond. Jefferson agreed that the boundary gap should be closed, but said that it should be done with the least possible change. He stoutly denied the validity of the British contention, insisting that the navigation clause had nothing to do with the definition of the northern boundary. The former, he said, was just a relic of the calculation that peace with Spain would have established Britain on the mouth of the river in Florida. On the following day, Jefferson reported to Madison the desire of the British for "such a slice of our Northwest Territory . . . as would admit them to the navigation and profit of the Mississippi." His words seem to suggest a desire to reduce the navigation clause to a nullity.

The discovery of this imperfection in the treaty raised the possibility of a bargain. Britain's willingness to observe the treaty by abandoning the posts might be bought by American willingness to revise the treaty to implement its promise of free navigation of the Mississippi by the British, and the American purpose behind the promise might be fulfilled by Britain's combining with the United States to free the Mississippi of its Spanish incubus. The idea of such a bargain began to take shape in the mind of Hamilton when Hammond, repulsed by Jefferson, discussed with him the closing of the boundary gap. Nearly four months later, on October 21, Hamilton opened his mind in a cabinet meeting held to consider a southern tangle with Spanish officials and Creek Indians, something comparable to that in the Northwest with British officials and the neighboring tribes. Hamilton favored peace with Spain; but he believed it could not last indefinitely and he wished to prepare for the coming crisis by securing the alliance of Britain. Knox also was willing to satisfy the British desire for access to the Mississippi, but Edmund Randolph,

41. For a good discussion of this subject see S. F. Bemis, "Jay's Treaty and the Northwest Boundary Gap," *The American Historical Review*, XXVII, 465–484.

then Attorney General, joined Jefferson in opposition, and Washington broke the deadlock by summarily condemning the proposal.

It has been said that his decision was fortunate for the future of the American West, which is another way of saying that it was unfortunate for the Canadian West; but it should not be forgotten that this proposal, unlike the barrier project, was bound to come up again, for the gap it was to fill remained open. What was more important than the President's decision was the subsequent agreement of Britain to relinquish the posts without insisting on access to "the father of waters," so that when the time came to fill the gap Britain had lost the springboard from which she might have leaped to the Mississippi. Washington's decision should also be related to the fact that Britain certainly overreached herself with the barrier project and to the possibility that she then missed her best opportunity for striking a bargain over the posts. In his conversations with Jefferson and Knox, as well as with Hamilton, Hammond discovered an American inclination to pay a good price for the recall of the British garrisons. The transfer of the posts did not necessarily mean the transfer of the power hitherto attached to them. The incoming American garrisons might be restricted in size, and the forts might even be razed. The control of the Great Lakes might be removed from consideration by a mutual limitation of armaments upon them. The British fur trade might be guaranteed against unfriendly interference by arrangements for freedom of intercourse. All these things and, in addition, even access to the Mississippi might have been secured on the one condition that Britain was willing to negotiate the transfer. But the members of the American administration knew from the beginning that Hammond had no power to negotiate. He had no power for the simple reason that the British government would not consider the surrender of these valuable pawns on the confused chessboard of America, unless the game was decided beforehand against the United States by the amputation of a huge territory and its erection into a neutral Indian barrier state.

Though Hammond refrained from pushing the barrier project in Philadelphia, he did not despair of a settlement that would please his government. He saw two possibilities, of which either or both might bring the desired end. One was a repetition of St. Clair's defeat, which he anticipated but could do nothing to effect. The other he might control. It was to force British mediation by bringing sufficient pressure from the Indians to bear upon the United States, the method contemplated by Dorchester. Accordingly, on July 11, 1792, Hammond wrote to Simcoe suggesting that he might engineer, without any appearance of "collusion" or "inspiration" on the part of British officials, a "spontaneous" demand of "all the Indian tribes bordering on the British possessions" for the good offices of Britain in establishing peace between them and the United States. In doing this, Simcoe was to avoid encouraging the natives to hope that Britain would support them with arms should her mediation fail. "It is neither the interest nor the inclination of His Majesty's Government to commence offensive hostilities against the United States," said Hammond, "though I think everything short of hostilities should be employed to give weight to our interference."[42]

Simcoe was just the man for the task, though he was not such a fire eater as some Americans have imagined him to be. It is true that this proud commander of a regiment of light horse, the Queen's Rangers, in the Revolutionary War boasted that he entertained a "military contempt" for "Washington and such like cattle," and the boaster dreamed of their overthrow; but he did not aspire to accomplish their downfall, for he knew that in the event of war his own military position was too desperate for anything but defensive measures,[43] and he had already been warned of impending danger. From various sources, including the captured instructions of Knox to St. Clair, he contracted the suspicion that Congress was lying in wait for a favorable opportunity for an offensive move. He also had a letter of April 21, 1792, from Hammond, informing him that Anthony Wayne, St. Clair's successor in the western command, was "the most active, vigilant, and enterprizing officer in the American service," and that his army, if successful against the Indians, might conceive or be inspired with the design of seizing the posts. The American government, said the letter, would hardly instigate it but would certainly sanction it if achieved.[44] The danger which he believed encompassed him was like the breath of life to Simcoe. He was burning with ambition. When the British government decided to send a minister to the United States, he had striven for the appointment not only before but even after he was chosen to govern Upper Canada. He believed that the two offices, though not the two salaries, might be combined because negotiations with the United States would chiefly concern Canada and he could conduct them from the seat of his government, leaving "common mercantile matters" to the care of consular hands.[45] Though remaining only lieutenant governor of an infant inland colony, such a man naturally felt upon his shoulders the whole weight of the Empire on this continent, and he jumped at the promising suggestion from Philadelphia. On August 20, he transformed it into orders to McKee, copying the exact

42. *S.P.*, I, 175–177.
43. *Ibid.*, p. 166.
44. *Ibid.*, pp. 131–132.
45. *Ibid.*, p. 21. Simcoe's high conception of the importance of Upper Canada appears strikingly in a letter of August 21, 1792, in which he said, "This country *must* be a great one, and sometime or other, from its position, govern internal America." *Ibid.*, p. 205.

words of Hammond and adding many of his own. The latter explained how the natives might be helped "with peculiar propriety." From British sources they might procure copies of pre-Revolutionary treaties and deeds of cession to substantiate their territorial claims.[46]

Here it may be well to pause for a glance at Simcoe's motives. His thought was of power and position, not pelts. In the spring, he had reported the "fur trade on its present foundation to be of no use whatever" to Upper Canada. The traffic would drain its population and debase its morals. Something might be gained by persuading the Indians to bring their furs "to our market places." Though the traders declared it necessary to go to the Indian villages, "the assertions of merchants," he said, were "always to be received with great caution." The natives had been pampered in their idleness.[47] In September he wrote to Hammond that Britain was bound to lose the trade of Detroit because the increase of western settlements would destroy it whereas the valuable northwest trade would never fall to the United States because of the cheaper Hudson Bay route into the country. What worried him was the fear that the Indians, if left to make their own peace with the Republic, would then fall like a scourge upon Upper Canada. What inspired him was the hope of strengthening and extending British influence in the interior of the continent.[48]

On September 30, 1792, exactly a month after Simcoe's order to McKee, a great council of tribes commenced its deliberations at "the Glaize," where the stream of that name emptied into the Maumee a few miles above the rapids. McKee of course was present, but he had not gathered the assembly. It was a by-product of the newly revived American policy of negotiating with the natives instead of trying to conquer them. The Six Nations were present as intermediaries between the western tribes and the United States, to persuade the former to meet representatives of the latter in a peace conference. Already the great native confederacy was cracking. The Six Nations, accused of deserting their brethren by "talking to the Americans," replied that they had been "two years past in council with Washington" and had heard from him "nothing false," nothing but a desire for "peace and friendship with all nations of our color." The retort came quickly that while the Americans were talking peace down east they were making war out west. "Their sweet speeches" must have "intoxicated" those who could hold such language. Nevertheless, after ten days, the council terminated with apparent harmony. The western tribes extracted from the Six Nations a

46. *Ibid.*, pp. 207–209.
47. *Ibid.*, p. 141.
48. *Ibid.*, pp. 215–216.

pledge of solidarity, they promised to meet American peace commissioners at Sandusky in the spring, they declared for the Ohio as their boundary, and they appealed to Simcoe.[49]

Three things the red men asked of the white chief. Two he promised without any question. One was to supply the coming conference with provisions, which was customary; the other was the production of official documents to support the native claims, which was his own suggestion. The third was his presence at Sandusky. This was the invitation that Hammond suggested, Simcoe ordered, and McKee got. Probably it was not so artificial as has sometimes been supposed, but whatever its nature it was useless. It merely provided Hammond with another opportunity to approach Hamilton and Jefferson informally on the question of British mediation. Of course they would have none of it, and Simcoe had to decline with regrets.

Of much greater importance was the declaration for the Ohio, which was made at the Glaize council. The change from the boundary demand of the previous year, the Muskingum-Venango line, was crucial. Those who made it admitted the sale of lands north of the Ohio, which underlay the more modest demand of 1791; but they justified the resumption of ownership without repayment, by balancing it against the abandonment of their claim for lands stolen from them on the other side of the river.[50] These Indians were obviously intoxicated, not by sweet speeches but by the sweeter taste of triumph in battle. Their victory over St. Clair advanced their price for peace so high that it became impossible. The United States would fight them rather than accept the Ohio line, and they would fight the United States if necessary to get it. War was therefore inevitable; yet nobody saw it because the Six Nations deceived everybody, including themselves, in what appears to have been a laudable effort to avoid war.

The confusion began in November, 1792, when the Six Nations gave an agent of the American government a garbled report of the council at the Glaize. The version that reached Philadelphia did not postulate the Ohio line, though it referred to the exchange of titles to lands on either side of the river.[51] Washington's government, thus notified of the Indian willingness to negotiate, but not of the Indian determination to make the Ohio line the basis of the negotiation, naturally thought that peace was at last within reach. In utter good faith, General Knox named June 1 as the date for the conference, and he issued what seemed reasonable instructions to the American peace commissioners. They were not to surrender

49. *Ibid.*, pp. 218–229.
50. *Ibid.*, pp. 242–258.
51. *A.S.P.I.A.*, I, 323–324.

lands bought from the red men and later granted to white men. Much greater compensation than had ever been paid to natives on this continent was to be offered for a confirmation of disputed titles. It was understood that there would be concessions on both sides, and it was definitely stated that the Indians might be allowed to retain everything north of the Ohio and west of the Great Miami save one block of land already given to an American general.[52] To the western tribes, on the other hand, the American agreement to treat at Sandusky naturally seemed like an acceptance of the Ohio line as the basis of peace, because they had made it a condition of their meeting. There was thus a fatal misunderstanding.

Brant, the brains of his people, evidently calculated to use the lever of native solidarity to undermine the western stand on the Ohio line before the two sides came together at Sandusky, and there is little doubt that his pressure soon stirred misgivings in the West. He also persuaded Simcoe that the natives would be reasonable about the boundary, that they would demand the 1791 line and were prepared to give up the few inhabited places on their side of it.[53] Even McKee was fooled. On April 11, 1793, he wrote from Detroit that all the western chiefs he had seen understood that the conference would "certainly take place" at Sandusky. His only doubt was of the time. He thought the natives would not be ready before the end of June.[54]

In this strange comedy of errors, all parties alike—the Americans, the British, the Iroquois, and the western tribes—were stumbling through an enchanted wood. They were looking for something that had a name but could have no existence—the conference at Sandusky. When Brant finally discovered his impotence to shake the determination of the western allies, he threw up his hands and the spell was broken.

The great illusion of 1793 gave rise to other misunderstandings, some of which have survived to our own time. Simcoe was anxiously working for peace, and yet was suspected of working against it. He was too sensible to resent the American veto of his mediation. True, he in turn vetoed an American proposal, backed by Hammond, to buy provisions in Upper Canada for the natives at Sandusky, and for this he has incurred American blame, quite unjustly. He had already undertaken, according to custom, to furnish the necessary provisions for the conference, so that American purchase would have been superfluous. The question was therefore whether he should turn over some of the responsibility to the Americans; and this he refused to do, on the advice of Butler

52. *Ibid.*, pp. 340–342.
53. *S.P.*, I, 317–318, 323.
54. *A.S.P.I.A.*, I, 343.

and Brant and with the approval of his immediate superior, General Clarke in Quebec.[55] The British sensitiveness to the Indian accusation of desertion has always been difficult for American comprehension. The only concession that Hammond secured, that British agents might appear to help explain the American offers, Simcoe reciprocated by offering to convey the American commissioners and their suite in one of His Majesty's vessels over Lake Erie to Sandusky. They reached Niagara in the middle of May, and a few days later a vessel sailed from Detroit to bear them to their destination. But McKee's letter about the Indians' not being ready persuaded them to tarry where they were, enjoying the abounding hospitality of the lieutenant governor in Navy Hall. It has been insinuated that they were his social prisoners and were thwarted by his guile; but they were not. He reported his guests wandering off to Buffalo Creek, "holding private councils and doing their utmost to seduce the Indians," though "with but little effect," as Colonel Butler told him. Of course the commissioners, like the lieutenant governor, were keeping their ears open, and from a Mohawk they heard that he had counseled the red men to make peace but to give up none of their lands. He denied having given such advice;[56] still they were not comforted, for they feared that it was being followed. Indeed he feared the very same thing, for rumors from the West were shaking his confidence in Brant's assurance.

Instead of repairing to Sandusky, the natives gathered at the foot of the rapids on the Maumee; and there Brant, whom Simcoe suspected of causing this "previous meeting," closed with the western tribes in a decisive struggle. They clung to the Ohio line, while he tried to pull them back to the Muskingum-Venango line. They had a double advantage: the disputed boundary was their own; and the Six Nations, having taken the lead in promoting unity among the tribes, would be most reluctant to break up this unity. But the great Mohawk chieftain who had fashioned the confederacy was about the cleverest child of his race, and the issue was long in doubt. When the British learned the nature of the council, their sympathy was on the side of Brant, who was fighting for peace and the preservation of his people; but the British were powerless to influence the debate, though their food sustained the debaters. The shrewdness of McKee had no scope except for reporting.[57]

55. *S.P.*, I, 277–278, 281, 286, 297–298.

56. *Ibid.*, pp. 350–351. Simcoe later said that they told him they could not agree to peace on the Muskingum line. *Ibid.*, II, 49.

57. See *ibid.*, pp. 5–17, for Brant's journal of the proceedings. Brant suspected McKee of fostering the resolution to defend the Ohio line. If McKee did so, he was not following orders. He told Simcoe that he had done his best to back the Six Nations' advocacy of the Muskingum line. *Ibid.*, p. 34.

At Niagara, hope rose or fell according to the uncertain news that came out of the West. On June 14, Simcoe wrote to Clarke that there was "little probability of effecting a peace," and he was inclined to believe the commissioners did not expect it. One of them had remarked to his host that there would be no point in going to Sandusky if the decision of the council by the rapids was to be "conclusive and binding."[58] Three days later, in a dispatch to the Secretary of State, Simcoe said the Americans would probably "proceed to the accomplishment of their mission" as soon as they received an express from Philadelphia, "of which they are in momentary expectation."[59] On the morrow they announced their desire to go to Detroit "to learn the true state of things" before landing at Sandusky. The lieutenant governor objected to their visiting the town[60] but said that they might stay at the mouth of the river, where they could find accommodation. The express arrived on the twenty-fourth, bringing a supply of wampum which had been strangely neglected; and on the twenty-ninth the Americans went to Fort Erie to embark for Sandusky.[61] Meanwhile, on the twenty-second, Simcoe had ordered Colonel Butler and Alexander McKee to attend the conference at Sandusky, warning them that they were not to consider themselves mediators. Their mission was solely to explain to the Indians at their request the nature of the American offers and the meaning of the maps, treaties, and other pertinent documents which he was then forwarding, and to influence the Indians to accept the American offers if they were consistent with their safety or to reject them if they were not. To guard against an abuse of this liberty to urge rejection, Simcoe cautioned them that they would be narrowly watched for any word or deed which might be interpreted in the United States as proof that peace was prevented by British machinations rather than by American injustice. In the event of failure, they were to guard the commissioners more carefully than they would himself, the personal representative of the King.[62]

On July 1, McKee wrote to Simcoe that if the commissioners went to Sandusky without being authorized to conclude a treaty on the basis of the message sent in the autumn—the Ohio line—their visit would bring no good and might cause much harm, by irritating some of the tribes and inflaming them to violence.[63] On the same day, a delegation of fifty chiefs led by Brant departed to seek the American commissioners, whom

58. *Ibid.*, I, 355.
59. *Ibid.*, p. 357.
60. Simcoe was very conscious of its defenseless state and he distrusted the French inhabitants. *Ibid.*, p. 311. His objection was upheld by his immediate superior, Clarke. *Ibid.*, p. 322.
61. *A.S.P.I.A.*, I, 348–349.
62. *S.P.*, I, 365–366.
63. *Ibid.*, p. 374.

they found on the fifth still detained at Fort Erie by contrary winds. All repaired to Niagara for a solemn interview in the presence of Simcoe on the seventh, eighth, and ninth.[64] Brant was obviously temporizing, for he misrepresented his principals and misled his hearers by the way he framed the main question the delegation had come to ask. He merely inquired whether the commissioners had power to run a new boundary, which of course they had, though they had no authority to consider anything like what McKee correctly reported they really wanted. The coming of the delegation was "a fortunate event," according to the commissioners. They then discovered that Anthony Wayne's quiet preparations for a military advance from the Ohio had disquieted the tribes on the Maumee, and at once they wrote to Knox and to Washington to keep the restless soldier absolutely still in order to ensure an "uninterrupted treaty." Having dispatched these letters, again they set out for Fort Erie, and again the wind was unfavorable. Their departure and their passage were so delayed that it was not until the twenty-first that they reached the mouth of the Detroit River, where they found lodging. Having decided to wait there until they heard the Indians were adjourning to Sandusky, they wrote McKee accordingly.[65]

A week later another deputation left the council fire on the Maumee, and this time Brant was left behind. The respite he had gained by his deception at Niagara had availed him nothing. Though strongly supported by McKee,[66] he was defeated, and he knew it. He wrote Simcoe a most despairing note[67] on the very day the new delegates departed. They were to explain that their predecessors had not put the question they had been sent to ask. On July 30, they faced the commissioners with a demand for a written answer. Were they empowered to make peace with the Ohio as a boundary? The American reply, submitted on the thirty-first, explained at length why this was impossible, and that the Indians as well as the United States must make concessions. The commissioners emphasized the enormous compensation their government was willing to pay, little imagining how this offer could be turned against them; and, as a crowning inducement to treat for peace, they made a startling announcement. The President repudiated the oft-repeated American claim that the United States had acquired ownership of the whole country by the treaty with Britain.[68]

At long last the American government had come round to the British

---

64. For the minutes of the council, see *ibid.*, pp. 377–382, and *A.S.P.I.A.*, I, 349–351.
65. *Ibid.*, pp. 351–352.
66. *S.P.*, II, 34. Brant, however, blamed McKee for the failure. *Ibid.*, p. 102.
67. *Ibid.*, I, 402–403.
68. *A.S.P.I.A.*, I, 352–354.

position that what had been transferred had not been the title to Indian territory but merely the exclusive right to acquire it from the natives by solemn treaty with them. If the American government had admitted this principle in the beginning, there need have been no Anglo-American entanglement over the posts, nor any Indian war in the Northwest; but these experiences were necessary to force this admission.

The conversion was too late to win the western tribes. They had drunk the strong wine of victory. On August 1, a Wyandot chief replied to the Americans that the Ohio had been made the boundary long ago and they could not change it. He was sorry no agreement was possible. "We shall talk to our head warriors. You may return whence you came and tell Washington." Captain Mathew Elliott, McKee's assistant and the Americans' host, leaped to the rescue of the dying truce by charging the interpreter, the famous Simon Girty, with translating falsely. Girty denied it, but the hint was taken and a respite given. The commissioners were told to remain until the delegation returned and consulted their "head warriors." [69] As the days passed without any further message from the Indians, the Americans grew impatient. A vessel had been placed at their disposal, and on the twelfth they asked the captain to carry them to the mouth of the Maumee that they might get a reply more expeditiously. He refused, pleading orders to wait.[70] They felt tricked, and they later voiced a bitter complaint that has been echoed today. They did not know that they were being purposely saved from thrusting their heads into the lion's mouth.[71] On the following day, the western tribes terminated the respite by a curt message. They spurned the offer of money; they wanted to keep their lands. Peace could easily be made by removing the white people who had settled north of the Ohio. All the American government had to do was to give them the money. They would eagerly take it and gladly depart. The treaty was over.[72]

Thus terminated a curious interlude which had two important results. One was the further embitterment of American feeling against the British, who were naturally though wrongly held responsible for snatching away a peace that was within the grasp of the United States. The other was something which exasperated Americans and yet benefited their country. Anthony Wayne's advance was held up for about a year. The delay strengthened him and weakened his enemies, so that his vic-

69. *Ibid.*, p. 354.
70. *Ibid.*, p. 355.
71. McKee had warned Simcoe that it would be dangerous for the Americans to go to Sandusky without power to conclude a treaty "agreeable to the tenor of their message sent last fall." *S.P.*, I, 374.
72. *A.S.P.I.A.*, I, 356–357.

tory became certain. Of all the parties involved in this baffling confusion of 1793, only one drew profit from it, and that was the United States.

The problem of the western posts entered upon its last and most critical phase as the suspension of hostilities between the United States and the western Indians came to a close. The crisis caught Britain in an awkward situation. She was embroiled in Europe and therefore, quite apart from the posts, was embarrassed in America. Having been drawn into the French Revolutionary War by the declaration of France on February 1, 1793, she had her first experience of the fundamental conflict with the United States produced by one country's being a belligerent and the other a neutral in a major war. In addition to this clash of interest—for such it is though its nakedness is always respectably clothed in the language of rights and principles—the French Revolutionary War imposed another serious strain upon Anglo-American relations. The United States felt a great pull toward France. It was the combined product of national gratitude for necessary aid in winning independence and of political sympathy for the next people to throw off the monarchical yoke. It might have been greater still if Citizen Genet, the French minister, had not tried to make it so. His wild efforts to involve the United States in covert if not open hostilities caused a certain reaction of American sentiment against France, making it that much easier for the American government to maintain the neutrality it declared. Meanwhile, however, the maritime measures adopted by Britain in her struggle against France were leading to more trouble with the United States.

The eventuality contemplated by Britain during the Nootka Sound crisis had at length come to pass; the time for the abandonment of the posts was at hand. She had to extricate herself from this entanglement with the United States in order to have free hands for the war with France. Yet it is necessary to exercise caution against overestimating the influence of this war in liquidating the problem of the posts. Apparently it only precipitated what was coming for other reasons.

The prime cause of the retention, Britain's failure to divest herself of the guarantee she had given the red men, showed signs of disappearing when the United States, after an interval of ten years, at last promised to assume it by adopting the British principle regarding the title to Indian lands. The two grievances advanced as excuses, debts and Loyalists, were being healed; the first by the American courts, the second by the British bounty, and both by time. However much, or little, the retention of the posts may have checked or reduced these grievances in the past, it could not much affect them in the future. The new excuse of damage accruing from the nonexecution of the treaty by the United States was a worthless improvisation which could easily be brushed aside by a counterclaim for damages caused by Britain's violation. The only other value of the posts, as pawns in a North American game of chess, was also dwindling as the consolidation of the Republic under President Washington steadily reduced the possibility of the game's being played at all. Britain had never considered the posts worth a war, and now they were worth less than nothing; from being assets they had become liabilities. The British garrisons were virtually hostages in the posts they had held as pledges. They could not long remain unless covered by another Indian triumph over American forces, and a smashing American victory was in the offing.

Before Britain agreed to withdraw from the posts, the American-Indian war nearly exploded into a British-American war on the Canadian border, partly out of the very nature of the situation and partly out of individual perversity. The condition which baffled Brant in the summer of 1793 greatly altered the situation, making it much more dangerous to the precarious peace between the British and the Americans. The western tribes, by their recalcitrance, threw away more than their doubtful chance of securing a treaty which would have saved themselves from destruction and their white allies from growing embarrassment. If they had agreed with Brant to unite on the Muskingum line, they might have missed their treaty and found themselves again involved in hostilities; but they would have preserved the great native confederacy and with it a chance of fighting their way through to a negotiated instead of a dictated settlement. By wrecking the confederacy, they threw away their red allies and resumed the war with no support except the British garrisons kept in the western posts for their protection. Thither they were bound to fall back, drawing on the army of the United States until it was at last face to face with British forces on American soil. The Indian buffer vanished.

The imp of the perverse which unnecessarily aggravated this crisis was apparently released by a death on the shores of the St. Lawrence. For years Dorchester had leaned so heavily on William Smith, whom he met as chief justice of the Province of New York and made chief justice of the Province of Quebec, that when the lawyer died in December, 1793, the soldier governor, recently returned from a two years' absence, was lost. His judgment floundered and his temper grew treacherous. Two months later, on February 10, 1794, he delivered an astounding speech to a group of Seven Nation Indians of Canada who came to him as delegates from the tribes who had been at the Glaize council. Referring to their boundary proposal of 1791 and his own vain hope of ending the native war by playing the mediator, he said that he had not been able to get any reply from the United States. "Since my return," he continued, "from the manner in which the people of the States push on, and act, and talk on this side,[73] and from what I learn of their conduct towards the sea, I shall not be surprized if we are at war with them in the course of the present year; and if so, a line must then be drawn by the warriors." He cautioned them against the sale of lands to the State of New York. The Americans, he said, had broken the peace and thereby had forfeited their right of preëmpting lands from the Indians. All encroachments or purchases made since 1783 he considered "as an infringement on the King's rights." He concluded with a menacing flourish: "I believe our patience is almost exhausted."[74]

Dorchester's statement was deliberate, for he had his words written down and circulated among the red men; and there is something to be said for what he was doing. He was undoubtedly emitting a trumpet call to resurrect the dead confederacy of the natives, that it might check the American advance and hold the door open for a negotiated settlement embodying the guarantee Britain had once given the Indians. This was precisely what the government in London still wanted,[75] and for this all the American efforts to argue Britain out of the posts had been stultified. It is not for the end he had in view that the governor is to be blamed.

It is for the means Dorchester adopted to achieve this end that we must hold him culpable. His speech, delivered at a time when American opinion was already dangerously inflamed by British maritime measures directed against French commerce, applied a strong draft to the smoldering fire. It has been said on his behalf that he intended his words to reach only red ears; for he angrily ordered an investigation when the leak occurred, as it did almost immediately. But such a defense would make

73. Dorchester was upset by reports of Genet's agents working among the French Canadians. See *infra*, Chapter IX.

74. *S.P.*, II, 149–150. Simcoe has been erroneously called the real instigator of Dorchester's bellicose conduct. To anyone familiar with the relations between the two men, the charge is absurd. As an illustration of how unsubstantial is the ground upon which it has been based, some statements about a certain offensive document ascribed to Simcoe may be examined. It has been said that, on hearing in the last week of May that France had declared war on Britain, he immediately sent his aide, Lieutenant Stevenson, from Niagara to London with the document in question, which, from internal evidence, was either dictated or written by Simcoe in Niagara at that time. Bemis, *Jay's Treaty*, p. 196. The facts are very different. Stevenson was a captain, not a lieutenant. He was not Simcoe's aide; Simcoe did not send him; nor did he cross to England in 1793. He went in the previous year, having got leave to return on family affairs. From time to time he discussed Canadian affairs with several great people in England, for he was a man of "influence," and reported his interviews to Simcoe. On August 1, 1793, he wrote: "I have been with Mr. Dundas and have had a long conversation with him. He requested on parting that I would write down my requisitions and observations. . . . I yesterday gave them to him at his own house." *S.P.*, II, 413. This is the document referred to. It may be interesting to add that Stevenson was a firebrand and repeatedly chided Simcoe for not assuming more authority.

75. A month afterwards Dundas again expressed the hope of achieving it. *Ibid.*, p. 187.

him a simple-minded fool. Who else could imagine that an important document copied many times and distributed through many tribes could be kept from curious white eyes? Dorchester must have known that he was running the risk of precipitating a war between Britain and the United States. It is true that Anthony Wayne, in setting out to crush the western tribes, was also running this very risk. But the two gamblers, though playing the same game and with the same enormous stakes, are not to be judged in the same way. Beneath the seeming similarity lay fundamental differences between the two men. The inequality of their chances of gaining their respective ends need not be taken into account. That could scarcely have been gauged with any accuracy in February, 1794, and it is relatively unimportant. Much more important is the fact that the American object did not extend to the British side of the boundary agreed upon in 1783, whereas the British object lay on the American side of that line. Still more important as a ground for establishing individual responsibility is a third difference, and it is decisive. Wayne had the backing of his government; Dorchester had not. For this reason alone, he merits condemnation; and he got it, from below as well as from above.

In Canada, it was soon the common belief that the governor would not have dared to utter such an inflammatory speech unless the home government had put it in his mouth.[76] Thus, quite unconsciously, did those who were under his authority pass judgment upon him. Nearly five months later, his chief in London wrote rebuking him for his outburst. It would rather provoke hostilities, said the Secretary of State, who had only indirectly received a report of the governor's words.[77] On receiving this dispatch a fortnight after the Battle of Fallen Timbers, when the crisis reached its head and then began to pass away, Dorchester penned a reply in which he unwittingly gave himself away. He admitted that he knew the friendly disposition of the British ministry and asserted that he had no contrary inclination. He agreed that it would be folly to provoke hostility. He had, however, observed the United States under French influence definitely pushing toward war with Britain, convincing him that a rupture was inevitable. Therefore, he said, it had been impossible for him to give the Indian deputies any hope of peace through British mediation, and he still did not see any reason for concealing his opinion.[78]

Meanwhile Dorchester had added to the offense of his wild speech. On February 17, 1794, just a week after he addressed the red deputation, he ordered Simcoe to guard Detroit and its communication with Lake Erie

76. *Ibid.*, p. 164.
77. July 5, 1794, Q, LXVII, 175.
78. *Ibid.*, LXIX, 176.

by advancing troops to hold the passage of the Maumee. The lieutenant governor was to judge what force was proper for the task and to pick the most advantageous positions without confining himself to the posts occupied in 1783.[79]

As for the speech, so also for this order was Dorchester censured both from above and below. The two indiscretions becoming known in London at the same time, the Secretary of State's rebuke, cited above, applied to both equally.[80] Of those who passed adverse judgment from below, the most important was Simcoe. He did not acknowledge the command to reoccupy the deserted sites on the Maumee until about a week after he received it, and then he included in his reply this cautionary note: "There appears to me to be little doubt but that the possession of these posts will be construed into hostility; whether such shall immediately take effect may depend upon the temper of Genl. Wayne and his force comparatively to the strength of the positions which may be taken." Simcoe's dubious attitude is also apparently reflected in the tardiness with which he obeyed the command of his superior officer. Instead of immediately

79. *S.P.*, II, 154. Simcoe has been unjustly blamed for "insulting" the United States by building Fort Miami on the Maumee, though he was merely obeying the command of his superior. As mentioned above on page 116, this forward step was first proposed by Alexander McKee in response to Dorchester's inquiry about the advisability of making such a move, and Dorchester contemplated it before he left for England in 1791. That was before Simcoe landed in Canada. A close examination of Simcoe's correspondence has revealed no evidence that he advised or even favored this advance before it was ordered. If he had done so, Dorchester might have vetoed it; for that was what he did, after his return in 1793, with practically all the plans submitted by the lieutenant governor of the upper province, whose appointment he had resented from the beginning.

Simcoe's letters clearly show that his mind was moving in the opposite direction. Though he advocated occupying Presque Isle to guarantee continued command of Lake Erie, he was for drawing in, rather than for pushing out. He repeatedly drew attention to the defenseless state of the two main posts, Detroit and Niagara; and he looked forward to withdrawing their garrisons to Chatham, London, Long Point, and York, leaving behind only "a few men sufficient to prevent Indian robbery and to certify the commission of hostilities should the United States venture upon so serious an undertaking." His decision to shift his capital from Newark to York had this end in view; and he stated that the American commissioners, whom he had entertained, regarded the removal of his residence to the north side of Lake Ontario as a preparatory step to the execution of this design.

Though Simcoe had earlier been plagued by nightmares of impending American aggression, which were perhaps as natural as the corresponding American nightmares of red devils hounded on by the British, his confidence increased as Wayne marched north in the autumn of 1793. It was not that he believed he could defend his province against attack, for that he admitted was impossible. He trusted that the attack would not come. As late as February 23, before he received Dorchester's order, he wrote the Secretary of State in England that the gradual retirement of the troops from the barrier forts would conciliate the Americans and convince them that national honor rather than commercial profit had held the British there. The order and the speech, which arrived together at Niagara about ten days later, were rather convincing evidence that war was imminent and naturally altered his outlook. Even so, he harbored doubts about the wisdom of the order. *S.P.*, II, 57, 63, 104, 105, 112, 163, 168.

80. In his defensive reply, however, the governor confined himself to justifying his speech.

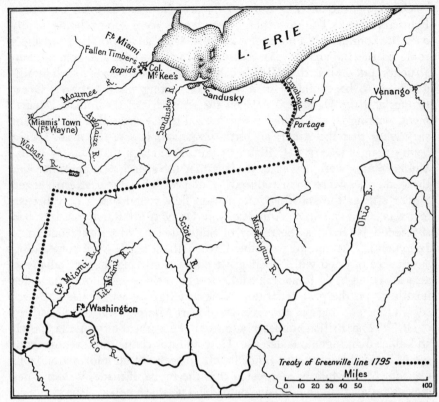

The Campaign on the Maumee, 1794, and the Treaty of Greenville, 1795

dispatching an express to Detroit to hasten the movement, he waited until he could go himself. Not until four weeks after the order reached him did he reach Detroit and start operations.[81] When Wayne was drawing perilously close in July, the Detroit commandant, who had sent almost all of his garrison to the newly built Fort Miami, wrote confidentially to Simcoe: "I ever apprehended the Americans would be extremely jealous of our establishing" this post, "and that it would expedite the rupture; I should not be surprised if the ministry mentioned their disapprobation of it to Lord Dorchester, as I don't believe they wish to provoke a war with the United States, and God knows this country is by no means in a situation to commence hostilities. We don't see anything from home that justifies His Excellency's speech to the Indians, or taking the post that seems to court offence."[82]

81. *Ibid.*, pp, 179, 219.
82. *Ibid.*, p. 334.

Great was the effect of the two shocks administered from Quebec in February, 1794. The governor's fiery words were soon echoing madly over the continent. "You cannot imagine what an alarm His Lordship's reply to the Indians . . . has occasioned in this town; the general construction put on it is that His Lordship must be possessed of such intelligence as to be confident of a war soon taking place between Great Britain and the U. States." When the secretary of the Indian Department, writing from Montreal, was moved to use these words,[83] it is not surprising that the American press screamed. It saw the mask falling from the ugly face of the villain, Britain. Friends of that country in the United States were driven to declare that the speech was spurious, but these skeptics were soon reduced to silence. The angry storm surged higher still as the startling information flew round that a new British fort was being run up on American soil. On May 20, Randolph, who had succeeded Jefferson as Secretary of State, demanded an explanation of Hammond. "At the very moment when the British were forwarding assurances of good will," their governor was stirring up the Indians to attack. Though, as Randolph said, Dorchester's speech "only forbodes hostility" on the part of Britain, "the intelligence which has been received this morning [of the erection of Fort Miami] is, if true, hostility itself."[84] The British minister admitted the authenticity of the speech and offered an ingenious defense. He could not confirm the report from the Maumee but promised immediately to seek official information from Canada. Meanwhile he suggested that the move, if made, was of a defensive rather than an offensive nature.[85] The sharp notes of the two men were at once submitted to Congress, and the wave of national indignation continued to rise in the United States. This naturally reacted to heighten the alarm in Canada.

With such a background it is almost a marvel that war did not break out by spontaneous combustion when Anthony Wayne finally triumphed over the Indians, reinforced by a contingent of British militia, within earshot of the new British fort on the Maumee. Three days before the battle, Simcoe said, "It is obvious that if Wayne attacks the Miamis post that a war commences between Great Britain and the United States";[86] and already, over in London where he was fighting to preserve the peace between the two countries, Jay had told Grenville that, though no attack would then be made upon the posts held by Britain in 1783, it was "highly probable that every new advanced post, and particularly the one

83. *Ibid.*, p. 164.
84. *A.S.P.F.R.*, I, 461.
85. *Ibid.*, p. 462.
86. *S.P.*, II, 386.

said to be taken by Mr. Simcoe on the Miami,[87] would be attacked."[88]

The Battle of Fallen Timbers, which cut the Indian knot, was fought on the north side of the Maumee rapids on the morning of August 20, 1794. As the noise increased, the listening garrison of the nearly completed Fort Miami, commanded by Major Campbell, closed up the gaps in their defenses and stood to arms. When the firing died down, the vanquished Indians fled by, and no Americans charged his walls, Campbell wrote: "It has been a great relief to my mind that the battle did not happen so near to this fort, so [sic] as to commit me." Perhaps he was not then aware of the fact that three score militiamen under William Caldwell had really committed him. In defiance of orders, they had imprudently joined in the fray, losing several of their number, among them the clerk of the court at Detroit.

Whatever Major Campbell may not have known, he did know that he would not sleep soundly that night. He could see some Americans feeding their horses on McKee's island, and on his own shore the victors were, as he said, "showing themselves in small bodies very near to us, beating their drums and sounding their horns."[89] Wayne's army occupied the heights opposite McKee's almost within reach of the fort's guns, but without communicating with the fort. Conceiving it a duty to his own "station" and to "the honor of the British colours," Campbell sent an officer with a flag of truce on the following morning to inquire "in what light" he was to view this near approach of an American army to the guns of His Majesty's garrison. He added that he knew of no war between the two countries. Late that afternoon he received Wayne's reply saying, "Were you entitled to an answer, the most full and satisfactory one was announced to you, from the muzzels of my small arms yesterday morning in the action against the hoard of savages in the vicinity of your post, which terminated gloriously to the American arms —but had it continued until the Indians &c were drove under the influence of the post and guns you mention—they would not have much impeded the progress of the victorious army under my command, as no such post was established at the commencement of the present war between the Indians and the United States."[90]

On the twenty-second, there was a further exchange of "courtesies." Campbell claimed that Wayne's letter of the previous day authorized him to commit hostilities, and he proclaimed his own forbearance in the face of insults offered the flag of his fort "by approaching it within pistol

87. The Maumee.
88. *A.S.P.F.R.*, I, 333.
89. *S.P.*, II, 396.
90. *Ibid.*, pp. 405–406.

shot of my works, not only singly, but in numbers with arms in their hands." He could forbear no longer; therefore let Wayne beware. The latter retorted that the erection of this fort was a hostile act, and he called upon Campbell to remove forthwith his garrison, artillery, and stores to the nearest post occupied by the British in 1783. Campbell closed the correspondence by refusing to discuss the propriety of his position. That, he said, was something "best left to the ambassadors." Meanwhile he would obey the orders of those under whom he served. He repeated his warning about the danger of approaching within reach of his guns.[91] When a party of horse later rode up within the prohibited range, a gun was pointed and the match was lighted; but it was not applied because the party wheeled round and made off.[92] The breath-taking crisis had passed. Wayne retired with his army, consoling himself for having failed to budge this British garrison by boasting in general orders that his forces had insulted the British flag "with impunity."[93]

Rarely have two countries come so close to war without plunging into it. Although no nervous finger touched off a fatal explosion on the Maumee, the catastrophe would probably have burst soon afterward in some other way, because American feeling was perilously tense and the dramatic meeting at Fort Miami was of itself more likely to aggravate than to assuage it, had not a restraint been already imposed by the dispatch of Jay's mission to London. That mission was launched with difficulty and just in time. Jay sailed from New York only eight days before Philadelphia was startled by the intelligence that this new British fort was rising on American soil. Had the order been reversed, which it would have been if Simcoe had not delayed executing Dorchester's command, the violent outburst of national feeling in the United States might have kept Jay at home and released hostile legislation that was suspended in Congress, thereby precipitating the country over the terrible brink on which it was poised.

91. *Ibid.*, pp. 406–408.
92. *Ibid.*, III, 232.
93. *Ibid.*, II, 410.

CHAPTER VIII
JAY'S TREATY

JAY's mission was born of desperation. When Congress assembled in the beginning of December, 1793, the President's opening speech focused attention on foreign affairs. His immediate submission of documents relating to the abortive efforts to make peace with the Indians, and of correspondence between the neutral United States and the belligerent European powers, provided an effective setting for the presentation of Jefferson's famous report on the privileges and restrictions of American commerce in foreign countries. Assailing Britain's tariff and navigation laws, and recommending vigorous retaliation, it let loose a storm of pent-up feeling against the supposed tyrant of the sea. The rapidly crystalizing political parties joined in the bitter struggle, the Federalists fighting hard to prevent the vengeful Republicans from passing legislation that would cripple American commerce and, by destroying the customs revenue, would undermine the government of the United States. Of course the Republicans made the best use of other ammunition that was lying around: Britain's refusal to surrender the western posts, her support of American Indians against the American government, and her order-in-council of June 8, 1793, stopping the American provision trade with France. The arguments flew back and forth with neither side sure of victory until March, when a quick and ominous change came over the debate.

The change was produced by the startling news of wholesale British captures of American vessels in the West Indies. The Caribbean was swarming with American craft eager to enjoy the French colonial trade which France, under pressure of the war, had recently opened; and Britain was applying the "Rule of 1756," which denied neutrals the right to relieve a belligerent by taking over its colonial trade prohibited in time of peace.[1] The British action, initiated without warning[2] and conducted in a harsh and undiscriminating manner, caused a great flame of anger in the United States. It transformed the issue before Congress into one of peace or war, and it seemed to cut the ground from under the feet of the Federalists. To make things worse, the newspapers then got hold of Dorchester's speech and blazoned it abroad. Did not that prove that Britain intended to attack the United States by land as well as by

1. For a fuller discussion of this issue, see *infra*, Chapter XI.
2. The first word Hammond had of the order-in-council of November 6, authorizing the action, came from the West Indies with news of the seizures.

sea, and with the horrible accompaniment of savage atrocities? A month's embargo was clapped on all shipping in American ports; the House of Representatives passed a bill to stop all intercourse with Britain until she satisfied American claims for these captures, paid compensation for Negroes carried off at the end of the Revolutionary War, and surrendered the posts; there was talk of following this up with a bill to sequester all British credits in the country; and Congress turned to strengthen the defenses of the country, with resolutions for fortifications, arsenals, and a greatly augmented army.

The Federalists were swept along in the general demand for preparatory measures; yet they desperately hoped to avert war. They believed it would be the undoing of their young country. As a last resort a group of Federalist senators[3] appealed to the President to send a special envoy, preferably Hamilton, to seek an accommodation with the British government; and meanwhile they fought to stave off the passage of legislation which would make reconciliation difficult if not impossible. Washington hesitated until the middle of April. Then he was persuaded by Hamilton, who wisely renounced any thought of going himself, to act quickly and to send the Chief Justice. John Jay promptly, though reluctantly, accepted the invitation of the President, who at once sent his nomination to the Senate. Three days later, on the nineteenth, it was confirmed. On the eighteenth, the embargo was extended for another month, but on the twenty-eighth the nonintercourse bill was defeated in the upper chamber by the casting vote of the Vice-President. The fever, which then reached its peak, would certainly have mounted higher and might have proved fatal if people in Philadelphia had known of the new British fort on the Maumee. Fortunately that exasperating news did not come for another three weeks, when it was too late to stir more than a third of the House to vote for a new nonintercourse bill.[4] The dove of peace was already far out on the Atlantic.

Until Jay landed in England on June 8, London was blissfully ignorant of this storm raging on the western side of the Atlantic, so slow and precarious was communication in those days. Almost immediately a pile of accumulated dispatches from Hammond descended upon Grenville, utterly crushing his fond dream of erecting a neutral Indian barrier between the United States and Canada, and awakening him to the peril in America. He must have breathed a sigh of relief on seeing the proffered olive branch. Its bearer did not reach the capital until the fifteenth, for

3. Hammond encouraged them by telling one of their members that he did not believe Dorchester spoke for his government.
4. The embargo was allowed to expire on May 25, to be replaced by a bill empowering the President "to lay, regulate, and revoke embargoes."

his poor state of health required him to travel by easy stages from Falmouth. During the next fortnight he had several interviews with the English minister, at whose house he dined with the cabinet. Jay encountered such friendliness and frankness combined that he concluded the auspices were favorable for a settlement even though Grenville would not commit himself in any particular.

The British hesitation to commence serious negotiations was probably due in part to two uncertainties of the moment, one concerning the war and the other domestic politics. The European coalition was beginning to fall apart, and French arms were advancing on the Continent; but on the sea the British navy had just won "the glorious First of June." At home, the government was flirting with the Portland Whigs, who had been supporting it from the opposition benches, and another ministry might take its place at any time. A weightier reason for caution lay in the very nature of the new maritime troubles with the United States. The American protests attacked principles that were vital to Britain. It was doubtful if even the threat of war could force their surrender.[5] Some delay was also inevitable because, as Jay was surprised to find, "not a single case" of seizure under the November order had been submitted to Grenville, none having been sent to Pinckney, the resident minister. Admitting that the facts when established might require some action of his government to satisfy the ends of justice, the British Secretary of State asked Jay "to furnish him with some of the strongest of those cases," and the American envoy had to scout for material. While there was still wide doubt whether Britain could appease American ire over what had been happening at sea, the British government was firmly determined to prevent American irritation by any action on land. Hence the obvious annoyance caused on July 1 by the receipt of a dispatch from Hammond, written on May 25, recounting the outburst of feeling caused by news of Simcoe's building the post on the Maumee. Only four days later, Henry Dundas sent off the rebuke to Dorchester, mentioned above.[6] It was intimated to the governor that his two indiscretions might handicap the negotiations just initiated in London.

On July 11 the formation of the coalition ministry was announced and Jay had another session with Grenville, who remained at the Foreign Office. The Englishman assured his guest that there would be no unnecessary delays and that a full discussion of all the points of difference between the two countries would be opened as soon as the members of the new ministry could be informed and consulted.

At this meeting, however, something definite was accomplished. It

5. These issues are examined in Chapter XI.
6. *Supra,* pp. 135, 136.

grew out of an informal discussion of Simcoe's recent move. It was an agreement to preserve the *status quo* on the Canadian-American frontier during the negotiations. "Both parties should continue to hold their possessions; . . . all encroachments on either side should be done away"; and if hostilities occurred they were to cease, prisoners captured were to be released, and property seized was to be restored. Both governments were immediately to give orders to this effect.[7] This agreement had two defects, either of which might have ruined its wise purpose. It was made too late to be conveyed to the banks of the distant Maumee before the dramatic meeting of Wayne and Campbell, and one may well wonder whether peace could have been preserved if these two soldiers had then broken it. It was also lacking in precision on one important point. What was the *status quo?* Jay was content with a general formula that did not stipulate whether Fort Miami was to be regarded as a "possession" or an "encroachment." Of course he understood it was the latter, and he simply took for granted that orders would be sent to Dorchester and Simcoe to remove it. But no such orders were issued because the British preferred the other interpretation. The misunderstanding, for which the American must thus share the blame, caused no little irritation in the United States; but fortunately this was not until the treaty was too advanced to be wrecked by it.

One dispute that had bedeviled other disputes between the two countries ever since 1783 was soon settled in the only way possible. It was the vexed question of which party was the first to violate the peace treaty. Jay and Grenville gladly agreed to bury it. The atmosphere was much healthier for the removal of this corpse.

The surrender of the posts then presented no difficulty. It was apparently taken for granted quite early in the discussions. On July 4, Dundas wrote to Simcoe that the presence of Jay had roused hopes of securing "a final termination of all disputes and a perfect good understanding" with the United States, and that "in all probability" the evacuation would be part of the arrangement.[8] As the negotiation of the other and more contentious points of difference proceeded, the details of the transfer of the posts were settled with little trouble. It was a simple matter to fix a date for the completion of the British withdrawal. Jay proposed June 1, 1795, but readily acquiesced in Grenville's firm demand for another year's grace, so that the treaty stipulated June 1, 1796. It also guaranteed to "all settlers and traders within the precincts or jurisdiction" of the posts the unmolested enjoyment of their property there, and the liberty to depart or remain. Those who remained were not to be compelled to be-

7. *A.S.P.F.R.*, I, 479.
8. *S.P.*, II, 300.

come American citizens or to take any oath of allegiance to the United States; but they were to be free to do so, and if this was their choice they were to declare it within one year after evacuation. These conditions were set forth in Article II. As the previous article was a mere declaration of amity, the surrender of the posts thus occupies the forefront of the treaty.

A clause inserted in this article late in the negotiation has since been condemned as "a curious impertinence."[9] Referring to the interval before evacuation, it reads: "The United States in the meantime, at their discretion, extending their settlements to any part within the said boundary line, except within the precincts or jurisdiction of any of the said posts." At first glance this interpolation may seem strange, but on closer examination it does not. It is linked with the agreement to maintain the *status quo*. This was originally to hold until the end of negotiation; but during the negotiation, as we have just seen, part of it was projected beyond the signature of the treaty by the adoption of a subsequent date for the evacuation of the posts. Until then the British were not to be disturbed. Hence the guarantee against the encroachment of American settlers. It was against American interests, however, and quite unnecessary to continue the whole *status quo* through this additional time. Therefore it was narrowed when lengthened.

The clause in question should also be particularly related to a disturbing piece of news which Jay received from America. This had its origin in a fear that had long worried Simcoe. He not unnaturally saw a menace in the advance of American settlement toward the posts, particularly Oswego. In that vicinity a certain Charles Williamson, an American magistrate and former British officer, was directing the colonizing activities of a British-American land company. The lieutenant governor of Upper Canada realized that he would soon have to withdraw the garrison or check the settlement that threatened to engulf it. After writing many letters to Quebec for a decision which he was loath to make, Simcoe at last received from Dorchester an order to cover any such situation.[10] In obedience to this order, he sent an officer[11] with a file of unarmed men to inquire by what authority the settlement was being made, to require a cessation from "such aggressions," and, in the event of a refusal to desist, to lodge a protest. The protest, drawn up by Dorchester, denounced "the taking possession of any part of the Indian Territory" during the inexecution of the treaty as "a direct violation of His Britannic Majes-

9. S. F. Bemis, *Jay's Treaty*, p. 256.
10. *S.P.*, II, 318.
11. Lieutenant R. H. Sheaffe, who was selected because he knew Williamson personally. *Ibid.*, III, 133.

ty's Rights." This "insult"[12] to the United States was delivered on August 16, just four days before the Fallen Timbers engagement; and by the end of the month it began to rouse angry echoes in Philadelphia, whence the indignant Randolph reported the whole business to Jay. When the latter was fully informed of it, he straightway agreed with Grenville to add this clause which repudiated the offensive British doctrine enunciated so formally in America.[13]

Another detail that was arranged without much difficulty was the special provision for freedom of movement across the international boundary, first proposed by Jay twelve years before in Paris, then lifted from the peace treaty to be inserted in a commercial treaty which did not materialize, and later discussed by Hamilton, Knox, and even Jefferson in conversations with Hammond.[14] This point was omitted from the first rough sketch of the treaty, which was the work of Jay and was dated August 6;[15] but it appeared in the next and fuller draft, prepared by Grenville and submitted to Jay on August 30.[16] As phrased by the Englishman it was designed to protect only British interests—that being the professed purpose of the original suggestion in the days of the Paris negotiations. But Jay objected to such a one-sided stipulation, and without any difficulty he persuaded Grenville to make it reciprocal. Therefore, Article III of the treaty stated that "at all times" British subjects, American citizens, and Indians dwelling on either side of the line should be free "to pass and repass by land or inland navigation into the respective territories and countries of the two parties on the continent of America, (the country within the limits of the Hudson's Bay Company only excepted,) and to navigate all the lakes, rivers and waters thereof, and freely to carry on trade and commerce with each other," with an exception to be noted below.

The exclusion of the Hudson's Bay Company's territories has since stirred American criticism on the ground that it "emasculated" the American equivalent for the British freedom to engage in the American fur trade.[17] This criticism is not very sound. The admission of Americans to those northern regions had never been considered and would have been absurd, for the simple reason that British traders were likewise excluded, the territory granted by the royal charter of 1670 being the close preserve of the English company.

12. In writing to Jay, Washington called it "the most open and daring act of the British agents in America."
13. *A.S.P.F.R.*, I, 500.
14. *Supra*, pp. 120, 123.
15. *A.S.P.F.R.*, I, 486–487.
16. *Ibid.*, pp. 487–490.
17. Bemis, *op. cit.*, p. 256.

The exception to the reciprocal liberty mentioned above had to do with the British navigation laws. It was apparently taken for granted that they did not, or should not, apply in the interior. But there was no question of their operation on the seaboard. Therefore, out of regard for these sacred laws, Article III went on to say that the concession just granted was not to be interpreted as allowing American vessels from the sea to enter the ports, harbors, bays, creeks, or rivers of British North America.[18] A corresponding American limitation forbade British vessels to ascend the rivers of the United States above the highest ports of entry for foreign ships from the sea. By this article, also, the mutual freedom to navigate the Mississippi was stipulated anew, though the value of the right thus given to British subjects was being obscured by the clarification of the geography of the interior.

The freedom accorded to persons to move to and fro across the boundary was greater than that which the same article gave to goods. The American suggestion that Britain might find a wide-open back door for the entry of her manufactures into the hinterland of the United States was a thing of the past. Grenville recalled it tentatively in his draft of August 30, which would have allowed British subjects and American Indians "to pass and repass with their goods and merchandises" free of customs duties or any other impediment; but apparently he did not press very hard for what he must have seen was then impossible. As originally intended, it was agreed that furs were to be exempt from the payment of duty on crossing the boundary; and red men carrying their own "goods and effects of whatever nature" were to enjoy the same privilege, but this was not to cover "goods in bales, or other large packages, unusual among Indians." It was also laid down that no duty should be paid on goods only temporarily crossing the border for transit over portages. Otherwise the two governments retained their right to collect customs, but this right was reciprocally limited. Neither was to demand more than it would require its own nationals to pay on the same goods if imported by sea. This prohibition of national discrimination was also applied to the levying of "tolls or rates of ferriage" on either side of the boundary.

The American vision of an unarmed frontier, which had inspired Adams during the Paris negotiations, was revived by Jay in these London negotiations. On September 30, he submitted to Grenville a new draft of the treaty[19] in which it was stated that neither party should keep any armed vessels "on the lakes or water thro' which the boundary line between them passes," and that as soon as possible arrangements should

18. With the possible exception of the St. Lawrence between Quebec and Montreal, where small American craft might be admitted under special arrangements.

19. Bemis, *op. cit.*, p. 243, and Appendix III.

be made for "diminishing or wholly withdrawing all military force from the Borders," because it was the "earnest desire" of both parties "to render mutual justice, confidence, and goodwill, a sufficient Barrier against encroachments and aggression."[20] We do not know what Grenville thought of this fine proposal, nor why Jay withdrew it. The time was not ripe for such a radical move, and we need not grieve over its elimination. Neither armed ships on the Lakes nor armed men on the borders contributed anything to the outbreak of the War of 1812. If they had been banned in 1794, the war would probably have come just the same. Indeed it might have come earlier, for the bad feeling between Britain and the United States arising out of the Napoleonic struggle might have precipitated a denunciation of the ban, thereby increasing the international tension.

The adoption of a new boundary for the northwest corner of the United States, to replace the impossible line of 1783 from the Lake of the Woods to the Mississippi, was naturally pressed by the English minister as a condition for the surrender of the posts. As early as 1790 he had thought of this bargain,[21] and now he was loath to let the opportunity slip away forever. He first broached the question in informal discussions with Jay, who fought shy of it and hoped it would not be raised again. The American had confidence in the logic and justice of his own solution for the problem. He proposed a joint survey to remove all doubt about how far north the river extended, and, if then necessary, a redefinition of the boundary by commissioners appointed for the purpose. To his dismay, he found the English minister's bold proposal set forth in the draft of August 30.

Instead of offering one substitute, as Hammond had done in 1792,[22] Grenville presented two alternatives, as the American peace commissioners had done in 1782.[23] One made the new boundary depart from the old one on Lake Superior to run to the westernmost extremity of the lake, by the modern Duluth, and thence straight west "to the river of the Red Lake, or eastern branch of the Mississippi." Though neither negotiator knew it, this was also an impossible line, for Red Lake River flows into the Red River which runs north to Lake Winnipeg. By Grenville's other option, which was free from this defect, the new boundary would leave the Mississippi at the mouth of the St. Croix, the present Minnesota-Wisconsin boundary, and strike straight north to the international boundary as defined in the peace treaty, eliminating all the line

20. *Ibid.*, p. 289.
21. *Supra*, p. 111.
22. *Supra*, p. 122.
23. *Supra*, p. 31.

to the west of the intersection. Grenville's contention, of course, was that some such redefinition was necessary to implement the purpose of the peace treaty, by which British territory was to reach the Mississippi and British subjects were given equal rights with Americans to navigate that river.[24]

Jay at once raised vigorous objections. He flatly told Grenville that he could not sign a treaty which ceded American territory, and that he believed the United States would reject it. He pointed out that the British proposition was premature, because it was not yet known how far north the Mississippi stretched, and until that was definitely known the impossibility of the line drawn west from the Lake of the Woods could not be established. Therefore, he repeated, an accurate survey should be made jointly. If it proved that the supposed gap really existed, then, but not till then, a revision would be necessary. Looking forward to that eventuality, Jay assailed Grenville's proposal. Like Jefferson in 1792,[25] he insisted that the gap should be closed with the least possible cession of territory; and that, he intimated, would be nothing like what either of Grenville's alternatives involved—more than thirty thousand square miles. He demolished the argument based on the stipulation for the free navigation of the Mississippi. That was in Article VIII of the peace treaty, and the boundary was described in Article II. There was not even an implicit connection between them. The peace treaty said nothing about British territorial access to the river where it was navigable; and there was good reason for believing that it was signed without any understanding about such an access. The British had given their case away in the beginning by rejecting the American offer of a boundary running along the forth-fifth parallel to the Mississippi. When they chose the alternative crooked line, it was well known, and the maps showed it, that the Lake of the Woods lay far north of•the latitude of the falls of St. Anthony, which interrupt the navigation of the river. How far it was navigable above those falls, or whether any, or how many, other falls intervened between them and its source, was then and even yet unknown. "Nothing," he said, "could be more obvious than that a *due* west line might terminate on the river at a place not navigable." If it had been intended to reach navigable waters, he continued, the treaty would certainly have contained some provision for inclining it as far as might be necessary to attain that end.[26]

The English minister's reply, dated September 5, challenged the American envoy's position on the cession of territory. It was quite as

24. *A.S.P.F.R.*, I, 488.
25. *Supra*, p. 122.
26. *A.S.P.F.R.*, I, 490–492.

reasonable, he argued, to maintain that Britain would be ceding territory by abandoning the due-west line to the Mississippi, as it was to assume that the United States would be surrendering territory by giving up the due-west line from the Lake of the Woods. Here he was on sound ground, but it did not justify the particular proposition he had made. Jay's objections to it were too strong for him to shake, and he showed signs of weakening. His only reference to navigation was an assertion that Article VIII of the peace treaty implied a possible access to the Mississippi without passing through foreign territory. Of Jay's suggestion that a survey should be made, his only criticism was that it would cause delay. "It cannot be desirable," he urged, "when all the interests of the two countries with relation to each other are under discussion, with a view to lasting friendship, to leave unsettled so material a ground of difference as that of an unascertained boundary." He was willing to consider an agreement for a final delimitation by joint commissioners, provided they were "distinctly enabled to take into their consideration the 8th article, and to give to that stipulation such effect as they shall think it ought in justice to have, in the formation of a new boundary line."[27]

Though involving the national ownership of the rich iron deposits long afterwards discovered in Minnesota, and also the latitude of the international boundary to be drawn toward the Pacific, Grenville's proposal of August 30, 1794, was nothing so momentous as the American offer of an alternative boundary in 1782. His proposal was not an ultimatum, and it had absolutely no chance of success. If Jay had weakly accepted it—and he was determined to have none of it—the Senate of the United States would certainly have rejected it offhand. Grenville wisely refrained from pressing it further, thereby reducing the difference to whether the joint commissioners' reference should include Article VIII of the peace treaty. On this point neither man would yield, but the Englishman soon[28] fell in with the American's suggestion that they postpone the discussion of it until the completion of the joint survey. Article IV of Jay's Treaty provided for this survey; and it also stated that, if the line of 1783 was found to be impossible, "the two parties will thereupon proceed, by amicable negotiation, to regulate the boundary line in that quarter, as well as all other points to be adjusted between the said parties, according to justice and mutual convenience, and in conformity to the intent of the said treaty." By these vague phrases, the difference between the negotiators was covered.

The settlement of the dispute over which was the St. Croix River at

---

27. *Ibid.*, p. 492.

28. On September 14, after further conversation with Grenville, Jay wrote home expressing the belief that his suggestion would be adopted. *Ibid.*, p. 496.

the other extreme of the boundary described in 1783, likewise due to a false geographical assumption, presented no difficulty whatever during the negotiations in London. The two men were of one mind in believing that it should be referred to three commissioners for a final decision, and so they stipulated in Article V. The British government was to name one commissioner, the American government another, and these two were to pick the third by lot if they could not do it by agreement. According to Grenville's draft of August 30, they were to meet in London. Jay asked why they should sit there, suggesting that "actual views and surveys, and the testimony and examination of witnesses on the spot" would probably be necessary. The Englishman replied that he had named the British capital because the great mass of evidence on the subject was supposed to be there, but that he was ready to let the commission adjourn to America if necessary.[29] It was finally stipulated that Halifax should be the meeting place and that the commissioners could sit anywhere else as they saw fit.

The treaty was silent on the question of the national ownership of the islands in Passamaquoddy Bay and the Bay of Fundy. Apparently the two negotiators ignored it entirely, and this they could easily do. Rufus Putnam, ten years before, had been the only official to point out the absurdity of the due east line which the peace treaty said should be drawn from the mouth of the boundary river to determine the nationality of the islands. The problem of these islands was of minor interest compared with that of the St. Croix on which it depended and which, in turn, seemed so relatively insignificant that it had been half forgotten. Indeed the provision for the solution of the St. Croix difficulty was not an essential part of the treaty, but rather a fortuitous inclusion.

The surrender of the western posts on the conditions already explained, however, was intimately linked with other parts of the treaty that had no direct concern with British North America. The bargain over the posts would have fallen through if it had not been embraced in a larger bargain, and the conclusion of the latter apparently saved British North America from being plunged into war. Therefore this discussion of Canadian-American relations has to include some consideration of extraneous disputes between Britain and the United States.

Little attention need here be paid to most of these differences. As the early removal of the futile controversy over the responsibility for the initial violation of the peace treaty cleared the way for an agreement on the posts, so also did it make possible a direct approach to a settlement of the quarrel over American obstacles to the recovery of British debts,

29. *Ibid.*, pp. 492–493.

which Grenville made a *sine qua non*.[30] By Article VI a mixed commission was to sit in the United States to judge the claims, and the American government was to pay in specie accordingly. To guard against any future recurrence of the trouble, Article X stipulated that private "debts" were never to be confiscated or sequestered in the "event of war or national differences." The protection thus given in the future, of course, benefited Britain more than the United States, because the former was a creditor and the latter a debtor country. It has been suggested that the provision to adjudicate existing claims was superfluous, because the courts of the United States were working out a solution. But it should be remembered that in Britain these courts then inspired little confidence. They were still new, they had not yet removed all the obstacles, they might reject claims that would be allowed in an arbitral award, and they could not guarantee full payment. The adoption of the more expeditious, more equitable, and more certain method of liquidation gave Britain a real satisfaction. It was one of the broader conditions of her willingness to surrender the posts and to make other concessions which averted the danger of war.

The whole treaty turned on this great question of avoiding war. The posts constituted only one of the issues that threatened to break the peace between Britain and the United States, and they all had to be settled together. There were two other major issues, and they were both maritime. The continuance of Britain's exclusive mercantile system had irritated the United States almost to the point of exasperation. Serious retaliation began with the American Navigation Law of 1789, and by 1794 Congress was ready to launch a strenuous trade war which, in the explosive temper of the time, might easily have led to an open breach between the two countries. One of Jay's chief objects in going to England was to conclude some commercial agreement that would ease the dangerous tension. It was utterly impossible for him to secure everything his countrymen wanted, which was the complete reciprocity that had intrigued the negotiators in Paris, for the commercial dependence of the United States upon Britain was much greater than that of Britain upon the United States, and the hostile legislation contemplated in Philadelphia would do more damage at home than abroad. Yet he was able to get something, because the government in London was most anxious to escape from the peril of war as well as to guard British commercial interests from the impending American blows. The consequent agreement was quite separate from the special arrangement for intercourse across the international border of the United States. Everything directly touching British North America was put in the first ten articles, the only

30. *Ibid.*, p. 503.

permanent part of the treaty. The general commercial agreement, which began with Article XI, was to hold for twelve years, though it might be terminated earlier by special circumstances.[31] The details need not be set forth here, because they did not affect sea-borne traffic with British North America. They dealt with trade between the United States on the one hand, and Britain, the British West Indies, and Britain's eastern Empire on the other. Their significance in this limited discussion is that they sufficed to forestall the threatening trade war.

The other crucial maritime issue was Britain's conduct in her war with France. Here was a distinct foreshadowing of the diplomatic strife which culminated in the War of 1812. Here, with the possible exception of the posts, was the greatest danger in 1794. Therefore more attention should be paid to this than to the general commercial issue in an examination of Canadian-American relations.

The order-in-council of November 6, 1793, headed Britain straight for war with the United States. Under that order, which directed commanders of warships and privateers to detain and to bring in for adjudication all vessels laden with the produce of, or supplies for, any French colony, there were hundreds of seizures in Caribbean waters and almost as many complete condemnations in the vice-admiralty courts of the British West Indies. The order was more sweeping than was allowed by the questionable principle on which it was based, and its execution was barbarous. The order outlawed all American trade with the French West Indies; but by the Rule of 1756, which was challenged in the United States, Britain had absolutely no right to interfere with a certain limited trade that had been legalized by French decree before the outbreak of the war. Britain stood forth as "the tyrant of the seas." Her public and her private cruisers in the region of the West Indies snapped up practically every American ship they sighted. The prizes were then as good as lost to their owners; for the local vice-admiralty courts were notoriously partial, and the conditions governing appeals to the superior courts in England were commonly prohibitive.

The most flagrant iniquity in this business was stopped by the time people in the United States knew that it had started. On January 8, 1794, a new order-in-council supplanted that of November 6. The new one did not go so far as it might have gone under the Rule of 1756. Yet wholesale damage had been done, and this threatened to cause a rupture until

31. With the exception of Article XII, which dealt with trade between the West Indies and the United States. This article, which the Senate rejected, was to continue in force to the end of the war then being waged with France and for two years after the signature of peace preliminaries. If at that time no new arrangement had been made to take its place and to regulate contraband and to settle the question of "free ships, free goods," all the articles of the treaty, save the first ten, were to expire even though the period of twelve years was not completed.

provision for redress was made. After Jay's arrival in England, Grenville quickly caught the point. On August 6, still another order-in-council waived an important part of the law restricting appeals, and before the month was out the Englishman fell in with the American's suggestion for settling all claims that could not be satisfied through the regular course of judicial proceedings. They were to be arbitrated by a joint commission sitting in London, according to Article VII.

At the same time another formidable obstacle on the path of peace vanished, and the claims for damages it left behind were handed over to the same body[32] by this Article VII. The obstacle was Britain's interruption of the American provision trade with France. Under an order-in-council of June 8, 1793, ships carrying "corn, meal or flour" to France were forcibly diverted to British ports, where they were released after the British government purchased these articles and paid for the freight, or after the masters gave satisfactory security to dispose of such food-stuffs in ports of any country friendly to Britain. To justify this early precedent for the well-known action of the Allies in the World War, Grenville referred to the principle "laid down by most writers, particularly by Vattel," that provisions were liable to be considered as contraband, and the Englishman pointed out that his country was more considerate than it needed to be. An angry altercation ensued, in which the American government denied the principle and denounced the practice, and the British government refused to budge. However, on August 18, 1794, still another order-in-council stopped this interference with neutral rights, stating that it was inexpedient to continue public purchase "for the present." It has been supposed that the practice was dropped out of regard for the bad effect in America, but more probably it was because of a good harvest in England.[33]

The principle, it will be observed, was not retracted; and its application was abandoned in a way that suggested it might be resumed, as it was in the spring of 1795, when the price of wheat was again high. With the advance of the season, however, the fear of a shortage receded and once more the practice was dropped. Indeed this was one of three important principles of maritime law on which no agreement between Britain and the United States was possible at this time. In addition to their fundamental difference over the definition of contraband, they were equally opposed, as already mentioned, on the Rule of 1756. They also clashed over the question of "free ships, free goods," Britain maintaining

32. It was also to adjudicate British claims for losses inflicted by French privateers fitted out in American ports.

33. W. A. Phillips and A. H. Reede, *Neutrality, Its History, Economics and Law, The Napoleonic Period* (New York, 1936), II, 62.

and the United States denying the belligerent right to capture enemy goods on neutral vessels. If Jay had insisted on the American interpretation of these principles, he would have wrecked the peace he was trying to save. On the other hand, a complete surrender would have led to the ruin of his handiwork after he sent it home.[34]

All the other conditions of the treaty hung upon this insoluble dilemma of a British or an American veto. Fortunately the negotiators found a temporary escape. They shelved the conflict for quieter times. Article XII of the treaty explicitly postponed the discussion of two questions, those of contraband and of enemy property on neutral vessels, until two years after the conclusion of the war with France. Meanwhile, to guard against "inconveniences and misunderstandings," this article declared that "provisions and other articles not generally contraband" were not to be confiscated as such but were to be preëmpted "with a reasonable profit thereon, together with the freight, and also the demurrage incident to such detention." The third question—the Rule of 1756—was put off indefinitely, the treaty saying nothing about it.[35]

There were other points of dispute, but they were minor and there-

---

34 The view expressed here differs from that of Bemis, as set forth at length in his *Jay's Treaty* and summarily in his *Diplomatic History of the United States*. He maintains that Jay might have wrung concessions from Britain in her conduct of the naval war if Hamilton had not told Hammond, who straightway informed Grenville, that the United States would not join the abortive Armed Neutrality of the North. I cannot accept this conclusion. The revival of the Armed Neutrality of the North, announced to the world in April, 1794, was only a hollow threat; and Britain knew it. It was the work of Sweden and Denmark alone. Neither Russia nor Prussia would have anything to do with it, and without their coöperation the closing of the Baltic to belligerent ships was absolutely impossible. Though the Swedish minister in London gave Pinckney a copy of the convention and suggested American adherence, the Danish government was frightened at the prospect of including the United States, and the Swedish government thereupon held back. Of course Grenville, on learning that the invitation had been extended through Pinckney, wrote to Hammond in May to use all his influence against American acceptance. This, apparently, was unnecessary. The English Secretary of State might certainly have been more concerned had he known of the curious coincidence that Jay's instructions contained an article advising collaboration with the representatives of the Baltic powers with the object of reviving the armed neutrality of 1780. But this article was abortive too. It had been inserted by the francophile Randolph, it had not the backing of the American government, and Jay paid no attention to it. If the government of the United States had tried to bluff Britain by flirting with Sweden and Denmark, the result would probably have been not a modified Jay's Treaty, but no treaty at all.

Bemis also says that Jay made "great concessions to British sea power." Strictly speaking, he conceded nothing for which his country, as a neutral, was contending. Actually, he gained something. As stated above, he extracted from Britain a sufficient recognition of the American position on the two points of contraband and "free ships, free goods," to agree to discuss them when the war with France was over; and in the meantime he bound Britain to abandon what she maintained was her right to confiscate as contraband "provisions and other articles not generally contraband." Otherwise the treaty left the conflict of principles between belligerent and neutral exactly as it was.

35. Some leading Americans recognized the validity of the rule.

fore, with one exception, need not be noticed here. The exception was the British impressment of American seamen. It had already roused resentment in the United States and had produced diplomatic representations in London, but it was not the burning question of later days. The British excuse for the press gang's gathering up a few Americans was that their language made it difficult to distinguish them from British sailors; and this was amply corroborated by the French government, which then gave exactly the same excuse for seizing American vessels and mistreating their crews,[36] for the French were not yet driven off the seas. Moreover, in 1794, long years of war had not imposed their terrific strain upon the personnel of the British navy, nor had the American mercantile marine attained anything like the size it reached in the time of Napoleon's greatest power. Jay's instructions were silent on the point, and so was his treaty.[37]

On November 19, 1794, Grenville and Jay signed this highly important treaty. For its successful conclusion both the United States and the British Empire owe them a great debt of gratitude. Each strove to protect the interests of his own country, but at the same time realized that the greatest of these interests was common to both countries: the establishment of harmonious relations between them. Together these two men worked for peace, not a peace at any price, but a peace based on justice. That, they knew, was the only sure foundation. Therefore their discussions from beginning to end were as frank as they were friendly. Many passages in the correspondence of both principals reflect the fine spirit in which they managed the business, and one quotation from each may here be given as illustrations. "I cannot conclude this letter," wrote the English Foreign Secretary to the American envoy on November 19, "without repeating to you the very great satisfaction I have derived from the open and candid manner in which you have conducted, on your part, the whole of the difficult negotiation which we have now brought to so successful an issue, and from the disposition which you have uniformly manifested to promote the objects of justice, conciliation, and lasting friendship, between our two countries."[38] On the same day, when forwarding the treaty to his government, Jay observed, "I do not know how the negotiation could have been conducted, on their part, with more delicacy, friendliness, and propriety, than it has been from first to last."[39]

36. *A.S.P.F.R.*, I, 359, 377.

37. Jay discussed the matter with Grenville, but I have found no authority for the statement that one of the points of agreement reached by September 13 was "an article to prevent impressment by either party of the other's citizens or subjects." Bemis, *Jay's Treaty*, p. 238.

38. *A.S.P.F.R.*, I, 504.

39. *Ibid.*

A meaner man in Jay's position might have harbored an unjust suspicion that the friendly atmosphere in which he found himself was specially prepared to warm him into a pliant mood, and this suspicion might have ruined his mission. He accepted at its face value the genial hospitality of the British, but he did it with his eyes and ears open for any evidence that it was not genuine, and he found none. Perhaps his judgment would not have been quite so sound had it not been for a memory of his Paris days, twelve years before, when Britain rejected the Franco-Spanish temptation to join in robbing the United States of its hinterland.[40]

The treaty of 1794 was epoch-making; and it appropriately bears Jay's name. Though both negotiators were equally anxious for a settlement of the disputes between their governments, the Englishman deserves less credit than the American. The former followed where the latter led, and he led along a memorable way. It was the way of arbitration, long neglected but by him established anew. For fifteen years he had been associated with the idea. Under his presidency Congress had proposed it in 1779, and as Secretary of State he had urged it in 1785. Now he gave it a wider application than he had earlier sought. By persuading Grenville to accept the joint-commission method as a cure for festering international sores, he did more than turn the difficult corner of that day. He ushered in a new era in the history of diplomacy. His treaty inaugurated the modern use of the judicial process in international affairs. It was a happy circumstance that this innovation occurred so early after the establishment of the United States. Nowhere else has it been so useful as in the regulation of Canadian-American relations, and here it has been indispensable.

Though now we see that Jay added a cubit to his stature by his negotiation in London, he was guillotined in effigy at home for what he had done abroad. He was execrated as a traitor to his country when he was actually saving it from rushing madly into a suicidal war. The original copy of the treaty was lost at sea,[41] and another copy did not reach the Secretary of State until March 7, 1795. Then the treaty itself was nearly lost in the storm that raged in the United States. The government did not give it to the public, for that would have been throwing it to the wolves; and the Senate adopted an order enjoining secrecy on June 8, when the President submitted the treaty and its supporting documents. The Republican opposition, confident of victory if only they could swing a vote or two, strove to gain their end by moving to rescind the order on secrecy. They would expose the Federalist senators to the hot blast of public opinion. The defeat of the motion saved the treaty. Behind closed

40. *Supra*, p. 29.
41. The packet *Tankerville*, to which it was entrusted, was captured by a privateer.

doors the fight went on until the twenty-fourth, when the Senate adopted the treaty without a single vote to spare, the division being twenty to ten.

Still fearful of the outcome, the majority renewed the injunction of secrecy, but in defiance of this action one of the minority gave the treaty to the press. Thereupon, in the words of Madison, "it flew with an electric velocity to every part of the Union," the President was bombarded with addresses to refrain from ratifying it, and it seemed as if those who favored it "were struck dumb by the voice of the Nation."[42] Then the speechless recovered their breath, and they sounded a note of caution. They pointed out that the treaty was not so bad as it was represented to be, and that the alternative was war. This appeal to reason was strengthened by a suggestion of treason. Randolph, the one member of the administration who opposed the treaty, was dismissed for doubtful dealings with the French minister. Though the country had by no means recovered from its spell of passion, President Washington went ahead with the treaty.

Even after the exchange of ratifications in London on October 28, the treaty was still in danger. In the spring of 1796, the House of Representatives threatened to destroy it. The formal proclamation of the treaty on the last day of February enraged the Republicans, precipitating a high debate in the lower chamber. For two months the strife raged. The members who were determined to kill the treaty had two strings to their bow. The first was the claim that the concurrence of the House, as well as of the Senate, was essential for the conclusion of a treaty requiring an appropriation of money, or regulating commerce, or necessitating the exercise of any other power specifically conferred upon Congress. This string broke. When the House by a considerable majority called upon the President to lay before them the instructions to Jay and other documents relative to his treaty, Washington refused to comply with the request out of just regard to the Constitution and to the duty of his own office. The other string was the undoubted right of the House to withhold the money for the operation of the vital terms of the agreement. This string could not break; but those who tried to pull it could not muster quite enough strength when the final test came. The appropriation for the joint commissions passed by the narrow majority of three votes.

Meanwhile peace was made between the western Indians and the United States. Though the Battle of Fallen Timbers knocked the bottom out of the native war, this was not seen in England. Therefore Jay's achievement owed nothing to Wayne's victory. Indeed the unpleasant vision of betraying the red men still haunted the British conscience. Dur-

42. *S.P.*, IV, 161.

ing the negotiations in London, Grenville sought to lay the old specter by again proposing British mediation. Jay deftly evaded the issue, saying that he had insufficient authority to deal with it and that, in his judgment, American feeling against Britain was too hostile to tolerate the proposal. This advice did not destroy the cherished hope of the British government, but it engendered caution. On the morrow of the signature, Grenville wrote Hammond urging him to sound out Hamilton privately on the possibility of mediation,[43] and copies of this letter were enclosed in dispatches to Dorchester and Simcoe that they might be prepared to coöperate with the British ambassador in seizing any opportunity he might discover. At the same time, these officials in Canada were instructed to make the most of the treaty. They were to persuade the Indians that it gave them full protection; and, to reinforce this persuasion, they were to be more liberal in distributing the usual presents.[44] If there was even the slightest chance of British mediation, which is highly doubtful, it was lost at sea with the original of the treaty, for all the November mail was entrusted to the same unfortunate packet.[41] Before duplicates of the above communications from London reached their destination, Wayne procured a preliminary treaty on February 11, 1795, which provided for a peace conference to meet at Greenville on June 15. In Niagara and Detroit there were doubts about Indian attendance at the conference, but these doubts melted away as the spring advanced. British traders, eager for new traffic, visited Wayne's posts, drawing red men after them. The seat of this movement was in Detroit, and there it was observed that the French had a particularly strong influence in inclining their old native allies toward the south. Gradually the news of the British treaty penetrated the forests of the interior, producing the same effect. It mattered naught whether Britain had finally deserted the Indians, as many of them naturally believed, or whether she had really protected their interests, as they were officially informed from Canada. They would go to the conference as arranged, because it was their only remaining hope or because they had nothing to fear there.

Thus did Jay's Treaty help to crown Wayne's victory by facilitating the conclusion of the treaty at Greenville on August 3, 1795. This treaty in turn smoothed the path for the execution of the other, for it completed the relief of the British conscience which had been sorely troubled by the blunder of 1783. The American government, abandoning the earlier disturbing claim to outright ownership of native lands, had offered to assume the old British guarantee to the Indians,[45] and now the

43. *Ibid.*, III, 188.
44. *Ibid.*, p. 185. *Q*, LXIX, 118.
45. *Supra*, pp. 130–131.

Indians added the finishing touch to the transfer by accepting the American terms and recognizing the exclusive protection of the United States.

Only the eighth article of the native treaty need concern us here. Like the recalcitrant majority in the House of Representatives, it threatened to hold up the execution of Jay's Treaty. It required every trader residing among the Indians to procure a license from the American government, and it bound the Indians to deliver every unlicensed trader to a superintendent that he might be dealt with according to the law of the United States. This meant a one-sided cutting down of the liberty of movement accorded by Article III of Jay's Treaty, and it might mean the complete destruction of that liberty. This breach of good faith on the part of the American government, apparently the result of oversight, disturbed the government in London, which was already worried by dark prophecies of the destruction of Jay's Treaty by a revolt in the lower chamber of Congress. Therefore the British government, in directing Dorchester to make arrangements with the American government for the evacuation of the posts, forbade him to carry out the arrangements until the American government repaired this fault, or if Congress in any way obstructed the operation of the treaty with Britain. To avoid unnecessary delay in the British execution of the treaty, he was to be guided by advice sent direct from the British embassy. At the same time the *chargé d'affaires* in Philadelphia[46] was ordered to require of the American government an explanatory article supplementary to the treaty, and to keep an eye on the House of Representatives.[47] He received these instructions toward the end of March, 1796; and immediately he submitted to the American Secretary of State a note, drafted in London, proposing the additional article. Days passed and he got no reply.[48] The House of Representatives was then in the midst of its high debate over the treaty, and there was no point in patching a torn garment that might be discarded right away. The end of April saw the crisis pass. At once the patch was prepared and applied. It stated that the third article of Jay's Treaty could not be impaired by any subsequent treaty between either signatory and a third party. It was signed on May 4, it went to the Senate on the following day, and on the ninth it was ratified.[49]

The western posts were not surrendered by June 1, 1796, the appointed date, for the simple reason that the United States was not ready to take them over, thanks chiefly to the opposition in Congress. The American officer who went to Quebec to procure Dorchester's orders

46. S.P., IV, 170–171. Hammond had departed, leaving Phineas Bond in charge.

47. *Ibid.*, pp. 172–175.

48. *Ibid.*, p. 225.

49. There is no mention of it in the *Annals of Congress*, but see *A.S.P.F.R.*, I, 551–553, and S.P., IV, 277.

asked him to delay their issue, and he did not depart with them until a week after the evacuation was to have been completed.[50] Still several weeks were required in those days of slow and difficult transportation to move American troops, with munitions and supplies, to their respective stations. Not until August 11 did the new garrison of Niagara arrive from Oswego and take over from a small contingent that had been left behind. These were the last of the British soldiers on the soil of the United States.[51]

Another article of the treaty which had to do with the interior was never carried out. This was Article IV, which provided for the joint survey of the Mississippi as a foundation for an agreement on the western boundary. There was some correspondence about it from the spring of 1796 until early in 1798[52] when, for some reason that is not yet clear, the subject disappeared from view. This neglect operated in a way that could not then be foreseen to benefit the United States at the expense of Canada. Because the peace treaty of 1783 bound the United States to accept a line *to* the Mississippi as much as it bound Britain to accept a line *from* the Lake of the Woods, such a line might have been drawn before the Louisiana Purchase entered the picture to change the whole face of the West.

Of the three arbitrations for which the treaty provided, only one was executed without a hitch. The commission which sat in the United States foundered on a disagreement of principle. It broke up in 1799, when the two American commissioners withdrew, and it never came together again. In 1802, the two governments finally compromised the dispute it was to have arbitrated. During this interval, the board which met in London was suspended, the British government retaliating by withdrawing its two commissioners; but it was quite successful after the sessions were resumed. Neither of these arbitrations really affected Canadian interests, but the third did.

The board which was to determine the identity of the St. Croix[53] was

50. *Ibid.*, pp. 280–296.

51. Russell to Portland, Aug. 6, 1796, *Q*, CCLXXXII, 559, and Aug. 20, 1796, *ibid.*, p. 572.

52. No American correspondence on this subject has yet been found, despite a search by the staff of the National Archives in Washington. Some of the British correspondence is in *Q*, Vols. LXXVIII–LXXX. Liston, Hammond's successor, appealed for guidance to Governor Prescott in Quebec, who sought advice from Montreal merchants engaged in the fur trade. Prescott reported home on the conditions that would have to be faced, the supplies and equipment that would be necessary, and the best man to undertake the job for the British. Prescott recommended a certain Captain Price, or Brice, and Portland communicated this recommendation to Grenville.

53. For this subject, see the definitive exposition in J. B. Moore, *International Adjudications* (New York, 1929).

smaller than the other two bodies, having only three members instead of five. The British commissioner, appointed on March 5, 1796, was Thomas Barclay, a man eminently fitted for the task. He was born in New York, the son of the rector of Trinity Church, was a graduate of King's [Columbia] College, had studied law in Jay's office, and had been called to the bar on the eve of the Revolution. During the war he had fought in the British army, rising to the rank of colonel. On the return of peace, he had retired as a Loyalist to Nova Scotia, settling in Annapolis. At the time of his appointment as commissioner, he was an outstanding lawyer of the province and the speaker of its assembly. In 1799, he returned to his native land as British consul general for the Eastern States. During the War of 1812, he was British commissary for the care and exchange of prisoners of war; and after the war, again as British commissioner, he participated in the arbitration of the eastern boundary under the Treaty of Ghent. General Henry Knox of Massachusetts was named American commissioner on April 1, 1796, but he declined to serve because he was personally interested in the outcome, and on May 21 the appointment was given to David Howell. He too was well chosen. A native of New Jersey and a graduate of its college, later Princeton, he had migrated to Providence, Rhode Island. There he became a pillar of Brown University, a prosperous lawyer, and a successful candidate for various public offices. Before this appointment he had been a member of the Continental Congress, a judge of the supreme court of his adopted state, and attorney general. He was later made United States judge for the district of Rhode Island; and, according to report, he was a great ornament to the bench. As third commissioner, Howell proposed Egbert Benson of New York who was related to, and accepted by, Barclay. He was of the same type as the two who appointed him. He had served his state as judge and as attorney general, and his country as one of the American commissioners for the withdrawal of British troops under Sir Guy Carleton according to the terms of the peace treaty; he was now a justice of the supreme court of New York, and was later a federal judge. Each government also appointed an agent to present and uphold its case before the board. Both these men, upon whom the chief burden of the investigation lay, were natives of Massachusetts and of course lawyers. James Sullivan, the American, was attorney general for his state and president of the Historical Society of Massachusetts. He had just published a history of Maine.[54] Ward Chipman, the British agent, was one of the Loyalist refugees who founded St. John and at this time was solicitor general of New Brunswick. He later mounted the bench and was subsequently promoted to be chief justice of his province.

54. Boston, 1795.

With such men collaborating, it is not surprising that this, the first of many arbitrations in the history of Canadian-American relations, was a model for all that followed. In the midst of the work, Sullivan was moved to remark: "Why shall not all the nations on earth determine their disputes in this mode, rather than choke the rivers with their carcasses, and stain the soil of continents with their slain? The whole business has been proceeded upon with great ease, candor, and good-humor."[55] The investigation lasted from the summer of 1796 until the autumn of 1798, the board meeting in Halifax, St. Andrews, Boston, and Providence, and collecting an enormous mass of papers which Howell, at the conclusion, declared would "remain a monument of the laborious researches, zeal, ability and fidelity of the Agents." His judgment has been confirmed by John Bassett Moore in his monumental *International Adjudications*. He says: "No one familiar with the labors of the agents can doubt that this encomium was well merited. Their immense industry, their tireless exploration of all available authorities, and their firm grasp and keen analysis of all the evidence that could be gathered, are attested by their arguments." He also points out that these arguments laid "the historical and legal foundations for further settlements."[56]

The American contention for the Magaguadavic[57] received two fatal blows in the summer of 1797. One was the collapse of the common belief in the United States that the plenipotentiaries of 1783 had definitely chosen the river named St. Croix on Mitchell's map even though it might not be the historical St. Croix, and that this intention could be proven by the testimony of the survivors, British as well as American. Of the American negotiators, only Adams, now President of the United States, and Jay, now governor of New York, were still living; and when their evidence was at last produced it became clear that there had been no understanding about the map's being decisive. The framers of the peace treaty had not contemplated the possibility of confusion. They had simply supposed that Mitchell had delineated the real St. Croix. This revelation exposed the American case so that the other blow could strike home. It was directed by Chipman. When the investigation was well under way, he procured a copy of the 1613 edition of Champlain's *Voyages* containing a map of St. Croix Island as well as a description of the buildings erected there in 1604. Following these clues, he had excavations made on an island known as Bone or Docea lying in the Schoodic. The spade disclosed remains of ancient buildings which, despite Sullivan's ingenious argument to the contrary, finally established the identity of the island

55. Amory's *Life of Sullivan*, quoted in Moore, *op. cit.*, I, 59.
56. *Ibid.*, p. 80.
57. See *supra*, Chapter V.

and the river. Barclay and Benson accepted the obvious while Howell remained skeptical. But before the hearings were concluded he too was convinced that the Schoodic was the St. Croix.

When the commissioners proceeded to trace the St. Croix to its source, they parted company where the river divides, one branch coming from the north and the other from the southwest. The former, known as the Chiputneticook, was chosen by Howell because it was of greater magnitude. Barclay and Benson followed the other, because it seemed to accord with the wording of James I's grant of Nova Scotia to Sir William Alexander in 1621, and because it had always borne the same Indian name as the united waters below. But these two commissioners could not agree on where to stop. Barclay went on to the most remote western spring of the chain of lakes from which their river emerged, on the authority of the 1621 grant; whereas Benson stuck at the point where the lowest lake emptied into the river, asserting that a chain of lakes could not be called a river. On the same principle Howell stopped at the first lake he encountered on his river.

Barclay's was the only one of the three "sources" which fulfilled the conditions of the peace treaty. That instrument prescribed a line drawn due north from the source of the St. Croix to the highlands which divide the rivers emptying into the St. Lawrence from those falling into the Atlantic Ocean. The British commissioner's line would do this, but the lines of his two colleagues would strike the highlands where they divide the rivers flowing into the St. Lawrence from those emptying into the Bay of Chaleur, which was not part of the Atlantic Ocean. Therefore, said Barclay and Chipman, the other two sources must be wrong. They also observed that the western line, which ran from a spring near the Penobscot, would have the advantage of giving each government the exclusive possession of the rivers rising within its territory, with the single exception of the St. John. Sullivan objected to the argument about conformity with the treaty's reference to the highlands. He insisted that it was invalid because it was based on a geographical supposition yet to be established. None of the three commissioners could draw the other two after him, but in the end they came together at a fourth point.

The return to unanimity began with Barclay, who abandoned his high position to rejoin Benson at the lowest lake on the southern branch. Sullivan did not claim credit for this shift, which he suspected was caused by a fear that Benson would run off to Howell. The remaining disagreement seemed likely to lead to a decision signed by only two of the board and open to practical objections. As the American agent observed, this decision would tend to breed trouble in days to come because it would establish as the boundary a long artificial line that cut across many waterways.

He was even more concerned over what had happened. His state had sold 150,000 acres of land in the territory that would be included in New Brunswick. This would certainly produce annoying difficulties. Then a Daniel came to judgment in the person of Robert Liston, the British minister, who happened to arrive in Providence. He dropped in upon Sullivan to learn how matters stood. Thereupon he sent for Chipman and was joined by Barclay. To the three men he proposed a new solution, for which he offered to assume full responsibility to the British government. It was to follow the northern branch to its remotest head, which had already been marked by the surveyors working for the commission. His suggestion offered an advantage to each side. Because the upper reaches of the Chiputneticook swung off to the west, New Brunswick would get more territory and a longer stretch of the St. John River. Massachusetts, on the other hand, would save the grants of land mentioned above. In addition, both would have a much longer natural frontier with its smaller opportunity for friction. Liston's judicious intervention produced the final move. Barclay and Chipman straightway agreed to make it, and so did Sullivan, who undertook to persuade Howell. His conversion made a unanimous award. It was signed on October 25, 1798.

On the previous day Sullivan presented the commission with a memorial which aimed at a solution of the problem of the islands. The board was to find the mouth as well as the source of the dividing river, and he rightly understood that the commissioners had decided to fix the mouth level with the town of St. Andrews. He suggested that it should be carried out, on either side of Deer Island, to make it conform with the peace treaty, which described the boundary as running "along the middle of the St. Croix from its mouth in the Bay of Fundy." There was good sense in his proposal but good reason for not adopting it then. The negotiators in Paris had obviously erred in their geographical reference. The mouth of the St. Croix is not in the Bay of Fundy. It is in Passamaquoddy Bay. Moreover, Article V of Jay's Treaty, which provided for this commission, limited its function to describing the boundary between the source and the mouth of the St. Croix. The members of the board quite properly refrained from following Sullivan's lead. Apparently they were little concerned over the question, thinking that it would be easy for ministers of the two governments, with maps before them, to fill in the gap through the islands. The task, however, was neglected until private interests added complications necessitating a later arbitration.

CHAPTER IX

OSMOSIS

A REACTION similar to that which chemists call osmosis has been at work between the United States and British North America from the foundation of the Republic. In this early period it was much more evident in the old Province of Quebec, and the two Canadas into which it was divided in 1791, than it was in the Maritime Provinces even though most of their population had come from the old colonies. The pre-Revolutionary pioneers and the much larger number of Loyalist refugees who followed them at the end of the war had all come by sea, the only possible way. It cut them off from their old home, and it enabled the surviving colonial system to close in and raise a great barrier behind them.[1] For all practical purposes, the Maritime Provinces were a group of islands out in the Atlantic. New England fishermen still haunted their shores; but these visitors' inclination to settle there was, if anything, even less than it had been. Occasionally they exceeded the bounds set by the peace treaty, but British fishing inspectors and customs collectors generally kept them at arm's length. The old Province of Quebec, even with its entirely different population, was not so severed. It could not be. The Revolution, in its very beginning, had thrust a fiery arm up into Canada and closed in upon the fortress of Quebec, while it had scarcely scratched the old Nova Scotia. Of course there were special reasons for the attempt to conquer the lower St. Lawrence Valley, but if there had been an equal urge to win the meager settlements on the northeast it would have made little difference. The Maritime Provinces, because they were maritime, were beyond the reach of a Revolutionary army. The St. Lawrence was not, for the great natural highway up the Hudson, over Lake Champlain, and down the Richelieu was too far removed from the range of British naval guns.

The outbreak of war between Britain and Revolutionary France loosed a French design to strike through the United States at British power in French Canada.[2] It was part of the larger plan to enlist the American Republic in the French crusade for liberty, a plan which Citizen Genet, who arrived in 1793 as minister to the United States, believed he could carry out. He would launch the righteous hosts of America against the wicked enemy of liberty in the north, and at the same time he would rouse the slumbering French population to throw off the hated yoke of

1. See *supra*, Chapter IV.
2. Gustave Lanctot, *Le Canada-Français et ses voisins du sud.*

tyranny. This flaming zealot soon burnt himself out, fortunately before the Anglo-American crisis of 1794. How he ruined the first part of his ambitious design, by antagonizing the government of President Washington into demanding his recall, is well known; but it cannot be said that he ruined the second part, and the story of what he did to effect a revolution in French Canada has never been told, for we have caught only the most fugitive glimpses of it. What defeated him there was the gulf, infinitely wider than the Atlantic, which separated the French people of the St. Lawrence from their cousins in France. The former had long since been emancipated by the physical conditions of life on this continent. The habitant was no downtrodden peasant. He was a free man, and he knew it. He was also devoted to his church, and most naturally, for it was not like that from which it had sprung. The frontier life, which had emasculated feudalism and autocracy, had invigorated the church in New France and preserved it from the corruption which ate into the church in old France. Moreover the French Revolution, by turning against the church and rending it, was already widening the breach between the Canadians and their parent stock.

Nevertheless Genet produced an uneasy stirring in the society that dwelt on the lower St. Lawrence. The very enthusiasm which blinded him to the obstacles in his way tended to drive him through them. The United States provided a convenient shelter for his plotting, and the American Revolution bequeathed some cunning instruments, for the ebb tide of the American invasion of Canada had drawn a number of compromised French Canadians into exile. These and other emissaries, some of whom seem to have been old-country Frenchmen, were well chosen, for they flitted in and out of Lower Canada like shadows, and their influence spread everywhere. Perhaps their most effectual appeal was to pride of race, for the news of how Frenchmen had stepped out on a victorious march in Europe quickened French pulses in America.

The ferment along the St. Lawrence was so obvious in the fall of 1793 that Dorchester was moved to issue a proclamation in November. He called upon all magistrates, militia officers, and other good subjects to seize the sowers of sedition who were abroad in the land. He cited their "false representations of the cause and conduct of the persons at present exercising the supreme authority in France," and he specified "particularly certain foreigners, being alien enemies, who are lurking and lie concealed in various parts of this province, acting in concert with persons in foreign dominions."[3] "Alien enemies" of course meant Frenchmen, but the vaguer phrase, "persons in foreign dominions," was probably intended to cover the governor's known suspicion of the American gov-

3. *P.A.C.R.*, 1921, Appendix B, p. 23.

ernment at that time. Instead of being checked, the seditious movement gathered momentum through the winter. The ominous rumblings which Dorchester heard all around him offer some excuse for his indiscreet speech of February, 1794, when he announced to the Indian delegation the present possibility of war with the United States. Thence came these new missionaries with their dangerous gospel. Genet and other individuals in the American Republic were responsible for the inflammatory pamphlets then circulating through the Canadian countryside. One, entitled *Les françois libres à leurs frères les canadiens*, fell into the governor's hands in January. Some time afterwards a man was convicted for publicly reading it at a church door in the neighborhood of Montreal. Another specimen of this revolutionary literature was generally known among the people as "le catéchisme." Though few habitants were literate, many received the forbidden fruit from the mouths of those who could read, and not a few found it delicious. Strange as it may seem, the clergy were commonly baffled in their persistent efforts to ferret out the growing evil. With the coming of spring it burst into the open.

Toward the end of April, 1794, a riot in Montreal temporarily paralyzed the local magistrates. On the following day, ignorant of what had just occurred nearly two hundred miles away, the governor in Quebec wrote a nervous letter to the Secretary of State in London. Dorchester's eye was on the United States, where he saw French influence playing fast and loose with American passions, and he feared what was coming. "Lower Canada," he said, "is much more exposed to inroads since the peace by the increase of population and mutual intercourse on all sides. Lake Champlain is the great and immediate inlet into this country from New York and Vermont, yet there are many paths through which troops might pass." He reported a current rumor that the people of Vermont had offered to conquer Canada if they were allowed to plunder it.[4]

The storm, such as it was, broke in May, when the governor called out a portion of the militia under an act which had just been passed by the provincial legislature. This measure, it should be noted, was not imposed by the government or by the English minority against the will of the French majority, for the Constitution of 1791 had established an assembly whose members were mostly French. The early attempt to apply the new law seemed to be wise. "The hostile conduct of the States afforded a good reason for trying the disposition of the King's subjects," Dorchester thought,[5] but the result astonished him. "He found the whole country so infected as scarcely to leave a hope of assistance from the new

4. *Q*, LXVII, 191.
5. These were not his own words but those of his attorney general in a letter to Dundas, the Secretary of State, May 30, 1794. *Ibid.*, LXIX, 256.

subjects,"[6] or French Canadians. Here and there the disturbance seemed rather alarming. There was wild talk of forcing the jails, of striking down the officers of governments and massacring the English, of attacking refractory habitants, burning their houses, tearing out their entrails, and carrying their heads on poles, and of a French expedition approaching. Seigniors were threatened, and there were outcries against the curés, the tithe, and the confession. Militia captains were seized by those who should have obeyed them; and at Charlesbourg, two miles from Quebec, an armed mob of several hundred controlled the community for a short while. Nowhere else, however, was there anything like this display of force, and it was apparently the result of a momentary panic.

The government quickly recovered its confidence; for the Vermont hordes did not descend, the mass of the Canadians did not rise, and the revolutionary movement collapsed. It might never have assumed such menacing proportions if Dorchester had not called out the militia. His order stirred widespread fear among the French Canadians when Genet's influence seems to have been dying, he having been obliged to surrender his office early in the year. This may help to explain what happened when the hand of authority in Lower Canada, guided by the church and strengthened by an alien act then passed by the legislature, reached out to grasp its enemies. There were scores of arrests, but most of those who were gathered into custody were poor, misguided folk who received little or no punishment. The dangerous birds had flown south to a safe refuge in the United States, where some converted Canadians entered the French service on ships of war.

The revolutionary fever, which had not touched the St. Lawrence until Genet injected the poison, showed no sign of recurring until another French minister to the United States repeated the process. Jay's mission had nothing to do with the disappearance of the disease from Lower Canada, for the first spasm was over before he landed in England. Genet's successor, Fauchet, was apparently responsible for the welcome change in the northern colony. His intercepted correspondence indicated at the time that he had little interest in revolutionizing Canada. He was much more concerned with the possibility of recovering Louisiana; and, when he learned what had been done in London, his one great object was to undo it in Philadelphia. He felt that he had to kill this treaty because, if it was allowed to live, it would destroy the vital Franco-American alliance. By fair means and by foul, he fought until Adet took his place in the summer of 1795; and then Adet continued the desperate struggle. Here one may see a possible connection between the treaty and the quiet in Canada, the fight in Philadelphia serving as a diversion. The treaty

6. *Ibid.*

emerged triumphant from the House of Representatives in the late spring of 1796, and then in the summer the symptoms of revolutionary fever reappeared in the north. The obvious conclusion is that Adet's defeat in the greater intrigue he had inherited from Fauchet drove him back to a revival of Genet's intrigue. But he did not know that he was beaten, he plunged into a more ambitious intrigue[7] to prevent the Franco-American divorce, and there is reason to believe that he had already set out to seduce Canada.

That the United States was an uncomfortable and possibly a dangerous neighbor to Canada was again forced upon the attention of the government in Quebec in the early autumn of 1796 by the outbreak of local violence. It was precipitated by an attempt to enforce another new piece of provincial legislation. This time it was a road act. Yet the situation was not quite the same as in 1794. Then Dorchester feared that the American government countenanced Genet's machinations, but investigation found scarcely a trace of any but French hands at work. Now, thanks to Jay, there was not the slightest suspicion in Canada that the administration of the United States was involved; but it was not long before many Americans appeared in the dark background of the new menace. The story is shrouded in mystery.

The dark background was Vermont. Of the Green Mountain Boys who had led the hue and cry down Lake Champlain into Canada in 1775, many were still living, and their old idea was by no means dead. The pioneers in those healthy hills were now much more numerous and just as sturdy. Because the Richelieu River provided their easiest access to the outside world, they looked north as well as south, and many of them cast covetous eyes upon the rich empty lands across the Canadian border. The rumor of Vermont hordes about to descend in 1794 was probably inspired by an effort of Genet to enlist them. He was later reported to have offered several hundred blank French commissions to a group of leading inhabitants of that state, all connected in some way or other with Governor Chittenden.[8] When Adet revived the project of overturning the British government on the St. Lawrence, it was only natural that he too should seek to employ the restless energy of the Green Mountain Boys, and it is not surprising that some of them fell in with his plans. Nor would it be surprising if the idea of a filibustering expedition from Vermont into Canada grew independently of his suggestion. Of course it would seek French support.

---

7. By taking an active part in American politics, he aspired to repeat in the United States what French representatives had done in Europe, where they had conquered for France by engineering revolutions in neighboring countries.

8. *P.A.C.R.*, 1891, Note C, p. 63.

That Ira Allen, "the founder of Vermont," was the central figure in an elaborate plot to overthrow British rule in Canada was soon suspected in many quarters—in England, on the St. Lawrence, and in the United States. In December, 1796, a British man-of-war stopped an American ship on the high seas somewhere west of the English Channel, and conducted her to England. Fifteen thousand stand of arms and some twenty pieces of artillery were stowed away in this ship, ironically named *The Olive Branch*. Allen, who was on board, had chartered the vessel to convey to America these implements of war which he had procured from the French Directory. He said that they were his personal property and also that they were for the Vermont militia. From that day to this, there has been a persistent suspicion that these muskets and bayonets and cannon were really intended for the conquest of Canada.

An adoring biographer has collected and presented an enormous mass of material to prove Allen's innocence, not only of this but of every other charge that has been made against him;[9] but he proves too much. He accepts Allen's every word as gospel truth. The British courts, where Allen and his guns were entangled in long litigation, were less credulous. Therefore the courts were corrupt, according to the hero-worshiper. He also takes for granted, without any shadow of proof, that a group of Londoners bought the prize rights and pursued Allen to France, when he went to get legal proof that he had bought the arms with which he was caught. There these hypothetical monsters, in order to prevent him from defending his case in London, bribed the French government to hold this long-suffering American in prison for many months without any charge against him. How they could do this when Britain was at war with France is not quite clear. When the arms were released on bail and shipped to New York in 1798, Vermont did not buy them, though its militia still needed them sorely. The proffered explanation of this strange denouement is that the political leaders, including the governor who had succeeded Chittenden, and the legislature of the state were out to ruin its founder. Indeed this biographer makes Allen appear white by blackening the public life of the whole of Vermont. Moreover he blandly insists that Ira's venture into the arms traffic was inspired by his local patriotism and by his solicitude for the poor militiamen whom the law required to provide their own arms; but what he proves, by abundant facts and figures, is that this fine public-spirited man was seeking to repair his broken fortune by mulcting these poor militiamen. His profit on the deal was to have been at least $50,000. Indeed a critical reading of

9. James Benjamin Wilbur, *Ira Allen, Founder of Vermont*, 1751–1814 (Boston and New York, 1928).

this uncritical biography confirms the old suspicion. Here is new evidence against Allen; and here is an extended account of strange and trying experiences through which it is difficult to follow him, unless we use the master key of his guilt. Then, instead of having to pick lock after lock, we pass right through.

The most damning evidence against Allen has been unearthed by the biographer who would exculpate him. It is a report which was prepared for the Directory and sent by Talleyrand at the request of the Directory to the Minister of Finance. This was at the end of August, 1798, when Allen was back in Paris on the quest already mentioned, a quest that proved vain. The gist of the story related by the report is as follows. In the early summer of 1796, Allen crossed from England to France and approached the Directory with certain propositions. After some investigation, the Directory adopted part of these and accordingly made an agreement with the American. By this agreement, a French army of several thousand men in French transports escorted by French war vessels was to reach Halifax in August, 1797. The expedition would seize "the English merchant fleet which leaves Quebec each year for this port," and, "with the aid of communications" which Allen was to "command in the place," would also take the town. Successful or unsuccessful, the French force was then to make for Quebec to effect a junction with Allen, whose movements were to be synchronized. At the time appointed for the Halifax *coup de main*, he was to pounce upon St. Johns on the Richelieu. He would do it at the head of troops secretly enrolled for the purpose but ostensibly for Vermont "and even a large part of the militia of this state, of which the principal officers shall second his plans." His entrance to the fort would be facilitated by "secretly armed persons . . . becoming part of the raft of shipbuilding timber" which he frequently sent down from Lake Champlain. He was then to advance down the St. Lawrence, and was "certain to raise part of the inhabitants (of French origin and inclination)." Quebec would fall before him, and the combined forces of France, Vermont, and Canada would clear the English out of the northeastern quarter of North America, where a new republic would arise. Meanwhile General Hoche's expedition would sail to liberate Ireland.

"The French government felt" that Allen, "in spite of his powerful influence" at home, and "in spite of his immense property and wealth," to prove which he displayed signed statements by Governor Chittenden and two Vermont justices of the peace, "could not alone furnish the funds necessary for an operation so large. A large amount of arms and money would be necessary." Thereupon the Minister of War undertook to supply him with 20,000 muskets and bayonets and two dozen pieces of light field artillery.[10] In return he promised to pay a stipulated price for these things at the end of seven years, with interest at 5 per cent, and pledged all his wealth as security. Anxious to avoid unnecessary risk, he observed that a British ship of war might stop the neutral vessel on which he proposed to load this precious cargo and might seize it as the property of the French Republic, "unless it appeared by some act" that he "had paid a part of the price." Thereupon the Directory ordered the Minister of War to prepare with him "two fictitious bills, one for the guns and bayonets, and the other for the cannons, effects and caissons." The bills were accordingly drawn to show that he had paid one-fifth down, 106,240 livres, and had given surety for the remainder. As for money to be given to Allen, the finances of the French government "did not permit them to pay . . . any considerable sums," but he was granted a loan for eight years without interest. The amount was 200,000 livres, and was furnished by bonds or treasury bills of the Batavian Republic, half of which were payable at the end of two months and the other half a year later. In 1798, having sold half this paper "at a very inferior rate," and still possessing the other half, "of which he cannot dispose without a great loss," he "hopes that the Directory will act at the time of reimbursement with the generosity the circumstances direct." Talleyrand's covering letter adds that the Directory desired to recover the half still in his hands. This confidential account, written by Frenchmen for Frenchmen in Paris in 1798 and long buried in the secret French archives,[11] speaks for itself. There can now be little doubt that Allen was engaged in such a plot, and should be classed with Burr and Wilkinson.

The seizure of *The Olive Branch* immediately paralyzed Allen and ultimately ruined him. It also forestalled the making of any plans for the French expedition as promised in Paris. That was now out of the question. Only echoes of the desperate scheme reached Canada. Not long after Allen's capture on the high seas, another dangerous individual disappeared from the American scene. This was Adet. He was recalled by his government, which was just as infuriated as he was with the "desertion" implied in Jay's Treaty. But the mischief he had started was continued by obscure agents. However, they seem to have been handicapped by insufficient support from home. Some of them appear to have flirted with a fantastic idea of a Franco-Spanish-Indian attack from the Missis-

10. When loading *The Olive Branch* at Ostend, Allen discovered to his dismay that she was too small to take all this. Therefore he left 5,000 stand of arms and a few pieces of artillery behind.

11. Wilbur has printed this report and its covering letter in his life of *Ira Allen*, II, 191–199. He introduces the story by saying that it "seems incredible," and later he dismisses it as manufactured out of the whole cloth. This is characteristic of the methods he has used to rehabilitate the character of Allen.

sippi region upon Upper Canada. There the only result was that government officials had an occasional bad dream inspired by a wild rumor floating in from the West.[12] Much more vulnerable was Lower Canada, with its French population and with Vermont next door. There the minions of France found a hospitable base of operations.

From September, 1796, when a group of old-country Frenchmen gathered at the foot of Lake Champlain by the international line, French influence was again at work in Lower Canada. These mysterious strangers, one of whom posed as a general of the French Republican army and remained in rather straitened circumstances after his fellows vanished, found a number of Canadians to further their dark designs. Quantities of blank French commissions and of inflammatory proclamations were smuggled across the border in the lining of at least one pair of breeches. There were secret meetings in Montreal, where the first and most serious outbreak of violence against the execution of the new road act occurred. Ten days later the movement spread to Quebec. These disturbances lasted on into the new year. As in 1794, there were scores of arrests but few severe judgments. It was an uneasy winter in Lower Canada. From Liston in Philadelphia came letters telling of Adet's agents in Canada. From Vermont came reports of Allen's alarming purchase of arms and other news of French comings and goings there; for, though some of the people of that state were willing to play the French game as their own, others were glad to betray it. Disturbing bits of information were picked up here and there in the colony. The deposition of a Massachusetts man who kept a large inn for travelers in Montreal may serve as a sample. One of Adet's emissaries told him that a French fleet was to come up the St. Lawrence to coöperate with a force from the United States and with insurgent Canadians. Then from London came word that Allen and his cargo of arms had been taken, but this reassuring intelligence was accompanied by a false report of another shipment of arms from France for the same purpose of turning Canada upside down. The government in Quebec knew that its enemies were passing in and out, and yet it groped for them in vain. On February 18, 1797, Prescott, Dorchester's successor, wrote that during the previous week Adet's proclamations had been traced to the hands of no less than ten persons but not a copy was to be found because they all said they had burned the documents when they saw what they were. One of Adet's Canadian tools, who had made at least one guilty visit to Montreal, was discovered living

12. Mathew Elliott, the deputy superintendent of Indian affairs, who resided in the southwestern extremity of Upper Canada, reported this French and Spanish tampering with the red men. He was inclined to think that it was designed as a diversion to cover an attack on the lower province. *Q*, LXXIX, 160.

in Burlington, Vermont, but the rascal fled to parts unknown just as the governor was about to apply through Liston to the United States government for his apprehension. The only principal to fall into the hands of the authorities walked into them in May when he mistook his man. His tale is perhaps worth telling briefly as an illustration of what was going on.[13]

He went by the name of David McLane[14] but occasionally borrowed that of a half brother, Jacob Felt, who accompanied him on a trip to Canada sometime in 1796. He came from Massachusetts or Rhode Island, had been with Adet in Philadelphia, and stayed with a married sister who resided in St. Albans, Vermont. The first glimpse we catch of him was at Alburg, hard by the border, toward the end of July, 1796, when he introduced himself to William Barnard. The latter, a native of Deerfield, Massachusetts, was on his way to Montreal where he had been a merchant since 1791. He did not know McLane, but McLane quickly proved that he knew a great deal about him and tempted him with the promise of making his fortune if he would assist in producing a revolution in Canada. Barnard was skeptical. He suspected some trick to effect his own ruin, for he had been threatened before. McLane parted from him with the remark, "When you know more of the business you will think differently." A few days later the two men met in Montreal, and McLane repeated his proposals. Barnard at once informed a magistrate of all that had passed, but the mysterious stranger remained at large. Early in November, Barnard again encountered him, this time at Laprairie, just across the St. Lawrence. McLane swore him to secrecy and confided that he was back on the same business and had just come from Montreal, where suspicions had been roused, that an army would come in the spring, and that no confidence was to be placed in the Canadians. He regretted the recent tumults and wanted Barnard to use his influence to keep the natives quiet. He also desired him to discover what money the seminary and all the principal persons in town possessed, where it lay, and who would be friends and who enemies of the scheme. He offered Barnard all the funds he wanted if he would take an active part, and promised protection if he only remained passive. He said he would return in the spring and send for him to meet him across the border. Again Barnard laid information with a Montreal magistrate, but McLane was gone.

In April, 1797, McLane reappeared with a full brother, Daniel, from Pittsburgh, and once more he moved about the northwest corner of

13. It is here summarized from the interesting collection of documents in *P.A.C.R.*, 1891, note D, pp. 57–84. See also *Le Procès de David M'Lane pour haute trahison* (Quebec, 1797).

14. Also spelled McClane and McLean.

Vermont, discussing his plans with various citizens of that state. There was talk of arms being deposited on the frontier and of a French fleet coming up the St. Lawrence in the summer. McLane openly spoke of accomplices in Canada, including Barnard and, report said, "one Black or Blake." One of his Vermont confidants, who kept a tavern in St. Albans and was reputed to be "the junto's treasurer," ran off to Philadelphia where he showed Pickering, the Secretary of State, some original papers from Adet and exposed the plot, or part of it.[15] The disclosure made no difference to McLane, who was already approaching the end of his last journey. Accompanied by Charles Frichet,[16] a Canadian of St. Johns whom he had found in the previous year and whom he now summoned through a St. Albans millowner, he skirted the fort of St. Johns during the night of April 30. Ten days later, having passed through the country disguised as a horse buyer, he hid in the woods outside Quebec while his guide fetched John Black from the city.

This man Black is something of a puzzle. He later overreached himself in trying to squeeze townships out of the government as a reward for his patriotism on this occasion, and on a previous occasion he had fallen under a cloud. That was in 1794, when he talked too freely in disaffected circles. Whether he was himself disaffected or was overdoing the role of *agent provocateur*, it is impossible to say. At any rate he then landed in jail, where he was held without bail for some time. His incarceration disrupted his business of shipbuilding, in which he employed many Canadians, and advertised him as one "oppressed by government." The upshot was that, in 1796, he was elected a member of the assembly for the County of Quebec.[17]

Frichet told Black that Adet had heard of his suffering under the British government and had sent "a French General" into the province to assist him and other friends of the French Republic to throw off the British yoke. When the Canadian mentioned the American's name, the Englishman seemed to know who it was that was waiting for him to come out. When Black arrived in the secret spot, McLane unfolded his design. Adet, he said, had gone back to France to arrange for an expedition to be sent against Canada. Meanwhile large forces, many of them Americans, were ready to burst across the border as soon as they received a call from within the country. To send out this call, it was necessary to seize Quebec, and that would be easy to do. He inquired after the disposition of various prominent inhabitants and wanted to make sure of a small group of individuals who had influence among the people. Fri-

15. Wilbur, *op. cit.*, II, 121–122.
16. Or Fréchette.
17. Q, LXXXI, 616–618.

chet quoted him as saying, "You, Mr. Black, can greatly facilitate the execution of our plan. You are well known to the soldiers in garrison. The sentinels will receive liquor from you, and in that you can mix laudanum." Black encouraged him and, with the promise of a safe lodging, lured him into town that evening. Arrest, trial, and conviction followed. On July 21, 1797, McLane was hanged, drawn, and quartered on the glacis outside the walls; Frichet was sentenced for life but was soon pardoned.

Though McLane's grim fate struck fear into the hearts of many on both sides of the line, the danger of a foreign invasion combined with a domestic rising still worried the authorities in Lower Canada for several months. They heard of spies running about but could not lay hands on them, and from Vermont they drew more information of how serious was the conspiracy there against the peace of Canada. But by the fall of 1798, Prescott was able to breathe a sigh of relief. Jules Le Fer, a French royalist sent up by Liston to investigate the situation in the colony, reported to the governor that though the Canadians generally were anxious to see their country restored to France they were inclined to be passive, and that the last republican emissary had been withdrawn pending a final decision by the Directory.[18]

The danger had passed. The Directory, having seen the bankruptcy of its plans to use Ira Allen and now finding itself involved in actual though undeclared war with the United States, turned its back upon Canada; and Napoleon, who overthrew the Directory in the autumn of 1799, scarcely ever turned his face in this direction. Thus deprived of any real hope of French support, the Vermont intrigue died.[19]

18. *Ibid.*, p. 21.

19. There was a slight attempt to revive it in 1801, when officials of Lower Canada discovered in Montreal a secret society whose object was to overturn the government in Quebec. There is a curious Irish suggestion about this mysterious organization, which was called the White Cap Club. Jonathan Sewell, the attorney general, pointed out some striking resemblances to the United Irishmen. He credited a certain Rogers, a schoolmaster who had come from the United States in the previous winter, with forming the club; and he was convinced that Ira Allen was the principal in the background. No French Canadians were implicated, and there was no outward disturbance. *Q*, LXXXVII, 297–298, 377, 417. In the spring of 1803, there were some indications that Napoleon was harboring a design against Lower Canada. A number of strangers reputed to be French officers and suspected of being French emissaries then entered the colony via the United States, and at the same time private letters from France suggested that the Napoleonic government was anxious to acquire Canada quite as much as Louisiana. *Q*, XCI, 161–173. The alarm in Quebec was not very serious; and the modern student may smile at it as absurd because Napoleon, having recently recovered Louisiana from Spain, was at this very time engaged in selling it to the United States. But it should be remembered that an important, if not the principal motive of Napoleon in making the sale was to break the growing bond between the United States and the British Empire. Therefore his American negotiation did not necessarily mean that he had renounced all interest in Canada. Indeed the above indications of such an interest coincided with the revival of Anglo-French hostilities after the Peace of Amiens.

In striking contrast to the military menace from the south, a peaceful American infiltration was building up both Canadas. This movement of people[20] was to exert a great influence on later Canadian-American relations, and might have had an even greater influence if there had been no War of 1812; but this migration of Americans to British soil, like other migrations, was quite independent of the political relations between the two countries at the time, until of course it was stopped by the war just mentioned. It began right after the recognition of American Independence and steadily gathered momentum right down to 1812, irrespective of the tension over the British holding of the western posts, of the appeasement wrought by Jay, and the years of growing strain which ended in the renewal of hostilities.

One area which was largely settled by Americans during this period was that since known as the Eastern Townships of Quebec. This large triangle of territory south of the St. Lawrence had been left vacant because Governor Haldimand refused to plant his Loyalists there, though many of them desired it and Lord North directed it. Haldimand suspected those who sought grants of land near the border of being more eager to engage in smuggling than in agriculture; he foresaw continued international friction if the Loyalists were allowed to live so close to their old foes; and he insisted that this district should be reserved for the expansion of the Canadians, whose different race, language, religion, and culture would provide a more effective barrier. With these arguments he persuaded the home government that the refugees should be settled elsewhere, and as soon as he found a place farther west he put them there That was in 1784, the year of his departure. Within five years the provincial government began to see the impossibility of locking up this portion of the country until the French needed it.

Reports that families from Vermont were clearing land and building huts on the Canadian side of the forty-fifth parallel raised alarming visions of American squatters attracting others to swarm in upon this empty land and appropriate it. There seemed to be only one way to hold it, and that was to fill it with loyal British settlers. But where could they be got? The nineteenth-century answer to such a question was impossible then. Not until a later generation did the home government abandon its opposition to emigration from the British Isles. The answer of the day was, curiously enough, the United States. There was then a common British belief that the American Republic contained countless numbers of people who were disgusted with their new government and still faithful

20. For a treatment of the whole subject of which this forms but a part, see M. L. Hansen and J. B. Brebner, *The Mingling of the Canadian and American Peoples* (New Haven, 1940).

to their old King. Only one obstacle to their coming was seen by the authorities in Quebec, and that was removed by the Constitutional Act of 1791. During the previous twenty years, all grants of land had to be made according to the ancient seigniorial system; but now freehold grants became possible.

In the closing decade of the century the district was thrown open, though internal quarrels at Quebec delayed the formal concession of titles. To speed the process of settlement, the government gave the land in large blocks, usually a whole township at a time to a single "leader" or a small group of enterprising individuals who assumed the responsibility of apportioning the lots among humbler "associates." Most of the "leaders" were genuine British and genuine speculators; most of the "associates" came from south of the line. A number were from New York, many from New Hampshire, and most from Vermont. Some came of their own accord; others were gathered wholesale by agents with the aid of newspaper advertisements. The government prescribed an oath of allegiance to guarantee the political character of the new settlers, but land-hungry men swallowed it with ease while in Quebec there was rejoicing over the salvation of so many sinners. For a while, however, when the shadow of revolution hovered over the country, it was sometimes difficult to distinguish between those who were spying out the land for a possible military conquest and those who were seeking land for peaceful settlement.[21] British tradition has tended to obscure the predominantly American character of the settlement of the Eastern Townships before 1812, though it is perfectly clear from the contemporary records. How many people were living there when war broke out, it is impossible to say, but we have a figure for the summer of 1805. Robert Shore Milnes, Prescott's successor, then reported that the population was more than five thousand, and he added that they were chiefly from the United States. Two years later a British traveler stated that fifteen thousand had crossed the line to settle in this region; and in 1812, according to the Anglican bishop of Quebec, the Eastern Townships contained about twenty thousand people, almost all Americans.[22]

Much larger was the American influx into what is now the old part of

21. Watchful eyes followed some of the visitors from the south, particularly Levi Allen in 1797. He dodged about in a suspicious manner, seldom sleeping twice in the same house. He denied any knowledge of his brother's doings except what appeared in the newspapers, and said he had come to obtain lands. His name was already on the books for the greater part of one township, Barford, right on the border, but he did not get it. In 1797, also, Ira Allen tried to get six townships as damages from the British government. It may be interesting to add that Barnard and Black each got a township, and when the latter lost his to his creditors he moved heaven and earth to get another.

22. *Q*, XCVIII, 109. Hansen and Brebner, *op. cit.*, p. 74.

Ontario. Only a general idea of its size is possible, but that is not difficult to get. We may deduce it from an examination of the size and structure of the population in 1812. Though no definite figure can be given for the total number of souls in the province at that time, it would appear to have been about eighty thousand.[23] Where did they come from? In the original Loyalist settlements in Upper Canada there were less than six thousand people, including babes in arms.[24] During the twenty-eight years that elapsed before the War of 1812, there was no appreciable addition to this population by immigration from other British provinces, beyond a mere handful of Loyalists who came up from the Maritime Provinces in search of wider opportunities. During this interval, also, there was only an occasional trickle of immigrants from the British Isles, with one exception. That occurred in 1786, when five hundred highlanders from old Glengarry came to live with their kinsmen, Loyalists, in the new Glengarry on the St. Lawrence. These small additions, together with the natural increase calculated rather generously, might account for an increase of the original population to twelve or perhaps even to fifteen thousand, but scarcely any more, by the outbreak of war. Immigration from the United States accounts for the large remainder.[25]

Why was this migratory movement much greater than that into the Eastern Townships? One reason was that there was much more room here. The old part of Ontario, in the eastern projection of the rich median plain of the continent, was the most extensive agricultural area of Canada until the Prairie Provinces were opened. The Loyalists could not begin to fill it. With the exception of a few hundred in a small corner at Niagara, they occupied only a narrow strip of land along the water front

23. On page 596 of his *Topographical Description*, published in 1815, Joseph Bouchette gave 95,000 as the population of Upper Canada in 1814. In his *British Dominions*, published seventeen years later, he produced a table (II, 235) giving 70,718 as the population in 1806, and he calculated from the assessment returns made to the provincial legislature that it was nearly 77,000 in 1811. *Ibid.*, I, 108. Other estimates run away up to about double this amount, but they may be ignored, Bouchette being the most reliable source of information, though inclined, perhaps, to be too conservative.

24. A. L. Burt, *The Old Province of Quebec*, pp. 362-363.

25. Michael Smith, a Baptist minister from Pennsylvania who lived in the London District from 1808 and gathered a lot of curious information for a book on the province, which he published in Hartford, Connecticut, in 1813, estimated that the Loyalists accounted for one-sixth of the population, and that natives of the British Isles were one-twelfth and, with their children born in Canada, amounted to one-fifth of the population. *A Geographical View of the Province of Upper Canada*, pp. 62-63. I am inclined to accept this analysis as approximately correct, though I cannot say the same for the figure he gives for the total population—136,000 in 1811. See E. Cruikshank, "Immigration from the United States into Upper Canada, 1784-1812—Its Character and Results," *Proceedings of the Thirty-ninth Annual Convention of the Ontario Educational Association* (1900), pp. 263-283.

of the upper St. Lawrence and the Bay of Quinte in 1784. There was also greater pressure behind this migration, and it began earlier. Little Vermont supplied most of the impetus that carried people north across the forty-fifth parallel, and they were held back for several years until the Eastern Townships were opened; but the Ontario peninsula was thrown open by the planting of the Loyalists, and the growing migration which followed with scarcely a break had its seat in the "Old Northwest" of the United States, the region just south of the Great Lakes. There the North American frontier was pushing out toward new land. Hostile Indians checked expansion westward, thereby increasing the pressure northward, and the movement in this direction was accentuated by another important influence. The Loyalist settlement pulled the American frontier into Upper Canada.

To explain this effect of the Loyalist settlement, it is necessary to enlarge a little upon its character, which was very different from that of the new settlements in the Maritime Provinces. There the refugees found it very hard to begin life all over again, for they came from the seaboard of the old colonies, where they had been accustomed to the amenities of an established society. Friends and relatives left behind felt little inclination to follow them and share their hardships. The Loyalists who founded Ontario were of another type. They were sturdy backwoods farmers from the interior of the old colonies, chiefly New York. They simply continued their old manner of living under more favorable circumstances, thanks to the generosity of the government. Having improved their lot by the remove, as they themselves admitted when the governor visited them in 1788, they naturally invited their friends and relatives whom they had left behind, frontiersmen like themselves, to come and do the same. They vouched for the loyalty of the newcomers, who also protested it. There were all kinds of excuses for not having fought for the King, and even for participating in the war on the American side. Without any hesitation, the government welcomed the "late Loyalists," as they were called. These friends and relatives of course had other friends and relatives, so that the process was repeated, and the small stream of "late Loyalists" insensibly grew into a flood of simple land seekers. Still the welcome held. The oath of allegiance, prescribed from the beginning for even undoubted Loyalists, was easy to take when the government gave land; and the government was glad to give land to prodigals who returned to their old allegiance. Far from resenting the intrusion, Loyalists of all shades were delighted at the coming of their own folk, and like the government they rejoiced at the prospect of a more rapid development of the country. They did, however, object to the presence of one individual during their first year. Posing as a Loyalist, he got provisions and land near Kingston; but he quickly disappeared when somebody happened to recognize him. He was none other than the man who had hanged Major André.[26]

When Upper Canada became a separate colony in 1791 and Simcoe came to rule it, he encouraged this American immigration, though not as such. To him it was at least potentially British. By the summer of 1795, "the rapid emigration[27] and influx of inhabitants into this colony from the United States," to quote Simcoe's own words,[28] was such that it raised interesting questions in the provincial legislature. What was the national status of these people who had lived at least part of their lives in the United States? Some were American citizens, some might still be British subjects, and some might be both. How was it possible to make a distinction so that only true British subjects would exercise full political rights? It was a badly tangled knot, and the legislature cut it by enacting that no one could be elected to the assembly unless he had been a bona fide British subject for seven years. These questions and this act were soon forgotten in the land-granting orgy which broke loose when Simcoe departed in 1796. He left the government in the hands of Peter Russell, of whom it was shortly said that he "would have granted lands to the devil and all his family as good Loyalists providing they were able to pay the fees." In 1799, to get money to build a road, the provincial government decided to sell land in blocks of four thousand acres and advertised it in the newspapers of New York, New Jersey, and Pennsylvania.[29] The men who did this were not even pretending to rescue submerged Loyalists from the Republic. They were simply thinking of developing Upper Canada from the United States, of speeding a process that was already at work. The extravagant granting of land to speculators was presently curbed, but there was no attempt to check the rising tide of immigration from the south. It had swamped the real Loyalists long before the outbreak of war cut it off suddenly in 1812.

One is tempted to wonder what would have happened to this part of British North America if that war had not come. The question does not concern the other parts, for there was no such movement into the Maritime Provinces and that into the Eastern Townships affected only a corner of Lower Canada. But Upper Canada was being flooded by immi-

26. C.O. 42, XVI, 265. Professor J. B. Brebner has drawn my attention to Winthrop Sargent, *Life and Career of Major André* (Boston, 1861), p. 393, where it is said that this fellow, "one Strickland, a tory of Ramapo Valley," was a prisoner who bought his freedom by undertaking the unpleasant job of hangman on this occasion.

27. This word was then commonly used for "immigration."

28. S.P., IV, 76.

29. Gilbert C. Patterson, *Land Settlement in Upper Canada*, 1783–1840 (Ontario Archives Report, 1920), p. 83. For a recent defense of Russell, see D. R. Plaunt, "The Honourable Peter Russell," *Canadian Historical Review*, XX, 258–274.

grants from south of the line.[30] Here a word of caution is in place. Too much emphasis should not be laid upon the American character of the movement, for it was primarily North American. It was land these people were after.[31] Few seem to have cared much whether they lived under the American or the British flag. For this reason the complacence of Simcoe and of other stout Britons was not entirely unfounded, though they based it upon the false assumption of the flag's taking precedence over the land. Yet we cannot overlook the fundamental fact that the human ties across the border were steadily increasing in number and in strength as the years passed by. With the single exception of its government, Upper Canada was becoming more and more American in character.[32] Even after the war, the largest religious body in the province was not just an offshoot of the church south of the line; it was a real part of it. Until 1824, when the Methodists of Upper Canada organized a separate conference, their preachers belonged to a conference in the United States, from which they came and to which they returned periodically. This is but one illustration of how the dividing waters did not divide. They were a common highway which tended to unite the people on either side, and the international line which ran along the middle of these waters might have become more imaginary if there had been no War of 1812.

30. Michael Smith reported in 1812 that two-thirds of the members of the Upper Canadian legislative assembly were natives of the United States. "Less than one-third of the justices of the peace are Americans, the sheriffs are either Europeans or loyalists; the jury, according to the constitution, must be taken in rotation from each township, as their names stand on the assessment roll or list of names; of course the majority are always Americans." *Op. cit.*, p. 72. On the outbreak of war, he observed, an attempt to suspend the Habeas Corpus Act was defeated in the assembly by a considerable majority. "Had this act passed," he said, "there is no doubt but that a rebellion would have taken place." *Ibid.*, p. 87. He also remarked: "Upon the declaration of war, the governor issued a proclamation making it treason for any one to attempt to cross the line. Had not this been done, one half of the people would have left the province." *Ibid.*, p. 88. Smith's statements, says General Cruikshank, "if not unbiased, are usually sensible and moderate, and show an intimate knowledge of local conditions." E. A. Cruikshank, "A Study of Disaffection in Upper Canada in 1812–15," *Transactions of the Royal Society of Canada*, Third Series, Vol. VI, Sec. II, p. 18.

31. Smith, *op. cit.*, p. 86.

32. Colonel Talbot, one of the pioneers in southwestern Ontario, wrote in 1802: "The present population consists of refugees from all parts, principally natives of the United States, who may be classed under the three following heads: 1. Those who were early enticed by a gratuitous offer of land, without any predilection on their part to the British Constitution. 2. Those who have fled from the United States for crimes or to escape their creditors. 3. Republicans, whose principal motive for settling in that country is an anticipation of its shaking off its allegiance to Great Britain." Talbot to Sullivan, Oct. 27, 1802, *Q*, CCXCII, 248.

Lieutenant Governor Francis Gore said in January, 1808, that excepting the inhabitants of Glengarry and the Loyalists, the inhabitants of the colony consisted chiefly of immigrants from the United States who "of consequence, retain those ideas of equality and insubordination, much to the prejudice of this government, so prevalent in that country." In the event of war, he said he could rely on the population living in the district between Kingston and the border of Lower Canada, but not upon those who lived around York, or Niagara, or Long Point. *P.A.C.R.*, 1896, Note B, p. 35.

The war suddenly stopped the peaceful American invasion of Upper Canada; it checked a renewal of this invasion after the return of peace, for the scales had fallen from British eyes; and it stifled the potentially American character of the population of the province, by purging it of the very small minority who were incorrigible republicans, and by corralling within the British fold the great majority whose political consciousness had not yet awakened. These changes draw an added significance from the fact that the tide of immigration from the British Isles, though beginning earlier to pour into this province, did not become a flood until a full fifteen years after the outbreak of hostilities. Then it might have been too late for these newcomers, themselves not very self-conscious politically, to impress a British character upon the country. Thus it would appear that the American declaration of war in 1812 severed the growing connection between the United States and Upper Canada as if with a knife.

CHAPTER X

TWO ABORTIVE CONVENTIONS

BEFORE turning to the causes of the War of 1812, we should examine two conventions negotiated in London in 1803 and 1807 to settle outstanding differences between the United States and British North America. They were designed to supplement Jay's Treaty, which had not wholly accomplished this end, but they accomplished nothing because extraneous circumstances blocked their ratification.

The convention of 1803 dealt only with boundaries that still required definition. Though Jay's Treaty effectively provided for a solution of the contentious St. Croix problem, it left a gap below the mouth of the river as determined by the joint commission in 1798. The question of the islands in Passamaquoddy Bay, then raised by Sullivan,[1] had to be settled. Above the source of the St. Croix, also, difficulties unknown at the time of Jay's Treaty were calling for a drastic revision of the boundary definition of 1783. These too had begun to dawn on the shrewd Sullivan when he objected to Barclay's and Chipman's argument for their particular source of the St. Croix because it alone conformed to the wording of the peace treaty,[2] which prescribed a line due north to the highlands dividing the rivers flowing into the St. Lawrence from those falling into the Atlantic. Less than twenty years after these highlands had been adopted as a boundary line, they turned out to be not a line at all, but a broad, rough plateau; and at the same time it was becoming evident that the line drawn north from the accepted source of the St. Croix would meet no highlands answering to the description in the treaty. Thus the boundary vanished at some unknown point north of the St. Croix and did not reappear until it approached the forty-fifth parallel of latitude. Out in the West it again vanished. As mentioned earlier,[3] a practical line was to have been substituted for the impossible line of 1783 between the Lake of the Woods and the Mississippi. The new boundary there was to have been based upon a joint international survey for which Article IV of Jay's Treaty had provided, but for some hidden reason this article had remained a dead letter.

The initiative which produced the convention of 1803 came from the American government, which was quite natural because these boundary questions were of much more remote concern to the government in

1. *Supra*, p. 165.
2. *Supra*, p. 164.
3. *Supra*, p. 161.

London; and it came apparently as the result of the closing of a new rift in Anglo-American relations. It will be recalled that the joint commission which, under Jay's Treaty, met in the United States to adjudicate British claims for debts had early reached an absolute deadlock which produced, by way of retaliation, a suspension of the joint commission sitting in England until a new solution for the old question of debts could be found. The negotiation of the new solution, which was the payment of a lump sum by the United States, was concluded in London in January, 1802.

In the summer of 1801, when this agreement was already in sight, Jefferson's Secretary of State, James Madison, raised the boundary problem in a letter to Rufus King, the American minister at the Court of St. James. Madison was then concerned only with the boundary in Passamaquoddy Bay. He was not yet prepared to make any definite proposal, but he had a suggestion for King to turn over in his mind. It was that the line should run around the west and south of Deer Island and north of Campobello, for a reason to be noted presently. He hoped that he would soon be able to send a commission and definite instructions for negotiating. Meanwhile, he intimated, King might "break the business to the British ministry." [4] On March 10, 1802, the legislature of Massachusetts memorialized the governor of that state to request the President of the United States to take steps to settle the dispute over the islands in Passamaquoddy Bay. Shortly afterward the Senate received and adopted the convention on debts, and then Madison turned to work seriously on the boundary question. For information and advice, he applied to James Sullivan, whose knowledge of the problem was probably unsurpassed and whose judgment upon it was untinged by any national bias. He was the real author of the convention of 1803, except the article on the northwest boundary gap. He deserves more credit than he has received. After many years and much negotiation, the boundary was at last made to follow the lines he advocated in his masterly reply of May 20, 1802, to the Secretary of State. [5]

Sullivan frankly admitted, despite the resolution of the legislature of his own state, that he knew of no dispute over the national ownership of islands in Passamaquoddy Bay, with the single exception of Moose Island. New Brunswick had recently granted lands in that island and the grantees had instigated the attempts of some officials of that province to exercise jurisdiction there; but the attempts had failed and had not been renewed. For a long time before the Revolutionary War, he said, people from Massachusetts had occupied the island. He insisted that it had

4. *A.S.P.F.R.*, II, 585.
5. *Ibid.*, pp. 586–587.

never been occupied by people who recognized the authority of Nova Scotia, and that Nova Scotia had never exercised any authority there. It clearly belonged to the United States, for the peace treaty had recognized as American all islands south of a due-east line from the mouth of the St. Croix and within twenty leagues of the United States unless they were or had been "within the limits" of Nova Scotia. Any shadow of a British claim would cover much that was not at all in question, because the claim would have to rest upon the ancient charter to Sir William Alexander. Under that instrument Nova Scotia had included all the country as far as the Kennebec. But this extension, nullified by the charter of 1692, which gave Massachusetts everything up to the St. Croix, could not have been contemplated in 1783. Deer Island, Sullivan now admitted to be British, though in 1798 he had been willing to see the line placed on either side of it; and Campobello, which Madison's suggested boundary would have included in the United States, he also renounced as "confessedly" British.

What worried Sullivan was not land but water. Across the channel between Campobello and the American mainland was a bar of rocks which, being dry at low water, blocked the passage for vessels of any considerable size. Only with a fair wind and at flood tide could they venture across the obstruction. If the two governments simply agreed to run the boundary along this channel, where he said it should lie, this whole corner of the United States would be locked in behind the barrier of rocks. It was this snag which had caught Madison's eye and had prompted his proposal to include Campobello in the United States, for there was a good channel around the north of that island and up the west of Deer Island. As a justification, he had said that the treaty apparently intended the line to follow navigable waters which both countries might use. Sullivan did not subscribe to this doubtful interpretation, nor would he override a British right in order to guard an American interest. Yet he was equally anxious to secure a navigable access to the American shores of Passamaquoddy Bay and the St. Croix River, and he had another solution for the problem. It was the equal right to navigate the waters of the bay. The British had never questioned it. Vessels of the United States had freely entered and traversed those waters. It was true that the British had seized a few American craft in the St. Croix, but that was for smuggling and they had all been released. This equal right to navigation, he argued, was implied in the treaty. That had recognized the jurisdiction of the United States up to the due-east line from the mouth of the St. Croix and out to a distance of twenty leagues from the shores of the Republic, and then had taken out the islands formerly belonging to Nova Scotia. This exception covered only the islands and such privileges as were necessary to their occupancy. These privileges did not include an exclusive British right to all the waters within the above limits. This argument of Sullivan was too ingenious, and it reached too far; but it may have been very useful in producing the compromise agreement which in the end gave the United States what he as well as Madison was intent on securing—a navigable access to this part of their country.

In the latter part of his letter, Sullivan directed Madison's attention to the boundary above the source of the St. Croix. Both Massachusetts and New Brunswick were granting lands in that quarter, and there might soon be trouble over interfering locations unless the due-north line was run and plainly marked "through a vast extent of wilderness where many known and unknown causes will affect the magnetic variations." Having urged this simple necessity, he proceeded to lay bare the difficult problem of how far the boundary followed this straight line and where it went on leaving it. In other words, he was presenting the problem created by the discrepancy between the imaginary highlands of the treaty and the real highlands of nature. A commission, he said, would have to decide arbitrarily upon some point as the treaty's "north-west angle of Nova Scotia . . . formed by a line drawn due north from the source of the Saint Croix River to the highlands . . . which divide those rivers that empty themselves into the River St. Lawrence from those which fall into the Atlantic Ocean." If no suitable mountain or natural monument could be found, an artificial one might be raised. From thence to the Connecticut River, the commission should fix the line through other artificial monuments they might establish; and he advised that this should be done soon because Canadian settlements ascending the Chaudière, and perhaps other rivers, were "approaching fast towards those of the United States."

Madison acted quickly. On June 8, less than three weeks after Sullivan had written from Boston, the Secretary of State in Washington sent off a commission and instructions for the American minister in London to negotiate with the British government a settlement of the undecided stretches of the boundary.[6] In Passamaquoddy, Rufus King was to regard Moose Island and the common navigation of the bay and of the channel between Deer and Campobello islands as "the essential objects to be secured to the United States." Madison referred to his own letter of the previous July in a way that suggests a lingering desire for the "trifling" island of Campobello, but he was obviously prepared to see Britain keep it. He did not press the point and he enclosed a copy of Sullivan's letter, in which the British claim was categorically upheld, with the remark that

6. *Ibid.*, p. 585.

"his information and his reasoning will be useful in the discussion."
Accepting Sullivan's advice on the necessity of running the straight line
up from the source of the St. Croix, Madison directed King to arrange
for this to be done by a surveyor appointed by two commissioners, one
selected by each government. He likewise accepted and passed on the
suggestion for fixing the termination of this line and for establishing the
boundary between that point and the Connecticut River by three commissioners, the two just mentioned and a third added in the same way as
provided for in Jay's Treaty.

As Sullivan's special interest in the boundary was limited to his own

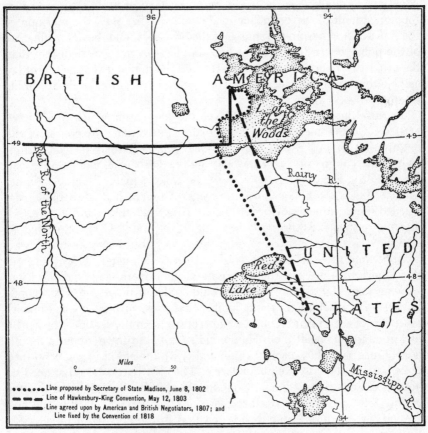

The Northwest Boundary Gap

Redrawn with permission of the American Geographical Society from Charles
O. Paullin and John K. Wright, *Atlas of the Historical Geography of the United
States.*

state, Madison looked elsewhere for guidance in approaching the problem of the gap in the northwest. He found it in the recently published *Voyages* by the great Scottish-Canadian explorer and fur trader, Alexander Mackenzie. That work made it quite clear that the Lake of the Woods lay to the north of every branch of the Mississippi. Madison then proposed the simplest solution. He did not see any necessity for a joint commission. A mere redefinition by agreement would suffice, and he suggested a line running straight from the source of the Mississippi nearest the Lake of the Woods to a point where it would reach the lake as a tangent on the west and then twisting along its shore line to the northwest corner. To illustrate this, he referred King to the map in Mackenzie's book. In conclusion, the Secretary of State intimated that the adjustment of the boundary in Passamaquoddy Bay, the marking of the line due north from the source of the St. Croix, and the determination of the point where this straight line should stop were more urgent than the other two boundary questions. He told the minister that he might lay aside either or both of these if he encountered difficulties or delays in his attempt to solve them.

Because the time element destroyed the convention which would have settled all these questions, it is important to examine the course of the negotiation in order that we may see what retarded its conclusion When the commission and the instructions reached London, King had departed for Harwich on his way to the Continent for a three months' holiday; but Christopher Gore, the *chargé* whom he had left behind,[7] forwarded the documents before he sailed. King then directed him to expedite the business. Accordingly, on August 24, 1802, Gore requested an interview with the British Foreign Secretary, Lord Hawkesbury, who later became the Earl of Liverpool and Prime Minister. They met, and the American presented the proposals of his government; but the Englishman asked for a delay until he could confer with George Hammond, formerly British minister to the United States and now permanent undersecretary of the Foreign Office, on his return from the seaside whither he had gone for his health. On Hammond's arrival in town, about a month later, Gore saw Hawkesbury again and, with the aid of maps, went into the details of the unsettled boundaries. The only particulars that need be noted here are that in Passamaquoddy Bay, following Madison's letter of July, 1801, Gore proposed to place the line west of Deer Island and around the north of Campobello, and that in the northwest he added a suggestion that commissioners be appointed to ascertain the relation of the Mississippi to the Lake of the Woods and to run the line according to

7. Gore was not one of Rufus King's official household, but was a member of the joint commission sitting in London under Jay's Treaty.

the treaty or, if that proved impossible, according to Madison's new suggestion. The last point made Hawkesbury shy. He hinted at a revival of the old British claim that the peace treaty promised Britain a territorial access to navigable waters of the Mississippi, and he intimated that the commissioners mentioned by Gore might be instructed to fix the line in accordance with this claim. It was then the American's turn to shy. He shut his eyes to this advance, merely replying that the line from the source was the natural correction of the mistake made in 1783; but he carried away an uneasy feeling that the British government would still press the embarrassing claim. On all other points the Englishman seemed to agree provided, on inquiry, the islands in the bay were found to belong to the respective countries to which the proposed boundary would assign them. He said he would have to seek information from several individuals, none of whom he named. Gore presumed that one of these was Barclay, then in England. One other matter which these two men discussed was a difference which had arisen over the interpretation of that section of Jay's Treaty which provided for the freedom of intercourse across the boundary in the interior.[8] But this did not appear in the convention of 1803, and therefore its examination may be deferred until we turn to the convention of 1807, by which time it had become a broader issue.

Hawkesbury halted the negotiation on October 4, 1802, when he sent Gore a short note promising to resume it either with him or with Rufus King "within as short a period as the circumstances of the case will conveniently admit." The Englishman was not prepared to complete the business, and Gore doubted if he could be ready before Rufus King's return, which he expected in November.[9] The American minister's absence had apparently nothing to do with the delay, which lasted on into the new year.

On February 28, 1803, Rufus King at last reported some progress. At Hawkesbury's desire he had conferred with Barclay, who seemed willing to cede Campobello if the inhabitants desired it. This condition was probably intended as a polite refusal, though the American did not recognize it at the time. He found no objection at all to Moose Island's being in the United States, and he could see nothing to impede a settlement of the boundary through Passamaquoddy Bay "except the difficulty of engaging the minister to bestow upon the subject sufficient time to understand it." For the same reason, he could give Madison no information of what might be done with the gap in the northwest and the line along the highlands; but he was fairly confident that nothing stood

8. *Ibid.*, pp. 587–589.
9. *Ibid.*

in the way of the American proposal for running the straight line up from the source of the St. Croix and for determining its end.[10]

In six weeks, during which he had more satisfactory conferences, King was able to draft the convention embodying an agreement he had reached on all the boundary questions sent to him from Washington.[11] In Passamaquoddy Bay the islands were to be divided as Sullivan said they should be; but the equal right of navigation was confined to one channel, the best, as suggested by Madison. The conflict which had worried these two men was resolved in a formula which might puzzle anyone not familiar with the local problem. The boundary was described as running from the mouth of the St. Croix down the west of Deer Island and up around the north of Campobello; and with the exception of the latter, which remained British, all the waters and islands on one side were given to Massachusetts and on the other to New Brunswick. No mention was made of Grand Manan, out in the Bay of Fundy, for the possession of that island was not yet in dispute. Here, however, it may be interesting to observe by way of anticipation that the United States probably lost Grand Manan by rejecting this convention.

Between the source of the St. Croix and the eastern end of the boundary on the forth-fifth parallel, the boundary was to be determined according to the American suggestion already explained, but with two slight alterations. Instead of two commissioners, a board of three was to undertake the marking of the due-north line from the St. Croix. The other change was to settle a new question that was being raised. The board was also to decide what was "the northwesternmost head" of the Connecticut River.

Article V of the convention would have closed the northwest boundary gap substantially as proposed in Washington. Because it was now supposed that the nearest source of the Mississippi lay west of the Lake of the Woods, the line was to run straight to the northwest corner of the lake without approaching it as a tangent and then following its shores.[12] It may seem surprising that the British government abandoned its insistence on a territorial access to a navigable portion of the river. Gore had suspected that this was impossible, but his report had drawn from

10. *Ibid.*, p. 590.

11. *Ibid.*, pp. 584–585.

12. "The source of the Mississippi nearest to the Lake of the Woods, according to McKenzie's [sic] report will be found about twenty-nine miles to the westward of any part of that lake, which is represented to be nearly circular. Hence, a direct line between the northwesternmost part of the lake, and the nearest source of the Mississippi, which is preferred by this Government, has appeared to me equally advantageous with the lines we had proposed." King to the Secretary of State, May 13, 1803, *ibid*, p. 590. At the desire of either government, commissioners were to be appointed for the purpose of running and marking this line, which, as the accompanying map shows, would not have followed the course that the negotiators anticipated.

Madison a supplementary instruction to King on December 16. The American Secretary of State then remarked that the President considered the offer of the United States a liberal one, inasmuch as the more obvious remedy of the error of the treaty was to draw a due-north line from the most northerly, rather than the nearest, source of the Mississippi and intersecting the due-west line from the Lake of the Woods. He added that if the British government did not see it in this light the settlement of this particular portion of the boundary should be indefinitely postponed because it was not likely to be of any material consequence for some time.[13] The American minister apparently made good use of this supplement.

On April 10[14] or 11,[15] 1803, King sent Hawkesbury the completed convention, drafted in accordance with the agreements they had reached in a number of conferences. Then ensued a delay of a month before they signed it, which they did on May 12. King immediately sent it home. There it was held up until the autumn, for the Seventh Congress had come to an end on March 3 and the Eighth Congress did not assemble until October 17, 1803. Then, one might expect, ratification would follow as a matter of course. The convention was not a negotiated compromise which would have to be examined to see if the terms insisted on by Britain were acceptable to the United States. It contained no such terms. In every particular it conformed to the instructions which the American Secretary of State had sent to the American minister. Britain had simply accepted the proposals of the United States. The Washington administration had a secure majority in the Senate, and President Jefferson's opening message to Congress referred to the convention as satisfactory to both signatories.

What wrecked the convention was Napoleon's sale of Louisiana to the United States by a treaty signed in Paris on April 30, 1803. The connection between the two transactions was not seen at the time, for the Americans were really surprised into purchasing this empire when all they had wished to buy was a city—New Orleans, which controlled the mouth of the Mississippi. This was Napoleon's doing. The master of France had dreamed of building a great American empire in which the Mississippi valley would be married to the French West Indies; and to this end, in 1800, he had wrung from Spain a promise to return Louisiana to France. But the yellow fever and the black population of St. Domingo, by ruining Leclerc's army, had wrecked the foundation of Napoleon's ambitious plan for the New World. Turning to liquidate his chief asset

13. *Ibid.*, pp. 589–590.
14. King, IV, 244.
15. *A.S.P.F.R.*, II, 591.

there, he hastily sold Louisiana even before Spain had made delivery. To him, on this occasion, it was more blessed to give than to receive. By selling what he could not hope to hold after the outbreak of another war —Britain being prepared to pounce on New Orleans—Napoleon put this rich prize forever beyond the reach of his great foe; he strengthened the United States, his prospective great friend and counterweight against Britain; and he applied a wedge to split the friendship that was drawing these two powers together.[16]

The conflict between the French treaty and the British convention did not develop until some time after the opening of Congress. The treaty was ratified on October 20, three days after its submission by the President. On the twenty-fourth he submitted the convention. It was read a second time on the twenty-seventh, and on the thirty-first a motion was made to ratify it with a verbal amendment of no particular consequence. A debate followed, ending in an adjournment. The debate was resumed on November 15, and then the convention was referred to a committee headed by John Quincy Adams. It would appear that his appointment was intended to lead to a removal of the objection that was arising, possibly inspired by the President himself. According to Timothy Pickering, the other senator from Massachusetts who also favored unqualified ratification, Jefferson "altered his mind" and "the Senate followed of course." [17]

16. See E. Wilson Lyon, *Louisiana in French Diplomacy* (Norman, 1934). On March 11, 1803, in a letter to Livingston, the American minister in Paris, King suggested that the United States might be glad "to see the English in N.O. not with the view of keeping it, but to prevent its going into the hands of France; or perhaps to assist us in acquiring a title to, and the possession of it." King, IV, 226. Three weeks later Addington, the Prime Minister, told King that Britain would probably occupy New Orleans on the outbreak of war with France. When King replied that his country would not like to see either England or France there, Addington hastened to add that his government's only object was to keep France out and this could best be accomplished by putting the United States in. "You may be assured," he said, "that nothing shall be done injurious to the interest of the United States." *Ibid.*, p. 241. In further conversation on May 12, when King mentioned "the probable cession of Louisiana by France to the U.S.," Addington expressed a "hope that it had been done" and remarked that then there would be no British expedition to New Orleans. Later in the same day, when they were signing the British-American convention, King discussed the matter with Hawkesbury who, according to the American minister, "seemed pleased with the prospect I held out to him that Louisiana would be ceded to the U.S." *Ibid.*, pp. 255–256. Three days afterwards King received word from Livingston and Monroe, announcing their signature of the treaty in Paris, and at once he informed Hawkesbury, who again expressed the pleasure of the British government. *Ibid.*, pp. 262–263.

An interesting contemporary American comment on the famous purchase is that of George Cabot in a letter of July 1, 1803, to his friend Rufus King on the latter's arrival home from his mission in England. According to Cabot: "The cession of Louisiana is an excellent thing for France. It is like selling us a Ship after she is surrounded by a British Fleet; it puts into safekeeping what she could not keep herself, for England could take Louisiana in the first moment of war without the loss of a man. France could neither settle it nor protect it; she is therefore rid of an encumbrance that wounded her pride, receives money and regains the friendship of our populace." *Ibid.*, p. 279.

17. *Ibid.*, p. 363.

The objection was to Article V of the convention. The Senate balked at the line from the Mississippi to the Lake of the Woods, fearing that its acceptance might operate to clip the top off the territory acquired by the treaty with France. Madison reported shortly afterwards:

There is reason to believe that the boundary between Louisiana and the British territories north of it were [sic] actually fixed by commissioners appointed under the treaty of Utrecht, and that this boundary was to run from the Lake of the Woods westwardly in latitude 49; in which case the fifth article would be nugatory, as the line, from the Lake of the Woods to the nearest source of the Mississippi, would run through territory which on both sides of the line would belong to the United States.[18]

The facts, as established long years later, were quite otherwise. It is true that British commissioners under the treaty of 1713 contended for the forty-ninth parallel as the southern boundary of the Hudson's Bay Company's territories, when the French claimed the country to within fifty miles of the bay; but the British and the French commissioners never reached any agreement, and they were discussing the northern boundary of Canada, not that of Louisiana at all. The distortion of these facts, however, was not swallowed by all the senators,[19] nor was it the sole basis for the fear that moved the majority. The reference to the forty-ninth parallel as a boundary in the West was not utterly wild. By the treaty of 1783, Britain had formally renounced the territory south of a line due west from the northwest corner of the Lake of the Woods and Mitchell's map, which was used by the authors of that treaty, correctly showed the forty-ninth parallel running through the bottom of that lake.

There would of course have been no objection to Article V if the convention had been completed in London in sufficient time for consideration by the Senate before March 3, 1803. For that delay the unpreparedness and the preoccupations of the British ministry were responsible. They were also responsible for the later delay which put the signature of the convention after that of the treaty, and it was the priority of the latter which caused the objection. This causal relationship deserves emphasis, for there is a temptation to reverse it and a reversal confuses the whole issue. The temptation is to imagine that the opponents of ratification, seeking a justification for breaking faith with Britain, found it in the priority of the French treaty. The real point is suggested in the attempt of John Quincy Adams to remove the objection. He had Madison apply

18. *A.S.P.F.R.*, III, 90.
19. Pickering's lament over the rejection of the fifth article does not mention this strange version of the past, but refers to the northern boundary of Louisiana as "not having been explicitly defined." King, IV, 363.

to King, now back in the United States, for information which might
make ratification possible. His committee wanted to know if the troublesome article "was concluded with any reference whatever" to the treaty
signed in Paris. King's reply, that the final draft of the convention was
made a month before it was signed, and was signed three days before he
heard that the other negotiation had been concluded,[20] satisfied some
senators that it would be safe to accept the fifth article. If only the convention had been signed before April 30, it could not have given away
what the United States had not yet got. That would then be secure. But
the convention was signed afterwards and therefore, even though it was
framed with no such intention, it might transfer to Britain some American rights that had just been gained from France. The fate of the fifth
article hung in the balance until February 8, 1804. Then the Senate by a
vote of 22 to 9 rejected a motion to advise its ratification and immediately, with the reservation of this article, passed the convention unanimously.

The division on this article is interesting. The New England senators,
with the exception of the two from Rhode Island, were solidly in favor of
unqualified acceptance of the convention. In a letter written three weeks
later, Pickering referred to the majority as Jefferson's "*magnanimous*[21]
partisans," and reported that some of them had since "openly avowed
the propriety of pushing G. Britain *now*[21] on any points we desire to
gain; because her present critical situation will dispose her to yield (as
they imagine) what in a time of peace she might refuse!"[22] But the
minority, who argued in favor of keeping faith with Britain, had no
monopoly of virtue. They were afraid that an American rejection of the
fifth article would precipitate a British rejection of the other articles, and
in these they were particularly interested. They were careless of American claims to the forty-ninth parallel away off in the west.[23] Indeed they
resented the whole Louisiana Purchase as tending to reduce their
"proper" influence in the Union by adding to the strength of the slave-
owning South. In this very spring, the bitterness of their feeling betrayed a number of New Englanders into indulging in quiet secessionist
talk.

American scruples were not alone to blame for the failure of the convention of 1803. They merely eliminated the fifth article. The other

20. *A.S.P.F.R.*, II, 590–591.
21. Italics in original.
22. King, IV, 363.
23. Pickering wrote to King on March 3: "Mr. Jefferson is not contented with the immense
extent of Louisiana as held by the French; . . . he wants to carry it to the parallel of the 49°
of North Latitude. To effect this end, he certainly supposes the suppression of the 5th Article
will contribute. For this object your *entirely satisfactory* convention is put in jeopardy." *Ibid.*

articles, comprising the main body of the agreement, were killed by the British government, which absolutely refused to ratify the mutilated convention. The reason for this refusal is obscure. It may have been only pique at the American government for first extracting consent to the fifth article and then striking it out. But it is just as reasonable to ask why the British would not welcome the removal of an article to which they had objected; and this question suggests that cold calculation rather than warm resentment inspired the refusal. The British ministers may have suspected that the American senators were right in refusing to ratify this article.

What were the results of the rejection of this convention? The acceptance of the line to the Mississippi might have given Canada a territorial access to the source of that river;[24] but of this we cannot be certain, for the American government might still have pressed to a successful conclusion the claim to the forty-ninth parallel. Though it was not finally conceded until 1818, the British government admitted it as early as 1807. The postponement caused little trouble. In the east, the division of the islands in Passamaquoddy Bay and the right of navigation were ultimately the same as what was agreed upon in 1803. The delay contributed some friction and possibly gave Grand Manan Island to New Brunswick. Much more serious was the failure to establish the line along the highlands to a point due north of the source of the St. Croix. It is impossible to tell how the boundary settlement of 1842 differs from what would have been adopted by the joint commission under the instrument of 1803; but the lapse of time allowed an international sore to open and fester, generating a poison that even yet has not died away. Here is the real tragedy of what happened to the hopeful convention of 1803.

THE convention of 1807, though of greater scope, is of lesser importance because it had no chance of life. It was never signed; nor, indeed, was it reduced to a form which the negotiators on both sides were prepared to accept. It reached the stage of being "nearly digested,"[25] to quote the words of the American commissioners who were engaged upon it; and then it was dropped. Yet it cannot be ignored in this study of Canadian-American relations, for it throws much interesting light upon the development of these relations.

The nearly completed convention was intended to be a supplement of a

24. Canadians who may regret the failure of the British government to secure a more southerly boundary in the west should study subsequent North American history, when the advancing tide of American settlement determined American territorial claims. If the British government had succeeded in getting more territory earlier, there might have been much less for the Dominion of Canada to get later.

25. *A.S.P.F.R.*, III, 160.

supplement to Jay's Treaty. The treaty of 1794, it will be remembered, was divided into two parts: one permanent and one temporary, the former including all the articles immediately concerned with British North America, and the latter containing the regulations for commerce and navigation between the United States and other parts of the British Empire, and provisions for the capture or detention of neutral vessels, and for contraband, blockade, privateers, pirates, and extradition. The temporary part of the treaty expired in the fall of 1803.[26] For various reasons which need not be examined here, the negotiation of a new treaty to settle all outstanding differences between the two countries was delayed until 1806. In London on the last day of that year the new treaty was signed by the plenipotentiaries, James Monroe and William Pinkney for the United States, and Lord Holland and Lord Auckland for Britain. Then almost immediately they plunged into the business of preparing this supplementary convention dealing with purely North American affairs, which they had left out of the general treaty.

Over boundaries the negotiators had little difficulty in reaching an agreement. They simply adopted the convention of 1803 with two amendments, one of which was a mere matter of form. Instead of running the line around the northeast corner of Campobello and then excepting that island from American jurisdiction, they chose the simpler and more intelligible method of accomplishing the same end by carrying the division down the west side of Campobello and then securing to the United States the use of the desired navigation channel through British waters. Grand Manan Island, hitherto neglected in discussions between the two governments, momentarily entered the picture, being drawn in by the Americans, who claimed it as lying within the treaty lines and not having been part of Nova Scotia prior to the peace. The British countered with an assertion that it had belonged to Nova Scotia, and they quickly pushed it out of the picture. They were so positive about the validity of their title, or perhaps so dubious, that they flatly rejected an American suggestion to have the question settled by adjudication.[27]

The second amendment of the defunct convention bears out the suggestion implied above,[28] that the British government might better have bowed to the will of the American Senate in 1804. The old unbending ministry was gone, and its successor seized the occasion to settle what would have been left unsettled by an acceptance of the deletion of the

26. Instead of continuing in force for twelve years, as contemplated, it expired at the end of nine, because Britain made peace with France in 1801 and did not make with the United States the new arrangement referred to in Article XII. See *supra*, p. 153n.

27. *A.S.P.F.R.*, III, 162–164.

28. *Supra*, p. 197.

fifth article. The British commissioners proposed a due-west line along the forty-ninth parallel from the Lake of the Woods, but yielded to American insistence upon a slight change at the eastern end of this boundary. There it was to follow a north-and-south line to the northwest corner of the Lake of the Woods, thus creating the curious "northwest angle" on the top of Minnesota. There was complete agreement upon a stipulation that nothing in this new article should be construed as applying to the northwest coast of the continent or to any territories possessed or claimed by either party west of the Rocky Mountains; but there was a difference over the definition of how far the boundary should run in this direction. An explicit statement that it should reach the mountains, the British were not prepared to admit and the Americans were not ready to demand. The former proposed to carry it "as far as the territories of the United States extend in that quarter"; the latter objected to this phrase, fearing that it might hold the door open for Britain to claim, by occupancy or conquest or a future bargain with Spain, some country south of the forty-ninth parallel. When the Americans demanded the elimination of this qualification, the British offered to substitute the words, "as far as their said respective territories extend in that quarter." To this reciprocal formula, the British urged, there could be no objection. It was neither accepted nor rejected when the negotiation ended.

There was only one other unresolved difficulty pertaining to boundaries. Holland and Auckland proposed a sixth article to allow British subjects with British goods free access by land or inland navigation to the Mississippi "in order to enjoy the benefit of the navigation of that river," as secured to them by the treaties of 1783 and 1794. Monroe and Pinkney were apparently inclined to allow this addition if it could be amended to exclude "waters flowing into the Mississippi from the westward,"[29] the significance of which phrase will appear presently.

The other articles which were to have been in this convention concerned intercourse between the United States and British North America. Friction had developed over the interpretation of the freedom of movement guaranteed by Jay's Treaty. Though legally reciprocal, this freedom was practically one-sided, not as the result of accident but out of deliberate design. It will be remembered that this condition was anticipated from the first discussions of reciprocity during the negotiations for peace in 1782 until it became the price promised for the evacuation of the western posts. This was really an international servitude imposed upon the United States, and it was legally permanent. Very naturally it grew more irksome as the years passed. It is not surprising, therefore, that the American government sought, by a strict interpretation of the treaty, to

29. *A.S.P.F.R.*, III, 162–165.

confine this right to the narrowest possible limits, and wished, by negotiation, to get rid of it entirely.

British traders felt the first American pinch at the opening of the new
century. On the Grand Portage route to the Northwest they ran into the
claim of the United States that they should pay customs duties. Of course
they would have had to pay if they had been going to trade in the Republic; but they were simply passing through American territory to reach
British territory beyond, and Jay's Treaty exempted goods which were
"carried over any of the portages or carrying places on either side" of the
line. The Canadians naturally resisted this new interference with their
old trade; but the Americans insisted, for their government had found
a hole in the treaty. If the pertinent clause gave exemption from customs
along this route, the portages and waterways of which continued for
many miles through wholly American territory, it might be stretched to
cover goods passing almost anywhere through the United States, which
was certainly not intended. By inference, therefore, the exemption applied only to land transits along boundary waters where their navigation
was interrupted. To forestall a probable British protest against an
American violation of the treaty, Madison wrote to Rufus King on July
20, 1802, to lodge an American protest against the pretensions of British
subjects to transport merchandise free of duty over certain rivers and
tracts of country in the northwestern parts of the United States. This
letter, which explained the strict American interpretation of the exempting clause, was received by Gore who, in Rufus King's absence, sent
Hawkesbury a note on September 22 presenting the American case.
Shortly afterwards the two men had a conference on the subject, and the
American reported that the Englishman acceded to this construction of
the loosely worded article.[30] Meanwhile the leaders of the Montreal fur
trade, foreseeing the necessity of abandoning this American route for a
British one, prepared to desert Grand Portage. In 1803, at considerable
expense, the North West Company shifted its headquarters to a new
post, soon to be named Fort William, at the mouth of the Kaministiquia;
and in the following year its vigorous but short-lived rival, the X Y
Company, made the same move.

Another matter of difference which, at Madison's request, Gore raised
in the above note was more important in principle than in practice. It had
to do with inland navigation, which the American government desired to
be as free as possible from national restriction. In its last session Congress had passed an act exempting from tonnage duties all vessels,
British or American, of not more than fifty tons burthen trading from
ports on the northern and northwestern boundaries of the United States

30. *Ibid.*, II, 588.

to Upper and Lower Canada. These American vessels, however, had to pay six cents a ton in Canadian ports. Madison requested an equalization, suggesting that it be accomplished by abolishing the duty rather than by imposing it on British craft. Hawkesbury admitted to Gore that the request certainly merited, and promised that it should receive, "all due consideration."[31]

Much more serious was a conflict over the interpretation of Jay's Treaty arising out of the Louisiana Purchase. General James Wilkinson started it. He was the first governor of the northern portion of the new American empire, and one of his first public acts was to issue a proclamation on August 26, 1805, excluding all but American citizens from the fur trade on the Missouri. In the autumn the news burst like a bombshell among the merchants of Montreal. At their behest the governor in Quebec wrote to Anthony Merry, the British minister in Washington, but he could do nothing. The American government upheld Wilkinson. The question was then discussed in London during the negotiation of the supplementary treaty signed on December 31, 1806. Monroe and Pinkney sought to include provision for a new regulation of commerce between the United States and the adjoining British colonies, but Holland and Auckland absolutely refused to consider it because of the exclusion of British traders from Louisiana.[32]

The British contention, as set forth by the commissioners in a written statement of several grievances of the Canadian merchants, was that this was a clear violation of the third article of Jay's Treaty. That article guaranteed the reciprocal right to engage in the fur trade in "the respective territories and countries of the two parties, on the continent of North America," with the single exception of the Hudson's Bay Company's domain. There was not a word about excluding territory that either power might acquire on this continent. The Americans would not deny that Louisiana was now a "territory" of the United States "on the continent of North America." Therefore the purchase of 1803 had automatically extended the scope of the guarantee of 1794 on the American side. But even if there had been a provision to confine the application of this article to the limits of 1794, still the Canadian merchants would have had a grievance, for by prescription they had prior rights in the country just taken over by the United States. They insisted that they were not seeking to gain something new, but to preserve something that was old. For years they had pushed their commerce in Louisiana without any interruption from the Spaniards, and in this traffic they had been

31. *Ibid.*
32. *Ibid.*, III, 147.

selling goods to the value of forty or fifty thousand pounds annually.[33]

The American contention was that the treaty did not apply to Louisiana because the article in question said nothing about future additions of territory. The argument was weak but the determination to uphold it was strong. Indeed it seems quite probable that a consciousness of this weakness intensified the natural American desire to exclude the British traders even from the territory to which they were admitted by the treaty of 1794.

This desire to escape from an international servitude found formal expression in a dispatch sent by Madison to Monroe and Pinkney on May 30, 1806. "This article," said the Secretary of State, referring to Article III of Jay's Treaty, "is found in its operation to be very seriously detrimental to the United States." It allowed British traders to gain an influence over American Indians which alienated them from the United States, and defeated the American government's efforts "to abolish the savage manners of those tribes." The mixture of British with American traders produced "collisions and heart-burnings, with mutual efforts to make the Indians their partisans," and the animosity against American traders tended to be animosity against their country. "These evils are not even attended with any real reciprocity of advantage to American traders" because they did not dare enter British territory, so great was the power of the North West Company over the natives there; and what made the situation worse was "the unlimited duration of the stipulation." Therefore, he said, it was the President's wish that they should urge a revision of the treaty which would allow the two governments "to confine the Indian trade within their respective limits to their own traders." To persuade the government in London, the American commissioners could point out "the valuable effect of cutting off forever one source of jealousy and ill-will," and how little the British would sacrifice. "The stipulated privilege does not extend to Louisiana, but is limited by the treaty to the small tribes eastward of the Mississippi, and by circumstances still further limited to those north-west of the Ohio." Echoing Shelburne's reasoning of years before, Madison observed that "the goods furnished will be of British manufacture" and the furs gathered would be freely exported to Britain, and from these conditions he concluded that it mattered little "whether this scanty portion of the Indian trade be carried on by American or British traders." He hoped that the British government, "in a moment of liberality and of general adjustment," would listen to his arguments and agree to the change;[34] but he was sadly mistaken.

33. *Ibid.*, pp. 152–153.
34. *Ibid.*, p. 126.

The American commissioners, far from being able to persuade the British to forgo the smaller right, were themselves persuaded that they would have to admit the larger right. This appears in their letter of January 3, 1807, when, having just completed the treaty, they were about to negotiate the convention on boundaries and commercial regulations in North America. They would see to it, they assured Madison, that the conditions on which British fur traders would be admitted to Louisiana would "render it impossible for them to do any injury." In any event the commercial articles would run for only ten years, and by then the American occupation of Louisiana would have so far advanced "as to supersede the necessity" of a renewal.[35] During the negotiations, however, they obeyed their instructions by fighting with all the arguments they could muster against the British demand for the opening of the country west of the Mississippi. But they could not shake the British conviction that their government was violating Jay's Treaty in this particular, and they reported home that they had abundant reason to apprehend that a continued rejection of the British demand "would be considered here as an unfriendly act, without adequate motive."[36] To satisfy the Americans, the British commissioners made two concessions in the article which they drafted to ensure their interpretation of the third article of Jay's Treaty. One opened the Hudson's Bay Company's preserve, except "the actual settlements" of the company and the immediate neighborhood of those settlements. The other, which was more important, provided for the expiration of this article after ten years.[37] Here was a suggestion, which will become clearer when we examine the other details of this seventh article of the new convention, that at the end of a decade the American government might make a long move toward getting rid of the objectionable article in the treaty of 1794.

Another Canadian grievance which this seventh article was designed to remove had to do with the execution of another clause of the third article of Jay's Treaty. It was that which bound each country to levy on goods carried across the border no higher duties than its own nationals would have to pay on importing the same goods directly from Europe. There was nothing ambiguous about the wording of this provision, so that there should have been no trouble over its execution. But customs officials are proverbially arbitrary, and those of the United States at this time were no exception. Inspired by the current American anxiety to curtail the freedom of British subjects to trade in the United States, they played a rather sharp trick. It was then the rule at the Atlantic ports of

35. *Ibid.*, p. 147.
36. *Ibid.*, p. 163.
37. *Ibid.*, p. 165.

the country to add one-tenth to the prime cost in Europe before estimating the duty, and there would have been no complaint had they done the same at the inland ports. There, however, they added one-third, that being the advance of value commonly recognized in Montreal. Thus they did what Congress could not do: they gave American merchants a tariff protection against Canadian merchants interested in the Indian trade. Early in 1806, Anthony Merry lodged a protest in Washington against this violation of the treaty; and later in the same year Holland and Auckland repeated it with circumstantial detail in their written statement on Canadian grievances mentioned above.[38] The American commissioners had no real defense for what, in their report home, they called a "doubtful practice";[39] and when the time came they seem to have readily acquiesced in a new statement that would prohibit it.

This seventh article also amplified the third article of Jay's Treaty to remedy what the British commissioners termed "minor grievances" in the written statement they submitted in 1806. Complaints had come from Canada that British subjects going to trade in the United States had to pay six dollars for a license and were "often compelled to dismiss their canoe men, and to hire others at a great expense and inconvenience." The corrective clause forbade the exaction of any toll, by way of licenses or passes, for traders of either power, or their employees, or their canoes. If licenses were to be required for administrative purposes, they were to be withheld only from those who had committed some offense or were guilty of some impropriety. Yet another clause prohibited national discrimination in the application of "restrictions or limitations" upon traders. This was to prevent another annoyance of which the Canadians had complained. It was the stoppage of Canadian bateaux at Michilimackinac by American revenue officers in an attempt to enforce on inland waters "regulations with regard to the approach to shores and ports" which were suitable only to ocean ports. It is interesting to observe that the convention contained no clause against the collection of customs duties at American portages, which had driven the Montreal traders from the Grand Portage route, though this was one of the "minor grievances" in the statement of Holland and Auckland.

More interesting, and much more important, is a generalization that may be drawn from all this discussion of what proved to be only a vain effort to give a more definite meaning to Article III of Jay's Treaty. What hits the eye is this: the limitation upon American sovereignty, though originally American in suggestion and the price promised for the emancipation of American soil from foreign occupation, was becoming

38. *Supra*, p. 201.
39. *A.S.P.F.R.*, III, 163.

more and more impossible; the British garrisons were gone but their ghost remained, and as long as it remained there was bound to be trouble. It too would have to go. Here is a nice illustration of the necessity for treaty revision to preserve international harmony.

Another light which this abortive negotiation of 1807 sheds is upon the relation between the United States and the adjoining Maritime Provinces. Although these neighbors were supposed to be completely severed by the closing in of the Old Colonial System, we have seen that they were not. In his instructions to Monroe and Pinkney dated May 17, 1806, Madison described the trade in two articles that had sprung up between the neighbors. Fish were going in provincial craft from Halifax to Boston, and thence in American bottoms to the West Indies; and plaster, or gypsum, from the Bay of Fundy was similarly delivered in Maine, whence it was distributed by American carriers down the Atlantic coast.[40] The American Secretary of State was not concerned with what was smuggled back to the Maritime Provinces in return for these cargoes. His interest was to put this precarious traffic on a secure basis, and to enlarge it. A strong jealousy between the shipping interests of New England on the one hand and of the colonies on the other threatened to destroy the trade. Massachusetts had clapped a lighthouse-money tax on provincial vessels, and had also placed a high duty on fish while canceling the drawback on reëxport. In the Maritime Provinces there was a retaliatory movement to prohibit the shipment of plaster to the United States, where it was of great importance to agriculture. Madison was particularly worried by the possible loss of this supply, which he estimated could not be less than thirty thousand tons and was perhaps fifty thousand. He cautioned his agents in London not to forget that the American commerce with New Brunswick and Nova Scotia was "more beneficial to the United States than to those colonies." He did not think it probable that London would be disposed to open the ports of the Maritime Provinces to American vessels, nor could he suggest any way to quiet the apprehension of Britain "that to open the trade to our vessels would destroy their own." Nevertheless he wished the commissioners to do their best to gain reciprocity with the Maritime Provinces, at least in domestic products.[41] Thus did the American government, while repelling British American trade with the left hand, reach out for it with the right hand.

40. Therefore his remark: "Notwithstanding our exclusion from their ports, we have in fact, as the trade has hitherto been carried on, a greater share of it than themselves." For this traffic, see G. S. Graham, "The Gypsum Trade of the Maritime Provinces," *Agricultural History*, XII, 209–223 (July, 1938).

41. *A.S.P.F.R.*, III, 123–124.

As was anticipated, the British commissioners pleaded the strong national prejudice against anything that would strike at the semisacred Colonial System. Yet the American commissioners gained more than their chief apparently expected. The eighth article of the convention, which like the seventh was to hold for ten years, provided for the present legalization of an exchange by sea "of gypsum, grindstones, and certain other articles of the produce of His Majesty's colonies in North America, and of British manufactures, and British West India produce, to be exported from the said colonies, in return for horses, cattle, grain, provisions, slaves, pitch, tar, turpentine, and certain other articles, the produce of the United States" in the vessels of either party.[42]

The British were certainly in an accommodating mood when dealing with the relations between the United States and the North American colonies. If only the times had been more propitious, this nearly completed convention might have been wholly completed and the result would have been wholly good. But a great war was then raging in Europe, bringing to a head an old quarrel between Britain and the United States. The inevitable failure of Monroe and Pinkney to force Britain to renounce the impressment of seamen from ships flying the Stars and Stripes let loose an American storm that blew away their treaty and their convention.

42. *Ibid.*, p. 165.

CHAPTER XI

THE WAR OF 1812: AN ANALYSIS OF ISSUES

IN 1812 the United States made war on Canada, having declared it on Britain, for Canada was the only part of the British Empire vulnerable to American attack. This statement may seem open to challenge for ignoring a recent tendency to regard the declaration against Britain as an excuse for the attack against Canada; but, as will be explained, further examination makes the traditional view appear sounder than the revision.

As Canada was caught between the United States and Britain, so was the United States caught between Britain and France. These two powers were the principals in the mightiest war the modern world had yet seen, and the United States was the greatest neutral. What happened seems almost, if not quite, inevitable. The remarkable thing is that it was delayed so long. Of the two periods into which the long war was divided by the short Peace of Amiens, the first passed and the second was nearly over before the United States was drawn in to fight Britain —nineteen years after Republican France had declared war on the island empire.

Why did not the American war come in the first period of the European conflict? As we have already seen, it very nearly did come at the beginning. The blow which Britain dealt at France also hit the United States so hard that it almost knocked the American Republic into the war on the side of the French Republic. The desperate mission of Jay averted the impending catastrophe by the narrowest margin. By reaction, however, it produced another tragedy which, though it drew the United States and Britain closer together for a while, throws an interesting light on the fundamental cause of the ultimate breach between them.

In veering off from war with Britain, the United States ran into war with France. Here was the other tragedy. When Washington sent John Jay to London, he also sent James Monroe to Paris,[1] for American relations with France were likewise strained. France too had hit the United States in an effort to injure Britain by interfering with sea-borne trade. She had done it from the beginning, and in flagrant violation of her treaty of 1778 with the United States. Monroe was to press American claims for damages and to procure the recall of the offending decrees. Because peace with Britain then seemed so precarious, he was also to

1. To replace Gouverneur Morris, who had become *persona non grata* to the Terrorists then ruling France.

cultivate the good humor of France.[2] It might be indispensable. The ardent Republican from Virginia overdid this part of his mission, kissing and hugging the president of the National Convention, and proclaiming to the assembled representatives of France how great was the love his country had for theirs. For such a country represented by such an emissary, the French did what was desired. They altered the decrees, promised observance of their treaty, and undertook to pay compensation for damage done. This sweet harmony between the two republics was no sooner restored than it was destroyed.

The French raged when they heard what Jay had done in London. In the heated atmosphere of Paris, it appeared as the betrayal of France by the United States. Monroe, who had unwittingly given the salute of Judas, saved his face by blowing hot against Britain. But the French did not need his prompting to raise heaven and earth first against ratification in Philadelphia and then for a political overturn in America. Out of exasperation, they renewed and intensified the decrees authorizing their cruisers and privateers to prey on American commerce, and they rudely severed diplomatic relations. What really happened was that France anticipated the modern practice of waging war without declaring it. As French captures of American vessels mounted, the United States was goaded into striking back in self-defense. During this "imperfect" war, which lasted from 1798 to 1801, the American navy was born. More than two score ships of war were equipped in American ports and sent cruising to capture French armed vessels, and about eight times as many private vessels were officially allowed to do the same. Others were permitted to arm to defend themselves, and they generally availed themselves of the privilege.

That neutrality was a counsel of perfection appears clearly in this first period of the great struggle in Europe. Neither Britain nor France would tolerate seeing the United States aiding its enemy by sharing in its trade, for belligerents are no respecters of neutrals, particularly weak ones. Lacking sufficient strength to resist, the United States was bound to be squeezed by both powers when they became locked in their deadly conflict. For two reasons, the international position of the American Republic was then essentially unstable: it was intolerable; and the pressure from both sides could not be equal. Some escape had to be found, and the inequality of pressure made for war with one and an accommodation with the other.

If Jay had failed, his country could hardly have avoided falling into the arms of France and plunging into war with Britain. This was what the Anti-Federalists wanted when they fought to block his mission and

2. *A.S.P.F.R.*, I, 678.

later to reject its fruit. They pinned their faith on the Paris mission of Monroe, one of their leading members, and he was very frank in his correspondence with the Secretary of State. Writing in September, 1795, while still hoping that "the most shameful transaction" would not be ratified, he urged cordial coöperation with France, then "willing to give us the fortune of its arms, in support of our claims against a common enemy." Only by compulsion, he said, would Britain be persuaded to acknowledge the just rights of the United States.

To secure success, by embarking this Government with full zeal in our behalf, and striking terror into England, it will be necessary to lay hold of her property within the United States, take the posts, and even invade Canada. This would not only secure to us completely our claims upon Britain, and especially if we likewise cut up her trade by privateers; but, by making a decisive and powerful diversion in favor of France, promote, and very essentially, a general peace.[3]

Here was the war of 1812, advocated seventeen years earlier by the spokesman of the party which was to bring on that war and the very man who was Secretary of State in 1812.[4]

Jay's Treaty, though barely sufficient to prevent the threatened outbreak of hostilities with Britain, led to hostilities with France; and the growing quarrel between the two republics thrust into the background the serious Anglo-American differences which the maritime war had raised and the treaty had not removed. The Royal Navy did not need to bear so heavily upon American commerce, now that the irate French were driving it away from their shores, and the United States drew even closer to Britain. The mouths of the Republicans were effectively stopped, and the minds of the Federalists began to cherish wild dreams of British sea power's being used in a combined onslaught of Britain and the United States upon the French and Spanish empires in the New World.

The key to the international position of the American Republic was in France. French folly had pushed things to this pass; French wisdom

---

3. *Ibid.*, p. 721.

4. In justice to Monroe's memory, we should here observe that he later changed his opinion. He would have done in 1806 what Jay had done in 1794. He strongly resented his own government's repudiation of the treaty which he and Pinkney concluded in London. In February, 1808, he wrote to Madison, "When I took into view the prosperous and happy condition of the United States, compared with that of other nations; that, as a neutral Power, they were almost the exclusive carriers of the productions of the whole world; and that in commerce they flourished beyond example, notwithstanding the losses which they occasionally suffered, I was strong in the opinion that those blessings ought not to be hazarded in such a question." *Ibid.*, III, 175.

might pull them back. On the receipt of definite suggestions from Paris that a reconciliation was possible, President John Adams sent over a delegation which achieved it in a treaty signed on September 30, 1800. The conclusion of this agreement reversed the direction in which the United States had been traveling. Escaping from the quarrel with France meant getting tangled up once more in the quarrel with Britain over her maritime conduct. Moreover, the wily Bonaparte saw to it that the treaty contained articles postulating maritime principles which were acceptable to the Americans but repugnant to the British. The logical consequence, however, did not follow, because the operation of the new treaty was suspended until after it could do its work. A hitch over the French payment of American claims delayed final ratification until December, 1801, nearly three months after the signature of the pre-liminaries which restored peace between Britain and France. Thus did the first period of the European struggle come to a close just as the United States was headed back toward war with Britain. It was the natural course from which, during the greater part of this period, France had compelled her to retreat.

The second period of the European war, which opened with the rup-ture of the Peace of Amiens in May, 1803, presents a striking parallel. Again the United States found that the equilibrium of neutrality was essentially unstable. Again the pressure from both sides was so intoler-able that she sought an escape by accommodation with either, which of course meant the abandonment of neutrality. This time, however, the United States rejected the treaty negotiated by Monroe and Pinkney which, like Jay's Treaty, might have pushed France against her. This time it was a fight to the finish between the powerful belligerents. Both scorned her potential resistance and resorted to more violent measures, thereby making it more difficult for her to find any basis of accommoda-tion with either. Neither would yield to her demands even to win her alliance, which was offered in the vain hope of playing off one against the other. She had an abundance of provocation for making war on both, but that was utterly impossible. Finally, so it has been said, Napoleon tricked her into declaring it against Britain. But we can see this end coming independently of his deception: for Britain, being in command of the sea, pressed much harder than France upon American neutral rights under international law; and France, having no foothold on the continent of North America, was much less vulnerable.

Before following in detail the evolution just outlined, it may be well to clarify the issues in the quarrel between the United States and Britain arising out of the latter's conflict with France. To accomplish this purpose, it will first be advisable to make some comments upon international law; for the quarrel was embedded in it, each side seeking to uphold its own "rights" under that law.

The nature of international law is perhaps the most important thing of all to remember in this connection. As a human institution, law implies some legislator and some tribunal capable of interpreting it and commanding its enforcement; but the sovereignty of the state has denied these conditions for international law, and therefore many careful authorities have insisted that it is not law at all. Strictly speaking, it has been a body of rules derived from common custom and consent. Private individuals, such as Grotius and Vattel, analyzed and expounded it in scholarly texts which became classics but nothing more. The principles thus set forth, being based on precedents which were by no means uniform, were necessarily very general and always open to conflicting interpretations to cover conflicting interests. Then the only solution was the superior force of one side. The whole structure was made more uncertain still by one principle, that of reprisal, which might undo any other principle, and by the insoluble problem of change. Consent is necessary for change, but consent becomes most impossible when change becomes most imperative—when war reveals new circumstances that undermine and destroy the old law governing the conduct of hostilities.

The relation between the "common law of nations" and specific treaties has also been fruitful of much trouble. Britain maintained that the former allowed her to do to the United States certain things which, under the latter, she could not do to certain European powers. The United States therefore insisted that Britain, by signing the latter, had inferentially abandoned her position under the former. Britain, on the other hand, insisted that she had inferentially strengthened it by concluding these treaties. They regulated only the relations between the signatories. By making an exception to the general rule as it applied among themselves, they confirmed its application elsewhere. The law of the world still governed the relations between Britain and America, and it would continue to do so until they agreed to change it. Finally it should not be forgotten that the law has undergone an evolution, and that the principles recognized at one time do not necessarily apply earlier or even later. The failure to recognize this evolution has often befuddled those who would explain old quarrels.

Impressment was the most baffling issue between the two countries. Though thrust forward by the war, it was not a question of the laws of war which define the balance between belligerent and neutral rights. It concerned something more permanent, more deep-seated—sovereignty. It was raised by the attraction of British seamen to the American service.

They deserted the navy, where life was too much like a floating hell; and they left the British mercantile marine, whence they were liable at any time to be impressed into the navy. There was only one place where they could go, and it was an inviting heaven where they would be at home right away. The merchant marine of the United States was hungry for sailors. Under the stimulus of the war, it was expanding so rapidly that it required four or five thousand additional hands every year. The increased demand tripled American wages afloat. This salvation of the British tar, however, threatened the destruction of Britain by draining the lifeblood of her sea power, the one thing that stood between her and downfall. To check this vital loss, British warships searched American vessels and removed British fugitives.

Necessity overrides law, and Britain was impelled by necessity. But she insisted that her action was not illegal. Though this may seem strange now, it was not then, for important developments in international law and usage have since taken place. One is in our concept of nationality. We have become accustomed to think of people changing their national status almost as readily as they change their shirts. Then nationality was commonly considered to be about as impossible to change as one's skin. It is the phenomenal growth of the United States by immigration that has made the difference, and even yet the new American-born principle has not gained universal acceptance. This principle, however, played no part in the quarrel over impressment. The American government did not pretend to throw the protecting cloak of American naturalization around the bodies of these British fugitives. The quarrel over impressment turned on the right of search for deserters, and on the abuses which inevitably accompanied the practice.

The right of search was the main point in the dispute, and here the clash between the past and the future stands out clearly. The British position rested on the prerogative of sovereignty to pursue fugitive nationals anywhere up to a line where another sovereignty barred the pursuit. The United States claimed no right to protect American vessels from search in British territorial waters; nor, on the other hand, did Britain claim the right of search within territorial waters of the United States. It was a question of jurisdiction on the high seas, over which there was of course no sovereignty, and there the difference was not over the immunity of government vessels. Though the *Chesapeake* incident has at times led people to suppose the contrary, Britain never asserted the right to search units of the United States Navy. What she did assert, and the United States deny, was the right to search private vessels because this involved no invasion of another sovereignty. Both sides were right, Britain by the old usage, and the United States by a new doctrine then only beginning to take shape: that a country's ships at sea are detached portions of its soil and therefore covered by its sovereignty. Though already admitted for public vessels, it was not yet really established for private ones. Even today this sovereignty is not as complete as that which exists on land or within the limits of territorial waters, and the United States admitted qualification then. The American government recognized, for example, the British right to stop and search private American ships for contraband in time of war.

It was the abuses which accompanied the practice of searching for deserters that inflamed the quarrel, and these abuses occurred on both sides. The British never claimed the right to impress American seamen, but they did impress them as British subjects. It was often impossible to tell the difference between the American and the British members of a crew, for there was no national distinction of language, physical appearance, dress, or manners. British deserters sailing under the Stars and Stripes would insist that they belonged to that flag; and the officers under whom they were serving, loath to lose valuable hands, would support their contention. A boarding officer in search of men whom he badly needed was judge in his own cause, and there was no real check upon his arbitrary decisions. No officer who seized goods as contraband could touch his share of the prize until it was brought into port and there condemned after a legal trial of the seizure, but there was no such procedure to protect human beings seized on the wide ocean. The only way to rescue an American thus carried off was to prove to the Admiralty that he was an American, and then an order for his release would be issued; but this was a difficult business and painfully slow. Early in the first period of the war the American government thought to check the abuse by what were known as "protections." These were certificates of American citizenship issued by magistrates at home and consuls abroad. But the granting of these papers was not hedged about by proper restrictions.[5] It was all too easy for a British tar to get one. They were often given out indiscriminately; sailors lost them and sold them; they were cheap. So notorious did the traffic become that the device made things worse instead of better. British officers naturally came to have nothing but scorn for these official documents of the United States. As the years passed, the number of kidnaped Americans serving in the Royal Navy mounted until it was several thousand. This right of search and practice of impressment was the British counterpart of the unre-

5. Grenville pointed this out in the spring of 1797, when he rejected an American proposal for a settlement of the impressment issue. According to the American proposal, British naval officers were to be instructed to respect the certificates. See Grenville's rather searching letter to Rufus King on March 27, 1797. *Ibid.*, II, 148–150.

stricted submarine campaign conducted by Germany a century later, for it touched American lives, and lives are more precious than goods.

Interference with American trade, the other great issue which the French war raised between the United States and Britain, was a complicated question. Though some references have previously been made to this problem, a fuller analysis is necessary here. The trouble springs from the very nature of war. It is a triangular affair. In addition to the clash of arms between belligerents, it precipitates a clash of interest between belligerent and neutral over intercourse with the enemy. The one would like to stop it completely and the other to continue it without any interruption. Long experience has tended to work out a rough compromise between them, for both have felt the restraint of prudence, the belligerent fearing to push the neutral to the point of open hostility, and the neutral shrinking from resistance that would mean fighting. Hence it came to be generally recognized that a belligerent could seize and condemn as legal prize any neutral vessel and cargo containing contraband being sent to the enemy country; and also, under the same penalty, could prohibit any neutral vessel, no matter what her cargo, from entering or leaving a blockaded port of the enemy.

All governments admitted that arms and accouterments of war constituted contraband, but there was no common agreement upon the further definition of the term. The textbook writers offered confusing advice. From the conflicting precedents which they recorded, they could deduce only the general principle that other things which might be used by the fighting forces could be treated as contraband when particular circumstances warranted such procedure. A few treaties gave greater precision to the meaning of the word; but there was conflict between them, and each had only a limited application. Thus the original clash of interest survived. Belligerents sought to expand the definition of the term, and neutrals to contract it. Both dressed up selfish interests as legal rights, and the decision between them was left as before to force tempered by prudence. Because the British soon chased the French from the sea, it was the interest of the latter to uphold the narrowest neutral view, and of the former to maintain the opposite, so that over this question the United States became embroiled with Britain and not with France. As we have already seen, however, prudential considerations moved Britain to qualify her seizure of provisions as contraband by purchasing them and paying demurrage. But this was only a mitigation of a principle which Americans regarded as evil; and when France and the United States made up their quarrel in 1800, Bonaparte apparently tried to revive the Anglo-American quarrel over the principle by inserting in his treaty with the United States a definition of contraband as warlike material only.

More exasperating difficulties grew out of the application of the other principle mentioned above. When was a blockade not a blockade? It was commonly conceded that a blockade had to be officially declared and had to be effective, but there was absolutely no consensus of opinion on what was "effective." Here treaties and classical authorities were of much less assistance than in the definition of contraband. Here Nature intervened to render impossible the formulation of any but a very general rule when it was at last adopted by the principal powers, with the exception of the United States, in the Declaration of Paris in 1856. So variable was the combination of such essential conditions as channels, currents, coasts, and weather, that each application of a blockade was a special problem. Here also Bonaparte tried to feed the starved Anglo-American quarrel by inserting into his treaty of 1800 a narrow definition of blockade. As long as the problem of blockade was confined to single ports, it was relatively simple; but, as will be noticed presently, that limitation soon disappeared in the titanic struggle between Britain and the Napoleonic Empire, and it has never returned.

From the ancient and undoubted right of a belligerent to capture private ships and goods of the enemy at sea, sprang other issues between the United States and Britain. One was the principle of "free ships, free goods," which would limit this right by giving immunity to enemy goods, other than contraband, on board neutral vessels. The limitation was so severe that, if enforced, it would have largely destroyed the value of the right, for an enemy could then trade with impunity under the protection of neutral flags. It was a doctrine made by neutrals in the interest of neutrals, to whom it would hand over the carrying trade of belligerents. Its advocates gave it a specious appearance of justice by coupling it with the converse, "enemy ships, enemy goods," which would likewise benefit neutrals by discouraging neutral use of belligerent bottoms. Free ships, free goods, was another of the principles laid down in the Declaration of Paris in 1856. At the time of the French Revolutionary wars, it was a subject of rather violent disagreement. It was already well on the way to establishment, for it had been written into a number of specific treaties. Even Britain had signed an odd treaty embodying it, but she had never admitted its general application, and she could not do so then without playing into the hands of France. For this very reason, France had lined up with the neutral powers; and she tried to use them, particularly her American protégé and ally, in forcing it upon Britain. It was the official doctrine of the United States government, but opinion in the country was far from being unanimous in support of it. When Jefferson was Secretary of State, he wrote to Genet: "It cannot be doubted, but that, by the general law of nations, the goods of a friend found in the vessel of an enemy are free, and the goods of an enemy found in the vessel of a friend are lawful prize."[6] Jay's failure to insert the principle in his treaty was to the French a violation of their treaty with the United States signed in 1778, and therefore one of the grounds of the subsequent Franco-American breach. In repairing this, Bonaparte revived the subtle French game. One of the maritime principles which he put into his treaty of September, 1800, with the United States was "free ships, free goods."

Of more serious consequence was the disputed right of neutrals in time of war to enter a trade that was shut to them in time of peace. This likewise threatened to destroy the value of the belligerent right to capture enemy property at sea. No compromise principle of any kind had arisen to regulate this issue. It involved two important branches of trade—coasting and colonial. Both were almost universally preserved as strict national monopolies in the period with which we are concerned. If a belligerent, exercising the clear right of capturing enemy ships and cargoes, could drive the enemy from the sea, the enemy would naturally seek relief by temporarily opening its monopoly to neutrals. If they took advantage of this indulgence they would certainly be bringing succor to the distressed enemy. Could neutrals do it and yet remain neutrals?

It was the colonial side of the question which first thrust itself forward, and therefore the first to get any answer. That was in the Seven Years' War, during which the British Empire devoured most of the French Empire overseas. Hard pressed by British maritime superiority, France was unable to supply her West Indies or to bring their produce to Europe under her own flag; and therefore she resorted to the expedient of relaxing her colonial monopoly in favor of neutrals. To counter this novel action, the British prize courts promulgated the novel doctrine which came to be known as "the Rule of the War of 1756," and later simply "the Rule of 1756," to which reference has already been made in a previous chapter. It was naturally a categorical negative to the question just stated. Made in Britain to support the interest of Britain, it was another illustration of law being the declared will of superior force. But there was justice in the contention that a trade prohibited by municipal law during peace should be prohibited by international law during war. It deprived neutrals of no right which they enjoyed prior to the outbreak of war, and it was necessary to preserve the value of an unquestioned belligerent right. It was a new rule called forth by new conditions, and it was promulgated in the only way possible. Yet, however just it might be, it ran counter to the interests of neutrals and of belligerents that

6. *Ibid.*, I, 266.

suffered from naval impotence; and they would not recognize the validity of this fiat of a single power.

The first American collision with this rule, as we have already seen,[7] nearly precipitated the United States into a declaration of war in the spring of 1794. Indeed Britain had overstepped her own mark by ordering the indiscriminate capture of American vessels trafficking in the French West Indies, for a limited trade in American vessels of small burthen[8] had been legalized before the war; and she drew back just in time. She then contented herself with only a partial application of the rule, ordering the capture of vessels laden in the French West Indies with produce of those islands and sailing thence for Europe.[9] The fruits of the naval superiority of the belligerent were being shared with a neutral.

The nature of this compromise is worth noting. It was confined to a single neutral, the United States, and it was wholly practical. Britain did not renounce any part of her full right under the Rule of 1756. What she did was done voluntarily, under no pressure from America, for the restrained practice was inaugurated long before people in the United States knew that the unrestrained practice had begun. When Jay went to London he found it impossible to extract a renunciation of the principle, as desired by his government. So intent were the British on retaining it that they persuaded him to accept a provision which, without formally according any recognition of the principle, would throw a legal cloak over the practical compromise until two years after the war ended. This was the price exacted for the opening of the much coveted British West Indian trade to American shipping during the same period. The bargain was made in Article XII of the treaty, which bound the American government to make it illegal for American bottoms to carry molasses, sugar, coffee, cocoa, or cotton anywhere except to the United States. These, of course, were the staples of the island colonies; and the object of this provision was to limit American intercourse with the West Indies, both British and French, to a direct trade. American ships were to be forbidden to supply Europe with any such produce even if it had first been landed in the United States. This article would have given an American guarantee, not only to the British

7. *Supra*, p. 141.

8. Limited to sixty tons in order to exclude vessels that might sail direct to Europe. In addition to this regulation, some ports had been opened before the war by Revolutionary assemblies and governors in the French West Indies. James Stephen, *War in Disguise*, 3d ed. (London 1806), p. 30.

9. These were not the only American vessels engaged in the West Indian trade that were liable to seizure under this order-in-council of Jan. 8, 1794. Any carrying contraband, or enemy goods, or trying to run a blockade were also liable.

monopoly of the transatlantic trade with British colonies, but also to the British prohibition of the same trade with French colonies under the Rule of 1756. The Senate rejected this article because it would outlaw a lawful and profitable American commerce between the French West Indies and France via the United States, recent decisions of British prize courts having legitimized it under the doctrine of the "broken voyage." The Senate's action saved the United States from winking at the Rule of 1756,[10] so that the nature of the compromise remained untouched. It continued to be a matter solely of British grace inspired by prudence.

The liberality of this compromise, and its adoption by unilateral action, may seem to imply a tacit admission on the part of Britain that the principle she had enunciated to meet new conditions in the Seven Years' War did not apply to the yet newer conditions created by American independence, and therefore should not be applied against the United States. The late Admiral Mahan was inclined to draw this deduction,[11] but it is not quite just. This particular British moderation was simply part and parcel of the regular British policy to keep the interference of belligerent rights with neutral rights down to the minimum necessitated by the exigencies of war. In this instance the interference was considerably less than landlubbers might imagine, for the trade winds blew away much of the hardship imposed on American vessels. They did not have to go very far out of their regular course to call at an American port when sailing from the West Indies to Europe. Yet the situation was fraught with danger. In the American treaty of reconciliation with France in 1800, Bonaparte committed the United States to a definition of commercial rights which condemned the British principle without naming it. But he could not rouse the American government over this issue. Only Britain could do that. The danger lay in the nature of the compromise. At any time the British prize courts might shift the basis of their rulings, substituting the "continuous" for the "broken" voyage, and the British government might decide to apply the Rule of 1756 in all its rigor. This decision was never made, but the shift did occur, upsetting the compromise and precipitating trouble.

American action, both public and private, was responsible for destroying the foundation of the British prize-court decisions favorable to the American interest. The doctrine of the broken voyage rested on the assumption that the goods in question were legally imported for use in the United States before they were reëxported. Importation meant the

10. As Bemis has pointed out, the Senate thus unwittingly rescued the export of American cotton from being stifled at birth, Whitney's cotton gin having just been invented. *A Diplomatic History of the United States*, p. 102, n. 3.

11. *Sea Power in Its Relations to the War of* 1812 (Boston, 1905), I, 92.

payment of customs duties, and the performance of such operations as unloading, checking, weighing, and storing, all of which involved time and expense. The corresponding operations attendant upon exportation of course added more to the cost. Here were hardships which the trade winds could not blow away, but American ingenuity might remove.

In 1799, Congress passed an act authorizing drawbacks which reduced to a nominal rate the duties paid on certain articles. These, it was observed, were "the ordinary and peculiar subjects of trade between Europe and the West-India colonies."[12] This piece of legislation, which would go far to mend what had been broken, remained unnoticed in England for some time, probably because the hostile relations then subsisting between the United States and France blocked its effect upon the operation of the Rule of 1756. But it could not escape attention after the rupture of the Peace of Amiens, when its effect was bound to be felt because Franco-American relations were once more friendly. This effect was enhanced by another mending process which, by contrast, was quite illegal and therefore conducted less openly. There was a constant temptation to cut corners with cargoes in port. Why go through all the motions of importing and reëxporting, when the same freight was put back in the same hold? Why should Americans suffer this absurd handicap for the benefit of British competitors? Patriotism pulled with profits, private shippers conspired with public officials, and proper papers covered improper performance. Some vessels even cleared with untouched cargoes. What was pious fraud in American ports became plain fraud under British questioning elsewhere. Thus, by congressional enactment and by official connivance, the Rule of 1756 was circumvented in the United States. But it was impossible to mend the broken voyage without ending it. That this was what Americans were doing, the British began to see when the war with France was resumed in the spring of 1803. Almost immediately the modern doctrine of the continuous voyage raised its head in the British prize courts,[13] though it was not until the spring of 1805 that it was finally established by a judgment on appeal. Its establishment doomed American ships and cargoes to capture and condemnation, thereby ruining a lucrative American trade.

Whether neutrals could engage in the coasting trade of an enemy— the other part of the question which had evoked the Rule of 1756— remained in the background much longer than the problem of colonial trade. Though it had not yet pressed for an answer, Bonaparte's treaty with the United States in 1800 supplied one inferentially. The definition

12. James Stephen, *op. cit.*, p. 223.
13. It had appeared before the Peace of Amiens. See the *Mercury* incident of 1800 in *ibid.*, pp. 52–53.

of commercial rights mentioned above stipulated the freedom of a neutral to navigate between enemy ports. Not until some little time after the renewal of hostilities in 1803 did this issue thrust itself forward,[14] and then it was soon obscured by other issues. As Napoleon's power spread on land and Britain's grew on the sea, he was relieved and she was frustrated by neutrals' taking over the coasting trade of his empire. Sooner or later she was bound to strike at their interference in this new sphere as she had struck at their interference in colonial trade during the Seven Years' War. She held her hand until January, 1807, when, finding a plausible excuse in Napoleon's recent Berlin Decree which was still little more than an empty threat, she outlawed all commerce between ports under his control. Apparently this extension of the Rule of 1756 was directed at northern Europeans, chiefly the Danes, rather than the Americans, but it was plainly recognized that they would feel the blow too. The American government promptly protested that the British action was illegal unless based on "actual blockades," and pointed out that it would ruin a trade which Britain herself recognized as wholly legitimate. The profits of a voyage commonly depended on dropping some cargo here and some there, and on picking up a return cargo in the same way. If an American merchantman had to make the whole exchange in one place, it might as well not go to France at all.[15]

Thus did the issue over the enemy's coasting trade come into the open when the issue over the enemy's colonial trade was finally chased out of its hole by the doctrine of the continuous voyage. Together they were capable of doing great damage to Anglo-American relations, and therefore it is easy to imagine the havoc wrought by the quarrel which soon swallowed them up along with all the other particular issues concerning trade—the quarrel over Napoleon's Berlin and Milan decrees and Britain's equally famous orders-in-council.

To understand these decrees and orders, we should remember that they accompanied the approach of the supreme crisis in the life-and-death struggle between the two powers which were then by far the greatest on earth. Napoleon had come to realize that his position in Europe would never be secure until he subdued Britain, and she that her freedom depended on his downfall. Having had to abandon his projected invasion of the island kingdom because British sea power effectively barred the way, he perforce fell back upon the use of his land power to accomplish by slow strangulation what was impossible by quick assault. Taking advantage of the fact that Britain had stretched her declaration of blockade to

14. In 1805, Stephen said, "As to the coasting trade, the employment of neutral vessels in it, is treated by our prize tribunals as illegal, though the extreme penalty of confiscation has not yet been applied." *Ibid.*, p. 166.

15. *A.S.P.F.R.*, III, 158–159.

cover a considerable length of his northern coast line, he stretched his declaration still farther and justified his action as a proper reprisal. He proclaimed the blockade of the whole of the British Isles.

This was a sort of fantastic and inverted blockade. Napoleon had no navy to enforce it, and his object was not so much to keep goods from reaching Britain as it was to prevent them from leaving. Because of this inversion, however, and also because of the wide extent of his power upon the Continent, he could undertake to enforce the blockade without a navy. This was what he was doing when he ordered the confiscation of all British goods and also, under pain of confiscation, the exclusion of every ship that touched at a British port. By depriving Britain of access to the European market upon which her economic life depended, he calculated that he could soon reduce the nation of traders and manufacturers to cry for mercy. Such, in short, was his Continental System which he began to enforce vigorously in the late summer of 1807.[16] Britain saw that, if he carried it through, she was done. The orders-in-council were her desperate reply. She extended her blockade to every port from which he excluded her ships; and she turned back upon him the provisions of his own decrees, declaring that she would treat as an enemy any ship which, without first going to Britain, sought to enter any port controlled by him.

The position of neutrals became impossible. It would have been much easier for them if they could have chosen to trade either with Britain or with the Napoleonic empire, but this was not the alternative that was forced upon them. The real issue was the Continental System. Would they coöperate with Napoleon in upholding it, or with Britain in undermining it? The question presented a perfect dilemma. A neutral vessel could not approach any European port that was under Napoleon's sway without being liable to seizure, either outside by a ship of the Royal Navy or inside by Napoleon's officials; inside, if it had touched at a British port, or had procured British papers; outside, if it had not. It was a choice between the devil and the deep sea.

Each belligerent was coercing neutrals to serve its own end; and as neutral rights disappeared under the combined pressure, each belligerent defended its departures from the traditional law oɩ nations by accusing the other of prior violations and by blaming neutrals for their non-resistance to these violations. Neutrals, however, could not accept the self-justification of either without shedding their neutrality, nor could they offer resistance to either without running the same risk. Resistance to both was unthinkable. It was then more terribly true than ever that

16. The standard work on this subject is Eli F. Hecksher, *The Continental System* (London, 1922).

law is what those who can and will enforce it say that it is; and that the principle of reprisal, once let loose, may destroy the other principles of the laws of war. Indeed, the "laws of war" is a contradiction in terms.

Both belligerents this time flouted the United States, and both professed eagerness to resume conformity to traditional law; but each insisted that the other should do it first, or that the Americans should resist with force the coercion of the other. Theoretically, the two belligerents were equally oppressive; but practically, legally, and psychologically they were not. Britain's control of the sea, being greater than Napoleon's control of the land, gave her greater power of enforcement. Much more important was the legal difference. Her seizures were made at sea and therefore, according to her own admission, were a violation of neutral rights under international law, her justification being that it was a necessary reprisal against Napoleon. His seizures, except an occasional capture by a fugitive French frigate or privateer at sea, were all made in port and therefore within the undoubted jurisdiction of his own or a subordinate government. Strictly speaking, his only violation of neutral rights under international law was confined to the occasional captures just mentioned. Napoleon also struck a responsive chord in the United States when he denounced the orders-in-council as designed to establish the economic supremacy of England upon the ruins of the industry and commerce of European countries. Here we approach another fundamental factor in the growing Anglo-American bitterness.

Between Britain and the United States there was a mutual suspicion mounting to a settled conviction that each was using the war to cheat the other out of its rights. The British were exasperated by the paradox of their position. Never had they possessed such complete control of the sea, yet more than ever the sea-borne trade of the enemy was escaping from their grasp. As already suggested, neutrals were running off with it and giving it their protection. They were climbing up on the back of the British navy, whose supremacy persuaded the enemy to hand over this trade; and they were throwing dust in the eyes of British judges, causing them to release as neutral what was really enemy property. By such means not only were they expanding their merchant marine while that of Britain shrank;[17] they were actually robbing her of

17. It suffered a serious drain of seamen by impressment into the Royal Navy and by desertion to vessels flying the Stars and Stripes. It was also burdened by higher insurance rates than neutrals had to pay, by the risks of capture which these higher rates reflected, and by the enforced obligation to sail under convoy and to pay for it. From 1792 to 1800, the total tonnage of British vessels entering and clearing from the ports of Great Britain declined from 3,151,389 to 2,825,078, while the corresponding figures for foreign vessels jumped from 479,630 to 1,448,287. David Macpherson, *Annals of Commerce*, IV, 262, 535.

the profitable prizes of war[18] and also of the crowning prize of a victorious end to the war. In other words, their cupidity had leagued them with the enemy and drawn them into an underhand war against Britain. The tricks by which they performed the daily miracle of transforming enemy into neutral commerce were publicly exposed, and a new British policy was demanded, by James Stephen[19] in his *War in Disguise, or the Frauds of the Neutral Flags*, a pamphlet of more than two hundred pages which appeared in the fall of 1805.[20] The author knew whereof he spoke, for he was perhaps the leading practitioner in the prize appeal court and he had earlier followed his profession in the West Indies. He probably shared the responsibility for the adoption of the principle of the continuous voyage, but this did not satisfy him. He was positive that there was only one cure for the evil, and that was a rigorous application of the Rule of 1756. Even if it drove neutrals into open hostilities, that would be preferable to this covert war. Britain would then be free to use her strength to strike down those who were injuring her.

Stephen gave forceful expression to a latent but growing feeling of hostility against neutrals in general and Americans in particular. It was directed against Americans in particular because they were gathering by far the greatest harvest at British expense, their mercantile marine having rapidly become the only great rival of Britain's. The pamphlet was very popular, running through three editions in four months. It undoubtedly had a great effect upon public opinion and may even have had some part, as has been supposed, in suggesting the famous orders-in-council. Be this as it may, the chief significance of Stephen's outburst would appear to have been symptomatic rather than causal. The logic of events was teaching Britain that she could not much longer allow neutrals to reap where she had sown.

As British people believed that Americans were abusing their neutral rights to the vital injury of Britain, so were Americans convinced that Britain was abusing her temporary belligerent rights to serve her permanent economic interests and that in doing so she was furtively dealing a dangerous blow at their country. They saw her trying, under cover of the war, to monopolize the commerce of the world. This may seem absurd when we remember that their mercantile marine had

18. Stephen emphasized their importance in preserving the navy. "As to the common seamen and mariners, the natural motives of dislike to the naval service, are in their breasts far more effectively combatted by the hope of prize money, than by such dazzling, but precarious prospects. They reason, however, and calculate on the chances and the value of success; witness the proverbial remark, that a Spanish war is the best mean of manning our navy." *Op. cit.*, p. 130.

19. Father of Sir James (Mr. Oversecretary) and grandfather of Sir Leslie.

20. On the very day Trafalgar was fought.

enjoyed a phenomenal expansion through the war while hers had suffered a contraction; but we should not overlook some other important considerations. Britain was in a position to do this very thing, international law being what it was and the Royal Navy being virtually supreme upon the sea; and there was no gainsaying the fact that measures which she took to win the war also tended to benefit her own carrying trade and commerce at the expense of others. In the United States this further effect was bound to be regarded as intentional and not just incidental. The adoption of the doctrine of the continuous voyage contained the suggestion that Britain would destroy what she could not appropriate; and the orders-in-council seemed to prove it.

The American reaction appears all the more natural when viewed in the light of the past. Britain had laid herself open to this suspicion by a policy which she, and she alone, had followed for generations. It was the policy of her navigation laws, by which she excluded foreigners from all but a corner of her carrying trade. This application of the monopolistic principle was purposely made to stimulate the growth of the country's merchant marine, and was commonly credited,[21] both at home and abroad, with having made it what it was—the greatest in the world. Another object of the exclusion of foreigners was to deprive them, particularly the Dutch, of their function as middlemen in international trade, and to transfer this function and its profits to England. Not unconsciously had she become the chief storehouse and clearinghouse of the world's commerce, or, to use the language of the day, the great entrepot. She had attained a position where she held the world in fee. It is not surprising, therefore, that non-British eyes saw in the orders-in-council a new and ruthless projection of the old and selfish design. To Americans, of all people, these orders-in-council were particularly offensive. The reason for their peculiar sensitiveness lay in their own history: they were being forced back into the dependence of colonial days. Once more Britain was insisting that they should have no trade of their own, that all their foreign commerce must be under her control. American Independence was at stake!

21. Whether rightly or wrongly makes no difference here.

CHAPTER XII

THE WAR OF 1812: THE EVOLUTION
OF CAUSES, TO 1809

THE Louisiana Purchase may be regarded as the first step, albeit an unconscious one, toward the War of 1812. Though the Peace of Amiens came when the Franco-American treaty of 1800 was heading the United States back toward war with Britain, the rupture of that peace would probably have seen the American Republic moving in the opposite direction if it had not been for the Louisiana Purchase. To prevent France from getting possession of New Orleans, Britain was waiting to grasp it as soon as the European war was resumed; and, far from intending to keep it for herself, she was anticipating its transfer to the United States.[1] It was to her own interest thus to provide a solution of the twenty-year-old American problem of the mouth of the Mississippi; and, had she proceeded to do so, there can be little doubt that the United States would have pulled with Britain against France. Indeed the cabinet in Washington had agreed to seek an actual alliance with Britain if the negotiation in Paris came to nought, and instructions to this effect were on their way across the Atlantic when the bargain was signed.[2]

Paradoxically, it was Britain's ability to control the fate of New Orleans which deprived her of the opportunity to do it. Her overwhelming superiority at sea decided Napoleon to sell what he had not yet got and could not hope to keep, so that he, rather than Britain, appeared as the benefactor of the United States. Moreover, he gave something in addition to what she could have given. He gave the whole of Louisiana, and not just the corner on which American eyes had so long been set. He thereby sowed seeds of Anglo-American discord which at once began to sprout. As we have already observed,[3] the conclusion of the bargain with France immediately upset the earlier-negotiated, but later-signed convention of 1803, spilling its hopes of an amicable settlement of troublesome boundary disputes between the United States and Britain; and the American acquisition of this empire in the West soon produced new friction over the application of Jay's Treaty. Also, as we have seen, it so embittered the strife between the Republicans of the South and the Federalists of New England that many

1. *Supra*, p. 194, n. 16.
2. *A.S.P.F.R.*, II, 555–556.
3. *Supra*, pp. 193–196.

of the latter began to dream and talk of secession from the Union. The split in the nation made the foreign policy of the country an affair of party politics, which is ever liable to be fatal when war is in the air. Finally, the Louisiana Purchase gave new self-confidence to the United States, with the exception of New England, by enlarging the country and increasing its security. The United States was thereby made more independent in attitude toward Britain. This effect became very noticeable in the autumn of 1803, as the news of the purchase spread from Washington;[4] and it led straight to the second step.

The British impressment of sailors from American ships, of so little importance in 1794 that it was completely ignored in the instructions to Jay and in the treaty which bears his name, became a more serious problem long before it was shelved by the cessation of hostilities in 1801.[5] Therefore in the spring of 1803, as soon as the American minister in London judged that the renewal of the European war was unavoidable, he approached the British government to secure if possible some working arrangement to avoid trouble over this question. The minister was Rufus King, who was about to return home. He had several conferences with Lord Hawkesbury, the Foreign Secretary, and with Henry Addington, the Prime Minister. Both avowed a sincere disposition to do everything in their power to prevent a recurrence of the late trouble; but they would conclude nothing without the consent of Lord St. Vincent, the head of the Admiralty, who was much more familiar with the practical details that might be involved. Therefore the retiring minister negotiated with the veteran seaman. On the very day before the former finally left London, they reached an agreement that for five years neither power would allow impressment "upon the high seas and without the jurisdiction of either party." As the Foreign Secretary had promised to sign whatever the admiral accepted, Rufus King drew up the agreement in the form of a convention and sent it to St. Vincent, who had undertaken to forward it to Hawkesbury. During the night, however, the First Lord of the Admiralty sent the American minister a letter saying that the narrow seas should be expressly excepted as "immemorially considered to be within the dominions of Great Britain" and that he had amended the draft accordingly. This stab in the dark[6] killed the negotiation. The American was loath to let it die, but he was helpless. Neither he nor any other citizen of the United States could bind the American

---

4. See Adams, II, 364–388.

5. By this time there were American applications for the release of some two thousand men, of whom more than half were ordered to be discharged. Eight hundred were held for further proof, and a hundred were detained as definitely British subjects. *A.S.P.F.R.*, III, 85.

6. This is what it seems to have been, though Castlereagh later tried to prove that Rufus King's zeal had caused a misunderstanding. *Ibid.*, p. 593.

government to recognize this British mare clausum.[7] The cure was worse than the disease.[8]

The second step toward the War of 1812, probably taken in the belief that it would lead away from war, was the decision of the American government to insist on a settlement of the impressment issue. On October 10, 1803, ten days before the Senate voted for the ratification of the Louisiana Purchase, Madison wrote to Monroe, who had crossed from Paris to fill the post vacated by Rufus King, requiring him to insist on orders being given to all British naval officers to stop the objectionable practice. The American Secretary of State backed his instructions by a warning that incidents were occurring daily and might "provoke the public temper into an irresistible impetus on the public councils."[9] By his own account submitted to the Senate a few weeks later, on December 5, the cases of impressment reported to his office during the year numbered forty-six: Britain had seized forty-three men, France and her allies the other three; twenty-seven of the forty-three were not Americans; twelve of the forty-six were said to have had American papers; and six of these twelve were taken on land under British jurisdiction. These figures are much smaller than those of a few years before;[10] but American opinion was now more sensitive. That was reflected in the debates of Congress, where a bill was introduced to punish violations of the American flag. To prevent unjust suspicion, it may be added that the administration disclaimed responsibility for the legislative proposal.

A more careful approach to the problem of impressment was made at the end of the year. Seeing danger ahead, and believing in preventive measures, President Jefferson set his heart on a convention with Britain to bury the war-born issues which might soon poison Anglo-American relations. Other matters, such as a new commercial treaty to replace the expired articles of Jay's Treaty, could wait for a more auspicious occasion. Monroe was to conduct the negotiations, and on January 5, 1804, Madison sent him a draft of the convention with voluminous comments. "The essential objects," he explained, "are the suppression of impressments, and the definition of blockade. Next to these in importance are the reduction of the list of contraband, and the enlargement of our neutral trade with hostile colonies." There were also some minor points which need not be specified here. The immediate cause of the prominence given to blockade was the British application of that principle to whole islands in the West Indies. It was impressment, however, which

7. The only recognition it still received from other powers was an occasional treaty stipulation that their vessels should pay the compliment of the flag in these waters. *Ibid.*, p. 86.

8. *Ibid.*, II, 501–502.

9. See Madison, VII, 65n.

10. *Supra*, p. 226, n. 5.

occupied the forefront of the projected convention and received most of Madison's attention. Diplomatically expressed in reciprocal terms, the formula manufactured in Washington forbade impressment, not only from American ships on the high seas, where British jurisdiction was challenged, but also of American sailors within British dominions, where there was no question of jurisdiction. Those taken under the latter category, which was added chiefly to protect Americans in England, were forthwith to be released and indemnified. Madison had as much to say about the opening article, which dealt with impressment on the high seas, as he had about all the other dozen articles of the convention. He did his lawyer best to prove that the British government was acting contrary to law and reason, and even to British interests, in taking fugitive sailors from neutral vessels on the high seas; and he tried to provide Monroe with arguments to combat the objections that would be raised in London. He remarked that the number of British seamen in American ships, "though considerable, is probably less than may be supposed." He contemplated little if any difficulty on the score of naturalization, because the law of the United States prescribed "conditions but little likely to be complied with by ordinary seafaring persons." What seems to have troubled him most was the memory of the condition postulated by Lord St. Vincent. If the British government insisted upon excepting the narrow seas, the Secretary of State told the minister, "your negotiation will be at an end." The United States could never purchase exemption from impressment on the high seas by admitting it in the British narrow seas, through which so great a proportion of American trade passed. There, because of "its peculiar exposure," was where protection was most needed.[11]

One country's right is another country's wrong; and the eternal problem of international affairs is not to find which side is right and which is wrong, for each is commonly both right and wrong, but to recognize and reconcile the conflicting rights. If the United States would press Britain to renounce the British solution for a British difficulty, the United States would have to supply a satisfactory substitute. Hence the provisions in another article of the draft convention. "No refuge or protection" was to be given to deserting seamen, and they were to be delivered up. Incidentally, there were also provisions for surrendering deserters from either army. There had been a few, and there were to be more, unpleasant little border incidents caused by British soldiers' yielding to American temptation.

Monroe, no longer the Anglophobe of ten years before,[12] was san-

11. *A.S.P.F.R.*, III, 81–89.
12. *Supra*, p. 209.

guine of signing a treaty in London; but the months slipped by without any treaty and he betrayed no great concern over his failure. The Addington ministry, which hospitably received his advances, was tottering. Then Pitt returned to power, and his Foreign Secretary, Lord Harrowby, was too busy with Europe to be much bothered with America. Harrowby was also very skeptical of the American solution for the twin evils of desertion and impressment. He would not rebuff the United States by a flat rejection of the proposal, but he pointed out a fatal defect. However willing the government in Washington might be to employ civil authority for the restoration of fugitive seamen, it would be frustrated by popular prejudice, which always shielded deserters. It was true in England, and it would be equally true in the United States. Monroe replied that the difficulty was exaggerated. His people, he said, "were very obedient to law in all cases," and would change their attitude toward deserters if the restoration of the latter became the price for exemption from impressment.[13] The Englishman was not convinced, and the negotiation was suspended in a friendly spirit in October, 1804, when Monroe had to depart for Spain on a special mission. He hoped to resume it on his return, but he was not impatient. He believed that Anglo-American relations were much better for his reluctance to press for a settlement, and he was little worried by the outlook. "Our commerce," he wrote, "was never so much favored in time of war, nor was there ever less cause of complaint furnished by impressment."[14]

Before Monroe returned in July, 1805, the atmosphere was much changed. Congress did what it had threatened to do a year previously. It passed a law to punish British officers who committed trespass or tort on American vessels on the high seas. This legislative blow at impressment, Madison followed up with another long and urgent letter to the absent minister. Much more disturbing was another development which coincided with the latter's return to London. A score of American vessels were seized,[15] for the doctrine of the continuous voyage was reviving the dormant Rule of 1756.

Monroe then became as importunate as he had been complacent, but he could get no satisfaction and he was filled with uneasy feeling. He reported that he could see no prospect of a settlement of this question, or of impressment, or of the boundary problem. He also expressed the belief that the British government was equally disposed to postpone a commercial agreement, though he was not so sure of this because it had

13. *A.S.P.F.R.*, III, 94.
14. *Ibid.*, p. 98.
15. By February, 1806, the seizures had increased sixfold. *Ibid.*, p. 114.

not been his business to make a definite proposition. Before leaving for Spain, he had received a British suggestion to extend the lapsed terms of the 1794 treaty, but now he suspected that it might have been advanced "only to obtain delay." Looking back over the whole conduct of Britain toward the United States from the beginning of the war, he said: "I am inclined to think that the delay which has been so studiously sought, in all these concerns, is the part of a system, and that it is intended, as circumstances favor, to subject our commerce at present and hereafter to every restraint in their power. It is certain that the greatest jealousy is entertained of our present and increasing prosperity, and I am satisfied that nothing which is likely to succeed will be left untried to impair it." A not uncommon opinion in England, he observed, was that the American government by its very nature was precluded from making "any great, vigorous, or persevering exertion." He thought that the late seizures were "probably an experiment" to find "what the United States will bear," and that the procrastination he had encountered was "only an expedient to give the Government time to see its effect." If it succeeded, more trials would follow; if it failed, he was equally confident that the attitude of the British government toward the United States would be reversed. Then it would be easy to adjust all differences.[16] This reaction of Monroe in the latter part of 1805 is an interesting anticipation of the official American position in 1812, when the minister in London had become Secretary of State in Washington.

The American minister was undoubtedly right in believing that the British government was following a policy of delay, but he could hardly be expected to see the principal reason for it. The two major issues then under discussion, impressment and the Rule of 1756, were more vital to Britain than to the United States. One country was at war and the other at peace. If it was impossible for the Americans to yield, how much more impossible was it for the British? The government in London had to refuse, and naturally wished to put off the evil day as long as possible. Something might turn up. It is not improbable, also, that British policy was influenced by the calculation that the essential character of the American government would cripple its action in the field of foreign relations, and by the jealousy which war profiteers naturally inspire in war sufferers. Furthermore it cannot be denied that the physical law of movement along the line of least resistance has its counterpart in international affairs.

A violent explosion should have been touched off in the United States when, without any warning or explanation, the news of these wholesale seizures arrived. Anthony Merry, the British minister, fully expected it

16. *Ibid.*, pp. 106–107.

and he dreaded the consequences. An explosion did occur, but it was dampened down. The administration was caught in an awkward plight. When the whole American seaboard was crying out for the President to do something against Britain, he and his Secretary of State were actually discussing the formation of an alliance with Britain. Determined to acquire Florida, which they had tried in vain to get included in the Louisiana bargain, they looked forward to possible war with Spain and her French ally. This they dared not contemplate without the aid of Britain.[17] Their predicament paralyzed them, and their paralysis stultified the rage of the nation. At the close of the year came another piece of intelligence which had a sobering effect upon the public mind—the news of Trafalgar. Britain was then so undoubtedly supreme upon the ocean that those who would challenge her upon that element were facing a terrible risk. Americans interested in the highly profitable neutral commerce saw that war with Britain would kill that trade, and therefore not a few were in favor of submission.

To provide an escape from the dilemma, Congress adopted a measure which inaugurated the policy of commercial restriction as a weapon against foreign powers, a policy that had roots in popular action on the eve of the Revolutionary War and was destined to bear bitter fruit not only for those who cultivated it most assiduously—Jefferson and Madison—but also for the nation at large. This measure was the non-importation act of April, 1806. To coerce Britain, it excluded a list of important British manufactures. To avert the risk of war, however, its operation was suspended until November 15, and a special mission was to negotiate a settlement of all differences with Britain, including the withdrawal of this legislative threat. The Republicans in 1806 were repeating the tactics of the Federalists in 1794. They were also repeating themselves. The instructions sent to Monroe on January 5, 1804, were confirmed and amplified by Madison on May 17, 1806; and though a new commission was at the same time issued to two American plenipotentiaries, Monroe was one of these. The other was William Pinkney of Baltimore who was to help him get an even better treaty than the one he had missed. The draft convention which had been given him as a model was to be improved upon in certain particulars. It was also to be expanded to include a broad commercial agreement between the United States and the various parts of the British Empire in the hope that this would seal the settlement of the issues arising out of the war.

In 1806, as in 1804, a considerable realism inspired the instructions. It was palpably impossible for the United States to persuade belligerent Britain to accept the full-blown neutral program. Hence a willingness to

17. See Adams, III, 96.

yield what was necessary in order to secure what seemed absolutely essential. The principle of "free ships, free goods" might go, though a formal renunciation was to be avoided if possible. The definition of contraband[18] was likewise subject to variable treatment; and even the Rule of 1756 might be allowed to apply to direct trade between a belligerent and its colonies. The neutral definition of blockade, having lost its urgency because Britain had soon ceased to violate it in the West Indies, was not made a *sine qua non* in 1806, as it had been in 1804. The only other essential of the earlier instructions, the British abandonment of impressment, was reasserted. Congress insisted upon it because the British practice seemed more offensive than ever; and, immediately after the session closed, its offensiveness was reinforced by a nasty incident. This was almost inevitable, for British warships were haunting American shores to uphold British "rights." The incident occurred just outside New York beyond the three-mile limit. An American citizen was killed by an ill-directed shot from the frigate *Leander* fired across the bows of an American merchantman to make it submit to the right of search. Here we should also note that this evil experience elicited a good proposal which, if accepted, would have prevented any *Chesapeake* affair. It was, to quote Madison's instructions, "that all armed belligerent ships should be expressly and effectually restrained from making seizures or searches within a certain distance from our coasts, or taking stations near our harbors commodious for those purposes." Jefferson's pet idea of making the Gulf Stream the western limit of belligerent activity was suggested; but this was apparently regarded as too ambitious, and a more modest American parallel of the British "narrow seas" was urged. Besides impressment, the only other absolutely indispensable condition of 1806 was the maintenance of the neutral trade disrupted by the application of the doctrine of the continuous voyage.[19]

Meanwhile the situation in London became more auspicious. The death of Pitt in January, 1806, gave birth to new hope in the mind of Monroe; for Charles James Fox, the "notorious" friend of the United States, then undertook to form a coalition ministry with Grenville and returned to the Foreign Office. In opposition he had attacked the Rule of 1756, but in office he found that he could not repudiate it. Nevertheless he seems to have modified the severity of its enforcement, and he certainly encouraged the American minister to believe that an accommodation was possible. Then, in a surprising move, he made it unnecessary.

18. Madison was hardly a realist when he suggested, as he did in these instructions, the possibility of abolishing contraband.

19. *A.S.P.F.R.*, III, 119–124.

On May 16, 1806, Fox sent Monroe a note stating that, as a consequence of extraordinary measures taken by Napoleon to distress British commerce, his government was declaring a blockade of the whole coast from Brest to the Elbe but would make it absolute only along the short stretch from the Seine to Ostend. Beyond these limits, along the coasts of France, Holland, and Germany, the right of capture would not be exercised against neutrals carrying neither contraband nor enemy goods, provided they were not entering from or leaving for enemy ports.[20] It will be observed that these prohibited categories included no provision against the neutral conduct of enemy colonial trade via American ports, so that its resumption was tacitly permitted and the question of the principle involved was simply brushed aside. Thus, on the very day before Madison sent off the new instructions, one of the two essentials disappeared from the field of controversy, leaving impressment as the only real bone of contention.

The declaration of the blockade, of May 16, 1806, must also be examined from another angle, for its chief significance in Anglo-American relations was not this opportunist evasion of a difficult problem. Napoleon soon seized upon it as a violation of international law which justified his irregular Berlin and Milan decrees, which in turn were made to justify the startling British orders-in-council. As charge and countercharge flew back and forth between the opponents, each trying to persuade the United States that the other was primarily responsible for the combined destruction of American rights, American statesmen naturally took refuge behind the position that neutrality was incompatible with passing any judgment upon the dispute. For them it was sufficient that both were guilty of breaking the law, and they did not hesitate to denounce the order of May 16, as well as the subsequent measures of both. Because they did not challenge the British blockade until after Napoleon's Berlin Decree, they created the impression, not only in the Old World but also in intelligent circles at home, that they were siding with Napoleon. More or less unconsciously, this was what they were doing, for they were supporting his basic contention. The delay of the American challenge is easy to understand. Monroe's relations with Fox were very friendly; the adoption of the blockade brought relief from the pressing question of the continuous voyage and the Rule of 1756; and, as Admiral Mahan has pointed out,[21] there could be no question of Britain's ability to make this an effective blockade, even along the coasts where it was only partial. At the time, there was

20. *Ibid.*, p. 125.
21. A. T. Mahan, *Sea Power in Its Relations to the War of* 1812, I, 111–112.

only one point, and that a very contentious one, on which there could have been any American objection. This was the blanket nature of the declaration. It applied to a coast line, whereas the American claim was that only specifically named ports could be blockaded. That the blockade was actually made effective, the only other point, could not be seen at once. However the six months which elapsed before the Berlin Decree afforded ample time for a test, so that the American silence throughout this period rather weakens the later American charge. To the very end, Britain insisted that it was a perfectly legitimate blockade, and we may suspect that the United States questioned it only as a pathetically constrained echo of Napoleon's bold challenge.

When Pinkney joined Monroe in London at the end of June, Fox was on his deathbed. He died in September. His illness and death delayed the negotiation, necessitating a further suspension of the nonimportation act. But the disappearance of Fox had probably little if any effect upon the outcome of the negotiation. Lord Holland, his nephew, and Lord Auckland, the former William Eden, were appointed British plenipotentiaries. Apparently they were selected because of their known friendly attitude toward the United States, which the ministry was anxious to conciliate. Late in August, right after their appointment, they opened discussions with Monroe and Pinkney, and at once they encountered the rock upon which the whole negotiation was to founder.

The abandonment of impressment from American ships on the high seas having been made a prerequisite to any treaty, the negotiators bent their best efforts to find some arrangement satisfactory to both parties. The basic problem, of course, was that of fugitive British seamen. When asked for their solution, the two Americans resubmitted the formula of 1804. The objection that Harrowby had then raised still remained, and others were added. These refugees, having been bred to the sea, would naturally prefer to remain afloat, where they would be beyond the reach of civil officers in the United States. An American undertaking to surrender "deserters" was not enough, because the word had too narrow a legal meaning.[22] What was necessary was not only to plug the leak in the Royal Navy but also to stop the huge drain from the British merchant marine. Then, too, there were the thousands of British subjects already sailing the ocean as members of American crews. In Britain's hour of peril, when her navy was all that stood between her and downfall, she could agree to nothing that might reduce her chances of recovering her sons of the sea. There was no possibility of an American solution for the British problem. Nor was there any possibility of a

22. *A.S.P.F.R.*, III, 138.

British solution for the American problem. The two Englishmen suggested that the impressment of American seamen could be prevented by furnishing them with "authentic documents of citizenship" to be determined by treaty and to be respected by British naval officers; but they would not give up the right to impress British sailors from American vessels outside the territorial waters of the United States. This, however, was the vital point of the whole dispute, and the Americans could not yield it. The discussions went on and on. Various other formulas were tried, such as parallel legislation making it penal for British naval officers to impress American citizens from American ships on the high seas, and for American officials to grant certificates of citizenship to British subjects; but the argument always came back to this vital point, and there it stuck. In their eager reaching after a friendly settlement, Holland and Auckland showed signs of weakening; but references to the cabinet, the heads of the navy, and law officers of the Crown made it clear that the deadlock was absolute.

What, then, was to be done? The Americans had repeatedly stated that it would be useless to touch other points of the projected treaty if they could not get this one settled. Were they to go straight home and report their failure? If they did, what would be the result? The outlook was ominous, and both sides saw it. The rare good will and mutual understanding with which the negotiators had labored together to lay the foundations for a lasting peace and friendship between their countries must have heightened the prospective tragedy of the two falling apart in renewed recriminations. Holland and Auckland pleaded with Monroe and Pinkney to remain and complete the rest of the treaty, which might help to heal the breach caused by their failure. The Englishmen pointed out that their government "gave at present no cause of offence to the United States by impressments," and they assured the Americans that this policy would be continued. They argued that each party could cling to its own rights and exercise them in such a manner as to preclude complaints from the other; and that this temporizing arrangement would be better than a treaty which ceded the point to one. The interests of each country would be just as "secure for temporary purposes, and much more so in respect to a permanent good understanding." The Americans hesitated and asked for a written statement, which they received two days later, on November 9. It was a formal diplomatic note conveying the most solemn assurances of the British government that instructions had been given, would be repeated, and would be enforced to observe the greatest caution in impressing British seamen; that the strictest care would be taken to preserve Americans "from any molestation or injury"; and that any complaint would bring "immediate and prompt redress." Expressing a desire for "drawing closer the connexion between the two countries," it invited the American commissioners to proceed to the completion of the remaining articles.[23]

Monroe and Pinkney decided that it was their duty to accept the invitation. They would thereby lose nothing and they might gain much. They knew that their government had been demanding the impossible, the surrender of the British principle. In its stead they had secured a documentary pledge, which time and circumstance invested with peculiar solemnity and binding force, that the British practice would be so regulated as not to hurt Americans; and they had not bought this pledge with any renunciation, even implicit, of the American principle. That stood unchanged. The only concession on the question of impressment was made by Britain. It was a great practical concession, and it could not be lightly withdrawn. Though not in the treaty, it was in another place that seemed quite as good. It was under it. The whole weight of the treaty rested upon it, for it was the price the British paid for the continuance of negotiations.[24] American writers have been prone to condemn Monroe and Pinkney for disobeying their instructions, and some have even insinuated that Monroe was swayed by political ambition and the hope of winning Federalist votes against his rival, Madison. But it is here submitted that the fault of the American commissioners was merely technical; that they displayed an unusually sound judgment of how international disputes should be handled; that they followed the only course to avert what might easily have been a serious crisis in Anglo-American relations; and that the real fault, if such is to be found with any individuals, lay with those in authority at home for their well-meaning yet narrow-minded repudiation of the wise decision made in London.

When the American plenipotentiaries accepted the British invitation, they found, as they had expected, that there was little difficulty in concluding a treaty. It was signed on December 31, 1806, and was to be binding for ten years. Together with the "nearly digested" supplementary convention of 1807, discussed in a previous chapter,[25] this treaty provided a settlement for almost all the outstanding issues between the United States and the British Empire.[26] Of what remained to be adjusted, there was nothing that was both complicated and urgent. Monroe and Pinkney were doing what Jay had done; and they were able to get terms which, generally speaking, were more favorable because

23. *Ibid.*, p. 140.
24. *Ibid.*, p. 139.
25. *Supra*, pp. 197–206.
26. *A.S.P.F.R.*, III, 147–151.

the intervening years had strengthened the relative position of the
United States. The outcome of this negotiation, however, was vastly
different from that of twelve years before.

Developments in the Old World, it may be argued, had doomed the
treaty before it was signed. On November 21, 1806, Napoleon issued
his Berlin Decree declaring a blockade of the British Isles and condemning all British manufactures and colonial produce as lawful prize.
The effect on the government in London was such that, for several days
after the news arrived, it seemed that the nearly completed negotiation
would have to be suspended indefinitely. Just as the Americans had
refused to ratify without qualification the boundary convention of 1803
because it was signed after the Louisiana Purchase instead of before, and
therefore might acquire a new and unexpected meaning, so were the
British fearful of concluding the treaty after they knew of Napoleon's
action. His decree might necessitate the invasion of neutral rights which
the treaty would recognize and the exercise of belligerent rights which
it would circumscribe. If, knowing this, the British went ahead and
signed the treaty without any qualification, they would have been more
foolish than Samson when he let Delilah cut off his hair. Therefore
they insisted upon a precautionary condition, likewise set forth in a
formal note.[27] Their government must keep its hands free to counteract
the designs of Napoleon, unless the United States made this unnecessary
by engaging to resist a violation of neutral rights under the Berlin
Decree. The second alternative, which meant an American willingness
to go to war against France, was simply out of the question. Monroe
and Pinkney would have none of it.[28] Their refusal, which they insisted
would be confirmed at home, shifted the basis of the treaty to the first
alternative. This weakened the treaty but did not destroy it. Whether it
would have done so, if given the chance, is a debatable question. It
never had the chance, because the treaty was wrecked right away—in
America.

The administration in Washington rejected the treaty offhand.[29] It
was not because the British had weakened it by appending the condition
in the accompanying note. When Madison read it he told Erskine, the
British minister "that the note itself would have prevented, he was
convinced, the ratification of the treaty," and Jefferson expressed the

27. *Ibid.*, pp. 151–152.
28. Their attitude toward the note on impressments has sometimes been confused with
their attitude toward this note, which they transmitted along with the treaty. To this they
gave no countenance whatsoever, whereas they had sent the former home in hopes that it
would be accepted as an equivalent for a treaty stipulation against impressments.
29. It arrived the day Congress adjourned, and the Senate was not recalled to consider it.

same opinion on the following day;[30] but the American Secretary of State soon came to hope that the occasion which had produced it would have vanished, and then he wrote to the American commissioners that, if it did not disappear, they might accept "a candid declaration that, in signing or ratifying a [new] treaty, it was understood on the part of Great Britain, that nothing therein contained would be a bar to any measures, which, if no such treaty existed, would be lawful as a retaliation against the measures of an enemy."[31] Nor was the rejection caused by any British violation of the treaty. Britain has been accused of doing it flagrantly within a week of signing, because an order-in-council appeared on January 7, 1807, outlawing neutral trade between ports under the control of Napoleon. But this action, which certainly curtailed the liberty allowed by the text of the treaty and dealt a severe blow at American commerce, was covered by the note which explained the condition governing the British signature of the treaty; and Madison himself said of this order, in a letter to Erskine, "No fair objection can lie against it, provided it be founded on, and enforced by, actual blockades, as authorized by the law of nations."[32] That the basic principle was not blockade but the Rule of 1756 was not known in Washington until long after the treaty had disappeared. Indeed its rejection was determined weeks before anyone in the United States knew of the existence of this note or of this order-in-council. The decision was made a month before Madison heard that the treaty was signed. It was made as soon as he received from the American commissioners their report, written on November 11, that they were about to proceed with the negotiation; and the reason for the decision was their confessed failure to make the British renounce the right to impress sailors from neutral vessels on the high seas. Without a clause to this effect, there would be no treaty.[33]

Such was the will of President Jefferson, who believed that he was

30. Erskine to Howick, No. 8, March 6, 1807, *F.O. 5*, Vol. LII.

31. *A.S.P.F.R.*, III, 168.

32. *Ibid.*, p. 159.

33. *Ibid.*, pp. 153–154. The British minister in Washington suggested a further consideration: "Notwithstanding the assurances of the French Minister of Marine that the American commerce will not be affected by the decree of blockade, yet doubts are evidently entertained in this country on that subject, and it is thought by many that Bonaparte will be offended with the United States for making a treaty with England, and will take advantage of his decree to injure the American commerce, and so great an alarm of the anger of Bonaparte is entertained by this government that, I fear, it might influence their determination on the subject of the treaty, unless the terms of it should prove to be so advantageous to the United States as to make it generally popular with the people." Erskine to Howick, No. 7, March 2, 1807, *F.O. 5*, Vol. LII.

reflecting the will of his people and of Congress. Whether he was right or wrong in this belief is a question that can never be positively settled;[34] yet it is possible to draw some pertinent conclusion from either alternative.

If Jefferson was right, and American opinion was inflexible on the point, then there was no possibility of a treaty: for it is clear, though he could not see it, that Britain would not accept such an article as he demanded. Then the trouble was an irreconcilable conflict of national wills; but they were not exact opposites. The British were willing, whereas the Americans were not, to let the other side cling to its principle and meanwhile to work out some practical compromise whereby neither would injure the other. There was thus a difference of intransigence. If Jefferson was right in his interpretation, and yet could have swung enough votes in the Senate to carry ratification,[35] then he threw away an irreplaceable instrument for stilling the growing strife between the two countries, and he also contributed to the increase of this strife. If he was wrong, then he was terribly wrong, for the same reason.

The second step had at last led to a much longer third step toward the War of 1812, and it was similarly taken without any consciousness of movement in this direction. The country was not thinking in terms of

34. That he was wrong, he appears to have implied, quite unconsciously, at a later date. Though the decision to reject the treaty was made weeks before he saw it and before he knew anything of the British note that was to accompany it or the order-in-council that was to follow it, he seems to have forgotten this by the autumn of 1808, when he told Erskine "we might have shoved along in the hope of some compromise on impressments if that had been the sole question." See Adams, IV, 351, 353.

35. The British minister in Washington analyzed the situation as follows: "Great anxiety prevails amongst the merchants to learn the provisions of the treaty which they have understood is favorable to the commerce of the United States, and which they therefore think ought to be promulgated that it might be supported.

"It is, perhaps, difficult to pronounce decisively as to what the public opinion in this country might be respecting the treaty when the terms of it become generally known, but my reasons for having ventured to suppose that, if the President should persist in his objections to it, he will be supported by the majority in Congress, arise from the state of parties in this country.

"It must be well known to Your Lordship that the present government has been hitherto supported by a very large majority of the people of this country, and although in the course of the two sessions of Congress preceding and in some instances, during the last session, differences have appeared to exist amongst the leading men of the ruling party, yet they have not as yet produced any serious disunion, nor do I think the rejection of the treaty on the grounds taken by the President would lead to such consequences. At the same time I feel it my duty to observe that there are many persons of great reputation for a knowledge of the state of politics and parties in this country who entertain a different opinion, and who think that the treaty would be ratified in its present form by the Senate, and that the President would not venture to reject it without laying it before them for their consideration.

"These opinions have, however, been held by persons of the Federal Party who are most respectable for character and talents, but few in number compared with the party now in power." Erskine to Howick, No. 10, March 28, 1807, F.O. 5, Vol. LII.

war,[36] nor were those responsible for the country's policy. Jefferson was a lover of peace, and Madison's logic banished the suggestion of war with Britain that flickered across his own mind. "The spoils of our defenceless commerce might enrich her greedy cruisers," and there might be "a temporary spasm . . . in the affairs of the United States." This the Secretary of State admitted, but the considerations in the opposite scale he found to be overwhelming.

To say nothing of the hostile use that might be made against Great Britain of fifty thousand seamen, not less hardy or enterprising than her own, nor of her valuable possessions in our neighborhood, which, though little desired by the United States, are highly prized by her, nor of the general tendency of adding the United States to the mass of nations already in arms against her, it is enough to observe that a war with the United States involves a complete loss of the principal remaining market for her manufactures, and of the principal, perhaps the sole, remaining source of supplies, without which all her faculties must wither. Nor is it an unimportant circumstance, though it seems to have engaged little of her attention, that in the loss would be included all the advantages which she now derives from the neutrality of our flag and of our ports, and for which she could find no substitutes in distributing her manufactures, and even her fish, to their necessary markets, and in obtaining the returns which she wants.[37]

Madison and his chief were inspired by a sublime faith that they could easily persuade Britain to see the error of her ways. They had only to stand firm, to reason with her, and, if that was not quite enough, then to threaten and possibly apply some economic pressure. Thereupon they commanded Monroe and Pinkney to arrange a new and proper treaty,[38] which was of course impossible. Thus did the American administration walk blindly on toward war without preparing for it.

36. "I feel persuaded," observed the British minister in Washington, "from everything that I have heard and from what I know of the sentiments of many persons who possess the most extensive influence amongst the people and are at present representatives in Congress, that the power of the dominant party could not engage this country in a war with Great Britain on the grounds of any of the complaints that have been urged, or, for the accomplishment of any of the objects included or omitted in the treaty lately signed by the respective commissioners.

"This opinion, I am satisfied, would be found fully confirmed by a reference to the transactions and debates in Congress during the most violent period of irritation against Great Britain in the two sessions of Congress before last, during which very few of the members of Congress most incensed at what they termed the unjust aggressions and insults of Great Britain ever hinted at the idea of going to war." Erskine to Howick, No. 9, March 7, 1807, ibid.

37. A.S.P.F.R., III, 172.

38. Ibid., pp. 166–173.

The famous *Chesapeake* incident, which soon precipitated an ugly crisis in the relations between Britain and the United States, appears to have been the direct consequence of the American government's repudiation of the agreement reached by its plenipotentiaries in England. This repudiation released Britain from her pledge of the previous November, and it had an exasperating effect. In a dispute over jurisdiction on the ocean, where the Royal Navy was supreme, the British government had gone to the limit, and perhaps even beyond it, in a desire to conciliate the United States; but the American government would not be satisfied with anything short of a complete surrender by Britain on her own element. It is not surprising that trouble ensued. It is conceivable that it might have come anyway: for it was already brewing in several American ports over a number of minor incidents;[39] and with the fall of Grenville at the end of March, 1807, the old unbending Tories, who had much less tenderness for American feelings, returned to office. But the unpleasant friction in American ports would most probably have been checked, and the train of circumstances which led to the attack on the *Chesapeake* would certainly have been broken, if Washington had grasped the hand stretched out in London.

A British squadron lay at anchor in Chesapeake Bay, ready to catch some French vessels as soon as they ventured forth from the protecting waters of the United States. This was a condition which Jefferson and Madison had hoped the treaty would prevent; but it only added two miles to the three-mile limit, so that if it had gone into force this addition would not have made much difference. But there would have been another difference, and that a crucial one, as will appear from the story of what happened.

While waiting for their prey, the British ships had to send ashore for water and supplies. This necessity was the sailors' opportunity to bolt for freedom, and a number seized it. Some seamen of the *Melampus* found another way of escape. While an entertainment was proceeding on board, they stole their captain's gig and away they ran, or rather rowed, to the nearby shore. Deserters who had thus got their freedom flaunted it before the very eyes of their officers; for they enlisted in the American naval service, and as American recruits they strutted up and down the streets of Norfolk. Commodore Barron had some of these men in the crew of the frigate *Chesapeake*; he knew they were deserters;[40] and the British knew that he knew, though they did not also know that he believed them to be American citizens impressed into the Royal Navy.

---

39. In which the haughtiness of some British naval officers played no little part.
40. *Ibid.*, p. 22.

Early in March, the British consul in Norfolk applied for them by name, only to meet with a refusal;[41] and at the end of the month the British minister in Washington sought their surrender, with a like result. Both refusals were flat, being accompanied by no intimation that the men were supposed to be Americans.[42] At the same time, as salt rubbed into a wound, the news spread from Baltimore that officers of the French vessels were pursuing their deserters on shore and were taking them with the aid of American constables.[43] Appeals flew to the British commander-in-chief in American waters, Admiral G. C. Berkeley in Halifax, who obviously concluded that he had to deal with a national insult.[44] Thereupon, on June 1, he issued a general order to all commanders under him to recover the men from the *Chesapeake* at sea, and outside the limits of the United States.[45]

It is inconceivable that the sequence of events would have been allowed to reach this fatal point if the American government had accepted the treaty with its underlying support, the "self-denying ordinance" imposed upon the British navy. A different spirit on each side would have called a halt somewhere between the escape of the men and the order for their recovery. But this reasoning does not absolve Berkeley from blame. The immediate responsibility for the *Chesapeake* incident rests squarely upon the shoulders of the British admiral. He ordered it.

On June 22, 1807, the frigate *Chesapeake*, commanded by Barron, left Hampton Roads and stood to sea.[46] The British ship *Leopard*, Captain S. P. Humphreys, then lying off Cape Henry, also got under way, and came within hail about three or four leagues from the cape. Humphreys sent an officer to the *Chesapeake* with Berkeley's order. The officer returned with a note from Barron denying knowledge of any such deserters as were described, presumably because the order referred to them as British subjects, and refusing to be searched. Humphreys hailed and remonstrated in vain. A shot across the bow of the *Chesapeake* being also without effect, the *Leopard* finally fired into the American frigate, killing and wounding about a score of her crew. After ten minutes or so,

41. *Ibid.*, pp. 16–17.

42. Erskine to Canning, No. 21, July 17, 1807, *F.O. 5*, Vol. LII.

43. Hamilton (British consul at Norfolk) to Erskine, March 17, 1807, enclosed in *ibid.*

44. "The insult which he conceived was offered to the honor of His Majesty's Flag by their being enlisted into the service of the United States, and put on board their frigate." Erskine to Canning, No. 24, Sept. 1, 1807, *ibid.*

45. *A.S.P.F.R.*, III, 12.

46. Barron must have known what he was running into, for practically everybody on board with him was familiar with a report circulated around Norfolk that the captain of the *Melampus* had threatened to take the men from the *Chesapeake*. *Ibid.*, p. 22.

having replied with only one wild shot, Barron struck. The search was made, and the four men were carried off.[47]

Insult was answered by insult, and the second was much worse than the first. If American officials had intended to thumb their noses at the British navy, at least they had not invaded British sovereignty; but the execution of Admiral Berkeley's order was a blow between the eyes, and a flagrant violation of American sovereignty. It was a hostile attack upon the United States.

The country raged, and wild cries of war resounded through the land. Not since the days of the Revolution had the United States been so united; and never again was it so solidly opposed to Britain. Even the "most temperate people and those most attached to England," reported the British minister, "say that they are bound as a nation and that they must assert their honor on the first attack upon it, or subject themselves to an imputation which it may be difficult ever to remove."[48] If Congress had been in session, or if the President had then summoned it, as he was strongly urged to do, there might have been a stampede into war; for it seemed that Britain had determined to provoke it.

The news of the attack sent General Turreau, the French minister, rushing back to Washington, which he had left for the summer. He went straight to the President and engaged him in a discussion of the affair. Jefferson told the Frenchman: "If the English do not give us the satisfaction we demand, we will take Canada, which wants to enter the Union; and when, together with Canada, we shall have the Floridas,

47. "Several other English subjects composed part of the crew," reported Humphreys, "but as they did not claim the protection of the British flag, and were not within the limits of my orders from the commander in chief, I therefore allowed them to remain." Humphreys to Douglas, June 22, 1807, enclosed in Erskine to Canning, No. 20, July 17, 1807, *F.O. 5*, Vol. LII.

Of the four who were removed, two were natives of Maryland. One was white and the other a mulatto born in slavery. The third, a black, was brought as a boy from South America by a Massachusetts mariner who duly registered him as his indentured servant. The two colored men were in the crew of an American brig when she was taken by the *Melampus* in the Bay of Biscay in 1805. Barron believed they were then impressed, but the records of the British ship showed that they volunteered in Plymouth, England, after they had been returned with the rest of the crew to the detained brig. The white man left an American brig in Liverpool to join an English vessel. According to Barron, he too was pressed at sea; but the books of the *Melampus* showed him as a volunteer who, like the other two, had been paid a bounty on enlistment. The fourth man, a deserter from the *Halifax*, was a native Englishman and unquestionably a British subject who, according to evidence submitted at his trial, had been advised by an American naval officer to change his name. The value of this evidence may be compared with that which satisfied Barron that the others had not volunteered but had been impressed, that is, their own assertions. *A.S.P.F.R.*, III, 13–17. Creighton to Hawkes, Aug. 11, 1807, enclosed in Erskine to Canning, No. 24, Sept. 1, 1807, *F.O. 5*, Vol. LII. Berkeley to Erskine, Sept. 1, 1807, enclosed in Erskine to Canning, No. 26, Oct. 5, 1807, *ibid*.

48. Erskine to Canning, No. 21, July 17, 1807, *ibid*.

we shall no longer have any difficulties with our neighbors; and it is the only way of preventing them." Nevertheless Turreau positively reported to Talleyrand "that the President does not want war, and that Mr. Madison dreads it now still more." He added that they would do everything to avoid it. If Congress should think itself bound to decide for war, its intention would be "crossed by powerful intrigues, because the actual administration has nothing to gain and everything to lose by war."[49] Turreau's judgment was sound.

Jefferson kept his head and preserved the peace in this trying crisis. As a precaution against further incidents that might precipitate an open rupture, he issued on July 2 a proclamation expelling all British armed vessels from American waters and prohibiting intercourse with any that refused to depart. He thus administered an emollient for wounded national pride. He also dispatched the United States schooner *Revenge* to demand satisfaction from Britain, and he put off the call to Congress.

The shots fired by the *Leopard* were the onset of the gathering storm which blew itself out in the war. The magic of electricity might have exorcised much of the evil done on the fatal day of June 22, but the means of communication were then too slow. The British government, in defiance of a considerable opinion that the affair only served the Americans right and that war with the United States would be good for England, was anxious to expiate the grave wrong committed by Berkeley. It disavowed the action and it denied the principle. It had not claimed, and would not claim, the right to search ships of war. It recalled the admiral; and it was willing to indemnify the wounded and the families of the killed, as well as to restore the abducted seamen still in custody.[50] Such was the basis on which the affair was finally liquidated, but not until long afterwards.

One of the conditions demanded by the instructions entrusted to the *Revenge* was a final settlement of the impressment issue. As "security for the future," Monroe was to insist upon a British renunciation[51] for which, if necessary, he might promise the return of deserters. Innocent as this demand might seem in Washington, it naturally appeared as blackmail in London. The United States was trying a game which only powers prepared for war can play successfully. The British government decided to call the American hand. If there was to be any settlement of

49. Turreau to Talleyrand, July 18, 1807, quoted in Adams, IV, 35–37, where, by an obvious misprint, the year appears as 1808.

50. There were three. The fourth, being unquestionably a British subject, was promptly tried and hanged in Halifax. Thereupon Madison complained that the execution added to the insult by making reparation impossible. Madison to Erskine, Oct. 9, 1807, enclosed in Erskine to Canning, separate, of same date, *F.O.* 5, Vol. LII.

51. This demand was an afterthought. See Adams, IV, 164.

the *Chesapeake* affair, it must be without any consideration of this extraneous[52] issue on which a deadlock had already been reached. In September the cabinet flatly refused to negotiate on Monroe's terms; in October it issued a proclamation reinforcing the right of search to recover British seamen, which was interpreted in the United States as adding insult to injury; and in November it dispatched a special envoy to Washington with instructions to settle the affair there without any reference to the question of impressments. Arriving at the end of the year, he found the American government willing to exclude it from the discussion; but then he discovered that the discussion could not be opened for another reason. He had also to require, as a preliminary, the recall of the President's proclamation closing the ports. This precautionary measure may have prevented some irritating incidents, but it certainly produced an irritating situation, to which the British squadron in the Chesapeake contributed not a little by defying the order to depart. By this time, however, these ships were gone, much to the relief of Madison, who had intimated to Erskine that British orders for their withdrawal must precede any discussion in Washington.[53] But the British complaint remained. To withhold from all armed vessels of Britain a hospitality continued to those of her enemy was an unfriendly act bordering on hostility. The American Secretary of State and the English emissary had a nice wrangle over the point until the former offered, and the latter refused, to compromise by making the signature of the recall coincide with the signature of the reparation settlement.[54] Thus the negotiation ended before it began.

Both sides were to blame for their failure to meet,[55] and therefore for the *Chesapeake* incident's remaining an open sore. But the effect of their failure should not be overdrawn. Before the negotiation stuck on the second snag in Washington, other influences had complicated the Anglo-American quarrel; and even before the first snag blocked discussion in London, the spark struck at sea had blown inland and there had started a sort of underground fire. Because this fire has sometimes been regarded as one of the causes of the War of 1812, it calls for careful examination.

The *Chesapeake* incident, by raising the specter of war between Britain and the United States, quickened the dead hopes of the Indians

---

52. Because Britain recognized the immunity of public vessels from search.

53. Erskine to Canning, No. 2, Jan. 28, 1808, *F.O.* 5, Vol. LVII.

54. *A.S.P.F.R.*, III, 213–220. See also Adams, Vol. IV, Chap. VIII.

55. Though the American attempt to extort a renunciation of impressments had a bad effect on British opinion, this attempt was less responsible for blocking negotiation than may be supposed. There is reason to believe that, if it had not appeared, the other obstacle would have taken its place in London, preventing discussion there and necessitating reference to Washington.

and the dead fears of the American frontier, disturbing the peace that had reigned in the Old Northwest for more than a decade. Again the red men looked to their old "white father" for salvation from advancing American settlement; and again the Americans saw the guilty hand of Britain behind a savage threat to their pioneer settlements. From out on the Wabash, Governor Harrison of Indiana Territory reported on September 5, 1807, that the Indian attack was only waiting for the signal from British agents. For some time he had been watching the spreading influence of that curious Shawnee leader known as the Prophet, and now he was sure that the British were employing this "vile instrument" to rouse the Indians against the United States.[56] His was only one of many such accusations which were believed in Washington.[57] Madison soon told Erskine that the government had "irrefragible proof" that the British were back at their old game.[58] As a matter of fact, the one-eyed Shawnee monster was plotting against the Americans, and the vanquished tribes were ripening for a new war on their own account; but the British authorities had then no hand in fomenting this movement in the western forests.

The British authorities had actually been neglecting the red men. During the years of quiet following Jay's Treaty, there seemed no point in cultivating the old attachment. Indian presents were cut down and the Indian Department in Canada was allowed to run down.[59] That was the situation when the international crisis burst upon the Western World.

56. Julius W. Pratt, *Expansionists of* 1812 (New York, 1925), p. 25.

57. For a British account of the alarm in Detroit, see the letter of August 7, 1807, by the commandant at Amherstburg to the military secretary at Quebec, printed in *P.A.C.R.*, 1896, Note D, p. 29.

58. Erskine to Canning, No. 27, Nov. 5, 1807, *F.O.* 5, Vol. LII.

59. On April 2, 1808, the lieutenant governor of Upper Canada wrote to the governor-in-chief in Quebec: "I feel some difficulty in conducting the Indian Department. The Indian Nations owing to the long continuance of peace have been neglected by us, and from the considerable curtailments, made in the presents to those people it appears that the retaining their attachment to the King's interest has not of late years been thought an object worthy of serious consideration." He also stated that the annual supply of stores reached St. Joseph's so late in 1807 that "the great body of Indians resorting to that post were under the necessity of going away to their wintering grounds without receiving their usual presents"; and he urged the revival of the former custom of keeping a two years' supply at that post. *Q*, CVII, 227–228. Three months later the governor-in-chief reported to the Secretary of State in London: "Among the various objects which have presented themselves to my consideration since my arrival here, that of the Indian Department has of course claimed much of my attention. It appears to me that it has been thought little probable that we should ever have occasion for their assistance again, and they have therefore been much neglected. A commendable principle of economy . . . has occasioned of late years a diminution of the establishment employed with them as well as a very considerable reduction in the usual supplies granted to those people. This has not only been productive of dissatisfaction among them . . . but it has lessened and almost destroyed that connexion with and influence over them that the remaining officers of the Department had before enjoyed." *Ibid.*, p. 202.

The effect upon the American Republic is well known, but the repercussion in the two British provinces adjoining on the north has received too little attention.[60]

The news of the attack on the *Chesapeake* reached Canada in July through the United States, bringing with it the hot blast of American opinion crying for war on Britain. According to reports from south of the line, every American town formed an association to attack the neighboring British provinces. It seemed that hostilities might break out at any time, if they had not already begun, and there was no doubt whatever that war would mean an American invasion. The acting commander-in-chief, Colonel Isaac Brock, was greatly alarmed, for he knew that the country was totally unprepared for the danger. He feared that all might be lost with Quebec. Its fortifications were seriously defective, and he had no force with which to prevent the Americans from closing in upon it. He had no thought for anything but a desperate defense, and the octogenarian who was then temporarily administering the government of the lower province exasperated him by refusing to see the necessity for rushing improvements in the works and for calling out the militia.[61] In a much more exposed position was Upper Canada, under Lieutenant Governor Francis Gore. Early in September he ran down to Montreal to meet Brock, his old friend and once his fellow officer, from whom he sought aid and advice. But Brock could spare only 4,000 stand of arms and declined all further responsibility for arrangements in the upper province.[62]

The war scare was soon intensified by the receipt of a letter from Admiral Berkeley in Halifax, later confirmed by a similar one from Erskine in Philadelphia. It was a circular informing the administrators of the various colonies that an American ultimatum had been sent to London and that hostilities were almost, if not quite, inevitable.[63] It reached Quebec on September 16[64] and York on October 1.[65] As a result of this startling message, Brock got some coöperation from the civil government, but this need not be detailed here because it was solely concerned with arming Lower Canada. Of more interest is Gore's

60. That upon the Maritime Provinces had no relation to the Indian problem of the West, and calls for no special attention.

61. *Ibid*. CIV, 54–64.

62. *Ibid*., CCCIX, 295–296.

63. It should be remembered that this warning was justified at the time, for not until toward the end of the year did Jefferson intimate to Erskine that the American government might back down on the question of impressments. Erskine to Canning, No. 29, Dec. 2, 1807, *F.O. 5*, Vol. LII. Erskine's circular dated August 10 is enclosed in Erskine to Canning, No. 24, Sept. 1, 1807, *ibid*. Berkeley's, written a week later, is printed in *P.A.C.R.*, 1896, Note D, p. 28.

64. *Q*, CIV, 175.

65. *Ibid*., CCCX, 2.

report from York, the present Toronto, for if there was any tampering with red men on American soil, Gore was responsible for it. The only political contact which the British had with the western tribes was through the Indian Department of Upper Canada headed by Colonel Claus, who took all his orders from, and made all his reports to, the lieutenant governor of that province.[66]

In a dispatch to Lord Castlereagh, the Secretary of State in London, written on October 7, Gore reported that, having been unable to procure a sufficient quantity of arms from Lower Canada, he was refraining from calling out any part of the militia, "that the Americans may not be made acquainted with our weakness." He also explained that, before receiving Berkeley's warning, he "had ordered additional supplies of provisions to be thrown into the posts of Amherstburg and St. Joseph's on account of the Indians who have neglected their corn fields in expectation of being called upon by the British government to take up the hatchet against the Americans." Here it should be noted that these two posts were the British substitutes for Detroit and Michilimackinac, and that Indians commonly resorted thither from near and far, even from the region of the Mississippi. Their coming and going had seemed innocent enough until the international crisis suddenly cast a dark shadow over it in the United States. But this letter by Gore shows that British influence was being exerted not to incite but to restrain the natives. They, he stated, would have "made war upon the Americans some time since" if it had not been for the "temperate and judicious conduct" of Colonel Claus and other officers of the Indian Department. He added that he had directed a general council of the western tribes to be held in Amherstburg and that before they could be assembled he hoped to know the issue of the crisis in Anglo-American relations,[67] the inference being that he would then know how to act.

On October 18, Lieutenant General Sir James Craig arrived in Quebec. The home government had suddenly realized that it had left British North America without its regular head. Hence the appointment of this veteran as commander-in-chief and "governor general" to give the leadership necessary in this crucial time. In sending him out, Castlereagh gave him a letter of instructions marked "secret." It was to guide him if the crisis ended in war with the United States. It said that American impotence at sea would probably dictate an American attack on the neighboring British provinces, that no military reinforcement of any account could be sent to them in the midst of the Napoleonic war

66. There had been only one Indian Department for both Upper and Lower Canada until 1796, when a separation was made.

67. *Ibid.*, pp. 2–3.

then raging, and that they were therefore in danger. Under these circumstances, the prime consideration was to retain the two places of outstanding importance—Halifax, "the most valuable naval station on the North American continent," and Quebec, the key of Canada. Passing by the problem of Halifax, presumably because it was largely naval and because Craig was a military man whose principal residence was to be in Quebec, the Secretary of State carefully instructed the new governor that he must subordinate all other considerations to the preservation of this fortress. There he was to hold out until succor could reach him from England. The only reference to Indian affairs in this letter was a short passage informing him that the department in Lower Canada was under his immediate control and that the lieutenant governor of Upper Canada, who had charge of the department there, would follow his directions.[68] The home government was evidently thinking as little as Brock or Gore of instigating the red men to attack the United States.

There came a time, however, when the protraction of the crisis turned responsible British minds toward the use of the savages. The object then was not aggression but defense—to parry the blow that the United States might strike at Britain in Canada. On December 1, 1807, Gore wrote to Craig asking, "Are the Indians to be employed in case of a rupture with the United States?" If so, he intimated that an additional supply of presents would have to be sent up in the spring when navigation opened; but he was far from eager to see this policy tried. From all the information he could gather, he doubted if these old allies were any better than a broken reed.[69]

Craig answered this letter before he received it. In his first communication to Gore, dated December 6, he enlarged upon the military problem of defending Quebec. He anticipated having to fight a delaying action, and he hoped that some of the Upper Canadian militia might be detached to strike at the American communications in Lower Canada. From this, he turned to the problem that would arise in the West, and he expressed the conviction that the Indians "will not be idle" in the event of war. "If we do not employ them, there cannot exist a moment's doubt that they will be employed against us." Therefore, if at all possible, they were to be prepared to act on the British side. He counseled great caution, and he wondered if it was "expedient to bring the subject forward at present until hostilities are more certain." It might be found that the Americans were "gaining so much ground" with the natives that it would be necessary to counteract this influence "by a direct address on our part"; and if the Americans made any public

68. *Ibid.*, CIV, 161–167.
69. *Ibid.*, CVII, 220–221.

proposal to the Indians to join them, no time should be lost in reminding the western tribes of Britain's "long subsisting friendship" and in pointing out to them that they "would only seal their own destiny" by aiding the Americans to drive the British out. Meanwhile there should be no commitments, but it would be advisable to insinuate on every possible occasion "that as a matter of course we shall look for the assistance of our brothers." Craig also sought information about the Prophet and his influence. If this was great, and if some of the Indian Department could "enter into an intercourse with him," he thought "it might be worth while to purchase it though at what might be a high price upon any other occasion."[70] Three weeks later, on the receipt of Gore's letter and of other advice from the West, the governor wrote again. He promised to rush up an additional supply of presents in the spring; and, though he confessed that his hopes of securing native assistance had been somewhat dashed, he urged the pursuit of the policy he had set forth, repeating his conviction that the Americans would employ the red men if the British did not.[71]

Gore was impressed by the soundness of Craig's conviction and he undertook to forward Craig's policy, though without great confidence in its success. He appreciated the delicacy with which the business would have to be handled, and so did his superior in Quebec.[72] The old dilemma of Haldimand, Dorchester, and Simcoe stared them in the face. To meet the danger of war and an invasion in which they might lose Canada, they were impelled to cultivate the neglected friendship of the western tribes; yet they knew that their effort to do this might precipitate the very catastrophe they dreaded. They had to steer between Scylla and Charybdis, and the wind was very fickle.

Only slowly and tentatively did the old policy get under way again, and the greatest care was exercised to keep it defensive. There could be no presents until some time after navigation opened in the spring of 1808, and the Indian Department had to be shaken up. Gore had little trust in the agent at Amherstburg, the dissolute son of the late Alexander McKee. He had been there for years, having ousted the reliable Captain Mathew Elliott, who had entertained the American commissioners in 1793.[73] It was imperative that Elliott be restored, but not until May could Gore persuade Craig to correct the mistake of a previous governor-in-chief.[74] Meanwhile Elliott, whose home was by

70. *P.A.C.R.*, 1896, Note D, pp. 30–32.
71. *Q*, CVII, 219–220.
72. *Ibid.*, p. 222. *P.A.C.R.*, 1896, Note D, pp. 34–37.
73. *Supra*, p. 130.
74. *Q*, CVII, 231.

the post, gave his services voluntarily, except when he had to attend to his legislative duties in York. As for the Prophet, Gore reported on January 5, 1808, that he was certainly hostile to the United States and presumably inclined to rely on British friendship, for he had lately sent messengers to Amherstburg to request clothing, which was immediately delivered, for a few of his people. The lieutenant governor's information was "that many of the Indians, especially those about St. Joseph's, who have had a meeting with him [the Prophet], now pay him little or no regard," and that his following numbered only eight hundred or a thousand. From Elliott, who knew the Shawnee personally, Gore hoped soon to get an opinion on whether "the purchase of this man is worthy of further consideration," and he promised to advise Craig accordingly.[75] Elliott may not have been enthusiastic, for no record of this advice has been found. With the coming of spring, a deputation of Shawnees appeared in Amherstburg and held a private council with Colonel Claus. They were humored with a promise that Elliott would send the tribe a message when their services were wanted. Gore was now led to believe that their influence was greater than he had supposed,[76] but the report he extracted from Claus about a fortnight later was not very encouraging. "The number of fighting men on the borders of the Miamies" and in the peninsula of Michigan was no more than fifteen hundred, and they would be "very backward" in lending assistance because of the obvious weakness of Amherstburg. If an adequate force were stationed there, Claus thought that enough of these Indians might be gathered to "keep our ground," as he said, "until the back Indians could be brought forward, I mean those on the banks of the Mississippi &c." He added that messages had been sent to these tribes beyond Lake Michigan "as long ago as October last and, from constant reports of their being on their way, I have deferred sending a second message, but I shall now lose no time in dispatching a confidential person to that country."[77]

Meanwhile down in the old Castle of St. Louis the man responsible for the fate of British North America was taking a larger view, and he descried a new danger which confirmed him in the pursuit of his policy. Napoleon might seize the opportunity to revive the French Empire in America! The suggestion was not so absurd as it may seem today. Rumors of some such scheme had just been flying around Washington.[78] We should also remember that Napoleon was then at the peak of his unprecedented power. He was the lord of Europe and was looking

75. *P.A.C.R.*, 1896, Note D, p. 37.
76. *Q*, CVII, 228.
77. *Ibid.*, pp. 233–234.
78. Erskine to Canning, No. 8, March 6, 1808, *F.O. 5*, Vol. LVII.

beyond. At Tilsit in the early summer of 1807, he had talked with the vanquished Czar of Russia about dividing the world between them. Craig saw Napoleon calculating that the risk of losing all the naval force he might employ to establish his power in the New World would be small compared to the possible gain. Instead of striking at the St. Lawrence, where the population was French, he would probably seek an even more favorable entry between Spanish America and the United States, and then he would reach up the Mississippi Valley to grasp Canada. How he could do this without quickly reversing the American attitude toward Britain was a question that does not seem to have occurred to Craig; but he could not understand why the United States was then bristling with hostility against Britain, and in this he was not peculiar. It is not the folly but the fact of his nightmare that is relevant here. He shuddered at the vision of French agents stealing up the interior of the continent. For captivating the allegiance of the natives, they had a genius the English never possessed; and they would hurl the savages upon the "defenceless frontier of Upper Canada."[79] Therefore, as he wrote to Gore on May 11, 1808, it was more than ever imperative to win the Indians and bind them to the British interest. Claus and Elliott should increase their efforts and extend them southward as far as practicable; but at the same time, he reiterated, "the means that are pursued should be such as are of general conciliation and attachment without any particular allusion for the present to any possible state of hostility with Americans."[80] As a further precaution against American misunderstanding, he straightway sent a long letter to Erskine so that the latter might be able to give any necessary explanation to the United States government.[79]

Craig's policy recalls that of Haldimand, nearly a quarter of a century before; and it was initiated in the same way, without any suggestion from London. American conditions forced it upon the governor in Quebec, and the home government merely sanctioned it afterwards. Like his predecessor, Craig observed that his policy supported the interest of the British fur trade, but he too was little moved by this consideration. What was of paramount importance was the defense of the country for which he was responsible, and this brought him to the same slippery slope leading down to war with the United States over British relations with the Indians.

In some respects the situation was not the same as in the years following the Revolutionary War. The balance of position and power in North America had shifted, Britain having become much weaker and the

79. Q, CVII, 261–266.
80. Ibid., pp. 229–232.

United States much stronger, so that it was now more dangerous for the former to interfere with the red men living in the latter. However, there was much less scope for interference. In the period before Jay's Treaty, this western imbroglio had been a primary cause of Anglo-American tension. Now it was only secondary, being released by the crisis which began at sea. Because this could not have occurred if the Monroe-Pinkney treaty had been ratified, and ratification was withheld because Britain would not yield to the American demand on impressments, the conclusion follows that the impressment issue was indirectly responsible for this revival of the old danger. Indeed the more the history of these years is studied, the greater appears the influence of this fundamental issue. Yet it was not wholly responsible for the British hand's reaching out into the American West.

This trouble stems from the entanglement of British and Americans in the interior of the continent over the plight of the doomed red race, an international phase of the old clash between a primitive people and white civilization. Jay's Treaty may have made the best arrangement possible at the time, but it effected only a partial disentanglement. The remaining limitation upon the sovereignty of the United States, as observed in a previous chapter,[81] inevitably roused American resentment. The consequent friction, however, was merely a minor irritant that if left alone would pass away, because the condition which produced it was essentially temporary, though it did not finally disappear until after the War of 1812.

Craig's solicitude for the friendship of the western tribes reached a highly dangerous point in May, 1808, when he issued the orders quoted above. He had just learned of the failure of the special mission sent to Washington to settle the *Chesapeake* affair. Shortly afterward the governor's apprehensions of an impending attack on Canada subsided, and his almost hysterical interest in the distant red men died away. This is reflected, though somewhat tardily, in the value of Indian presents shipped from England. As already suggested, it was slightly less in 1807 than in 1806; but it leaped up about fourfold in 1808, in answer to the appeals from Canada. In 1809, however, it fell back to nearly the old level,[82] London as well as Quebec having come to the conclusion in the summer of 1808 that the United States was not about to declare war.[83] This conclusion may seem strange in light of the fact, already mentioned

---

81. *Supra*, pp. 199–205.

82. Tables in *Q*, CCCXIV, 256–257. Another table (p. 258) shows, as might be expected, that the issue of provisions in 1807 was double that in 1806.

83. See Castlereagh's dispatches to Craig, of May 7, June 3, July 7, and Nov. 23, 1808, in *G*, III, 32, 48, 65, 98; and Craig to Cooke, Aug. 25, 1808, *Q*, CVII, 322.

and now to be explained, that other influences had complicated the Anglo-American quarrel during the months following the attack on the *Chesapeake*. What brought relief to Craig and Canada was not an improvement in Anglo-American relations but a sudden deterioration in Franco-American relations.

The whole international situation rapidly became much worse in the latter part of 1807 as a consequence of French, British, and American action. The change came before there was any possibility of liquidating the *Chesapeake* affair and quite independently of it, though there can be no doubt that things would not have been so bad if that unfortunate incident had never occurred.[84] The new turn of events grew out of the mighty struggle in the Old World, which then reached its central climax, and the initial impetus came from France.

Napoleon's smashing victory over Russia at Friedland led him to believe that he had completed his mastery over Europe and could therefore make his Continental System work the destruction of England's power. Having persuaded Alexander to apply it in Russia, he proceeded to enforce his Berlin Decree vigorously in the rest of the Continent. His orders were issued in August, and by the end of the month the news of wholesale seizures startled London. There it became practically impossible to get insurance for shipments to the Continent, so that they ceased for the time being. Ostensibly in retaliation for the way Britain then struck back at him, Napoleon tightened his system on December 17, 1807, when he issued the Milan Decree. This announced that any neutral ship, together with its cargo, sailing from a British port or having submitted to British search had lost its neutral character and become lawful prize.

The British action which thus stirred his ire was the issuance of the famous orders-in-council of November 11, 1807, modified and developed by subsequent orders, declaring a blockade of all countries in Napoleon's system, together with their colonies, and condemning their produce as lawful prize. This was precisely the weapon he had aimed at Britain in his Berlin Decree. She claimed that she had a right to do to him what he would do to her; and at the same time she prided herself on being more considerate of neutrals, for she made a number of important exceptions in further provisions to be noticed presently.

Such assertions were delusive. There were fundamental differences between the two belligerents and what they were trying to do to each other. Napoleon would have stopped all trade from anywhere with Britain, but he could not; whereas she could have prevented all inter-

84. It is also possible that the change contributed to the failure of the special mission to Washington.

course with the French Empire and its dependencies, but she would not. He could not, because he had no navy and she possessed a mighty one; she would not, because she felt that her life and liberty depended on continued access to the European market, from which he would exclude her utterly by means of his land power. In one respect their sweeping declarations of blockade were alike. Both were dishonest, being designed to cover only a partial though effective execution. Her object, however, was the opposite of his. Hence her tenderness toward neutrals.

Britain announced that neutral vessels might pass with impunity through the blockade of Europe if they were cleared from, or bound for, a British port in the Old World. They would serve her purpose. The strong continental demand for her wares would see to that; and she revised her navigation and customs laws to legalize the introduction of return cargoes comprising goods of enemy origin for domestic consumption or reëxport. Another "concession" to neutrals was that of direct trade with enemy colonies; for the British fleet effectively isolated them from Napoleon's dangerous system, and the British government was anxious to avoid unnecessary pressure upon neutrals lest she lose their indispensable aid in European waters. Even the produce of enemy colonies might thus find its way to their mother country, Britain collecting equalizing duties[85] to protect the produce of her own colonies. No concession, however, was to protect ships complying with a new regulation of Napoleon, by which his agents abroad certified that their cargoes contained nothing of British origin. Such ships and cargoes were to be confiscated.

The American action was the imposition of the embargo of December 22, 1807. This was before the news of the orders-in-council, and of course of the Milan Decree, had reached America. Of all the above European developments affecting neutrals, the only thing that was positively known to the government of the United States was that Napoleon had commenced to enforce his Berlin Decree against even Americans in violation of the treaty of 1800; and this information had just arrived. It might thus appear that the American action was rather precipitate, but no judgment on this point should be passed without an examination of the background.

Both Jefferson and Madison, as well as other Americans, had long cherished a comfortable belief that Nature had placed in the armory of the United States a most effective weapon that might be produced at any time to coerce an offending power such as Britain and France. Their rapidly expanding country imported almost all its manufactured goods from Europe, and it provided the West Indian colonies with supplies on

85. Which were soon abandoned.

which they were vitally dependent. By shutting this market and by cutting off this source of supply, the American government could suddenly release an economic pressure that would be much more telling than any possible military or naval pressure. It would also be cheaper than war. The confidence inspired by this homespun theory was so complete that, as already observed, the administration walked blindly on toward war without making any preparations for it.

From the spring of 1806 the nonimportation act had remained on the statute book without being applied against Britain, suspension being followed by suspension, even though the complex quarrel between the two countries was aggravated by the unsuccessful efforts of Monroe and Pinkney to compose it and by the order-in-council of January, 1807, condemning American vessels plying between enemy ports. But the *Chesapeake* "outrage" made any further suspension impossible; and when the last one expired on December 14, 1807, the punitive act was finally allowed to come into operation, over strong mercantile remonstrances. The exclusion of many principal articles of British manufacture hit producer and consumer on opposite sides of the Atlantic and widened the breach between their governments. This American blow at Britain was no sooner launched than a British blast hit the United States. It was the October proclamation on impressments, likewise produced by the mounting quarrel and further embittering it.

The conclusion is obvious: by action and reaction, the degeneration of Anglo-American relations was developing a dangerous momentum toward some new crisis without any assistance from France. If Napoleon had not provided the impetus mentioned above, the near future would probably have seen the United States giving a further twist to the economic screw against Britain, for such was the logical sequel; and Britain might have proceeded to destroy the American trade with the enemy's colonies by blockading them or by canceling her relaxation of the Rule of 1756, for such was the recommendation submitted by a House of Commons committee at the end of July. It would thus appear that Napoleon might have maneuvered the United States into war with Britain long before 1812 if he had scrupulously observed the Franco-American treaty of 1800, but his mind was set on crushing England with his Continental System.

It was in the middle of December, 1807, just as the nonimportation act went into force and the impressment proclamation arrived, that the *Revenge* returned with startling news from Paris. Napoleon was laying violent hands on American commerce! Consternation and confusion seized Washington, where men now saw double. Two great potential foes, instead of only one, confronted the United States. Though weeks were yet to pass before anyone in the country knew of the orders-in-council, there was every reason to believe that Britain had already struck back in some way most damaging to American interest. Within a day or two of the *Revenge*, some vessels arrived from England bringing London newspapers of November 12, two days before the orders were published; and these papers unanimously predicted some such move immediately.[86] Quick action in the American capital seemed imperative, and there was no question of what it should be. Hastily Jefferson drafted, Madison revised, and the cabinet sanctioned a message to Congress calling for an embargo. In four hours, the Senate rushed through a bill supposed to have been drawn by the President, but the House required two more days to pass the embargo.

A twofold motive inspired the measure. American merchandise, vessels, and seamen were in peril on the sea, and elsewhere abroad, because of the predatory behavior of the belligerent powers; and therefore the embargo was necessary to preserve "these essential resources." This was the only argument of the presidential message and the only official explanation in the United States. Madison straightway assured Erskine, and instructed Pinkney to tell Canning, the British Foreign Secretary, that the act was purely a precaution and devoid of offense. It was not to be regarded as in any way tinged with hostility.[87] These professions of innocence were repeatedly renewed, but they rang hollow. Here we may detect a certain likeness to the dishonest blockade declarations of Napoleon and Britain. Neither Jefferson nor Madison nor any other responsible American believed the embargo had a single motive. They knew it was also designed to coerce the powers that were oppressing American commerce. Its punitive purpose was unwittingly revealed in negotiations over its possible repeal and also in its enforcement along the international boundary of the adjacent British provinces.

The rigid enforcement of the embargo all along this boundary would have been quite superfluous if the sole object of the act was to prevent the illegal seizure of American ships, cargoes, and sailors; yet the attempt was made to sever all commercial intercourse with the northern neighbors of the United States.

The only exception was that the fur trade, despite the alarm over British support of Indians on American soil, was legally allowed to continue. As originally passed, however, the law did not make this exception. When the Montreal merchants of the Michilimackinac Company, recently organized to conduct the British traffic in the

86. The American government believed that it was a complete prohibition of trade with any enemy country or colony.
87. *A.S.P.F.R.*, III, 206.

American West, heard of what was afoot in Washington, they saw ruin staring them in the face. For the slow strangulation of this trade, by the requirements for passes, by the arbitrary calculation of customs duties, and by other vexations, the Americans seemed to be substituting sudden extinction by means of the embargo. This meant that the violation of Jay's Treaty, which had been furtive, was to become open and flagrant. The merchants appealed to Craig and, with his warm sanction, they sent a mission to the American capital. There Erskine interceded; and just before Congress adjourned at the end of April he procured the insertion of a saving clause in an amending act.[88] It stipulated that neither the embargo nor the nonimportation act should be construed to prevent the export by land or inland navigation of furs bought from the Indians by British subjects, or the import in the same way of British merchandise solely intended for the native fur trade. But what was thus allowed legally was soon stopped practically.

On May 21, 1808, five bateaux, manned by French Canadians who did not understand English, entered the mouth of the Niagara River. At once they were accosted in a strange tongue, and then they were fired upon by a party of American soldiers in a boat. Three of the five craft, pursued by musket shot, reached the Canadian shore, but the other two were taken. Learning that more were coming, the captors went out and seized six in the open lake, and pursued nine more for about thirty miles before giving up the chase. This flotilla of twenty bateaux belonged to the Michilimackinac Company and contained the year's supply of trading goods to be distributed from St. Joseph's Island, the company's western base. As usual, on leaving the St. Lawrence the boats had skirted the shorter southern shore of Lake Ontario, which was American. Therefore, apparently, the United States customs collector at Niagara believed that it was his duty to stop them, and he had to invoke the aid of the garrison to do it.

The eight bateaux thus gathered in were straightway declared confiscated, along with their cargoes, and the frightened crews were left to shift for themselves. The company suffered a crippling blow.[89] The direct loss was over six thousand pounds, and the indirect was estimated at twenty thousand, being caused by the disruption of the year's trade. Far from receiving any warning, the Montreal merchants had just received assurance that the embargo was not to stop their trade across the international line. Nor had there been any witting contravention of a legal technicality. In British eyes, the affair seemed to be a violent

88. Craig to Erskine, March 8, 1808, Q, CVIII, 16. Erskine to Canning, No. 18, May 3, 1808, F.O. 5, Vol. LVII.
89. From which it never recovered.

interference with the freedom to navigate boundary waters guaranteed
by Jay's Treaty, a right which had been taken for granted as unassailable
even under the unamended embargo. The partners of the company cried
out in dismay, Gore and Craig wrote indignantly to Washington, and
Erskine made strong representations against this "gross and unprovoked
outrage" upon unarmed British subjects and "flagrant insult" to His
Majesty's government in Canada.

The Secretary of the Treasury, Albert Gallatin, did not know why
the seizure had been made. If these boats were really British, had only
British cargoes on board, and had not attempted to engage in smuggling,
he could discover only two provisions of the law which might catch them,
one forbidding departures from the United States without clearance
papers and the other requiring all arrivals with dutiable goods to make
formal entry; but he added that "sailing on the American side of the
boundary line" was not of itself enough to require either formality. He
ordered the collector at Niagara to release the boats and cargoes, if such
was the cause of their detention, taking sufficient security to cover possible judgment by the proper tribunal. The collector would have obeyed,
but the company refused to pay the double surety demanded for the
recovery of property which had been "illegally" captured and, because of
many weeks' delay, could not be used that year. Meanwhile Madison complained to Erskine of the "tone" of the company's complaint, and Erskine
stoutly defended it.[90] The whole incident created bad blood in Canada.

Though it was thus possible to stop a legal traffic, it was impossible
to stop what was illegal, and the attempt to do it produced other more or
less violent incidents. Down in Passamaquoddy Bay, where the boundary
was still undefined,[91] American vigilance offended British susceptibilities
by the military occupation of Moose Island and the forcible seizure of a
flour-laden boat after it had touched at Deer Island. When Canning
heard of this, he ordered Erskine to lodge a protest on both counts.
Though the convention of 1803 had anticipated the future settlement of
the dispute over these islands by assigning the first to the United States
and the second to New Brunswick, the rejection of the convention had
technically preserved the British claim to Moose and the American claim
to Deer Island. Madison therefore might have made the balanced
retort; but the two governments were not in quite the same position,
for what had occurred was a unilateral alteration of the *status quo* in

90. Erskine to Canning, No. 23, July 5, 1808, and voluminous enclosures, *ibid*. See also
Forsyth to Inglis, Aug. 4, 1808, *Q*, CVIII, 213–214, and Memorial of the Merchants of
Montreal, Oct. 20, 1808, *ibid*., pp. 3–15.

91. As a consequence of the failure of the conventions of 1803 and 1807. See *supra*, Chapter
X.

disputed territory, and the American Secretary of State preferred the surer ground for the more positive action. He stoutly defended the American claim to Moose Island, citing the convention as confirmation; and he evaded the point about the fugitive invasion of Deer Island.[92]

The summer of 1808 saw serious disturbances at Oswego and Sackett's Harbor, especially the latter. At the former place, the arrival of a detachment of soldiers enabled the customs collector to make some show of doing his duty; but when this little military contingent went on to unruly Sackett's Harbor, the bold commanding officer was roughly handled as a "Jefferson tory, scoundrel," and "one of Bonaparte's men." Led by the local constables, the mob took him prisoner. After being rescued by the man he had come to support,[93] he was apparently a little more circumspect, for he was able to report that he sent out armed boats which "fired on British and American boats after they had refused to come to and when they were actually escaping to Canada with cargoes of potash, etc."[94] Ineffectual efforts were made to check the delivery of lumber rafts from Lake Champlain to Montreal merchants who, as usual, had supplied the money for cutting operations in the previous winter. Craig had his eye on this situation, lest some "scuffle" spill over the border; but when he heard that some of the many French Canadians who were regularly employed in the business, "a lawless set," had been caught and landed in jail, he refused to lift his little finger on their behalf.[95]

On the whole, British North America benefited, rather than suffered, from the embargo. It was easier to shut the ocean ports of the United States to overseas commerce than it was to prevent intercourse with the neighboring provinces, with the result that a tremendous internal pressure forced an abnormally large trade through these provinces. Passamaquoddy Bay, which had always been a good place for smuggling, now became a marvelously good one. Vessels crowded into it. Furious gales of wind, overriding the American law, carried New England coasters into the friendly harbors of Nova Scotia.[96] The frontiers of Vermont and New York poured their produce into the Canadas, raising the exports from the St. Lawrence in 1808 to double the average of the

92. Canning to Erskine, No. 7, July 9, 1808, F.O. 5, Vol. LVII. Erskine to Canning, No. 37, Oct. 6, 1808, ibid., Vol. LVIII, and No. 39, Nov. 2, 1808, enclosing Erskine to Madison, Sept. 11, 1808, and Madison to Erskine, Oct. 4, 1808, ibid.

93. Hart Massey, who had recently been appointed collector of customs.

94. The story of these doings in Oswego and Sackett's Harbor was set forth in a letter of October 21, 1808, from the officer, Lieutenant Joseph Cross, to the Secretary of War, with a confirming note signed by Massey. This document was published in the Albany Register, and the clipping was enclosed in Erskine to Canning, No. 13, Feb. 13, 1809, F.O. 5, Vol. LXII.

95. P.A.C.R., 1896, Note B, p. 47. Q, CVII, 265.

96. See A. T. Mahan, op. cit., I, 194–195.

previous five years.[97] The Canadian merchants were not entirely pleased
with what was going on, for they would like to have seen less specie and
more manufactures recrossing the interior border, and they found a new
fault in Jay's Treaty. They complained that the freedom it accorded to
the entry of goods from the United States was allowing the two Canadas
to be inundated with tea, cotton, and other East Indian produce, as well
as many articles of European production and American manufacture,
particularly bar and cast iron, shoes, and saddlery.[98] Here it may be
observed by way of anticipation that the artificial stimulus to commercial
intercourse between the United States and the neighboring provinces did
not cease with the embargo in 1809, for the nonintercourse act, which
was then substituted, had the same effect.[99]

In the negotiations between the United States and the two great
belligerents of the Old World, the hostile character of the embargo
became more obvious as its failure became more apparent. It failed
because it did most injury to the nation it was supposed to protect.
Apparently the small region adjoining the Canadas throve, particularly
upper New York, and the sparsely populated West was not much
affected. But the rest of the Union suffered deeply. The planter South
was half ruined by the stoppage of the outlet for its produce, yet the
people there were patient under the severe strain. Their own leaders,
who controlled the government in Washington, assured them that it
was necessary. Complete ruin, however, faced the group of states in the
northeastern corner of the country, where the population was least
agricultural and most urban. There was the home of American shipping
and the seat of American commerce. Both were paralyzed. For economic
reasons, the people of this section were the least capable of sustaining
the embargo and they had to bear most of its weight. For political
reasons, also, they were the most inclined to resist. This crushing
measure was the work of their political foes, the Republicans, who had
got control of the national government in 1801, and had consolidated
their victory in 1803. The Louisiana Purchase had given New England
a little impetus toward rebellion, and now the embargo gave it a big
one. The increasing tension within the country turned politics upside
down. To enforce the embargo, the Republicans had to ride roughshod
over their own principle of state rights; and to resist the hated law, the
Federalists repudiated their doctrine of the superior authority possessed
by the central government.

The legislation designed to prevent a foreign war was working to

97. *Q*, CIX, 10.
98. *Ibid.*, p. 239.
99. See Jackson to Wellesley, No. 44, Sept. 15, 1810, *F.O. 5*, Vol. LXIX.

produce a domestic war, one with nasty foreign complications. From each party rose hot accusations that the other would betray the country, the Federalists by submitting to Britain and the Republicans by submitting to France. There was much truth in both charges. The split within the United States was following the lines of the division between the belligerents across the ocean. New England sympathized with old England in the hour of her trial, and believed that she was fighting the battle of liberty against the tyrant of Europe. On the other hand, Jefferson and his supporters denied having any partiality for France, but the policy on which they insisted was practically and definitely pro-French: for the issue in the Old World then turned on whether neutrals would coöperate in upholding the Continental System or in breaking it, and the embargo was enlisting the United States on the Napoleonic side of this issue. Fortunately for Britain a large number of American vessels were abroad when the law was passed and they refused to come home to be caught by it. Many of them now sailed the seas with British licenses.

Before Congress adjourned in the spring of 1808, internal pressure produced a law empowering the President to lift the embargo for whichever belligerent removed its restraints on American commerce, or for both belligerents on this condition. The government then tried to play one off against the other, hoping desperately that the embargo would succeed abroad before it failed at home. The desperation was inspired by the belief that war was the only alternative method of defending American rights and honor; and therefore it was suggested to both belligerents that either might oblige the United States to commence hostilities against the other. It was a pitiful attempt at an international auction with the American Republic on the block. It brought no bids and it exposed the country to scorn. Napoleon did not hesitate to say that he regarded the United States as automatically at war with Britain since the issuance of the orders-in-council.[100] His words stung. He would like to have seen the embargo continued as a reinforcement of his Continental System. It assisted him by keeping American bottoms at home; and as for those it kept from coming home, it gave him an excuse for treating without mercy any that fell into his clutches.[101] He did not even deign to reply to the American overture. The British were more polite but no less shrewd in rejecting it. On Madison's instructions, Pinkney urged Canning to repeal the orders-in-council, pointing out that this would "entitle" Britain to a suspension of the embargo. From their conversation in June, 1808, the American minister thought that Canning was inclined to yield. If any such inclination existed, it was discouraged

100. *A.S.P.F.R.*, III, 249.
101. Hence his Bayonne Decree.

in July by news from France and from America. From across the Channel came reports of the stubborn French attitude, reflected in Napoleonic orders to condemn more American ships. From across the ocean came strong echoes of the rising outcry against the embargo. Erskine wrote that it was ruining the popularity of the administration; and he advised Canning that, if England and the West Indies could sustain the privation of their usual supplies from the United States, Britain might let the American government teach the American public a wholesome lesson. He also reiterated an opinion he had already sent home: that though the orders-in-council had given great offense, "Congress would never dare to consider them as justifying hostilities" if the *Chesapeake* affair could be amicably settled.[102] Pinkney's hopes sank when he resumed his conversation with Canning at the end of July. The Englishman complained of the Passamaquoddy Bay and Niagara incidents, and his general attitude was much stiffer. In September, he delivered his final answer, in which he laid bare the American inconsistency. If, as asserted, the embargo was an innocent domestic regulation, why was its suspension tied to a repeal of the orders-in-council? It did not alter the reason for their promulgation—the decrees of Napoleon. Because the Emperor would not yield, the British government could not.[103]

Looking more critically at the conditions underlying this effort to play one power against the other, we can detect that the scales were not evenly balanced. What happened in 1812 was distinctly foreshadowed in 1808. Britain had to do more than France to effect a *rapprochement* with the United States. Beyond the orders-in-council lay other obstacles that would have to be surmounted and for which there was no French counterpart. Of those raised by the United States, the nonimportation act might have gone with the embargo: but there would still have been the discriminating presidential proclamation, which Canning's final answer to Pinkney described as amounting "nearly to direct hostility."[104] More formidable was the list of American charges against Britain that had been piling up before the orders-in-council and would still have to be cleared away: the blockades, the Rule of 1756, the impressment of seamen, and the attack on the *Chesapeake*. There was yet another difference between what was required of the two belligerents, and this might have been more serious. The American price for lifting the embargo was theoretically the same for Britain and France, but practically it was not. Not without destroying the orders-in-council could Britain exempt

102. Erskine to Canning, No. 20, June 4, 1808, *F.O. 5*, Vol. LVII.

103. For Madison's instructions to Pinkney and the ensuing discussions in London, see *A.S.P.F.R.*, III, 221–239.

104. *Ibid.*, p. 232.

American vessels from their operation, and that meant abandoning the struggle against Napoleon's Continental System. But, as Madison and even Jefferson confessed to Erskine, the Emperor could refrain from applying his decrees beyond the territorial waters under his control and yet preserve his system, because the government of the United States could not challenge another government's right to enact and enforce "municipal regulations."[105] Napoleon therefore had a trick he might have played on both the Americans and the British, and one is tempted to wonder why he did not employ it.

Though the scales were thus loaded in favor of France, it was the British refusal to budge which seems to have stirred the greater surprise of Jefferson and Madison. They leaped to the conclusion that the hopes reported by Pinkney in June had been dashed by a British reliance on support from New England; and they were more than ever irritated at the two members of this combination.

A thoroughly disillusioned and dejected President faced a bewildered Congress when it assembled in November, 1808. The embargo was a complete and disastrous failure. The only alternative that Jefferson could see was war, and from that he shrank in horror. Out of sheer despair he clung to the doomed embargo, but he dared not officially urge Congress to continue it. He yearned for the arrival of March when he would depart from office, and meanwhile he regarded himself as no longer responsible for the direction of the country's affairs. His chief remaining interest was purely personal—to avoid the crowning humiliation of being forced to sign the repeal of his own measure. He had to do it in the end, but not before he had made confusion worse confounded by struggling to prevent the passage of the repeal. Seldom has a country been in a more miserable plight than was the United States during the winter of 1808-9. It had been brought to the brink of war without any preparation for it; the national revenue was destroyed by the embargo; and government was reduced to a negation.

The painful alternative of peace or war was squarely presented in the report of a House committee on November 22, 1808. "Every European power having become a party to the contest" in which Britain and France were trampling under foot the rights of neutrals as established by international law, "the whole of our commerce with Europe and European colonies becomes liable to capture by either one or the other." Referring to the transit charges on trade forcibly diverted through British ports, the report continued, "If there be any nominal exception, it is made on a condition of tributes, which only adds insult to the in-

105. Erskine to Canning, No. 17, May 2, 1808, *F.O.* 5, Vol. LVII; No. 44, Nov. 10, 1808, *ibid.*, Vol. LVIII.

jury."[106] The execution of the Berlin Decree and the order-in-council of November 11, 1807, were, "as they affect the United States, contemporaneous aggressions of the belligerent powers, equally unprovoked and equally indefensible on the presumed ground of acquiescence," and "together with the Milan Decree of December, 1807, which filled the measure, would, on the principle of self-defence, have justified immediate hostilities against both nations." Instead, the embargo had been passed "to avoid war, at least for a season." The subsequent appeal to the belligerents, involving even an offer to become "a party to the war," having provided no escape, the people of the United States should face the facts. "The pressure of the embargo, so sensibly felt, and the calamities inseparable from a state of war, naturally create a wish that some middle course might be discovered, which should avoid the evils of both, and not be inconsistent with national honor and independence. That illusion must be dissipated." The reasons were clearly stated. A general repeal unaccompanied by the arming of merchant vessels would mean submission to both powers. A general repeal with arming "would be war with both, and war of the worst kind, suffering the enemy to plunder us without retaliation upon them." A partial repeal to allow trade with any territories not belonging to Britain or controlled by Napoleon would be tantamount to submission to Britain[107] and war with France. There was "no other alternative but war with both nations, or a continuance of the present system." A permanent suspension of commerce would really be submission. "The aggressions of England and France . . . are, to all intents and purposes, a maritime war waged by both nations against the United States. It cannot be denied that the ultimate and only effectual mode of resisting that warfare, if persisted in, is war." Because the country was then in no condition to face it, an obvious and humiliating fact which the committee took for granted and would change as soon as possible, war was ruled out as a question for the time being. What was left was a choice between submission, which the committee would bind the House to reject, and a temporary perseverance in the existing system.[108] The logic of the report was inexorable. War must come soon unless both Britain and France abandoned their oppressive edicts.

The report was a bitter pill. It was swallowed with difficulty, but it could not be kept down, for it contained one false ingredient that made

106. *Supra*, p. 255 and n. 85.

107. "But the true effect of the proposition would be to open an indirect trade with Great Britain, which, through St. Bartholomew and Havana, Lisbon, Cadiz, or Gottenburg, would receive at prices reduced by glutted markets, and for want of competition, all the provisions, naval stores, raw materials for her manufactures, and other articles which she may want."

108. *A.S.P.F.R.*, III, 259–262.

the legislature gag. This was the assumption that the "continuance of the existing system" was possible. Congress had a prolonged fit of convulsions. At the very outset Gallatin aggravated the disease. Two days after the presentation of the report he wrote a letter demanding stiffer legislation to enforce observance of the embargo. Seven weeks later, after chaotic debates, he got it; but nothing could save the embargo, and this reinforcement only hastened the end. It had to be repealed to save the Union. That became more and more evident, but the great question was when and how. Madison was for keeping it until the new Congress could be called together some time in May to undertake measures for war. But the dying Congress writhed and squirmed, apparently unable to reach any conclusion. Finally, by the end of February, 1809, it was decided that the embargo would end on March 4, motions for allowing merchantmen to arm and for issuing letters of marque were rejected, and a nonintercourse law was substituted.

The nonintercourse law of 1809 excluded, under heavy penalties, all ships and goods of the belligerents and their dependencies; and it forbade American vessels, under heavy bonds, to enter French or British ports, or to engage in any trade with either power; but it allowed the President to suspend its operation against a repentant belligerent. The last provision was a repetition of the implied offer, made under the embargo, to join one side against the other.

Though the new law was carried by a majority of two to one, few members liked it. It was accepted, rather than supported, by a company of strange bedfellows. Some voted for it as the only way to get rid of the embargo; some as the most hostile, and others as the least hostile step then possible; some because it could, and others because it would not be applied; some to benefit New England at the expense of the South, and others to unite these two parts of the country by exposing New England's shipping and commerce to the depredations of Britain. John Randolph of Virginia called it an excuse "to sneak out" of the trap in which they were caught.[109] What the outcome would be nobody could tell. One member wrote, "The Lord, the mighty Lord, must come to our assistance, or I fear we are undone as a Nation!"[110]

That the country had been, and still was, reeling on the brink of a war for which it was totally unprepared, Madison and others in the administration frankly admitted to Erskine.[111] Though the United States had scarcely any fighting forces fit for service, this did not seem to matter much. Regular naval warfare was not contemplated.

109. Quoted in Erskine to Canning, No. 14, March 9, 1809, *F.O. 5*, Vol. LXIII.
110. Macon to Nicholson, Feb. 28, 1809, quoted in Adams, IV, 453.
111. A number of his dispatches reporting this are in *F.O. 5*, Vols. LXII and LXIII.

"War on water must be carried on by private armed vessels, and whenever we did wage war it must be as much on land as possible," declared one member of the House on January 11, 1809, according to one of the many newspaper clippings sent home by Erskine. John W. Eppes of Virginia, who was the President's son-in-law, and another member expressed a similar idea. Eppes condemned the common talk of allowing government frigates to rot in port. "He was not for sending out these vessels to force a war before a single soldier was ready to march where they ought. So soon as our troops were ready to send to Canada, he said, he was ready to send the frigates."[112]

The British minister was neither shocked nor surprised. The idea was quite current. Already he had written to Canning about it. In a dispatch of December 7, 1808, he said that "the United States would rely altogether on privateers and very small vessels of war, for the purpose of annoying their enemies at sea," and upon fortifications and gunboats for defense. The military force, he noted, would have "two great objects." One was the defense of New Orleans, which "could not however be defended against a strong force (ten thousand men for instance) if the superiority of naval force was also with the assailants." The other object was "the attack upon Canada and Nova Scotia, which would be a favorite project with the Democratic Party." He doubted if "it could be attempted for a year at least," because of the large number of troops that would be required; and he was not unduly concerned over the possible result. "The people of this country entertain generally an opinion that the conquest of His Majesty's Dominions on this continent might be more easily accomplished than I believe it would be found to be."[113] Four weeks later he wrote, "I know that a strong idea prevails that the militia of the adjacent states aided by a large volunteer force would be sufficient to take possession of Upper Canada, and that an attack might be afterwards made with the aid of a regular force upon the fort of Quebec." It was "hardly possible it could happen very soon, yet as it might be attempted in the next summer," he had warned Sir James Craig to be on his guard against a surprise.[114]

Here was the War of 1812 accurately anticipated at the close of 1808 and the beginning of 1809. The one surprising thing about this alarm is that it did not reinvigorate Craig's efforts to gain Indian support, though it inspired him to send home an urgent appeal for twelve thousand men.[115]

112. Enclosed in Erskine to Canning, No. 13, Feb. 13, 1809, *ibid.*, Vol. LXII.

113. Erskine to Canning, No. 48, Dec. 7, 1808, *ibid.*, Vol. LVIII.

114. Erskine to Canning, No. 3, Jan. 3, 1809, *ibid.*, Vol. LXII.

115. Craig to Castlereagh, Feb. 13, 1809, *Q*, CIX, 10. In April, Castlereagh sanctioned Craig's policy of cultivating the Indians, echoing his own statement that the important consideration was not the use of the natives as allies but their destructiveness as enemies. *Ibid.*, p. 99. Before this reached Craig, he had learned of Erskine's agreement (*infra*, pp. 269–271) which seemed to banish all thought of war.

The war might easily have come at this time if Napoleon had played his possible trick. Erskine knew what held the United States back. Early in the session, Madison had told him "that she would be fully justified in having recourse to hostilities with either belligerent, and that she only hesitated to do so from the difficulty of contending with both."[116] The British minister analyzed the baffling situation a little more fully on New Year's Day, when he wrote, "The project of engaging in hostilities with both powers seems so chimerical, and so little likely to be attended with any advantages, as the commerce of the United States would be thereby excluded from the whole world as much as by an embargo, and the evils of war added to it, that it has caused the greatest embarrassments to determine what course ought to be pursued."[117] What course would be pursued, he could not prophesy. He observed that the bellicose forces might burst their bonds. "Although a war with Great Britain would be far from being popular in the Eastern States, yet as the Southern States are almost unanimous and the Eastern States divided in their sentiments, I cannot help thinking that a war might be brought on by Congress authorizing an armed resistance to the enforcement of His Majesty's orders-in-council."[118] On the very next day he was told by Madison, already selected as Jefferson's successor, that if the belligerents continued their restrictions on neutral commerce, the government intended to ask Congress for a law "to allow merchant ships to arm and also to issue letters of marque and reprisal."[119]

116. Erskine to Canning, No. 46, Dec. 2, 1808, *F.O. 5*, Vol. LVIII.
117. Dana made sport of the idea of war under these circumstances, as the following quotation from a newspaper report of one of his speeches shows. It was sent home by Erskine, enclosed in No. 13, Feb. 13, 1809, *ibid.*, Vol. LXII. "As to war with G. Britain and France, I should wish to delay that till I could understand how it was with two nations at war with each other, I should like first to make some enquiry on the subject. I wish to know if any gentleman of military talents has drawn up any system of fighting three armies together. One against two on the same side, is no new thing, sir, but three against each other is a perfect novelty. I really do not know how they could draw up their troops in order of battle, supposing three armies to meet. They could not be drawn up in parallel lines, for each army must be opposed to two others. It is a sort of *prismatic or triangular thing;* for I cannot take three lines and form a square of them, or any other regular body. How would they form a line of reserve? The only way that I could think of arranging an army on this principle, was to draw up the three armies in a triangular form, the angles at 120 Degrees, the whole making 360 degrees, or a whole circle; but in this case you must keep them there, not let them move, or you destroy the principle. This is a new thing which I wish to have explained. It is not the old fashioned way of fighting at all."
118. Erskine to Canning, No. 1, Jan. 1, 1809, *ibid.*
119. Erskine to Canning, No. 3, Jan. 3, 1809, *ibid.*

CHAPTER XIII

THE WAR OF 1812: THE EVOLUTION OF CAUSES, FROM 1809

THOUGH the war did not come in 1809, that very year saw the precarious peace seriously damaged by a bungled effort to patch it. Sometime about the beginning of December, 1808, Gallatin pointed out to Erskine that the nonintercourse law, which had just been proposed in the House, would "remove two very important grounds of difference with Great Britain." By excluding impartially all ships of both belligerents, it would obliterate the anti-British discriminations of the nonimportation act and the *Chesapeake* proclamation. From this he went on to suggest that the impressment issue might cease from troubling, because the employment of foreign seamen on American ships of war had been forbidden and now the extension of the prohibition to all American vessels "under heavy penalties or forfeitures" was being considered. He also intimated a willingness to tolerate the application of the Rule of 1756 to direct trade between belligerents and their colonies; and he observed that all points of difference between the two countries might be "smoothed away" in this manner. Furthermore, he would apply to commercial intercourse with Great Britain the principle of reciprocity or of the most favored nation; and he led Erskine to believe that, with the accession of Madison, American policy would swing from a pro-French to a pro-British course if London would only supply a fair wind. Erskine was greatly impressed, though he saw that the American's eagerness was inspired by a desperate desire to extricate the United States from a terrible predicament; and he cautiously suggested to Canning the sacrifice of the orders-in-council to purchase American good will.[1] This conversation in Washington was supplemented in London, where Canning discussed with Pinkney the delicate problem of enforcing the embargo against France should it be lifted for Britain; and, according to the Englishman, the American agreed that the Royal Navy might undertake the task, for otherwise the law "must be altogether nugatory."[2]

Canning reacted immediately to Erskine's dispatch and Pinkney's acquiescence. On January 23, 1809, just a fortnight after receiving the former, he directed the minister in Washington to open negotiations for a settlement with the United States. If he sent back a favorable report, a special minister would be hurried off to America for the formal

1. Erskine to Canning, No. 47, Dec. 4, 1808, *F.O.* 5, Vol. LVIII.
2. Canning to Erskine, No. 4, Jan. 23, 1809, *ibid.*, Vol. LXII.

completion of the business; and meanwhile the resident minister was authorized to fix a date for the reciprocal suspension of the British orders-in-council and the hostile American legislation. Finally, Canning heartily approved Gallatin's suggestion of a commercial treaty and asked Erskine to explore the question.[3]

Canning's orders reached Erskine on April 7, and in less than a fortnight a complete revolution of policy seemed to have been effected by a simple exchange of notes in Washington. According to instructions, the minister began with the *Chesapeake* affair as "the best test" of the American disposition. He formally stated his sovereign's desire to make "an honorable reparation for the aggression," which had already been disavowed and for which the admiral had been recalled. His Majesty would restore the seized sailors and, if acceptable to the American government, would make "suitable provision" for the widows and orphans of those who had been killed. Robert Smith,[4] the new Secretary of State, replied that the President accepted the offer "as a satisfaction for the insult and injury."[5]

For the recall of the orders-in-council, three conditions had been laid down in London. The first two were based on Erskine's reports of suggestions from Gallatin and Gallatin's colleagues. One was the withdrawal of the *Chesapeake* proclamation "and all non-intercourse and non-importation acts, so far as respects Great Britain, leaving them in force with respect to France and the powers which adopt or act under her decrees." The second was the recognition of the Rule of 1756. The third was the use of the British navy to enforce American legislation prohibiting intercourse with France. In an informal discussion, Erskine presented all three to Smith. It was agreed that the nonintercourse act provided for the first. The President had only to issue a proclamation under that act to relieve Britain from its operation. The second condition, said Smith, would occasion no difficulty. The United States would satisfy Britain on this point when the two countries arranged their commercial treaty. Meanwhile an official recognition of the principle had been rendered unnecessary for Britain and impossible for the United States by the nonintercourse act, which had outlawed all American trade with France and her dependencies. The third condition, Smith added, was likewise unnecessary for the former and impossible for the latter. It was self-evident that American citizens could never require their government to support them in violating their own law. This, however,

3. Canning to Erskine, Nos. 3, 4, 5, 6, all of Jan. 23, 1809, *ibid.*

4. It is understood that Robert Smith did little more than sign what Madison wrote. The former, who was utterly incompetent, had been forced upon the latter by a factional intrigue.

5. *A.S.P.F.R.*, III, 295–296.

could not be officially proclaimed, because a stipulation for a foreign execution of a domestic law would be degrading to the United States.

Erskine hesitated to depart from the letter of his instructions. But these had been framed in ignorance of the terms of the nonintercourse act; and circumstances would again change before advice could be procured from London. The delay might be fatal, for the new Congress was shortly to assemble in special session to deal with the emergency in the country's foreign relations. The wiser course, he decided, was to fall back upon the spirit of his instructions and effect a reconciliation before it was too late. Thereupon he closed with Smith. The American government was assured that, as far as the United States was concerned, the orders-in-council would cease to operate on June 10; and the President issued a proclamation suspending the anti-British application of the nonintercourse law from the same date. The notes exchanged were straightway published, so that not a day might be lost in relieving the tense anxiety of the American people; and in one of these notes was the British minister's announcement that his government would dispatch "an envoy extraordinary" to cement the new accord with a formal treaty.[6]

Before noting the effect of this agreement, we may turn for a moment to the Canadian-American border. Gallatin had followed up his conversation with Erskine by a display of consideration for the unfortunate Michilimackinac Company. In January, 1809, with the support of the attorney general, he procured a presidential order to discontinue the prosecutions for the forfeiture of the boats and cargoes seized at Niagara[7] and to restore them immediately. At the same time he gave some quiet advice to comfort the new fears of the Montreal merchants aroused by the nonintercourse bill. He assured Erskine that it would not interfere with the export of peltries, and though it would prohibit all imports, the merchants could slip their goods in before the law came into force. They could do it, he said, by entering them at Oswego, whence they might be forwarded as desired.[8]

A few months later a tragic incident occurred on the St. Lawrence at Brockville, then called Elizabethtown. There, on May 1, 1809, an American schooner from Ogdensburg anchored. On board was a detachment of the Sixth United States Infantry under Captain William P. Bennett. Having heard that an American deserter was living somewhere near, he sent a sergeant and two men ashore to apprehend him. They

6. Erskine to Canning, No. 19, April 18, No. 20, April 20, and enclosures, separate, April 22, 1809, *F.O.* 5, Vol. XLIII. The notes and the proclamation are printed in *A.S.P.F.R.*, III, 295–297.

7. See *supra*, p. 258.

8. Erskine to Canning, No. 4, Jan. 17, 1809, and enclosures, including his correspondence with the merchants, *F.O.* 5, Vol. LXII.

went to the schoolhouse, seized the schoolmaster, Isaac D. Underhill, bound his hands, and marched him off. On reaching the King's highway, he made a dash for liberty, only to be shot down in his tracks, mortally wounded. His "murderers" ran for the schooner and, with their officer, escaped in a boat across the river. The schooner was held for investigation and Bennett wrote back demanding its release, praising his sergeant and men for the spirit and promptness with which they had executed his order, and boasting that he would again do his duty "on like occasion." It was evident that the British were not the only ones who could perpetrate a *Chesapeake* "outrage." This affair, however, should not be regarded as typifying the relationship between the people and the civil officials living on opposite sides of the international river. A few days afterwards, the local British justices of the place wrote to the magistrates at Ogdensburg requesting the surrender of the culprits, and the Americans replied in a friendly note. They regretted the occurrence, hoped it would not disturb the good understanding between the two countries, and explained that the accused, being up at Sackett's Harbor, were beyond their jurisdiction.[9] Down in Washington the news of this American violation of British territory reached Erskine through the Secretary of State, who hastened to assure him that the offending officer, sergeant, and men had been arrested, that reparation would be made, and that the President deeply regretted what had been done.[10] But the American captain, like the English admiral, escaped with only a nominal punishment. After a formal court martial, he received back his sword with honor.[11] Apparently the wheels of American justice were clogged by the collapse of Erskine's peace structure.

The collapse was a rude awakening from a sweet dream that lasted for three months. During this period the United States had the illusion of being near unto heaven. The bitter party strife was stilled, as Federalists and Republicans joined in a hymn of praise to the newborn peace, though each claimed the credit for securing it.[12] A new life stirred in the dead forest of masts that had been crowded together in the country's ports for nearly a year and a half, as ships and cargoes were being prepared for a resumption of trade with all the world save France.

Napoleon's decrees were the only cloud on the American horizon, and that cloud was not very menacing. A war with France was something remote in space if not in time, and it might not come after all

9. *Q*, CCCXII, 74, 77.

10. Erskine to Canning, separate, June 5, 1809, and enclosures, *F.O.* 5, Vol. LXIII.

11. *Interesting Political Discussion, The Diplomatic Policy of Mr. Madison Revealed,* by a Bostonian, p. 43. This pamphlet was enclosed in Jackson to Bathurst, separate, Jan. 25, 1810, *ibid.,* Vol. LXIX.

12. Erskine to Canning, No. 22, May 4, 1809, *ibid.,* Vol. LXIIII.

because the Emperor might be constrained to follow the British example. He had been dealt a heavy blow in the repeal of the embargo, for thereby the United States deserted his Continental System; and the nonintercourse law was another blow, for everybody could see that it would allow American supplies to pour through devious channels into the lap of England. Such was the effect, though not the intention, of the hectic voting in February. There had been no thought of committing the incoming administration or Congress. They would have to work out the country's salvation.

Only a short life had therefore been given to the nonintercourse law. It was to expire at the end of the next session, which began in May. By that time the executive and the legislature found their task marvelously simplified by Erskine's agreement. There could be no question of what to do. By an overwhelming vote the nonintercourse act was extended, with one amendment, to the end of the next session, namely, to the spring of 1810. The amendment repealed the exclusion of foreign ships of war from American ports. When the British minister looked askance at this, Smith explained it by saying that to continue the exclusion of French war vessels while admitting those of Britain would be "an open" and "a premature act of hostility" against France and would also be unnecessary because the Royal Navy would prevent France from taking advantage of the restored privilege.[13] This unwitting commentary on the *Chesapeake* proclamation appears to have been sound. The only concession to Napoleon was one to appease his *amour-propre*, and it was made in the avowed interest of Britain as well as the United States. It was designed to facilitate what both countries wanted—the repeal of the Napoleonic decrees. Beyond continuing the nonintercourse act against France, the special session adopted no hostile measure. This restraint was just. Both belligerents had been given a chance to reform. Napoleon should not be condemned unheard because his opponent had anticipated the offer. Quite properly, therefore, the question of peace or war with him was put off until the regular session.

Anglo-American relations had yet to be established on a regular footing; but, thanks to the restoration of amity by the exchange of notes, this problem seemed neither urgent nor unpleasant. Both before and after Congress adjourned at the end of June, Erskine had several interviews with Smith, in which they discussed the proposed negotiation. Madison was about to retire to his estate and planned to remain away until Congress assembled in November, unless he should be compelled to return "in order to cause some preparations to be made against hostilities with France which might become inevitable." The American

13. Erskine to Canning, No. 24, June 6, 1809, *ibid.*

Secretary of State hinted that the negotiation had better be postponed until after the congressional recess because of the President's absence, but he hastened to assure the British minister that "delicacy would prevent" the American government from refusing to negotiate before November if the British government did not wish to wait. At the same time Smith told him that the impressment issue, which was commonly regarded as the greatest obstacle, could be removed by American regulations against the employment of British seamen and for the surrender of deserters from British ships. According to Erskine, the American Secretary of State "added that the United States would be ready to pass any laws which the ablest English lawyer could frame to carry such regulations into operation, and would make it the duty of the magistrates to lend their assistance to the King's agents in this country for that purpose. It would not be contended for by the United States that Great Britain should abandon the principle, but only the practice of impressment out of American ships."[14]

The crash came at the end of July, when the United States was stunned by the news that Canning had repudiated and recalled Erskine. The settlement of the *Chesapeake* incident, the cancellation of the orders-in-council, and the hope of burying the impressment issue along with the other differences between the two countries were all cast to the winds. Canning's action was the source of a great tragedy and still remains a mystery.[15] It is true that the minister had stepped outside the letter of

14. *Ibid.*; Erskine to Canning, Nos. 28, 29, July 3, 1809, *ibid.*

15. British writers have failed to observe the mystery, being satisfied with an uncritical acceptance of Canning's severe indictment of Erskine for departing from his instructions. Half a century ago, Henry Adams grasped the puzzle, but he did not find a satisfactory solution. Adams, Vol. V, Chap. V, "Disavowal of Erskine."

The reasons Canning gave for repudiating the settlement of the *Chesapeake* affair are best stated in his dispatch to Erskine of May 22, 1809, No. 10, *F.O. 5*, Vol. LXIII. They are obviously only excuses, for they are suspiciously superficial. He had required, as a preliminary, the exclusion "in point of fact" of French war vessels from American ports. He accused Erskine of neglecting this, observing that the nonintercourse act was only prospective and did not provide for a warning to French vessels in American ports to get out. As a matter of fact there were no such vessels there. His second point was that Erskine had disobeyed the injunction to procure a formal withdrawal of the presidential proclamation or a formal declaration that its operation was at an end; but he already had a letter from Erskine, endorsed "*Highly Important*," stating that the nonintercourse act had repealed the law upon which the proclamation rested. Erskine to Canning, No. 18, March 18, 1809, Recd. April 15, *ibid.* His third point was that Erskine had omitted to reserve His Majesty's right to reclaim the restored seamen afterward if they were natural-born British subjects or deserters from the British service; but he had to admit that this omission was not vital because it did not impair the right, that being "founded on public law." His fourth point was that Erskine had made the offer of pecuniary compensation a part of the reparation instead of representing it as "an act of spontaneous generosity," as the instructions had intimated. Finally, he condemned Erskine for allowing the American Secretary of State to conclude his accepting note with expressions of disrespect to His Majesty. This point was well taken. The offensive passage stated that the President, while forbearing to insist on a further punishment of Berkeley, was nevertheless "sensible of the justice and utility of such an example" and "persuaded that it would best comport with what is due from His Britannic Majesty to his own honor." Madison, who added these words to the note, should have known better than to use such language; but he was only giving Canning a dose of his own medicine.

Equally lame were Canning's excuses for denouncing the agreement to suspend the orders-in-council. He put them most forcibly in his dispatch to Erskine, No. 11 of May 23, 1809, *ibid*. He denounced the publication of the notes exchanged, calling it a "singular and offensive step," though it was neither; and he rebuked the minister for not having remonstrated against it. Erskine, he said, had violated his instructions when he opened this discussion, because he had been forbidden to proceed without proof of the good disposition of the American government and the offensive passage just quoted proved the absence of that disposition. He also reprimanded the minister for promising the dispatch of an envoy extraordinary empowered to conclude a comprehensive treaty, because he was not authorized to hold out the expectation of such a mission until His Majesty had received from the United States "an authentic and official recognition of the conditions." Canning rated him severely for neglecting these in promising the withdrawal of the orders-in-council. "Nothing," he said, "can be more clear than that not one of these three conditions has been adopted by the American government, nor any engagement taken for their adoption."

To say the least, Canning was not candid. His first condition was "that the interdiction of the harbors of America to the ships of war of Great Britain, and all non-intercourse or non-importation acts should be withdrawn so far as respects Great Britain, leaving them in force with respect to France and the powers which adopt or act under her decrees." But did not American legislation (the nonintercourse act and the President's proclamation exempting Britain from its operation) do this very thing? Canning, however, declared that this was unsatisfactory because (1) it was not consigned to "a formal and written agreement," (2) the nonintercourse act was passed for only a short period (to the end of the special session), and (3) Holland was exempted. None of these objections had any validity as a reason for repudiating Erskine. The first took for granted that the executive could bind the legislature, which was notoriously impossible under the Constitution, and it implied that the American government was not to be trusted, which was insulting. The second, resting on a similar insinuation, was already removed by the continuance of the nonintercourse act. The third was inconsequential, as Canning later admitted to Pinkney, because the British blockade could stop trade with Holland.

At the same time the American minister in London extracted from him a confession that his second condition, which was the recognition of the Rule of 1756, had no necessary connection with the orders-in-council, could have been left to future discussions, and had been inserted in the instructions because Erskine's reports of conversations in Washington suggested that there would be no difficulty over it. In the same interview Canning gave himself away on his third condition—the American recognition of the British right to enforce the American nonintercourse act on the high seas. He said, to quote Pinkney, "that he was himself of opinion that the idea upon which that condition turns could not well find its way into a stipulation; that he had, nevertheless, believed it proper to propose the condition to the United States; that he should have been satisfied with the rejection of it; and that the consequence would have been, that they should have intercepted the commerce to which it referred, if any such commerce should be attempted." Pinkney to the Secretary of State, June 23, 1809, Extract, *A.S.P.F.R.*, III, 303.

"Nothing can be more clear than that" Erskine was Canning's scapegoat. If Canning had been an incompetent fool, one might dismiss the whole business as ghastly blundering; but the English Foreign Secretary was one of the cleverest men of the day. There is some evidence to support the view that, when he ordered the negotiation, he intended Erskine to fail; but this seems almost incomprehensible. It is possible that the serious troubles within the cabinet, which were soon to lead to his long political eclipse, may offer some clue to the mystery. It is also possible that between January and April he changed his mind. Perhaps he concluded that he had miscalculated the probable outcome of a reconciliation with the United States; that if it produced an American war with France then Britain could not so easily use American vessels to pierce Napoleon's Continental System; or that it might induce Napoleon to play his trump his instructions, but he had not compromised the spirit and he had accomplished a great thing. Yet he got the disgrace which, it would seem, his superior richly deserved. The War of 1812 might have been avoided if Canning had completed what Erskine had begun. So far as one can judge today, the friendship and at least the virtual alliance of the United States was genuinely offered to Britain in 1809, only to be flung away as if worth nothing. Whatever blame may attach to Jefferson for refusing to ratify Monroe's treaty, still more must be heaped on this English Foreign Secretary. The relations between the two countries had since grown much more critical, and Canning did more than Jefferson had done. He rubbed salt into the wound he uncovered. As Erskine's successor, he sent out Francis James Jackson, who had been employed to browbeat the Danish government before the British fleet battered the Danish capital in 1807, and to whom George III was reported to have expressed surprise that the Prince Royal had not kicked him downstairs; and to this man Canning gave instructions which threw the whole responsibility for the tragedy on the American government by accusing it of fraud. It had purposely tricked Erskine into an unauthorized bargain in order to ensnare the British government. The latter, not the former, had every right to complain. So said Canning.[16]

The insufferable Jackson therefore bluntly charged Smith and even Madison with having known that Erskine was violating his instructions; and on receiving a denial he repeated the charge. In other words, he called them liars. He was then figuratively kicked not downstairs but out of the house. Madison wrote and Smith signed[17] a curt note of November 8, 1809, saying, "No further communications will be received from you." Diplomatic relations were half severed. The offending and offended minister shook the dust of Washington off his feet, but he lingered on in the country, not sailing for home until September, 1810. Meanwhile he sunned himself in Federalist favor and appealed to the people against their government. With the support of his powerful government, he would force himself back upon Madison.[18]

card, which was to buy off American hostility and turn it against Britain by restricting the operation of his decrees to a domestic scope. Though he did not know that General Armstrong, the American minister in Paris, had already written the French government a note suggesting reconciliation by this means (Armstrong to Champigny, April 29, 1809, *ibid.*, p. 324), Canning certainly saw the danger. He had read Erskine's dispatches which pointed it out (*supra*, p. 264), and he discussed it in a dispatch which he addressed to Erskine's successor on July 1 and marked "Secret." *F.O. 5*, Vol. LXVIII.

    16. Canning to Jackson, No. 1, July 1, 1809, *ibid.*

    17. *Supra*, n. 4.

    18. See Adams, Vol. V, Chap. VI, for Jackson's mission. His voluminous official correspondence, some of which is printed in *A.S.P.F.R.*, III, 308–314, is in *F.O. 5*, Vols. LXIV, LXVIII, and LXIX.

Canning gave the United States a big push toward war, and yet it seemed farther away than it had been before April. A nonplussed President rode back to Washington to sign, on August 9, a proclamation restoring the nonintercourse act against Britain, and then he departed again. He returned on October 1 to receive the new British minister, with whom he entered upon the above unpleasant correspondence under the name of Robert Smith.[19] Madison could not fathom the ways of Canning, and he knew not what to do except to wait for something to turn up. Meanwhile the fortuitous unity of the country, produced by the Erskine agreement, began to crack. The Republican organs broke forth in fury against the perfidy of Britain; and the Federalist press, slowly recovering from the numbing shock of the repudiation, groped its way back to a defense of Britain. At the end of November, Congress was in session again; but it was of as little aid to the President as he was to it. The blind led the blind, and they went round in a circle.

Sheer impotence restrained the United States from war, for which it was even less prepared than it had been in the previous winter. "No department of the government was fit for its necessary work."[20] The condition of the army and of the navy was enough to make a patriot weep. The Secretary of State did not know how to write his own letters, and the President had to do it for him. The able Gallatin, cornered by a pack of intriguers, clung to an empty treasury. The embargo had ruined the revenue, and the nonintercourse act left it in that state. Though trade was somewhat restored, it brought nothing to the government; for it was a trade the law could not recognize, and therefore it avoided the customhouses. The country was leaking at every pore. About the only hope was to be found in news from England. The execrated Canning resigned in September because he would not work with Castlereagh, who then wounded him in a duel, and the ministry went to pieces. There would be some respite until the new ministry got firmly into the saddle and decided what course to take with the United States. New negotiations might yet be possible, and they would at least put off the evil day of a fateful decision.

For five months Congress floundered helplessly. A resolution hurling epithets at the British government for the recent "outrageous" insult offered by Jackson was passed with enthusiasm. All the "aggressions" of Britain, which did not include plotting with American Indians,[21] were indignantly aired. A special report on the state of impressments was called for and submitted, showing hundreds of new cases since the close

19. *Supra*, n. 4.
20. Adams, V, 163.
21. Julius W. Pratt, *Expansionists of* 1812, pp. 38–39.

of 1807,[22] which may account for the eagerness Smith had expressed for a settlement of this issue. Many and vehement were the displays of hostile feeling against Britain, but they were all confined to words. No steps were taken to uphold the damaged national honor. The President recommended the enlistment of twenty thousand volunteers for a short period, advised a reorganization of the militia, and suggested that the legislature consider whether anything should be done to fit out the navy. These things meant new taxes, which were not to be borne, and the members of the House actually voted to cut down the alarming deficit by cutting down expenditures on the armed forces, which many members admitted were no good. When bills were introduced to effect this saving, their clauses were successively struck out. All in all, it was a topsy-turvy session, with curious somersaults in debates and divisions, and with little party cohesion.

Most of the time of this session of 1809–10 was spent in squabbling over a substitute for the nonintercourse act which, like the embargo a year before, was clearly doomed. It had never been intended to be more than a makeshift of a few weeks. The Erskine "incident" had unexpectedly riveted this impossible law upon the country. It would expire with the end of the session; but in April differences over what should be adopted in its stead brought the two houses back to where they had been in November. Then they began again, only to reach another deadlock by the end of the month. On May 1, a few hours short of adjournment, committees produced a compromise. It was substantially the old measure turned inside out. It freed commercial relations with all the world, but authorized the President to prohibit intercourse with either belligerent if the other ceased "to violate the neutral commerce of the United States" before March 3, 1811. The prohibition was to come into force three months after its proclamation. Of Jefferson's and Madison's doctrine, that commercial restrictions were an effective substitute for war, this was all that was left in 1810, but the American government clung to it as a drowning sailor clutches a spar of his shipwrecked vessel.

This was the third successive year in which Congress had held out the offer to side with one belligerent against the other, in the hope that the latter would then follow the former's example of respecting American neutral rights and the United States would not have to declare war after all. There was no other way of escape from submission to both, for resistance to both was unthinkable. Each time the offer was made it had an appearance of impartiality which the conditions belied. In 1808, the embargo enlisted the United States on Napoleon's side, for it was an extension of his Continental System. In 1809, the nonintercourse act

22. A.S.P.F.R., III, 348.

withdrew this support and favored England, though its authors had no such purpose. Now, by throwing off all shackles on trade, the act of 1810 was a national humiliation, for it was a virtual surrender to the mistress of the seas. By a weird inversion, the new law was passed by men who were cursing her. All the Federalists and only a few insurgent Republicans voted against it. Congress was standing on its head.

The independence of the United States was being frittered away. The country was losing its self-respect, the most precious possession a nation can have, as it failed to command the respect of the belligerents. More and more the feebleness of the American government's policy had been teaching these embattled giants of the Old World that they could trample with impunity upon American rights, American interests, and American feelings. The result was strikingly apparent in the negotiations of 1810.

A pathetic effort was made to heal the widening breach between the United States and Britain. It was made in London on orders from Washington; and for a while Pinkney thought he might succeed, because the new British Foreign Secretary, the Marquis of Wellesley, reciprocated his anxiety for a reconciliation. The first business they had to discuss was the repair of the half-severed diplomatic relations. The President demanded Jackson's immediate recall, expected it would be accompanied by a reprimand for his extraordinary behavior, and anticipated no delay in the dispatch of an acceptable successor. As early as December, 1809, Wellesley assured Pinkney, as he was to assure him again and again, that everything would be satisfactorily arranged. Months passed before the useless official was summoned home, with honor; and his place was left vacant. The Foreign Secretary could not convert his cabinet colleagues. They seem to have believed that the United States should swallow its pride and Jackson too, or else do without a British minister. In February, 1810, Pinkney began to importune Wellesley about another matter. He thought he could grasp the key to the revocation of the Napoleonic decrees and the British orders-in-council. According to a tip he had just received from Paris, he had only to procure an official statement that no British declaration of a blockade of France made prior to the Berlin Decree was still in force, and then the locked doors would open in succession, releasing the United States from prison. In conversation Wellesley seemed to agree with Pinkney's argument that it would be easy to give such a statement on the understanding that the blockades had been superseded by the orders-in-council; but every time the American received the promised note there was a flaw in it, the writer's hand having been tied by his colleagues or restrained by his conscience. There is no indication of any suspicion on

Wellesley's part that Pinkney was chasing a will-o'-the-wisp. The relations between these two men were so friendly and even so intimate as to excite comment in London. Pinkney may therefore be excused for imagining, as he did for some months after his first interviews with Wellesley, that in discussing these and other questions he was perhaps laying the foundations for a better understanding between the two countries.[23]

There is no such excuse for the fatuity of a dispatch signed by Robert Smith on January 20, 1810, directing the minister in London to resume negotiations for the restoration of amity. He was to be guided by the instructions issued to him and Monroe in 1806. But first of all he was to secure satisfaction for the attack on the *Chesapeake*, and then he was to begin with an arrangement for the withdrawal of the orders-in-council. Until Congress reached some conclusion, the President could not "state the precise condition to be annexed to the repeal of the orders-in-council." He could merely assure the British government of his "cordial disposition" to do his best according to whatever the legislature might prescribe.[24]

When these orders reached Pinkney on the last day of March, he could not see their futility. He was still in high hopes that Wellesley's many and obviously genuine assurances would soon bear fruit. He expected almost any day to possess the magic key mentioned above, and already he had informally broached the subject with which he was now to begin. The two men soon put their heads together and easily agreed upon a settlement of the *Chesapeake* affair which was practically the same as that for which Canning had condemned Erskine. Wellesley promised to put it in writing, and from time to time he led Pinkney to suppose that the document was about to be produced.[25] As late as July 23, the American reported home that the famous affair would "soon be brought to a conclusion."[26] Presently, however, he expressed surprise at the procrastination, and misgivings began to assail him. There were grave misgivings in Washington too. A dispatch addressed to Pinkney and signed by Robert Smith on July 5, 1810, reveals a clear consciousness that Congress had delivered the United States into the hands of Britain. It stated that the British government might "feel a temptation" to leave things as they were, enjoying American intercourse to the full and denying it to France. "If the unworthiness and unfriendliness of such a course" did not divert Britain, "she ought not to overlook the oppor-

23. See *ibid.*, pp. 349–364.
24. *Ibid.*, p. 349.
25. *Ibid.*, p. 364.
26. *Ibid.*, p. 363.

tunity afforded her enemy of retorting the inequality . . . or the necessity to which the United States may be driven by such an abuse of their amicable advances, to resume, under new impressions, the subject of their foreign relations."[27] In other words, Britain had better be careful because, if France did not change her course and come to the rescue, the United States might still do something.

Just as pathetic was the American helplessness against Napoleon. He had been proceeding from violence to violence, utterly reckless of American susceptibilities. Under his orders, American sailors were plunged into prison, American goods were condemned and sold, American ships were confiscated, and some were even burned at sea by French frigates. American property worth many millions was thus lost. During the embargo, the Emperor used the excuse that every American ship abroad was really British and therefore lawful prize. When the repeal of the embargo robbed him of this excuse, he continued to rob citizens of the United States. He had discovered a new excuse in the nonintercourse law, which threatened French ships with confiscation if they entered American ports. What Americans would do to him, he would do to them. It was a reprisal, he said. But it was neither just nor legal. He purposely avoided imitating the American formality of enacting a public law to cover such action and to give due warning, so that he gathered a considerable American harvest whereas not one of his vessels was seized under the American law. Even when this excuse in its turn was no longer valid, he could not desist from his profitable plundering. He then justified it with specious arguments that need not be noticed here, or with none at all. General Armstrong, the American minister in Paris, was forever protesting; but he might as well have prayed to Neptune for the restoration of ships from the bottom of the sea.

The American government and people were exasperated. Before the news of the last spoliations crossed the Atlantic, Armstrong's reports of the seizures under the plea of reprisal for what the nonintercourse act might but did not do, and of the brazen justification offered by the Duke of Cadore, Napoleon's Minister of Foreign Affairs, stung the President into action. On June 5, after expressing his "high indignation," he ordered Armstrong to inform the French government that he would not revive the punitive act against Britain if these seizures were followed by a confiscation that barred restoration; and a month later he stiffened this order by insisting that "a satisfactory provision for restoring the property . . . must be combined with a repeal of the French edicts."[28]

27. *Ibid.*, p. 362.
28. *Ibid.*, pp. 384–385.

It was all useless. On August 5 Napoleon signed a secret decree[29] condemning without trial or judgment all the ships and cargoes still sequestered. Though no American knew of this outrageous command until years after the war,[30] its outrageous effect was soon felt in the United States.

Truly the United States was caught between the devil and the deep sea. The situation was so intolerable that it could be borne no longer. Indeed the country was already escaping by plunging into the arms of the sea. Though nominally at peace, the United States was really at war, fighting on Britain's side. There was a grand rush of American ships and cargoes to revel in trade under the protection of the Union Jack, while scarcely any craft were fitted out and laden in the United States for ports of Napoleon's empire.[31] Some American bottoms still found their way thither, but generally by devious routes and with British licenses. The United States was sinking into an appanage of the empire from which it had revolted. There was rejoicing in New England, where Napoleon was a robber-tyrant, England was the champion of liberty, and trade was the life-giver; but there was gnashing of teeth in Washington over the loss of American independence. The country had betrayed itself into abandoning its rights and its neutrality. It had sold itself back into slavery for a mess of pottage. This sense of national ignominy has attracted less attention than it deserves. It is highly important, being essential for an understanding of the tragedy that was about to be enacted in the United States.

Through the darkness of despair thus deepening over Washington, a new light burst from Paris. Napoleon had been hit hard by the American act of May 1, and he quickly saw the necessity of turning it about and directing it against Britain. This he proceeded to do in a rather surprising way. He did not attempt to play the trick which, as already observed,[32] was placed at his disposal. To satisfy the condition pre-

29. Incidentally it also ordered the release of American crews from the dungeons where they had been held as prisoners of war.

30. When Gallatin was American minister in Paris, he discovered it and, in a rare outburst of anger, he declared that its publication would have prevented the War of 1812.

31. "Previous to and since the cessation of the non-intercourse law, so many American vessels have sailed for England that there is hardly freight to be found for the goods and produce that it is still desirable to ship from the ports of the United States.

"Such accounts have been received of the unpromising appearance of the crops in England, that great purchases of flour have been lately made in expectation of a rise of that article in the British markets.

"No shipments are made to France, and altho' the intercourse with the Baltic is not quite closed, the merchants in general of this country prefer sending their goods to England as the only place of entire safety. In consequence, large quantities even of colonial produce have of late been sent there for re-exportation." Jackson to Wellesley, No. 39, New York, July 10, 1810, *F.O. 5*, Vol. LXIX.

32. *Supra*, p. 264.

scribed by Congress, he did not have to repeal his Berlin and Milan decrees. He had merely to modify them by renouncing his pretension to lay hands on American ships and goods outside his territorial waters, and he could keep his Continental System intact. But he probably saw a danger of being hoist with his own petard. Because the Americans were submitting to Britain, could she not afford to recall her orders-in-council, thereby transforming the private and passive coöperation of the United States into a public and active Anglo-American alliance? For the same reason he could not hope to accomplish his end by repealing his decrees, because Britain had often stated that she would then withdraw her offending orders. It would thus appear that Napoleon was determined to do the impossible. He could not satisfy the American condition without opening the way for Britain to do the same. But this master of psychology had taken the measure of the American government of that day, and he calculated that he could gain his end by deceit. He would make the Americans act on the false assumption that he had withdrawn his decrees, and to this end he dictated and revised the famous note which the Duke of Cadore sent to General Armstrong on August 5, 1810, and was published in the *Moniteur* four days later. It declared "that the decrees of Berlin and Milan are revoked, and that after November 1 they will cease to have effect; it being understood that, in consequence of this declaration, the English shall revoke their orders-in-council, and renounce the new principles of blockade, which they have wished to establish; or that the United States, conformably to the act[33] you have just communicated, shall cause their rights to be respected by the English."

The trap Napoleon thus laid for the United States was crude and clumsy. It could not work without the aid of egregious blundering in Washington. The government there would have to accept an unsupported statement that the Emperor had done what he had not done. Not even fictitious proof was forthcoming. That might have led Britain to spoil his game by withdrawing her orders-in-council. It will also be observed that the American condition was not met by what Cadore said the Emperor had done, for the note of August 5 reversed the order stipulated by Congress. Congress had required the Emperor to act before the President could revive the nonintercourse law against Britain, but the Emperor required the President to move first,[34] again to

33. Of May 1, 1810.

34. The letter of the American law did not preclude the possibility of a preconcerted arrangement for simultaneous action at the end of the three months that were to elapse between the presidential proclamation and the operation of the revived nonintercourse law, but Cadore's letter reserved to Napoleon the right to judge if the United States did "cause their rights to be respected by the English" before he would stop the operation of his decrees.

block Britain's possible escape. In other words, the President would have to exercise an authority which Congress had not conferred upon him.

Madison walked right into the obvious trap and he carried Congress with him. On November 2, the President proclaimed "that the said edicts of France have been so revoked as that they ceased on the 1st day of the present month to violate the neutral commerce of the United States," so that the nonintercourse law would be automatically revived and applied against Britain on February 2, 1811, unless she rescinded her orders-in-council before that time. If Madison entertained any serious hope that Britain would yield, he evidently did not communicate it to his cabinet. Two of the members, Smith and Gallatin, told the French minister the day before the proclamation appeared that it meant war,[35] on the supposition that Britain would strike back. In thus committing the country, the President swept aside the instructions he had sent to Armstrong in June and July, he abused the authority given him by Congress, and "he made himself a party to Napoleon's fraud."[36]

This action was impulsive[37] and may suggest that of a drowning man clutching at a straw. But the comparison is not quite fair to Madison. It was two years since he had told Erskine that the United States "would be fully justified in having recourse to hostilities with either belligerent, and that she only hesitated to do so from the difficulty of contending with both."[38] The strain of their combined pressure had since reached the breaking point. Already the resistance of the nation had broken where the pressure had been greatest. The commercial element was submitting to Britain and dragging the United States into the struggle against Napoleon. As guardian of his country's honor, the President would save it while yet he could.[39] The note of August 5 might be deceptive, but if he waited until he had definite proof that it was supported by an appropriate decree, the United States might be committed to side with Britain against American principles upheld by France. It should also be said on his behalf that he could hope to bind Napoleon by catching at his word, and then the American position would be correct. Nor should we forget the truth of his words quoted above. The United

35. Adams, V, 303. See also Robert Smith's conversation as reported by the British chargé, Morier to Wellesley, No. 15, Oct. 26, 1810, F.O. 5, Vol. LXX.

36. Adams, V, 304.

37. He issued the proclamation on the earliest possible date and without having heard directly from Armstrong. He based his action upon an unofficial copy of Cadore's note received from Pinkney in London.

38. Supra, p. 268.

39. Here is the simple explanation of what has often been referred to as a suspicious anomaly—that the American government should quarrel with Britain over her oppression of American commercial and shipping interests though these very interests were most opposed to any such quarrel.

States had ample justification for declaring war on either belligerent, and he might well have added that the count against Britain was greater than the count against France. Bearing these considerations in mind, one may conclude that his issuance of the proclamation was natural under the circumstances and was also quite rational. His critics have been too severe.[40]

Congress did not meet until a month after the proclamation. Back in May, Madison had anticipated that "the passive spirit which marked the late session" would "at the next meeting be roused to the opposite point."[41] The reaction had not gone that far; but a popular demand for more energy in government, already expressed in the elections for the Twelfth Congress, was reflected in this final session of the Eleventh. The bold lead given by the Chief Executive roused no challenge from either chamber before February 2, 1811, the very day his proclamation made nonintercourse the law. Then a lively debate began in the House. No decree to confirm the statement of Cadore's note had come from France; and it was now known that American vessels had been sequestered there as late as December. This was a whole month after the date when Cadore said the decrees would, and the President proclaimed they had, ceased to operate. The old Federalist fury against the embargo and its successor flamed forth again, fed by righteous indignation against the swindle that had been perpetrated. The Republicans were chagrined by the strange conduct of France, and at least some of them favored delay in applying the screws to Britain until they could see what they were doing. John Randolph, the political nonconformist from Virginia, at once moved for the repeal of the law on which the now dubious proclamation rested. He professed to be striking at the rotten branch; but he was really laying his axe at the root of the tree, for he abominated the whole policy of commercial restriction and he said so. Thus challenged, the majority closed their ranks, and member after member boldly asserted that Cadore's note had sealed an American contract with France.[42] For all their brave words there was fear in their hearts. They saved their law by voting Randolph down, but the courts might kill the proclamation by denying that France had satisfied the condition of the law. The conflicting evidence caused some bitter clashes in the House.

On the ninth the debate was suspended by the announcement that a

---

40. They have damned him for placing the issue of peace or war on a bad foundation when he had a perfectly good one. But he was not declaring war on November 2, 1810, and when the time for that came he used the good foundation. Racial bias, an equally natural prejudice against Napoleon, and a knowledge of later events have unconsciously warped the minds of those who have sat in judgment upon him.

41. Quoted in Adams, V, 210.

42. Randolph mocked them by calling it a "bargain which, like the bargains of old with the devil, there is no shaking off; . . . a bargain which credulity and imbecility enters into with cunning and power." *A.C.*, Eleventh Congress, Vol. III, col. 892.

new French minister, Serurier, was arriving. Surely he would settle the point. The administration and its supporters expected him to bring convincing proof of their contention that Napoleon had actually revoked the decrees. But the new minister came empty-handed. To obscure this embarrassing fact, Madison would not let his Secretary of State send Serurier an official note asking for information; and to supply the deficiency, he presented Congress with a pair of documents which, at this awkward juncture, he had just received from Jonathan Russell, the American *chargé* at Paris. They were copies of two French departmental letters, both written on Christmas Day, 1810, one from the Minister of Justice referring to the Berlin and Milan decrees as "suspended" and ordering a stay of proceedings against seized American vessels until February 2, and the other from the Minister of Finance directing the customs officials to refrain from enforcing these decrees against American vessels.

The production of these documents intensified the strife in the House, for while they supported the majority's argument that the decrees had been revoked they also upheld the opposition's charge that the revocation had not occurred on November 1. But arguments had ceased to count for anything with the angry members. The Republicans were determined to drive on with the President's policy, insisting that they must keep faith with France; and to steer this policy around the courts they forced through a legislative measure which supplanted the proclamation.[43] To do it, they had to gag the loquacious Federalist representatives when the end of the session drew near. Amidst considerable uproar, the House passed the bill about five o'clock in the morning of February 28. Two days later it slipped quietly through the Senate and received the President's assent. Congress had followed him into the trap.

One might imagine that Congress would have been made more cautious by the news that had come from France since November 1. But there was reason in the madness of the majority. Randolph's motion was bound to fail because it cut at the root of the only policy that the country had, he offered no substitute, and the policy was beginning to show at least some signs of producing results. When the country, pulled by that part which the Federalists represented, was toppling over into the arms of Britain, the President had tried to jerk it back; but he lacked the necessary power and the Republican members of Congress naturally felt compelled to come to the rescue. The opposition, which accused both

43. One British vessel was seized under the proclamation, but its release was soon ordered, "I imagine in order to avoid the award of the courts, which would certainly have been against the seizure, and in direct contradiction to the principle of the proclamation of the 2nd November," wrote J. P. Morier, the British *chargé*, to Wellesley on March 26, 1811. *F.O. 5*, Vol. LXXIV.

alike of flagrant partiality to France, were quite as guilty of partiality to Britain and would have cast away immediately what the majority would fain preserve—a fighting chance[44] of escape by playing off one belligerent against the other. Moreover the Republicans were right in shutting the mouths of the Federalists in order that Congress might exercise its undoubted power to govern the foreign policy of the country instead of leaving it for the courts to decide, as the minority would have done in this crisis. Finally, the new law corrected a dangerous fault in the old one, which contained no provision for suspending nonintercourse after it became operative. If Britain now withdrew her orders-in-council the President could immediately lift the penalty by a proclamation which was not to be subject to judicial review.

Neither the executive nor the legislature at this time took any steps to prepare for hostilities. Indeed Congress in this very session cut the country's sinews of war by destroying the Bank of the United States and by rejecting Gallatin's plea for new taxes to cover at least some of the enormous loss of revenue that was sure to follow the application of nonintercourse against Britain; it only slightly increased the naval appropriation over that of 1810, which was scarcely more than half that of 1809; and on the eve of adjournment it abandoned a bill to raise a military force of fifty thousand volunteers.

This neglect of the country's fighting needs does not imply a refusal to see that the country might soon need to fight. It rather recalls Erskine's reports of the popular American illusion about the conduct of hostilities. There can be little doubt that the President and his cabinet realized that the bold course on which they embarked in the fall of 1810 would carry the United States perilously close to war with Britain; and Congress knew it too. Though it was not unusual for a member on rising to profess a desire to keep to the point of the debate, namely, whether the nonintercourse was justifiable, the discussion frequently burst beyond and ranged over the general field of American grievances against Britain.[45] There were no references to any British backing of

44. That it was a fighting chance seemed to be confirmed by news from England, where government was paralyzed by the final insanity of the King. The confusion lasted until February, when the Prince of Wales became Prince Regent and confirmed the Tory ministry in power, much to the surprise of many people who expected him to inaugurate a Whig regime with a new policy. Hence the reference in Quincy's fighting speech in the American House on February 25. "I know," he said, "that great hopes are entertained of relief from the proposed law, by the prospect of a British regency. Between a mad monarch and a simpering successor, it is expected the whole system of that nation will be abandoned." He scouted the idea. *A.C.*, Eleventh Congress, Vol. III, col. 1024.

45. The grievances against France were likewise fully aired, but only by the opposition members, who did their best to exculpate Britain. A reading of the whole debate as reported in the *Annals of Congress* leaves the impression that the party division coincided with, and was embittered by, a split between the partisans of France and the partisans of Britain.

troublesome Indians in the West, for the scare of 1807 had so died down
that the President's annual message in December, 1810, could include a
pleasing passage on the growing tie of peace and friendship with the
native tribes. Some hot things were said about impressments and the
detention of ten thousand American sailors, and more than one attempt
was made to withhold from the President the power to restore intercourse until he had secured a satisfactory settlement of the impressment issue.[46]

That both branches of the government were consciously steering the
country much closer to hostilities becomes clearer when viewed in the
light of another grave commitment undertaken at this time. At the end
of October, 1810, Madison gave orders for the occupation of West
Florida, still held by Spain, proclaiming that it belonged to the United
States as part of the Louisiana Purchase. Congress backed him in this,
too, and in the middle of the session it granted his request for power to
add East Florida. This revival of an old scheme, which had slept since
Napoleon had vetoed it some years before, had an unmistakable meaning. It was the present possibility of an armed clash in the south. The
danger that Britain might support Spanish resistance in Florida was
implied by the protest which J. P. Morier, the British *chargé* in Washington, made in December against this strange proceeding, and also by
an exchange of documents between President and Congress. He sent a
confidential message covering Morier's note, stating in so many words
that the United States should not allow Britain to acquire any portion of
this Spanish territory; and in reply he got a resolution echoing his own
proposition.

There is an obvious connection between the two commitments made
by the President and sustained by Congress, but we need not here
digress to explore it, intriguing as it may seem. Though Federalists[47]
believed that Florida was the bait which made Napoleon's trap work,
this hypothesis has never been proven and is not necessary for an understanding of why Madison and the Republican majority accepted Cadore's
note at its face value. From the explanation already given, we may

46. Henry Adams has smiled at this effort to load the stick with which Congress was about
to strike Britain, saying that "the subject had somewhat fallen out of sight" and observing
that the proposed amendment secured only twenty-one votes. Adams, V, 351–353. But this
excellent historian has here missed the point. As remarked by Eppes of Virginia, the sponsor
of the bill under consideration, its object "was to remove doubts in the minds of some as to the
operation of the law of May last." By that law Britain had only to revoke her orders-in-council
to be assured of commercial intercourse; it was not yet known whether she had done so before
February 2, and the proposed amendment was "irrelevant to the question at issue." *A.C.*,
Eleventh Congress, Vol. III, col. 1035. That it got as many votes as it did in spite of this
argument is startling.

47. Notably Senator Pickering.

conclude that they would have done it, Florida or no Florida; and therefore we may return to the main thread of the story.

The United States had again joined Napoleon's Continental
System, and the great question of the day was how Britain would meet
this blow. Within Madison's cabinet there was a belief that she would
strike back, and in Congress it was suggested that she might follow the
Emperor's retaliatory example by confiscating American ships and
cargoes. But that would have been playing straight into the hands of
Napoleon, for it would have precipitated war with the United States and
this was precisely what he wanted.

Britain's game was to hold back and, if possible, to avert the war.
She could afford to wait because Latin America was providing her with
a market to compensate for that which was lost in the United States;
and she could hope for an early reëntry into the latter. The strong
British suspicion that Napoleon was deceiving the United States must
soon turn out to be true or false. If true, the discovery of Napoleon's
treachery would oblige the American government to reopen the doors
of the United States; if false, a repeal of the orders-in-council would
have the same effect. Even though this calculation were to fail, as a
result of influences at work in Washington to produce an open break, it
would have been arrant folly for Britain to hasten the evil day by the
retaliation mentioned above. The United States was visibly splitting
under the terrific pressure of the long-continued world war. In the
wealthiest and most compact part of the country, whose representatives
formed the opposition in Washington, Britain had a solid ally which
might be counted on to hamstring a hostile American government. It
was to Britain's interest to cultivate this alliance and not to destroy it by
an attack on American shipping and commerce. Moreover Downing
Street had known for years that the Canadas could not withstand a
resolute American attack. If this war was really coming, the greater
part of British North America could be saved only by a divided United
States.

The British government decided in February, 1811, to check the
dangerous drift of Anglo-American relations by sending a minister to
Washington, where none had been since the repulse of the impossible
Jackson in the fall of 1809. It was high time that such a decision was
reached, because there would soon be no American minister in London.
The reciprocal withdrawal of Pinkney, delayed at first by his vain hope
of negotiating a general settlement with Britain and then by his equally
vain hope of using Cadore's note to force a repeal of the orders-in-
council, was about to take place. In January, 1811, he had notified
Wellesley that, in compliance with his instructions, he was now waiting

for a formal audience of leave, which he secured on the last day of February. No other American minister went to London until after the War of 1812.

Anglo-American relations drifted still closer to the rocks before the new British representative reached Washington at the end of June, 1811. Again it was the impressment issue which was at the root of the further trouble. About the beginning of May, the British frigate *Guerrière* impressed an American under circumstances which magnified the offense. He was taken from a coasting vessel, and just off Sandy Hook. If, as it may appear, the incident was a naval backfire against the exclusion of all British ships from American waters, it was unofficial, for the orders of the British admiral on the North American station enjoined particular caution against friction with the United States. These orders, of course, were not known in the United States, where the incident produced such a violent explosion of public opinion that Morier was startled. On receiving a demand for the release of the captured seaman, he forwarded it to Herbert Sawyer, the admiral, with a private note deploring the affair and urging the immediate discharge of the man. "The subject of impressment, as you well know," he said, "has always been one by which the popular feeling of this nation has been kept alive in its animosity against Great Britain. . . . Were I to venture to give an opinion on the subject of impressment in general, it would be [for] . . . its abandonment in practice (except in cases of absolute certainty as to person or desertion) because I am confident that no possible advantage, which can accrue to the service, even if five hundred men were annually procured in that way, can compensate for the evil which a constant state of irritation between the two nations must create."[48] When writing these words, Morier did not know that on the ocean the incident had already touched off an explosion of something more than words. This was the fight between the American frigate *President* and the British corvette *Little Belt*. It was a belated reply to the attack on the *Chesapeake*, which was likewise a product of impressment; so that this issue was thus both the remote and the immediate cause of the new bloody encounter.

To understand what happened, we have to go back to the summer of 1810. An American squadron under Commodore Rodgers was then sent out to patrol the coast of the United States, with orders to protect American shipping within territorial waters, using whatever force was necessary. The Secretary of the Navy underlined these orders by recalling the *Chesapeake* affair as an example of the intolerable insults that

48. Morier to Sawyer, May 20, 1811, enclosed in Morier to Wellesley, No. 25, June 4, 1911, *F.O.* 5, Vol. LXXIV.

had been heaped on the Stars and Stripes. What had been perpetrated, he said, might be attempted again and it was "therefore our duty to be prepared and determined at every hazard to vindicate the injured honor of our navy, and revive the drooping spirit of the nation." Nothing untoward happened in 1810, but when the precaution was repeated in 1811 conditions were different. French privateers, which still infested the Caribbean, might now seek a safe shelter and base in American waters. This attraction of belligerent activity toward American shores, an unintentional by-product of a discriminating nonintercourse, worried both the British and the American governments. Before the new minister left England he was ordered to investigate reports that French privateers were bringing British prizes into American ports and were also fitting out there;[49] and on May 10 Rodgers in the *President* got under way from his anchorage off Annapolis to proceed to his station off New York under an order from the Secretary of the Navy, who had been informed that the trade of New York was interrupted by British and French cruisers. "At this time," Rodgers said, he learned from the newspapers that during his absence a British frigate supposed to be the *Guerrière* had impressed a man as mentioned above.[50] Six days later the tragedy occurred.

At noon on May 16, 1811, when about fifty miles off Cape Henry, Rodgers discovered a sail far to the eastward. It stood straight for him under a press of canvas, and then it turned away. It was the *Little Belt*, Captain Bingham, a light vessel lately come from Bermuda to join the *Guerrière*, which it had not yet found. Spying the strange sail, Bingham had given chase until he recognized it as an American frigate, whereupon he resumed his course. Thereupon Rodgers chased the retreating stranger, which he had been able to identify only as a man-of-war of some kind. Not having heard of any other ship of the Royal Navy being on the American coast, he concluded that this was the *Guerrière* and he was determined to speak to her that he might demand the release of the imprisoned seaman.[51] The *President* overhauled the *Little Belt* shortly after nightfall, when the darkness prevented Rodgers from recognizing

49. Wellesley to Foster, No. 4, April 10, No. 9, May 2, 1811, *ibid.*, Vol. LXXV. Shortly after he sailed, another dispatch was sent after him directing him to lodge an immediate protest on the subject. *Ibid.*, No. 10, May 16, 1811.

50. *A.S.P.F.R.*, III, 496.

51. This is his own explanation as given to the court of inquiry in September, but it is not certain that this was the real reason for his hot pursuit of the *Little Belt*. On July 2 the newly arrived British minister, who had just discussed the affair with Monroe, reported the latter as saying "that Commodore Rodgers defended his conduct, and had asserted that Capt. Bingham had given the provocation, maintaining that the circumstance of the English officer's having chased first was of a nature to have piqued the pride of the American commander, and to induce him to chase in return." Foster to Wellesley, No. 2, *F.O. 5*, Vol. LXXVI.

his chase as only a corvette. Both ships were cleared for action, but how it began we know not, for the conflict of evidence has never been resolved. Apparently each commander hailed the other with "What ship is that?" and got only the same question in reply because each hailed first; and straightway the guns took up the argument, each ship firing the first shot. The frigate, being far superior in strength, soon silenced the corvette. The *Little Belt* was terribly crippled and lost nine killed and twenty-three wounded. The *President's* rigging was a little damaged and only one of her crew was wounded. The *Chesapeake* was avenged, with interest. Mahan says the engagement was an accident, but perhaps it would be truer to call it spontaneous combustion.

Something similar nearly occurred three weeks later, again just after nightfall and off Cape Henry. Two British men-of-war met an American frigate, and when the captain of H.M.S. *Eurydice* was "in the act of verbal communication" with the *United States* a gun of the latter fired a shot. Fortunately it fell clear, and the British captain received an immediate apology with a solemn protestation that "the gun went off by accident."[52] When guns speak without orders, as they did on May 16 and again on this occasion, they utter a warning that war is very close.

Could the impending disaster be averted by the new British minister then on his way across the Atlantic?[53] There was certainly no fault to be found with the man selected for the desperate mission. Augustus John Foster had the right personality, the right political complexion, and the right experience. He had none of Jackson's truculence: everyone spoke well of him. He was no Tory; his affiliations were Whig, and therefore a distinct asset in Washington. Nor was he a stranger to the American political scene and the role he was there to assume; he was returning to take charge of a legation in which, not long since, he had served as secretary. But he was expected to do the impossible—to persuade the American government to withdraw its demand for a repeal of the orders-in-council and to reverse its action against Britain because this demand

52. Bradshaw to Hamilton, June 11, 1811, enclosed in Morier to Wellesley, No. 27, June 26, 1811, *ibid.*, Vol. LXXIV.

53. One is also tempted to ask what might have been the difference if there had been no delay in his coming. It would seem that he should have been sent as soon as England heard of the President's proclamation. But an appointment was then impossible, because of the King's insanity, and did not become possible until the Regency was established in February, when it was made. The appointee did not sail until early in May, and his voyage, being via Bermuda, took nearly twice the time commonly required for a trip from England direct to the United States. If he had been rushed off in February, he might perhaps have averted the tragedy of the *Little Belt* by an earlier settlement of the *Chesapeake* affair (see *infra*, pp. 296–297); but against this suggestion it may be argued that he could not have done it because he had no control over the direct cause of that explosion, which was impressment.

and this action were founded on an American error.[54] The repeal of the Berlin and Milan decrees, which Washington had officially accepted as genuine, London insisted was spurious; and London called upon Washington to eat its own words. What independent government is ever willing, at the behest of another, to swallow such an indigestible morsel? Even if Foster could convince Madison that he had done a wrong which he should make right, the President could not correct it. His hands were tied by the Constitution. He would have to wait till Congress met, and then he would have to convince both houses that they too had made a first-class blunder which they must undo by repealing the nonintercourse act. The obstacles in Foster's way appear all the more insuperable when we remember that this act, taken by itself, was a just retaliation for the orders-in-council which, by Britain's own admission, violated American neutral rights, and that it had been adopted as the only hope of American salvation.

Turning to what the United States demanded of Britain as the price for the resumption of intercourse, we have to notice that the price had been raised. To the withdrawal of the orders-in-council, which was all that the law of May 1, 1810, stipulated for British immunity from nonintercourse if Napoleon dropped his decrees, Madison had added a demand for a renunciation of Fox's blockade of May, 1806. This may seem strange in view of the fact that in 1809 he had eagerly accepted Erskine's agreement, by which the recall of the orders-in-council sufficed to lift the ban from Britain and leave it on France; and his critics on both sides of the Atlantic assailed him for unfair dealing. But his enhancement of the price was the natural result of Pinkney's pressure on Wellesley to state that, of the British blockades declared before the Berlin decree, none was still in force. It then developed that the blockade of May, 1806, though "comprehended" in the subsequent orders-in-council, would be automatically revived by a simple repeal of the latter; and when this fact was brought to the President's attention he instructed Pinkney to present this further demand. Thus thrust forward, the blockade became a matter of warm dispute, the American government denouncing its legality and the British government defending it. In the midst of the dispute came Cadore's note, which stiffened the American attitude by tying Britain's "new principles of blockade" to the orders-in-council. From the end of August, 1810, when Pinkney received a copy of this note direct from Paris, he had threatened Wellesley with

54. The first four dispatches addressed to him are dated April 10, 1811, more than three weeks before he sailed. These constitute the chart of his mission; and the first of them, which is nearly twice as long as the other three together, is devoted to the problem of the nonintercourse snarl. *F.O. 5*, Vol. LXXV.

American nonintercourse unless Britain gave up the blockade as well as the decrees, until at last the blow fell. No British government could surrender the belligerent right of blockade, which Americans of a later day were to use most successfully against other Americans in the Civil War. All the arguments with which Wellesley had tried to prove to Pinkney how unreasonable was this extra demand were repeated in his instructions to Foster, who was to use them in procuring an American retraction. The blockade had been effective, and it would certainly be effective if it were ever revived. Unlike the orders-in-council, it was in perfect accordance with international law, and therefore it gave the United States no claim whatever against Britain. Here too the new minister faced an impossible task. The American government could not yield on this point without sacrificing its claim on France and thereby undermining its whole position.

The peremptory demand for the repeal of the orders-in-council which Pinkney had advanced in London was certain to be repeated to Foster in Washington, and he was to meet it by renewing the British offer to withdraw them as soon as Napoleon did the same with his decrees. But the terms attached to the offer, as set forth in Foster's instructions, reveal more clearly than ever the half-hidden weakness in the British position to which reference has earlier been made. These terms envisaged a possible continuance of the orders-in-council after the French decrees ceased to violate American rights under international law. The mere exemption of American vessels from the operation of the decrees would not satisfy Britain. She must have complete repeal. Even this was not enough. She would not tolerate an imperial move to accomplish the purpose of the decrees by means of municipal regulation although, as we have seen, the American government could not challenge this evasion. "Nor can we ever," continued the instructions, "deem the repeal of the French hostile decrees to be effectual, until neutral commerce shall be restored to the condition in which it stood previously to the commencement of the French system of commercial warfare as promulgated in the decrees." In simple language purged of all euphemism, Britain insisted that the American government stretch American neutral rights to cover the admission of British goods into the French Empire in Europe. Therefore we may conclude that Napoleon, without resorting to deception, had it in his power to reduce the triangular quarrel between himself, Britain, and the United States over neutral trading rights into a straight quarrel between Britain and the United States. From this it follows that the two powers thus pitted against each other were fundamentally the victims of circumstance and only superficially the victims of fraud.

In concluding this analysis of the conditions under which Foster's mission was undertaken, we should notice an ominous change in his instructions which was made shortly before he left England. The British government had halted the condemnation of American vessels which ran foul of the orders-in-council as a consequence of the President's proclamation, which led some Americans to believe that it would induce a prompt British repeal; and the minister had been directed to wave this olive branch in Washington. Now it was taken from him, and in its stead he was given a stick to shake. When London heard that Congress had substituted an act for the proclamation, the stay on proceedings in the prize courts was removed and Foster was told to inform the American government that a perseverance in its hostility would compel a "resort to adequate means of retaliation."[55]

The deadlock between the British and the American governments was thus complete, though neither knew it, before the new minister sailed; and therefore it is not necessary to follow him through all his discussions and exchanges of notes in Washington. He quickly exhausted the armory of arguments he brought with him, but fresh orders from home conveyed new arguments and spurred him on to continue the attack. He challenged the American government to prove its contention that the French decrees were revoked by producing a copy of the instrument which revoked them. He pointed out that the orders-in-council in no way affected American warships and therefore the United States was guilty of hostile conduct in excluding British warships while admitting those of France.[56] But in all his negotiations over nonintercourse and the orders-in-council, he was knocking his head against a stone wall.[57]

Another unpleasant duty imposed on Foster was to lodge protests against the fitting out of French privateers in American waters and against the unscrupulous schemes of the United States government to steal Florida from Spain. He was much relieved to find that the American government, though allowing French privateers to come and go freely, was exercising all reasonable precautions to keep them from being

55. Wellesley to Foster, No. 8, April 29, 1811, *ibid.*
56. Privateers.
57. In April, 1812, he was instructed to make a new offer for the withdrawal of the nonintercourse law. Trade between Britain and the Continent had been increasing by leaps and bounds under the protection of the license system adopted by Napoleon as well as by the British Board of Trade, thereby giving color to the American charge that the orders-in-council were really designed to give Britain a monopoly of the world's commerce and shipping. The offer was to abandon this system entirely or, if Washington preferred, to adjust its operation so that Americans might share freely with the British; but it made not the slightest impression on the American government when Foster presented it late in May. Castlereagh to Foster, No. 9, April 10, 1812, *ibid.*, Vol. LXXXIII. Foster to Castlereagh, No. 41, June 6, 1812, *ibid.*, Vol. LXXXVI.

fitted out in American ports. An occasional vessel cleared as an innocent merchantman and then quickly bristled with arms that had been concealed as cargo, but such tricks were only to be expected. The other business, however, greatly worried the British minister and also the American government. Though he carefully observed the caution enjoined upon him not to commit his own government over Florida, his remonstrances, being directed at guilty consciences, suggested a veiled threat of British intervention to defeat the American design and perhaps to run off with the prize.

One thing, and one thing only, did the British minister achieve by way of conciliation. He effected a settlement of the *Chesapeake* affair, but not as quickly as he had hoped. His original instructions contemplated an agreement substantially the same as that which Canning had rejected in 1809, and he was to have broached the subject immediately after his arrival. This he could not do until some smoke had cleared away from the engagement of the *Little Belt*. At once he sought an official denial of an ugly and persistent rumor that Rodgers' chase and attack were in obedience to orders from the government, and he requested an examination of the officer's conduct. He would secure satisfaction for the loss of so many British subjects "wantonly slaughtered" and the insult to His Majesty's flag in this "outrage." Monroe, now Secretary of State, did not hesitate to assure him verbally that no such order had been issued; but he delayed a fortnight before he put this assurance in writing, and then his words implied that such an order might have been justified. "Although the excitement which had been produced by previous and recent aggressions, particularly by the impressment of American citizens from American vessels, even on the coast of the United States, was great, yet no order had been given by the Government for the recovery by force of any citizens so impressed from any British ship of war."[58] As for the official examination into the affair, Foster intimated to Monroe in their first conversation that it was holding up a settlement of the *Chesapeake* incident, but the American suggested that the attack which had occurred first should be atoned for first, and he left the impression that he was little concerned about the removal of this old grievance.[59] Nevertheless he unofficially informed his caller, either then or shortly afterward, that there would be a court of inquiry. Foster was therefore surprised to find that the above note completely ignored his request for an investigation, and he soon learned from Monroe's own mouth that there was to be no court of inquiry. The Secretary of State told him that the government had abandoned the idea on discovering that he had no

58. *A.S.P.F.R.*, III, 472.
59. Foster to Wellesley, No. 2, June 2, 1811, *F.O. 5*, Vol. LXXVI.

power to satisfy the demand for a repeal of the orders-in-council.[60] However, a few days later, a court was called. It sat from the end of August to the middle of September, and it turned Foster's hopes into fears. The British inquiry in Halifax had proven that the frigate had fired the first shot, but now the American investigation proved that the sloop commenced the fight, so that the United States would not offer reparation and might even demand it. At least the formality required by the British minister had been fulfilled, and when in due course Monroe sent him a copy of the proceedings he came forward with his proposal to close the *Chesapeake* account. He formulated it on November 1, and Monroe accepted it on the twelfth.[61] The settlement came years too late, when it could no longer do any good. It deprived some Americans of a talking point, but that seems to have made no real difference.[62]

The root of the trouble was still there, and though Foster saw it he could not touch it—the British impressment of sailors from American ships. This was what was responsible for the bloodshed on the *Chesapeake* and the *Little Belt*. At any time it might cause other violent clashes, and all the time it was producing little incidents which had a great cumulative effect. As Morier reminded Admiral Sawyer, and Monroe told Foster, it was ever feeding American bitterness against Britain. The longer the Napoleonic War lasted, the greater grew this evil for which there was no cure. Very naturally, therefore, the American outcry against it rose in a marked crescendo during the last year of the troubled peace between the United States and Britain. Some historians, American as well as British, have believed that this discordant note was artifically stressed, and for confirmation they have pointed out that those parts of the country which were most affected by the practice, the maritime

60. Foster to Wellesley, No. 7, July 18, 1811, *ibid.*

61. Of the four seamen taken from the *Chesapeake* in 1807, one had been promptly hanged in Halifax as a British deserter and another, a mulatto born in Maryland, had died in hospital in Halifax in 1809, leaving only two survivors—a white native of Maryland and a colored sailor who had been brought as a boy from South America. There was considerable delay in the return of this pair, orders for their delivery chasing them to and fro across the Atlantic. See Foster to Wellesley, No. 16, March 13, 1812, *ibid.*, Vol. LXXXV. They had not arrived when war was declared, and Foster then made a special arrangement for the admission of the schooner bearing them. They were finally placed back on the deck of the *Chesapeake* in Boston harbor on July 11, 1812. The war also intervened to prevent the United States government from accepting payment of damages, which had not yet been arranged.

62. The *New York Evening Post* said: "The democratic editors are not a little embarrassed at this arrangement; on the one hand, they are loath to find fault with the administration, just at this moment, when things seem to promise a rupture with England, notwithstanding the settlement of this item in the list of controversy; on the other, it robs them of the best bone in their picking; they can no longer snarl and be pathetic about the slain and the prisoners." The *Baltimore Whig* said that the reparation was "like restoring a hair after fracturing the skull." Newspaper clippings enclosed in Foster to Castlereagh, No. 25, Nov. 21, 1811, *ibid.*, Vol. LXXVII.

constituencies, did not complain. But this interpretation, which mini-mizes the importance of impressments as a cause of the War of 1812, needs revision.

In January, 1812, the legislature of New Jersey adopted strong warlike resolutions denouncing the "flagitious conduct of the rulers of Great Britain," and particularizing two intolerable grievances. The orders-in-council came second. The first charge was "the abominable practice of impressing native American seamen while in the pursuit of a lawful commerce, forcing them on board their ships of war, and com-pelling them, under the lash, to fight against nations with whom we are at peace, and even against their own country."[63] Foster, a very discern-ing man in close touch with the political currents around him, likewise bracketed impressments with the orders-in-council as the two outstand-ing grounds of quarrel. Referring to the former, he reported home that the members of Congress "who are friendly to peace assure me that it is a much more difficult task for them to explain this point to their con-stituents than the orders-in-council."[64] In another dispatch he wrote, "It is to be observed that the federal party, however they may for the purpose of getting into power press lightly on the points of dispute between the two countries for the moment, yet do not fail on all occasions to complain of the interruption of their direct trade with France and of the practice of impressment exercised by us on board American ships." A few lines later, he asserted that this practice "certainly creates more irritation than any other [difference] between the two countries"; and he repeated his favorite prescription for easing the pain. It was that the government in London should occasionally collect and send out batches of impressed Americans with some money in their pockets.[65] These are but a few of many passages in his letters to London which show that he regarded the American outcry against impressments as both genuine and serious. There is still more to be said on this cause of the War of 1812, but it is better to reserve it until we have examined some other developments.

From all we have seen, it would appear that Mahan was right when he said, "Conditions were hopeless, and war assured, even when Foster arrived in Washington, in June 1811."[66] Yet a whole year, all but a few days, elapsed before war was declared, and this long delay casts some doubt on his conclusion. Was there something more that was necessary to prod a lethargic country into taking the last step? Further influences

63. *A.C.*, Twelfth Congress, Vol. I, col. 908.
64. Foster to Castlereagh, No. 28, April 23, 1812, *F.O. 5*, Vol. LXXXV.
65. Foster to Castlereagh, No. 37, May 22, 1812, *ibid.*, Vol. LXXXVI.
66. *Sea Power in Its Relations to the War of 1812*, I, 255.

were certainly at work in the United States to produce war, and these call for examination.

The Federalists, who had been more or less openly pro-British, began to throw their weight into the opposite scale. When Foster studied the state of political parties in the summer of 1811, he discovered that even the warmest Federalists were disposed to resist the British "pretension that, as a condition of the revocation of the orders-in-council, France would repeal her system so as to admit articles of British origin, when owned by neutrals, into her ports and those of the countries under her influence."[67] This disposition was probably genuine, Britain's cloven hoof having been at last revealed even to her friends. But the startling change of policy adopted by the party in the autumn was admittedly a *ruse de guerre*.

Shortly after Congress assembled early in November, 1811, a Boston paper sounded a new clarion call, said to have been written by one of the leading Federalists of Massachusetts. "The alternatives presented to the people of this country are a continuance and more rigorous enforcement of the restrictions upon commerce, or a British war. The last is probably intended as a bug-bear to terrify the country into patience and toleration under the former." This seems to be a fair statement of Madison's attitude still, for his faith in the efficacy of commercial restrictions took an unconscionably long time to die. Having stated the alternatives, the anonymous author blasted the "withering experiment" which would reduce the people of the United States "to the condition of the Chinese." He insisted that there was only one choice, and that was war. The country, he said, "may probably" be defeated but it could not be conquered; and he strongly hinted that war would overthrow the administration and restore "the best men" to power. They would prosecute the war with vigor or make the best possible peace, the implication being that the Virginia dynasty could do neither. "It is then the duty of the Federalists to prepare for the war they have endeavored incessantly to avert."[68]

Rallying to the call, the Federalists pushed war measures so zealously that they embarrassed the hesitant government and alarmed the British minister. In December he reported that it was doubtful if the administration possessed sufficient influence to prevent Congress from recommending an immediate declaration of war. Leading members of the party told him they would vote for war, and they shrugged their shoulders at his "observations on the strange and dangerous nature" of their game. They assured him that they would have a short war, a political

67. Foster to Wellesley, No. 22, Nov. 9, 1811, *F.O. 5*, Vol. LXXVII.
68. Newspaper clippings enclosed in Foster to Wellesley, No. 29, Nov. 29, 1811, *ibid*.

revolution, and a solid peace.[69] But the party lacked the courage and the discipline to play the game through to the end. Deserted by a considerable number of their followers, some of the leaders urged Foster to advise his government against any concession lest it spoil everything. Incidentally he did the opposite.[70] At the end of January, 1812, he reported that the desperate tactics were being dropped. "Many of the federal leaders mean to push their support of war measures no further," he wrote home, and he added that the party representatives on the foreign relations committee, "although they have agreed to join with the most violent democrats . . . have explicitly stated their intention to oppose the resolution for war when it shall be brought into Congress."[71] This is what they did in the end, and we may conclude that their earlier aberrations contributed little or nothing to the advent of war.

The publication of the Henry correspondence early in March came like the bursting of a bomb which threatened to blow the United States into war right away. John Henry was a charming and insinuating Irish adventurer who, after living for some years in the United States, moved to Canada and was then employed by Governor Craig as a confidential agent in the United States when the war cloud caused by the *Chesapeake* incident hung heavy over Canada. When the cloud passed, terminating his delicate mission, Henry sought extravagant rewards from the authorities in Quebec and London. When dejected over his failure, he fell into the hands of a French rogue who negotiated the sale of his papers to the American government for $50,000 and ran off with the money. The letters thus procured were turned over to Congress and straightway published. At first glance they seemed to prove that the British government, working through the representative of the Crown in Quebec, had been intriguing with the Federalists to disrupt the Union. Great was the consternation in New England and the patriotic uproar in other parts of the country. But the bomb soon proved to be a dud. The excitement died down before the month was out because, on closer examination, the papers did not bear out the first impression. Even the United States government had been swindled.[72]

Other Irishmen contributed much more to the Anglo-American quarrel at this time. Though we are accustomed to think of their anti-

69. Foster to Wellesley, No. 30, Dec. 11, 1811, *ibid.*

70. Foster to Wellesley, most secret, Dec. 28, 1811, *ibid.*; No. 3, Jan. 16, No. 8, Feb. 1, No. 14, March 12, 1812, *ibid.*, Vol. LXXXIV.

71. Foster to Wellesley, No. 7, Jan. 31, 1812, *ibid.*

72. The British government knew nothing of Henry's mission until after Craig had recalled him. The bulk of the correspondence was made up of Henry's reports to Craig, of which only badly garbled copies were sold to the American government. For the fullest account of the episode, see E. A. Cruikshank, *The Political Adventures of John Henry* (Toronto, 1936).

British influence in the United States as commencing with the mass migration in the middle of the nineteenth century, rotten potatoes were not at the root of the trouble. That can be traced back to the disturbed state of Ireland in the latter part of the eighteenth century, and particularly to the Rebellion of 1798. Not a few Irishmen then sought heaven in America. It took another Irishman of contrary political principles to smell them out. This was the British minister himself. Foster found an astonishing number in places of power. "America is governed by the Press which is conducted principally by Irishmen," he wrote. "Binns who was of the Corresponding Society owns one of the bitterest papers against us at Philadelphia."[73] He might also have mentioned Henry's successor as editor of the *Aurora*, William Duane, an American-born Irishman who had been reared in Ireland and deported from India. On the day after the British minister wrote the words just quoted, Randolph of Virginia said much the same thing in the House. "The war spirit is principally stimulated at this moment by those who have escaped from the tyranny (or justice as it may be termed,) of the British Government, long since the war of independence. Almost every leading press in the country is conducted by persons of that description . . . who, in resentment of the wrongs they have recently received from the Irish and British Governments, are now goading us to war; talking about American spirit: the spirit of the Revolution: and of tarring and feathering the 'Tories.' " He scornfully called them "these second founders of the Republic."[74] Perhaps the two men had been comparing notes. Foster also commented upon the presence of Irishmen in Congress. John Rhea of Tennessee, one of the members who was most persistent and outspoken in crying for war with Britain, was a native of the unhappy island;[75] and the Pennsylvania delegation, which ultimately voted almost

73. Foster to Castlereagh, private, May 5, 1812, *F.O.* 5, Vol. LXXXV.

74. *A.C.*, Twelfth Congress, Vol. I, col. 1401. Wright of Maryland was the only member who took any exception to Randolph's statement, and he admitted its general truth. "We are charged by the same gentleman with being governed by certain ministerial prints in our Congressional measures; that the Aurora, The Democratic Press, the Whig, and the Intelligencer, are edited by foreigners, who have come here to disturb our repose by goading us on to war measures. Sir, I feel the impropriety of that suggestion, as inapplicable not only to myself, but to the whole House. We, Sir, have been governed by an honest zeal to represent our constituents in avenging the wrongs of our country, and a firm conviction of the wisdom and policy of the measures adopted for that purpose. But I feel it due to those printers who cannot be heard in their own defence, to say that they have just claims on the gratitude of their adopted country for their patriotic exertions in supporting the principles of our glorious Revolution, and defending the measures of the Execution and Legislation departments. . . . I wish the Representatives on this floor, elected by the American people, would test their devotion to their country's cause, with half the practical patriotism of these foreign printers." *Ibid.*, cols. 1412–1413.

75. Foster to Castlereagh, No. 28, April 23, 1812, *F.O.* 5, Vol. LXXXV.

as a solid block for war, contained several Irish members. Referring to the latter some weeks before this vote was taken, the British minister hopefully commented, "It is not to be supposed that the mass of the population will suffer their interests to be sacrificed to please the passions and prejudices which such individuals may have imported from the country which they have deserted."[76] As might be expected, he also found "Irishmen of the lowest order" in the popular crowd that clamored for war.[77] But Foster, who was no fanatic, did not attempt to prove, or even to suggest, that his embittered fellow countrymen decided the issue that was hanging in the balance.

Another impetus toward war was given by the renewal of hostilities with the Indians in the Northwest. At the battle of Tippecanoe, which coincided with the meeting of Congress in November, 1811, the savage strife burst forth again. Henry Adams and others have cast upon Governor Harrison of Indiana Territory the blame for breaking the peace. By his menacing march up the Wabash, right to the village of the Prophet, he really asked for the battle the Indians gave him. But he only hastened the beginning of a war which was most certainly coming. The Prophet and his abler brother, the warrior Tecumseh, had been scheming for years to make a last valiant stand for the freedom of their race. At the time of the opening fight, Tecumseh was off on a tour among tribes to the south, trying to rally them for the great blow he was about to strike. Though the prime cause of this war was the relentless advance of the American frontier, which robbed the red men of their only way of life, the British in Canada were believed to be at the bottom of it, and therefore it is interesting to turn to the Canadian correspondence dealing with developments in the American Northwest.

At Amherstburg on the east side of the Detroit River, Captain Mathew Elliott of the Indian Department kept in touch with the western tribes as in the days of the alarm raised by the *Chesapeake* incident. Things were still quiet in the summer of 1810 when he was visited by some six score braves from the West. They unanimously said they would await the royal commands for peace or war; and he advised them to keep the peace, supporting his advice by a liberal distribution of presents. But in the autumn his reports to his superior were a cry of distress. The Indians were "ripe for war." They would begin it themselves, and the British would be accused of encouraging them. Already they were demanding supplies. He had just held a private conference with the Prophet's brother. What was he, Elliott, to do?[78]

76. Foster to Castlereagh, No. 30, April 24, 1812, *ibid*.
77. Foster to Castlereagh, No. 39, May 26, 1812, *ibid*.
78. *Q*, CXIV, 65–79.

At this very time, down in Quebec, Sir James Craig was writing home for permission to resign his command. A communication from Morier in Washington and other intelligence from the United States had convinced him that an American declaration of war was probable. That would require an exertion which he could not put forth, for he was well past sixty and his health was broken.[79] But his mind was as clear as ever, and it was dead set against giving any aid or encouragement to the natives in the American Northwest. Before Elliott's disturbing letters reached him, he had heard that the Indians were about to appeal to arms, and, anxious to avert the horrors of an Indian war on the American frontier, had advised Morier to warn the government in Washington in order that necessary precautions might be taken. The warning was duly delivered.[80]

The orders which Craig sent back for the guidance of the Indian Department in Upper Canada were categorical. The projected native hostilities would expose the British in Canada to American suspicions of their complicity, would sooner or later involve Canada, and the result would be disastrous. The red men must be impressed with the certainty of misfortune to themselves if they attacked the whites, and they must be made to know that it was their "father's" regard for them which made him urge the preservation of the peace. From Quebec another letter went to Morier repeating the warning.[81] Craig's policy won the entire approval of the government in London, and in July, 1811, about the time he arrived home, a dispatch was addressed to his locum tenens directing a continuance of this policy.[82]

In September Sir George Prevost landed in Quebec and took over the government. One of his first acts was to send Major General Isaac Brock to preside over the administration of Upper Canada in the absence of Gore, who had been granted a year's leave;[83] and Brock's first care after his arrival in the upper province was to direct the officers of the Indian Department to exert their whole influence against the impending attack of the natives upon the American frontier. But the "infatuation" of the savages was such, he reported on December 3, that they "refused to listen to advice and they are now so deeply engaged that I despair of being able to withdraw them from the contest in time" to save them from their doom. "A high degree of fanaticism which has been for years working in their minds has led to the present state of things."[84] On

79. *Ibid.*, CXIII, 95.
80. *A.S.P.F.R.*, III, 463.
81. *Q*, CXIV, 80–82, 106–109.
82. *Ibid.*, p. 110.
83. *Ibid.*, pp. 170, 172.
84. *P.A.C.R.*, 1896, Note B, p. 65.

March 23, 1812, when more fully apprised of the situation, Brock wrote to Lord Liverpool a dispatch in which he reported that "the most scrupulous attention has been given by the officers of the Indian Department to the instructions issued by Sir James Craig and subsequently enforced by your Lordship . . . to avert the commencement of [native] hostilities with the United States, and although their unjust aggression compelled about 300 to have recourse to arms, yet the officers so far succeeded in their endeavors as to persuade numerous tribes to remain neutral, which I firmly believe saved the western country from destruction."[85]

Though the old American tradition that British officials in Canada fomented this native strife is groundless, it can hardly be called a myth. There was still an international problem centering around the Indians of the American Northwest, in spite of the obvious contrast with the winter of 1807–8. Then Craig used all the influence he could, short of rousing American hostility, to wean the western tribes from their dependence upon the United States, for he wanted their alliance to parry the threatened American attack on Canada. Now the British authorities there did their utmost to check the hostility of these tribes toward the United States, lest it provoke the American attack which again menaced Canada. But the governor in Quebec and the lieutenant governor in York could now be sure of the native alliance if they should need it. American ineptitude, rather than British solicitude, had seen to that. The international problem was the disentanglement of British and American interests in the interior of the United States. Until this was solved, every strain on Anglo-American relations arising from other causes was liable to be aggravated by American suspicions of British intrigues with red men in the United States. The problem was baffling. No mere law passed in Washington could stop the British traffic with Indians on American soil. That was protected by something stronger than the violated guarantee of Jay's Treaty. The American government had to wink at this particular trade because it furnished the red men with the articles which they must have and Americans could no longer supply, thanks to the ban on intercourse with Britain.[86] But there was another solution, one which had often been suggested in years gone by and was now urged vociferously in the press and advanced in Congress. It was war with Britain to drive her out of Canada. That would quench the native war forever! It would thus appear that the Indian situation in the Northwest was perhaps an efficient cause of the War of 1812; but it is

85. *Q*, CCCXV, 4.
86. See *A.C.*, Twelfth Congress, Vol. I, cols. 53–56.

better to suspend judgment upon this point until we have examined another development with which it has been associated.

According to a thesis which has been widely accepted in recent years, we cannot understand why there was a War of 1812 unless we look inland. This thesis[87] may be summarized as follows. The quarrel over neutral rights on the sea brought the United States to the verge of war with Britain but did not do more than that, for the maritime constituencies voted against war. The force that induced the last fatal step was largely, though not wholly, an urge to conquer Canada. This urge was chiefly inspired by the determination to uproot the British-Indian evil but was also compounded of the old jealousy of the British fur trade and a new lust for territorial expansion that anticipated "Manifest Destiny"; and it found abundant "righteous pretexts" in the maritime quarrel. "By the end of the spring of 1812, the whole frontier country from New Hampshire to Kentucky was insisting that the British must be expelled from Canada."[88] But the people of the Northwest might have clamored in vain for war if they had not found fortuitous allies in the people of the South, who were likewise impatient to take Florida from Spain, the weak ally of Britain. This combination, which promised to preserve the balance between North and South by adding territory and population to both, brought on the war. This explanation is supported by the much quoted words of John Randolph delivered in the House on December 16, 1811.

Sir, if you go to war it will not be for the protection of, or defence of your maritime rights. Gentlemen from the North have been taken up to some high mountain and shown all the kingdoms of the earth; and Canada seems tempting in their sight. That rich vein of Gennesee land, which [sic] is said to be even better on the other side of the lake than on this. Agrarian cupidity, not maritime right urges the war. Ever since the report of the Committee on Foreign Relations came into the House, we have heard but one word—like the whip-poor-will, but one eternal monotonous tone—Canada! Canada! Canada! Not a syllable

87. Julius W. Pratt, *Expansionists of* 1812, an interesting book in which the author tries to explain the paradox, "which apparently gave little concern to the older historians," of the United States' going to war to uphold maritime rights despite the stout opposition of maritime New England. He carefully explains in his preface that his work "makes no effort to give a full account of the causes of the War of 1812, but deals with one set of causes only. The exclusion from all but briefest mention of the maritime grievances against Great Britain is with no wish to belittle them." Ignoring this caution, many readers have leaped to the conclusion, which he never intended to suggest and does not, that the traditional causes were of relatively minor importance and that the real causes of the war are to be found in the West. He admits, however, that he "feels safe in saying that without the peculiar grievances and ambitions of the West there would have been no war." This conclusion, I have been driven to reject. But at the same time I would like to pay tribute to the author for having made an important contribution to the history of Manifest Destiny.

88. *Ibid.*, p. 58.

about Halifax, which unquestionably should be our great object in a war for maritime security.[89]

Confirmation has also been found in the division of Congress on the war issue, "most of the navigating interests voting nay, and the interior, particularly the whole frontier in a great crescent from Vermont to Louisiana, voting aye," with "only a small majority for war."[90]

There is more than one *non sequitur* in this argument. Does the voting of the maritime constituencies prove that neutral rights alone could not have produced the war? Their votes were divided, as a glance at the map shows; and the division would have been more equal if it had truly reflected the opinions of the people. Nor should it be forgotten that this was the part of the country that stood to suffer most in a trial of strength with British sea power. Much more serious is another consideration which we have already seen. The American government had to champion the maritime interests not only in spite of their opposition but also because of their opposition. The commercial and shipping elements had been betraying the national honor. They would have sold neutral rights and the country's independence for selfish profit and sectional welfare.

The southern pressure for war is also misconstrued. Why should Americans want war with Britain in order to seize Florida? Part had already been taken without it, and the obstacle that seemed to stand in the way of getting the rest was the possibility of British intervention. Britain ruled the waves, and the waves nearly surrounded Florida. Moreover the administration's schemes for acquiring this weakly held Spanish possession were well under way long before the "War Hawks" flocked to the Twelfth Congress. The one reason why the South should welcome war with Britain to aid in getting Florida was to buy off sectional opposition within the United States by letting the North have its *quid pro quo* in Canada;[91] but, as already suggested, this meant running the obvious danger of the means' defeating the end. The reports of the debates in the *Annals of Congress* contain no suggestion of Florida's being a motive for war; but they do reveal another material motive which has attracted too little attention. It was a strong one.

The planters were being badly pinched. "Our cotton is reduced to seven cents, and our tobacco to nothing," cried old Robert Wright of

89. *A.C.*, Twelfth Congress, Vol. I, col. 533.

90. S. F. Bemis, *A Diplomatic History of the United States*, pp. 156–157. Louisiana, however, did not vote. The final vote in the House was 79 to 49, and in the Senate, 19 to 13. One of the names in the last list is omitted from the report in the *A.C.*, Twelfth Congress, Vol. I, col. 297.

91. This motive was suggested in a speech by Grundy, a Virginian who had moved to Tennessee. *Ibid.*, col. 427.

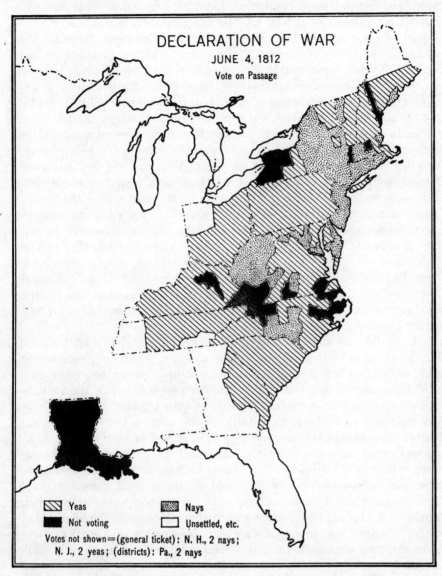

DECLARATION OF WAR
JUNE 4, 1812
Vote on Passage

Yeas
Nays
Not voting
Unsettled, etc.
Votes not shown = (general ticket): N. H., 2 nays;
N. J., 2 yeas; (districts): Pa., 2 nays

The Vote in the House of Representatives on the Declaration of War, 1812

Redrawn with permission of the American Geographical Society from Charles
O. Paullin and John K. Wright, *Atlas of the Historical Geography of the United
States.*

Maryland in the House. He denied Randolph's assertion "that our own restrictive system has undone us," pointing out that restrictions on the export of these articles had ceased and if they had been the cause the effect should have ceased too. "The price of cotton depends on the demand for the manufactures of that article; the English-made cottons depended on the continental markets, from which the British manufactures are excluded. The price of tobacco never was materially varied by the consumption in England, but depended on the foreign demand from Great Britain, which, by their exclusion from the continent, is almost entirely arrested." The retaliatory system of the two great belligerents, he said, had ruined the market for these American staples, and since Napoleon had revoked his decrees the blame now rested on the British orders-in-council.[92] Wright put his finger on the sore spot of the South. This was the one section of the country that was vitally dependent upon the markets controlled by Napoleon. It was not a commercial region; but its very life was tied up with commerce. Here was a further reason for championing the maritime interests in their own despite. Maritime New England would have deserted the planter South; and the rural North would have done the same thing, for it was attracted by the fabulous price of wheat in England and the market for provisions created by the Peninsular War.

The voting of the frontier constituencies from Kentucky to New Hampshire also calls for more careful analysis. Another glance at the map shows that the unanimity was broken in Vermont and more particularly in New York. But if there had been no such break, the attitude of the members from the interior would be quite understandable without any reference to Canada. Practically all the members of Congress, no matter what part of the country they represented or how they voted in the end, admitted that the United States had just grounds for declaring war on Britain. This being so, it stands to reason that those who came from the interior were least inhibited by the fear of consequences.[93] Their electors had little direct interest in the sea-borne commerce which would be disrupted; they had no settlements which might be bombarded by British naval guns; and, if we except inhabitants of New York and Vermont, they were about as secure from a British military attack. This immunity was the common contemporary explanation of the pronounced bellicose attitude of the interior. It was also said that the western members saw in a war a lever to raise the price of hemp and of other produce which their people wished to sell but could not.

92. *Ibid.*, cols. 470–471.
93. "When a man rises in this House, you may almost tell how ardent he will be, by knowing how far distant he lives from the sea." Stow of New York, on Jan. 6, 1812, *ibid.*, col. 677.

Though the Indian menace, which was played up by the Republican press, haunted the minds of some members of Congress, there is a good reason for doubting if it had any appreciable influence in bringing on the war with Britain. The seat of the native strife lay off in a remote corner. Relatively few whites lived anywhere near it, and they had no representatives in Congress. There it was openly said that Americans had stirred up the hornets' nest, and the aggressive character of Harrison's advance on Tippecanoe was so obvious that it was difficult to deny. A close study of all the debates from the opening of the session until the declaration of war shows that very few members, and they only very occasionally, pointed to the red peril or accused Britain of instigating it. If the old nightmare turned any vote from peace to war, there is no evidence for it in the *Annals of Congress*. In the President's historic message of June 1, 1812, recommending a declaration of war, Britain is charged most positively with "a series of acts, hostile to the United States as an independent and neutral nation," and after the enumeration of these acts, which are a catalogue of the maritime grievances, a short paragraph insinuating that there was some connection between the hostility of the savages and their intercourse with the British is inserted as a sort of afterthought. This is the only reference to the Indian troubles and it makes no definite charge.[94] Apparently the administration did not consider the native hostilities to be a cause of war any more than did the majority in Congress.

The conquest of Canada was frequently mentioned in the debates, but the suggestion that it was desirable for its own sake was made so rarely that a reader of the debates might miss it if he did not look for it. Randolph's words which have been quoted above should not be taken at their face value. This Virginian stood out from among his fellow members of the House as the most persistent opponent of war. He denounced it eloquently, at great length, and often. If he really believed that the effective cause of the pressure for war was agrarian cupidity, rather than maritime grievances, we might expect to find that he directed his invective at this dishonorable motive again and again. But he did not. His words which have been so aptly used to support this thesis constitute only a short passage in a long speech delivered six months before the war, and there is hardly an echo of them in the records of his many other speeches during these six months. In the reports of what was said by all the other speakers who opposed war, there is equally little to support the startling charge he flung at the warmongers in December, 1811. Evidently it was not considered to have much point.

This conclusion is confirmed by a careful reading of Foster's letters.

94. *Ibid.*, cols. 1624–1671.

They reveal him not only as most interested in whatever was going on but also as one of the best-informed men in the country, and they do not even suggest that an urge for the conquest of Canada was a cause of war. At the very end, during the secret session in which Congress passed the act declaring war, the idea did creep into one of his dispatches. He wrote that Harper of New Hampshire, a member of the committee on foreign relations, was reported as saying that "it would be advisable to go to war for Canada alone" and "he would be for never laying down arms until Canada should be taken."[95] The British minister's only comment was, "It is supposed that this was a manoeuvre by which to get rid of the question of war altogether, as it would be impossible ever to get the House to agree to so great an absurdity."[96] He was perfectly familiar with the talk of an attack on Canada, but he saw war coming as a consequence of what had happened at sea and not because of what was expected to happen on land.

This concept of the war dominated the discussions in Congress, and it was not the product of the "War Hawks." Erskine had described it before their party was hatched.[97] It was simple, logical, and honorable. Britain had injured the United States on the high seas, where she was invincible. To challenge her there would be to court defeat. Britain had a thousand warships; the United States had not a single ship-of-the-line and only a half dozen frigates. A swarm of American privateers might prey upon British commerce, but a few heavy vessels of the Royal Navy might bombard American cities and even capture American ports. The only way to make Britain submit was to strike her where she was vulnerable—in the provinces adjoining on the north. Quebec might be too hard a nut to crack, but the United States could easily overrun the two Canadas right down to that fortress, and Quebec without the country back of it would be of little value to Britain. The small attention paid to Halifax is explained by the plain fact that it was beyond the American reach. The prevailing thought was that the United States was potentially supreme on land, as Britain was actually supreme on the sea. Each country had its own element, though only one had used it; and Britain would cease from her oppression at sea rather than lose her share of the land. If the worst came to the worst and, as one senator pointed out, Britain should get possession of New York and New Orleans, they could be recovered by an exchange of conquests.[98] The conquest of Canada was anticipated as the seizure of a hostage rather than as the capture of a prize.

95. This is not reported in the *Annals of Congress*.
96. Foster to Castlereagh, No. 43, June 9, 1812, *F.O. 5*, Vol. LXXXVI.
97. *Supra*, p. 267.
98. *A.C.*, Twelfth Congress, Vol. I, col. 41.

Why, then, did the war not come in 1811, shortly after Foster's arrival, when according to Mahan the breach was assured? Why the delay of a year? The answer is threefold. For one thing, the government in Washington was gravely worried by the possibility that American honor might also require a declaration of war against Napoleon.[99] He seemed determined to ruin American trade with the whole continent of Europe; his minions confiscated American ships and cargoes, they were still burning them at sea, and they even impressed American sailors. Repeated representations in Paris brought no redress nor any promise of it. The President's temper grew very bad as he saw more and more clearly that the Emperor had been making sport of him and his people. Monroe was furious. In defiance of notorious evidence to the contrary, he tried again and again to persuade Foster that the Berlin and Milan decrees were repealed; and then he turned to Serurier and used this evidence to prove the opposite. The outrageous behavior of France was aired in Congress, where it found scarcely an apologist. Members who advocated war with Britain commonly admitted that hostilities against France would likewise be justified. In his opening message and again in his war message of seven months later, Madison referred to the American grievances against France. It is quite conceivable that, if the French Empire had been as vulnerable as the British, the United States might have made war on Napoleon too.

In the second place, the administration cherished a dying hope that Britain would yet surrender her orders-in-council and thereby open the door for an accommodation of other difficulties, particularly impressment. The discovery of Foster's impotence, which followed almost immediately upon his arrival, was a hard blow, but it did not kill this hope, for Monroe told him in the summer of 1811 that the United States would soon send a minister to London. The appointment was put off until it could be submitted to the Senate for confirmation, and when Congress met he confessed that the appointment had to be abandoned because the Senate would not give its consent.[100] Still the hope was not dead.

The third reason for the delay in declaring war was that the country was absolutely unprepared to wage it, thanks to the sublime faith of Jefferson and Madison in the efficacy of commercial restrictions. Before the United States could begin to fight, an army had to be found and before an army could be found, special legislation had to be passed. This required time, and then more time was needed because it was difficult to

99. See Madison to Jefferson, May 25, 1812, in Madison, VIII, 190–192.

100. Foster to Castlereagh, No. 24, Nov. 12, No. 25, Nov. 21, 1811, *F.O. 5*, Vol. LXXVII.

find the men and the money. As it was, the declaration came long before the country was ready for it.[101]

Though the President opened Congress with a request for war preparations, he had not yet given himself over to despair. Preparations for war are sometimes the only way to avoid it, and he seems to have believed that London might repent when it heard the rattling of the saber in Washington. The faint hope lingered through the winter and on into the spring, showing signs of life at the approach of every dispatch vessel from England. The end came on May 27 or 28. On those days Foster had several interviews with Madison and Monroe, and to them he communicated a long note he had just received from the British Foreign Secretary.[102] Its categorical insistence on the maintenance of the orders-in-council, supported by new proof that the Napoleonic decrees were still the law, at last convinced Madison that further discussion with the British government was impossible.[103] Thereupon he drafted the war message which he submitted to Congress on June 1.

Reviewing the hostile conduct of Britain only since the renewal of Anglo-French hostilities in 1803, the President made four definite charges. The first was impressments. The second was that British cruisers violated the peace of American coasts, hovering over and harassing entering and departing commerce. The third was the employment of "pretended Blockades" to plunder American commerce. The fourth was "the sweeping system" of the orders-in-council. He said nothing of the *Chesapeake*, for that account had been settled. Nor did he mention the contentious Rule of 1756, for this question had been liquidated by conquest. There were no French colonies left, and therefore there was no enemy colonial trade. Nor did he refer to the contract with France, for France had patently failed to live up to it.

Henry Adams has accused Madison of "inverting the order of complaints previously alleged," and he says that "this was the first time that the Government had alleged impressment as its chief grievance."[104] But it is just as reasonable to conclude from a study of this document that the discussion of the orders-in-council was intended to be a climax of the indictment. In fact, there appears to have been no intended relation between the order of the charges and Madison's view of their relative gravity. He was proceeding chronologically. It should also be pointed out that he had long since committed himself officially on the importance of the impressment issue. When he was Secretary of State

101. Madison, VIII, 242.
102. Castlereagh to Foster, No. 8, April 10, 1812, *F.O.* 5, Vol. LXXXIII.
103. Madison, IX, 272–273.
104. Adams, VI, 222.

his instructions to Monroe made it the crux of the negotiations in London, and as soon as he learned that Monroe was completing a treaty without requiring Britain to abandon impressments from American vessels on the high seas he notified him that the United States must reject the treaty for this very reason. There had been no subsequent negotiation over the question simply because it seemed so hopeless. The blood it caused to be spilled while the two countries were nominally at peace is grim testimony of its fundamental importance.

The bill declaring war was passed by the House of Representatives on June 4, the Senate passed it in an amended form on the seventeenth, it was returned with the approval of the House on the eighteenth, and the President signed it immediately. On the following day Foster proposed a suspension of hostilities until the declaration of war reached England, and he offered to hurry home with any proposition the American government might wish to make. He met with a refusal.[105] When taking his formal leave on the twenty-third, he asked if a repeal of the orders-in-council would restore peace, and he again urged a suspension of hostilities "until further intelligence should be received from Great Britain." Once more he met with a rebuff. He was told that the repeal would have to be accompanied by a promise to negotiate on impressments in order to halt the war, and that there was no prospect of repeal.[106] But on that very day, over in London, the orders-in-council were repealed—conditionally.

To explain this surprising reversal of British policy, it is necessary to go back a little. The orders-in-council had stirred opposition in England from the very beginning, and a rising tide of public opinion blamed them for the growing distress of the country. To allay the discontent, the government clothed its oft-repeated promise in an official form on April 21, 1812. This was a new order-in-council repealing its objectionable predecessors. It was to come into force immediately the Berlin and Milan decrees were unconditionally revoked by some authentic act of the French government, publicly promulgated. Armed with this document, the American minister in Paris, Joel Barlow, presented a stiff note on May 1 to the Duke of Bassano, Cadore's successor. It demanded the publication of an authentic act declaring the decrees had ceased to apply to the United States in November, 1810. Barlow later had "a pretty sharp conversation" with Bassano. Then came an astounding climax. The Frenchman produced a decree exactly fitting the American requirement. From the date it bore, April 28, 1811, it was more than a year

105. Foster to Castlereagh, No. 47, June 20, 1812, *F.O. 5*, Vol. LXXXVI.
106. Minute of Interview, June 23, 1812, enclosed in Foster to Castlereagh, No. 49, June 24, 1812, *ibid.*

old. How it could have been kept secret all this time is still a mystery. When asked if it had been published, Bassano had to admit that it had not; but he blandly asserted that it had been communicated to Jonathan Russell, then American *chargé* in Paris and since transferred to London, and also to Serurier with orders to give it to the American government. Both men denied they had ever received it, and it appears to have been spurious. However that may be, Barlow secured what he had demanded and he sent it posthaste to Russell, who immediately presented it to Castlereagh with a request for corresponding British action. This was on May 20, when no action was possible. Britain was without a government. Only a few days before, a lunatic had assassinated the Prime Minister, Spencer Percival. In the middle of June, almost as soon as the ministry was reconstituted under Lord Liverpool, he announced the provisional repeal of the orders-in-council. Some days were consumed in working out the provisions, and then the requisite order was passed on the twenty-third. The pressure which had produced the order of April 21 had also forced the government to give up its prerequisite of a complete restoration of neutral rights as they existed prior to the Berlin Decree.

Three days later, Foster's suggestion bore fruit in Washington. On June 26, Monroe wrote to Russell informing him of the declaration of war and at the same time authorizing him to arrange an armistice immediately, "if the orders-in-council are repealed, and no illegal blockades are substituted for them, and orders are given to discontinue the impressment of seamen from our vessels, and to restore those already impressed." As an inducement for Britain to yield on impressments, he was instructed that he might "give assurance that a law will be passed (to be reciprocal) to prohibit the employment of British seamen in the public or commercial service of the United States."[107]

Neither of the two doves of peace which were simultaneously sent forth from opposite sides of the Atlantic could find a resting place. The nature of the British repeal, it is important to note, was not absolute. It was to apply to American vessels and cargoes, being American property, from August 1, and was to operate retrospectively to such vessels and cargoes seized since May 20 as had not already been condemned. But there was to be no repeal at all unless the government of the United States revoked the legislation prohibiting British intercourse as soon as possible after the communication of this order; and even after American compliance nothing in this order was to be understood as precluding a revival of the orders-in-council "if circumstances shall so require."[108] When inspected in Washington, the offer was quickly

107. *A.S.P.F.R.*, III, 585.
108. *Ibid.*, p. 433.

rejected. It wiped out an unknown number of American claims arising since May 20 and all claims of a previous origin. More serious was another objection. The very act which offered to withdraw the intolerable offense stipulated the right to repeat it at any time. This, said Monroe, the government of the United States "cannot admit." The outbreak of war had also raised an insuperable obstacle to American compliance, for the restoration of intercourse would have meant the admission of British fighting vessels[109] along with British commercial bottoms into American ports. The repeal was therefore null and void. The American government felt little or no regret when repelling this British effort at conciliation. There was consolation in the thought that, if any satisfactory arrangement was possible, Russell was already procuring it in London.

Of the three conditions in the American proposal for an armistice, one was already met. In communicating the repeal order, Castlereagh had informed Russell that it was to be interpreted as extinguishing the blockade of 1806 and that there was no intention of reviving it or any other blockade.[110] But Russell realized that the repeal of the orders-in-council, having been adopted in ignorance of the declaration of war, could not be effective under the new circumstances; and therefore he demanded a reënactment which would make it effective. Castlereagh refused. The British government had acted in good faith and expected the American government to do the same. One may be tempted to condemn this lack of imagination, or obtrusion of national pride, but it appears probable that the British government would have accommodated the American government on this point had it not been for the third condition posed by Russell. That touched a vital British interest, and on that Castlereagh was adamant. "You," he said to the American *chargé*, "are not aware of the great sensibility and jealousy of the people of England on this subject; and no administration could expect to remain in power that should consent to renounce the right of impressment, or to suspend the practice, without the certainty of an arrangement which should obviously be calculated most unequivocally to secure its object. Whether such an arrangement can be devised is extremely doubtful, but it is very certain that you have no sufficient powers for its accomplishment."[111] The impressment issue was the rock that wrecked the last hope of peace.

Years afterwards Madison wrote, "Had the repeal of the orders been

109. This could have been avoided only by legislation excluding French vessels of the same description.

110. *Ibid.*, p. 434.

111. *Ibid.*, p. 594.

substituted for the declaration that they would not be repealed, or had they been repealed but a few weeks sooner, our declaration of war as proceeding from that cause would have been stayed, and negotiations on the subject of impressments, the other great cause, would have been pursued with fresh vigor & hopes, under the auspices of success in the case of the orders in council."[112] He did not venture to say that peace would have been preserved, for he was wiser than the later dogmatists who have confidently asserted that there would have been no War of 1812 if there had been an Atlantic cable in 1812. That will always be a debatable question.

112. Madison, IX, 273, where the word "improvements" appears instead of "impressments." This is an obvious typographical error.

CHAPTER XIV

THE WAR OF 1812: ITS OPERATIONS[1]

THE fighting of the War of 1812 is a story so well known to Canadians and Americans, having been so often told, that it would be tedious and superfluous to repeat it here. Moreover it would be out of place in this study of Canadian-American relations, to which it would make little or no contribution. But it is very pertinent to try to find the explanation and significance of what happened in this war, which calls for an analytical rather than a descriptive treatment.

Most Canadians are prone to ignore the fact, which Americans can never forget, that the War of 1812 was oceanic as well as continental. The distinction is fundamental. It should not be confused with that between naval and military operations, which in this war is purely artificial. The naval operations on the Lakes, which were completely separate from those on the sea, were subsidiary to the military operations around the Lakes and therefore should be considered with them in an examination of the war on land. The struggle on the sea stands by itself and was of vital importance. It conditioned the war on land but was not conditioned by it.

The nature of the war on the sea had often been predicted. The United States Navy being then negligible and the Royal Navy invincible, no battle between fleets was possible. Each side therefore sought to reduce the other by crippling its commerce in the only way it could, the Americans by raiding and the British by blockade, the natural method of warfare between a strong naval power and a weak one.

The United States had no ship of the line, nor any use for one. The American task called for numbers rather than size, speed rather than strength. Numbers could scatter to prey more widely, and speed spelled safety from capture by superior force. The marauders appeared on every sea, and were particularly active where the lines of communication from all over the world converged upon Great Britain. British trade and shipping suffered severe damage. Most of it was inflicted by privateers,

---

1. Of the numerous accounts of the War of 1812, large and small, early and late, special and general, the best is probably that found in Adams, Vols. VI–IX, and the next best is A. T. Mahan, *Sea Power in Its Relations to the War of* 1812. C. P. Lucas, *The Canadian War of* 1812 (Oxford, 1906), is also excellent.

For documents, see *A.S.P.M.A.*, Vol. I (Washington, 1832); William Wood (ed.), *Select British Documents of the Canadian War of* 1812, 3 vols. (Publications of the Champlain Society, 1920–23); and E. A. Cruikshank, *Documentary History of the Campaigns upon the Niagara Frontier*, 1812–1814 (Lundy's Lane Historical Society Publications, Vol. III, Parts I–VIII, 1902–7).

small light vessels, of which a total of some five hundred at one time or another went out to cruise. About three hundred returned empty-handed or not at all, but the remainder gathered over thirteen hundred prizes. United States frigates and smaller seagoing craft of the navy were a more efficient destructive force; but they were pitifully few, twenty-two in all, and four of these took nothing. The other eighteen accounted for one hundred and sixty-five prizes. A handful of the latter were plucked from the Royal Navy in a series of single-ship engagements, and Americans remember with just pride that the British lost all these duels save one. These, however, had no military value, for their reduction of the power of the British fleet was infinitesimal.

On the British side there was privateering too, though on a much smaller scale. It was a poor business except for those who could take advantage of the location of Nova Scotia, overlooking the American seaboard. To the people of that province, fighting in the War of 1812 meant sailing under letters of marque—a wartime projection of their traditional rivalry with Americans. A total of some three thousand "Bluenoses" tried their luck at this game at least once during hostilities, and the forty-four privateers on which they sailed reported over two hundred prizes. But this had no appreciable effect upon the issue at sea.

The naval war was won by the fighting ships of Britain without much actual fighting. Before the return of peace, American privateers as well as merchantmen were pretty well swept from the ocean and the United States Navy had practically ceased to exist. The decisive factor was the British blockade of the American coast. Growing tighter with the continuance of hostilities, it strangled the maritime activity of the United States. Nor is this all it did. It strangled the ability of the American government to continue the war on land; and, what has sometimes been overlooked, it was doing this even before the fall of Napoleon released a powerful British army for use in North America. Another thing which should not escape attention is that, as a last resort, British sea power could have been used to make the United States disgorge even a considerable land conquest. Here was an ultimate guarantee, not called upon because not needed, that British North America would survive the war.

The war on land passed through two very distinct phases, one long and the other short. In the first phase, the initiative lay with the United States. Though having gone to war out of self-defense, the American government waged it as if for an aggressive purpose—the conquest of Canada while Britain's hands were tied in the Old World. This seemed the surest way to wring from Britain a recognition of the American rights which she had violated. It was a means to an end. Potentially, however, it was something more, for success might easily have elevated the means into an end. The British in Canada were strategically on the defensive, though tactically they were occasionally able to assume the offensive, and, in one quarter, to maintain it throughout. Their object was to parry the American blows, and to stave off the threatened conquest. Their military dispositions were governed by those of the Americans. The second phase of the struggle began in 1814, when this little war in America was turned inside out by the collapse of the big one in Europe. Then the offensive and defensive roles were reversed, except in the West where the Americans had been on the defensive from the beginning, and the purpose of the fighting changed from the expansion to the contraction of the United States.

The first phase of the war on land proved to be a surprise to both sides. In the United States there had been great confidence, and in England grave fears, that American forces would swarm over the greater part of British North America, conquering it easily. How could Britain save these colonies where less than five thousand of her regular troops were stationed in scattered garrisons? How could she reinforce them when her army was engaged in the much more important struggle against Napoleon? What could the population of the British provinces, totaling scarcely half a million, do against the people of the United States, who numbered about seven and three-quarter million? The majority of the former were French, who, having remained sullenly neutral when British and Americans had last fought each other, were now openly resenting the rule of their British masters. The minority contained a large proportion of Americans, who occupied the Eastern Townships and formed the bulk of the Upper Canadian population. British North America was a thin line of settlement, broken here and there, stretching over a thousand miles and more along a notoriously indefensible border. There had been some American doubt if the rock of Quebec would fall, and the British government had warned Craig to subordinate everything to the retention of that fortress. The Americans had besieged it once and they might do it again. A British army of ten thousand men had crossed the ocean and driven them away in the spring of 1776, but the spring of 1813 could see nothing like that. The agreement between British and American anticipations extended to Halifax, the only other strong place of the Empire on this continent, but there was little chance of any surprise there. This all-year naval base, unlike the winter-bound citadel of the St. Lawrence, was generally and properly recognized as quite beyond the American reach.

Turning to the actual war as it was fought while Britain's military power was still absorbed in Europe, what do we find? At no time was there even the slightest attempt to strike at the Maritime Provinces. The peace between them and their neighbors was broken at sea but not on land, and profitable peaceful intercourse continued between them, even by sea. Some soldiers who were stationed in the Maritime Provinces and others who were raised there did fight, but that was far away in Upper Canada. The second American siege of Quebec was a forgotten dream. There were plans for the invasion of Lower Canada, but they collapsed at a touch. This province also continued to enjoy trading with neighboring Americans.

It was on Upper Canada that the brunt of the war fell, but not on the oldest and most solid part. That was the district along the upper St. Lawrence where most of the Loyalists who founded the province were planted. No real attempt to conquer them was made, nor did the war stop all friendly dealings across the river. The fighting was centered on Niagara and scattered between the eastern end of Lake Ontario and the western end of Lake Erie. There was little but skirmishing beyond these limits. What was at stake in the fighting between them was the possession of this remote portion of British territory, where the population was largely American in origin, and the control of a wider American region beyond, the land of red men who were again open allies of the British. These two objectives, it will be observed, were at the very extremity of the British line; and yet when 1814 arrived the British still exerted their sway out to the Mississippi, and the only territorial loss they had suffered was the little corner of Upper Canada between Lakes St. Clair and Erie, as a consequence of a small but decisive naval encounter on the latter. No decision had been reached at Niagara or on Lake Ontario. In short, the war on land was a misfire. It did not go off against the eastern flank of British North America, it scarcely reached the outer edge of the center, and it expended its whole force on the western flank with astonishingly little result. Why the misfire?

The immunity of the Maritime Provinces may be ascribed to British sea power. This explanation clearly holds for little Prince Edward Island and for Nova Scotia too. In a military sense, the latter was also an island, the narrow Isthmus of Chignecto being nothing more than a bridge. New Brunswick, however, was in a different position. Sea power could have protected it if there had been an available army to throw into it; but there would have been none to spare if the United States had launched a determined drive against Quebec. The wilderness of Maine could not have saved New Brunswick from invasion, for American forces penetrated a much greater wilderness in the West. What shielded this province was New England, and it shielded much more.

OPERATIONS OF THE WAR OF 1812

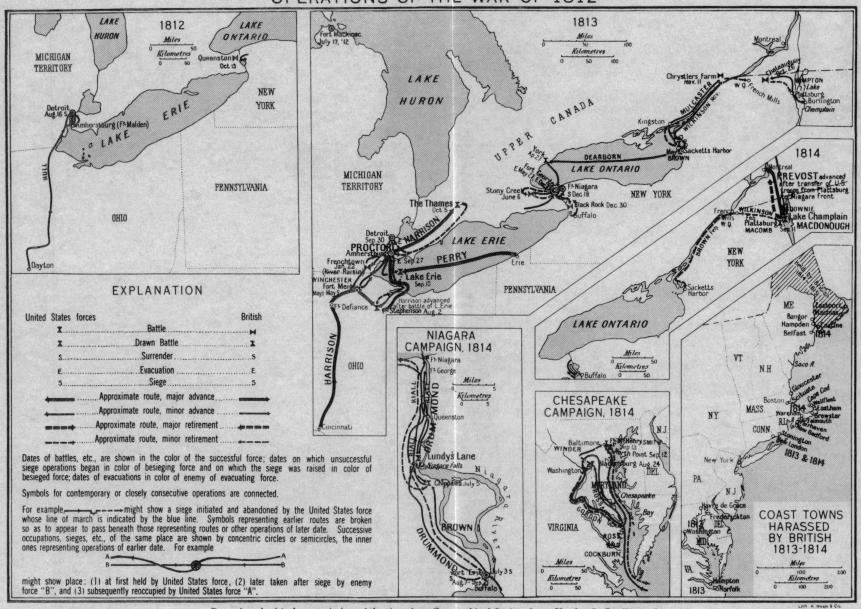

Reproduced with the permission of the American Geographical Society from Charles O. Paullin and
John K. Wright, Atlas of the Historical Geography of the United States, Plate 162

Lith. A. Hoen & Co.

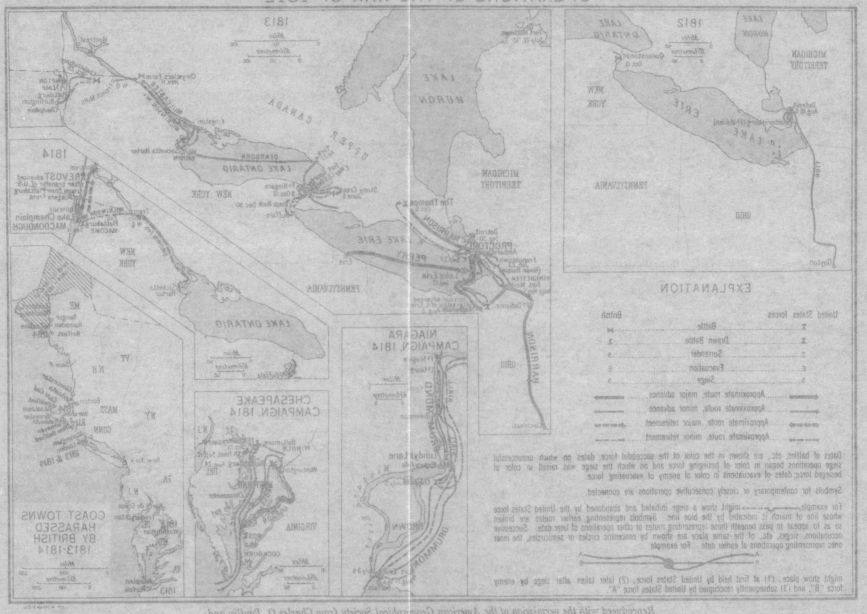

There would probably have been little left of British North America before Napoleon fell, if the division in the United States had not offset the distraction of Great Britain. The American nation was split as it had never been before and, with the exception of the Civil War period, has never been since. The opposition to the war was quite as intense as it had been before the declaration; and it was largely sectional, being concentrated in the North. It divided New York and, what was much more important, it dominated New England, the home of the Federalists. It was natural that they should be hysterical in their hatred of this war. To them it was the climax of a policy designed to ruin their particular part of the country. To them it was the betrayal of the whole country, its interests, and its honor, by the party in power, who had sold out to France. To them, also, it was the consummation of a secret alliance with the international monster. So strong was this feeling that it burst out in all sorts of ways, bearing down the local minority who had held opposite opinions. Flags flew at half-mast in Boston; the governor of Massachusetts proclaimed a public fast; state legislatures, county conventions, and town meetings passed resolutions; and the pulpit, still a power in the land of the Puritans, thundered against the awful thing that had been done in Washington. This desperate opposition exasperated the President and his supporters. They naturally saw it as downright treason, and they were impotent to deal with it. The mere suggestion of coercion was enough to raise the specter of secession.

There was only one thing that might have welded the two halves of the nation together in this war. That was a British attack on New England. But the British, who had long counted on this breach to save their colonies by paralyzing a hostile United States, did their best to cultivate it. They were discriminating in their hostility. They attacked the West with soldiers and savages, and with their ships they bottled up the ports of the South, but they kept the war away from New England. Shortly after the outbreak of hostilities, the commander-in-chief in Canada reported home that his policy was "to avoid committing any act which may even by a strained construction tend to unite the eastern and southern states."[2] It is possible to discount his prudence by pointing to his military weakness; but the British had New England at their mercy in another quarter. New England was left outside the blockade which might have completed its ruin. The pointed exemption of this part of the country from hostilities deepened the cleavage in the United States.

New England returned the compliment—and the curses—with disastrous effects upon the United States. It was able to do this because

2. Quoted without reference in C. P. Lucas, *op. cit.*, p. 23. For the dispatch in which these words occur see *Q*, CXVIII, 39.

it was the section of the country which had the most concentrated population, the greatest wealth, and the most strategic location. The refusal to place its militia, the best in the land, at the service of the federal government hit the weak spot in the latter's military policy. Dictated by political fear reinforced by financial necessity, this policy was to raise only a small number of regular troops and to rely on the state militias for the mass of the fighting forces. The militia from the other parts of the Union, available for six months' service at the outside, proved to be little better than an armed mob. The refusal of New England to subscribe to federal loans was also a crushing blow. It reduced the government to insolvency, for though there was plenty of liquid capital in this corner of the United States there was not enough in all the other sections of the Republic to finance the war. To make matters worse, New England was acting like a leech upon the rest of the country, sucking all the good money out of it; for the commercial restrictions imposed by Virginian leaders had incidentally established industries in the northeast, and the blockade, by driving transportation inland, made it difficult if not impossible for distant consumers, engaged in producing bulky raw materials, to pay for their manufactures with anything but cash. The drain of specie from the middle and southern states, which had begun as early as 1810, gathered great momentum from the commencement of the war, producing economic exhaustion in the depleted regions. These of course were the regions which supported the government and its war.

In addition to this indirect aid to the enemy, New England gave positive assistance by lending money to the British government and by trading with the British provinces. With capital seeking employment, it freely invested in British Treasury notes, for the purchase of which a considerable quantity of coin was sent out of the country. Much more important was the trading, which continued almost as if New England was a friendly neutral. Upper Canada might have fallen for lack of supplies to sustain the British war effort there, if Americans had not furnished them by the roundabout route of Halifax, which then enjoyed an unprecedented prosperity, and by more direct overland trails to Lower Canada. Even in the concluding phase of the war, when the British forces were multiplied as a consequence of the peace in Europe, their commander-in-chief was able to report home that two-thirds of his army "were eating beef provided by American contractors, drawn principally from the States of Vermont and New York."[3] Finally, as suggested above, the geographical position of New England permitted it to serve as a buffer for much of British North America.

3. Prevost to Bathurst, Aug. 27, 1814, *ibid.*, CXVII, 183, quoted in Adams, VII, 146.

The difficulties created by New England do not wholly explain the poor showing made by the United States in this war. That was also caused by the failure of the rest of the country to throw its heart into the struggle. The popular attitude is reflected in enlistments. Even the small regular establishment, numbering 36,000 in 1812 and raised at the end of that year to 58,000, was scarcely ever half filled, despite all that the government could do. More discouraging was the response to the call for volunteers who would serve for twelve months. The President was authorized to raise 50,000, but all he got from first to last was a bare 10,000. Henry Adams has pointed out that, in proportion to population, the effort put into the Civil War was ten times greater.[4] Why was there so little now?

As a partial answer to this question, a recent writer has argued that the fiasco in the region of the Great Lakes and St. Lawrence was connected with a fiasco elsewhere, that the South lost interest in the conquest of Canada when most of the northern members of the Senate, irrespective of party, combined in February, 1813, to block the acquisition of East Florida.[5] The incident referred to was the emasculation of the immoral bill, which had been introduced with the blessing of the government, to authorize the occupation of the Spanish province, then held by a garrison so weak that it could have offered no effective resistance. But this frustration of the South cannot explain the shockingly lax prosecution of hostilities prior to the vote, which was a stunning surprise, and it did not prevent a more vigorous prosecution afterwards. Indeed there is no evidence that it had any practical effect on the conduct of the war. As a matter of fact, this defeat of the South was not accepted as final. The government, controlled by Southerners, still cherished hopes of getting the whole of Florida by more honorable means before the termination of the war, by negotiating a recognition of the American claim for insertion in the peace treaty. The same writer has also alleged that Monroe, one of these Southerners, never showed any enthusiasm for taking Canada.[6] But why should he itch, as he certainly did, to command the armies in the field if he was not eager for their success? His instructions to the peace commissioners, detailed in the next chapter,[7] are further proof of his anxiety to round out the United States by the addition of Canada. We must look elsewhere for the answer to the above question, and we do not have to look far.

The plain truth is that the mass of the people, even outside New

4. *Ibid.*, p. 385.
5. Julius W. Pratt, *Expansionists of* 1812.
6. *Ibid.*, p. 267.
7. *Infra*, pp. 346–347, 348.

England, were not convinced that their vital interests were in any grave danger, nor were their passions roused by any flagrant national insult, such as had stirred them to fever heat in 1807. No two wars are waged, nor do opposing belligerents fight, with the same intensity; and for Americans generally, this war was very close to the border line where a mere severance of diplomatic relations suffices to preserve national integrity and honor. If any part of the country was keen for war, it was Kentucky; and Henry Clay affirmed at the end of July, 1812, when he had gone home, that he was almost alarmed at the ardor of his state. Yet what did this ardor then amount to? Service in the militia quota, four hundred recruits for the regular army, which was less than one recruit per thousand of the population, and not one volunteer! Clay's explanation was that the structure of society, being wholly agricultural, would keep its men home from springtime until harvest. What kind of a war was this, in which most of the fighters on one side would not fight during most of the fighting season? It is clear that the nature of the issues was such that they made little appeal to the people at large.

The feebleness of the popular response may also be traced to the unformed character of the nation. It had a loose, sprawling body, and an undeveloped spirit. Though there was much sturdy independence in the country, it was chiefly individual and local. The national government, even apart from considerations of party and personality, commanded small respect or confidence. It was born weak and it remained weak, attempts to strengthen it only provoking dangerous resistance. In the abstract, it was commonly regarded as a necessary evil. This general attitude tended to stifle the American war effort. Descending to particulars, we find further reasons for failure in the government of the day.

The men who directed the Republican administration had left undone those things which they ought to have done, they had done those things which they ought not to have done, and there was no health in them. For years they had been wrestling with the danger of war, and how had they prepared the country to meet it? They had saved money by cutting down the army and the navy, but had squandered it on useless gunboats. They had ruined the trade, wrecked the revenue, and strained the unity of the Republic by their fatuous and obstinate belief in the efficacy of American economic pressure to stop the embattled giants of Europe from trampling on American rights. When the war came, it was soon evident that two members of the cabinet would have to go, the men who were in charge of the fighting services. Paul Hamilton, the Secretary of the Navy, was a nonentity who was of no more use than his gunboats; and there was an almost universal outcry against William Eustis, the Secretary of War, as utterly unfit for the office he held. His generals also promptly demonstrated their appalling incapacity to lead in the field. More serious still was what lay behind this shameful array of incompetence. One man was responsible for it all, the man who had appointed these hopeless individuals, the President himself. Madison had fine qualities, but these did not include the ability to head the national government in this war, even though he was reëlected in the fall of 1812. Four years earlier, though handicapped by the embargo, he had won by a big majority; but now he got little more than half of the votes, and he might have got less if his party supporters had not shrunk from condemning themselves by denying him a second term.

Madison and his crowd had thus crippled the country before they let it enter the contest, and then they weakened it still further. By their obvious shortcomings they inspired such a widespread distrust of the Executive that the people would not rally to support the war nearly as much as they might otherwise have done. In these two ways, which need no further comment, they contributed greatly to the American failure. But these were not all. They added a third and crowning contribution in the actual conduct of the war. The fighting resources at their command were wasted by misuse. They were spent where they would bring the least rather than the greatest return.

The colossal blunder of this war, a blunder that dwarfs all others into insignificance, was in American strategy. The forces of the United States struck at the leaves and branches of British power in the north instead of attempting to cut it down by attacking the trunk, on the lower St. Lawrence. The capture of Quebec would have given all that the seizure of Montreal could give, and a great deal more. With the ancient capital, the whole of Lower Canada as well as everything British out to the Mississippi would have fallen into American hands, and Britain would have had no foothold for recovering any part of this enormous loss. Quebec, however, was a much more difficult objective than Montreal. The fortifications of the former were many times stronger than they had been when the previous generation of Americans closed in upon it, whereas the latter had no fortifications at all. The numerical odds would also have made Montreal much easier to take. The Americans could collect more troops there and the British fewer—the Americans because it was nearly two hundred miles nearer their base, and the British because they would sacrifice the open city to hold the fortified one, but never the reverse.

Though Montreal was not the key to all Canada, it was the key to all that lay above. British agents could not have supported the Indian war in the American Northwest without supplies forwarded from Montreal over the old and expensive route of the Ottawa River and Georgian Bay, or over the newer and cheaper one of the upper St. Lawrence and Lower Lakes. Upon the latter line of communication, all the British forces in Upper Canada, land and lake, were also vitally dependent for supplies and reinforcements. It was a single line along the water, and severance at any point meant the loss of everything above. The British had to withdraw from Detroit, which they had seized in August, 1812, and from the adjoining corner of Upper Canada when their little fleet on Lake Erie was destroyed in September, 1813. But there was no need whatsoever for the Americans to undertake a naval contest there, or to launch a military attack on Niagara. If they had only concentrated upon winning the control of Lake Ontario, that gain would have carried with it all the fruits of their victory of Lake Erie and much more than any military triumph at Niagara could win. Upper Canada from Kingston to Amherstburg would have been theirs. But they would have got all this without exerting any naval or military effort on or around these lakes if their military forces had merely cut the line below. Montreal was the place to strike. There the two routes from the west came together. There, with one fell swoop, the Americans might have killed the native war in their own country and sliced off the whole of Upper Canada and the richest portion of Lower Canada. There success would have given a strong impetus toward success at Quebec, which, if realized, would have locked Britain out of the whole land. The government in Washington wanted to conquer as much of Canada as possible, and this was obviously the only way to do it; but the military energies of the United States were dissipated in scattered and desultory fighting over the wide region of the Lower Lakes.

Why was not everything else sacrificed to strike a decisive blow down Lake Champlain and the Richelieu, over which many armies had passed in previous wars? New England could not block the way, and New York did not. Was it that the memory of the ignominious retreat in 1776 rose like a warning ghost? There is no evidence of it. Everyone knew that this time Britain could send little or no reinforcements across the sea. Did the recurrence of the hideous Indian nightmare serve as a distraction to pull the war westward? If so, the military operations give little indication of it, for they were centered on Niagara.

There is a better suggestion in the proclamation which General Hull issued in Sandwich on July 12, 1812, calling upon the Canadians to exchange British "Tyranny and Oppression" for the blessings of American liberty. He and many of his countrymen, in high station as well as in low, were thinking in terms of a triumphal progress of liberation rather than of regular warfare, and this seemed the proper place to begin such a pleasant crusade. Lower Canada was much less inviting. The French, who formed the great mass of the population, might have little love for their British rulers but they had less for their American neighbors, as had been demonstrated a generation before; and the Americans who were settling the Eastern Townships were off in a pocket by themselves, away from the highroad into the heart of the country. In Upper Canada, the situation was very different. The only part of that province which was strongly British in sentiment was along the Upper St. Lawrence and the Bay of Quinte. The rest of it, with the exception of Niagara, where a small Loyalist outpost had been established, was predominantly American, and this fact was well known in the United States.

That the national character of this colony was trembling in the balance is borne out by evidence supplied by the British officer in charge of the government in York. In February, 1812, so many settlers had openly professed a determination not to act against their countrymen that Brock felt it "highly necessary" to extract from every militiaman an oath abjuring any foreign power, and he tried to get the legislature to adopt this amendment to the militia act. The assembly rejected it. Two-thirds of the members came from the United States.[8] At the same time and for the same reason, he sought the suspension of the habeas corpus, but the same obstacle defeated him. "The great influence which the fear and number of settlers from the United States possess over the decisions of the Lower House is truly alarming," he reported.[9] The ground shook under his feet at the approach of war. Without the presence of troops to rally the loyal and to restrain the disaffected, he feared for the outcome. Hull's invasion and proclamation must have made him feel like the commander of Jericho. Half the militia assembled in Amherstburg promptly deserted, some of them enlisting under the American general. "Numbers have already joined the invading army," wrote Brock on July 20, 1812, "commotions are excited and late occurrences have spread a general gloom." It enveloped him a week later, when he learned that the Norfolk militia as a body refused to march and that the legislature, which he had called for an emergency session, was about to refuse his repeated request for a suspension of the habeas corpus. Had it passed, there would have been a rebellion, according to one competent observer; and Brock was informed that if he had recourse to martial law "the whole armed force will disperse."[10] On the following day he confessed:

My situation is most critical, not from any thing the enemy can do but from the disposition of the people—the population, believe me,—is essentially bad—

8. *Supra*, p. 183, n. 30.

9. E. A. Cruikshank, "A Study of Disaffection in Upper Canada in 1812–15," *Transactions of the Royal Society of Canada*, Third Series, Vol. VI, Sec. II, pp. 16, 19.

10. *Ibid.*, pp. 20–22.

a full belief possesses them all that the Province must inevitably succumb—this prepossession is fatal to every exertion. Legislators, magistrates, militia officers, all have imbibed the idea, and are so sluggish and indifferent in their respective offices that the artful and active scoundrel is allowed to parade the country without interruption and commit all imaginable mischief. They are so alarmed of offending that they rather encourage than repress disorders and other improper acts. I really believe it is with some cause that they dread the vengeance of the democratic party, they are such a set of unrelenting villains.[11]

The common American belief that Upper Canada was ripening to fall into the lap of the United States was not mere wishful thinking, and the attempt to pluck the fruit might have succeeded if American confidence had not been so overweaning as to scorn proper military preparations. If the American forces gathering at Detroit and Niagara had been real armies directed to carry out a pincer movement, Brock's military genius could not have prevented them from nipping off the southwestern peninsula of his province by a painless operation. They gave him his opportunity. With only a handful of regulars, a few companies of militia, and a body of Indians under Tecumseh, he cut off Detroit and took it with Hull and his army in it; and he dashed back to Niagara before the Americans who were collecting there even thought they were ready to cross that river. When at last, some weeks later, they thought they were ready, they were hurled back in a bloody encounter at Queenston Heights. Brock, who fell on the field of battle, had changed the whole face of things in Upper Canada. It was no longer ready to fall. This was now obvious, though there was considerable disaffection to the end of the war.[12]

According to the American plan of campaign for 1812, suggested by Eustis' predecessor, Henry Dearborn, and loosely adopted by the government, Upper Canada was not the only objective. The main army, which was collected on the Hudson and moved up to Plattsburg, was to have advanced on Montreal under the command of this man Dearborn, who was now commissioned senior major general of the United States. But he evinced so little enthusiasm for the task that he had to be ordered to his post, and there he found that his forces were not fit to take the field. They proved it in November, when some of them crossed the frontier on the Richelieu, just fifty miles from Montreal, and at once retired in confusion. Incidentally, as characteristic of American arrangements in the beginning of the war, it may be observed that Hull's command was quite independent of Dearborn and the latter did not know for some time that his authority extended to Niagara.

11. *Ibid.*, p. 23.
12. *Ibid.*, pp. 25–65.

The invasion of Lower Canada to take Montreal, which was impossible in 1812 because the United States had declared war without being ready to wage it, should not have been impossible in 1813; but confused counsels prevented it. In January, 1812, General Armstrong wrote Eustis a letter in which, referring to the dependence of Canada upon the St. Lawrence, he said, "This outlet forms your true object of attack." A year later, when he became Secretary of War with the intention of directing operations himself, he was incapable of following his own clear admonition. He lacked the commanding intelligence and the bold daring to expose the western flank, once it had been engaged, in order to win the war in the center, the only place where it could be won. In the previous autumn, Captain Chauncey of the United States Navy had been sent inland to secure control of the Lower Lakes, and a naval race had begun on Lake Ontario. It had not yet really started on Lake Erie, but no time was now lost in building there for the purpose of recovering Detroit, which Harrison, Hull's successor, had found impossible to accomplish by land. Armstrong forbade the victor of Tippecanoe to advance again until a decision had been reached on the lake.

Viewed locally, this plan was excellent, though it had a defect which luck covered. With more available resources, the Americans could outbuild the British above Niagara, and they did. The American flotilla was constructed at Presque Isle, now Erie, Pennsylvania, in a harbor which was safe from attack but was also a trap, for the mouth was closed by a bar over which the clearance was only between five and seven feet. Here was the flaw. The fighting vessels within could not come out with their guns on board nor without their hulls' being lifted by floats. They would have been exposed to certain destruction if the inferior British force, which was blockading the place, had caught them crossing the bar; but for some reason which is not yet clear the British disappeared on a Friday and did not return until the following Wednesday, just when the delicate operation was completed, and then they had to retire to the protecting guns of Fort Malden by Amherstburg. Five weeks later, when the stoppage of water transport reduced that place to the verge of starvation, the hiding squadron came out to fight and the result was a foregone conclusion. On September 10, the British lost their little fleet, and with it their foothold on the Detroit River. In three weeks Harrison was chasing their retreating soldiers up the Thames. The American victory was decisive locally, but that was all.

There was a much larger sphere in which this battle on Lake Erie might have been decisive, but was not. That was in the whole region from the Great Lakes to the Mississippi, where the sudden seizure of Michilimackinac by a small British force in July, 1812, had awakened the Indian war to its full fury.[13] The effect was tantamount to a sweeping British conquest of American territory and it revolutionized Governor Prevost's concept of the struggle against the United States. It was no longer wholly defensive, as is seen in the directions which he issued in the winter of 1812–13. The British agents, while restraining the natives from inhuman methods of warfare, were to encourage them to fight for their exclusive possession of all the lands which they had not ceded at Greenville in 1795 or by any subsequent treaty. Already, inspired by the rapid turn of the tide in the West, Brock had written to Prevost,[14] and Prevost to Bathurst,[15] urging the inclusion of the Indian allies in any peace negotiation; and Bathurst, who heartily concurred, replied that he had passed the suggestion on to the Foreign Secretary to make sure that the natives would not be forgotten when peace was made.[16] Thus was the old idea of an Indian buffer state revived as a consequence of the American declaration of war in 1812. The idea was practically accomplished in 1812, and 1813 saw no change. Through the Indians, the British were in control of the American Northwest, the American military efforts in that direction being confined to the limited objective of protecting frontier settlements, thanks to the local dread of massacre by savages and to the pitifully inadequate support provided by a harassed Washington. Then came the destruction of the British fleet on Lake Erie, which potentially undermined the whole British position in the interior. That rested on Michilimackinac, which was now uncovered because the British had no fleet on Lake Huron and the victor could move at will from the lower to the upper lake. But the Americans did not seize the great prize they had won.

The British, undaunted by the loss of the main route over Lake Erie and spurred by the desperate plight of their little garrison in the key to the West, rushed supplies and reinforcements north from York to Georgian Bay, where they improvised a supporting depot at the mouth of the Nottawasaga, and across to Michilimackinac in the spring of 1814. Colonel McDouall, the energetic officer who then took charge of this strategic post, soon made his presence felt hundreds of miles away, out on the Mississippi. Hearing that Prairie du Chien, an important center of Indian influence, had fallen, he hurried off an expedition which quickly took the fort the Americans had then constructed. Until the end of the war McDouall's empire extended south to the mouth of the Rock

13. For this important but rather neglected aspect of the War of 1812, see the excellent article by Julius W. Pratt, "Fur Trade Strategy and the American Left Flank in the War of 1812," *The American Historical Review*, XL, 246–273.

14. Sept. 28, 1812, Wood, *op. cit.*, I, 597.

15. Oct. 5, 1812, Q, CXVIII, 265.

16. Dec. 9, 1812, Wood, *op. cit.*, III, 719.

River, and his capital was threatened only once. That was almost a year after the battle on Lake Erie, and then he drove off a force that was twice the size of his own. Though the disappointed Americans retired to attack his communications at Nottawasaga, obliging the commander of the depot to blow it up, he and his men escaped in boats to Michili-mackinac, whence they shortly afterwards took by surprise two of the American vessels that had returned to that vicinity, so that the British communications with the West were not severed after all. The American victory on Lake Erie, thus deprived of its logical sequel on Lake Huron, did not rescue the American Northwest from the British.

The American failure to win control of Lake Ontario is another interesting commentary upon the American naval effort on Lake Erie. The rival fleets, which were built in Kingston and Sackett's Harbor, were so nearly equal in strength that, though they were frequently in presence of each other and three times came to blows in 1813, neither Chauncey nor his opponent, Sir James Yeo, would engage in a decisive action except under conditions favorable to himself. Being on the defensive and not compelled to fight, the British commander rightly declined to run unnecessary risks. But the American had to fight to gain his end, which was offensive, and Admiral Mahan has severely blamed him for excessive caution. Another criticism cuts much deeper. Chauncey might have been bolder had he been stronger, and this he might have been. When he was transferred to fresh water, the United States had only one vessel below Niagara and none above it, whereas the British had begun the war with fighting craft both above and below. The Americans had thus overtaken their opponents in the naval race, and they might have won it if, instead of dividing their effort between Lakes Erie and Ontario, they had spent it all upon the latter. The British, being already divided, would have lost both lakes.

An analysis of the operations on and near Lake Ontario in 1813, which were governed by the American initiative, reveals a confusion of counsel which confounded the whole campaign. Armstrong had not been a week in office before he compromised his original plan, which was to strike at Montreal. He did not abandon this project. He merely postponed it, as he thought, for a few weeks to gather victories elsewhere. To this end, he ordered four thousand troops to Sackett's Harbor and three thousand to Buffalo. The former were to be embarked on boats and escorted by the fleet to Kingston, where they would destroy the British ships, navy yards, and magazines. That done, they were to sail to York to take two vessels known to be there. Then they were to cross the lake and, in co-operation with the force assembled at Buffalo, fall upon the British on the Niagara front. Armstrong was following the advice of Chauncey, who three weeks earlier had proposed an attack on Kingston as soon as navigation opened. The naval man had promised success if he had only a thousand picked soldiers to aid him. There was merit in the first part of the scheme drawn up by the Secretary of War, for next to Montreal the best objective was Kingston. But the rest of the scheme looks like a movement in the wrong direction. If the British lost Kingston they would have been helpless above it, and the Americans could have neglected them to proceed against Montreal. The plan adopted in Washington, however, was soon emptied of its only virtue by being turned upside down.

Dearborn and Chauncey, who were to execute this circular movement around the lake, decided to reverse it, Dearborn out of stupid funk and Chauncey because of stupid reasoning. The latter still admitted that they could capture Kingston, but he thought it would be a difficult job and therefore he concluded that it would be better to do the easier things first. He would begin with York, the easiest, and then sweep the British from Niagara River before tackling the strongest position of all in Upper Canada. In other words, he did what no commander should do; he subordinated strategy to tactical considerations. Dearborn had an acute attack of imagination. Reports which suddenly multiplied the strength of the British in Kingston, he accepted as true though common sense should have told him they were false, for no considerable movements of troops from Lower Canada could have taken place without definite observation from the American side of the river; and when he learned that Sir George Prevost was in Kingston, whither he had gone on a rapid tour of inspection, the American general was seized with panic. He had wild visions of the British governor-in-chief leading a great host against Sackett's Harbor. This hasty visit of Prevost was the most valuable military service which this mediocre general ever rendered in Canada. In a few days Dearborn recovered some of his senses. He realized that Sackett's Harbor was not about to be attacked, but he would not go near Kingston, at least for a while. His statement that there were between six and eight thousand men collected to defend it persuaded Armstrong to invert the plan as desired by Chauncey. Thus was Kingston saved, the descent on Montreal indefinitely postponed, and the war carried westward.

The capture of defenseless York, which occurred at the end of April, was in a military sense nothing but a passing incident in the opening of the campaign. The Americans could not hold the place so long as Yeo's fleet was still in being, and they reëmbarked four days after they landed, having lost as much as they gained. They caught only the smaller of the two birds they were after, the larger one having just flown home to

Kingston; they found another vessel on the stocks and left it in ashes; and they took more military and naval stores[17] than they could carry away, so that they destroyed the remainder. They lost three hundred men, most of them blown up in the accidental explosion of a powder magazine. One of the dead was "the best brigadier then in the service."[18] This raid had an important result that was not military, for the parliament buildings were burned and looters entered private houses, the public library, and the church. A year and a half later Dearborn protested that the burning was done without his knowledge and against his orders; and after the war was over Chauncey, at his own expense, sent back all the plundered books and plate that he could collect. But the words of the former and the deeds of the latter could not alter the fact that their men had begun in the capital of Upper Canada[19] a nefarious game which led to the more famous destruction in the capital of the United States.

The next step in the American campaign, the attempt to drive the British from Niagara, has to be related to the naval situation above and below. It influenced but was not influenced by the struggle on Lake Erie, which was not decided until September, when the design on Niagara had been abandoned. The land attack did not begin until Chauncey brought more troops from Sackett's Harbor and landed them exactly a month after the descent on York. The landing, a mile to the west of the river mouth, turned the British position all along the Niagara, forcing a general retreat inland and toward Burlington. This increased the disparity between the two flotillas on Lake Erie, strengthening the American one by releasing a few small vessels nearly completed at Black Rock on the upper river, and weakening its British opponent by checking the flow of necessary naval stores over the Niagara portage. This double effect, however, seems to have been more incidental than intentional. The object of the military operation was to get possession of the Niagara Peninsula, and that had to be abandoned because of the naval situation on Lake Ontario. By a significant coincidence, the landing which turned the British position occurred on the very day that Prevost and Yeo emerged from Kingston and appeared before Sackett's Harbor. Though this amphibious expedition was so irresolutely conducted that it withdrew after inflicting little damage, the lesson was obvious. The British navy on the lake might at any time snatch victory from the American army on the Niagara front. There the westward thrust of the

17. Some of which were intended for the British vessels on Lake Erie.

18. Adams, VII, 155.

19. For these few mad days, see W. B. Kerr, "The Occupation of York (Toronto), 1813," *Canadian Historical Review*, V, 9–21.

American forces was checked in a little engagement at Stony Creek some ten miles short of the head of Lake Ontario; but this was not responsible for the ensuing American retirement, which the British followed up, to the line of the river. Dearborn ordered it because, on the appearance of Yeo's fleet near the mouth of the river, he feared that his men might be cut off by the British slipping back by water. Throughout the whole of June, Yeo, with a new vessel which gave him temporary superiority, ranged the lake at will, while Chauncey lay tight in his base waiting for the completion of another vessel with which he hoped to turn the tables. Meanwhile the American communications along the southern shore of the lake were disturbed, and the Americans holding the Niagara River ventured little beyond their line.

When July came, the War Department at last began to turn in the right direction, enjoining a continuance of this inactivity on land until control of the lake could be recovered. Knowing that the new vessel in Sackett's Harbor would soon be ready for service, as it was before the end of the month, and expecting that Yeo would then hide in his base until his yet newer vessel would be completed, Armstrong pondered over what should be done. The regular troops divided between Niagara and Sackett's Harbor should be united at one of these places when Chauncey could transport them, but for some time the Secretary of War could not decide which.[20] He hesitated for a whole month before ordering a concentration eastward for the reduction of Kingston. In making this decision, he again wavered between two alternatives. The fall of the British naval base, he said, might be effected by direct assault, or it might be encompassed by cutting the British communications lower down. The main army could descend the St. Lawrence and cross a few miles below Ogdensburg, there fortify and garrison a commanding position which would stop all movement by road or river, and then march on to Montreal while the army on Lake Champlain, commanded by Wade Hampton, moved simultaneously on the same goal. Armstrong was gravitating back to his original sound conception. He had discarded Niagara, but he was loath to renounce Kingston as an immediate objective. Unable to make up his own mind, he left the choice to the new military commander, who likewise wobbled. Kingston was ultimately passed by, but then it was too late to carry out the plan, which was attempted, of closing in on Montreal.

The fatal delay in shifting the direction of the war away from Niagara to the strategic city on the lower St. Lawrence began with Armstrong's hesitation between concentrating westward or eastward on Lake Ontario. He thereby threw away a precious month, the first half of

20. Armstrong to Lewis, July 3 and 9, 1813, *A.S.P.M.A.*, I, 451.

which might have been used to make the necessary preparations for the withdrawal from Niagara and the second half to carry out the movement down the lake; for Chauncey's new vessel was ready on July 20, he sailed on the morrow, and Yeo did not come out for another fortnight. From then until the end of September the two fleets dodged around in their confined ring of water, exchanging occasional blows but, as already observed, avoiding a conclusive battle. It might be imagined that this condition would prevent the transfer of the troops, but it did not. It merely postponed the embarkation for four days at the end.

The chief cause for the further delay was in the military command. Dearborn, at first professionally and at last physically an invalid, had been retired in July; and his successor, who had been summoned from New Orleans and did not reach Sackett's Harbor till August 20, was worse. He was James Wilkinson, that unsavory man whom Winfield Scott described as an "unprincipled imbecile." On the way to his new headquarters, he rudely stirred up an old feud with Hampton, who detested him, and when he arrived in Sackett's Harbor, he called a council of war whose decision in favor of descending the St. Lawrence made him dependent upon the loyal coöperation of that general. Following this decision, orders were issued to provide river transport for seven thousand men and sixty pieces of artillery to be ready by the middle of September; and in the beginning of that month he went up to Niagara to complete the arrangements for the movement of the troops from there. This began on October 1, while Yeo, who had just suffered considerable punishment in a sharp encounter with Chauncey, lay at the head of the lake; and by the middle of October the last of the three thousand regulars from Niagara were coasting eastward.

While the main expedition was thus being assembled at the foot of the lake, Hampton was already in position with his four thousand men. Abandoning the Richelieu route, he had moved some forty miles westward to the Chateauguay River where, close to the Canadian border, two roads met, one running northeast to a point opposite the island of Montreal and the other west to St. Regis at the boundary on the St. Lawrence, so that, as desired, he could join Wilkinson at either place. But Wilkinson did not then know whither he was bound, to Kingston, or to Montreal, or to both, or to neither: for the Secretary of War had arrived on the scene and the two old comrades-in-arms were having an unseemly wrangle over the purpose of the campaign. Apparently both saw failure ahead and each strove to make the other shoulder the responsibility for it.

The collapse came quickly. Hampton advanced down the Chateauguay in obedience to orders from Armstrong, and then he retired. The turning point was a little check inflicted by a much smaller force under Colonel De Salaberry on October 26, but the deciding factor was the receipt of further orders from Armstrong—to prepare huts for winter quarters. These orders, he wrote, "sunk my hopes." The descent of the St. Lawrence by the main army of nearly eight thousand did not begin for another week, and then it was retarded by the fire of musketry and artillery from the Canadian bank, along which eight hundred British regulars, supported by gunboats, followed. From Ogdensburg, Wilkinson wrote Hampton to forward two or three months' supplies and to join him at St. Regis. Twenty miles below Ogdensburg, he called a council of war to consider whether his expedition should proceed, and the vote obliged him to go on. At the same time, to protect his movement, he landed a division on the north shore. That led to a rearguard action on November 11 at Chrystler's Farm, where two thousand Americans were badly defeated by half their number of British. On the morrow, at Cornwall, Wilkinson was much relieved to find his own hopes sunk by the receipt of a reply from Hampton stating that he had no supplies to send and was on his way back to Plattsburg. With extraordinary energy Wilkinson moved his men into winter quarters a day's march east of St. Regis on the American side of the line; and there they lay while the Niagara front, guarded by only militia, was driven in before the year was out. In December, the British established themselves astride the mouth of that river; and, in return for the burning of Newark and Queenston by the retiring Americans, they lit avenging fires from Lewiston to Buffalo.

Though the United States still had the advantage of the initiative until the summer of 1814 was well advanced, and though the American army at last developed real fighting quality under real fighting generals who replaced broken-down creatures like Hull, Dearborn, and Wilkinson, yet this superior weapon and the respite to use it were thrown away in futile effort, thanks to the incompetence that ruled in Washington. From Montreal to Kingston to Niagara, and then back through Kingston to Montreal, the American objective had vainly wandered in 1813; and in 1814, it staggered back to Niagara, where it had no business to be. Montreal was now definitely out of the picture, though at the end of March a division of more than three thousand men made a feint in that direction, crossing the line on the Richelieu. The invasion, which ended about as soon as it began, was Wilkinson's last exploit, undertaken on his own responsibility when an order had already been signed, though he did not know it, terminating his inglorious military career. At this time, Armstrong had once more fixed his gaze on Kingston, the capture of which would deliver the whole of Upper Canada with the exception of the settlements on the St. Lawrence. He had suggested to the energetic General Jacob Brown, whom he sent to Sackett's Harbor with two thousand regulars, that he might seize the prize while another force, assembled at Buffalo under Winfield Scott, distracted the British by a feigned attack on Niagara. But the Secretary of War did not make his purpose unmistakably clear, and history repeated itself. After consulting Chauncey, who persuaded him that the move against the British naval base was impracticable, Brown marched his men off for Buffalo. Kingston was thus removed from the picture too. Indeed there was now no picture of any kind for many weeks. After the disruption of Armstrong's plan, another was not adopted till June, such were the uncertainty and confusion in Washington.

Meanwhile it was as evident as ever that naval operations on Lake Ontario would govern military operations around it. By putting off the attack on Kingston, Chauncey exposed his own base: for his new building was not quite so forward as that of Yeo, who was able to sail in the beginning of May with two vessels just finished. He and Sir Gordon Drummond, who had assumed the command in Upper Canada, would have attempted to take Sackett's Harbor right away, and they might have done it, if Prevost had been able to supply a few more troops for their expedition. Instead, they made for Oswego to cripple Chauncey by intercepting guns and stores on which he counted to fit out his squadron. The town, a large stock of provisions, and nine heavy cannon fell into their hands; but the bulk of the armament, being deposited at the falls twelve miles up the Oswego River, eluded their grasp. Yeo then blockaded Sackett's Harbor, but the heavy guns, which had to go by water, were smuggled along the shore and in to their destination while the lighter equipment went by road. As this circumvented the object of the blockade, the British fleet returned to Kingston early in June. By this time it was known that large reinforcements were coming from England, and Yeo decided that his proper policy was to avoid battle until he could make sure of victory by the completion of another vessel on the stocks, a ship of one hundred and two guns, about twice as strong as any other on the lake.

Simultaneously, the American cabinet adopted a plan of campaign on the northern front where, for a brief interval, superior numbers would enable the forces of the United States to push offensive operations. It was too late to think of winning Montreal, which British arms could quickly recover. There was only one objective that was worth any effort to gain. That was Kingston, which would give the United States absolute control of communications above the rapids on the St. Lawrence. With characteristic perversity, however, the rulers in Washington chose

Niagara. The concentration was ordered at Buffalo, where Scott had been forging an efficient weapon. The command of Lake Erie would permit a turning of the British position at the entrance to the river, where the movement was to start; and then, supported by the fleet which was nearly ready in Sackett's Harbor, the army would clear the British out of the peninsula and march on York via Burlington. The one uncertainty was the date when Chauncey could come out, but it was not long before he promised to "sail the first week of July to offer the enemy battle." Such was the plan. It foundered on the lake.

The invasion began on the night of July 2 at the southeastern corner of the peninsula. Under General Brown the American army rolled north, defeating the British who made a stout stand at Chippewa on the fifth, and forcing them back to the mouth of the river, where Brown expected Chauncey to appear. But the days passed and no Chauncey came. On the thirteenth, the general wrote him: "For God's sake, let me see you. I have looked for your fleet with the greatest anxiety since the 10th." He received no reply for several weeks, but on the twenty-third he heard from Sackett's Harbor that no one knew when the fleet would sail. Meanwhile the British received reinforcements, their communications across the lake being undisturbed; and Brown could not reduce the forts at the mouth of the river without siege artillery that was to have been brought by water from the other end of the lake. He therefore decided to risk leaving these hostile garrisons in his rear while he struck across to Burlington, where he could cut off their line of retreat by land; and he recoiled to prepare for this forward spring. His apparent retreat drew the British on, with the result that on the twenty-fifth at Lundy's Lane, the beginning of the road to the west, the two armies fought their bloodiest battle. From afternoon until midnight the roar of the Falls was drowned by the sound of the firing. When it ceased, the Americans had lost more than a quarter of their men and one-third of the British had fallen. Tactically the engagement was a draw; but strategically it was not, for it stopped the American drive to the west. It is also important to observe that the British alone could not have done it. They were much beholden to the man who did not sail from Sackett's Harbor for yet another week.

What is the explanation of Chauncey's inactivity, which ruined the American campaign on the Niagara? Some excuse may be found in the fact that he was sick during part of the time. But there was something wrong with his mind as well as his body. He was afraid to leave Sackett's Harbor exposed to an attack from Kingston. His mission, he said, was to seek the enemy's squadron and defeat it. But he was now so superior in strength to Yeo that he could have blockaded Kingston and also dispatched enough vessels to coöperate with Brown; and if he really wanted a naval battle, the only way to get it was to entice the British squadron out by threatening to act against the British army at the other end of the lake. The government was also partly to blame for his strange behavior, for apparently he had received no positive directions to do what was expected of him. But he should not have needed them to pry him loose from his base. When duty stared him in the face, he was blinded by an obsession. The best that can be said for him is that he was consistent. He had always allowed Kingston to hypnotize him.

The subsequent operations on the Niagara, where Lundy's Lane marked the turn of the tide without being a "decisive" battle, are of relatively little interest. There were thrusts and counterthrusts between the Americans who held both sides of the entrance to the river until November, when they closed the campaign by withdrawing from the Canadian shore, and the British who continued to possess the forts on either side of the mouth. Meanwhile the control of Lake Ontario shifted back and forth without any naval fighting. From the first of August, when Chauncey finally ventured forth, too late to retrieve his error, he cruised up and down at will, interfering seriously with the movement of men and supplies to the British at Niagara, so that at one time they were too short of ammunition to attack. But when Yeo's big ship was completely equipped in the middle of October, the American fleet had already flown home to its nest, leaving the British in undisputed possession of the lake for the short remainder of the navigation season. The main interest in the war had been diverted elsewhere. Indeed the invasion of the Niagara Peninsula in July was of little real importance, being only the last desperate fling of the American offensive which was already doomed to failure. Before it expired at Lundy's Lane, the general British offensive, not to be confused with the local British offensive which had been sustained in the Indian territory of the United States, was swinging into action.

In the final phase of the war, as already observed, the roles of the belligerents were reversed and the issue was the contraction instead of the expansion of the American Republic. There was rough justice in the purpose for which Britain was now fighting. It was not to smash the United States. It was rather to impose upon the United States a revision of the peace settlement of 1783 in accordance with what seemed to be the dictates of experience since then—the American treatment of Britain's native allies, boundary disputes, and the attempt of the United States to steal Britain's colonies when her hands were tied in Europe. To induce the United States to accept such a treaty, British arms struck in four quarters.

In Washington, alarmed by the news from Europe, the cabinet met on July 1 to plan the defense of the capital. Wellington's veterans were coming across the ocean to put a British end to the American conflict, and some of them were sure to strike at the seat of the government which had begun it. Though seven weeks elapsed before the impending blow fell, the preparations to meet it were pitiful. The only naval force available was a flotilla of gunboats and armed barges manned by four or five hundred stout fighters. The Secretary of War, who thought he might provide a thousand regulars, could collect only four hundred. The chief reliance was placed upon the militia, and a call was issued for nearly a hundred thousand men from the surrounding area—a paper force, of which a paltry five thousand appeared on the only field of battle and, at the first attack, were blown away like paper. The seamen and the regulars, though fighting valiantly, were too few to stem the rush of the four thousand British professionals at Bladensburg on August 24.

That night the victors burned the Capitol, the presidential mansion, and several other government buildings. For this incendiarism the British have been roundly cursed by Americans who have ignored what had happened at York. On this occasion too, the captors departed almost immediately, and for a corresponding reason. As the Americans had to abandon the Upper Canadian capital because they might be cut off by water, the British could not think of holding the American capital because they were separated from their supporting fleet. But the significance of the two temporary seizures was vastly different. York was not London. Its nearest counterpart was Detroit. The President, who was terribly shaken, hoped that the national disaster would at last rouse the lethargic national feeling. It did, but not in quite the way he thought it should. It disgraced him and his administration in the eyes of the American people.

Of a similar nature was the expedition against New Orleans. No conquest in that region was intended. The object was to put pressure on the Republic by temporarily plugging the outlet of the whole Mississippi Valley. Because the forces detailed for this task were slow in getting under way, the famous Battle of New Orleans, where they were disastrously defeated, was not fought until a fortnight after peace was signed several thousand miles away. It may be suggested that the delay affected the treaty by depriving the American negotiators of a great victory to wave in the faces of their opponents. But it is by no means certain that the military decision at this vital spot would have been the same if it had been reached in time to influence the discussions at Ghent; and even if it had been the same, it is difficult to see how the American plenipotentiaries could have got a better treaty.

On the northeast corner of the United States, the virtual truce which had prevailed was broken in July, 1814, when a regiment of the line sailed from Halifax and landed in Eastport, taking possession of the disputed Moose Island. Frederick and Dudley, its two small neighbors over which Massachusetts had also exercised jurisdiction, were occupied at the same time, so that all the islands in Passamaquoddy Bay were brought under the Union Jack. The plan, of course, was to terminate with the sword the American claim to any of these islands.

Much more far-reaching was the British design set forth in orders from London received in August by the governor of Nova Scotia, Sir John C. Sherbrooke. He was to occupy as much of the district of Maine "as shall insure an uninterrupted communication between Halifax and Quebec." The exigencies of war had suggested this move as a measure of security. A regiment raised in New Brunswick, where it was not needed, had been badly wanted in Canada for the beginning of the 1813 campaign, and it took this unit nearly four weeks to march on snowshoes from Fredericton to Quebec. Exactly a year later, a battalion of British regulars that had been stationed in Halifax was made to plod over the same route. To end the dangerous separation of these two parts of British North America, Sherbrooke sailed with two thousand troops in ten transports, accompanied by nine men-of-war.

On September 1, the expedition arrived at the mouth of the Penobscot and occupied Castine. A detachment went thirty miles upstream to where the United States frigate *Adams* was being repaired. The militia which had been gathered to defend the vessel fled, obliging the captain to fire her. The invaders then pressed on to Bangor, where there was an unconditional surrender, the militia disbanding and the officer commanding it taking his parole. Another detachment was sent back to Machias and occupied it without opposition. A British garrison was planted there, and another at Castine. "All the province of Maine east of the Penobscot was then in Sherbrooke's hands. The people formally submitted. One hundred miles of Massachusetts sea-coast passed quietly under the dominion of the King of England. The male citizens were required to take, and took, the oath of allegiance to King George, and showed no unwillingness to remain permanently British subjects."[21] It is also worthy of note that this conquest, far from interrupting, actually facilitated the commercial intercourse between supposed enemies. New Englanders no longer had to go to Halifax. The new "British" port of Castine was much more convenient. The customs duties collected on goods entered there for an American destination amounted to some £13,000. They formed the so-called Castine Fund, which was carried off

21. Adams, VIII, 96–97.

to Halifax and there made possible the establishment of Dalhousie University.

Another corner of the United States was also to be lopped off, according to the plans now matured in London, but it did not have to be conquered at this time because it was already under British control. This was the Indian territory in the northwest, which Britain would erect into an independent native state under her tutelage, thereby making amends for the desertion of 1783 while also giving effective protection to the western flank of Canada. But to cover this flank and to provide a territorial link between Lower Canada and the Maritime Provinces was not enough.

The long southern frontier of the two Canadas had been perilously exposed and would have to be guarded by some arrangement which would guarantee British control of the navigable boundary waters; and to achieve this, the imperial government saw the necessity for a stunning blow in that quarter. Hence the government's humble request of the Iron Duke himself that he go to take charge of the war in America, and the dispatch to the St. Lawrence of the largest body of his famous soldiers, sixteen thousand of them, in the summer of 1814. Wellington said he was willing to do it, but he thought it better to tarry yet a while where he might be of greater service. He suggested, and the ministry hoped, that he might go in the spring of 1815. Meanwhile Sir George Prevost was to do his best with the mightiest armament that Britain had ever sent overseas. Apparently his instructions,[22] which have been lost, directed him to undertake vigorous offensive measures, including "the entire destruction of Sackett's Harbor, and of the naval establishments on Lake Erie and Lake Champlain."[23] As the first two of these objectives were for the time being eliminated by Yeo's inability to stir out of Kingston, Prevost focused his attention on the third.

If there was one "decisive" action in the War of 1812, it was on September 11, 1814, at Plattsburg, the American base on Lake Champlain. The War Department in Washington did its best for Prevost. While his host was gathering on the border, some twenty-five miles away, the bulk and the pick of the regulars in Plattsburg set out for Niagara, leaving a poor fifteen hundred behind. At the last minute, a call for militia brought a doubtful reinforcement of about twenty-five hundred from the neighborhood. With seven thousand of the best trained soldiers in the world, the governor of Canada crossed the line on September 1 and, brushing aside what little opposition he encoun-

22. Dated June 3, according to his acknowledgment on July 12, *Q*, CXXVIII, 33.
23. *Some Account of the Public Life of the late Lieutenant-General Sir George Prevost, Bart.* (London, 1823), p. 136.

tered on the way, he reached his destination five days later. There he waited for his little fleet, which had not been quite ready, to coöperate in the reduction of the place by engaging the American flotilla which was anchored in the bay.

Though the Americans improved the time by strengthening their works, these appear to have been of such little value that they could not compensate for the enormous disparity between the land forces. The diminutive squadrons were about the same size, but there was an important difference between them. The American had the advantage at short range and the British at long range, the former having more carronades and the latter more long guns. It would therefore appear that the proper tactics for the invaders to adopt was to attack by land when their vessels were approaching and before they would have to fight at close quarters. There has been some doubt whether the American vessels were anchored close enough to support the defense on land, but this does not really matter. They were either at the mercy of the long guns alone, or they were subject to the combined fire of these guns and of the British artillery from the land. It should also be remembered that the prime object of the expedition was the destruction of the American flotilla, which would thus seem to have been almost inevitable. If the anchored vessels cut their cables to escape from the trap, the British could chase and engage them out of carronade range. Yet it was the British flotilla that was destroyed because it came into the bay and fought at close quarters.

Prevost, who watched the whole proceeding without doing anything, then marched his army back again to Canada. Who was responsible for this astounding outcome has never been determined, for the two trials that might have cleared up the mystery never came off, the British naval commander being killed in action and the military commander dying before his case was ready for the court martial that was ordered. There is a lot of evidence, but it is ex parte and it is colored by professional jealousy between the two services. Though most British writers have exculpated the naval man and thrown all the blame upon the general, their arguments are unconvincing. However that may be, the complete failure of this powerful expedition had not a little to do with cutting short the war.

The end came just in time to scotch the secessionist movement which was coming to a head in New England. Neither the governor nor the legislature of Massachusetts would lift a finger to help the helpless national government to expel the enemy from Maine,[24] for his very presence there was too good an argument for changing the constitution

24. Which therefore grew much more anxious to become a separate state.

of the country. In the middle of October, the newspapers published the demands which the British had made at Ghent, and the Federalists, bent on peace at any price, blamed the American plenipotentiaries for rejecting it. New Englanders were resigned to the loss of territory in the northeast, hoping that thereby they might buy the retention of the fisheries, which they feared might be lost too. Their resentment was bitter, but it was against Washington rather than London. They expected the West to suffer great losses by the treaty, but this did not concern them. Should not the West be made to pay for its own sins? Throughout New England, the Republican candidates were routed in the November elections, and in the middle of December representatives of the New England states met in the famous Hartford Convention. Three weeks later, when this body adjourned, it seemed that the dissolution of the Union was at hand.[25] But it was already saved by the American delegation in Ghent, who, for all their ability and patriotism, might not have been able to serve their country so well had not a long absence from the United States prevented them from realizing how great was the weakness at home.

25. Though it was not known that Governor Strong of Massachusetts had sent an agent to Sir John Coape Sherbrooke in Halifax to broach the subject of a separate New England peace and an alliance with Britain. This episode has recently been brought to light in J. S. Martell, "A Side Light on Federalist Strategy," *American Historical Review*, XLIII, 553–566.

CHAPTER XV

THE TREATY OF GHENT

UNTIL the fall of Napoleon knocked the bottom out of the War of 1812, the American government sought peace in vain and rather pathetically. The first move, after the abortive armistice discussions, was the passage of the foreign seamen act, which the President signed on the last day of the session in March, 1813. Upon the termination of the war with Britain, it would exclude all foreigners from service in any public or private vessel of the United States. Though it was a sincere effort to persuade Britain that impressment was no longer necessary, we need not regret that it was delayed so long. There is no ground for believing that it would have prevented the war which it could not stop. The problem of deserting sailors was too vital to Britain for her to trust any foreign solution, and her own solution was not yet repugnant to international law.[1] As for the United States, the cure would have been about as bad as the disease. The injury it would have wrought to American commerce and shipping, as well as to the national character,[2] is a measure of the desperate hope with which it was initiated.

The second move was the acceptance of the Tsar's offer to mediate between the United States and Britain, which coincided with the completion of the first move[3] and was dependent upon it. The acceptance was eager, for the offer came when Madison's world was falling about his ears. He had counted on a Napoleonic victory over Russia to bring Britain to terms, but now the country was learning of Napoleon's catastrophic failure. The mediation proposal had been sent during the French occupation of Moscow, when Alexander was most anxious to relieve his new friend and only ally of this embarrassing American war, and it was unaccompanied by any intimation of how Britain would regard it. But the black news from Europe vetoed any suggestion of delay in seizing the helping hand held out from Russia. John Quincy Adams, the resident minister in St. Petersburg, Albert Gallatin, and James A. Bayard, a patriotic Federalist leader from Delaware, were appointed

1. See *supra*, pp. 212–213.
2. Adams, VI, 457.
3. The offer was presented and accepted informally in February, and then formally in March. C. M. Gates, "The Peace Negotiations between Great Britain and the United States, 1812–1814," an unpublished thesis deposited in the Graduate School of the University of Minnesota, 1934, p. 35. The Russian minister suggested mediation in January. Elizabeth Donnan (ed.), "Papers of James A. Bayard, 1796–1815," *Annual Report of the American Historical Association*, 1913, II, 204, n. 3.

commissioners to negotiate under the Tsar's mediation; and as soon as possible Gallatin and Bayard left to join their colleague.

The instructions governing this mission reveal how little the American government was in touch with international reality. The commissioners were to exact from Britain a formal renunciation of impressment. If they failed to secure it they were to drop all negotiations and return home, but it was confidently expected that they would succeed. As the adjustment of this controversy, "though very important, would leave much unfinished," they were also to seek a settlement of the other maritime issues. They were to strive for a definition of blockade which would limit it to ports and prevent it from being applied to stretches of coast; for an abandonment of the Rule of 1756, which might regain its importance through a restoration of conquered colonies; for a stipulation that the prohibition of neutral trade between enemy ports in one country, and more particularly between such ports in two countries, was illegal; for a restriction of contraband to specified implements and materials of war; and for "indemnity for losses."[4] They were explicitly forbidden to renew Article III of Jay's Treaty, which had imposed an international servitude upon the United States in order to provide for the continuance of the British fur trade on American soil. They were to avoid any agreement "which might restrain the United States from increasing their naval force to any extent they may think proper on the Lakes held in common, or excluding the British traders from the navigation of the Lakes and rivers exclusively within our own jurisdiction." The last clause meant that the treaty right of freedom to navigate the Mississippi, accorded to Britain in 1783 and renewed in 1794, would be tolerated no longer. The territorial settlement was to be a reciprocal restoration of conquests.[5] Such was the gist of the instructions, dated April 15, 1813, with which Gallatin and Bayard sailed for the Baltic on May 9. A few weeks later, inspired by the American capture of York and the expulsion of the British from the Niagara front, Monroe amended his instruction about the mutual exchange of territory. If that took place there was to be a revision of the boundary from the forty-fifth parallel to the northwest corner of the Lake of the Woods to determine the ownership of all islands in the international waterways, but he hoped it would not take place. He had visions of winning all Upper Canada that season, and then his country would have to restore much more than it could recover. Therefore he sent a dispatch after the travelers telling them that Britain would have to compensate the United States by being

---

4. *A.S.P.F.R.*, III, 695–700.

5. Donnan, *op. cit.*, p. 205. This is the gist of the confidential paragraph No. 2 referred to but not printed in *A.S.P.F.R.*, III, 700.

"more liberal on other points," and he further suggested that Britain should realize "the advantages to both Countries which is [sic] promised by a transfer of the upper parts and even the whole of Canada to the U.S." This would remove "a fruitful source of controversy"; it would relieve Britain from the burden of supporting her possession "which must be considerable in peace or war especially in war"; and it would merely anticipate a severance which she could not long postpone.[6] One might imagine that it was not Napoleon but Britain that was falling.

If ever a government sent envoys on a wild-goose chase, it was the American government in 1813. It counted on strong diplomatic support from Sweden and Russia; for the Baltic powers were the senior champions of neutral rights against Britain, and this, so it seemed in Washington, was their great opportunity. But Sweden was reserving all the little weight she then possessed in order to use it in getting Norway; and Russia, though beginning to stand out as the greatest power on the Continent, had had her fill of neutral rights while she was Napoleon's ally. Alexander had only one thought now, and that was to destroy the European monster. He would not even shake a finger at Britain from whom all blessings flowed in the hour of trial. It was enough for him that she had returned a polite though firm refusal to his offer, suggesting instead a direct negotiation in London or in some foreign place that was near at hand. Her heart had been suddenly hardened. Here also the calculation of the United States administration was all wrong. The growing opposition to the government's anti-American policy, instead of being stimulated, was utterly killed by the American declaration of war. The blow fell like no ordinary stab in the back, for it came at a time when Britain was conscious of facing the greatest peril in her history and of bearing the whole weight of Europe on her shoulders. The United States might prate about fighting for liberty, but it struck dangerously at the cause of liberty in the Old World. By merely stopping the stream of supplies that had fed Wellington's peninsular army, the American government had given Napoleon the equivalent of a military reinforcement, and all the while Washington was pursuing the old quarrel with Paris. Truly the United States was an Ishmael among the nations.

The members of the American peace mission kicked their heels and wracked their brains in St. Petersburg until early in 1814, unable to verify rumors that Britain had rejected mediation and had suggested direct negotiations. Apparently it was Alexander who kept them in suspense.[7] He was embarrassed at having brought them across the world for nothing; and he was far from home, engrossed in the business

6. Monroe to Gallatin and Bayard, June 23, 1813, Donnan, *op. cit.*, pp. 227–228.
7. Gates, *op. cit.*, p. 122.

of conducting military operations against the enemy and negotiations with his allies. Meanwhile London was puzzled over the long tarrying of the Americans in the Russian capital,[8] and on November 4, 1813, Castlereagh wrote direct to Washington conveying the suggestion that had been held up by the Tsar.[9] The letter arrived at midnight on December 30; and Madison, having received no report from the frozen trio in St. Petersburg, decided to accept at once.

For the direct negotiation, a new commission and new instructions were necessary. The new commission was the old one reinforced by the addition of Henry Clay, to represent the West, and Jonathan Russell, who was also appointed to be the first American minister to Sweden. Gallatin, whose name was omitted as the result of a misunderstanding, was later included in the new commission.

The new instructions, dated January 28, 1814, expressed as confidently as ever the hope of getting diplomatic support in Europe, with a specific reference to the double roles which Adams and Russell were to fill.[10] These new instructions bound the commissioners to use the old ones, and added a few particulars to make them even more ambitious. Britain should pay all impressed American sailors, on their discharge, the amount of the wages they might have earned in the American merchant marine. The provision for "indemnity for spoliations" should be enlarged to cover "the destruction of all unfortified towns, and other private property, contrary to the laws and usages of war," by either side, and the return of, or full payment for, every Negro taken from the South.[11] In a paragraph omitted from the copy later submitted to Congress, the commissioners were strongly urged to secure the cession of the two Canadas to the United States as the only way to prevent another war which would certainly wrest these provinces from Britain. "Experience has shown that Great Britain cannot participate in the dominion and navigation [of that part of North America] without incurring the danger of an early renewal of the war. It was by means of the Lakes that the British Government interfered with and gained an ascendancy over the Indians." American settlement would soon crowd round the Great Lakes, and "collisions may be daily expected between the Inhabitants on each side, which it may not be in the power of either Government to prevent."[12] Three months later, at the instigation of John Jacob Astor, Monroe issued a further direction about the disposi-

8. *Ibid.*, pp. 124–125.
9. *A.S.P.F.R.*, III, 621–622.
10. Donnan, *op. cit.*, pp. 264–265.
11. *A.S.P.F.R.*, III, 701–702.
12. Donnan, *op. cit.*, pp. 263–264.

tion of territory in another region. Astor had founded a fur-trading post at the mouth of the Columbia River in 1811. In the fall of 1813, shortly before the arrival of a British sloop of war sent to capture it, the place changed hands, Astor's local representative selling out to agents of the North West Company. On March 22, 1814, while it was still difficult to tell what had happened in that far corner of America, the Secretary of State ordered the commissioners in Europe to insist, if necessary, upon the restoration of this post. "It is not believed," he added, that the British "have any claim whatever to territory on the Pacific ocean."[13]

"Their terms were those of a Conqueror to a conquered People." This seems an apt comment on the American instructions, though it was the lament of Bayard over the British demands when presented at Ghent.[14] A swift glance at what was happening in Europe reveals how absurd were the official aspirations of the United States. The giant war came to an end before the two parties of the pygmy war could meet at the conference table. In 1813 Germany leaped to arms, and, with the aid of Russian men and British gold, hurled Napoleon back across the Rhine, while the Iron Duke finally cleared the French out of Spain. Pressing into France, the allies closed in on Paris, which they entered on March 31, 1814, forcing Napoleon's abdication eight days later. Britain's hands were at last free to deal with America, and she had reached the pinnacle of her power.

The news that the European war was over made surprisingly little impression upon the government in Washington. On June 25, Monroe sent an additional instruction authorizing the conclusion of a treaty without a positive stipulation against impressment, for he now knew that the practice had ceased; but the condition he laid down for this omission was the inclusion of a clause binding Britain to negotiate for a settlement of the principle "without delay." In the same letter he noted a report that "the late events in France" might encourage the British government to demand a surrender of American fishing rights. These, he said, "must not be brought into discussion," and the negotiations must stop if the British insisted on this demand.[15] Within two days, however, the scales began to fall from official eyes in the American capital. From Gallatin and Bayard, who had gone to London on a scouting expedition, came a letter stating that the British were adamant on impressment; and on the twenty-seventh Monroe wrote a letter empowering the envoys, if necessary, to accept a treaty without any

13. *A.S.P.F.R.*, III, 731. For the history of this post on the Pacific coast, see K. W. Porter, *John Jacob Astor* (Cambridge, 1931), Chaps. VII and VIII.

14. Donnan, *op. cit.*, p. 318.

15. *A.S.P.F.R.*, III, 703–704.

reference to it.[16] This, with the dispatch of two days before, arrived in the nick of time at the close of the first day's conference.[17]

Meanwhile the American commissioners were face to face with hard facts which left them with no delusions. They knew that the United States had not a friend in Europe. Their frantic efforts to find one proved that. They knew that the British public lustily demanded vengeance for "the great betrayal," and that the British government was sending seasoned veterans to America. They knew that though one state may make war upon another it takes two to make a peace. They knew how impossible was almost every condition which they were instructed to put in a treaty. They knew that if they were so fortunate as to get one at all, it would have to be silent on every maritime issue. They knew that Britain would press demands which they could never entertain and they believed their government would never accept. They knew how desperate was their country's plight. They knew that the best they could hope for was a peace based on a restoration of the *status quo ante*, and they did not see how they could get it. But they were grimly determined to stand firm, confident that, if Britain preferred to go on with the war, the United States would become really united and would fight as it had never fought before.

The British objectives in the peace negotiations were all designed to secure British North American interests against the United States. They amounted to a more or less drastic revision of the settlement of 1783 and its supplement of 1794. As far as possible, the mistakes of the past were to be corrected and precautions for the future were to be taken. By striking at Britain where she was vulnerable, the United States had taught her the necessity for protection in that quarter. The embarrassing and costly blunder of 1783, when she forgot her red allies, was at last to be repaired by the creation of an Indian buffer state. The project which had been dropped in 1794, when an American war threatened to come on top of the French war just begun, was thus revived twenty years later by the collapse of the long French war coming on top of the delayed American war. For a boundary, Britain would take that which the United States had accepted in the Treaty of Greenville in 1795, and she would make it permanent. The establishment of this native reserve under the joint guarantee of the two powers, which would preserve the Indians from further American encroachment and would also cover the most exposed part of Canada, was to be a *sine qua non* of any treaty. Wildly extravagant as this demand may seem today, it was then in general accord with the military situation in the West, as observed in

16. *Ibid.*, p. 704.
17. *Ibid.*, p. 706.

the last chapter. Of course the government in London also determined that Article III of Jay's Treaty must be renewed. To eliminate annoying disputes and to guard against another American attack when Britain was again involved elsewhere, the British North American boundary was to be revised. All the islands in Passamaquoddy Bay were to be British; to substitute a solid bond for the tenuous land connection between New Brunswick and Lower Canada, the northern limit of Maine was to be run along the forty-seventh parallel; the British communication over the Great Lakes was to be assured by the cession of Michilimackinac and a strip of land on the east side of the Niagara River, and by the prohibition, which might be made reciprocal, of American war vessels on those waters; the international line from the Lake of the Woods was to go straight to the source of the Mississippi, if a better boundary from Lake Superior could not be gained; and the northern limit of Louisiana was to be so set as to leave the British on the Columbia River. Another fundamental was that the right of fishing in British territorial waters and of drying on British shores, accorded by the Treaty of Paris in 1783, was to be at an end. The continuance of this international servitude without a just equivalent was intolerable. The British determination on this point was the counterpart of the American determination to throw off the yoke of Jay's Treaty; and the Indian buffer state, together with the readjustment of the international boundary, matched the American design of a proper territorial settlement. To sum up, the Americans were to be treated with a good dose of their own medicine.

These objectives were set forth in a sketch of intended instructions prepared by Castlereagh, the Foreign Secretary, and an almost identical document entitled "Points to be insisted upon in any Treaty of Peace to be entered into with the United States" in the papers of Lord Bathurst,[18] who had charge of the Colonial Office and, after the departure of Castlereagh for Vienna, of the Foreign Office also. The British negotiators were plenipotentiaries only in name and therefore they received from time to time only such partial and particular instructions as the government in London, to whom everything had to be referred for decision, thought wise to send.

The negotiations at Ghent in 1814 resemble the Paris negotiations of a generation before, in that the American delegation of five was composed of uncommonly able men whereas the three British representatives were men of no particular distinction. This was natural because the former, being far from home, had to shoulder a responsibility which the latter, being in constant communication with their government, did not have to bear. They were Lord Gambier, an old naval officer who was

18. Gates, *op. cit.*, p. 279.

the nominal head of the mission, Henry Goulburn, a member of Parliament and undersecretary to Lord Bathurst in the Colonial Office, and William Adams, a doctor of civil law. Goulburn was the spokesman, because of the personal limitations of his colleagues and the restriction of the discussions to his own special field.

It was tacitly agreed, after a little preliminary skirmish, that the issues which had produced the American war should be ignored in the peace settlement. Having arisen out of the European war, they were buried with it; and though the American government would have liked to take out some insurance against a resurrection, the American delegation saw that it was impossible. Of what they had been told to demand, they could get nothing; and they knew it. The only tactics they could follow with any chance of success was to refuse the demands of their antagonists until they became reasonable; and, if a break seemed inevitable, to make it come in a way that would unite and inspire the American people. The game of the British, on the other hand, was to take the initiative but not to present their whole program at once. The changing fortunes of war might suggest favorable alterations, and the Americans had to be sounded to discover what they might be forced to accept. Thus, though the two programs were so utterly disparate that one might expect an early and complete breakdown of the conference, it was to the interest of both sides to keep the negotiation simmering; and the discussions all turned on North American questions which would have given a new meaning to the war if it had not been stopped when it was. Here is an important clue to the outcome.

At the opening meeting on August 8, armed with only limited instructions,[19] Goulburn announced that his government would make no peace that did not include the Indians and give them security by marking off their territory "as a permanent barrier between the dominions of Great Britain and the United States"; that the "revision of the boundary line between the British and American territories, with the view to prevent future uncertainty and dispute," was a proper subject for negotiation; and that the privilege of fishing and drying within British jurisdiction would not be renewed gratuitously. The Americans were asked if they were authorized to treat upon these points, and they replied on the following day that they had instructions on the second but not on the other two because they had not been matters of controversy. Nevertheless they expressed a willingness to discuss them and a desire to know the British views upon them. They stated that their government had already appointed commissioners to treat with the Indians, and known lines of demarcation separated the Indian country from the lands

19. Dated July 28, 1814. Castlereagh, X, 67.

of the United States. The British, having advanced the Indian pacification and boundaries as a *sine qua non*, declined to enter upon the discussion unless the Americans would say that they considered it within their discretion to make a provisional agreement upon this subject; and the Americans declined to give any answer previous to the discussion. After some little parleying, in which it was made quite clear that the United States would be expected to surrender sovereignty over the Indian barrier state, the meeting adjourned.[20] That evening a courier departed for London with a report of the deadlock, for Gambier's delegation was powerless to proceed without further orders. Then followed "the first of the ten-day intervals which were to become so regular a part of the routine of negotiation."[21]

The second round, which opened on the nineteenth, was also short but much livelier, and it looked like the last. The new instructions,[22] which Goulburn explained to his opponents, were peremptory and far-reaching. The Indian barrier must be established, and the continuance or suspension of the negotiation was made to turn on whether the Americans would sign a provisional article. To meet their objection that the proposition was not sufficiently explicit, it was stated that neither Britain nor the United States should ever have the right to acquire any part of the territory thus recognized as belonging to the Indians and that its delimitation should be based on the lines laid down in the Treaty of Greenville. When Gallatin asked what should be done with the hundred thousand Americans who had settled beyond these lines, Goulburn suggested that modifications of the proposed frontier might take care of some but the rest would have to take care of themselves.[23] His admission, when reported in America, stirred hostile feeling. Had he been quicker-witted, he might have observed that Gallatin's question strengthened the British cause by admitting the frailty of American treaties with the Indians.

It was now avowed that the principal object of the British was something more than the tranquillity of the red men. The Americans were informed that the erection of this native state was also designed to give protection to Canada, and then they learned what further provisions were to be made for this purpose. According to the instructions imparted by Goulburn, the joint possession of the Great Lakes, with the common right of maintaining armed forces upon them, had proven and would continue to be a danger to peace; and as the British were much

20. *A.S.P.F.R.*, III, 708.
21. Gates, *op. cit.*, p. 303.
22. Dated Aug. 14, 1814. Castlereagh, X, 86.
23. *A.S.P.F.R.*, III, 709.

weaker on their side of the dividing waters than were the Americans on the other, the former were exposed to sudden invasion and conquest as the latter were not; therefore, as a necessary measure of security, there must be American disarmament in this region. Free commercial navigation was to continue unchanged.[24] One might almost imagine that Castlereagh had had a peep at the American instructions which, going much further, called for the total exclusion of the British from the Lakes by the cession of at least Upper Canada.

These British instructions rather ostentatiously disclaimed any desire for territorial acquisition and said nothing about a transfer of the strip of land along the Niagara, but they pointed out that the impossible line of 1783 would have to be replaced by a new line from Lake Superior to the Mississippi and that the unsettled northeastern boundary of the United States would have to be adjusted to allow direct land communication between Halifax and Quebec without going over American soil. By a question about the disposition of Moose Island, Gallatin elicited the remark that all the islands in Passamaquoddy Bay were undeniably British; and when Bayard suggested that the new western line should run from the Lake of the Woods, Lake Superior was again named as the beginning. While attention was turned in that direction, the Americans were also told that the treaty right to the free navigation of the Mississippi was to be revived. Finally, they were warned that if they felt obliged to refer home for further instructions the British government would not feel obliged to adhere to the above terms but might alter them in accordance with the changed state of the war when the negotiation was resumed.[25]

At the close of this conference on August 19, the Americans faced a crucial decision. Should they reject the British proposals and risk a continuance of the war? Should they write home for instructions and leave the British free to raise their terms? Or should they proceed to treat on the basis of the program just presented? A week before, Henry Clay had shrunk from the prospect of breaking off negotiations; and, burning patriot and ardent champion of the West as he was, he had contemplated referring home for new instructions if the British government insisted on its *sine qua non*.[26] But now, with one mind and with no hesitation, he and his colleagues decided for rejection, and in the letter they wrote to Monroe that evening they said "there is not, at present, any hope of peace."[27]

24. *Ibid.*, p. 710.
25. *Ibid.*, pp. 708–710.
26. Gates, *op. cit.*, pp. 310–311.
27. *A.S.P.F.R.*, III, 709.

Considering the momentous nature of what they were doing, the Americans desired the British to reduce their demands to writing, which was done immediately; and then they took four days to frame their reply, which was completed late in the evening of the twenty-fourth and delivered on the following day. In this document they asserted that the British *sine qua non* was contrary to acknowledged principles and established practice. "No maxim of public law has hitherto been more universally established among the Powers of Europe possessing territories in America, and there is none to which Great Britain had more uniformly and inflexibly adhered, than that of suffering no interposition of a foreign Power in the relations between the acknowledged sovereign of the territory and the Indians situated upon it." By the treaty of peace in 1783, Britain had acknowledged, without any qualification whatever, American sovereignty over the immense territory which she would now require the United States to surrender to twenty thousand Indians, who had themselves acknowledged the same sovereignty by the Treaty of Greenville in 1795 and every subsequent treaty down to the last in 1810. The proposition was also "utterly unnecessary" for the pacification of these Indians. The United States wanted nothing but peace for them. That was already being arranged, and all that was needed to complete it was peace with Britain. The American commissioners might sign with the British a provisional article following the precedent of some former treaties, engaging each party to treat for the Indians in its own territories; and they would also propose, "for the purpose of securing the duration of peace, and to prevent collisions which might interrupt it," a stipulation to prohibit the nationals of either from trading with the Indians residing in the territory of the other.[28] There was a touch of irony in this, as perhaps there was in the reference to there having been no qualification in 1783, which was the very reason why Britain was set on getting it now.

Equally out of the question was unilateral disarmament on the Lakes. Disregarding the great potential difference in strength between the parties on opposite sides of the waterway, the Americans argued that the British had ever been the stronger because of the fortifications and forces they had maintained there; and, taking advantage of the secrecy of their own instructions, they pointedly asked the British how they would have received such a proposal from the United States. They also observed that the proposals for revising the boundary, here for "the alleged purpose" of giving direct communication between two British provinces, and there "without purpose specifically alleged" to run the line west from Lake Superior instead of from the Lake of the Woods,

28. *Ibid.*, pp. 711–712.

meant ceding territory belonging to the Union, for which they had no authority and to which they could never subscribe.

The British conditions, the reply went on to say, were "founded neither on reciprocity, nor on any of the usual bases of negotiation, neither on that of *uti possidetis* nor of *status ante bellum*." They would dismember the American Republic, arrest its natural growth, expose its northern and western frontier to British invasion and Indian aggression, deprive its people of natural rights on their own shores and waters, and admit foreign interference in their domestic concerns. "A treaty concluded on such terms would be but an armistice." It could not "be supposed that America would long submit to conditions so injurious and degrading," or would hesitate "at the first favorable opportunity, to recur to arms for the recovery of her territory, of her rights, of her honor. Instead of settling existing differences such a peace would only create new causes of war, sow the seeds of a permanent hatred, and lay the foundation of hostilities for an indefinite period." The causes of the war had ceased, and the war should cease with a mutual restoration of territory and rights. A peace on this basis, the Americans were ready to make; and they were also willing to improve it by amicably discussing all differences and uncertainties that had arisen and might disturb the harmony of the two countries.[29]

That this note would kill the negotiation, both delegations expected; but the British government decided to preserve it, at least in a state of suspended animation. The American publication of the documents exchanged at Ghent was sure to follow as soon as possible; and then, if a breach occurred, the onus would rest upon Britain. It was important to avoid this because of the revolution in the nature of the armed conflict in America. As already explained, the United States had declared war for defensive reasons and, under the compulsion of circumstance, had waged it as if for an aggressive object. There are clear indications that military success would have glorified the means into an end, transforming appearance into reality; but failure checked this development, preserving for the United States the defensive purpose of the war. For the British it was likewise a defensive struggle until victory in Europe promised victory in America. Then an aggressive motive appeared in the determination to revise the old settlement between the United States and the adjoining parts of the Empire. In British eyes it seemed only just that the United States, having made the appeal to arms, should accept the arbitrament of war, and, having acted aggressively against Britain's allies and possessions, should give them security against a repetition of this action. With true British hypocrisy, an aggressive object was

29. *Ibid.*, pp. 711–713.

represented as being defensive, just as, with true American hypocrisy, the desire to get Canada was justified on the ground that it was necessary for the protection of the United States. But the American desire had ceased to be a practical question, whereas the British object had become the crux of the negotiation and the real reason for continuing the war. If this fact had been advertised by a breach, it might have affected the outcome of the war by making it more popular in America and less popular in England. The British game, now that the attempt at bluff had failed, was to stall the negotiation until news came of a military decision on the other side of the Atlantic. Therefore the British tossed the ball back to the Americans in Ghent in a note of September 4, which was more argumentative and less peremptory than its predecessor;[30] and when the ball came bouncing back on the ninth[31] there was another reference to London followed by yet another return of the play on the nineteenth. Now, however, a change was beginning to appear. The British were showing signs of weakening.

It seems that the real pressure behind the proposal for an Indian barrier came from the Colonial Office,[32] headed by Bathurst and Goulburn. Castlereagh, the Foreign Secretary, was not strongly back of it. When he heard of the stout American resistance, he was in Paris on his way to participate in the European settlement about to be undertaken in Vienna, and at once he wrote home suggesting new ideas for an American settlement. Liverpool, the Prime Minister, had never been enthusiastic about the *sine qua non*, and he was worried over the prospect. Public interest in the war was flagging, in the coming session of Parliament the opposition would seize every opportunity to attack him on the peace negotiations, and he would miss Castlereagh, his able leader of the House of Commons. A stubborn insistence on the Indian barrier would apparently prolong the war indefinitely, and he concluded that it was not worth it.[33] Therefore the British note of September 19 implicitly abandoned the project of a buffer state, reducing the *sine qua non* to a treaty provision which would include the Indians in the peace and would restore to them the rights and privileges which they had enjoyed before the war began. This note also stated that the exclusive military possession of the Lakes was not an ultimatum; and it promised, on the settlement of the Indian question, "a final proposition on the subject of Canadian boundaries, so entirely founded on principles of moderation and justice" that the Americans would doubtless find it acceptable.[34] As

30. *Ibid.*, pp. 713–715.
31. *Ibid.*, pp. 715–717.
32. Gates, *op. cit.*, p. 376.
33. *Ibid.*, pp. 367–377.
34. *A.S.P.F.R.*, III, 717–718.

a matter of fact, the British government was contemplating a proposal based on the principle of *uti possidetis*, following the suggestion in the American note of August 24, and was calculating that military successes would make it seem reasonable. The possibility that these successes might also revive the neutral buffer, the wording of the note did not preclude; but there is no evidence that it was even considered in London.

The demand that the Indians be included in the peace treaty, even without the objectionable feature just eliminated, set the American delegation by the ears. Curiously enough it was not Henry Clay of Kentucky but John Quincy Adams of Boston who was the most outspoken for rejection. He maintained that if this was not a good point on which to break they would never find one.[35] This attitude was dangerous, for the British government was determined to keep the solemn pledge it had given the red men through Sir George Prevost that they would not be forgotten at the peace. Fortunately the New Englander was calmed by Gallatin. He and Bayard believed that their government would immediately delete any Indian article but would be forced to admit it as the only escape from a continuance of the war. In a note completed on September 26, the envoys gave such a grudging acceptance that Goulburn read it as a refusal. What worried the authors was the principle involved in the British intercession on behalf of Indians living on American soil. They would lay this old ghost so that it could never return to threaten the integrity of the United States. They vigorously repudiated the British contention that a clause was necessary because the war had abrogated the Treaty of Greenville, by which the Indians had placed themselves under the protection of the United States. The right of protection, they asserted, did not spring from that treaty but was an attribute of American sovereignty. Tribes residing in the United States could not be included in the treaty "in any manner which will recognise them as independent nations, whom Great Britain, having obtained this recognition, would hereafter have the right to consider, in every respect, as such." The utmost that could be offered was a reciprocal and general stipulation of amnesty covering all persons, red as well as white, in the enjoyment of rights possessed at the commencement of the war.[36]

The amnesty suggestion was rejected in London. It did not go far enough, and it went too far. Liverpool feared that such an article would have the appearance of slighting the Indians, who must be satisfied, and he objected to pardoning British traitors. He would have an article restoring to the Indians everything to which they were entitled in 1811,

35. *Memoirs of John Quincy Adams*, III, 37–38.
36. *A.S.P.F.R.*, III, 720.

and he was willing to satisfy the Americans by making it reciprocal. Bathurst, who framed the article, easily persuaded him to advance it as an ultimatum. If the Americans refused it, they were to be told that the negotiation was at an end.[37]

It is possible that the British government's firm stand owed something to the news, which had just arrived, of the easy victory at Bladensburg and of the conflagration that made the White House white; but the Prime Minister's letters suggest otherwise. Writing to Castlereagh on September 23, shortly before that news came, he said, "I think we have now gone to the utmost justifiable point in concession, and if they are so unreasonable as to reject our proposals, we have nothing to do but to fight it out";[38] and four days later, after receiving the news, he wrote to Wellington and Castlereagh, "I am satisfied that if peace is made on the conditions we have proposed, we shall be very much abused for it in this country; but I feel too strongly the inconvenience of a continuance of the war not to make me desirous of concluding it at the expense of some popularity."[39]

The British ultimatum, conveyed in a note of October 8,[40] revived the warm debate in the American camp. Again Adams was for breaking on this point. The news that had cheered London and depressed his colleagues had apparently stirred in him a feeling of despair unmingled with resignation. After holding out for several days, he submitted to the pleasant persuasions of Bayard and the promises of the others that they would yield nothing of importance. The implication is amusing. What were they yielding now? This article was most carefully framed to preserve British honor without doing any damage to American honor. It was completely reciprocal, and all it bound the United States to do was to terminate hostilities with the Indians and restore them to their status of 1811, provided the Indians promised to desist from hostilities and kept their word. As the Americans pointed out in their reply of October 13, the article accorded with their own views, because it did not make the Indians a party to the treaty and it prescribed only what the United States would do anyway.[41] As a matter of fact they doubted if it would ever mean anything; for only a fortnight before they had heard of a new Treaty of Greenville which made peace with the Shawnees and other tribes, and Adams had not yet hit upon the meaning which he was to read into the article a few weeks later.[42]

37. Gates, *op. cit.*, pp. 401–404.
38. *Wellington's Supplementary Dispatches*, IX, 278–279.
39. *Ibid.*, pp. 290–291.
40. *A.S.P.F.R.*, III, 721–723.
41. *Ibid.*, p. 724.
42. *Infra*, p. 366.

Thus was the first agreement reached, and this was in the tenth week after the opening of the negotiation. Meanwhile there had been much disagreement, for all the notes exchanged between the delegations were swollen with controversial material, each side trying to prove that the stand taken by the other was utterly unreasonable. But we do not need to follow them through the maze of their arguments, for none of them had any effect upon the progress or outcome of the negotiation.

The American acceptance of the Indian article was a great turning point. It decided whether the British government would proceed with the discussions or would drop them and push on with the war. The messenger bearing the acceptance reached London on October 17, and there on the following day new and detailed instructions were issued directing the British mission to get down to business, eschewing the fruitless controversy just mentioned. In reply to an American request for a project of a treaty, now that the initial obstacle was cleared away, they were to remind their opponents that the inshore fisheries could not be reopened to Americans, and they were to broach the boundary question.[43] They obeyed in a short note of October 21. This stated that, from the discussions that had taken place, the line from the Lake of the Woods to the Mississippi as arranged in the convention of 1803 "will be admitted without objection," and proposed a settlement of the other boundaries on the principle of *uti possidetis*, mentioned in the American note of August 24, "subject to such modifications as mutual convenience may be found to require."[44] A recognition of this principle was to have been followed immediately by the presentation of the British plan. The American posts of Niagara and Michilimackinac and all the territory of Maine east of the Penobscot were then in British control, while the Americans held only the British forts Erie and Amherstburg; and it was supposed that the latter could be recovered in exchange for Castine and Machias. Moose Island was to remain part of New Brunswick, and the connection with Lower Canada was to be secured by carrying the boundary from the point where the due-north line intersected the Aroostook, up that stream to its source, and thence in a westerly direction until it reached the highlands. Britain would retain Niagara and Michilimackinac, which were obvious keys to the Great Lakes.

At the very moment that these instructions of October 18 were being sent from London a ship arrived from across the ocean bringing a report of Prevost's disastrous failure on Lake Champlain, but this only stiffened the British back. Apparently Bathurst would now have transformed the boundary proposals into an ultimatum had he not been restrained by

43. Castlereagh, X, 168–170.
44. *A.S.P.F.R.*, III, 725.

Liverpool, who agreed with him, however, that they should not reduce their demands as a consequence of what had happened at Plattsburg.[45] In further instructions dated October 20, Maine was not to extend beyond the forty-sixth parallel; Carleton Island, at the head of the St. Lawrence and then in dispute, was to be made British; the cession of Niagara was to include the land for at least five miles around it; and the island of Michilimackinac was to go with the fort.[46] This dispatch of course had not arrived when the British delegates drew up their note of October 21. To the Americans at Ghent, still depressed by the disgrace of Bladensburg and the capture of Washington, this more recent news was wonderfully welcome: but it was not needed to dictate their equally short reply of the twenty-fourth, abruptly refusing to treat on the basis of *uti possidetis*. They reiterated that the *status quo ante* was the only principle they could accept. Repeating their request for a draft of a treaty, they added that they had no objection to a simultaneous exchange of drafts.[47] They made no comment on the British reminder that the fisheries privileges could not be renewed. That question would come up in due time.

Again the negotiation had reached a deadlock, and it seems to have been inevitable. If Prevost had won, it is difficult to conceive how the British could have been willing to consider making peace on the only principle the Americans could accept; and his failure had so piqued British pride that the government could not contemplate the adoption of this principle. How could the vicious circle be broken? The United States plenipotentiaries believed that the issue of peace or continued war would turn on military events in America or diplomatic developments in Vienna, or on both;[48] and Liverpool hesitated between breaking off the negotiation immediately or continuing to play for time in the hope that something would turn up. He called a meeting of the cabinet, which chose the latter course.[49] Hence the British note of October 31 calling upon the American commissioners to present their project of a treaty.[50]

Something did turn up to break the deadlock, but it was not in favor of the British. It occurred while the Americans were completing their

45. Gates, *op. cit.*, pp. 425–426.
46. Castlereagh, X, 172.
47. *A.S.P.F.R.*, III, 725.
48. Gates, *op. cit.*, pp. 430–431.
49. *Ibid.*, p. 438. The above paragraph may suggest that the engagement at Plattsburg was in no way "decisive" (*supra*, p. 342); but the destruction of the British flotilla on Lake Champlain was one of the factors which Wellington took into consideration when he persuaded the government to make peace right away. See *infra*, p. 362.
50. *A.S.P.F.R.*, III, 726.

project of a treaty, though they knew nothing about it until more than a fortnight afterwards. Difficulties over the European settlement had not a little to do with the conclusion of an American settlement. Tsar Alexander's desire to restore Poland with himself as king led to a complicated international intrigue which split the principal powers into two armed camps with Britain and Russia on opposite sides. As the intrigue proceeded, it was obvious that Alexander had an advantage over Britain because she was still involved in America; and the Prime Minister felt the growing strain between the New World and the Old World phases of British policy. In the end he was glad to escape from the American embarrassment in order to face the European crisis squarely, but in the beginning he leaned the other way. On October 28 and again on November 2, he cautioned Castlereagh to walk warily in Vienna lest he hamper the cause of his country in America. At the same time Liverpool was looking forward to a more vigorous prosecution of the war against the United States. Everyone knew that if anyone could win success there, it was the great military hero of Britain. Accordingly an appeal was sent to Wellington in Paris, where he was serving officially as British ambassador and unofficially as a much-needed prop to the restored Bourbon monarchy.

The Duke of Wellington replied on November 7 and 9, discouraging the move. He suggested that he might be wanted in Europe; he pointed out that his going to America would give European powers an exaggerated notion of British defeats there; and, what was to have a decisive influence, he frankly expressed his fear that it would be futile to send him across the ocean. "That which appears to me to be wanting in America is not a general, or a general officer and troops, but a naval superiority on the Lakes." Without that, he said, he could do little more than "sign a peace which might as well be signed now." He was almost brutal in his condemnation of the government's hopes.

You have not been able to carry it [the war] into the enemy's territory, notwithstanding your military success and now undoubted military superiority, and have not even cleared your own territory on the point of attack. You cannot on any principle of equality in negotiation claim a cession of territory excepting in exchange for other advantages which you have in your power. . . . Why stipulate for the *uti possidetis?* You can get no territory; indeed, the state of your military operations, however creditable, does not entitle you to demand any.[51]

The judgment of Wellington was final. His words ended the war in a few weeks, by forcing the British cabinet to adopt the American princi-

51. *Wellington's Supplementary Dispatches*, IX, 422, 425–426.

ple. Now the government swung round in favor of peace in the New World to gain freedom of action in the Old World. It is conceivable, of course, that the great Duke only hastened a revolution which other causes were about to effect. The European situation was growing worse; awkward questions about the peace negotiations were being raised in Parliament; the first installment of the Ghent correspondence, published in the United States, arrived in England, stimulating criticism of a war conducted for territorial aggrandizement; and the government was finding that the cost was going to be much greater than anticipated and that resistance to the payment of high taxes was growing. But it is also conceivable that these considerations would not have induced the cabinet to reverse its policy, at least for some time; and the fact remains that the change was dictated by the Duke of Wellington.

So it came to pass that the American project of a treaty turned out to be what those who requested it had not at all intended—the actual basis of the peace agreement. It was sent to the British with a covering note on November 10.[52] This draft contained fifteen articles of which, in a more or less amended form, the first seven,[53] the ninth, and the fifteenth constituted the whole of the Treaty of Ghent, with the exception of one short article on the slave trade inserted by British request. Articles I and II of the draft established peace and stipulated the reciprocal restoration "without delay" of all territory and possessions taken by either party during the war. Articles III to VIII provided for a settlement of boundary questions from the Bay of Fundy to the Rocky Mountains. Following the precedent laid down in Jay's Treaty, international commissions were (III) to decide the ownership of Grand Manan Island and the islands in Passamaquoddy Bay, (IV) to find the historic "northwest corner of Nova Scotia" and the northwesternmost head of the Connecticut River, to have the boundary between these two points surveyed and marked, (V) to determine the middle of the international waterway through the St. Lawrence and the Great Lakes in order to allocate every island to one or the other power, (VI) to do the same from Lake Superior to the northwest corner of the Lake of the Woods, and to have such portions of the last-mentioned section as required it surveyed and marked. Article VII regulated the functioning of the commissions. Article VIII described the boundary from the Lake of the Woods to the Rocky Mountains in the very words of the abortive convention of 1807, and as it was finally established in 1818. Article IX was that already agreed upon for the pacification of the Indians. Article X bound each party to restrain its Indians from committing hostilities

52. *A.S.P.F.R.*, III, 733–734.
53. Expanded into eight by splitting one.

against the other and to refrain from using them against the other in any future war. Articles XI, XII, and XIII were on impressment, blockade, and indemnities for losses, in obedience to the instructions from Washington. Article XIV provided for a general amnesty, and XV for ratification.[54]

One omission is striking: the fisheries were not mentioned. But they were not forgotten. Gallatin prepared an article renewing the American privilege of sharing in the inshore British fisheries and the British privilege of free navigation of the Mississippi. Britain had served notice that she would not allow the continuance of the former without an equivalent, and this was all that the United States had to offer. Moreover Gallatin realized that these two privileges, having been granted by the same instrument in 1783, would have to stand or fall together. If the United States insisted on shutting the British out of the Mississippi, Britain could insist on shutting the Americans out of the fisheries within her jurisdiction.

Gallatin's article roused the Westerner. Clay would keep the river closed. Its character had been changed. What had been an international stream in 1783 had become a purely national stream twenty years later. To open it now would be to grant a greater concession in return for a smaller one. He would have sacrificed the East for the West, just as the article would have sacrificed the West for the East. Adams, strange to say, was not quite so intransigent on the other side. His own state was the only one that was greatly interested in the fisheries; and his own father was the man who, almost singlehanded, had secured the privilege in 1783. He admitted that the mere mention of the subject would invite the British to submit their counterclaim to the Mississippi; and he was willing, if necessary, to rely on the theory that the right to share in the inshore fisheries had been recognized in 1783 as part of the independence of the United States and therefore, like independence itself, was not abrogated by the war and needed no new stipulation for its survival. But he was extremely reluctant to incur an avoidable risk of losing this right by default. Clay, however, forced his hand. When the mission voted three to two for the inclusion of Gallatin's article, the citizen of Kentucky declared that he would refuse to sign the covering note to the British delegation. After more warm debate, he suggested a way out of the impasse, and his colleagues adopted it. They dropped the article and in its stead they inserted in their covering note a paragraph which, replying to the British notification, stated that they were not authorized to bring the subject into discussion and that "the peculiar character of the treaty of 1783" provided for the continuance of the right without a

54. *Ibid.*, pp. 735–740.

formal renewal. Clay had the better of the argument, for this method of handling the subject was in accord with Monroe's instructions whereas the deleted article was not. Nevertheless he feared that he would have to capitulate in the end; and he intimated that, if the British insisted on free navigation of the Mississippi, he might sign a treaty that was not otherwise objectionable.[55]

The government in London received the American draft on November 15, two days after Liverpool had written to Wellington, "I believe I can assure you that we shall be disposed to meet your views upon the points on which the negotiation appears to turn at present."[56] In other words, the British territorial demands advanced under the principle of *uti possidetis* would no longer stand in the way of peace. On the twenty-first, Bathurst returned the American text with marginal comments, and he wrote privately to Goulburn urging every effort for an early conclusion of the treaty. The comments contained the British suggestions of the changes which seemed necessary. Articles X to XIV, on the use of Indians in war, impressments, blockade, indemnities, and a general amnesty, were marked "inadmissible." All the other articles were to remain substantially as they were with only three amendments of any importance. One was intended to continue the British occupation of all the Passamaquoddy Bay islands pending an award, though this was not explicitly stated in the British amendment. Incidentally it might also have covered the permanent retention of Astor's post on the Columbia, which seems to have been almost entirely neglected during the negotiation.[57] The second British amendment revised the provisions for the boundary commissions to obviate the danger of a breakdown. Instead of three members, as in the American plan, each commission was to have only two, and if they failed to agree a final decision was to be secured by the arbitration of a friendly sovereign. The third amendment was a rider attached to Article VIII. It would give British subjects free access

55. *Memoirs of John Quincy Adams*, III, 62–65.

56. C. D. Yonge, *Life of Lord Liverpool* (London, 1868), II, 61.

57. A possible explanation of the British neglect is contained in the following statement made in Canada in August, 1815, by Simon McGillivray: "The writer of this had the honour of an interview with Lord Bathurst on the subject, after the ratification of the treaty was known . . . when His Lordship declared decidedly that the country in question was not considered as a conquest to be restored under the treaty, but as a British territory to which the Americans had no just claim; and the reason which His Lordship assigned for this country not being mentioned in the treaty was, that requiring from the Americans any recognition or guarantee of His Majesty's rights thereto, might lead to cast doubts upon a title which was already sufficiently clear and incontrovertible." Statement relative to the Columbia River, undated, enclosed in Simon McGillivray to Bagot, Nov. 15, 1817, enclosed in Bagot to Castlereagh, No. 74, Dec. 2, 1817, *F.O. 5*, Vol. CXXIII. The date of this memorandum may be found by collating McGillivray's covering letter with Drummond to Baker, Aug. 14, and Aug. 31, 1815, in *C*, MCCXXXVI, 35, 41.

from British territories to the Mississippi "with their goods, effects, and merchandise" and guaranteed the free navigation of that river.[58]

Great was the rejoicing in the American lodgings in Ghent on November 27 when, with the addition of the above marginal comments, the project of a treaty was returned to its authors. The British having seemed as determined on the principle of *uti possidetis* as the Americans were on that of the *status quo ante*, the latter had pretty well despaired of getting peace; and now the object of their mission was suddenly placed within their grasp. But there was one of their company who was by no means pleased.

Again Clay was up in arms to exclude the British from the Mississippi, and to gain his end he was apparently ready to throw away the peace that was offered. In the rider to the eighth article, he maintained, the British were demanding something much more than they had been granted in 1783, for the Louisiana Purchase had altered the character of the river. The Westerner also had his eyes on the Indians, whose dangerously intimate relations with the British would be preserved by this concession, in spite of the fact that Article III of Jay's Treaty was not being renewed. Adams, on the other hand, was eager to swallow the revised version of the treaty. The British silence on the question of the inshore fisheries—for no reply had been made to the American argument on this point in the note of November 10—seemed to imply acquiescence in the American claim, as indeed both Bathurst and Goulburn privately thought; and the New Englander belittled the proposed American sacrifice in the amendment to Article VIII of the draft. He pointed out that this was a just compensation for the British renunciation of a boundary running to the upper waters of the river; and he observed that it would make no difference to the British influence over the Indians, because the agreement on Article IX, which restored to the Indians all the rights and privileges of 1811, placed the old traffic on the prewar footing.[59] He would not sign a treaty that balanced the new stipulation on the navigation of the Mississippi with another on the fisheries, for that might be taken as an admission that the American right had been forfeited by the war and would be liable to forfeiture by another war. There were some heated passages between the two antagonists; but, as Adams reported in his diary, "Mr. Gallatin brought us all to unison again by a joke." The shrewd humorist prevailed upon his colleagues to keep the two questions together, either in the treaty or out of it.[60]

A joint conference of the two delegations was held on December 1 at

58. *A.S.P.F.R.*, III, 735–740.
59. See *supra*, p. 359.
60. *Memoirs of John Quincy Adams*, III, 71–77.

the request of the Americans that they might discuss the British proposals and present their own criticisms. When the eighth article came up for examination, Adams divided the British addition into its two parts, navigation of the river and access to it, and he dealt with each in turn. He declared that the British right to navigate the Mississippi stood on the same foundation as the American right to share in the inshore fisheries, and that according to the American view neither was canceled by the war. If this view was correct, the new provision for navigation was unnecessary. If it was incorrect, and both rights had lapsed, which was to be inferred from the British demand, this could not be granted without an equivalent provision for the fisheries; and therefore the Americans had prepared an article to renew both privileges. The British could take it or leave it, but they could not have their rider. As for the access through American territory to the river, if the navigation was to be granted, this was a matter which would require a special arrangement, as Adams pointed out. A road must be allowed and it would have to be guarded by a provision for the collection of duties. This passage, according to the article just mentioned, was to commence at some place within three hundred miles of the Lake of the Woods and to the west of it. If the access was to be general, without limitation of place, then the people of the United States should be allowed a reciprocal right of access through British territory to the St. Lawrence and of free navigation of that river.

It then came out that the British silence on the fisheries might have a sinister meaning, for the British envoys confirmed the opinion already expressed by Adams to his own colleagues that the demand for a clause on the navigation of the Mississippi was balanced by the abandonment of the British claim, based on the treaty of 1783, to have the boundary reach the Mississippi. If the navigation question was to be tied to the boundary instead of to the fisheries, what might happen to the latter? The unspoken question apparently troubled Gallatin, who suggested that they strike out the whole of the eighth article.

As a matter of fact the British were quite innocent of any design to entrap the Americans, who knew nothing of Bathurst's and Goulburn's private thoughts on the fisheries. Actually the British envoys found relief in the American suggestion of a parallel provision for the fisheries, because that would definitely establish the American privilege on a conventional basis and they had been greatly worried by the language of their opponents whenever the question had been mentioned. The United States delegates had taken pains to refer to the treaty of 1783 always as recognizing, never as conferring, the right of their people to share in the British fisheries.

With most of the other British proposals, the Americans were content. They declined to press for anything in the deleted articles except compensation for the confiscation of American ships and cargoes in British ports at the outbreak of the war. This they sought in return for the United States' having allowed the departure of British vessels in American harbors at that time. But the British replied that there was a material difference in the consideration of which party declared war. More strenuous was the American objection to the continued British occupation of all the disputed islands below the mouth of the St. Croix. The great bone of contention was Moose Island. There lay the town of Eastport, whose elected representative had sat in the legislature of Massachusetts. The trouble was over the wording of the clause on the mutual restoration of territory, the American text having called for the return of all that had been taken by one party from the other whereas the British amendment required the surrender only of what belonged to one and had been taken by the other. Though the Americans argued strongly for their version, their opponents gained the impression that the original form would not be insisted upon if the rest of the treaty was satisfactory.[61]

Another reference to London followed immediately. The report from Ghent reached Bathurst on December 4, and it pleased him. It dispelled his fear that the United States had imposed a perpetual servitude upon British sovereignty in the matter of fishing and drying, but he was very cautious. On the sixth, he wrote to the British commissioners informing them that the Americans' substitute for the rider to Article VIII was impossible because it proposed "a limited and restricted renewal of our former privileges, in return for an unlimited and unrestricted renewal of their former liberty." Another article, which he enclosed, was to be offered in its stead. This would reserve for a future negotiation a settlement of the conditions on which the fisheries and navigation privileges were to be renewed. Bathurst's object was twofold. He was impatient for peace and he foresaw long discussions on the fisheries. He was also apprehensive of yielding, even by implication, more than was necessary. Therefore he warned the British commissioners that if the Americans declined this new proposition "you will not consider yourselves as authorized to sign the Treaty with the omission of the amended *project* of the 8th Article, and still less with the omission of the latter part of it." They were to refer home for further instructions if the Americans would

61. *Ibid.*, pp. 79–90. The British to the American ministers, Nov. 26, 1814, *A.S.P.F.R.*, III, 740. The American to the British ministers, *ibid.*, p. 741. Protocol of a conference held on the 1st Dec., 1814, *ibid.*, p. 742. The British Commissioners to Castlereagh, Dec. 1, 1814, *Massachusetts Historical Society Proceedings*, XLVIII, 151–155.

neither accept what was now offered nor otherwise make it clear "by some written document that they consider the stipulations of 1783, with respect to the liberty given them of taking, drying, and curing, fish on our coasts, as no longer in force." By the same dispatch, the British commissioners were allowed to meet the American criticism of the British rewording of the clause on the restitution of territory provided they realized the purpose of this amendment, which was the retention of the islands in Passamaquoddy Bay during the adjudication of their national ownership.[62] Though Bathurst's eye was fixed on the east coast of America, his pen also touched the west coast. This concession involved the restitution of Astor's establishment on the Pacific. It is doubtful if he realized it,[63] but his carelessness was probably of little consequence in the long run.

Dissension among the Americans again broke out when they received the British proposals in a conference on the tenth.[64] Only two things stood in the way of peace: the temporary disposition of Moose Island and the adjustment of the fisheries question. Both concerned Massachusetts alone, and Adams found himself standing alone. The insistence on an exception to the restoration of conquests sprang from a fear of compromising what the British believed was their unassailable claim to the possession of Moose Island. Their contention was that it had been part of Nova Scotia in 1783, that New Brunswick had exercised jurisdiction there, and that the subsequent exercise of American authority over it was an aggression which would have been resisted at the time but for the danger of provoking hostilities. Adams, being equally convinced that the island was an integral part of his state, would admit of no exception; but his colleagues were inclined to allow it, and some of them confessed to him that they thought the British claim was sound.

The fisheries article, as framed in London, meant that the privilege of 1783 had been abrogated in 1812, which he could never admit but his fellows could not reject. Some of them frankly told him that his theory about fishing and drying within British jurisdiction was quite untenable. He succeeded in persuading the rest of the delegation to join in resistance to both demands at another conference on the twelfth, but their opponents, being bound by strict orders, could not budge. In the privacy of the American lodgings, Adams continued his wrestling match. He weakened on the question of Moose Island, expressing a willingness to accept the British condition; but he was as defiant as ever on the fisheries. At last he told his colleagues to go ahead and sign without him, for

62. Castlereagh, X, 214–217.
63. *Supra*, n. 57.
64. When the article on the slave trade was accepted.

they were determined to yield the point in the end and he so distrusted the British that he was afraid another reference to London would upset the treaty. Thus challenged, they agreed to make one more effort before giving way.[65]

By his resistance Adams prevented a positive surrender of the American claim to share the British inshore fisheries. In a note of December 14, the delegation accepted the British amendment affecting Moose Island but rejected the clause on the fisheries and the Mississippi. They were secretly a little embarrassed by the fact that they were refusing a formula because it contained an implication which they themselves had allowed in the article they had proposed for a renewal of both privileges; but this, they now asserted, would have been merely declaratory. They offered silence on both points or a reference to future negotiation so expressed as to imply no abandonment of any right.[66] Their offer required yet another reference to England. Bathurst replied on the nineteenth. Observing that there was no apparent prospect of a satisfactory arrangement for the fisheries, he ordered the acceptance of the American suggestion, made by Gallatin at the conference on the first, that the whole of Article VIII be dropped; but the acceptance, he was careful to state, must be preceded by a reminder of the British determination not to renew the American privilege gratuitously.[67] When the contents of this dispatch were communicated at Ghent on the twenty-second, Clay had another fit of bad temper. He was apparently annoyed by the disappearance of the British article, which would have confirmed his principle that the war had canceled the navigation privilege. He cared nothing for the corresponding fisheries privilege, and he had not quite thrown off the war fever. Only a few days previously he had been talking of continuing hostilities for another three years, adding that this would make the Americans a warlike people and enable them to terminate the struggle with honor. Now he was for breaking off the negotiation at the very moment when the last difficulty disappeared. He appealed to Adams for support, but the New Englander said it was too late.[68] At a conference on the twenty-third, the last touches were put to the treaty, and on Christmas Eve it was signed and sealed.

The nature of the peace settlement was negative. What the United States had hoped to get out of the war became both unnecessary and impossible with the overthrow of Napoleon. That is why the treaty

65. *Memoirs of John Quincy Adams*, III, 94–191.
66. *A.S.P.F.R.*, III, 743–744.
67. Castlereagh, X, 221–223.
68. *Memoirs of John Quincy Adams*, III, 101, 120–122.

contained not one word about the causes of the war. This silence did not imply a British victory, for the United States retired from the struggle without sacrificing any principle for which it had fought. What Britain had hoped to get out of the war was unnecessary because, as the Americans at Ghent observed in one of their controversial notes, her security against an attack on the Empire in the interior of the continent was her undoubted ability to strike a more damaging blow on the Atlantic seaboard of the United States.[69] She had held her hand to avoid antagonizing New England. Had she elected to continue the struggle in order to win a territorial revision, she might have found it impossible. She would have been sorely embarrassed at home and in Europe, and she would have had to face a long war against a nation in arms instead of a short war against a paralyzed country. In the end, she might have lost much, if not all, of Canada. Such seems to have been the calculation in London, where the grave internal weakness of the United States was little appreciated.

As neither side had won the war or wished to continue it, neither could enforce its will upon the other. The fisheries question was left wide open, each party having served notice that the other's interpretation was not to be allowed. Their failure to reach any agreement on this point led them to discard their agreement on the boundary from the Lake of the Woods to the Rockies, leaving this question wide open too. As for the boundary beyond, they did not even attempt to settle it. The British might perhaps have kept Astoria if they had been as intent upon it as they were to keep Moose Island; but, as already suggested, it is doubtful if this would have made any difference in the end. The navigation of the Mississippi, entangled with the western boundary and the fisheries, was left in the same uncertain state. Though a formal renewal of Article III of Jay's Treaty was out of the question, there was no understanding on whether the British trade with tribes on American soil was to be stopped or continued; for this question was tied up with the fisheries, the Mississippi, and the western boundary questions; and, as Adams had discovered, it might be governed by the general terms of the article on the pacification of the Indians. Except for the provisions to establish boundary commissions to remove some friction over what was the line prescribed in 1783, the only definite achievement of the Treaty of Ghent was the termination of hostilities. Both sides were deeply disappointed in the result, but the stalemate was fortunate. The treaty did nothing that had to be undone, which is more than can be said for many treaties of peace: and though it left much undone, the differences

69. On September 9, 1814. *A.S.P.F.R.*, III, 715–716.

between the two countries were to be settled in an atmosphere of peace rather than of war.

Tempestuous weather delayed the Atlantic passage of the Treaty of Ghent. It reached New York on the evening of February 11. Four days later the President sent it to the Senate, and on the next day, the sixteenth, that body accepted it unanimously. As soon as the American ratification was completed, which was late in the evening of the seventeenth, just four hours after the arrival of the new British *chargé d'affaires* with the British ratification, the two documents were exchanged and the treaty became binding. Before the next day dawned, a messenger was speeding to Quebec, where he arrived on March 1, and immediately the peace was proclaimed in Canada.[70]

The tidings of peace spread immense joy throughout the United States from Maine to Louisiana even before the people knew anything about the terms of the treaty. It was enough for them that at last they had peace. In British North America, the popular reaction seems to have been much less hearty. The Maritime Provinces had thriven on the war, Halifax in particular enjoying a prosperity such as it had never known; the night of fear had been banished from Canada by the overthrow of Napoleon; and the fur traders felt that they and their red clients had once more been betrayed by a careless government across the sea. But, in the ensuing relations between British North America and the United States, the grudging acceptance of peace on one side of the line did not offset the enthusiastic welcome it received on the other, for British North America had little to say in the management of these affairs. They were regulated in Washington and London. In England the treaty stirred "feelings of mixed anger and satisfaction":[71] satisfaction over having got rid of the war and anger over the humiliation of the terms. But the latter feeling was soon stifled by two items of news that arrived together early in March. One was of the crushing defeat at New Orleans, and the other was of Napoleon's escape from Elba. His return to France led to Waterloo, and in the glory of that day Britain found compensation for her American peace without victory. Then the government in London became as anxious as the government in Washington to transform what was little more than a truce into a lasting peace, and the relations between the United States and British North America entered upon a new era.

70. Baker to Castlereagh, No. 1, Feb. 19, 1815, and to ————, of same date, *F.O. 5*, Vol. CVI. Prevost to Bathurst, March 13, 1815, *Q*, CXXXI, 75.

71. Adams, IX, 54.

CHAPTER XVI

THE ESTABLISHMENT OF PEACE: BORDER FRICTION AND DISARMAMENT ON THE LAKES

THOUGH the War of 1812 was like a thunderstorm that clears the air, it would be a mistake to imagine that the spirit of hostility suddenly vanished from all along the northern border of the United States. But it was not long before the strong will to peace that prevailed in Washington and London made itself felt. Underlings might bicker but they could not involve their principals in a quarrel. This is the dominant feature of the relations between British North America and the United States in the postwar years.

The old problem of British relations with Indians living within the borders of the United States raised its head for the last time at the close of the war, and soon disappeared forever. For a brief moment in 1815, Michilimackinac threatened to become what the western posts had been a generation before. When the nature of the treaty was disclosed in Canada, the chief director of the North West Company, William McGillivray, approached Sir George Prevost to persuade him that Michilimackinac should not be given up. He advanced the well-worn argument that the security of Upper Canada depended on the friendship of the western tribes, which in turn depended on their trade with Montreal. But he had gloomy forebodings that it would be impossible to retain this door to the American West, and therefore he urged that at least the United States should not be allowed to close it. He contended that the British government still had the power to insist on the continuance of the trade to the Mississippi through the straits guarded by this post. It would be necessary, he said, to force a reduction of the American customs duties on trading goods, and to base the traffic on a new fort built in some strong position near by. The new substitute for Michilimackinac, which would then "dwindle away," should not be on the site of the old substitute, destroyed during the war, for St. Joseph's Island was "very unfit for a military station."

The governor inclined an ear to the fur baron and asked him to commit his ideas to paper.[1] McGillivray submitted the desired memorandum[2] on March 28, and on that very day an order went forth to Lieutenant Colonel McDouall, the commander at Michilimackinac. Though he was immediately to withdraw the contingent he had posted

1. *Q*, CXXXII, 35.
2. *Ibid.*, p. 20.

at Prairie du Chien on the Mississippi, he was not to move from his own station until shelter was provided for his garrison.[3] Within a week Prevost was gone, having been summoned home, and his place was temporarily filled by Sir Gordon Drummond, upon whom the fur traders got to work immediately. They tried in vain to convince him that Michilimackinac was one of the disputed islands in the international waterway and therefore did not have to be surrendered until the commissioners to be appointed under the Treaty of Ghent allotted it to the United States; but he agreed with them that there should be no American customs jurisdiction in the island while the British garrison remained, and he was so much influenced by their general argument that he undertook to delay the evacuation of this important place until he could get advice from England.[4] Having already notified the British *chargé* in Washington, Anthony John Baker, that the garrison could not move until a place was prepared for them,[5] Drummond allowed this to become the official excuse for his contemplated violation of the treaty, which called for the surrender of occupied territory "without delay."

Drummond did not wait to hear from London. His sly policy almost immediately provoked a reaction that forced his hand. The United States had not yet succeeded in making peace with the tribes dependent on Michilimackinac, where the presence of British troops was a serious obstacle to the pacification of these Indians, but the American army had a good lever with which to pry the British loose. The Stars and Stripes still waved over Fort Malden, and American orders forbade its evacuation until arrangements were made for a simultaneous departure from Michilimackinac. Apprised of this fact on May 4, Drummond ordered the immediate removal of the British garrison. He was eager to clear his own frontier out of regard for the Indians.[6] The Americans retired from the southwest corner of Upper Canada on July 1, and on the eighteenth the British withdrew from Michilimackinac to encamp on Drummond Island. But the cloud which hung over the region beyond was not yet dissipated.

Serious questions had already been started by the refusal of the northern tribes to bury the hatchet as soon as the United States government notified them of the Treaty of Ghent and its stipulation in their favor. Were the British still at their old tricks? The Americans suspected it, and bits of evidence gathered by government agents scattered all the

3. *Ibid.*, p. 7.

4. Drummond to Bathurst, April 25, 1815, and enclosures, *ibid.*, pp. 18–37.

5. Drummond to Baker, April 6, 1815, enclosed in Baker to Castlereagh, No. 12, May 2, 1815, *F.O. 5*, Vol. CVI.

6. Drummond to Bathurst, May 20, 1815, and enclosures, *Q*, CXXXII, 104–115.

way from Detroit to St. Louis seemed to prove it. Monroe complained
to Baker and sent him the evidence. Baker replied that most of it was
worthless, but he would ask Quebec for an investigation.[7] Over against
this American suspicion of British machinations stood a British suspicion
of American bad faith. How could the movement of American troops to
occupy Prairie du Chien and other strategic points in Indian territory
which they had not held in 1811 be reconciled with the treaty? McGillivray advised Drummond that this was a violation of Article IX,
which promised the Indians a restoration of their position in 1811.[8]
Down in Washington, Monroe's complaints directed Baker's attention
to another clause in that article. "It is evident," the *chargé* reported,
"that one object of this government is to shew that these Indians, by
not agreeing to desist from hostilities against the United States, lose
the benefit of the stipulation in their favor." He observed that renewed
hostilities were expected at any time and that American preparations
were being made accordingly.[9] Here were familiar symptoms of the
trouble that had been chronic for a generation, but it was already beginning to clear up.

The inquiry ordered by Drummond at the request of Baker brought
to light a story that explains much. Because a rascal wasted several
weeks in carrying a dispatch from York to Michilimackinac, McDouall
had not known until May 1, 1815, that the war was over. Meanwhile he
had been broadcasting orders in anticipation of an impending American
attack; and though, when he learned the truth, he instantly sent out
countermanding orders, these took another three weeks or more to
cover the territory of which he had charge. Thus it happened that, quite
innocently, he continued to fan the flames of war for some considerable
time after he should have been extinguishing them. Small wonder the
Americans had failed to pacify the northern Indians and had blamed the
British for their failure! In due course Baker was able to provide Monroe
with this satisfactory explanation of the mystery:[10] and by this time the
elusive peace had already been made, the reversal of McDouall's orders
having removed the obstacle. In August, representatives of the tribes
living in what is now Michigan and Indiana met the United States
commissioners near Detroit; and on September 8, 1815, they concluded
the Treaty of Spring Wells. This was but one, though the most important, of fourteen treaties signed between the middle of July and the end

7. Monroe to Baker, July 10, 1815, and Baker to Monroe, July 12, 1815, enclosed in Baker
to Castlereagh, No. 22, July 19, 1815, *F.O. 5*, Vol. CVII.

8. *Q*, CXXXII, 47.

9. Baker to Castlereagh, No. 22, July 19, 1815, *F.O. 5*, Vol. CVII.

10. Baker to Monroe, Dec. 15, 1815, and enclosures, enclosed in Baker to Castlereagh, No.
1, Jan. 18, 1816, *ibid.*, Vol. CXII.

of October. They all guaranteed to the red men the rights and privileges of 1811—in accordance with the Treaty of Ghent.

The old nightmare of the West was now finally banished, as the British connection with Indians on American soil was finally cut. It was cut by stopping the fur trade which had been its life. As already observed,[11] this trade was doomed; but, instead of being allowed to wither away, it came to a sudden end as a consequence of the War of 1812. That let the knife fall.

The War of 1812, having been terminated without a specific renewal of Article III of Jay's Treaty, released the United States from the international servitude imposed in 1794. That it had been implicitly revived by Article IX of the Treaty of Ghent, as Adams had privately argued,[12] Washington would never admit and London did not claim. That it might be restored by subsequent agreement was a British hope that was soon dashed. During the negotiations which led to the signing of an Anglo-American commercial convention on July 3, 1815, the American plenipotentiaries announced that their instructions forbade them to concede any right to intercourse with Indians living within the borders of the United States; and when the British plenipotentiaries submitted a draft that might be interpreted as giving this right, an American hint extracted a British disclaimer of any intention thus to recover what had been lost.[13]

The United States quickly stopped the compromising trade which had thus lost its treaty protection. Seeing that the end was near, some British traders rushed goods into the country through Michilimackinac while it was still in British hands; but the end was nearer than they thought. When their furs came down to Michilimackinac, American officers seized them all because the goods had evaded the United States customs.[14] The protective tariff, born of the war, was an effective barrier. It would not have been, if Americans still had to import the articles necessary for the Indian trade; but the war had also given a stimulus to domestic manufactures. To make doubly sure of the British exclusion, Congress passed an act in the spring of 1816 prohibiting, under severe penalties, all foreigners from trafficking with the natives; and in the same year the government began to establish fortified posts along the routes that the Canadian traders had been wont to follow.[15]

The severance of the historic tie between Canada and the American

11. See *supra*, pp. 202–205, 253.
12. See *supra*, p. 366.
13. *A.S.P.F.R.*, IV, 15–16.
14. McDouall to the Military Secretary, June 17, 1816, *Q*, CXXXII, 18.
15. See E. B. Wesley, *Guarding the Frontier* (Minneapolis, 1935), Chap. VIII.

Northwest naturally produced some strain, but this was not economic. The commercial loss to Montreal was a mere bagatelle. The main seat of the fur traffic had long since shifted beyond the northern bounds of the United States, and the material prosperity of that city had ceased to depend on furs. Equally negligible was the number of British traders who had settled in American territory and now had to become American citizens to preserve their occupation. Most of the scattered population of Canadian origin living in that region seem to have become Americans after the military evacuation of 1796.

The tension which accompanied the disentanglement of 1815 affected the red men but it was not allowed to affect the relations between the two white peoples. It is revealed in dispatches written in June, 1816, by Lieutenant Colonel McDouall, who had enjoyed in Michilimackinac a brief rule over an extensive empire and was now cooped up in Drummond Island. There he frequently had to entertain Indians who came from the lost territory, sometimes in considerable numbers. They visited him, as they also did the commandant in Fort Malden, because they knew they would not be turned away with empty hands, or stomachs, and they still hoped that the British would somehow rescue them from the fate closing in upon them. He described as "inconceivable the horror they entertain" at the thought of no more British traders going amongst them, and he told of their fierce resentment against the building of new forts in their country. That this was an infraction of the Treaty of Ghent, a quixotic idea which did not occur to practical Americans, he had not the slightest doubt. The most ominous of McDouall's reports was that the natives were forming a new confederacy to strike another blow for freedom. He dreaded the prospect. He was evidently infected by the old fear that the Indians, feeling themselves betrayed by the British, would fall upon them as well as upon the Americans. Though he provided his visitors with presents enough for themselves, he observed that they were "highly dissatisfied" because he could give them nothing for their people at home. He was also sure that "the extremely moderate supply of powder which they received" would be "blazoned forth as supplying them with the means of war."

There was a cooler head down in Quebec. Sir John Coape Sherbrooke, the new governor who had just been promoted from Nova Scotia, immediately sent McDouall fresh orders to spread the gospel of peace. He was to tell the Indians "distinctly and explicitly" that the British government would neither assist nor countenance them in any hostilities against the United States. At the same time he was to assure them that any grievances they might have would immediately command the attention of the governor, who would refer them to His Majesty's minister in Washington. This, McDouall was to explain, would "be a much more likely way for them to obtain their reasonable objects than by acts of indiscreet hostility." Sherbrooke also sent copies of these orders, along with the disturbing dispatches that inspired them, to Charles Bagot, who had recently commenced his remarkable work as British minister in the American capital. He straightway communicated to Monroe the contents of these documents, and the Secretary of State expressed his great obligation for this intelligence.[16] Already these two gentlemen in Washington had turned their backs on the suspicions of the past, and were at work on the famous agreement for disarmament on the Lakes. Indians from across the line continued to frequent Fort Malden and Drummond Island, but their visits had no international significance.

Before examining disarmament on the Lakes, which further revolutionized international relations in the interior of this continent, we should note another, and very different, legacy of the War of 1812. For a couple of years after the fighting ceased, the spirit of hostility lingered along the border, particularly in the region of Detroit; and there was quite a crop of unpleasant local incidents which might have produced still more friction if, as before 1812, the two powers had been drifting toward war.

The flight of deserters across the line was like a running sore. Many were the complaints sent to Baker and Bagot that Americans were seducing British soldiers. "Sergeants of the most unblemished characters, without a single grievance absconded with many of their men." One such sergeant on a march from Kingston to Montreal "deserted accompanied by no less than 50 soldiers, horses being stationed on the

16. Bagot to Castlereagh, No. 26, Aug. 12, 1816, and enclosures, including McDouall to the Military Secretary (see *supra*, n. 14), *F.O.* 5, Vol. CXV. On August 8 Sherbrooke sent Bagot another alarming dispatch from McDouall, and this time the governor urged the officer's more explicit charge that the Americans were violating Article IX of the Treaty of Ghent by their military occupation of the Indian territory; but Bagot, having received no "precise instructions" on the point, wisely refrained from mentioning it to Monroe. The only step he took on this occasion was to give the American Secretary of State "a general assurance that the Indian Nations would receive from His Majesty's Government no countenance or assistance whatever in committing acts of hostility against the United States; although His Majesty's Government would always feel deeply interested in obtaining for them the redress of any grievances under which they might really labour." Bagot to Castlereagh, No. 31, Sept. 1, 1816, and enclosures, *ibid.*

This later dispatch from McDouall enclosed the report of an Indian council at Drummond Island on June 29, in which a Winnebago chief addressed an officer of the Indian Department as follows: "I detest the Big Knives from the bottom of my heart, and never took from them a glass of whiskey nor a needle, which is a convincing proof of my dislike to them. Father, I know of no other Father but you, and never will be considered or taken for a Bastard, which would be so if I acknowledged the Big Knives to be my father also."

American side of the River St. Lawrence to favour their escape, on which they immediately mounted on gaining that bank."[17] Other instances occurred on the New Brunswick frontier and along the Detroit River. According to evidence collected by local British authorities and forwarded to Washington, representatives of the United States Army were enticing the men with bribes and promises of promotion; and it was notorious on the British side of the line that absconders enlisted under the Stars and Stripes. Though American soldiers also escaped to the British side, there were no counteraccusations that they were admitted to serve under the Union Jack.[18] The complaints were all British, and it should be observed that they were not all reserved for transmission to the American capital, for they stimulated local bickering across the border. Sailors likewise fled from one flag to the other on the Lakes, and though these nautical fugitives were less numerous they were the cause of no less trouble. In addition to desertion, smuggling was a distinct irritant. Yet another was the interpretation of the treaty provision for the restoration of what had been taken during the war; and last, though not least, was bad-tempered officiousness. Such were the influences that produced a certain state of local tension which now and then found expression in border incidents.

On the New Brunswick frontier, where feeling was nothing so bitter as it was in the West, occurred the boldest effort to recover military fugitives. At the end of April, 1815, a British sergeant and half a dozen privates were dispatched from Moose Island in the garrison boat to catch some deserters at Machias. There a genial American lieutenant met the invaders, learned their business, sent a messenger to keep the hunted out of the way, invited the sergeant to breakfast, and tried to lure the men along with their leader into the ranks of the American army. The sergeant and one private succumbed, apparently along with the boat. The faithful remnant of the party were left to find their own way back to Moose Island, where they told their story and supported it with affidavits. When these reached Halifax, they were transmitted to Baker as convincing proof of American iniquity. As such, he presented

17. Baker to Monroe, July 7, 1815, enclosed in Baker to Castlereagh, No. 27, Aug. 14, 1815, *ibid.*, Vol. CVII.

18. "Upwards of three hundred American deserters have passed through this district, yet not one of them has been taken into the British service. On the contrary, and in order to give as little cause of representation as possible to the American Executive, I have given orders that no deserter should remain more than twelve hours after landing without proceeding from this part of the country, which order was most particularly obeyed." Thus wrote the officer commanding at Sandwich when, on March 2, 1816, he reported that a score of his runaways, of whom he mentioned a dozen by name, were then doing duty as American soldiers in Detroit. James to Harvey, enclosed in Bagot to Castlereagh, No. 15, June 4, 1816, *ibid.*, Vol. CXIV.

them to Monroe with a request for orders to stop it.[19] To complete the story, which reads more like comic opera than sober history, the Secretary of State does not seem to have retorted by asking what these foreign soldiers were doing on the soil of the United States. On this occasion American forbearance matched British effrontery.

There was also a little difficulty over the application of the treaty in Moose Island, but it was quickly and easily settled without reference to London. On taking possession of the island in the summer of 1814, the British captors had respected the property of residents but not of others. When peace returned, these nonresident owners, living in various parts of Massachusetts, sought the return of their property as guaranteed by the treaty. It was a question of only a few lots and buildings in Eastport. The local military authorities refused to surrender them without orders, whereupon the dispossessed applied to Monroe. He turned their petitions over to Bagot in the summer of 1816. Bagot agreed that the request was just, and so did Sherbrooke, whom he consulted, with the result that a restoration was effected in a few weeks.[20]

On the frontiers of Lower and Upper Canada, there was more trouble; but most of it, with the exception of what happened at the western extremity, was rather petty. Five deserters from Kingston were followed to Sackett's Harbor by an officer who persuaded them to return;[21] but when two dragoons fled from Montreal with horses of the regiment, and an officer was sent across the line to redeem the animals, he could not get them. This irritated Drummond, who expected reciprocity for what he had recently done under similar circumstances, when three American soldiers turned up at Ile aux Noix with the six-oared gig of the commanding officer at Plattsburg. Drummond had then ordered the immediate restitution of the boat and issued instructions that this decision was to be a binding precedent on future occasions.[22] More serious was an incident on the waters of Lake Ontario in the autumn of 1815, according to the report of the British commander-in-chief of the

19. Baker to Monroe, July 28, 1815, and enclosures, enclosed in Baker to Castlereagh, No. 27, Aug. 14, 1815, ibid., Vol. CVII.

20. Bagot to Castlereagh, No. 20, July 4, 1816, and enclosures, ibid., Vol. CXIV; also No. 32, Sept. 1, 1816, and enclosures, ibid., Vol. CXV; and No. 36, Nov. 9, 1816, and enclosures, ibid.

21. Drummond to Baker, Aug. 10, 1815, C, MCCXXXVI (Military Secretary's Letter Book), 24.

22. Drummond to Baker, Feb. 10, 1816, ibid., p. 60. This was apparently the same boat as that which was detained by the British after being seized by a United States customs boat, as Captain W. F. W. Owen complained, "by force under the guns of Ile aux Noix, ten miles on our side of the border." Bagot Papers, Canadian Correspondence, II, 2. For a further reference to this incident, see Drummond to Baker, Jan. 6, 1816, C, MCCXXXVI (Military Secretary's Letter Book), 59.

lake forces. The American schooner *Lady of the Lake*, he said, "waited the sailing of one of our merchant vessels from Niagara, whence she chased her for a very considerable time, firing canon shot at her repeatedly to bring her to, and this for the purpose (as avowed by the American naval commander-in-chief)[23] of searching for deserters."[24]

This affair, however, occasioned less concern than the American seizure of the British schooner *Julia* in October, 1815, at the mouth of a creek two miles from Sackett's Harbor. She belonged to the naval dockyard at Kingston, and was under orders to procure hay for the dockyard cattle during the winter. Sir Edward Owen, who had charge of the British naval forces on the Lakes, appealed to Baker, who vainly pressed Monroe for the surrender of this government vessel. According to the report of the customs collector at Sackett's Harbor, ever since the opening of navigation she had been plying back and forth from Kingston, to which place she carried large quantities of hay, oats, butter, cheese, and livestock, "without paying the least attention to the port of entry" though in the spring she had been warned to comply with the law. The master, on being apprehended, claimed exemption from the law requiring formal entry, because the schooner belonged to His Majesty and was on public business; and the *chargé* in Washington argued that the craft should be allowed the privileges of a naval tender going ashore for supplies. But this vessel had "frequented the most suspicious places, and these in the night." Apparently the master had been abusing his position as a government servant to indulge in private business which was not all cash transactions. There was an enormous amount of smuggling across the lake and the river which drained it.[25]

In the region of Detroit, the war spirit still pervaded the atmosphere. Perhaps the chief reason for this may be found in the Indian background, to which attention was drawn by the hitch over the evacuation of Michilimackinac. Before the surrender of that place was arranged, but not because the British clung to it, the American commander at Detroit, Colonel Anthony Butler, developed correspondingly free ideas about yielding occupied territory. He decided that when he gave up Malden he would keep the little island of Bois Blanc, which lay close to the Canadian shore in front of that fort and the village of Amherstburg; and he began

23. Verification for this has not yet been found.

24. Baumgardt to Bagot, Sept. 5, 1816, enclosed in Bagot to Castlereagh, No. 46, Dec. 3, 1816, *F.O.* 5, Vol. CXV, citing a letter of November, 1815, by Baumgardt's predecessor, Sir Edward Owen, to Baker. This letter is missing from Baker's correspondence in *F.O.* 5, and has not been found in the Canadian correspondence.

25. Baker to Castlereagh, No. 3, Jan. 18, 1816, and enclosures, *F.O.* 5, Vol. CXII; No. 10, March 2, 1816, and enclosures, *ibid;* No. 25, April 7, 1817, and enclosures, *ibid.*, Vol. CXXII.

to fortify it. His action roused the British, who had occupied the island from the delivery of Detroit in 1796 until the retirement of Proctor in 1813. Their local protests were unavailing. Butler would accept no proof of British occupation, which would oblige him to withdraw in accordance with the treaty. The root of the trouble was that the narrow passage along the east of the island was then the regular navigation channel, which he insisted must be the boundary, the much wider passage on the west being little used. Fortunately the treaty had also provided for an international commission which would determine where the boundary ran; Drummond was willing meanwhile to leave the place unoccupied by either party; and Baker persuaded Monroe to check Butler in the summer of 1815.[26] Otherwise there might have been a dangerous explosion.[27]

Another nasty dispute began in September, 1815, when Lieutenant Alexander Vidal, a British naval officer, landed on the American side of Lake St. Clair and was arrested. A few nights before, while the schooner on which he was serving lay at anchor, some of the crew ran off with two of her boats, carrying with them some stolen stores and clothing. In the morning one of the boats was found abandoned, but the other was nowhere to be seen. Vidal was sent to search for it. On landing, he found the missing boat and learned that some of the stolen property was in a public house a little distance off. Walking thither while the boat skirted the shore, he met one of the missing seamen, who willingly obeyed his order to return in the boat. At the public house, where he discovered some of his own clothes with other loot, a crowd gathered and he was arrested. Thereupon a spirited correspondence sprang up between Governor Lewis Cass in Detroit and Sir Edward Owen who was on board a vessel in the river. Owen demanded Vidal's release. Cass offered to restore as much as he could of the stolen goods, but he demanded the return of the man whom Vidal had "seized and trans-

26. Baker to Castlereagh, No. 19, June 21, 1815, and enclosures, No. 22, July 19, 1815, and enclosures, No. 29, Aug. 16, 1815, and enclosures, *F.O. 5*, Vol. CVII. Butler asserted that he was carrying out the will of his government, that an American vessel had once landed goods on Bois Blanc to evade the duties levied at Amherstburg, and that the attorney general of Upper Canada had ruled against the collection of duties on the island because it was part of the United States. He was soon forced to admit that it was not the attorney general but a local lawyer named Woods who had given the ruling. Woods denied it, and the customs collector at Amherstburg could not recall the transaction at all. Nor was Butler carrying out the will of his government, as Monroe assured Baker when the latter protested.

27. "I frankly declare that had the American Government much longer allowed their officer at Detroit pertinaciously to retain possession of this island, in open and direct violation of the existing Treaty of Peace, that such an act would have operated with me as strongly as any decided declaration of war." Drummond to Baker, Aug. 11, 1815, *C*, MCCXXXVI (Military Secretary's Letter Book), 26.

ported" from the United States. Owen refused because the sailor had returned of his own free will. Indeed the poor fellow declared that he had not deserted at all, that he had fallen into a drunken sleep in the boat before the deserters made off with it, that he knew nothing until he woke in the morning, and that he was going along the beach looking for the schooner when he encountered his officer. When Vidal was tried, he was found guilty of riot[28] and fined $631; and, according to the report sent to Washington, the nonappearance of two witnesses who had been summoned saved him from being condemned for forcible abduction. In the American capital, Baker interceded with Monroe[29] for the unhappy officer;[30] and in London, John Quincy Adams denounced him to Castlereagh.[31]

This episode cannot be dismissed as a comedy of errors inspired by a sailor's thirst. No one can read the local correspondence it occasioned without being impressed by the pent-up bitterness on both sides of the Detroit River. "Some time must elapse before the passions excited by the late war will entirely subside," was the comment of Cass in one of his letters to Owen.

The violent death of a Kickapoo Indian on the Detroit River, just four weeks after the arrest of Vidal, further inflamed the local international feud. The unfortunate red man and a few companions had been hunting squirrels on Grosse Ile when a boatload of American soldiers arrived and chased them off. When the retreating canoe was a few rods from the shore, and therefore still within the United States, one of the soldiers shot and mortally wounded the Indian seated in the stern. According to the later American story, the victim was "in the act of presenting his gun," but according to a chief of his own tribe, an eye witness, he had given no provocation whatever, and was actually steering the canoe when he was shot. This witness said that the soldier had twice leveled his musket at the deceased before firing, a man who appeared to be an officer stopping him the first time and the chief himself the second time. The canoe made for the Canadian shore, where the stricken man died.

28. Apparently he was not wholly to blame for whatever riot occurred, for the leader of the crowd, the man who seems to have arrested Vidal, had an account of his own to settle. Owen observed "that the improper conduct of that person within British territory had sometime back obliged the commanding officer at this place [Sandwich] to make complaint of him to Colonel Butler, the then commanding officer at Detroit."

29. Who promised to have the fine remitted if possible. It proved to be impossible because the money had been paid. Cass to Owen, June 6, 1816, Bagot Papers, Canadian Correspondence, II, 17.

30. Baker to Castlereagh, No. 38, Dec. 6, 1815, and enclosures, *F.O.* 5, Vol. CVII.

31. *Memoirs of John Quincy Adams*, III, 286.

A coroner's jury brought in a verdict of murder by someone unknown, and the magistrates of the Western District of Upper Canada offered a reward of $500 for the apprehension of the murderer. Though this applied only within the British province, Cass issued a proclamation which accused the Canadian magistrates of attempting to violate the sovereignty of the United States and called upon all people within his territory "to repel by force" any such attempt on land or water west of the middle line of the river and to seize the offenders that they might be dealt with according to law. There was great excitement in Detroit and Amherstburg. National insults had been exchanged! But there was more than this to the affair. What made it explosive was the Indian background. There were many Kickapoos about, having come to visit their old friends; and Cass was obviously startled by what he took to be an effort to revive the British protectorship over Indians of the United States, while the British across the river were exasperated by the thought of Americans murdering Indians with impunity. This affair likewise inspired opposite and ineffectual diplomatic representations in the two capitals.[32]

More serious was a storm brewing on the water. The *Lady of the Lake* was not the only naval vessel that chased or stopped foreign merchant shipping on the Lakes in order to recover deserting sailors. Though Captain Baumgardt, Sir Edward Owen's successor, asserted in September, 1816, that on these inland seas American officers claimed and exercised the right of search more frequently than did the British, the evidence that has survived all points the other way. With the exception of the Niagara incident just referred to, all the specific complaints were American and were confined to what happened above the Falls. On Lake Erie, the British boarded American vessels and fired on at least one craft that flew the Stars and Stripes. At last, in September, 1816, Adams' repeated complaints evoked peremptory orders to stop the offensive practice;[33] but already the local situation had reached and passed a crisis.

In the spring of this year, the attorney general of Upper Canada scotched another dangerous development of British naval activity on the Lakes. There being some doubt whether the navy could enforce the revenue laws without a special deputation from the civil government of the province, for which application had just been made, he ruled that the operation of the British statutes, on which the question turned, was confined to the sea and did not extend to the Lakes, which were "free to

32. *Ibid*. Baker to Castlereagh, No. 4, Jan. 18, 1816, and enclosures, *F.O. 5*, Vol. CXII.
33. Castlereagh to Bagot, No. 17, Sept. 7, 1816, *ibid*., Vol. CXIII.

the navigation of vessels of the United States."[34] Lieutenant Governor
Gore then declined the request because, in his opinion, the civil authority
was sufficient.[35] Captain Bourchier, who commanded on Lake Erie and
blamed the bad character of people on the Grand River for an inordinate
amount of smuggling, was responsible for raising this delicate point.
He was also responsible for pressing the right of search to a climax.

Bourchier made it a rule[36] that American vessels passing through the
narrow channel east of Bois Blanc Island should be boarded and their
crews examined for British deserters. To him, it was the port of Malden,
wholly under British jurisdiction; but to Americans, it was an international waterway. If they admitted it to be British, they might compromise their country's claim to the island. For this reason, as well as
because this was the only place where American vessels were regularly
searched, the storm centered there. It began to break on July 24, 1816,
when two indignant passengers on a brig that had just been visited
wrote protesting letters to Governor Cass and to General Macomb,
then commandant of the district. According to one passenger, a military
man, "two field pieces were brought out from the fort at Malden, to the
edge of the bank, and trained on this vessel, accompanied with a detachment of troops etc." while the search was being made. The other, a
civilian, did not observe anything in this direction until the brig was
freed, and then he "perceived a field piece hawling off from the beach,
surrounded by ten or fifteen men, which appeared to be artillerists."
Cass and Macomb immediately forwarded these letters to Washington
with warm comments of their own. "It goes to exhibit the determination
of the British commanders, if not to make open war, at least to break the
peace which has so happily been accomplished," the general wrote to
the Secretary of War; and the governor's report to the Secretary of
State concluded with the remark that "from the tone and temper of
public sentiment, if this practice is continued, I am confident, it will
terminate in blood." There was an angry outburst in the American
press; but Monroe did not explode to Bagot, with whom he was on
friendly terms and had already discussed similar incidents. On August
11, he simply turned the correspondence over to him with a note in

34. As authority for the concluding part of this statement, he cited "the last treaty of commerce." This is curious. As a matter of fact, there was then no conventional provision for the
free navigation of the waters through which the boundary ran. Omitted from the treaty of
peace in 1783, it had been inserted in the treaty of 1794, only to expire with it in 1812. The
American negotiators tried in vain to revive it as one of the terms of the commercial convention signed in London on July 3, 1815, which was "the last commercial treaty." See *infra*,
p. 396.

35. Gore to Bathurst, May 23, 1816, and enclosures, *Q*, CCCXX, 210–222.

36. By verbal order on May 31, 1816, and by written order on July 23 following.

which he expressed a fear that such incidents would produce still greater mischief, a belief that British officers in Canada had mistaken the policy of their government, and a confident hope that Bagot would take effective measures to put an end to the trouble.[37]

Bourchier was a firebrand. Knowing what he had done and what the consequences might be, on July 29 he appealed to Baumgardt, his commander-in-chief down in Kingston: "I hope to have the honor of instructions from you in case of falling in with the United States vessels of war, as I am well aware we are placed on Lake Erie on a very ticklish footing." Evidently Cass's reference to blood was not very wide of the mark. But the outburst in the newspapers of the United States, whatever harm it may have wrought in that country, had a wholesome effect in Canada. It startled Baumgardt into ordering an explanation immediately, and it prepared him for quick action as soon as he heard from Bagot, who, on the very day he received Monroe's representation, wrote directly to the commander-in-chief on the Lakes requesting an inquiry.

On receiving this communication, Baumgardt promptly countermanded Bourchier's order, reprimanded him for issuing it, and forbade him to stop or board any vessel not in His Majesty's service until he was commanded to do so; and on the same day he replied to Bagot that nothing in the orders given to Bourchier could have justified "his assuming a right to bring to, board, and search American vessels in any case." At the same time, he offered two excuses already mentioned. One was that Americans had likewise followed the practice on the Lakes, and the other was "the customs of our service on the ocean." "That we were not within the jurisdiction of the Admiralty, was unknown to the officers and, until very lately, even to myself," he added. He also scouted the report of "aggravating circumstances," because it came only from "two officious passengers, not at all concerned in the transaction, and apparently very ignorant in such matters." Either the guns trained on the brig were quite imaginary, or the sworn testimony of the British commander in Amherstburg was a brazen lie. In the middle of November, 1816, the British minister was able to turn over to the American Secretary of State a mass of documents from Canada which confirmed the belief and justified the hope that Monroe had expressed to Bagot in August; and, by a happy coincidence, Bagot now received and communicated to Monroe, along with these documents, the result of Adams' agitation in London—the peremptory orders of the British government to stop the offensive practice on the Lakes.[38] That was the end of the trouble there.

37. Bagot to Castlereagh, No. 31, Sept. 1, 1816, and enclosures, *F.O. 5*, Vol. CXV.
38. Bagot to Castlereagh, No. 46, Dec. 3, 1816, and enclosures, *ibid.*

Meanwhile desertion from the troops along the border, though still occurring, ceased to be an international problem. At first the complaints seem to have given Monroe some secret pleasure, for he saw in them a weapon that might be useful to the United States. Writing to Baker in July, 1815, he intimated that the proper remedy was a treaty which would finally dispose of the great question of impressment. The American government was most eager to kill that dragon while it slept. But at the same time, Monroe promised to do everything possible to remove the grounds of the British complaints. The documents supporting them, he said, would be sent to the commander on the northern frontier with instructions to investigate the charges, to "prevent any interference of the kind suggested, and to punish for disobedience of orders any persons under his command who may be guilty of it."[39] When Bagot arrived in the spring of 1816, one of his first tasks was to present more circumstantial evidence of the American enlistment of British soldiers who slipped across the river to Detroit. In an interview with the Secretary of State, and also in a formal note, he earnestly remonstrated against "a proceeding so irreconcilable with what was due to a neighbouring and friendly state." He reported that "Mr. Monroe appeared to acknowledge that the case, as it was represented, afforded a just ground of complaint, and assured me, that in his belief it was in direct breach of the general orders of the War Department."[40] This was apparently the last occasion on which such a protest was made. In a few days, Bagot's note, the accompanying evidence, and an order for an inquiry were on their way to General Macomb. He replied that in his department there had been no recruiting since the war, that British deserters had frequently offered themselves and had "uniformly been ordered away," but that some might have crept into the service under a general regulation allowing substitutes. To close this loophole, he forbade the acceptance of any substitute without permission from headquarters.[41] When Monroe gave this letter to Bagot in July, 1816, the subject disappeared from the diplomatic correspondence.

A new day was dawning on the international frontier in the interior of America with the negotiation for disarmament upon the Lakes.[42] The idea was old, having been advocated first by John Adams in Paris and later by John Jay in London. After lying dormant, it had been awakened

39. Monroe to Baker, July 22, 1815, enclosed in Baker to Castlereagh, No. 27, Aug. 14, 1815, *ibid.*, Vol. CVII.

40. Bagot to Castlereagh, No. 15, June 4, 1816, and enclosures, *ibid.*, Vol. CXIV.

41. Bagot to Castlereagh, No. 27, Aug. 12, 1816, and enclosures, *ibid.*, Vol. CXV.

42. For this subject see J. M. Callahan, *The Neutrality of the American Lakes* (Johns Hopkins University Studies, 1898), Chap. IV.

in a rather unpleasant form by the War of 1812, when the British government, and also the American, hankered after a one-sided arrangement to prevent naval competition on these confined waters. But that was made impossible at Ghent. Immediately peace was restored, the United States took the initiative to secure this disarmament, and to her belongs the honor of persuading Britain to agree to it.

On February 17, 1815, the very day after the Senate voted for the ratification of the Treaty of Ghent, a resolution looking forward to the reduction of the fresh-water navy was introduced into the House; and ten days later an act was passed authorizing the President to have it all laid up or sold, except such vessels as he deemed necessary to enforce the revenue laws, "such vessels being first divested of their armament, tackle, and furniture, which are to be carefully preserved." Parsimony may have inspired but did not dictate this move, for the seagoing navy was maintained. There was a genuine American belief that armaments on the lakes would be folly unless Britain made them necessary. If she would follow suit, common sense would reign; but on August 29, 1815, Adams wrote from London that she would not. He enclosed newspaper reports to prove that the cabinet had determined "not only to maintain, but to increase the British naval armament upon the lakes." Though he professed the belief that no immediate rupture was intended,[43] his news presented the American government with the alternative of rearming or of drawing the British government into an agreement to stop it. Therefore, on November 16, Monroe replied to Adams directing him immediately to propose a mutual limitation of armed vessels, in order to avoid a struggle for ascendancy which would entail vast expenditure and a corresponding danger of collision; and on the twenty-seventh, when discussing with Baker the predicament of Vidal, he threw out the same suggestion, observing that such an arrangement would prevent unpleasant things like this from happening again.[44]

The discussion between the two governments on this question was opened in London on January 25, 1816, when Adams had an interview with Castlereagh, in which they dealt with a number of other matters of interest to both powers. Adams explained that the President, while leaving Britain to determine the extent of the reduction, wished it to be

43. The Writings of John Quincy Adams (New York, 1913), V, 360.

44. Baker to Castlereagh, No. 38, Dec. 6, 1815, enclosing Monroe to Baker of same date, F.O. 5, Vol. CVII. According to Callahan (op. cit., p. 67), Monroe had apparently made a similar intimation to Baker in a letter of July 22, but on rereading this letter I am convinced that Monroe was not referring to this but to an agreement for the restoration of deserting seamen. This letter is enclosed in Baker to Castlereagh, No. 27, Aug. 14, 1815, F.O. 5, Vol. CVII.

as great as possible, the optimum being a confinement of armaments to what was necessary for the protection of the revenue. Castlereagh was apparently surprised by the American proposal. He wavered between welcome and rejection. The best way to preserve peace on the Lakes, he said, would have been to give them to Britain, according to the proposition made at Ghent. Becoming more practical, he argued against mutual disarmament as placing far-off Britain at a great disadvantage. But almost at the beginning of the conversation, he agreed that "everything beyond what is necessary to guard against smuggling is calculated only to produce mischief," and he promised to consult the government, which would sincerely reciprocate the "pacific dispositions" of the United States.[45] He was too cautious to give more encouragement to Adams, who, on the thirty-first, reported home that disarmament "will not be accepted."[46] Two months later, the American reiterated this opinion, supporting it by references to recent debates in Parliament, where, as he said, a Lord of the Admiralty declared to the House of Commons "that bumboat expeditions and pinchback administrations would no longer do for Canada," Castlereagh talked of "the great and growing military power" of the American Republic, and "the prospect of a new war with the United States has been distinctly held up by the ministers and admitted by the opposition as a solid reason for enormous and unparalleled expenditure and preparation in Canada and Nova Scotia."[47]

Adams had made a mistake, as he learned ten days afterwards; and this was to shift the negotiation across the Atlantic. On April 9, 1816, when calling on the Foreign Secretary at the latter's request, he was informed that the British government was willing to meet the American proposal and wished to keep no ships in commission on the Lakes save what might be necessary for the occasional transportation of troops. Castlereagh wanted to know if Adams had instructions or power to conclude anything on the subject, and the latter had to admit not only that he had no such authority but also that the instructions which he was expecting might not give it to him. He was probably thinking of the discouraging effect of his adverse reports. It must have been obvious to him that the negotiation could begin in Washington long before he could enter upon it in London, and he readily assented to Castlereagh's suggestion that Bagot should be directed to undertake the business. Meanwhile, to anticipate the result and to smooth the path for its accomplishment, the two men entered into an unwritten agreement that

45. *Memoirs of John Quincy Adams*, III, 285–286.
46. *The Writings of John Quincy Adams*, V, 496.
47. To Monroe on March 30, *ibid.*, p. 555.

neither government would commence new armaments on the Lakes.[48]

Monroe was determined to press for an agreement though Adams had said it was impossible; and he broached the subject to Bagot on May 2, 1816. Both men were still ignorant of the favorable response in London, and Bagot apparently did not even know that the proposal had been made. Monroe professed to be moved solely by a "desire to remove every point of collision between the two countries, of which he conceived this to be the most prominent." Bagot's reply added to the cold water that Adams had thrown. He said he was "totally unprepared to speak," having no instructions on the matter and no knowledge of how his government would regard it. Nevertheless he observed that the American Secretary of State seemed to have overlooked the fact that, by such an agreement, Britain would surrender to the United States the potential control of the Lakes in the event of war. Monroe appeared to admit it, according to the Englishman's report of the conversation, and suggested that both parties might be allowed to lay down the keels of ships and take other precautionary measures to preserve the balance of power on these waters. Bagot also confided to Castlereagh that Monroe's anxiety, coupled with the cessation of American building, "seems to confirm the opinion of the inability of this government to continue at present the expense of these equipments."[49]

The suspicion that the United States was trying to steal a march on Britain was natural, but it was brushed aside in London, and it is not difficult to see why. If Washington could pay for defense on the high seas, it could afford, if necessary, to match Britain on the Lakes, to which no ships of her great navy could ascend,[50] and the strategic importance of these waters was such that American public opinion would not long tolerate British superiority there even in peacetime, for Britain would then be able to strike a deadly blow whenever she willed. In short, the dice were loaded against Britain on the Lakes, where American equality in peace meant potential American superiority in war. The conclusion is obvious. By attempting to establish a lead on these inland seas, the British government had entered upon an expensive, a dangerous, and, what was most important of all, a losing game. Why keep any fighting forces on the Lakes? They would be of no use there or anywhere else. In

48. *Memoirs of John Quincy Adams*, III, 329. *The Writings of John Quincy Adams*, VI, 17. The above formula of the gentleman's agreement is that reported by Adams. Castlereagh put it differently when reporting it to Bagot. He mentioned only a British engagement to "keep in commission the smallest number of vessels that was compatible with the ordinary routine of a peace establishment." No. 7, April 23, 1816, *F.O.* 5, Vol. CXIII.

49. Bagot to Castlereagh, No. 8, May 3, 1816, *ibid.*, Vol. CXIV.

50. The later building of the shallow Rideau Canal from Ottawa to Kingston was obviously no solution. Its purpose was military rather than naval.

accepting the principle propounded by Washington, London bowed to the inevitable. There was only one effective way to protect Canada on the Lakes, and that was not by British arms but by American good will.

On April 23, 1816, just a fortnight after Castlereagh found from Adams that it would be more expeditious to treat in Washington, the former wrote to Bagot informing him of what had taken place in London and instructing him to confer with Monroe upon the subject. Bagot was to accept *"ad referendum* any precise proposition" which the American Secretary of State might advance for a permanent regulation, but Castlereagh suggested that it might be "an easier course for both" governments "to act in the spirit of confidence and of abstaining from exertion in that quarter than to reduce their system to positive stipulations." Lest this suggestion be construed as a preference, he added that there was no disinclination to negotiate for a definite and permanent agreement. Though this dispatch gave Bagot no power to conclude anything, it implied a possible extension of the informal understanding reached in London: for he was told to keep in touch with "His Majesty's servants in Canada," who would be instructed "to frame their measures" according to any information he might supply regarding American intentions.[51]

Early in July,[52] in Bagot's first interview on the subject with Monroe, the latter discouraged Castlereagh's suggestion that they could achieve the desired end without a formal agreement. There had been too much irritating friction on the Lakes for the American government to be satisfied with such an arrangement. Here it is interesting to note another American preference. Bagot was in no hurry to negotiate for disarmament on the Lakes, now covered by the informal understanding that both governments would refrain from new activity there. He proposed to deal first with the fisheries, which had simultaneously been referred to him. But the President was impatient at this prospect of delay, insisting that the more urgent question was that of the naval forces.[53] Thereupon the British minister and the American Secretary of State proceeded and by the end of the month, after further conversation and the private submission of a draft of a note from Monroe to Bagot, the two men agreed on what they should do. The Englishman was to address the American in a formal note expressing the Prince Regent's disposition to act on the principle advanced by the United States government, the American would reply stating the precise views of the President, and the Englishman would undertake to submit these views to his government,

51. Castlereagh to Bagot, No. 7, April 23, 1816, *ibid.*, Vol. CXIII.

52. Bagot received the above dispatch on July 3. Bagot to Castlereagh, No. 23, July 6, 1816, *ibid.*, Vol. CXIV.

53. Callahan, *op. cit.*, p. 73. Madison may have had an ulterior motive for postponing the fisheries question.

at the same time offering to enter "a general agreement to suspend *ad interim* any further exertion upon the Lakes." These communications were duly written on July 26, August 2, and August 6, respectively. Monroe's note of August 2 contained the formula finally accepted: neither power to maintain more than two armed vessels on the Upper Lakes, one vessel on Lake Ontario, and the same on Lake Champlain, each vessel to be limited to one hundred tons burden and one eighteen-pound cannon; all other armed vessels on these waters to be dismantled forthwith; each naval force to be so restricted in its services as not to interfere with the other; and either party to be free to terminate the agreement after giving notice.[54]

On August 12, 1816, Monroe sent for Bagot and explained a difficulty in the way of the proposed interim agreement for the suspension of all building and equipment. That would expose him to the imputation of giving the British an advantage because the United States had "in fact" no force upon the Lakes. He therefore wished to reply to Bagot's note of the sixth by requesting his provisional acceptance of the terms set forth on the second, or, if this was impossible, that Bagot would furnish him with a statement of the British force, in return for which he would offer to confine the American force to the same standard. Bagot said he would have to refuse the first alternative but would comply with the second. Accordingly there was at once another exchange of notes and Bagot wrote to Baumgardt directing a suspension of further augmentation and requesting the promised statement. Incidentally, he reported to Castlereagh that the motive assigned by Monroe was genuine, there being not the slightest intention of increasing the American strength on the Lakes to equal that of the British. On November 4, having procured the necessary document from the British commander on the Lakes, Bagot sent it to Monroe with the assurance that there would be no addition before the home government's reaction to the American project of August 2 was known; and three days later Monroe formally completed the provisional arrangement.[55]

54. Bagot to Castlereagh, No. 24, Aug. 12, 1816, and enclosures, *F.O. 5*, Vol. CXV. The enclosures are printed in *A.S.P.F.R.*, IV, 203 *et seq.*
55. *Ibid.* Bagot to Castlereagh, No. 39, Nov. 9, 1816, and enclosures, *F.O. 5*, Vol. CXV.

Statement of His Majesty's naval force on the lakes of Canada, September 1, 1816.

ON LAKE ONTARIO

St. Lawrence, can carry 110 guns, laid up in ordinary.
Psyche,   do.   50   do.   do.
Princess Charlotte, do.   40   do.   do.
Niagara,   do.   20   do.   condemned as unfit for service.
Charwell,   do.   14   do.   hauled up in the mud; condemned likewise.
Prince Regent,   do.   60   do.   in commission, but unequipped, being merely used as a barrack or receiving ship, and the commander-in-chief's head-quarters.

Montreal, in commission, carrying 6 guns; used merely as a transport for the service of His
    Majesty.
Star, carrying 4 guns; used for current duties only, and unfit for actual service.
Netley, schooner, carrying no guns; attached for the most part to the surveyors, and con-
    veying His Majesty's servants from port to port.
There are, besides the above, some row-boats, capable of carrying long guns; two 74 gun
ships on the stocks, and one transport of four hundred tons, used for conveying His Majesty's
stores from port to port.

ON LAKE ERIE.

Tecumseh and Newark, carrying 4 guns each; and Huron and Sauk, which can carry 1 gun
    each. These vessels are used principally to convey His Majesty's servants and stores
    from port to port.

ON LAKE HURON.

The Confiance and Surprise schooners, which may carry 1 gun each, and are used for purposes
    of transport only.

ON LAKE CHAMPLAIN.

Twelve gun-boats; ten of which are laid up in ordinary, and the other two (one of which
    mounts 4 guns, and the other 3 guns) used as guard-boats. Besides the above, there
    are some small row-boats, which are laid up as unfit for service.
Keel, stem, and stern-post of a frigate laid down at the Isle aux Noix.

J. BAUMGARDT,
Captain of His Majesty's ship Prince Regent, and senior officer.
(*A.S.P.F.R.*, IV, 204–205.)

*Exhibit of the United States Naval Force on Lake Champlain shewing the Names and condition of
the respective Vessels.*

	NAMES	FORCE	CONDITION	
Ship	Confiance	32	Laid up at	White Hall
	Saratoga	22	Do	Do
Brig	Eagle	12	Do	Do
	Linnet	16	Do	Do
Scho^r	Ticonderoga	14	Do	Do
	6 Galleys (each)	2	Do	Do

*Exhibit of the United States Naval Force on Lake Ontario shewing the names of the several Vessels
their force and condition.*

	NAMES	FORCE	CONDITION	
Brig	Jones	18 guns	Retained for occasional service	
Schr.	Lady of the Lake	1	Employed in aid of the Revenue laws	
		RATE		
Ship	New Orleans	74	On the stocks building suspended	
	Chippewa	74	Do	Do
	Superior	44	Dismantled	
	Mohawk	32	Do	
	General Pike	24	Do	
	Madison	18	Do	
Brig.	Jefferson	18	Do	
	Sylph	16	Do	
	Oneida	18	Do	
Scho^r	Rewen	None	Do	Receiving Vessel
	15 Barges (each)	1	Laid up for preservation.	

*Exhibit of the United States Naval Force on Lake Erie shewing the names of the respective Vessels
their force and condition.*

	NAMES	FORCE	CONDITION
Scho^r	Porcupine	1 gun	Employed in transporting stores
	Ghent	1	Do
Ship	Detroit	18	Sunk at Erie
Brig	Lawrence	20	Do
	Queen Charlotte	19	Do
	Niaga [*sic*]	18	Dismantled at Erie.

(Enclosed in Bagot to Castlereagh, No. 39, Nov. 9, 1816, *F.O. 5*, Vol. CXV.)

London was pleased with what had been done in Washington. On September 30, a fortnight after receiving Bagot's report enclosing the American plan, Castlereagh wrote Bagot commending him warmly for the course he had pursued and informing him that final instructions would be sent as soon as possible. The permanent settlement, he observed, required "some consideration," the members of the cabinet were dispersed, and he was about to cross to his native Ireland.[56] Four months later he directed Bagot to close with Monroe's offer and to conclude the business with a formal exchange of notes.[57] The delay had no significance, and its only consequence was purely nominal. When this dispatch arrived from England, Monroe had become President and Richard Rush was acting as Secretary of State until Adams could arrive from London to assume this office, so that Rush's name was fortuitously attached to the final transaction. His only contribution was his signature. The one point that had previously to be settled was the period to be required for abrogation. Monroe then suggested either three or six months, and Bagot chose the longer term in order to reduce the British handicap of distance if a naval race on the lakes should ever begin.[58] The exchange of notes which comprised the famous Rush-Bagot agreement took place on April 28 and 29, 1817.[59] It was implemented immediately.[60]

One little hitch occurred over the status of the agreement, which was not regularized for some time. When Congress assembled toward the end of the year, Monroe in his opening speech referred to the arrangement between the two governments without, however, submitting the official notes that had been exchanged. His failure to do this surprised Bagot, who requested Adams to jog the presidential memory. Weeks passed without any apparent result and the British minister, growing somewhat uneasy, repeated his request. The Secretary of State then confirmed his suspicion "that the President had felt some difficulty in

56. Castlereagh to Bagot, No. 16, Sept. 30, 1816, *ibid.*, Vol. CXIII.

57. Castlereagh to Bagot, No. 2, Jan. 31, 1817, *ibid.*, Vol. CXX. This is endorsed as sent on February 4, and Bagot referred to it as dated February 5.

58. Bagot to Castlereagh, No. 32, May 5, 1817, *ibid.*, Vol. CXXII.

59. *A.S.P.F.R.*, IV, 204–205.

60. For the American orders, see *ibid.*, pp. 205–206. The British orders were issued by Sir Robert Hall, who had succeeded Baumgardt, without waiting for orders from the Admiralty. He accepted Bagot's communication of the agreement as sufficient authority. Bagot to Castlereagh, No. 37, June 3, 1817, enclosing Hall to Bagot, May 18, 1817, *F.O. 5*, Vol. CXXII. A few days after writing the letter just cited, Hall received from the Admiralty an order, issued in anticipation of the conclusion of the agreement, to pay off the whole of His Majesty's vessels on the lakes. Writing to Bagot on June 4, he expressed his surprise at the unnecessarily drastic nature of the order. "In place of leaving a small vessel of 100 tons on each lake," he said, "we are reduced to a boat's crew on the civil establishment." Bagot Papers, Canadian Correspondence, II, 112.

laying before the Senate a correspondence which amounted substantially to a treaty, and which therefore could not, according to the strict letter of the Constitution, have been made binding in the manner in which this had been, without their previous approbation and ratification." Bagot at once assured Adams that he had no wish to raise any embarrassing question of this kind, and, though he certainly desired the agreement to be made public in some formal mode, he would not press the point in any manner which might inconvenience the government.[61] Not until April 6, 1818, did Monroe communicate the documents to the Senate, which promptly approved; and on the twenty-eighth, a year to the day from the official British acceptance of the American offer, the agreement which had already been carried out was published by presidential proclamation.[62]

This complete mutual disarmament has been, and still is, held up in self-righteousness by Canadians and Americans as a shining light for a dark world to follow. But Canadians had nothing to do with this achievement in the beginning or for a long time afterward. Half a century passed before they inherited it, and then it would have been suicidal for them to change it. Under the strain of the Civil War, the United States did contemplate abandoning it; but there was no need to do so, because the American desire to acquire Canada by force had died in the War of 1812. Only a faint echo of the old cry was ever heard, and that only very occasionally. Canadians owe a debt of gratitude to American restraint in later years though not, perhaps, at the time of the original agreement. No special merit attaches to London for deciding to accept the proposal from Washington. As already explained, there was really no alternative. The complete break of navigation between the ocean and the Lakes reduced the naval command of the latter to a question of local building, in which the Americans were bound to have the advantage. Armaments exist elsewhere, and will exist, as a promise of gain or a guarantee against loss; but here they had no such value. This was true not only for Britain but also for the United States, because, as the Americans had pointed out at Ghent, Britain could do more damage to them on their seaboard than they could to her in the interior of the continent. Peculiar conditions rather than peculiar national virtue, American or British, were primarily responsible for producing this agreement; and those who do not analyze its origin and the reasons for its continuance can never understand the perverse course of other benighted peoples.

Economic disarmament between British North America and the

61. Bagot to Castlereagh, No. 41, May 6, 1818, *F.O. 5*, Vol. CXXXII.
62. *A.S.P.F.R.*, IV, 202, 207.

United States was, as it still is, more difficult to arrange. The question was discussed in London during the negotiation of the commercial convention of July 3, 1815, which freed intercourse between the United Kingdom and the United States from discriminating duties on goods and tonnage, and permitted American ships to trade with India under certain restrictions. The American plenipotentiaries, like their government, had hoped to gain more than this in an economic supplement to the political Treaty of Ghent. Their first project of the convention contained an article which they took with a small but important modification, from the defunct provision of Jay's Treaty. It declared that the navigation of the international waterways was "at all times" to be free to British subjects and American citizens; that they might freely carry on trade and commerce "with each other," and to this end might freely pass and repass by land as well as by water between the adjoining territories of the two powers; and that on each side there would be no national discrimination in toll, ferriage, or customs charges. The British counter-project omitted the words, "with each other," and added a clause which prevented the freedom of navigation from extending to those parts of the international waters "where the middle is not the boundary." Each of these two changes was a body blow to an American purpose. The deleted phrase had been inserted to plug a hole through which British traders might crawl to regain contact with Indians living in the United States, which the American negotiators had said would not be allowed. The additional clause raised a barrier against Americans' bringing their own produce down the Richelieu to the lower St. Lawrence or down the upper St. Lawrence to Montreal, thereby defeating a design which the same negotiators had cloaked in general language but now openly avowed. Their insinuation that the British plenipotentiaries had attempted a sharp trick evoked an immediate denial accompanied by an offer to reword the provision accordingly. Though satisfied on this point, the Americans were not satisfied on the other. Meeting with a flat refusal to open the two rivers, they threw out the whole article as useless.[63]

Intercourse across Lake Ontario and the upper St. Lawrence, where there was a great deal of smuggling, was difficult to regulate. The

63. *Ibid.*, pp. 7–18. It reappeared in a draft convention of four articles, the other three dealing with Bermuda and the West Indies, which Castlereagh gave Adams in the summer of 1817 (*ibid.*, pp. 367–368) in reply to the American minister's continued pressure for a colonial supplement to the agreement of July, 1815. Again suspicious American eyes detected an underhand move to recover the lost Indian trade, but the chief objection to the British offer, which Washington rejected offhand, was to the niggardly concessions in the other three articles. There were hopes that the American Navigation Act, when passed, would force Britain to grant much more. Bagot to Castlereagh, No. 59, Aug. 3, 1818, *F.O. 5*, Vol. CXXXIII.

government of Upper Canada applied a drastic measure in the spring of 1816, clapping heavy duties on a long list of American articles, a surcharge on imports in American vessels, and a tonnage tax on the latter, which had been admitted free.[64] But the effect was much less than desired. Smuggling became more profitable, and it was practically impossible to keep American bottoms out of Upper Canadian harbors. Sir Edward Owen's brother and successor wrote from Kingston on September 3, 1816, that vessels, men, and even the flag of the United States were daily seen employed in carrying from port to port on the British side of Lake Ontario.[65]

Trade between the Maritime Provinces and the United States did not enter into the above discussions in London. The chief interest in this traffic, apart from what was illicit, was in the export of gypsum, or plaster of Paris, from the Bay of Fundy to New England, where it was much in demand to repair a depleted soil.[66] The transportation of this article became an international question, though a very minor one, in 1816. In the spring of that year, the legislature of New Brunswick passed a law to make it a British monopoly. The act was to come into force when Nova Scotia followed suit and the home government gave its consent. The legislature of the sister province promptly obliged, tying its law to that of New Brunswick; and a proclamation issued in Fredericton on New Year's Day, 1817, put both laws into operation. The exclusion of American vessels from this particular business precipitated a diminutive trade war with the United States.

The government in Washington, with an eye chiefly on the West Indies, had long contemplated an assault upon the Old Colonial System by applying to American intercourse with British colonies restrictions corresponding to those imposed by Britain. Monroe had privately warned both Baker and Bagot, and Congress had given public warning. It is not surprising, therefore, that this pinprick by the Maritime Provinces was quickly returned. On March 3, 1817, President Madison approved a bill prohibiting the importation in foreign bottoms of plaster of Paris, "the production of any country or its dependencies, from which the vessels of the United States are not permitted to bring the same article." This act, which applied immediately, was to remain in force for five years or until the foreign ban was lifted. The retaliation struck home. The Nova Scotian law was repealed early in 1818, the New

64. This provincial order-in-council was the ground of one of Adams' complaints to Castlereagh in September, 1816. *A.S.P.F.R.*, IV, 363.

65. Bagot Papers, Canadian Correspondence, II, 80.

66. See G. S. Graham, "The Gypsum Trade of the Maritime Provinces," *Agricultural History*, XII, 209–223.

Brunswick legislation was suspended a few weeks later, and then the American ceased to operate. Meanwhile, however, the principle embodied in the last measure was given a general application in the American Navigation Act of 1818, which excluded foreign vessels coming from ports shut against the Stars and Stripes. It happened that the adoption of this policy coincided with a slight relaxation of the British system by the creation of colonial free ports, including Halifax and St. John; but Adams informed Bagot that British ships would not be admitted from thence because the entry of American bottoms was there permitted only under an order-in-council and for a limited period, not "by the ordinary laws of navigation and trade."[67] The truth of the matter is that the United States would pry open the British oyster to get the West Indian pearl rather than the meager meat of trade with the neighboring provinces. This became more evident later in 1818, during the negotiation which settled the dispute over the British inshore fisheries.

67. Bagot to Castlereagh, No. 70, Sept. 2, 1818, *F.O. 5*, Vol. CXXXIII. See also Bagot Papers, Canadian Correspondence, I, 115.

CHAPTER XVII

THE ESTABLISHMENT OF PEACE:
THE CONVENTION OF 1818

THE fisheries question, which had raised its head at Ghent, thrust itself forward in the spring of 1815, when American fishermen rushed back to their old haunts. On May 6, Baker reported from Washington that a Salem vessel had been ordered away from the coast of Nova Scotia and had returned to port without a cargo. "This is the first instance of the kind which has occurred; the subject has never been mentioned in any conversations which I have had with Mr. Monroe," wrote the *chargé*.[1] Not until more than two months later did the Secretary of State break this silence, though meanwhile other Americans were driven away from British shores; and when he at last complained he displayed a surprising restraint.

The British government was also curiously silent, after having served notice on the United States at Ghent. This attempt to enforce the exclusive claim to the inshore fisheries was initiated without any direction from London. Rear Admiral Edward Griffith, the commander-in-chief on the Halifax station, did it on his own authority Seeing the Americans pressing in, he determined to keep them out lest he give a tacit acknowledgment of their claim. He dispatched a sloop of war to Labrador and detailed another, the *Jaseur*, to cruise along the coast of Nova Scotia with orders to warn off foreign fishermen under pain of confiscation and to seize those that might be found in any port or harbor unless they had been driven in by distress. He "cautioned the captains against using violence towards any American fishing vessels, except such as are found in our harbours, whence by law all foreign vessels, are excluded." To the Admiralty, as a matter of course, he reported what he had done; and, thinking that he might get official advice from Washington earlier than from London, he wrote to Baker.[2]

Toward the end of June, in a little harbor near Shelburne, the captain of the *Jaseur* came upon nine American fishing schooners, one of which he had previously warned away and had offered to supply with water if necessary: and he detained them all. Still without any instructions, Griffith judged it advisable to release the captured craft with a warning

---

1. Baker to Castlereagh, No. 14, May 6, 1815, *F.O. 5*, Vol. CVI.

2. Griffith to Croker, July 4, 1815 (referring to an earlier letter of June 16), and Griffith to Baker, June 18, 1815, both enclosed in Baker to Castlereagh, No. 24, July 19, 1815, *ibid.*, Vol. CVII.

endorsed on each register. The skippers were also told that, though they might not have known it, the war had canceled their privileges on British coasts and they would certainly suffer confiscation if they were again caught fishing in these waters.[3] This incident, or another like it, might have roused Washington if the rear admiral had not already done it by assuming an exclusive authority on the high seas.

American fishermen were not to come within sixty miles of the British coast, according to Griffith, and a few days before the above seizure the master of a Barnstable vessel had an endorsement to this effect written on his license by the captain of the *Jaseur* some forty-five miles off Cape Sable. The poor fellow returned home without his fare and complained to the Barnstable customs collector, whose report precipitated the diplomatic discussion of the fisheries. Monroe's initial protest to Baker was verbal and it raised the general question, the Secretary of State insisting that the interruption of American fishing off British shores was a violation of rights still in force and the British *chargé* replying with an argument to prove that it was not. But when Monroe put his protest on paper he surprised Baker by avoiding this issue and by challenging only the warning to keep sixty miles away from the coast, which he presumed was not authorized by the British government.[4] Baker received this note right after the appeal from Griffith, to whom he wrote immediately. He confirmed the rear admiral's belief that the war had annulled American fishing privileges within British territorial waters; but he pointed out that these, in the absence of any particular stipulation, extended only one marine league from the coast and that Americans had an indisputable right to fish on the high seas beyond British jurisdiction. Enclosing Monroe's note, he asked for information explaining the sixty-mile limit, if it had been actually prescribed in orders to the *Jaseur*. Until he got an answer he would not reply to the Secretary of State. Six weeks later Baker was able to assure Monroe that the offending order had been "totally unauthorized by His Majesty's Government," and that steps had been taken by the proper authorities to prevent any further interruption of American fishing on the high seas.[5]

Griffith had blundered. The excuse he offered was that the Americans, who swarmed around the coast, were ruining the inshore fisheries by throwing their offal overboard and thereby drawing the fish out into

3. Lock to Griffith, June 28, 1815, and Griffith to Croker, July 4, 1815, both enclosed in Baker to Castlereagh, No. 24, July 19, 1815, *ibid.*

4. *A.S.P.F.R.*, IV, 348–349.

5. Baker to Griffith, July 19, 1815, enclosed in Baker to Castlereagh, No. 24, July 19, 1815, *F.O.* 5, Vol. CVII. *A.S.P.F.R.*, IV, 349.

deeper waters, that the twenty-league limit was necessary to protect the fishermen of Nova Scotia, and that he had considered it legal. With complete irrelevance, he said he got the twenty leagues from the treaty of 1783, which gave the United States, with certain exceptions, all the islands within that distance of her shores. As supporting evidence for the legality of his order, he cited the treaties of 1713 and 1763, by which French fishermen could not approach within fifteen leagues of Cape Breton or thirty leagues of the rest of Nova Scotia. His crowning argument was that the war had canceled, as purely conventional, all American rights to participate in the British fisheries, "even on the Banks of Newfoundland, which extending to 50 leagues from the land must be considered on the *high seas.*" However, his future conduct would be governed by the instructions issued to the cruisers on the Newfoundland station, from whose commander, Sir Richard Keats, he had recently received a copy.[6]

London had somewhat tardily sent directions, and these instructions were the first result. They forbade any interference whatsoever with Americans on the high seas, because there they had a permanent right which Britain had simply recognized in 1783. What the Americans had forfeited by the war and failed to recover by the peace, said the instructions, was the privilege which Britain had granted of fishing within British jurisdiction and of using certain British shores. Therefore they were to be excluded from British territory and from "bays, harbours, creeks, and inlets of all H.M. possessions," but not immediately. As American fishermen might have invaded these waters and shores, and might yet do so, believing that they still enjoyed the privilege, they were not to be driven off or molested *"during the present year,"*[7] unless, by attempting to engage in smuggling, they rendered themselves unworthy of the indulgence which the Prince Regent was thus willing to extend to the citizens of the United States. But they were to be distinctly told that they were not to expect it "in any future season."[8]

Both the British and the American governments seem to have felt some embarrassment in approaching the issue, as if each side recognized the strength of the other's contention. Monroe talked but did not write to Baker on the general question, and, according to the latter's report of their conversation, made no attempt to reply to the British argument. More striking is the hesitation of the authorities in London. They left

6. Griffith to Baker, Aug. 10, 1815, enclosed in Baker to Castlereagh, No. 33, Sept. 15, 1815, *F.O. 5*, Vol. CVII.

7. Italics in original.

8. Bathurst to Keats, June 17, 1815 (two dispatches), *Q*, CXXXVIII, 112, 115. General Orders, July 24, 1815, enclosed in Baker to Castlereagh, No. 33, Sept. 15, 1815, *F.O. 5*, Vol. CVII.

the commanders on the Halifax and Newfoundland stations to face the difficult and important problem without any guidance until late in the season, and then directed them to refrain from enforcing British rights during the remainder of that year. Neither side, however, was aware of the reluctance of the other until the issue was formally joined in London.

John Quincy Adams was an American Daniel. It was notorious that he was not afraid to enter the lions' den; and three days after Monroe sent his limited protest to Baker, the Secretary of State wrote to the minister in London, telling him what had happened and calling upon him to make a bold stand against the threatened exclusion of Americans from the inshore fisheries. Already the doughtiest champion of this cause, Adams obeyed with gusto. In September, 1815, with voice and pen, he subjected Bathurst[9] to a long and strong exposition of the American doctrine, which he reinforced with extralegal considerations. He made a humanitarian appeal against taking away the only means of subsistence which people had possessed for ages. He observed that Britain would suffer economically. By depriving New Englanders of their traditional livelihood, she would drive them into industry and at the same time would cut off the means of paying for British manufactures. He also hinted at the possibility of force being met by force,[10] remarking that it was not for him to say whether, or for how long, Americans would tamely submit to the loss of what they held to be an unquestionable right.[11]

Bathurst was firm but conciliatory. At the very outset he disavowed the warning given by the *Jaseur* to the Barnstable vessel, of which he had just heard from Baker; and he assured Adams that Britain had "by no means" any intention of interrupting American fishing "anywhere in the open sea, or without the territorial jurisdiction, a marine league from the shore." Within this limit, however, he insisted that Americans had now no claim whatsoever. In developing his argument to prove it, he made good use of the distinction, neglected during the discussions at Ghent, which the treaty of 1783 had carefully drawn between *right* and *liberty*. It will be recalled that the American plenipotentiaries had then succeeded in applying the former label only to fishing on the high seas and had been obliged to substitute the latter for what their countrymen might do within British territorial waters.[12] Here was the fatal flaw in the American case, and the Englishman made it quite clear that his government would not yield on the question of principle. This firmness

9. Who was again acting for Castlereagh during the latter's absence.
10. Compare his father's lusty shout of a generation previously, *supra*, pp. 49-52.
11. *A.S.P.F.R.*, IV, 349-354.
12. *Supra*, p. 51.

was right. No government will accept an international servitude that can be avoided, as Americans had already discovered.[13] Britain, however, had no desire to stir up unnecessary trouble by playing the dog in the manger. As evidence of her liberal disposition, Bathurst cited the indulgence granted for the rest of the season, and he offered to negotiate for a new arrangement which would reconcile British and American interests. The old arrangement, he explained, was impossible. It had allowed Americans to preëmpt the best fishing, drying, and curing grounds, to the exclusion of British fishermen from across the Atlantic, with the result that there had been many disputes which sometimes led to violence; and it had encouraged smuggling into the British provinces. A simple renewal of the expired liberty would produce discord rather than harmony between the two powers. Some modifications were necessary, and Bathurst invited the United States government to coöperate in devising them.[14]

This British proposal to compromise was the basis of the convention signed three years later, and it is interesting to inquire why it was made and why it was accepted. According to the man who announced it, His Majesty's ministers were strongly moved by a genuine concern for the interests of the United States and of her fishermen, whose existence for generations had depended on access to these inshore fisheries.[15] There was some truth in this—about as much as there would have been in a similar American profession. But it was not the whole truth. The alternative policy, that of rigid exclusion, was out of the question for certain obvious reasons. It could not have been implemented without a large naval force patrolling extensive shores throughout the fishing season, and the great expense of maintaining this force would be only a small part of the probable cost. What would happen to British manufactures in the American market was likewise of little consequence compared with the grave risk of provoking another war with the United States, this time with maritime New England acting as the propelling force instead of the brake. And what would have been the fate of Canada? But there were limits to what the government in London would yield. The concession should not allow Americans to oust British fishermen nor permit foreigners to break into the Old Colonial System.

As common sense thus dictated the British offer, so also did it dictate the American acceptance. Many Americans thought their government's claim was bad, and anyone could see that the only way to make it good

13. In the application of Jay's Treaty.
14. *A.S.P.F.R.*, IV, 350–351, 354–356.
15. *Ibid.*, p. 356.

was to fight and win another war against Britain.[16] The country had been too glad to escape from a war dominated by sectional interests to relish another such struggle, though it might be necessary if Britain refused to compromise. Moreover the United States would have been stultified by fighting on opposite sides of a single issue. How was it possible to insist on an American right to inshore British fisheries without admitting the British right to navigate the Mississippi? In short, the servitude imposed in 1783 could be neither wholly restored nor wholly rejected. The logical conclusion was the negotiation of a new agreement.

The negotiation hung fire for a considerable time. Adams and his government were willing to discuss practical remedies for "abuses," but they clung to their principle, which the minister again expounded in a long note to the British government.[17] Castlereagh made no attempt to refute it. He was impatient of prolonging a futile controversy. He would terminate it by requiring a renunciation of all claim to the old liberty as the price for the concession of a new and more restricted one. Not until the spring of 1816 was he prepared to make a definite offer, for he and his colleagues were distracted by "the press of parliamentary business" and they wanted to get the advice of Keats. Then Castlereagh sounded Adams, and, finding him unreceptive, he referred the business to Bagot, whom he empowered to offer three alternatives in succession. The transfer of this negotiation, which coincided with that of disarmament on the Lakes, was likewise accompanied by the delegation of authority to restrain naval action. As soon as the minister reached an agreement, he was to notify the commanding officers, who would conform; or, pending discussions, he could give them such instructions as he deemed expedient.[18]

Before Admiral Griffith received advice to hold his hand for another season, he again ordered the exclusion of foreign fishermen from the harbors of Nova Scotia, and there was another batch of seizures. He was moved, he said, by repeated complaints of Nova Scotian fisherfolk. The Americans were coming in to take bait, to get wood and water, and to refresh their crews, that they might continue to fish throughout

16. Because of the nature of international law. See *supra*, p. 211.

17. On January 22, 1816. *A.S.P.F.R.*, IV, 356–359. On February 27, Monroe authorized Adams to treat for a convention which would satisfy the British complaints without sacrificing the American claim. The latter was to be preserved intact "either by the reservation of mutual rights, or making the instrument a remedy for abuses." *Ibid.*, pp. 360–361.

18. Castlereagh to Bagot, No. 8, April 24, 1816, enclosing Melville to Castlereagh, April 8, 1816, *F.O.* 5, Vol. CXIII. This dispatch from Castlereagh, like all the other out dispatches in this series, has been preserved only in the draft form. This there appears as No. 7, April 16. According to the endorsement, the correct date is the twenty-fourth. The dispatch on disarmament is No. 7, and is dated the twenty-third.

the season without returning to their home ports. Their crews "so completely overawed the inhabitants of the coast, forcing those of the smaller harbors to assist in setting their nets, and report says even going to the length of breaking open houses . . . that at Shelburne the people did not consider themselves safe, whilst these people remained in harbor, without the protection of a war vessel." The seizures occurred while he was off in Bermuda, and the captain who made them sent one of the detained vessels to Halifax for a test case. But he soon released them all with a warning, because the provincial attorney general was not sure of the law on the point. When the admiral returned, he decided to renew his rigid order.[19] Then came the contrary advice from Washington.

Bagot's conferences on the subject with Monroe began on July 5, 1816, only two days after the receipt of Castlereagh's dispatch, and they dragged on for months. At their commencement, the British minister informed the American Secretary of State of the order to carry out the warning of the previous year, but he undertook to suspend its operation during the discussions.[20] By thus extending the indulgence allowed to American fishermen, he displayed the conciliatory disposition of Britain. This may have contributed to a more amicable settlement in the end, but it did not expedite the negotiation.

The first alternative, which Bagot presented at the opening interview, was the use, for fishing, drying, and curing, of the gulf shore of Labrador from Mount Joly, opposite the eastern end of Anticosti, to the Esquimaux Islands, at the western entrance to the Strait of Belle Isle. On the following day he received a note from Monroe saying that, being unable to obtain in Washington any circumstantial information about that coast, he would have to write to the Secretary of the Navy, then in Salem, asking him to make the necessary inquiries. Seven weeks passed, during which men were sent to examine the shores in question; and on August 10 Monroe told Bagot that these would not afford the accommodation that was necessary.[21] He intimated that his government wished an allotment either on the Labrador coast outside the strait, or along New Brunswick in the neighborhood of the Bay of Chaleur, or upon the Magdalen Islands. Bagot discouraged all three suggestions. He said that he knew of insuperable objections to the first,[22] that he believed they would hold against the second, and that the third would be difficult because the Magdalen Islands were private property.[23]

19. Griffith to Bagot, June 20, 1816, Bagot Papers, Canadian Correspondence, II, 10.
20. *A.S.P.F.R.*, IV, 361.
21. Keats admitted that the harbors on that coast were not good. Melville to Castlereagh, April 8, 1816, enclosed in Castlereagh to Bagot, No. 8, April 24, 1816, *F.O. 5*, Vol. CXIII.
22. Keats had been very decided on this point. *Ibid.*
23. Bagot to Castlereagh, No. 2, Jan. 7, 1817, *ibid.*, Vol. CXXI.

The second alternative, which the minister at once offered, was the use, for the same purposes, of the southern shore of Newfoundland from Cape Ray to the Rameau Islands, where Americans had not been allowed to dry or cure since the Revolution. Again Monroe pleaded for time in which to have a local survey made. Not until the latter part of November was he ready to give even a tentative answer. He then informed Bagot that he was doubtful if either proposition would be worth accepting, but he would have to consult the New England delegation to Congress who would appear within ten days after the opening of the session. A fortnight or so after the legislature convened, he informed Bagot that his doubt had been confirmed, and on December 30 he sent him a formal note rejecting both propositions as inadequate.[24]

The third alternative, submitted by Bagot on the following day, was the use of the two shores, which Monroe likewise declined a week later. He said that American vessels did not, and were not likely to, frequent these shores.[25] As Bagot had exhausted his power to negotiate, he could pursue the subject no further without new instructions from home.

Though the six months' discussion which thus ended on January 7, 1817, had not brought the two governments to an agreement, it had brought them a long way toward one. Monroe had concurred in the sentiment expressed by Bagot that it was desirable to avoid controversy over respective rights and to proceed in a spirit of conciliation. In this spirit the British offers had been presented, received, and examined. In this spirit the discussion closed. When Monroe wished to make a definite counterproposal in December and again at the beginning of the new year, Bagot had felt obliged to dissuade him; but the American took this refusal with a good grace, and in his concluding note of January 7 he invited further offers and promised meanwhile to make further investigations. The negotiation was not terminated. It was only halted.

The next step had to be taken by Britain, and it was not long delayed. Instead of preparing another British proposition, which might have taken some time, Castlereagh directed Bagot, on March 22, 1817, to procure the American proposition which Monroe had desired to make and believed would satisfy Britain as well as the United States. Castlereagh also told Bagot that the navy was at last to enforce the exclusion of American fishermen from British territorial jurisdiction in America, and he suggested that the government of the United States should be informed of this fact.[26]

24. *Ibid.*, and Monroe to Bagot, Dec. 30, 1816, enclosed in *ibid*.

25. Bagot to Monroe, Dec. 31, 1816, and Monroe to Bagot, Jan. 7, 1817, both enclosed in *ibid.*

26. Castlereagh to Bagot, No. 5, March 22, 1817, *ibid.*, Vol. CXX.

The British government was clearly in a quandary. As long as the indulgence continued, it was to the interest of the Americans to avoid an agreement, because the latter would give them less than what they got under the former. But a withdrawal of the indulgence might also defeat the negotiation, because the ensuing friction might make any agreement impossible. For the moment, it seemed that this risk was unavoidable and might be reduced to a minimum by a diplomatic word spoken in Washington. In a few weeks, however, London reverted to the more cautious policy. On April 21, pleading the possibility of a satisfactory arrangement within a few months, Adams strongly urged a further suspension of the disturbing orders; and on May 7 Castlereagh replied that instructions to this effect would be sent across the Atlantic.[27] On the thirteenth, he sent Bagot copies of these instructions and told him to endeavor to extract from the American government, as soon as possible, such reasonable terms as he thought might be approved in London.[28]

Domestic political considerations blocked the communication of the American proposal for which Bagot asked, directly he received Castlereagh's dispatch of March 22, 1817. A fortnight after he applied to Rush, the acting Secretary of State, the British minister learned with some surprise that President Monroe wished to gather further information on the subject and would probably not be able to shape a proposition until after his return from a tour he was about to make in the north of the country which would occupy at least three months. Though Bagot realized that there was therefore little prospect of any arrangement's being made before the close of yet another fishing season, he appreciated the cause of the delay and he reported it to London. The President was eager to heal the breach that the war had opened in the Union, and the surest way to court sullen New England was to consult its wishes on the fisheries question, which concerned that part of the United States solely and vitally.[29] Bagot's report must have allayed the natural impatience of London at this repeated procrastination by Washington.

Twenty American fishing vessels, found under very suspicious circumstances on the shores of Nova Scotia, were seized and sent to Halifax for adjudication early in June, 1817. From Sir David Milne, recently appointed naval commander-in-chief in North America, Bagot received a detailed report at the end of the month. The minister was not at all perturbed. Writing home on the following day, he observed that the two years' warnings to American vessels, his own statement to the

27. *A.S.P.F.R.*, IV, 368.
28. Castlereagh to Bagot, No. 8, May 13, 1817, *F.O. 5*, Vol. CXX.
29. Bagot to Castlereagh, No. 40, June 3, 1817, *ibid.*, Vol. CXXII.

American government that the rejection of the British offers ended the suspension of the British naval orders, and the notice he had since served on Rush, as suggested by the instructions of March, would furnish so obvious and complete an answer that he doubted if any remonstrance would be made. He was inclined to think that the news of the captures, which might reach Monroe in Boston, would have a beneficial effect.[30] He did receive a formal complaint, but not for some weeks and then it was rather perfunctory. This was about the beginning of August, when he waited upon Rush to communicate the contents of Castlereagh's dispatch of May 13. The acting Secretary of State then protested against the detention of American fishermen who, he contended, had been driven in by stress of weather. Bagot promptly told him that the facts had been misrepresented and "would at all times warrant a similar measure." Rush replied that it would nevertheless be necessary for him to address an official note on the matter.[31] This he did on the fourth, and Bagot answered it on the eighth, enclosing a document which gave circumstantial details. It was the report of the captain who had made the seizures.[32] On the twenty-ninth the judge of the vice-admiralty court at Halifax came to the rescue of the unfortunate Americans. In a decree containing a curious assortment of reasons and suggesting a strong personal desire to close this international incident, he ordered the restoration of the vessels on payment of costs.[33]

Monroe's trip in the summer of 1817 was of more than national significance. Traveling along the border of the United States as far as Detroit, he was gratified to learn at first hand that all symptoms of irritation had disappeared from each side of the frontier, and he pointedly said so to Bagot as soon as they met again in Washington on September 20. He also remarked "how sensibly he had felt, as indicatory of this state of things, the personal civilities which had been offered to him upon every occasion by His Majesty's officers and subjects."[34] One instance may sufficiently illustrate this pleasing attention. The British

30. Bagot to Castlereagh, No. 47, June 30, 1817, *ibid.*

31. Bagot to Castlereagh, No. 51, Aug. 8, 1817, *ibid.*

32. Enclosed in the dispatch just cited and printed in *A.S.P.F.R.*, IV, 369–370.

33. *Acadian Recorder*, Sept. 6, 1817. It was copied in the American newspapers. Bagot to Castlereagh, No. 62, Oct. 6, 1817, *F.O. 5*, Vol. CXXIII.

The judgment astonished Milne who, at the request of Lord Dalhousie, the governor, had attended a meeting of the council of Nova Scotia, where the judge was present, and produced all the pertinent documents in his (Milne's) possession, including his instructions from London and his correspondence with Bagot. Milne to Bagot, March 2, 1818, enclosed in Bagot to Castlereagh, No. 29, April 7, 1818, *ibid.*, Vol. CXXXI. The captors apparently initiated appeal proceedings but subsequently dropped them, allowing the time limit for an appeal to expire during the negotiation of the convention of October 20, 1818. *A.S.P.F.R.*, IV, 399.

34. Bagot to Castlereagh, No. 59, Oct. 6, 1817, *F.O. 5*, Vol. CXXIII.

commander at Niagara, who might have ignored the distinguished presence across the river, sent an officer with a letter in which he said he would pay his personal respects if the President would "condescend" to let him, and he undertook to accord him the honors due to his "exalted situation" if he wished to visit the Canadian shore. Incidentally, Monroe did not cross the river; he stayed only three quarters of an hour at Niagara and was already embarked to continue his journey when he received this letter.[35]

For all his friendliness, which was genuine, Monroe still withheld his formula for the fisheries. He departed for his home in Virginia on September 22, only five days after returning from this tour, and during his short stay in the capital he told Adams, who arrived on the twentieth to take over from Rush, that he had gathered all the information he required and would have the proposition ready when he came back from Virginia about the end of October. But no proposal was then forthcoming, and during the months that followed Adams put Bagot off with various excuses. At one time his plea was the need for further information; at another, it was a difference of opinion among those who were most interested in the business; and at yet another, it was the failure of Castlereagh to furnish a promised report on the "real injuries and inconveniences" caused by American fishermen. The minister supplied what he judged to be the wanted document, a letter from the Shelburne customs collector which had been forwarded from London in 1816; but the communication produced no apparent effect.[36]

The intervention of the intractable Adams, reinforced by the judgment of the vice-admiralty court in Halifax and the renewal of the British indulgence, seems to have held up the negotiation. In the spring of 1818, Adams gave Bagot to understand that it had been found impossible to make any proposal based, as had been intended, on the assignment of any particular coast, because the small fish used as bait, without which the cod fishery could not be pursued, migrated constantly and often deserted whole stretches of coast for years.[37] At the same time the American let slip a more significant remark which the Englishman did not report home, perhaps because of its inflammatory nature. Adams recorded it in his diary as follows: "I was afraid we should have to fight for this matter in the end, and I was so confident of our right, I was for it."[38] He was probably inspired by what Bagot had told him at the be-

35. Grant to Bagot, Aug. 15, 1817, enclosing Grant to Monroe, Aug. 5, 1817, both enclosed in Bagot to Castlereagh, No. 57, Sept. 1, 1817, *ibid.*

36. Bagot to Castlereagh, No. 29, April 7, 1818, *ibid.*, Vol. CXXXI.

37. *Ibid.*

38. March 18, *Memoirs of John Quincy Adams*, IV, 61. This was the course that Adams favored.

ginning of the conversation: that according to a letter he had just received from Milne all foreign vessels found fishing on the coasts of British North America during the season just opening would be seized and brought into port for adjudication. The New Englander meant what he said. Two months later, he repeated it to the same ears, again using the little fishes as an introduction. "For my own part," runs his entry of the words he used on this occasion, "I had always been averse to any proposal of accommodation. I thought our whole right, as stipulated by the Treaty of 1783, so clear that I was for maintaining the whole, and if force should be applied to prevent our fishermen from frequenting the coast, I would have protested against it, and reserved the right of recovering the whole by force whenever we should be able." He admitted, however, that it had been determined otherwise. Monroe had prevailed over Adams. The American government would keep the promise it had given. What the proposal would be, Adams did not yet know. "Perhaps," he told Bagot, "we should ultimately offer to give up the right of drying and curing on the shore, and reserve the whole right of fishing."[39] Adams was mistaken in this forecast and when the negotiation was finally resumed, it had passed out of his hands. But even then he instructed the American plenipotentiaries that "not a particle of these rights will be finally yielded by the United States without a struggle, which will cost Great Britain more than the worth of the prize."[40]

Meanwhile the naval orders to exclude American fishermen were again put into operation, but only a few vessels were caught before the arrival of another suspension which the vacillating home government sent on May 26.[41] One of the captured craft escaped from Halifax; Milne released several without trial; and the vice-admiralty court again confounded the captors. It found some guilty of having violated the laws of trade and navigation, but did not condemn them for fishing in prohibited waters.[42]

The inshore fisheries question was to be settled not by itself nor in Washington but in London and along with other questions. In only one of these was British North America really concerned, and that most vitally. It was the national possession of the territory lying between the Lake of the Woods and the Pacific Ocean.

The fate of Astoria, half-forgotten at Ghent and attracting little attention from either government for some time afterwards, was be-

39. May 15, *ibid.*, pp. 96–97.
40. *A.S.P.F.R.*, IV, 378.
41. Castlereagh to Bagot, No. 12, June 9, 1818, *F.O. 5*, Vol. CXXIX.
42. Bagot to Castlereagh, No. 58, July 24, 1818, *ibid.*, Vol. CXXXII; and No. 81, Nov. 2, 1818, *ibid.*

coming a pressing problem; and it suggested the advisability of ending the uncertainty over the international boundary in the West before other disputes arose out of it to make an agreement more difficult. In July, 1815, Monroe informed Baker that, under the treaty provision for the restoration of places taken during the war, the United States would reoccupy the post on the Columbia River "without delay," and he asked for a letter to the British commander there to facilitate the restitution. The *chargé* replied that he could give no instruction of this kind, having himself received no communication from His Majesty's government on the subject. He added that he was doubtful if anyone was there, for he was under the impression that when the establishment was captured it had been broken up and that the site was deserted; but for more definite information he referred him to Vice-Admiral Dixon on the Brazil station, which included the Pacific.[43] To prepare this officer for an appeal from Monroe, Baker at once sent him copies of the latter's request and his own refusal, and in his covering letter he observed that the claim of the United States rested solely on the words of the treaty and that Great Britain had never recognized an American title to any possession on that coast. In conversation with Monroe, he had said much the same thing.[44] For his own information, Baker also wrote to Quebec, where Sir Gordon Drummond procured for him a long statement from the North West Company, explaining the British claim to the Pacific coast and how Astor's establishment had been acquired by purchase instead of conquest. It came from William McGillivray, the principal director, but it was largely, if not wholly, the work of his brother Simon, who usually resided in England and had been chiefly responsible for the company's adventures to the Columbia River. He said Bathurst had recently told him that His Majesty's title to that coast was "clear and uncontrovertible." Simon McGillivray later saw Baker in Washington and tried in vain to draw him out upon the subject.[45]

Over in London, at the very time when Baker replied to Monroe, agents of the North West Company applied to the Colonial Office for

43. *A.S.P.F.R.*, IV, 852. The determination to reoccupy the post on the Columbia "seems to have been taken partly at the instance of Mr. Astor, who was anxious, if possible, to recommence operations on his former plan in North-West America," according to Robert Greenhow, *The History of Oregon and California*, quoted in K. W. Porter, *John Jacob Astor*, p. 240. Three weeks after informing Baker of this determination, Monroe wrote Astor for more definite information. Astor's reply (*ibid.*, pp. 583–585) indicates that he too was not well posted on what was then the situation at the mouth of the Columbia. This letter, moreover, does not reflect the anxiety mentioned above. He "seems by the end of 1816 to have given up his intention of renewing his establishment on the North West Coast."

44. Baker to Castlereagh, No. 26, Aug. 13, 1815, enclosing Baker to Dixon, July 24, 1815, *F.O. 5*, Vol. CVII.

45. See *supra*, p. 365, n. 57.

protection on the Columbia, whither £150,000 worth of goods had been sent for the Indian trade, where it was proposed to develop a settlement, and whence furs were to be shipped to the China market. Without some assurance from the government, they were afraid of being forced either to combine their interests with American merchants or to abandon them entirely, for their goods might be seized on the plea that British subjects had no right to traffic with Indians on the soil of the United States, "now said to extend to the shores of the Pacific." Receiving from Goulburn a noncommittal answer, carelessly or cunningly based on the assumption that they asked for Bathurst's opinions on a commercial speculation, the petitioners reframed their question in unequivocal words: "Whether we may rely upon the protection of His Majesty's Government in carrying on a legal trade as British subjects, within what we have always considered British territory from the mouth of the Columbia to the Russian settlements on the coast of the Pacific and from the coast in the countries between the sea and the Rocky Mountains."[46] No reply to this has yet been found.

For two years after this warning in Washington and this appeal in London, the problem slumbered. During this interval, Simon McGillivray heard nothing more about it, and the company continued undisturbed in the pursuit of its activities on the Pacific coast with headquarters at Fort George,[47] the old Astoria. Then an ominous rumor began to circulate in the United States.

Early in October, 1817, the *Ontario*, an American sloop of war mounting eighteen guns, sailed from New York bearing an American government agent bound for Peru; and it was said that she was also to proceed to the mouth of the Columbia to retake possession. Bagot passed the gossip on to Governor Sherbrooke in Quebec, that he might put the partners of the North West Company on their guard.[48] Simon McGillivray, then passing through New York on his way home from a visit to Canada, heard the rumor too and, being credibly informed that it was true, he wrote to the minister in Washington.[49] His letter made Bagot so uneasy that he at once sought a conference with the Secretary of State to inquire if the report had any foundation.

"Mr. Adams appeared to me to be considerably embarrassed by my

46. Inglis, Ellice & Co. to Goulburn, July 25, 28, and Aug. 2, 1815, *Q*, CXXXIV, 385, 388, 390.

47. This name was given by Captain Black when he arrived to capture the post only to find that it was already in British hands. Memorial of the North West Company, Dec. 23, 1817, enclosed in Bagot to Castlereagh, No. 18, Feb. 8, 1818, *F.O. 5*, Vol. CXXXI.

48. Bagot to Castlereagh, No. 65, Nov. 7, 1817, *ibid.*, Vol. CXXIII.

49. McGillivray to Bagot, Nov. 15, 1817, enclosed in Bagot to Castlereagh, No. 74, Dec. 2, 1817, *ibid.*

question," wrote Bagot after the meeting;[50] and well might the American be embarrassed, for his government had secretly sent a ship of war in time of peace to occupy a place known to be already occupied by the subjects of another power and claimed as a rightful possession by their government. After a short silence, Adams admitted that the *Ontario* had been sent to reëstablish the settlement at the mouth of the Columbia. He excused the failure to notify the British government by citing Baker as having expressed the belief that there was nobody there, and he assured the minister that no orders had been given to destroy or disturb the trade of the North West Company. But he did not say that orders had been given not to destroy or disturb this trade, and the excuse which might have passed in 1815 was no longer valid. Moreover he disputed with Bagot the title to the Pacific coast, and he asserted that Great Britain would hardly find it worth while to have any difference with the United States over such a remote territory.

The British minister was properly alarmed, and he saw an urgent necessity to checkmate the United States at the mouth of the Columbia. He thought of having Milne detach a vessel to race the *Ontario;* but, considering the time it would take for him to get into touch with the admiral and for the latter to prepare a ship for such a long voyage, and also the time the *Ontario* might lose on the Peruvian business, he concluded that the home government, to which he dashed off a ciphered dispatch, could just as well assume this responsibility. He realized, however, that it might be too late to overtake the American expedition by sea. Therefore he addressed a secret dispatch to Sherbrooke, suggesting a rapid overland communication of the startling intelligence, so that the men of the North West Company might be ready to prevent the intrusion of American settlers. He was afraid that the traders might find the settlers there and drive them off, thereby embarrassing any negotiation on the subject, if not occasioning yet more serious consequences. Meanwhile, he wrote Adams a formal note in which, after pointing out how the company had secured Astoria and had ever since retained peaceful possession of the coast and how that territory had always been regarded as British from the time it "was early taken possession of in His Majesty's name," he called for an explanation of the object of the voyage of the *Ontario.*[51] Adams left this note unanswered.

This ugly-looking affair, which suddenly arose when the British minister was becoming worried over the nonappearance of the promised

50. *Ibid.*

51. Bagot to Castlereagh (ciphered), Nov. 24, 1817, and No. 74, Dec. 2, 1817, enclosing Bagot to Adams, Nov. 26, 1817 (printed in *A.S.P.F.R.*, IV, 852), and Bagot to Sherbrooke, Dec. 1, 1817, *F.O.* 5, Vol. CXXIII.

fisheries proposal, was presently brushed aside by the two governments, for they were set on peace, and they soon came together in a memorable agreement. Bagot's report reached London on January 8, 1818, and before the month was out orders were issued to "obviate a very unpleasant collision" by anticipating the purpose of the *Ontario*. In obedience to these orders, a British sloop of war picked up an agent of the United States on the west coast of South America and carried him to the mouth of the Columbia, and there the settlement of Fort George was formally handed over to him by the captain of the sloop and a representative of the North West Company on October 6, 1818.[52] The company, however, was not disturbed in its possession of the post.

Though Bagot had argued that the restitution prescribed by the Treaty of Ghent did not include this post because of the peculiar circumstances, his government had not adopted this position. On February 4, 1818, Castlereagh wrote him that there could be no doubt of the American right to the reoccupation of the place. The Foreign Secretary, however, directed him to protest against the brusque way in which Washington had raised the issue, and to register a caveat against this question of *seizin* being interpreted as a question of ownership. The British government was not prepared to admit the validity of the American title, for it regarded the establishment of Astoria as an encroachment on British soil.

Having made this point clear, the minister was to propose a settlement, by means of commissioners, of the boundary from the Lake of the Woods all the way out to the Pacific, as the Treaty of Ghent had provided for the undetermined portions of the line from the same lake to the Atlantic. Fixing the western line would foster amicable relations between the two governments by forestalling disputes over the right of possession, said Castlereagh, and he added that it was always easier to reach such an arrangement when the territory in question was little known or cultivated than when it contained settlements. Bagot was to invite the American government to furnish Rush, who had succeeded Adams in London, with the necessary powers to sign either a supplementary treaty or additional articles to the Treaty of Ghent which would provide for a settlement of this boundary and also for the settlement of a dispute over American slaves carried off at the close of the War of 1812, Castlereagh having just accepted a proposal Rush had made for the latter purpose.[53] His object in wishing the discussion to be in London was professedly to avoid the delay of another communica-

---

52. *A.S.P.F.R.*, IV, 854–856.
53. To refer the matter to the decision of some friendly sovereign or state.

tion across the Atlantic,[54] but one may wonder if he did not privately think it better to deal with the new minister than with the old one.

Washington gladly grasped the hand held out from London. On May 6, 1818, Bagot complained that no English mail of February or March had yet reached him.[55] Three days later, he received the above instructions; and then important things began to happen rather quickly. It would be misleading to suggest that Adams suddenly fell into Bagot's arms at a.push from Monroe; for in the middle of the previous winter, when the American Secretary of State and the British minister were discussing the affairs of Latin America, the former had stated that a material influence in preventing the United States from interfering in that region was the President's fear of an unfavorable effect upon American feeling toward Britain. "He," said Adams, "had seen with peculiar satisfaction the rapid decline of that animosity which had formerly subsisted," and one of the chief objects of his administration was "to cherish and improve this state of public sentiment."[56] But this avowal did not jibe with the dispatch of the *Ontario* nor with Adams' neglect of Bagot's note on the subject. In May, however, the American received the British remonstrance "in good part." He obviously wished to wash his hands of the affair, and so did the President.[57] The reception of the British proposal suggests that it brought a sense of relief. Almost immediately the American government improved and expanded it. Why not also throw in the fisheries dispute, the question of colonial trade, the problem of what should be done with the commercial convention of July, 1815, which would expire in July, 1819, and any other point which either government might wish to add; and settle them all, or as many as possible, by one direct negotiation without further delay?[58] This was

54. Castlereagh to Bagot, No. 7, Feb. 4, 1818, *F.O.* 5, Vol. CXXIX.

55. Bagot to Castlereagh, No. 36, May 6, 1818, *ibid.*, Vol. CXXXII.

56. Bagot to Castlereagh, No. 14, Feb. 8, 1818, *ibid.*, Vol. CXXX.

57. "Mr. Adams appeared to receive what I said in good part. He stated that in fact the American Government put very little value upon the post of Astoria; that the Ontario had received her orders before he had entered upon the duties of his office; but that he could assure me, that she had been instructed not to commit any act of hostility or force whatever; and that, with regard to her having been dispatched without previous concert with me, he could take upon himself to say, that it was entirely owing to a belief, founded upon the statement formerly made by Mr. Baker, that there was no person upon the spot by whom a formal surrender could be made." This explanation does not quite accord with another which Adams gave, apparently some days later. It is reported in the same dispatch by Bagot as follows: "Mr. Adams informed me that he had been directed by the President to assure me, that the circumstance of the Ontario having been dispatched to the Columbia River without any intimation being given to me of her destination, was entirely accidental, that she had received her instructions whilst he was at New York on his tour to the northern frontier, and that, in the pressure of his business there, he had omitted to direct the proper communications to be made to me upon the subject." Bagot to Castlereagh, No. 48, June 2, 1818, *ibid.*, Vol. CXXXII.

58. *Ibid.*

what Monroe's administration wanted and at once prepared to do. Less than a fortnight after Bagot received Castlereagh's dispatch, the President commissioned Rush and Gallatin, then minister in Paris, to arrange and sign a general treaty or convention with Britain.[59]

The negotiation was to be in London, rather than Washington, to save time. The American plenipotentiaries could get to work as soon as the Prince Regent's government had consented to this larger proposal, and they were instructed to lose no time. The President wanted to have the result for submission to Congress at the opening of the next session. Time was likewise a consideration, though only one, in the substitution of negotiation for the judicial process. The demarcation of the original boundary by commissioners was proving to be so slow that it aroused criticism in the United States. It was also attacked as expensive. To draw a line in this manner "through the depth of deserts, and to an indefinite extent, would be still more liable to censure." Moreover it would be less suitable, because there had been no previous treaty definition of the line, and because London would have the same board adjudicate the dispute over slaves. The British and American commissioners would barter concessions to reach a final settlement, and such decisions should be made by the governments themselves. Finally, by adopting the judicial method, the United States might bring "British territory again in contact with the Mississippi."[60] It should also be observed that, though Adams and then Rush had been pressing in London for a solution of the war-born issues which had poisoned Anglo-American relations during the European upheaval, the American government was now willing to leave these things out of the pot lest they spoil the broth.[61]

The British cabinet welcomed the American suggestion of a general negotiation. On July 22, 1818, Rush received a note requesting him to call at the Foreign Office, which he did on the following day. Castlereagh then told him the good news and reciprocated the American eagerness to get at the business. "The sooner the better," was his comment when Rush informed him that Gallatin would come from Paris as soon as wanted. The British plenipotentiaries, he added, were already selected—Frederick Robinson,[62] the President of the Board of Trade, and Henry Goulburn. The Foreign Secretary said that he himself would have to leave in about a month to attend the Congress of Aix-la-Chapelle, but the negotiation could go on in his absence. He would

59. May 22, *A.S.P.F.R.*, IV, 372.
60. Extracts, Adams to Rush, May 21, 1818, and Adams to Gallatin, May 22, 1818, *ibid.*, pp. 370–372.
61. The instructions gave the American plenipotentiaries discretionary authority to include or omit these subjects. *Ibid.*, p. 378. See Extract, Adams to Rush, May 30, 1818, *ibid.*, p. 372.
62. Later Viscount Goderich and Earl of Ripon.

like, however, to see the discussions begin before he departed.[63] He was present at the informal beginning, when he entertained the four plenipotentiaries at his country seat, a dozen miles out of London, on August 22 and 23. "Nothing could have been more cordial than the reception given to us," Rush reported home. "The several subjects of the negotiation were talked over in general terms, and in a spirit which, we think, promises well for the friendly manner in which, at all events, it will be conducted."[64] The formal conferences opened on August 27 and closed with the signature of the convention on October 20, 1818.

So great was the British desire to accommodate the United States that the Foreign Secretary himself introduced the question of impressment at the first informal meeting,[65] and during the formal negotiation the British plenipotentiaries went very close to a substantial surrender of their country's position. The formula they offered was based on the persistent American proposal. Each power would bar its public and private marine to the native-born subjects or citizens of the other, except such as were already naturalized, of which lists, specifying places of birth and dates of naturalization, would be prepared and exchanged; there would be a mutual renunciation of impressment on the high seas "on any plea or pretext whatsoever"; and the agreement would run for ten years unless previously abrogated after six months' notice by either party.[66] Gallatin and Rush rejected it because the British refused to amend it to meet their objections. They pointed out their list would necessarily be very imperfect and therefore they could not agree to prohibit the maritime employment of all previously naturalized citizens who might be omitted. They would also extend the ban on impressment to anywhere outside the ordinary jurisdiction of either government—to foreign waters as well as to the high seas.[67] Their failure entailed the abandonment of a hopeful effort to secure a joint definition of maritime rights in time of war, into which they had been drawn at the very outset by the conciliatory gesture of the British on impressments. American policy made security for American sailors on American ships a *sine qua non* for any settlement of the rights of neutral trade.[68]

The question of colonial trade, after much discussion, was also dropped. The American navigation act, which the United States hoped

63. Extract, Rush to Adams, July 25, 1818, *ibid.*, p. 375.
64. Extract, Rush to Adams, Aug. 28, 1818, *ibid.*, p. 379.
65. *Ibid.*
66. *Ibid.*, pp. 386–387.
67. *Ibid.*, pp. 389, 393–397. On November 2, Adams wrote them raising other objections which would have been effective. *Ibid.*, pp. 399–400.
68. *Ibid.*, pp. 383, 387–388, 396–397.

would persuade Britain to see the folly of her way, missed its mark. The government in London accepted with complacency this American counterpart of the British system. Robinson and Goulburn offered to permit, on a reciprocal basis, American ships to conduct a general trade in the products of American or British dominions between the United States and the Maritime Provinces; but the only concession they would grant to American bottoms plying directly to the West Indies was so limited that the American plenipotentiaries would not accept it.[69] They shared the good old American belief that the British planters could not long prosper without free access to American sources of supplies, or, to put it differently, shared the American eagerness to break into the rich and convenient British market in the Caribbean. As for the general trade which the British were willing to allow Americans to enjoy with the Maritime Provinces, Gallatin and Rush suspected that it would allow British ships to bear to British planters American supplies which should be held back to force open the coveted market.[70] Intercourse between the United States and the Canadas was practically ignored in this negotiation.

Only the first three articles of the convention need concern us here. They dealt with Canadian-American relations. The other three did not, and therefore may be dismissed with a mere mention: the fourth renewed the commercial convention of 1815, the fifth provided for some friendly sovereign to determine the indemnity which Britain should pay for abducted slaves, and the sixth made April 20, 1819, the last day for the exchange of ratification.

Article I settled the dispute over the inshore fisheries. It stated that the inhabitants of the United States should have "forever" the liberty (1) *to fish, dry, and cure* on the southern coast of Newfoundland from Cape Ray to the Rameau Islands and on the whole coast of Labrador from Mount Joly through the Strait of Belle Isle and northward indefinitely, saving the exclusive rights of the Hudson's Bay Company, the liberty to dry and cure being limited generally to unsettled bays, harbors, and creeks of these coasts, the prior consent of "the inhabitants, proprietors, or possessors of the ground" being necessary for the exercise of this liberty in places where there was any settlement; (2) *to fish*, but not to dry or cure, on the west coast of Newfoundland from Cape Ray around through the strait to Quirpon Island, and on the shores of the Magdalen Islands; and (3) *to enter* any bays or harbors of British North America "for the purpose of shelter and of repairing damages therein, of purchasing wood, and of obtaining water, and for no other

69. Except *ad referendum.*
70. *Ibid.*, pp. 381–385, 391–392, 397.

purpose whatever," under such restrictions as might be "necessary to prevent their taking, drying, or curing fish therein," or in any other manner abusing their liberty. In return for these British concessions, though it was not so stipulated, the United States renounced "forever, any liberty hitherto enjoyed or claimed by the inhabitants thereof to take, dry, or cure fish on or within three marine miles of any of the coasts, bays, creeks, or harbors of His Britannic Majesty's dominions in America, not included within the above-mentioned limits."

The American plenipotentiaries were pleased with what they got,[71] which was more than their instructions required. These authorized them to surrender the liberty of fishing, drying, and curing within British jurisdiction generally, if they secured its perpetuation on the coasts specified in the first of the above three categories.[72] The addition of the Atlantic coast of Labrador to the rejected British offer would have contented the United States government. The initial draft of the article[73] was the work of Gallatin and Rush, who included the second and third categories because, according to papers which accompanied their instructions, these additions would be of great benefit to American fishermen. Without the right to enter Nova Scotian bays and harbors, for example, Americans might be seriously handicapped in working the fishing grounds of Nova Scotia which, unlike those of Labrador, were outside the three-mile limit.[74] Incidentally this explains the American willingness to surrender the claim to share in the inshore fisheries of that province.

It is indicative of the spirit in which the negotiation was carried on that the British did not set to work to pare the American demand to the bone, which they might have discovered by exploratory offers. They readily adopted the American draft with only a few changes. One, which the Americans accepted as of no importance, was the addition of the saving clause about the exclusive rights of the Hudson's Bay Company. With this exception, they made no alteration to the first category; and they made none to the second. From the third, they cut out bait, a valuable item which the Americans had included as one of the objects for which their countrymen might enter any British bay or harbor; to it they added another object, that of repairing damages, which the Americans had overlooked, and the final clause, "for no other purpose whatever."[75]

From all this, some may draw the conclusion that the Americans

71. *Ibid.*, p. 380.
72. *Ibid.*, p. 378.
73. *Ibid.*, p. 384.
74. *Ibid.*, p. 380.
75. *Ibid.*, pp. 390–392, 395.

overreached the British. But did not the American government make the mistake, corrected by its representatives, of fixing too low a minimum? One might as well argue that the British overreached the Americans because the latter did not get all they might have got. This is implied by the behavior of Robinson and Goulburn. They were obviously pleased that the Americans had not demanded more.[76]

The one difficult thing in the preparation of this article was the stipulation not of the geographical, but of the temporal, extent of what American fishermen were to possess. Gallatin and Rush were instructed to perpetuate the modified liberty "as a permanent right, not liable to be impaired by any war";[77] but they soon discovered that it would be "impracticable" to put this explicit declaration in the text. Therefore they fell back upon an implicit declaration. This is why the article says that Americans are to have the liberty "forever." The word appeared in the original draft submitted to the British. They strenuously fought for its elimination, but yielded when the Americans insisted that they would sign no fisheries article without it. This was one of those points in international affairs which occasion great concern at the time but none afterwards because the contemplated eventuality never materializes. The same is true of the American renunciation of the general liberty. This likewise appeared in the initial American draft and was omitted by the British when they redrew it. At first glance it might seem that the Americans were gratuitously surrendering what their government had so stoutly defended, and that the British were carelessly satisfied with a virtual admission that the American principle had been wrong. But the former took pride in having persuaded the latter to restore the clause which implied that the old liberty continued up to the moment of renunciation and that the liberty now to be possessed was not a new grant but a survival from ancient days.

Though conscious of having served their country well in securing what they did in this article, the American plenipotentiaries anticipated the possibility of criticism at home because they had not preserved all the liberty recognized in 1783. But this does not seem to have worried them much. As they observed in the dispatch transmitting the completed convention, they had gained a liberty denied in 1783, that of curing on the southern shore of Newfoundland, and they had rid their country of "an inconvenient privilege" which had been tied to the fisheries in 1783, the British bogy on the Mississippi.[78]

76. I have been unable to find how far the British government was willing to go if necessary.
77. *Ibid.*, p. 378.
78. *Ibid.*, p. 380.

Article II drew the boundary from the northwest corner of the Lake of the Woods along the meridian to the forty-ninth parallel and along this to the Rocky Mountains. This definition was taken from the abortive negotiation of 1807, when, as already explained, it was based on the doubly false belief that the forty-ninth parallel had been accepted as a boundary by Britain in a negotiation with France under the Treaty of Utrecht.[79] The legend being still unchallenged,[80] it was almost a foregone conclusion that the two delegations should come together on the line their predecessors had nearly fixed over eleven years before. It appeared in the first American and the first British drafts of the article. But the British, as might be expected, coupled it with another article guaranteeing to British subjects the free navigation of the Mississippi and free access to it "from such place as may be selected for that purpose, in His Britannic Majesty's territories," along with "their goods, wares, and merchandise" on payment of the same duties as were charged at Atlantic ports of the United States.[81] The Americans knew how to deal with this ghost. It vanished[82] when they shot an ultimatum at it. They declared that they could accept no article on the navigation of the Mississippi nor any that brought the British in contact with the river.[83]

Article III dealt with the new problem that had arisen over the mountains. It was shelved for ten years, during which, for the prevention of disputes, the country claimed by either party on the northwest coast of America up to the Rockies was to be free and open to British and Americans alike. This article, of course, allowed the North West Company to remain in the post which Astor had founded. It was not for lack of trying to get a final settlement that the negotiators agreed to postpone it. The British apparently sought to force the issue by refusing to fix the boundary east of the mountains. The Americans countered by proposing, in their initial draft of the second article, to extend the line of the forty-ninth parallel over the mountains and down to the sea. They "did not assert that the United States had a perfect right to that country, but insisted that their claim was at least good against Great Britain." What it might be against Spain and Russia was another question; for the Americans, like the British, recognized undefined Spanish and Russian shadows on the Pacific coast. Gallatin and Rush supported the American claim to the region of the Columbia by citing the discovery of the mouth of the river by Captain Gray, the exploration of the course of the river by Lewis and Clark, and the building of Astoria as the first

79. *Supra*, pp. 195, 199.
80. Gallatin and Rush referred to it in their report of Oct. 20, 1818, *A.S.P.F.R.*, IV, 381.
81. *Ibid.*, p. 391.
82. *Ibid.*, p. 395.
83. *Ibid.*, p. 392.

permanent settlement in that quarter. Their arguments made as little impression as those of their opponents, who took their stand on previous voyages, with particular reference to Captain Cook, and on pre-Revolutionary purchases of land from natives south of the Columbia. The closest the British came to proposing a boundary running to the Pacific was to suggest that the river would be the most convenient one. They would not agree to any which did not give them the harbor at the mouth, to be held in common with the United States. The Americans replied that they could not agree to this, but expressed a readiness to insert a proviso similar to what had been proposed in the past, which would simply put off any agreement on the territory to the west of the mountains. The British said they would not have it.[84] They were determined to get some agreement.

As it was patently impossible to dispose of the issue finally, the Englishmen sought to confine it within definite limits and to render it harmless there. To this end, they revised the American draft of the second article by making the territory west of the Rockies between the forty-fifth and the forty-ninth parallels free and open for an indefinite period.[85] The third article thus began to take shape as a British amendment of the second. Gallatin and Rush at once objected to this one-sided arrangement, which would prevent their country from claiming anything north of the forty-ninth parallel but not Britain from claiming everything south of it. They said they could not "consent to throw in a common stock that part of the country to which the United States deny the claim of Great Britain, and which lies within the same latitudes as their own territories" east of the mountains. However, they welcomed the British provision for the prevention of disputes in the territory where the national claims overlapped, and they would have accepted it right away if the British had been willing to divorce it from the definition of the overlapping.[86] For nearly a fortnight Robinson and Goulburn fought shy of the question. They gave in reluctantly on the very day before the signature of the convention. The alternative was no agreement on what lay beyond the Rockies. They may have seen an advantage in an amendment which the Americans made at the last minute. It limited the operation of the article to ten years.[87] Thus was concluded a convention which stands out as one of the major international agreements in the history of Canadian-American relations.

As we examined in the beginning of this volume the definition of the

84. *Ibid.*, p. 381.
85. *Ibid.*, p. 391.
86. *Ibid.*, p. 392.
87. *Ibid.*, p. 397.

eastern half of the dividing line between the two countries, it is perhaps fitting that we should return to the same subject at the end. We have yet to notice the work of the boundary commissions appointed under the Treaty of Ghent,[88] of which little need here be said because not much of this work lies within the period under discussion.

The criticism mentioned above[89] does not apply to the commission which, as provided by Article IV, terminated the dispute over the islands below the mouth of the St. Croix. Again Thomas Barclay served as commissioner and Ward Chipman as agent for the British government. The former was paired with John Holmes, a member of Congress from that part of Massachusetts which soon became the State of Maine. The American agent was James T. Austin, a leading lawyer and later attorney general of the Bay State. They finished their task in about a year from the first meeting. Though they went over all the old ground from the grant to Sir William Alexander in 1621, each side claiming all the islands, their task had been simplified by the negotiation of the abortive conventions of 1803 and 1807, which divided the islands in Passamaquoddy Bay.

The one real problem the commissioners faced was the disposition of Grand Manan Island, which had been left out of the earlier discussions, and the way they solved it suggests that Barclay could have beaten Holmes in a game of chess. The old Loyalist studied the moves ahead. The Treaty of Ghent provided, in the event of a disagreement, for a separate report by each commissioner and then arbitration by a friendly sovereign who, Barclay foresaw, would naturally adopt the division of 1803 and 1807, the mutual acceptance of which had been prevented by extraneous causes. But what would he do with Grand Manan, which was worth more than all the islands in Passamaquoddy Bay, when he examined the arguments advanced in support of the opposing claims? All islands south of an east line from the mouth of the St. Croix and within twenty leagues of the United States were given to that country by the treaty of 1783, except such as belonged to Nova Scotia. As Grand Manan lay within this geographical limit, the crucial question was whether it belonged to Nova Scotia in 1783. The foundation of the British case was the original grant in 1621, which gave Alexander the territory lying east of a line from the entrance to St. Mary Bay, at the western extremity of the Nova Scotian peninsula, to the mouth of the St. Croix. This line cuts through Grand Manan, about two-thirds of the island being west of it. The grant also included all islands within

88. This subject has been definitively treated in J. B. Moore, *International Adjudications*, *q.v.*

89. *Supra*, p. 416.

six leagues, but whether this distance was to be measured from the above line, as the British now contended, or from the coast, as the Americans argued, was a moot point. The Latin text might be interpreted in either way. To strengthen their case, the Americans appealed to subsequent royal commissions given to governors of Nova Scotia in 1763, 1765, and 1773, which specifically included all islands within six leagues of the coast elsewhere but said nothing of islands westward of this line. In the light of all this, Barclay saw that an arbitral award might give the United States two-thirds of the island or even the whole of it. He discussed the matter with Chipman, who agreed with him, and the upshot was an offer to surrender the British claim to Moose, Frederick, and Dudley islands if Holmes would let Britain have the remaining islands, including Grand Manan.

The American appeared to be astonished to discover that the British claim to Grand Manan was serious, and he said he could never join in a decision recognizing it. Barclay replied that a rejection of his proposal, which was his ultimatum, would necessitate arbitration. It was a bold move, but he probably calculated that Holmes would be afraid to take advantage of it lest it lead to the imprisonment of Eastport: for an award which copied the division contemplated in 1803 and 1807 would give Britain the ownership of the ship channel to that harbor, and the friendly sovereign would have no power to qualify his award by guaranteeing to Americans the use of this passage. This was precisely what Holmes feared, and to obviate it he offered to abandon Grand Manan for Campobello. Barclay would not budge from his ultimatum, but he was willing to join in a letter to both governments expressing the opinion that the channel in question was common to both nations. On this condition Holmes yielded "with great reluctance" on October 9, 1817. Thus Moose, Dudley, and Frederick islands were finally allocated to the United States, and the other islands in Passamaquoddy Bay, along with Grand Manan, to Great Britain.

The commission appointed under Article V of the Treaty of Ghent, to fix the boundary between the source of the St. Croix and the point where the forty-fifth parallel strikes the St. Lawrence, took a long time to settle nothing. Barclay and Chipman served in the same capacities as in the adjudication of the islands below the mouth of the St. Croix. The American commissioner was Cornelius P. Van Ness, later chief justice and governor of Vermont, and the agent of the United States was William C. Bradley, also of Vermont. The task they faced was the most formidable of all, and it depended upon lengthy surveys which had yet to be made. The commissioners did little but direct this work until the fall of 1820, when they decided that no further surveys were necessary and ordered the agents to present their arguments at the next meeting in the spring of 1821. When these were heard, the board came to a deadlock. The final session was held in the spring of 1822, when the commissioners presented their conflicting reports, which were transmitted to their respective governments.

Three points of disagreement had emerged. In 1818, Dr. Tiarks and F. R. Hassler, the British and American astronomers, made a startling discovery at Rouses Point, where the United States had built a fort costing a million dollars and had commenced the construction of a new fortification. Both works, regarded as of great strategic value, were on British soil! Fearing a local uprising if the discovery were known, the scientists kept it a profound secret except from the agents. Prompted by Hassler, Bradley met the emergency by claiming that the geocentric latitude rather than the observed latitude should be taken. This meant the correction of a minor error by a major one. The geocentric calculation, ignoring the varying curvature of the earth, would have put the boundary another twelve miles north. Van Ness did not sustain the claim, but he did not commit himself in any way until the fall of 1821, when he informed Barclay that he would report no opinion on it. A second point of difference was over the northwesternmost tributary of the Connecticut, the British claiming one stream and the Americans another. But the territory involved in this dispute was insignificant compared with the area at stake in the third difficulty.

What was "the northwest angle" of the old Nova Scotia, the intersection of the line drawn due north from the source of the St. Croix with the highlands dividing the waters of the St. Lawrence from those of the Atlantic? According to the British contention, it was Mars Hill, forty miles north of the source of the St. Croix. According to the American case, it lay one hundred and three miles farther north—across the St. John and the Restigouche rivers, just beyond the forty-eighth parallel. As the location of the "angle" was the commencement of the boundary along the watershed, there were therefore two lines, one British and the other American. The area between them was about twelve thousand square miles.

Five years passed before arrangements were made to submit the work of this commission to arbitration. The King of the Netherlands, who was chosen, rendered his award in January, 1831. Britain accepted but the United States Senate rejected it. Finally, after some dangerous frontier strife, a solution was reached by the negotiation of the Webster-Ashburton Treaty in 1842.

The designation of the boundary through the St. Lawrence and the Great Lakes to the communication between Lake Huron and Lake

Superior, under Article VI of the Treaty of Ghent, had likewise to wait upon surveys which were not completed until late in 1821. In the following June, the commissioners reached an agreement, of which the most important detail was the allocation of Wolfe Island, opposite Kingston, to Canada in exchange for Grand Island, above Niagara Falls, and a few islands near Cornwall. Under Article VII, the same board then proceeded to fix the boundary from Lake Huron to the northwest corner of the Lake of the Woods, and again they had to wait for the surveyors. Then the commissioners ran into difficulties which they reported in 1826 and the Webster-Ashburton Treaty settled along with the much greater difference over the northern boundary of Maine.

By 1820, the truce which had closed the War of 1812 had been transformed into a real peace, and it may be appropriate to conclude this volume by noting a most pleasant incident which occurred on February 26, 1819. It was a ball in honor of the British minister, who was about to return to England. General Philip J. Schuyler, Commodore Stephen Decatur, and other leading men arranged it. Almost everybody of consequence in Washington and the neighborhood made a point of attending, including the Secretaries of State, of War, and of the Navy, the Chief Justice and all his associates, and a large number of senators and representatives from all states and of all parties. At each end of the ballroom, the names of Mr. and Mrs. Bagot were "written in transparency"; and at supper, the company found something which would be taken for granted today but was then unprecedented. The tables were decorated with "little flags of the two countries united." Then too, for the first time, music expressed the sentiment represented by the combination of the flags. "Upon drinking our healths," Bagot wrote to a friend, "the band, to my infinite surprise and somewhat to my apprehension for the effect, played 'God Save the King,'[90] which the company heard standing. As this was a pierre de touche, I hinted to one of the managers to tell the band to play 'Yankee Doodle' the moment 'God Save the King' was finished, in order that it might be understood as a union of the two national airs, which I believe it was, for not a murmur was heard."[91] Truly a new era had begun.

90. "My Country, 'Tis of Thee" was not yet written. It was first published in 1832.
91. Bagot to Planta, private, March 5, 1819, F.O. 5, Vol. CXLII.

INDEX

Adams, Henry: criticism of Madison's war message, 312–313; comparison of War of *1812* with Civil War, 323

Adams, John, 24, 31, 108, 110; the St. Croix boundary, 39; successful champion of American fishermen in negotiations of *1782*, 46–54; consulted on identity of St. Croix, 75 n; minister to Great Britain, interest in St. Croix problem, 77, 79, 80; demands surrender of western posts, 97–98; calls for American navigation law as lever against Great Britain, 99; despairs of getting western posts till United States observes the treaty, 100; withdrawal from London, 106; procures release of impressed seamen in *1785*, 110; advice in Nootka Sound crisis, 113; casting vote defeats nonintercourse bill, *1794*, 142; fails to uphold claim based on Mitchell's map, 163; makes peace with France, *1800*, 210

Adams, John Quincy: convention of *1803*, 194, 195; minister to Russia, 345–346; appointed peace commissioner, *1813*, 345–346; instructions, 346–347; appointment renewed and new instructions, *1814*, 348; outspoken against inclusion of Indians in Treaty of Ghent, 358; favors breaking off negotiations, 358, 359; argues that Indian article revived Article III of Jay's Treaty, 359, 366, 371, 376; on fisheries and the Mississippi, 364, 366–367; contention for Moose Island, 369; defiant on fisheries, 369–370; complaints against British searching Americans on Lakes, 384, 386; disarmament on Lakes, 388–390, 394–395; protests exclusion of American fishermen, 402; unyielding on fisheries, 404; urges further suspension of excluding orders, 407; intractable on fisheries, 409–410; yields under Monroe, 410; discussions with Bagot on Columbia River region, 412–415

Adams, Samuel: champion of American fishermen, 44, 53

Adams, William, 352

Adams, United States frigate, burned, 341

Addington, Henry, Prime Minister: discusses New Orleans with Rufus King, 194 n; discusses impressment with Rufus King, 226; ministry tottering, 229

Adet, Pierre Augustus, 176; fights ratification of Jay's Treaty, 169–170; revives effort to revolutionize Canada, 170, 174; recalled, 173

Alexander I, Tsar: offers to mediate, 345; cares less for neutral rights, 347; against Great Britain over Poland, 362

Alexander, Sir William: grant of Nova Scotia to, 37, 164, 187

Allan, John: stirs up dispute over St. Croix, 71, 74, 78, 80

Allen, Ira: plot for conquest of Canada, 171–174, 177; attempts to get land in Eastern Townships, 179 n

Allen, Levi, 66, 69; attempts to get land in Eastern Townships, 179 n

Amherstburg and Fort Erie to be exchanged for Castine and Machias, 360

André, executioner of Major John, 181–182

Aranda, Count of: suggestions for western boundary of United States, 17, 28–29

Arbitration: proposed by Continental Congress to determine eastern boundary, 38–39; proposed by Jay to settle dispute over St. Croix, 77, 78–79; and to fill northwest boundary gap, 148; Grenville accepts with condition rejected by Jay, 150; provisions in Jay's Treaty for, 151–152, 154; importance of Jay and his treaty in history of, 157; failure with debts and delay over damages, 161, 186; successful in determining St. Croix, 161–165; convention of *1803*, 188–189, 190–191, 192; convention of *1807*, 198; Treaty of Ghent, 363, 365, 369, 416, 423–425

Armed Neutrality of the North, 155 n

Armstrong, General John, 283, 284, 335; American minister to France, 267 n; fruitless demands in Paris, 281; confused direction of American strategy in War of *1812*, 329, 331, 332, 334, 336, 337